Robert Jan van Pelt

The Barrack 1572–1914

Chapters in the History of Emergency Architecture

The Barrack 1572–1914

Chapters in the History of Emergency Architecture

Robert Jan van Pelt

PARK BOOKS

Contents

Acknowledgments

This project goes back to a semester that I spent at the Netherlands Institute for Advanced Study in the Humanities and Social Sciences (NIAS) in Wassenaar as part of the Terrorscape project conceived and organized by Rob van der Laarse and Georgi Verbeeck. I thank them, NIAS rector Aafke Hulk and her staff, and our both formal and informal Terrorscape colleagues—Hans Citroen, Caroline Sturdy Colls, Gerry Kearns, Władysław Malarek, Francesco Mazzucchelli, Carlos Reijnen, and Karen Till—for their friendship and inspiration.

The project to research the history of the barrack was made possible by two generous grants from the Social Sciences and Humanities Research Council of Canada (SSHRC). I am deeply grateful for Tom Barber's assistance in preparing the grant proposals, and to the anonymous reviewers and the merit review committees that deemed the project worthy of financial support. The SSHRC remains the most important source of federal research funds for Canadian historians, and having received its support for thirty years, I consider myself also for this reason blessed to have found a home in this vast and plentiful country as it stretches *a mari usque ad mari* (from sea to sea).

At the University of Waterloo, Anne Bordeleau encouraged my research in this field, and students Shalal Ahmed, Mayassah Akour, Shaina Coulter, Charlotte Damus, Tracey Elasmar, Oliver Green, Lisa Huang, Cindy Lan, Courtney Lee, Janet Li, Janet Lin, Laura Matos, Justin Park, Rushali Patel, Nicholas Puersten, Amanda Reyes-Martin, Ali Salama, Vanessa Sokic, Alina Turean, Owen Yang, and Sarah Zeng joined me in an early exploration of contemporary use of the barrack in refugee camps, detention centers, and emergency hospitals.

Philipp Oswalt organized for a visiting professorship at the University of Kassel (Uni Kassel), funded by the German Academic Exchange Service (DAAD), which gave me the opportunity to test and fine-tune my findings in a course on the history of the barrack. I am deeply grateful to Philipp, DAAD, Uni Kassel, colleagues, students and members of the public who attended my public lectures, and students Enise Biqkaj, Frederika Bücher, Rukija Dacic, Julia Gamm, Betül Gülmez, Jessica Henkel, Sebastian Hofmeier, Hilal Imanci, Yasmina Kirsch, Oliver Knopp, Sina Kupillas, Matti Niles, Annabelle Oeste, Laurin Queck, Axel Rellensmann, David Sadowsky, Jannes Schmidt, Adeline Stapel, Hilal Tasdemir, Zichen Wen, and Emma Westheide who participated in my research seminar for this invaluable opportunity. Special thanks also to Philipp's collaborator Andreas Buss, who, following my stay in Germany, secured an important barrack for posterity, and to Katja Weckmann, Secretary of the Division of Architectural Theory and Design in the Faculty of Architecture, Urbanism and Landscape, who made everything easy—or at least appear easy.

In the long course of this undertaking, I have received the assistance of many colleagues, librarians, archivists, curators, historians, photographers, artists, and other professionals who helped me negotiate the collections entrusted to them and, when necessary, obtain research materials and photographic images—or who helped me to make contact with others who might be able to help me in my research, or who allowed me to publish their own work. I recall with gratitude the help provided by Sheila Anirudhan, Peter Baetes, Eva-Maria Bergmann, Patricia Biggs, Sander van Bladel, Philipp Bockenheimer, Anne Bordeleau, Ulrich Blortz, Tristan Broos, Peter Bruns, Carlos Bunga, Richard Dabb, Melissa Davis, Elke Edlinger, Andreas Ehresmann, Silke Geiring, Ainhoa González Graupera, Alan Hawk, Silvia Hiechinger, Lisbeth Hollensen, Malin Joakimson, Anna Kamyshan, Ann Kilbey, Martin Kleinfeld, Dietfrid Krause-Vilmar, Micha Krüger, Elsa Lam, Janis Langins, Astrid Ley, Bo Lundström, Piotr Malarek, Władysław Malarek, Olaf Matthes, Eve McAuley, Edward McParland, Marian Miehl, Alice Mountfort, Frank Neupert, Erwin Nolet, Rikard Nordström, Jenny Odell, Bertil Olofsson, Itohan Osayimwese, Reinhard Otto, Gottfried Pahl, Simon K. Bering Papousek, Geoffrey Parnell, Emeline Perrin, Janet Rabinowitch, Tobias Reinel, Luigi Ricciari, Peter Rogiest, Rainer Salzmann, Holger Scheerschmidt, Antje Senarclens de Grancy, Ann Sheppard, Therkel Straede, Ann Verdonck, Alexander Veryovkin, Eva Vreeburg, Miriam Ward, Kai Wenzel, and Andrea Wulff.

A very special thank you goes to my research collaborators Marina Androsovich, Suhaib Bhatti, Mark Clubine, Albina Krymskaya, Anna Longrigg, Polina Nilova, Martin Overby, Zaven Titizian, and Victor Tulceanu. Too much of the work done by all of you did not find a place in this incarnation of the story to be told, for which my apologies. I trust that in subsequent publications it will find its way into the public domain.

My long-time friends Robert Baldock and Bob Wiljer read the whole manuscript and provided both vital critical feedback and very helpful suggestions. Claire Crighton copy-edited an early version of the first six chapters, and Amy Hughes applied with considerable empathy her sharp editorial skills to the final product.

Thomas Kramer, Managing Director and Chief Editor of the renowned Swiss publishing houses Scheidegger & Spiess and Park Books, invited me to submit what he labeled as my “big Barrack oeuvre,” considered it while holidaying amidst the gorgeous scenery of Graubünden—or was it Ticino—and undoubtedly mellowed by the splendour of the Alps, graciously accepted it into his care. His decision to entrust the design to Sandra Doeller was inspired: our collaboration was, from the arrival of a pdf showing the first concept of the book to the production of the final design, full of happy surprises. Colette Forder subjected the print proof to a final round of corrections, while Patrick Schneebeli began to plan the sales trajectory of the finished product, and Dave Prout extracted a brilliant index from the text, ensuring that every reader will be able to easily access its contents. And, as I am writing this, the printers at the renowned Altenburg Printing Works, established over four centuries ago by Duke Friedrich Wilhelm of Saxony, are ready to receive the final print file to feed it into essentially pre-digital offset lithography machines that will give this book a material presence in our persistently physical world. Given the fact that the story told begins in 1572, the choice of a printer founded in 1594 seems utterly pertinent.

My penultimate thanks go to Miriam Greenbaum, who has provided indispensable, energetic, and critical support of this project from the very beginning to the, admittedly provisional, end represented by this book. Miriam was throughout the project involved as a fellow researcher, reader, and editor, ensuring not only that the project remained on course, but also that it proved doable for its author, manageable for its publisher, and we hope pleasurable for its readers.

Finally, I would like to express my deep gratitude to my father, Willem Diederik (Wim) van Pelt, for having introduced me to this topic in my early youth. In the oldest photo that shows us together—Wim at age 28 a recently licensed physician gently holding my couple-of-days-old self—my father wears the uniform of a First Lieutenant in the Netherlands Army Medical Corps. His two-year sevice as a medical officer in the mid 1950s introduced him to the science and art of anesthesiology, which shaped his civilian career in the four decades that followed. Moreover, his annual recall as a reserve officer brought him between the mid 1950s and the early 1980s the repeated pleasure of meeting old comrades during two-week training stints in a Dutch field hospital pitched near the Weser River in Germany. These highly anticipated absences from ordinary pressures of family life resulted upon his return in tall tales about both the pleasures of a couple of summer-weeks' sojourn in the field and the problems of working in the improvised setting known to me through the weekly *M*A*S*H* TV episodes. And it also resulted in a small library of manuals on military medicine that included richly illustrated instructions on how to construct and manage temporary medical facilities in combat zones. My father's stories and these books mark the true beginning of the now partially completed journey that is embodied in this book.

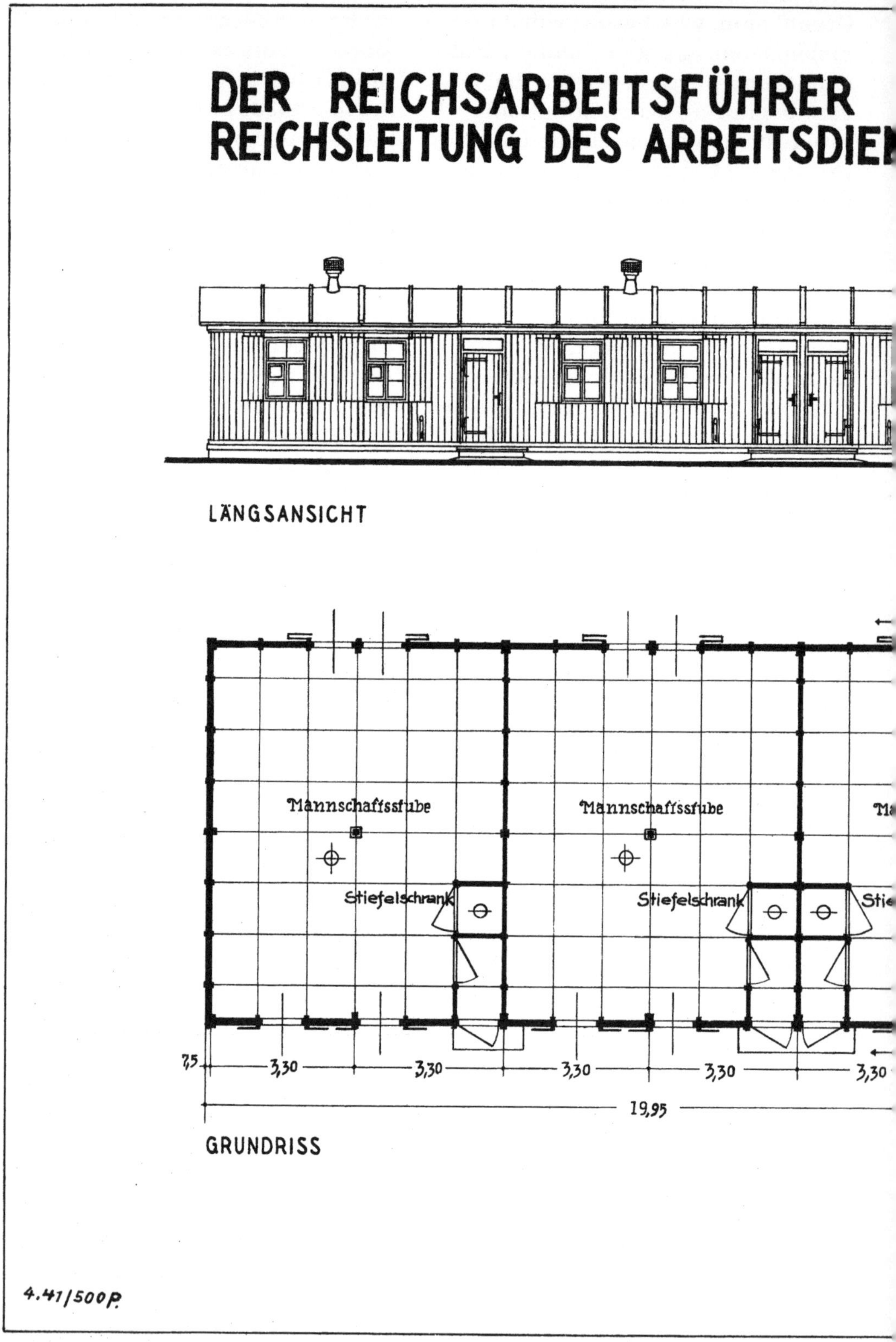
DER REICHSARBEITSFÜHRER
REICHSLEITUNG DES ARBEITSDIE
LÄNGSANSICHT
Mannschaftsstube
Mannschaftsstube
Stiefelschrank
Stiefelschrank
7,5
3,30
3,30
3,30
3,30
3,30
19,95
GRUNDRISS
4.41/500P.

→ p. 17

S

OBERKOMMANDO DES HEERES (BDE:) VA. (R A D.)

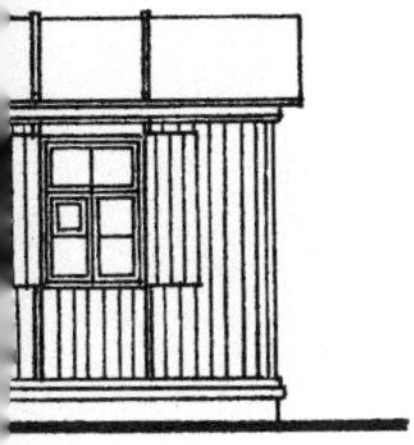

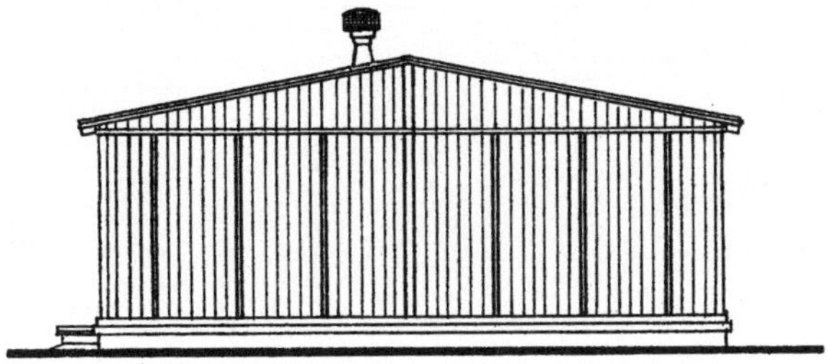

GIEBELANSICHT

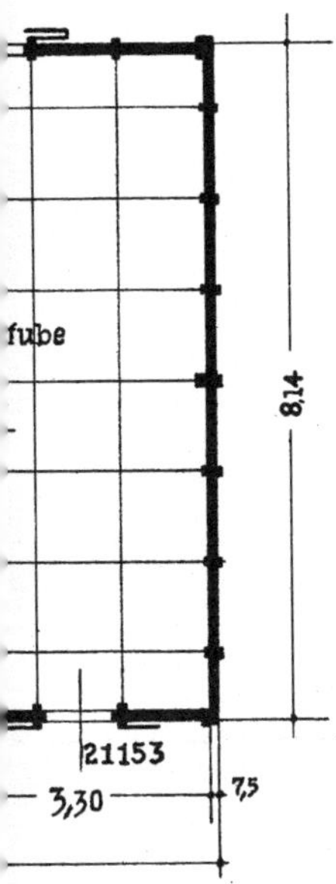

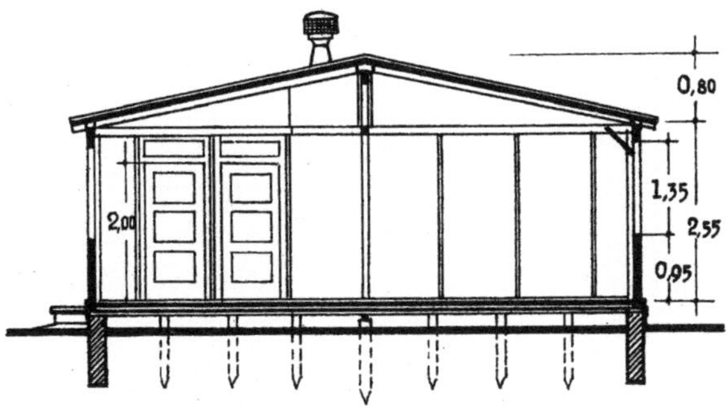

QUERSCHNITT

M. 1 : 100

1. 10. 1939

gezeichnet: Nal. | geprüft:

geändert: am 2.10.39 | durch | geprüft: Hz.

TYPENBLATT RL IV/3 (OKH.)
MANNSCHAFTSHAUS

„TANNERA", DRESDEN-A.1

Introduction

The Most Beautiful Place in the World

A decade ago, I found myself in Poland on the threshold of a ruined barrack near the former Auschwitz concentration camp, constructed and operated by Germans between 1940 and 1945.

Fig. 1
Ruined barrack in Monowice, Poland, December 2012. Photo: Carlos Reijnen.

I was leading a group of academics as part of a project to analyze key sites of twentieth-century terror and mass violence and their place in local, national, and transnational identity. Formally educated as an architectural historian, I had also become a Holocaust historian in the years following my doctoral defense in 1984, and one of the focal points of my research since 1990 had been the construction history of Auschwitz. For almost a quarter century I had visited the remains of Auschwitz annually, and I was convinced the place did not hold any more surprises. As we set out to visit the site of the former IG Farben Buna synthetic rubber factory, built by Auschwitz prisoners, my friend Hans Citroen suggested we make a detour and visit a small farmhouse not far from the factory site in the village of Monowice. A Dutch artist whose grandfather had been imprisoned in Auschwitz, Citroen had been married to Polish architect Barbara Starzyńska until her death in 2010. Starzyńska had grown up in Oświęcim, the Polish town that the Germans renamed Auschwitz in 1939, and Starzyńska and Citroen had identified many wartime-related artifacts located outside the boundaries of the professionally preserved parts of the Auschwitz concentration camp included in the Auschwitz-Birkenau State Museum (ABSM). Their work had culminated in the 2011 book *Auschwitz-Oświęcim/Oświęcim-Auschwitz*.[1]

At the back of the farmhouse, we found a partly ruined addition, 12 meters long and 8 meters wide, that, on close inspection, turned out to be made of wooden panels typical of German barrack construction between 1933 and 1945. At the point where the wall of the addition touched the house, we saw a door, carefully opened it, and entered a space that clearly preserved the basic architecture of the barrack originally conceived and produced for the Reichsarbeitsdienst (RAD; Reich Labor Service) camps, a national institution in Germany since 1934. Young men were sent to these camps to undergo the obligatory six-month-long third stage of Nazi socialization, begun in the Deutsches Jungvolk in der Hitler Jugend (German Youngsters in the Hitler Youth) and amplified in the Hitler Jugend proper. The time in the labor service camps was to prepare them for their induction into the Wehrmacht (armed forces).

"Good, an authentic *Reichsarbeitsdienst-Mannschaftsbaracke* [RAD

1 Hans Citroen and Barbara Starzyńska, *Auschwitz-Oświęcim/Oświęcim-Auschwitz* (Rotterdam: Post Editions, 2011).

crew barrack]," I muttered, clutching for the safety offered by identifying our discovery with its proper label. The barrack was now being used as a storage place for farm tools, old windows and doors, lumber, and hay. Remarkably, the owner, or perhaps the various owners since 1945, had not considered it necessary to paint over various German-language inscriptions, written in Gothic script on the beams and walls, summoning the original occupants not to drink the water and to adhere to certain standards of hygiene.

We speculated on the original location and purpose of the building. Citroen and I agreed that it more than likely had come from the Auschwitz-Monowitz camp, a satellite of the main Auschwitz camp created to provide slave labor to the IG Farben corporation for the construction of the synthetic-rubber factory. In 1941 the Germans had forcibly expelled the Polish inhabitants from the original village of Monowice—renamed Monowitz—and demolished the village to create a building site for the plant. When the original inhabitants returned, in the summer of 1945, the newly established Polish government had taken over the factory, which was to be an essential part of the new postwar economy. The returnees were given lots located in a large field adjacent to the plant and were told to build a new village. Each family was offered two, three, or four bays (a bay measured 27 square meters) of the *Reichsarbeitsdienst-Mannschaftsbaracken* that stood empty in the nearby Auschwitz-Monowitz camp. Easily taken apart, transported, and re-erected in the new location of Monowice, these partial barracks were to provide a temporary home and, as such, mark a new beginning.

It was only minutes before Citroen mentioned Primo Levi, who had been an inmate of the Auschwitz-Monowitz camp for almost a year. Levi's memoir *Se questo è un uomo* (*If This Is a Man*), first published in 1947, was a key testimony about life in the German concentration camps. The surviving inscriptions on the beams and above the doors of the ruined barrack in which we found ourselves suggested that it might have served as a camp infirmary, and one of the most powerful chapters in Levi's book describes his ten-day sojourn in such a place, which the inmates called "Ka-Be," short for *Krankenbau* (literally, "building for the sick"). In Ka-Be, Levi and a few comrades found shelter and security in January 1945 after the Germans evacuated the camp and before the Red Army's arrival. Ka-Be had started out as limbo but slowly became a site of a new beginning, as men who had lived for themselves began to share food and act with a measure of civility—marking, as Levi remembered, "the beginning of the change by which we who had not died slowly changed from Häftlinge [prisoners] to men again."[2] Somehow, as I told the story of the ten days in Ka-Be, a universe of the imagination composed in words began to merge with the actual place in which we stood, and the concatenation of narrative and architectural structure took on a life of its own. From that moment onward, we referred to this barrack as either "Primo Levi's barrack" or "Ka-Be."

2 Primo Levi, *If This Is a Man*, trans. Stuart Woolf (New York: Orion Press, 1959), 190.

When I was asked more detailed questions about the architectural history of Ka-Be, I felt embarrassed because I knew little about the history of its design and production. While I had conducted extensive empirical and forensic research on the construction history of Auschwitz, my primary focus was on those buildings that had been specifically designed for use in the camp—most importantly, the five gas-chamber-equipped crematoria.[3] As the prefabricated demountable wooden barracks had been ordered by the camp management as ready-to-erect commodities, I had largely ignored the design and production history of these buildings. In December 2012, standing in "Ka-Be," I was finally confronted with the limitations of my knowledge, and this suggested that I had more work to do.

Eight months after our visit, I received an email from Citroen, who was visiting his in-laws in Oświęcim. The message was terse and to the point: "Primo Levi Barrack. Demolished? Or perhaps preserved? Do you know anything about it?" Attached were two pictures: the first he had taken during our visit in December, and it showed the sagging barrack; the second was taken the day the message was dispatched, and it showed a clearing next to the farmhouse, with only the foundations of the building that had created so much excitement that December day.

I was shocked by the disappearance of the structure, especially as our discovery of "Ka-Be" had triggered my commitment to learn more about the history of that building type. But I was not surprised. In the more than twenty years that I had been a regular visitor to Oświęcim, I had noticed garden shacks and other accessory buildings located on private properties in and around the city that appeared to be constructed from German barrack parts. With every visit, some of them had vanished; most likely their owners had decided that they had become a safety hazard because of rot. As I felt little relation to, or responsibility for, those structures, their disappearance had made little impact. But things were different with the barrack in Monowice—undoubtedly, the fact that I had stood in that building, and the lingering association with Primo Levi expressed in the fact that I continued to think about it as "Ka-Be," made me investigate its demolition. With the help of a local friend, Piotr Malarek, I learned that a newly established nonprofit, the Fundacja Pobliskie Miejsca Pamięci (Foundation of Memory Sites), created to purchase, preserve, and exhibit privately owned camp-related artifacts, had purchased and stored "Ka-Be."

In 2015 I returned to Monowice. I had become involved with the Spanish production company Musealia in a project to create a large traveling exhibition on the history of Auschwitz. In the discussions of the curatorial team, I had mentioned our discovery of "Ka-Be" and suggested that we might seek to purchase another original barrack. Our driver, Piotr Malarek, knew of one standing in a nearby garden owned by a retired railway engineer who lived in Krakow. A couple of telephone calls led to a meeting with the owner and an inspection of the barrack, which

3 Déborah Dwork and Robert Jan van Pelt, *Auschwitz: 1270 to the Present* (New York: W. W. Norton, 1996).

his parents had received in 1945 as compensation for a farmhouse demolished to create space for the Buna plant. It turned out to be in better condition than "Ka-Be," and in addition, the owner provided a complete and satisfactory provenance. With the help of the ABSM, we negotiated the legal hurdles involved in the purchase and export of a historically important artifact, and also arranged for its preservation by the company responsible for the maintenance and preservation of the wooden barracks on the museum's grounds. When Musealia opened its exhibition *Auschwitz. No hace mucho. No muy lejos.* (*Auschwitz: Not Long Ago. Not Far Away.*) in Madrid in December 2017, the barrack was its largest artifact, providing a dramatic environment for many smaller ones.

Fig. 2
Barrack exhibited at *Auschwitz. No hace mucho. No muy lejos.*, in Madrid, 2017. Photo: José Barea.

The discovery of "Ka-Be" in 2012 had already motivated me to investigate the history of the whole range of *Reichsarbeitsdienst-Mannschaftsbaracken*. By 2015 my ambition had expanded: to write a comprehensive history of barracks. While Musealia was negotiating the purchase of the railway engineer's barrack, I submitted a research proposal to the Social Sciences and Humanities Research Council (SSHRC), the main granting agency for the humanities in Canada. In my submission, I stressed not only the academic value of my enterprise but also its existential resonance: many people have experienced, for shorter or longer time periods, life in a barrack, and for all of them it represented life on the edge, for better or worse. For military veterans or labor service graduates, life in the barrack was usually remembered as a romance of a comradely existence, while for those once made homeless by natural disasters and for former refugees lucky enough to make new beginnings elsewhere, the memory of the instant shelter provided by the barrack was closely linked to the experience of survival. And for the survivors of the concentration camps, the barrack remained the stuff of nightmares, past and present.

As this grant proposal moved from the desks of peer reviewers to the meeting room of the SSHRC adjudication committee, the Museum of Modern Art in New York included the flat-pack Better Shelter, developed by IKEA for use in emergencies, in its permanent collection. MoMA's decision suggested that a project to research the history of this building type was both viable, necessary, and possibly even urgent. In April 2016 I received the news that my request had been honored.

With this research, as with so many enterprises, an increasing excitement about the topic under investigation emerged from a close look at its details. Other works of architecture are typically rooted in the place where they were built and tied to the community they serve. As such, they provide an effective mise-en-scène for the exits and entrances of the players, who are

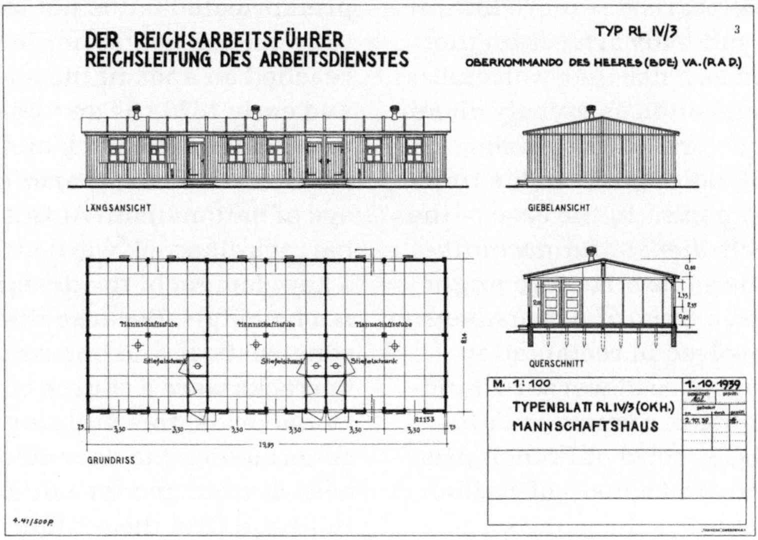

Fig. 3
Plan, elevations, and section of a three-room *Reichsarbeitsdienst-Mannschaftsbaracke*, 1939. The dormitory version of this barrack Type RL IV came in different sizes: the smallest contained one room designed for a troop of seventeen *Arbeitsdienstmänner*, and was numbered RL IV/1. The most popular sizes, RL IV/3 and RL IV/4 contained three and four rooms. Collection: Bundesarchiv, Berlin.

DER REICHSKOMMISSAR FÜR DEN FREIWILLIGEN ARBEITSDIENST
REICHSLEITUNG DES ARBEITSDIENSTES BERLIN N 24 FRIEDRICHSTRASSE 110—112

Typ RL IV/5
Mannschaftsbaracke
(Baubeschreibung siehe Seite 26 und 27 — Barackenquerschnitt siehe Seite 3)

Zeichnung Nr. 18019/5

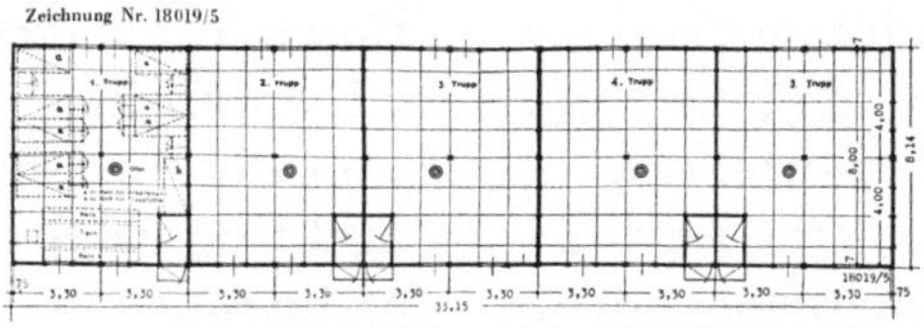

Preise bei Abnahme von:	1—5	6—8	9—11	12— aufwärts Stück
	RM	RM	RM	RM
Kosten der Baracke frachtfrei Bestimmungsbahnhof bis zu einer Entfernung von 500 km vom Lieferwerk	9140,—	9005,—	8865,—	8685,—

Zuschlag für Fracht bei einer Entfernung von:
500—600 km . . . . RM 50,—
600—700 km . . . . RM 90,—
700—800 km . . . . RM 120,—
800—900 km . . . . RM 145,—

Gewicht der Baracke rund 25000 kg

Bei einem Transport der Bauteile durch Lastkraftwagen werden benötigt 9 Lastkraftwagen je 3 to

Mehrkosten für zusätzliche Lieferungen:

(Baubeschreibung der zusätzlichen Lieferungen, sowie Hinweise auf die betreffenden Technischen Mitteilungsblätter siehe Seite 28).

Die nebenstehenden Mehrkosten für zusätzliche Lieferungen verstehen sich bei Lieferung für 1—5 Stück Baracken. Es treten Ermäßigungen ein:
Bei Lieferung für 6—8 Baracken . . . 1,5 Prozent
Bei Lieferung für 9—11 Baracken . . . 3 Prozent
Bei Lieferung für 12 und mehr . . . 5 Prozent

Pos. 1) **Pfahlrostfundament,** bestehend aus Rundpfählen und äußerer Sockelverbretterung . . . . . RM 325,—
Pos. 2) 5 Blech-**Schornsteine** . . . . . RM 110,—
Pos. 3) **Doppelfußboden,** als Fehlboden zwischen den Lagerhölzern mit einer Abdeckung aus teerfreier Pappe . . . . . RM 575,—
Pos. 4) **Isolierplatteneinlage** in den **Umfassungswänden** . . . . RM 270,—
Pos. 5) **Isolierplatteneinlage** in den **Dachflächen** . . . . . RM 425,—
Pos. 6) **Doppelfenster** für alle Räume . . . . . RM 490,—
Pos. 7) 10 **Fliegenfenster** . . . . . RM 30,—
Pos. 8) **Fensterläden** für alle Fenster . . . . . RM 450,—
Pos. 9) **Lignatbekleidung** für die Innenseite der **Umfassungswände** RM 540,—
Pos. 10) **Lignatbekleidung** für **Dachuntersichten** . . . . . RM 820,—
Pos. 11) Beiderseitige **Lignatbekleidung** für alle **Scheidewände** . . RM 720,—
Pos. 12) Durchlaufende **Dachrinnen** mit Abfallrohren . . . . . RM 175,—
Pos. 14) 4 Querscheidewände **schalldämpfend** zu verdoppeln . . . RM 440,—

7 10. Preisliste vom 16. 6. 1935

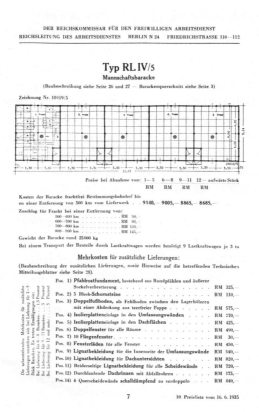

Fig. 4
Plan and price list of a core RL IV/5 *Mannschaftsbaracke* of the *Freiwillige Arbeitsdienst*—the predecessor of the *Reichsarbeitsdienst*. This page from a catalogue of standard barracks offers an all-included price for deliveries up to 500 kilometers, and specifies extra charges for larger distances and various upgrades. In addition, it also offers quantity discounts. Germany, Reich Management of the Labour Service, *10. Preisliste*, 1935. Collection: Staatsbibliothek zu Berlin.

human. The barrack is more like an actor who suddenly arrives on the stage, often as a not-that-welcome stranger, and often as quickly disappears—a performer who, in the words of Shakespeare, “in his time plays many parts.” In the case of the *Reichsarbeitsdienst-Mannschafts-baracke*, the same structure might have housed a troop of *Arbeitsdienstmänner* involved in reclamation work, a team of road workers building an autobahn, a squad of Luftwaffe pilots, a crowd of French prisoners of war, and a mass of civilian prisoners. Always the same structure, wearing different masks—and as a result it is uncanny, provoking at times a strong response, more appropriate to the way we deal with a hated criminal than with what remains, from a formal point of view, just a piece of scenery.

← Figs. 3, 4

When I set out to study the history of the barrack, I aimed to write a monograph that would cover the topic from the early seventeenth century to the present—the period that provides both a historic continuum and an increasing abundance of evidence. It was clear from the beginning of my research that I would have to leave the use of the barrack in classical antiquity outside of the project. As I engaged the material and began to articulate a narrative, I realized the plot of the tale to be told was a classic rise-and-fall story. The main protagonist is a makeshift building type, designed as a temporary dwelling for soldiers in the field, that existed for centuries at the margins of society. Pushed in the 1850s into the limelight of publicity and scientific attention, the stationary barrack—that is, the version that might be prefabricated but is not intended to be reused at another location—reached an apex in the late 1860s and early 1870s as an important tool in the care of sick and wounded soldiers of the mass armies of the age of nationalism. At this time, the barrack-like sick ward also became a key element of the design of civilian hospitals. Because the design, construction, and operation of barracks were a source of professional pride, this building type generated ample documentation, both written and visual.[4] Between 1890 and 1914 the prefabricated portable barrack reached its zenith when a technically sophisticated model revealed the potential of this building type as a key instrument of humanitarian intervention. The prestige of the barrack declined from 1914 onward when, in combination with barbed-wire fences, it became the implement of mass internment. In the 1930s the reputation of the barrack recovered somewhat, but in 1945 it stood quite literally condemned as an essential building block of the concentration camp universe.

Figs. 5, 6 →

As I began to produce early drafts of chapters, it became clear that it would be impossible to do justice to both the scope and depth of the topic in a single book. Therefore, I decided to focus on the origin and the rise of the barrack as a prescribed building type, with the outbreak of World War I in 1914 marking a good end for this tale. God willing, I’ll have

4 A primary guide to the use of barracks and barrack-like wards in nineteenth-century military and civilian hospital design can be found in Friedrich Oswald Kuhn, *Handbuch der Architektur, Vierter Theil, 5. Halb-Band, Gebäude fur Heil- und sonstige Wohlfahrts-Anstalten, 1. Heft: Krankenhäuser* (Stuttgart: Arnold Bergsträsser, 1897), 245–306, 591–635.

Fig. 5
Three of the eighteen barracks of the emergency military hospital constructed in August 1870 in the Sachsenhausen suburb of the German city of Frankfurt am Main to nurse soldiers wounded in the Franco-Prussian War (1870–71) back to health. The photograph, erroneously dated 1866, was given to one of the attending physicians, Dr. Jakob Hermann Bockenheimer, on his seventieth birthday, in 1907. Collection: Archiv Familie Bockenheimer.

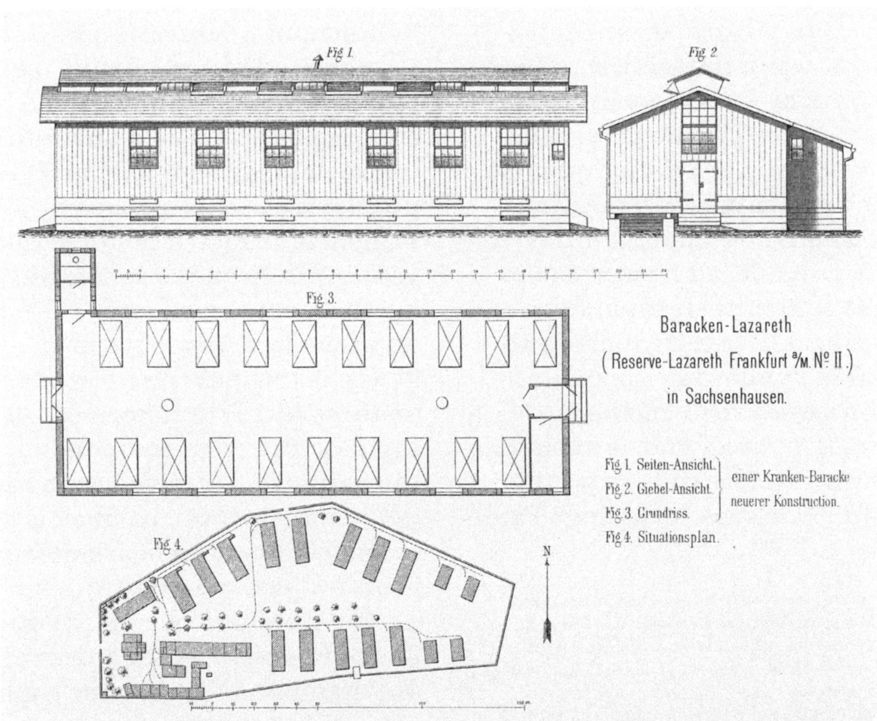

Fig. 6
Site plan of the emergency military hospital constructed in 1870 in Sachsenhausen, Germany, and plan and elevations of one of the larger barracks, 1870, from Prussia, Royal Prussian Ministry of War, *Der Sanitätsdienst bei den deutschen Heeren im Kriege gegen Frankreich 1870/71*, 1884. Collection: Staatsbibliothek zu Berlin.

the energy and opportunity to chronicle the decline and fall of the barrack at some future date. Writing in a time of a pandemic, when we are reminded that in life we are in death, makes one aware of the Latin phrase that aptly summarizes in three words not only the condition of human life but also the very meaning of the barrack as a form of accommodation: *Ut migraturus habita* (Dwell as if about to depart).[5]

The history of the barrack is anchored in historic intervals when seemingly dormant energies in society or nature suddenly awaken, in the form of wars, earthquakes, volcanic eruptions, pandemics, and economic depressions. When these human-generated or natural catastrophes overwhelm, damage, and often destroy the carefully planned, built, and maintained buildings and physical infrastructures that shape our precious cityscapes and landscapes, or when they throw millions out of work or force them into battle, the barrack has, in the past, come to the rescue by providing instant shelter amid ruins or in faraway places where new opportunities beckon. Considered from the perspective of architectural history, the barrack is akin to the capable and determined underdog in popular children's tales such as *The Little Engine That Could*, and as such it is also at times a favorite toy for the powerful, who seek to demonstrate their concern for the afflicted. German emperor Wilhelm II used prefabricated barracks produced by Christoph & Unmack as a tool of international politics. In January 1904, when the Norwegian town of Ålesund was destroyed by fire, Wilhelm dispatched four ships loaded with aid, including a dozen barracks. And in the wake of the 1908 earthquake that killed so many and destroyed so much in southern Italy, German naval units dropped off many barracks in the Sicilian capital Palermo, ostensibly to shelter survivors from Messina but more importantly to show German munificence and solidarity.

The barrack is the oldest and remains the most potent example of emergency architecture. As such, it is an architecture of the present as crisis, of that gap between a past as, paraphrasing writer Franz Kafka, a force pressing us from behind and a future as a force blocking the road ahead.[6] Political philosopher Hannah Arendt argued that this gap between past and future, between tangible reality and general perplexity, is experienced by all and is, hence, "a fact of political relevance."[7] In Arendt's sense, the barrack, conceived and created as an immediate response to an emergency, is the most political of architectures hitherto conceived. And as architecture is an embodiment of the political, conceived as the art of living together, the barrack is the most architectural of architectures, present, past, and future.

For members of civil societies like our own, in which works of architecture articulate the sophisti-

5 This saying derives from an admonition made by Seneca the Younger in letter 70 to Lucilius, in which he advises his friend to live with a full acceptance of the prospect of death: *Vis adversus hoc corpus liber esse? Tamquam migraturus habita.* (Would you be free from the restraint of your body? Live in it as if you were about to leave it.) It was made famous by William Makepeace Thackeray in his description of a traveler's inn in Londonderry, Ireland; *The Irish Sketch Book, 1842* (Boston: Houghton Mifflin, 1889).

6 Quoted in Hannah Arendt, preface, *Between Past and Future: Six Exercises in Political Thought* (New York: Viking, 1961), 7.

7 Ibid., 14.

Fig. 7
Italian postcard showing Christoph & Unmack barracks erected at the Piazza Indipendenza in Palermo, Sicily, 1909. In the wake of the severe earthquake that destroyed Messina and Reggio di Calabria, Italy, on December 28, 1908, and killed between 75,000 and 82,000 people, prefabricated (or partly so) barracks sent from many countries provided provisional shelter. Collection: author.

cation and complexity of the art of living together, a sojourn in a barrack clearly shares an essential dimension with a stay in a simple hut, which often becomes an essential part of a fantasy of a return to origins. Nearly 180 years ago, the American writer Henry David Thoreau decided to construct such a primitive, one-room dwelling in a forest with the aim, in his own words, "to live deliberately, to front only the essential facts of life."[8] Many who are forced to live for some time in a barrack experience something like what Thoreau sought, but they do so in a standard shelter that is ready-made and typically crowded with people, most if not all of whom are strangers but, as the result of the experience, may turn into comrades. To them the barrack is not part of a fantasy project but a situation into which they are thrown, most often against their wishes and inclinations, and it becomes, therefore, the setting of an intensity of experience that, when one tries to account for it, when memory and a poetic imagination meet in a temporal clearing, cannot but assume a surreal and at times even a psychotic dimension.

This is perhaps most powerfully expressed in the writing of Mary Borden. The heir of a fortune made by her father in the Colorado silver mines, she was twenty-eight and living in England when World War I broke out. Borden immediately volunteered to help the Allied war effort by financing and equipping a frontline hospital, where she worked as a nurse. In the scarce time she had for herself, she wrote poems, vignettes, and prose sketches. Living and working in a landscape of destruction and survival, in which life was reduced to its barest dimensions, energized Borden. "I enjoyed the War," she wrote in her novel *Jane—Our Stranger*, in which the protagonist is a nurse

8 Henry D. Thoreau, *Walden; or, Life in the Woods* (Boston: Ticknor and Fields, 1854), 98.

in a military hospital who felt liberated by the savage conditions in the field. "In a wooden hut, on a sea of quaking mud under a cracking sky, I lived an immense life. I was a giant—I was colossal—I dwelt in chaos and was calm. With death let loose on the earth, I felt life pouring through me, beating in me; I exulted."[9]

Many of the pieces Borden had written during the war years remained unpublished until 1929, when she bundled them in a book, entitled *The Forbidden Zone*, which easily ranks among memoirs of World War I in a year that produced two more famous autobiographical novels: Erich Maria Remarque's *Im Westen nichts Neues* (*All Quiet on the Western Front*) and Ernest Hemingway's *A Farewell to Arms*. She described her work setting up and running a barrack that served as a reception and triage center for the wounded, the pivot of a group of twelve barracks that housed the operating rooms, a group that in turn was the core of an immense barrack emergency hospital close to the front lines. Borden and a group of elderly medics had been entrusted with the task to keep the men alive until they could reach the operating table.

> It wasn't much to look at, this reception hut. It was about as attractive as a goods yard in a railway station, but we were very proud of it, my old ones and I. We had got it ready, and it was good enough for us. We could revive the cold dead there; snatch back the men who were slipping over the edge; hoist them out of the dark abyss into life again. And because our mortality at the end of three months was only nineteen per cent., not thirty, well it was the most beautiful place in the world to me and my old grizzled Pépères, Gaston and Pierre and Leroux and the others were to me like shining archangels.[10]

Certainly, life in that barrack was not easy—in fact Mary likened it to a "dream-hell"—but there her life made sense, *there*, not in a comfortable drawing room in a manor house, where society believed she belonged.

> How crowded together we are here. How close we are in this nightmare. The wounded are packed into this place like sardines, and we are so close to them, my old ones and I. I've never been so close before to human beings. We are locked together, the old ones and I, and the wounded men; we are bound together. We all feel it. We all know it. The same thing is throbbing in us, the single thing, the one life. We are one body, suffering and bleeding. It is a kind of bliss to me to feel this. I am a little delirious, but my head is cool enough, it seems to me.[11]

Fig. 8 →

As an architecture of the present as crisis, the barrack also has a powerful hold on the imagination of those of a less delirious disposition who have faced predicament and survived to tell the story. In 1947 KLM pilot Adriaan Viruly reflected on the

9 Mary Borden, *Jane—Our Stranger* (New York: Knopf, 1923), 317

10 Mary Borden, *The Forbidden Zone* (London: William Heinemann, 1929), 148–49.

11 Ibid., 155–56.

Fig. 8
Reception room of a field hospital at Cugny, France, c. 1916. Collection: Library of Congress, Washington, DC.

Fig. 9
Construction of a barrack at Schiphol airport, the Netherlands, summer 1945. Collection: KLM Fotohistorisch Archief | MAI, Amsterdam.

great difficulties the Dutch airline had faced in 1945. A market leader in the 1920s and 1930s, after the catastrophic German occupation of the Netherlands that brought its European operations to a halt, KLM had to rebuild its fleet and network from scratch. And it had to do so from an airport in ruins. In 1940 Schiphol had been a paradigm of contemporary airport design. Used by the German Luftwaffe from 1940 onward, it had been bombed to smithereens by the British Royal Air Force and the US Army Air Forces. Five hastily erected barracks marked a new beginning. "In the summer it looked quite nice," Viruly observed in 1947, when conditions at Schiphol had already improved dramatically and KLM had become, again, a major airline with a network connecting Amsterdam to the United States, South America, South Africa, and the Dutch East Indies. It had been a very difficult time, yet also one filled with a strong romantic appeal. Viruly wrote:

> It is to this barracks camp, to this collection of primitive huts with their smoking potbellied stoves and their drafty walls, that in later years the thousand KLM employees who worked there after the liberation will think back with nostalgia in their hearts. In the years to come, Schiphol will have risen as a modern airport. People will work there in spacious, heated hangars and in bright, pleasant offices. But the time when, with numb fingers, the first engines had to be made ready to fly, and when the manifests almost ran away from cold hands in woolen mittens, will have retained a strange luster. [...]
>
> In those barracks or in the open air in all weather conditions, civil aviation was set up again, sputtering and protesting, but at the same time with speed and determination.[12]

A photograph, taken in the early summer of 1945, shows this new beginning in different ways.

← Fig. 9

The Dutch flag, forbidden during the five years of German occupation, proudly flies over the modest structure, the top of a fir tree extending skyward from its pole, heralding that, with the erection of the trusses, the building has reached its greatest height. Several men, dressed in military uniforms, are carrying a truss to be lifted into position. The already erected panels seem to be worn, the result of earlier use somewhere else. In the foreground are piles of prefabricated boards and precut beams, ready to be assembled. The description of the photo is: *Barakken in aanbouw op Schiphol. Wederopbouw* [Barracks under construction, Schiphol. Reconstruction]. The noun *Wederopbouw* was used at the time to designate not only the rebuilding of destroyed buildings, roads, railway tracks, bridges, ports, and airports but also the repair of a society that had been split apart by the pressures of conflict: friend and enemy, hero and traitor, victim and perpetrator. While the barrack in the making symbolizes the repair of the physical fabric of society, the ten men visible in the picture, joined in a common physical and moral effort, show

12 Adriaan Viruly, *Kleurenvlucht* (Joure and Utrecht: Douwe Egberts, n.d.), 6. *Note*: All translations from sources in Dutch, Danish, French, and German are made by the author.

another kind of repair: some are wearing the Dutch army beret and battledress, while others are wearing the German side cap and Wehrmacht shirts and pants. Mortal enemies a few months earlier, they now collaborate—be it under order from high.

The first chapter of the book of Genesis teaches that the secret of beginnings lies with God, but the fourth chapter, describing the story of Adam and Eve after the expulsion from paradise, teaches that humans were given the secret of how to begin again. As Auschwitz survivor Elie Wiesel believed, the "beginning again" is in many ways a greater secret than mere beginning.[13] While the case of Auschwitz shows that the barrack is a powerful symbol of catastrophe, the building under construction in Schiphol, or the one that allowed the railway engineer's parents to make a new beginning in Monowice, or the one where, during the Battle of the Somme, the wounded were kept alive so they could reach the operating table and have a fighting chance for a new life, also reveal that other, more hopeful dimension.

13 Elie Wiesel, *Messengers of God: Biblical Portraits and Legends*, trans. Marion Wiesel (New York: Summit Books, 1976), 32.

Faciat och grund

der Öfwer officerare. 1

gen såsom han här u

a, Kammar för Fältwäbeln, Sergianten, Mönst

för Corporaler. c, dito för twå Trummeslagare, ...

ras uthi. e, Rum, der i spisar att Koka uthi. f, Sänt

dare, giör Etthundrade fyratiofyra Man. g, Gången

emindan derast Soldaternas gewär pro-

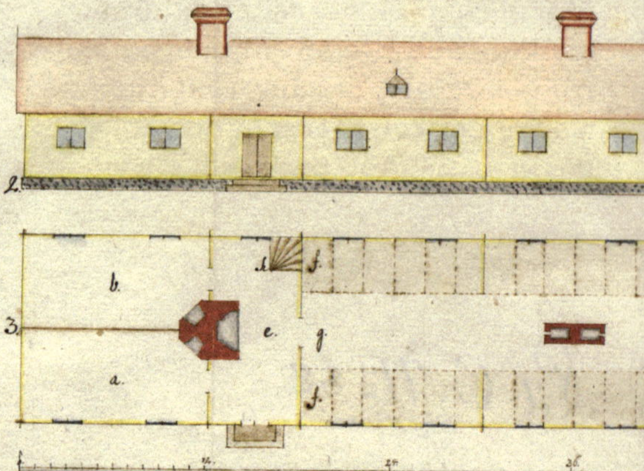

Project, hwad materialier, som requireras till En

antrellnas hwad att sådant uthi penningar ma

384. st. Sollhugne furuträ, till wäggar af 13 aln: längd

69. st. Trossning bialkar af furu af 13 alnars läng

380. st. Sparr af 10 alnars längd till taakresning

... och upståndare samt ... - á 12 ör

66. Tolfstaks läcktar, af 6 alnars längd - á 8 öre tol

160. Tolfstaks bräder af furu, af 7 alnars längd, till

rer, gaflar, Kojer, Trappor, golf, dörar, fönsterkarmar

10000. st. läcktspijk till band: läcktors och bräders fastfästande -

500. st. 6 tums spijk till Kojarnes underredning och upst

ståndares fästande - á 2 öre spijket -----

12. laß måss till wäggarnes mossning - á 8 laß

230. laß blålera och sand att älta till ...

på trossningen till ... bibehållande - a

Arbets penningar till dem som lera att älta och upläggia a

300. laß Kampstenar till tomptning och förstallens grund,

8 arbets löhn för tomptning - á 4 öre famnen ... giör ---

För sand för fall till fyllning up under fotaträn ... noga

20000. st. Murtegell till 10. spisar och 4. Kakallungar

14. st. ... till ... spisar och Kakallungar.

Summa ----

→ p. 30

fen Baraqve för Ett Compagnie footfolck, undantagan.
Baraqven såsom han är att anse för ändan. 2. faciat af bara,
, Grundrytningen, dess explication med literis marqverat. Nembl:

van, förman, furiarner och Rustmästaren. b, Kammar för
profossen. d, Vinkelstuga, som Nÿo personer kunna accommode.
Rum eller Kojer der Soldaterne kunna ligga twå uthi hwar
one, mitt uthi Kalallungar twå tillsammans. h, Trappor till
vinet och andra saker kunna förwaras.

opbyggande, efter denna åfwan stående Faciat och grundrytning, hwar med och så
, och här å ortan för nogaste prÿs upkiöpas kan, medmera som följer. Nembligen

	Dl:	öre
t	280	
ll.	69	
m		
	142	16
	16	16
ll		
till	200	
ge	72	
mt		
	7	26
	3	
ge		
t	14	12
t	7	6
at	56	8
	11	
	43	14
	311	8
t	21	
	1263	20

	Dl:	öre
Transport	1263	20
16000. st:r Taaksten till hölfwa taket och Kurornas tähkning à 25 D: tuss.	400	
13. läst: Kalk till spiys och Kalallungarnas upmurande samt tak-		
ketz understrykande — à 8 D: lästen	104	
46. Lass murusand à 3 öre lasset	4	10
30. Lass hwytler att blanda uthi murkalken à 5 öre lasset	4	12
48. üsd: swinhåår att sättia uthi understrykning kalken à 2 öre üsd:	3	
94. st:r fönster uthi wäggar, gaflar och kurar — à 1 D: stycket	94	
Smeden för 94. st:r fönster beslag, dito gångiern och låssar till 15 st:r dör-		
rar, item 14 jernankar till spiys och Kalallungar	75	
Timmermäns arbetz löhn, för upbyggning och takresning	160	
Snickarnas dito för tröskning, golf och behörig inredning	150	
Murmästarnas, Kalkslagarnas och handlangarnas löhn tillsammans	210	
Förselöhnen för murteglet och taaksten från ään till byggningplatzen à ört:	9	
Summarum Sölfwermynt	2477	20

Alt detta efter högwälborne H:r General Major och Landzhöfdingens Hans von
Delling Hausens gunstiga ordres, ödmiukeligen insinuerat. Halmst: d: 28 Feb: A:o 1699

J. Hoffman

Note on the Word "Barrack"

The *Oxford English Dictionary*, which is generally recognized as the definitive record of the English language, records the oldest meaning of the English noun "barrack" as "a temporary hut or cabin; e.g. for the use of soldiers during a siege, etc." (1617). A bit later one, "usually in plural (collective), sometimes treated as a singular," denotes "a set of buildings erected or used as a place of lodgement or residence for troops." At least in British English, the oldest meaning, while still valid, is eclipsed by the second one—also because the British Army customarily refers to a temporary soldiers' lodging as a "hut." This offers a potential source of confusion, because in many European languages the noun *barraca* (Catalan, Spanish, Portuguese), *baracca* (Italian), *baraque* (French), *Baracke* (German), *barak* (Dutch, Danish, Polish), *brakke* (Norwegian), *baracă* (Romanian), барак (Russian) signifies a temporary, mostly single-room soldiers' dwelling constructed without permanent foundations.

The *OED* suggests that the origin of this word can be found in the Spanish or Catalan noun *barraca*. More detailed investigations have established that this word emerged in Occitan, a language that was spoken in southern France and is closely related to Catalan. Most likely, it referred to a hut made of *barro* (adobe).[1] The Eighty Years' War (1568–1648), which ended with Dutch independence from Spain, and the Thirty Years' War (1618–48), which tore up central Europe and initiated the formal end of the Holy Roman Empire, brought many soldiers from southern France and Spain to the north. They carried the word *barraca* with them, which now came to be associated with a soldiers' hut. The rapid penetration of versions of *barraca* into the vocabularies of the chief European languages between 1600 and 1700 illustrates the universal importance of the architectural innovation it represented. Known as an "internationalism" in linguistic theory, the word *barraca* and its derivations suggest that it represented a technology that was widely shared in early modern Europe and that showed little variation from country to country.[2] While there are significant differences between the architectural form and technology of the barrack before and after the 1850s, within each of these two epochs, a carpenter trained to build a barrack in France would have had little difficulty constructing one in Italy or Austria.

As the derivative of the Occitan *barraca* entered various European vernaculars, it showed in general a constancy of meaning, denoting a soldiers' dwelling that was prescribed in military manuals and that was meant to shelter between

1 See Friedrich Dietz, *Etymologisches Wörterbuch der Romanischen Sprachen* (Bonn: Adolph Marcus, 1853), 43, also 47; Hensleigh Wedgwood, *A Dictionary of English Etymology*, 4 vols. (London: Trübner & Co., 1859–65), 1:115f; Hensleigh Wedgwood, *A Dictionary of English Etymology*, with notes and additions by George P. Marsh, 4 vols. (New York: Sheldon and Company, 1862), 1:77; Friedrich Kluge, *Etymologisches Wörterbuch der deutschen Sprache*, 5th ed. (Strassburg: Trübner, 1894), 28f; Friedrich Kluge, *Etymologisches Wörterbuch der deutschen Sprache*, 6th ed. (Strassburg: Trübner, 1899), 31; Gottfried Baist, "Zum 'Stamm' barr," *Romanische Forschungen* 32, no. 3 (Jan. 1913), 895; Aalto Pentti Aalto, "Contribution à l'étymologie de 'baraque,'" *Neuphilologische Mitteilungen* 39, no. 4 (1938), 375–86.

2 See Marcel Cohen, *Pour une sociologie du langage* (Paris: Albin Michel, 1956), 340–43; Paul Wexler, "Towards a Structural Definition of 'Internationalisms,'" *Linguistics* 7, no. 48 (Jan. 1969), 89–92.

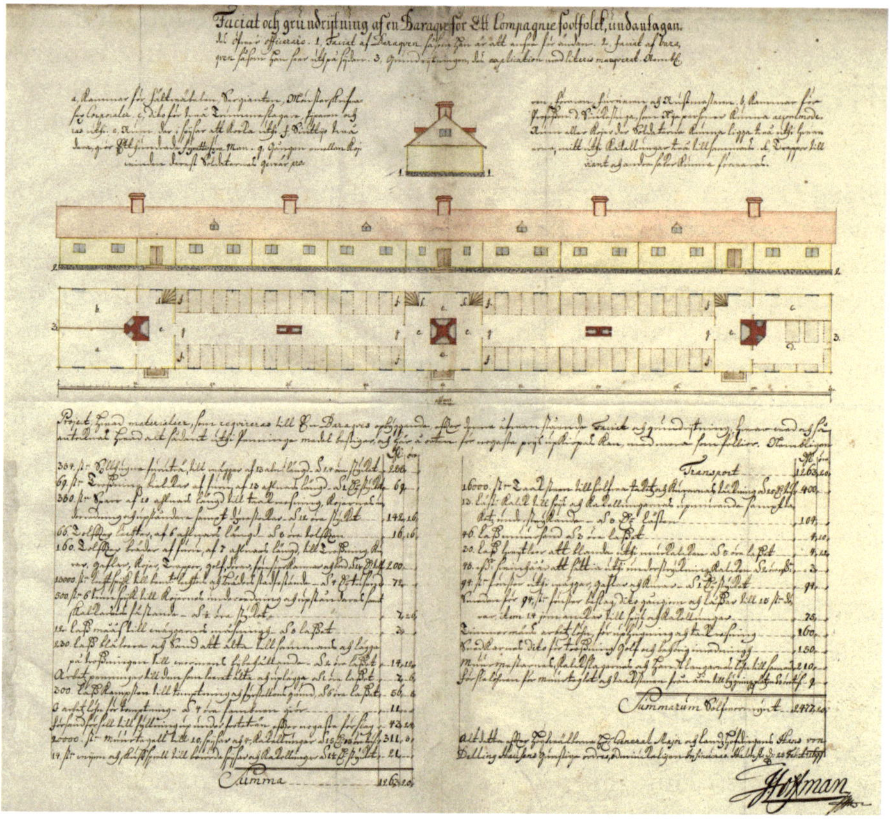

Fig. 1
Jacob Loffman, Plan and elevations of a *Baraque* in Halmstad, Sweden, 1699. Collection: Riksarkivet, Täby, Sweden.

two and twenty soldiers during sieges of fortified places or during a lengthy sojourn in the field. The *barraca* was thus less permanent than military accommodations offered in brick or stone casemates or caserns that were part of the ramparts of a fortress or walled city, and it was less temporary than a bivouac or a tent. In some languages, the meaning of the derivative of *barraca* underwent a semantic shift—often permanent but sometimes also temporary. For example, in Sweden and Denmark the words *barrack* (Swedish) and *barak* (Danish) do not refer typically to temporary dwellings built by soldiers; these were commonly known as *hydda* (Swedish) and *hytte* (Danish)—that is, huts. In general, *barrack* and *barak* denote in Sweden and Denmark more substantial, permanent single-story dormitories for soldiers constructed within fortifications. In 1699 Jacob Loffman, a military engineer from Gothenburg, drew a design for substantial timber-framed soldiers' lodgings, housing one infantry company, to be built in the city of Halmstad. The drawing identifies the structure as a *Baraque*—appropriating the French spelling—yet it clearly exceeds in scale whatever was understood as a barrack elsewhere in continental Europe.[3]

The most dramatic shift in the meaning of the derivative of *barraca* occurred in English—which causes a particular problem in any English-language book that deals with the topic of the building type that has its origin in the soldiers' dwelling.

3 Ejnar Berg, *Kaserner, baracker och hyddor: Svenska soldatboningar under fyra århundraden* (Stockholm: Almqvist & Wiksell, 1981), 77–78.

Initially, English assigned in its adoption of the word *barraca* a meaning that was in line with the use of the word elsewhere. In the beginning of the seventeenth century, when English lexicographer John Minsheu included the Spanish noun *barraca* in the Spanish–English vocabulary printed at the end of his *Ductor in Linguas, The Guide into Tongues*, remembered as the first etymological dictionary of the English language, he described *barraca* first in Latin, as (in translation) "a soldier's hut made from a sail or canvas," and subsequently somewhat loosely translated this as "a souldier's tent, or a booth, or such like thing made of the sayle of a shippe, or such like stuffe," to which he added, "properly speaking, it is a hut by the sea for fishermen."[4] Minsheu did not suggest an anglicized version of the word. In the seventeenth century some English authors make occasional references to barracks as soldiers' huts. In his *History of the Campagne in the Spanish Netherlands, Anno Dom. 1694*, military chaplain Edward d'Auvergne mentioned that in September of that year, English soldiers campaigning in what is today Belgium had received orders to prepare their winter quarters by taking down their tents and making "Baracques or Huts of straw."[5] The English philologist John Kersey did not list an English derivate of the Occitan *barraca* in his *New English Dictionary* (1702), which focused on words in common usage. However, he did include the noun "Barrach or Barraque" in his expanded and revised seventh edition of the more comprehensive *New World of Words: or, Universal English Dictionary*, by Edward Phillips, originally published in 1658. In Kersey's 1720 version, a barrack is defined as "a Hut like a little Cottage for Soldiers to lodge in a Camp, when they have no Tents, or when an Army lies long in a Place of bad Weather."[6] This definition still matched the one current at that time in the languages of the continent.

By 1720 an expanded meaning that referred to the plural "barracks" as a set of buildings used as a permanent place of lodgment for troops, constructed out of brick or stone, had become the dominant meaning in English. A first instance of this semantic shift is found in a document concerning the construction of permanent soldiers' lodgings north of the Tower of London, in the yard of the Irish Mint. In 1685 the Board of Ordnance ordered a contract to be drawn up "with all possible speede for ye building ye Barracks in ye Comptrollers Garden in ye Mint."[7] These barracks were substantial and permanent buildings. At that time, many other European languages had adopted for such buildings a derivative of another word from Occitan, *quazerna*, originally meaning a room that holds four people. The modernization of fortifications in sixteenth- and seventeenth-century continental Europe, which prompted the construction of first four-person, and later more-person, soldiers' lodgings in the bastions and curtain walls, led to the adoption of derivatives

4 John Minsheu, *Ductor in Linguas, The Guide into Tongues* (London: John Brown, 1617).

5 Edward d'Auvergne, *The History of the Campagne in the Spanish Netherlands, Anno Dom. 1694, With the Journal of the Siege of Huy* (London: Matt. Wotton and John Newton, 1694), 75.

6 Edward Phillips, *The New World of Words: or, Universal English Dictionary* (London: J. Philips, 1720).

7 Quoted in Geoffrey Parnell, "Putting the Barracks Back in the Tower of London," *London Archaeologist* 12 (Spring 2011), 328.

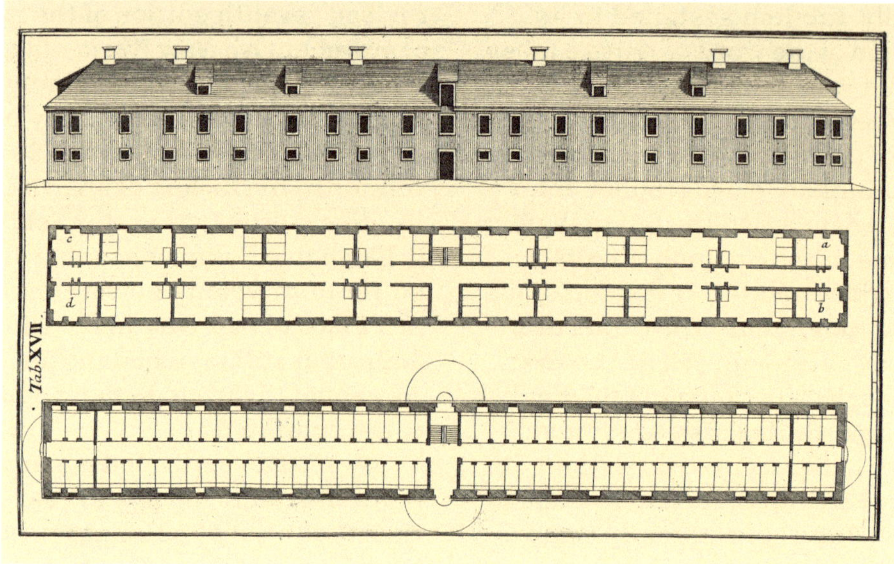

Fig. 2
Leonhard Christoph Sturm, Design for a Kaserne accommodating a cavalry squadron of 100 men and 100 horses, from his *Architectura Civili-Militaris*, 1719. Collection: Sächsische Landesbibliothek, Dresden.

of *quazerna* in many languages: *caserma* (Italian), *caserne* (French), *Kaserne* (German), *kazerne* (Dutch), *kasern* (Swedish), and so on. The term also penetrated into English, as *cazern*, *casern*, or *caserne*, but it never became common. Inhabiting a relatively unified island nation safe from foreign invasion, the English did not experience sieges of their cities and hence could afford to forgo the construction of fortifications with four- or more-person soldiers' quarters. Consequently, the noun *casern* never got traction in English.

Great Britain's position as a military outlier relative to the nations on the continent had another unique linguistic result: instead of the noun "barrack," the word "hut"—commonly denoting a normally single-room dwelling of simple construction, without foundations, fireplace, or fenestration, fabricated from readily available building materials such as boards, logs, branches, loam, or stones for walls, and boards, shingles, straw, turf, skins, canvas, matting, or cardboard for the roof—came to refer to the provisional dwelling for soldiers known, for example, in German, as *Baracke*. And the more spacious, permanent soldiers' quarters known as *Kaserne* in German came to be known in Great Britain as "barracks."

In an English-language study of a building type that had such a divergent linguistic history, it is helpful to clarify the use of terminology. English texts will be quoted without any modification, which means that the noun used to denote a provisional soldiers' dwelling will usually be "hut." However, outside of quotations, I will consistently use the noun "barrack" when referring to the building type named after the Occitan *barraca*, relying for justification on the fact that it is, as the *OED* acknowledges, the oldest meaning of the word that denotes the building type commonly referred to as *barraca*, *baracca*, *baraque*, *Baracke*, *barak*, *brakke*, *baracă*, and барак in various continental European languages.

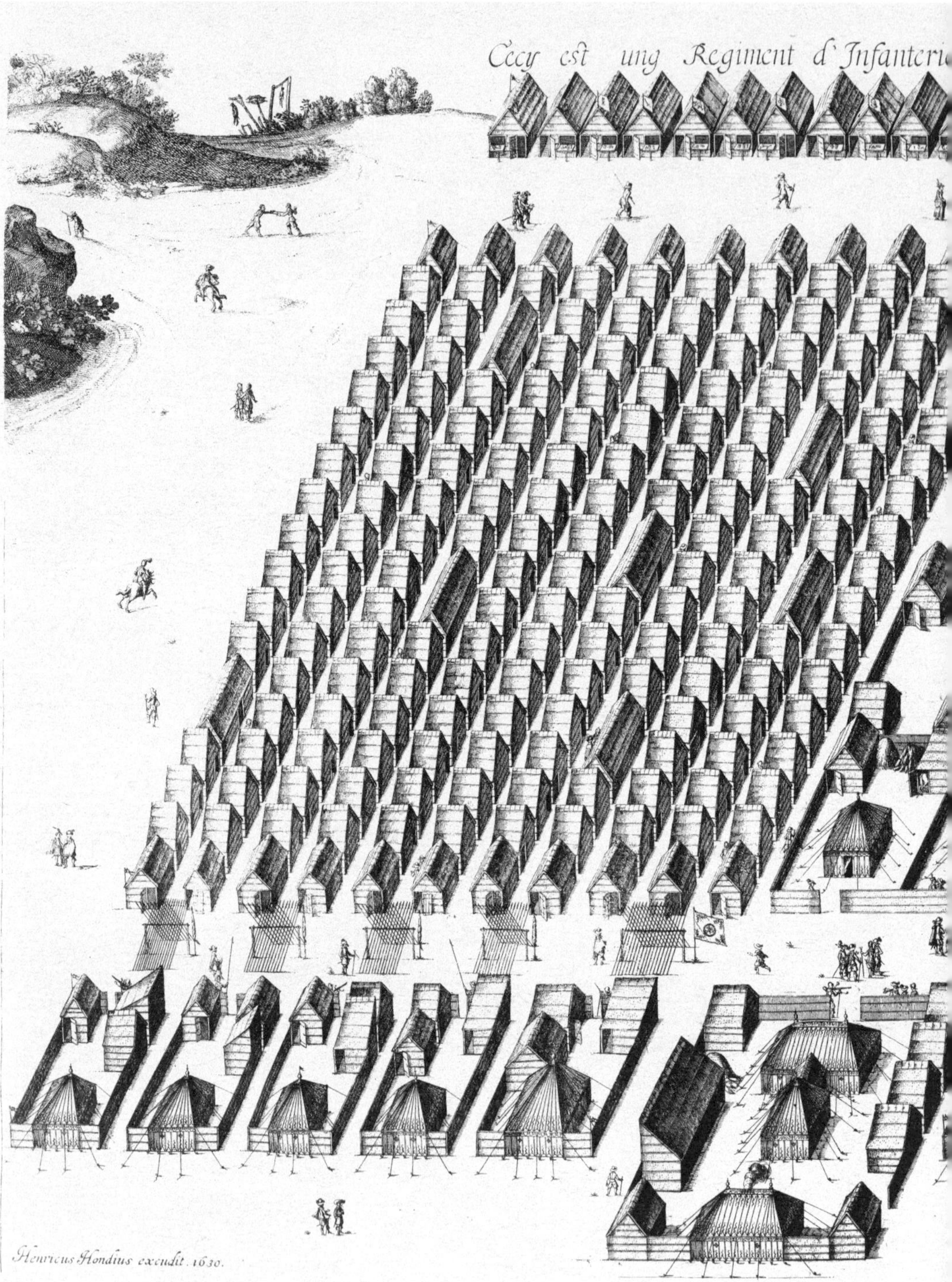
Cecy est ung Regiment d'Infanteri
Henricus Hondius excudit. 1630.

→ p. 51

Dit is een Regiment Voet-volck,

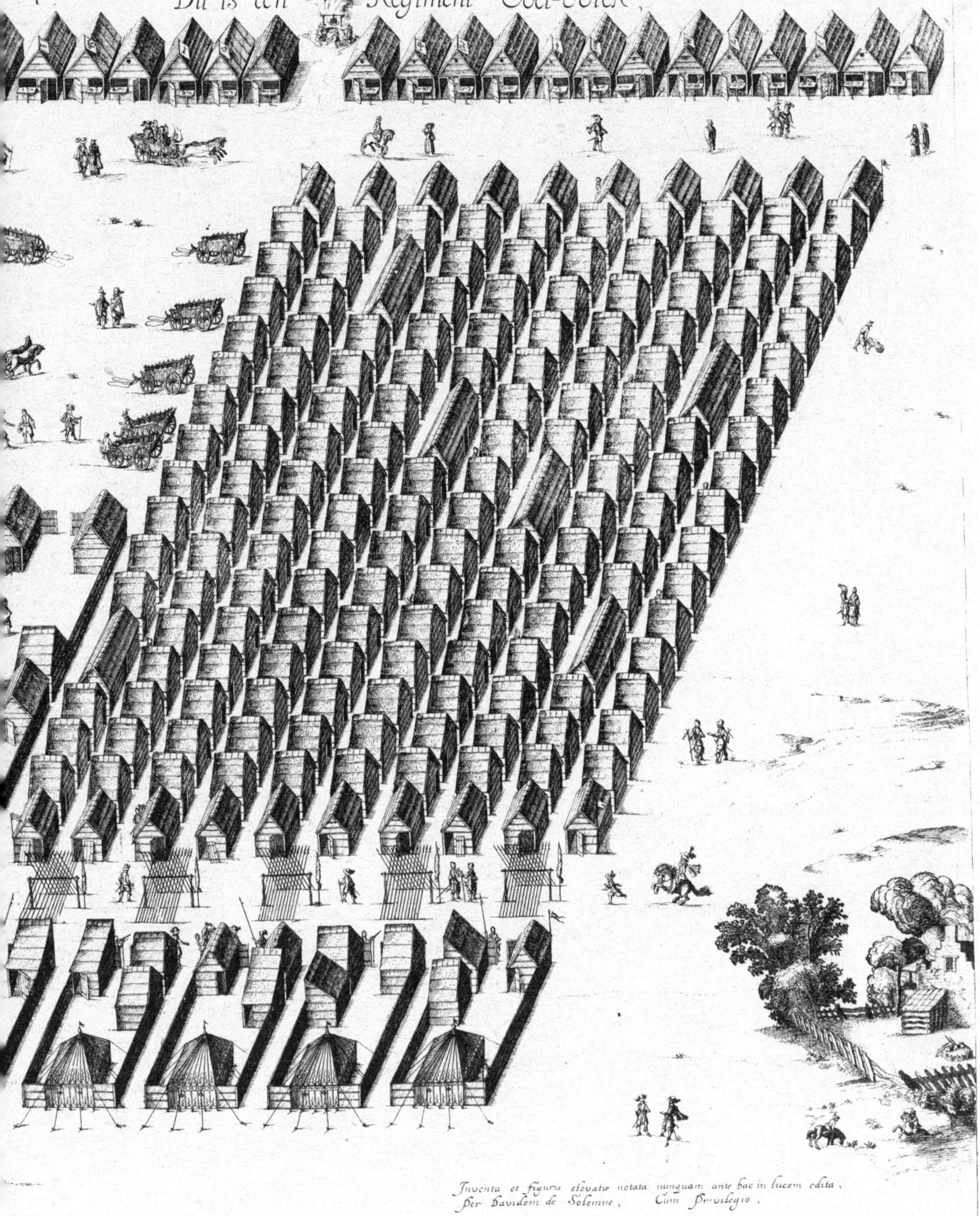

Inventa et figuris elevatis notata nunquam ante hac in lucem edita,
Per Davidem de Solemne, Cum Privilegio.

One

With the Means at Hand

On November 7, 1850, Frederik Christian Lund sketched the interior of a Danish field-guard *barakke* (barrack) erected in the Duchy of Schleswig. Two years earlier, the twenty-four-year-old graduate of the Royal Danish Academy of Fine Arts had volunteered for service in the Danish army to fight an insurgency by German nationalists in both Schleswig and the adjacent Duchy of Holstein. Both territories were ruled by the king of Denmark, and provided half of the tax revenue of Danish unified monarchy, but neither territory was fully integrated in the Danish state.

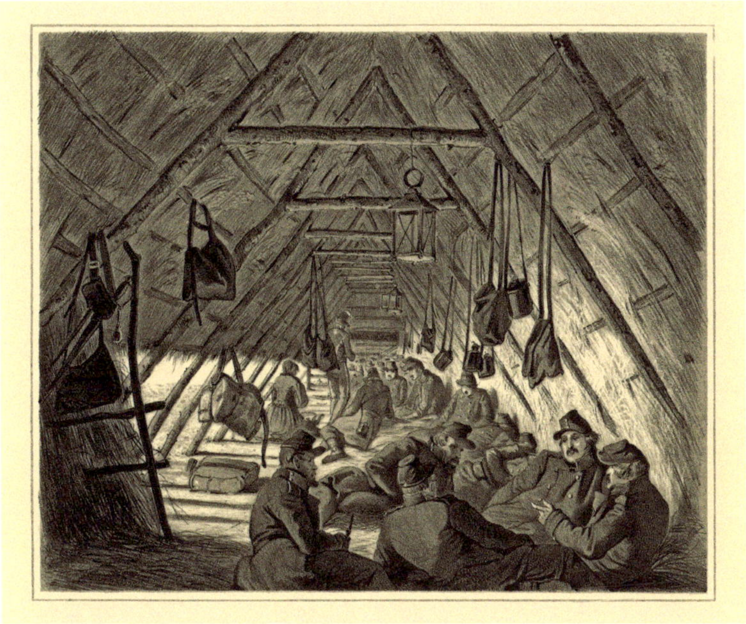

Fig. 1
Frederik Christian Lund, Interior of a Royal Danish Army field-guard barrack in Cugraben at Danevirke, November 7, 1850. Collection: Kongelige Bibliotek, Copenhagen.

Half of the population of Schleswig, and almost all of the inhabitants of Holstein, spoke German as their mother tongue. To complicate matters even more, Holstein was also part of the German Confederation—a loose alliance of German states centered on the Kingdom of Prussia and its traditional rival, the Austrian Empire. In 1848, a year of nationalistic revolutions all over Europe, King Frederick VII of Denmark declared Schleswig to be an integral part of his kingdom, triggering an uprising in which the German-speaking rebels aimed for an immediate severance of all political ties between the two duchies and the Danish Crown, their unification and a full integration into the German Reich proclaimed by a newly constituted National Assembly in Frankfurt. The Royal Danish Army mobilized to counter a Prussian invasion force, and Lund was one of many young men who saw it as his patriotic duty to protect the *fædreland*. For three years, making sketches as circumstances allowed, he lived the life of a soldier in a skirmish known in the English-speaking world as the First Schleswig War.

Erected at the age-old Danevirke earthwork fortifications, Lund's *barakke*, constructed from wooden trusses connected by purlins and covered by straw, is both simple and efficient. The relaxed postures of the soldiers, who had built their temporary shelter on the basis of a simple set of instructions issued in an army manual, suggest that it provided a sense of comfort on what might have been a cold fall day. The barrack drawn by Lund was of a standard type used by many armies, including that raised by the rebels who had taken up arms against the Danish king. The simple A-frame structure, with a straw-covered roof and board-covered gables that incorporate a door and a small window, provided an obvious solution to the problem of instant shelter in the field.

Fig. 2
Frederik Christian Lund, The Royal Danish Army picket at Rønhave on Als, May 27, 1849. Collection: Kongelige Bibliotek, Copenhagen.

While in the eighteenth-century armies in the field had been generally equipped with tents, these forms of instant shelter had been abandoned first by the French Revolutionary Army, in the early 1790s, and by the middle of the first decade of the nineteenth century no major European army used canvas to house soldiers. Barracks, made with whatever construction material was at hand, but which followed a limited number of standardized designs, were the go-to solution when billeting soldiers in existing buildings or bivouacking in the open air proved impossible, impractical, or inadvisable.

In the course on military construction during campaigns that he taught at the Royal Danish Military Academy (established in 1713), Captain Ehrenreich Christopher Ludvig Koefoed, a military engineer, described the construction of the barrack in considerable detail, providing also a section and a plan of the building type that had housed Lund and his comrades.

Drawings, Koefoed's Danish Standard Barrack
→ p. 508

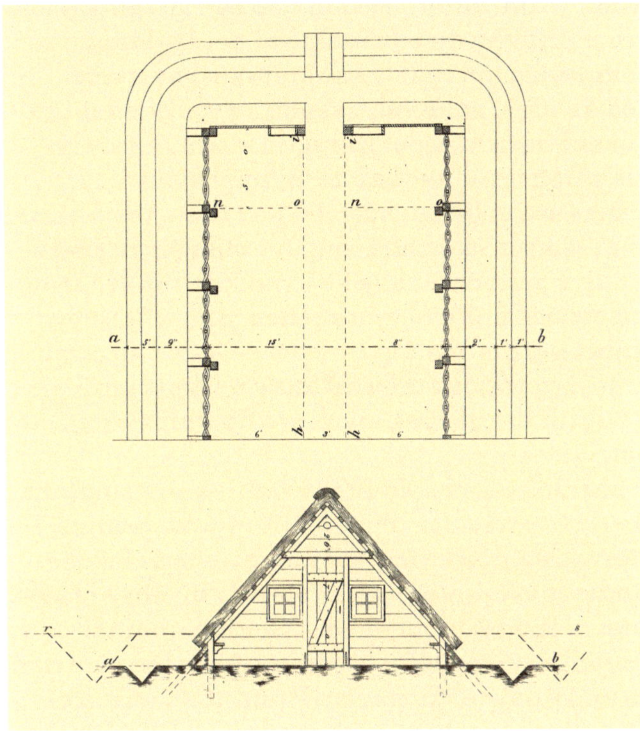

Fig. 3
Ehrenreich Christopher Ludvig Koefoed, Design for a standard Danish barrack, from his *Krigsbygningskunst for Officersskolens naestaeldste Klasse*, 1868. Collection: Forsvarsakademiet, Copenhagen.

The base was 5 meters wide, and at intervals of 1.5 meters, the soldiers were to erect frames consisting of two beams, each 12 by 12 centimeters across and 4.5 meters long, which, spaced 5 meters from each other, were to be rammed 90 centimeters into the ground, at an angle of around 45 degrees, in such a manner that they met at the top. The full height inside was 2.6 meters, and at around 1.8 meters, a collar tie was to connect the two beams. Up to seven of such frames, connected by purlins, were to create a framework for a barrack that measured in plan 5.2 by 9 meters, providing accommodation for a platoon of thirty soldiers in two rows of fifteen, with each soldier assigned a sleeping space of 0.6 by 1.8 meters. While in principle the number of A-frames was unlimited, Koefoed counseled against increasing the length of the building, as cross ventilation, provided by means of the door, windows, and a special air opening at each end, would be insufficient at the greater length. The roof was covered with either thatch or straw, and if the former material was used, a layer of turf was to be added,

Koefoed advised: "Roofing with straw is always preferable to roofing with thatch; it is less hot in summer, less cold in winter, and more resistant to rain; it takes less time, but requires more people and much straw.[1]

Koefoed offered two versions of this standard barrack: the first was to be constructed on grade, and the second required an excavation of 60 centimeters into the ground. The latter version had the advantage of being warmer and the disadvantage of being damp. Koefoed acknowledged that these standard barracks represented an ideal solution, assuming the availability of dimensioned beams—something that would rarely be available when a shelter had to be improvised: "If, therefore, huts are to be built for a short time, to be used only in the milder season, and only for shorter period of time, simpler materials may be used: the timber may be replaced by logs and thick branches, the rafters by thinner branches, the roofing by wattles, etc."[2] In other words, his design was, in the end, only a license to improvise within the general parti set by Danish military custom.

The barrack described in the Danish instructions belonged to the vernacular of many European armies. Yet it is interesting to see how the conditions of its use might be understood somewhat differently in other places. For example, in the main field construction manual issued between 1850 and 1900 to officers from the Austrian (until 1866) and Austro-Hungarian (from 1866 onward) army, the A-frame structure appears in exactly the same dimensions, holding the same number of soldiers, as described in the Danish manual. Yet, depending on the solidity of construction, the name for it varies. The more permanent version constructed from lumber is designated the status of *Nothbarake* (emergency barrack) and considered to be the lesser version of the *gewöhnliche Barake* (ordinary barrack), which in contrast to the A-frame *Nothbarake* has regular walls. The lighter version of the A-frame barrack, created out of lighter poles and whatever material may be at hand, is known as a *Feldhütte* (field hut) and, depending on the roofing material, also as either a *Reisighütte* (brushwood hut), a *Schilfhütte* (reed hut), or a *Strohhütte* (straw hut).[3]

The first edition of the Austrian manual was published in 1850—the same year Lund drew the interior of the *barakke* at the Danevirke. Eight editions followed over the next forty years, in which the instructions concerning the construction of barracks during military campaigns did not change. It is remarkable that the dramatic advancements in both military and architec-

1 Ehrenreich Christopher Ludvig Koefoed, *Laerebog til Brug bed Forelaesningerne over Krigsbygningskunst for Officersskolens naestaeldste Klasse* (Copenhagen: F. S. Muhle, 1868), 277.

2 Ibid., 278.

3 Konstantin Wasserthal Edler von Zuccari, *Technischer Pionier-Dienst im Felde* (Vienna: Carl Gerold und Sohn, 1850), 162–64.

tural technology in those four decades, which radically transformed warfare, did not touch this most domestic part of a soldier's existence in the field. The same can be said for the most modern and technologically advanced army in the second half of the nineteenth century, the military force maintained by Prussia and, from 1871 onward, the German Reich. The *Lager- und Wegebau-Anleitung* (Camp and roads construction guide), published by the end of the century for use in the German army, provided by and large the same models as those in the Danish and Austrian manuals and offered more or less the same instructions.[4]

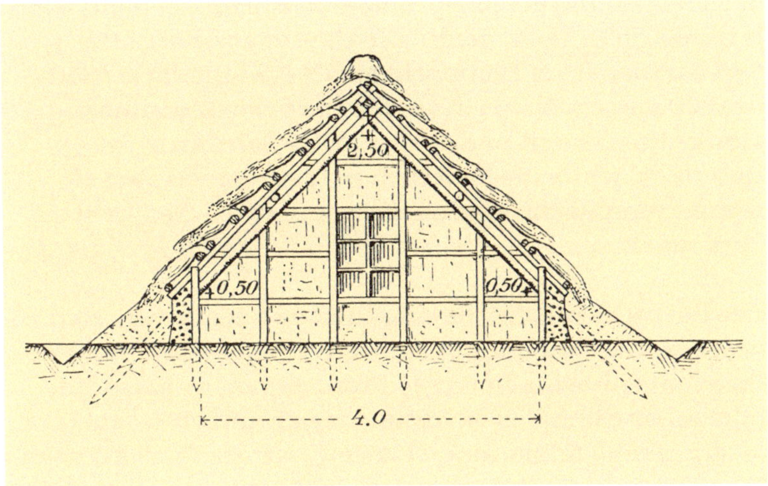

Fig. 4
Section of a German Army barrack made from poles and covered with straw, from German Reich, German Army, *Lager- und Wegebau-Anleitung*, 1896. Collection: author.

Lund's drawing of the barrack on the Danevirke is the very first depiction of the *interior* of a barrack. Before 1850, we have a relatively limited body of drawings and engravings that illustrate the exterior of this modest architectural type, but no draftsman thought the interior space of enough importance to spend time and effort on recording it. Since the late nineteenth century, when the German art critic August Schmarsow defined architecture as the art that creates space, many architects have rightly understood their primary contribution to society in terms of space making—if only because it is the part of their profession in which they can claim preeminence; as far as construction is concerned, architects typically defer to engineers; in terms of craftsmanship, architects must acknowledge cabinetmakers as their betters; and in artistic content, the skills of the painter or sculptor trump those of the architect. But in terms of space making, architects are without equals. When Lund decided to preserve, in a quickly drawn sketch, the interiority of the barrack in which he and his comrades found shelter at the end of a day of patrols in a hostile environment, he might have intuited that his

4 German Reich, German Army, *Lager- und Wegebau-Anleitung* (Berlin: W. Bath, 1896), 13–31.

time within that structure marked a symbolic passage in the history of this building type—one that was to be confirmed in the next decade, when the barrack both formally and dramatically entered the stage of history in a blaze of publicity.

As to the First Schleswig War, it ended inconclusively. In 1851 the major European powers forced Denmark, the insurgents, and their German backers to restore the situation to the *status quo ante*, in which Schleswig and Holstein were both part of the kingdom of Denmark but not integrated within the state. The Schleswig-Holstein Question remained, for the next decades, an intractable problem in European politics. It flared up in 1864, leading to the separation of the two duchies from Denmark, and it was finally settled in 1920 when a plebiscite led to the permanent inclusion of the Danish-speaking part of Schleswig in Denmark, while the southern part remained part of the German Reich—the successor state of the German Confederation.

The barracks created during the First Schleswig War represented examples of a military vernacular architecture that served to house soldiers during a campaign. Like other examples of vernacular architecture, its origin can be found in a relatively straightforward need for shelter, in a particular geography with a particular climate, locally available materials, and existing building practices. Its beginning, like the beginning of most vernacular architecture, is lost in what Thomas Mann labeled as the bottomless well of the past. One of them may be located in the camp of the Spanish Army as it besieged, in 1572, the Dutch city of Haarlem. The investment of Haarlem was a direct result of the messy aftermath of a badly considered division of the Habsburg lands following the abdication, in 1555, of the Holy Roman emperor Charles V. Born in 1500 as heir of the Netherlands and Austria through his father's lineage, and heir of Spain through his mother's, Charles had expanded his heritage into an empire that included a significant part of Europe and large holdings in the Americas. Yet the glory inherent in *el imperio donde nunca se pone el sol* (an empire on which the sun never sets) did not bring much happiness to its ruler. The Protestant Reformation, which began even before his ascent to the imperial dignity, destroyed his peace of mind—as did epilepsy and gout. Worn out at the age of fifty-four, he divested himself of his sovereign powers and dignities in 1555. His brother, Ferdinand, received

Austria, Bohemia, and Hungary, and also obtained the dignity of Holy Roman emperor; Spain and the Spanish Empire in the Americas went to his son Philip, as did the Kingdom of Naples, Duchy of Milan, and the Netherlands. King Philip II believed in unifying his far-flung realm through centralized policies and standardized procedures. This did not work in the Netherlands, where the seventeen lands that made up the territory enjoyed a decentralized administration rooted in the high level of autonomy of its numerous towns and cities. In addition, the devoutly Roman Catholic Philip's inflexible approach to dissent did not prove an effective way to address the tensions created by the Reformation in the Netherlands. When, in 1566, Calvinist mobs attacked churches and monasteries, defacing religious statues, Philip II appointed his most successful and trusted general, Fernando Álvarez de Toledo, 3rd Duke of Alba, as *Stadhouder* (literally, "city-holder," or governor) of the territory. The Duke of Alba initiated a ruthless policy of religious suppression, which triggered an uprising in 1568. The rebels found a leader in German-born William I, Prince of Orange and Count of Nassau.

In July 1572, Haarlem, located 16 kilometers west of Amsterdam, joined the rebellion. In response, the Duke of Alba ordered his son Fadrique Álvarez de Toledo, a ruthless senior commander of the Ejército de Flandes (Army of Flanders), to return Haarlem to the fold. Don Fadrique had a good track record in such matters. He had just forced the surrender of the rebel city of Mechelen, and before turning his attention to Haarlem, he "pacified" the towns of Zutphen and Naarden, killing most of the civilian population. On December 11, 1572, the Army of Flanders arrived at the gates of Haarlem. It was very late in the year, and with the onset of winter, the fighting season had effectively ended. However, Don Fadrique wanted to crown the year with the subjection of the largest rebel city in the Netherlands; he expected that a single, massive assault would crumble Haarlem's defenses. This did not happen; the soldiers of the Army of Flanders, many of whom had been forced to bivouac in the open air while the army assembled and made camp, proved ill prepared for a decisive assault, and after the news of the massacres in Zutphen and Naarden, the 3,000-man garrison and citizens of Haarlem were highly motivated to defend the city. The defenders prevailed in the first battle. With the honor of both his father and the monarchy at stake, Don Fadrique ordered a siege: the army was to stay where it was. Soon soldiers began to freeze in their tents. Army paymaster Alonso de Alameda, who was responsible for supplies, reported that soldiers left their positions around the city, "in search of firewood to burn and tables and beams for shelter, tearing down houses and making *barracas*.[5]

Haarlem-born cartographer Thomas Thomaszoon visited the Spanish positions in 1573. On four joined sheets of paper, he made a large drawing, sketching Haarlem Lake (now the site of Schiphol airport), with the besieged city of Haarlem in the background, and Huis ter Kleef, the castle that served as Don Fadrique's headquarters, in the foreground. He also depicted the hutted camps that housed the Army of Flanders, showing that the *barracas* were simple structures made of wood and straw, of approximately 1.8 by 3.7 meters.

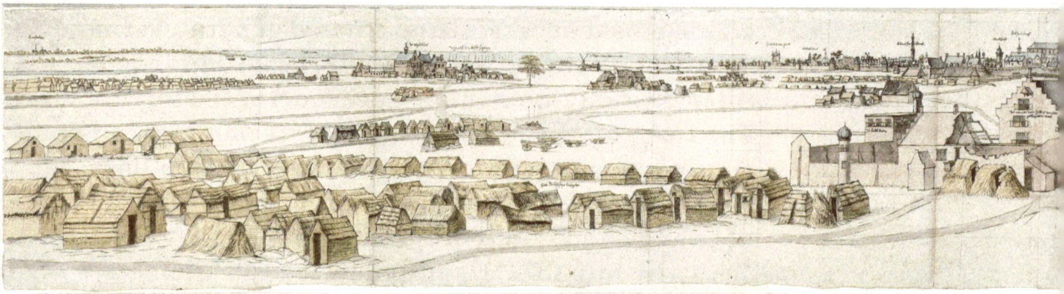

Fig. 5
Thomas Thomaszoon, View of the headquarters of the Spanish in the Huis ter Kleef during the siege of Haarlem, 1572–73. Collection: Noord-Hollands Archief, Haarlem.

The siege of Haarlem proved successful: after eight months, the citizens ran out of food and negotiated a surrender; a payment of 240,000 guilders was to save their lives and the city from pillage. Don Fadrique violated the agreement and ordered the execution of most of the garrison and forty civilians. In response, the rebels produced broadsheets depicting the hangings, beheadings, and drownings, propaganda that strengthened the resolve of other rebel-held cities not to surrender on any terms. As a result, the Army of Flanders proved unable to blockade nearby cities like Alkmaar and Leiden into submission, and by the end of the sixteenth century, the Low Countries were effectively cut into two equal parts, with the independent, Protestant-dominated Republic of the Seven United Netherlands (also known as the Dutch Republic) in the north, and the Roman Catholic Royal Netherlands (also known as the Spanish, Habsburg, or Southern Netherlands) in the south.

In the Southern Netherlands, the inhabitants were forced to billet the Army of Flanders, which had effectively become a permanent army of occupation. King Philip II did not care much about the resulting bitterness of the local population, but in May 1598, months before his death, he granted sovereignty to the Southern Netherlands under the rule of his daughter Isabella Clara

5 In Geoffrey Parker, *The Army of Flanders and the Spanish Road, 1567–1659: The Logistics of Spanish Victory and Defeat in the Low Countries' Wars* (Cambridge: Cambridge University Press, 1972), 166.

Eugenia, infanta of Spain, and his son-in-law-to-be Archduke Albert of Habsburg. The transfer of sovereign authority from Madrid to Brussels was conditional on the continued presence of the Spanish-controlled Army of Flanders. Seeking support for his rule, Albert sought to lessen the burden of the army on the civilian population and ordered the soldiers to leave the houses where they were billeted and house themselves by constructing small *baracques* in the towns and cities.[6]

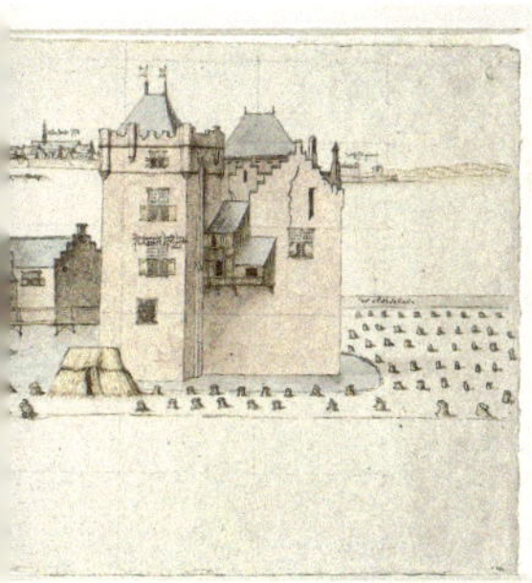

In the history of the barrack, Thomas Thomaszoon's drawing marks the beginning of a transition from a period characterized by an unregulated and relatively irregular use of the barrack to one defined by first prescription and then, from 1850 onward, rapid technological development. It marks a beginning but not an origin, which is, as historian Marc Bloch articulated in a reflection on the "Idol of Origins," "a beginning which explains" or "a beginning which is a complete explanation."[7] The history of the barrack as a significant building type begins only in the mid-1800s—in fact, three years after the conclusion of the First Schleswig War—when the seed represented by the barracks created by the soldiers of the Army of Flanders, the *barakker* erected by soldiers of the Royal Danish Army, and the *Baracken* used by the Schleswig-Holstein insurgents (and all the other vernacular barracks described in this chapter) falls into a fertile soil of nineteenth-century nationalism, communication, transport, and construction technologies. The barracks created in the 280 years that separate the siege of Haarlem from the Crimean War (1853–56), in which the barrack became of central concern to soldiers, officers, journalists, politicians, and the public at large, do not represent a dormant future ready to unfold in 1854. If the barrack had not become a vitally important building type in the second half of the nineteenth century, or later, the earlier history described in this chapter would have been forgotten and deservedly so. But as it did become important in 1854, it created, *ex post facto*, a series of precursors, among which those depicted by Thomas Thomaszoon are examples of the earliest we have in a contemporary visual account.

6 Ibid.
7 Marc Bloch, *The Historian's Craft*, trans. Peter Putnam (New York: Knopf, 1953), 30.

Barracks are anomalous works of architecture. They are similar to the most basic of dwellings—simple, single-story and single-room buildings constructed without stone foundations out of readily available building materials. But they are different from the typical dwellings of so-called primitive cultures because barracks represent only one form of shelter among many other more sophisticated ones. And they are different from the hovels, shacks, or shanties built as cheap abodes for the poor at the margins of towns and cities or as quick shelters in fields, forests, and wilderness and at edges of rivers and seas for hop pickers, peat cutters, shepherds, hunters, foresters, loggers, charcoal burners, bark peelers, prospectors, fishers, and adventurers. The difference is located in the circumstance that barracks are constructed to serve the needs of soldiers who live and operate within a less or more developed command hierarchy that imposes many rules and prescriptions to ensure a predictable operation in the chaos of combat. The soldiers who constructed and inhabited those apparently primitive *barracas* outside of Haarlem were anything but primitive: highly trained professionals, they knew that they belonged to the most accomplished army in the known world.

The Army of Flanders represented a perfected form of a new kind of fighting force that fought a new kind of war. In the sixteenth century armies had changed from small, fast-moving, and relatively expensive cavalry formations dominated by nobles, for whom fighting was one of many other activities—running an estate, administering a territory, attending court, and so on—to the large, slow-moving, and relatively cheap infantry formations consisting of commoners who had chosen the (quite literally) fashionable career of *Landsknecht* (pikeman) and served in the army under standard contracts that gave them specific rights and obligations within a well-defined chain of command and the promise of regular pay. These new armies did not only operate during the short fighting season that defined medieval warfare. In response to the increasing use of guns, architects and engineers had developed new ways of fortifying cities by means of bastions, low curtain walls, and systems of ravelins and crown works. These new fortifications made it almost impossible to conquer a city by creating a breach in the wall and following it up with a direct assault. Now a blockade leading to famine among the besieged became the only means to conquer a fortified place. A siege could last very long—seven months in the case of Haarlem, a year in the case of Leiden and

Antwerp, three years in the case of Ostend. Prolonged sieges necessitated the creation of more permanent shelters for the soldiers of the besieging army. In the second half of the seventeenth century, Roger Boyle, Earl of Orrery, summarized this transformation in his *Treatise of the Art of War*: "In ancient times they used tents, instead of huts, for then the way of making war was in the field, and armies were daily in motion, and in such cases, straw, rushes and flags to cover, and wood to make stakes and roofs, were not always at hand, nor to form the roof easie, but now that for the most part war is made in the besieging of strong places, or in standing camps, both officers and soldiers use to hut, which is more warm and lasting than tents."[8]

In the late sixteenth century, Roman antiquity was the main source of inspiration for confronting apparently novel problems—the adverb "apparently" is used here because, in the view of Renaissance scholars, the course of history does not generate new things because human nature does not change. Historical recurrence means that general rules for current behavior can be found in the past. Niccolò Machiavelli articulated this view in his *Discorsi sopra la prima deca di Tito Livio* (Discourses on the first ten [books] of Titus Livy): "Wise men say (and perhaps not unjustly) that in order to form an impression of what is yet to come, we ought to consider what is already passed; for there is nothing in this world at present, or at any other time, but has and will have its counterpart in antiquity; which happens because these things are operated by human beings who, having the same passions in all ages, must necessarily behave uniformly in similar situations."[9] The practices of antiquity were not only relevant but also authoritative, because the ancients were superior to the moderns.

In the case of warfare, one did not need much demonstration to grasp the superiority of ancient Rome. Conducting its wars with professional armies deployed in a determined fashion without irresolution and without halfway measures, Rome had been triumphant in every conflict, causing the permanent subjection of its enemies. Of course, the invention of gunpowder and the introduction of guns had made some aspects of Roman military tactics obsolete. But as to Roman army organization and its logistics, important lessons could be—and were—learned. In his Ἱστορίαι (*Histories*), the Greek historian Polybius had deemed the standardized arrangement of Roman march formation, army camps, and battle order both "noble" and "great" and "genuinely worth observation and knowledge."[10] Descriptions of a

8 Roger Boyle, Earl of Orrery, *A Treatise of the Art of War* (London: Henry Herringman, 1677), 86.
9 Niccolò Machiavelli, *Discourses on Livy*, trans. Leslie J. Walker (London: Routledge and Paul, 1950), 43.
10 Polybius, *Histories of Polybius*, 2 vols., trans. Evelyn S. Shuckburgh (London and New York: Macmillan, 1889), 1:481.

Roman camp by Polybius, Hyginus Gromaticus, Aelianus Tacticus, or Flavius Vegetius provided descriptions of the key principle that guided the general arrangement of the Roman camp: facility in finding one's way. Because every camp is laid out in the same fashion, every soldier, even after a long march, will know where to pitch his tent.

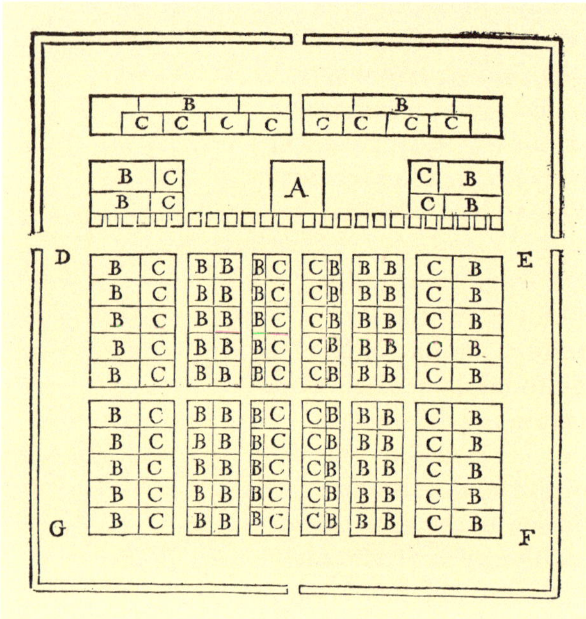

Fig. 6
Simon Stevin, Plan of a Roman military camp as described by Polybius, from Stevin's *Castrametatio*, 1618. (A) indicates the headquarters, (B) the lodgings for infantry, and (C) lodgings and stables for cavalry. Collection: Bibliothèque Nationale de France, Paris.

All these accounts concerned a *castra aestiva* (summer camp), created in the field during a campaign and designed to be used for sometimes as little as one night. As the fighting season typically began in the early spring, to last into the fall, the soldiers sheltered in a summer camp *sub pellibus* or *sub tentoriis* (under tents). When cold set in, soldiers would take up residence in a *castra hiberna* (winter camp). This was a mostly permanent fortress, equipped with solid timber or brick dormitories. Neither Polybius nor the other authors found a need to describe them; to the soldiers, they were quite literally a given.

When soldiers had to create a *temporary* winter camp because they had not been able to return to a permanent one in time, they had to construct barracks. Livy's *Ab urbe condita libri* (Books from the founding of the city) reports that the Romans used barracks when the generals decided to conquer Veii, not through a direct assault but through what turned out to be a lengthy siege (c. 400 BCE). In Rome, the tribunes representing the common people protested the, at that time, unprecedented decision to maintain the army over the winter. "Perennial war"—lasting beyond the usual fighting season of late spring, summer, and early fall—was tantamount to “slavery.”[11] Yet the generals had cleverly anticipated the protests by the tribunes, and when the cold weather set in, ordered “the erection of winter quarters—a new thing to the Roman soldier.”[12]

The oldest description of such winter shelters can be found in Livy’s account of the Roman occupation of Capua (211 BCE) during the Second Carthaginian (or Punic) War (218–201 BCE). The soldiers had been billeted in town, but Proconsul Quintus Fulvius Flaccus feared that “the great charms of the city might weaken his army also, as they had Hannibal’s. Accordingly he had compelled them to build their own shelters soldier-fashion at the gates and along the walls.” Most of these were “made of wickerwork and planks, others of reeds interwoven, all of them thatched with straw.”[13] Julius Caesar also used straw-covered barracks, in 51 BCE, when he ordered his men to create winter quarters in Cenabum (today’s Orléans, France) by applying a layer of straw to the walls of tents and covering their roofs with thatch.[14] The accounts by Livy and Caesar were well known in the sixteenth century, and Paymaster Alonso de Alameda might have taken some comfort from the fact that when Don Fadrique ordered the creation of improvised winter quarters for the Army of Flanders in December 1572, he could point to the example given by the ancients. Yet the detailed descriptions of Roman camps offered by Polybius and the others did not offer any guidance as to the size, shape, or materials of their barracks, nor did they provide instructions for their construction.

But a more systematic approach to the construction of barracks was ready to make an entrance. While the fall of Haarlem almost brought the rebels to their knees, the successful defense of first Alkmaar and subsequently Leiden in 1573–74 marked a turning point. By 1579 the rebels had formally established a new state, which, in 1581, declared itself, following Roman precedent, as the Republic of the Seven United Netherlands. This state achieved a measure of security and stability thanks to the outstanding military leadership of William of Orange’s second son, Prince Maurice. As captain general of the republic’s army, he created a professional standing army that, due to a stable financing system, could be maintained throughout the year. The army used the winter for drills and training—or to engage in sieges of fortified cities still under Spanish control. This effort was overseen by some remarkable experts, such as the mathematician, architect, and engineer Simon Stevin, who encouraged Prince Maurice to

11 Livy, *Ab urbe condita*, 14 vols. (London: Heinemann, 1919–ongoing), vol. 3, trans. Benjamin Oliver Foster, 5.
12 Ibid., 7.
13 Ibid., vol. 7, trans. Frank Gardner Moore, 211.
14 Caesar, *The Gallic War*, trans. Henry John Edwards (London: Heinemann, 1958), 523.

follow the instructions found in the Roman treatise *De munitionibus castrorum* (On the fortification of a military camp).

Initially, Maurice insisted that the Dutch Republic's army would establish the sorts of camps prescribed by the Romans. When senior officers objected that there were substantial differences between the operations of the Roman legions and those of the republic's army, Maurice commissioned Stevin to develop models and procedures that combined the authority of Roman precedent with the new circumstances created by guns and muskets.[15] In 1617 Stevin published his system of camp design as *Castrametatio: dat is, legermeting* (Castrametation: that is, the measurement of the army). The book included a two-page justification for why he had modified the instructions given by the Roman writers, in which two issues stand out: first, the modern form of siege warfare, and second, the fact that, unlike a Roman cohort, a modern regiment came with artillery, a large baggage train that carried supplies, and many camp followers, including family members, merchants, sutlers or victualers who sold provisions, and craftspeople who attended to the maintenance and repair of equipment.[16] Stevin provided precise plans for various camps and instructions on the arrangements and sizes of the dwellings for soldiers and subaltern officers, which were to be not tents but *hutten* (huts), each measuring 2.4 by 2.4 meters and accommodating three soldiers or one junior officer—field officers were to be housed in spacious marquee tents that resembled pavilions. Stevin did not describe the barracks in detail.[17]

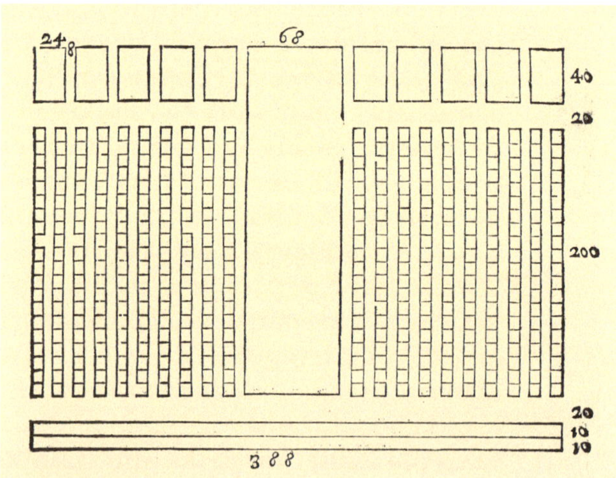

Fig. 7
Simon Stevin, Plan of a military camp of an infantry regiment, from his *Castrametatio*, 1618. Collection: Bibliothèque Nationale de France, Paris.

15 See Kees Zandvliet, ed., *Maurits, Prins van Oranje* (Amsterdam: Rijksmuseum; Zwolle: Waanders, 2000); Olaf van Nimwegen, *"Deser landen crijchsvolck" Het Staatse leger en de militaire revoluties (1588–1688)* (Amsterdam: Bert Bakker, 2006); and Marco van der Hoeven, ed., *Exercise of Arms: Warfare in the Netherlands, 1568–1648* (Leiden: Brill, 1997).

16 Simon Stevin, *Castrametatio: dat is, legermeting* (Rotterdam: Waesberghe, 1617), 42–44.

17 Ibid., 38.

In 1631 Quartermaster General David de Solemne of the Dutch Republic's army published *La Charge du mareschal des logis* (The responsibility of the quartermaster), in which he defined barracks as the principal building block of the camp. De Solemne described the manner of construction in some detail, providing an illustration of the basic structural frame and the straw-covered walls and roofs.

Fig. 8
Hendrik Hondius, The construction of a soldiers' hut, from David de Solemne, *La Charge du mareschal des logis*, 1631. Collection: Bibliothèque Nationale de France, Paris.

A couple of large engravings drawn by the well-known Dutch artist and publisher Hendrik Hondius showed the ordered arrangement of barracks in the context of the camp.[18] One of these plates offers a bird's-eye view of the field quarters of an infantry regiment of some 1,250 men.

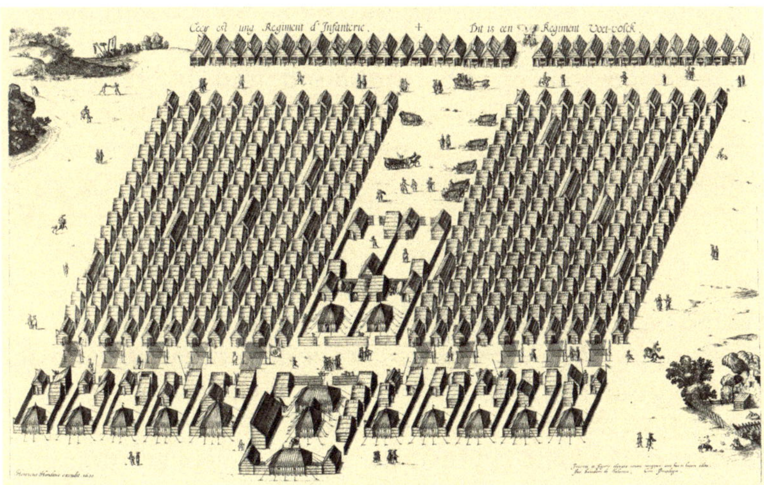

The camp measures 135 by 90 meters. From the foreground to the background, we see three zones: the first one numbers eleven compounds, each with a marquee tent and a few barracks. These are the lodgings for the higher officers: the colonel occupies the largest compound in the center, and the lieutenant colonel the one to its left. The seven other inner compounds are occupied by captains, while the compounds at the corners each house a sergeant major—an officer senior to the captains

Fig. 9
Hendrik Hondius, Camp for an infantry regiment, from David de Solemne, *La Charge du mareschal des logis*, 1631. Collection: Bibliothèque Nationale de France, Paris.

18 David de Solemne, *La Charge du mareschal des logis* (The Hague: Hondius, 1631), 21f.

but junior to the lieutenant colonel (in the eighteenth century, the title was changed to "major"). Separated by a broad avenue is the second zone, which consists of twenty-one rows of barracks that house the soldiers: each compound of the captains and sergeant majors faces two rows housing the 120-man companies under their command; the compound of the lieutenant colonel faces three rows, housing his 150-man company. At the near end of each row, we see a building, measuring 3 by 2.4 meters and turned toward the avenue, which houses either a lieutenant or an ensign. The building at the farthest end of each row is also turned toward an avenue; this houses the sergeants. On the other side of that avenue are the booths of the sutlers, merchants who sell provisions; given the possibility of trouble when soldiers and sutlers meet, the sergeants are well positioned. In the center, along the main avenue, are the two compounds for the pastor and the regimental quartermaster, each housed in a marquee tent. The two compounds that face an open area used to park carriages are occupied by the regimental surgeon and the provost marshal, who policed the regiment.[19]

The engraving represents a model layout, to be adjusted to circumstance. The image has a very practical purpose: it brings to life a set of instructions that provides not only the precise location of each officer, noncommissioned officer, soldier, and sutler, but also the exact dimensions of each compound, tent, barrack, road, path, and passage. This was to avoid "great disorder and confusion in the housing of a regiment," the text explains. "The very illustrious Maurice, Prince of Orange, of exalted memory, has so delightfully ordered the housing of his army that everyone, from the highest to the lowest officer, and both common infantrymen and cavalrymen, will have, when needed, a place to stay, as no one is allowed to take more or less than the place allocated to him."[20]

De Solemne referred to the temporary dwellings constructed by the soldiers as "huts." However, the adoption in the languages of northern Europe of the internationalism derived from the Occitan *barraca* was well underway by the time *La Charge du mareschal des logis* appeared. In 1630, Adam Freitag, a Lithuanian-born designer of fortifications employed in the Dutch Republic's army, introduced a derivative of the Occitan *barraca* into the German language when he used the noun *baracke* in his treatise on military architecture: "For the soldiers one arranges the *baracken* close to the wall." When the work—and the word—was translated

19 Ibid., 19–20.
20 Ibid., 16.

into French, the translator found it necessary to illustrate the meaning of the French equivalent, *baraques*, by adding the words "or huts."[21] Interestingly, while de Solemne had reserved *baracken* for the ranks and the lieutenants, Freitag also assigned this building type to all field officers—except their *baracken* were considerably larger, approaching the size of a small house.

Only occasionally did a third kind of dwelling appear in a camp: a mostly small, prefabricated, and portable wooden habitation to provide, in addition to tents, more secure and private lodgings for the commanding general or the monarch. Generalissimo Albrecht von Wallenstein, who was in charge of the armies of the Holy Roman Empire during the Thirty Years' War, used such a temporary home in the immense Zirndorf camp, pitched in 1632 near Nuremberg to host 50,000 soldiers, 10,000 sutlers and other noncombatants, and 15,000 horses. No details as to the form or construction of this temporary home survive.[22] King Louis XIV of France had use of a prefabricated palace—as every abode of a French king or prince is by definition a *palais*—during the Franco-Dutch War (1672–78). The core of the palace consisted of a single room made up of a frame covered with wooden panels attached to the structure and locked into place by means of hooks. "The king is camped like us," the official chronicler of Louis' deeds observed during the French army's siege of the Dutch city of Maastricht. "He sleeps in his wooden room, to which one added a kind of large portico, being used as an antechamber and chamber, of which the small one is the cabinet of the king. He dresses and undresses in what I call portico, because it is made with large arches closed by curtains only."[23] As the anticipated quick victory over the Dutch remained elusive, the war dragged on, and the tiny wooden palace expanded: the first addition was a wrought iron chimney, followed by "a rather long gallery, divided like those of Versailles in three or four small cabinets, very neatly floored, each furnished with a table and other furnishings in different colors."[24]

After the end of the war, which ended with some minor territorial gains for France at the expense of the Habsburg-ruled Southern Netherlands, the various sections of this miniature palace were stored in the Château de Vincennes. Parts of the king's private room and the larger council chamber were rediscovered and drawn in 1744, at a time of the War of Austrian Succession, which pitted a Franco-Prussian-Bavarian alliance against a coalition of the Habsburg monarchy, Britain, the Electorate of Hanover, and the Dutch Republic.

21 Adam Freitag, *Architectura militaris nova et aucta oder newe vermehrte fortification* (Leiden: Elseviers, 1631), 50; Adam Freitag, *L'Architecture militaire, ou La Fortification Nouvelle* (Leiden: Elseviers, 1635), 50.
22 Helmut Mahr, "Historische Wanderung um Wallensteins Lager 1632 und über die Stätten der Schlacht an der Alten Veste," *Fürther Geschichtsblätter*, vol. 56, issue 4 (2006), 139.
23 Paul Pellisson-Fontanier, *Lettres historiques de M. Pellisson*, 3 vols. (Paris: Barios, 1729), 1: 300, as quoted in Paul Bastier, "Les tentes de guerre de Louis XV: résidences royales éphémères aux armées (1744–1747)," *Bulletin du Centre de recherche du château de Versailles* (May 2019): 54. http://journals.openedition.org/crcv/17907.
24 Ibid., 1: 359, as quoted in Bastier, "Les tentes de guerre de Louis XV," 55.

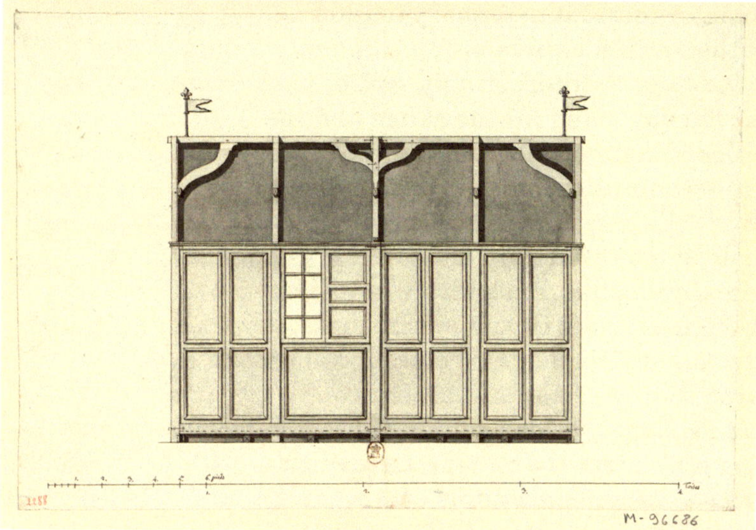

Fig. 10
Section of the private room used by King Louis XIV in the field and restored for the use of King Louis XV, 1744. Collection: Bibliothèque Nationale de France, Paris.

Repaired on orders of King Louis XV, who appreciated any direct association with his more august grandfather, the tiny wooden palace was brought in use again in the summer of 1744 to accommodate him when commanding the army during the defence of France's eastern frontier against an Austrian invasion force.[25] In an application of the trickle-down effect on construction, the prefabricated wooden dwelling, invented in the seventeenth century to accommodate the mighty in the field, became two centuries later the quarters of first soldiers, then the sick and wounded, prisoners of war, and finally anyone made homeless as the result of a man-made or natural catastrophe.

The simple construction of the soldiers' barracks stipulated by Stevin, de Solemne, and Dilich remained common practice for 150 years—if and when they were built at all. Monarchs, politicians, and generals all tried to avoid campaigns that extended beyond the traditional spring-to-fall fighting season, and tents were the preferred means of temporary housing when the army was in the field. When the troops were withdrawn into their winter quarters, they now found permanent two- or three-story stone or brick barracks that had become a required part of every fortified city or citadel. But on the rare occasions that barracks were required, they were typically constructed from whatever materials the soldiers found nearby, and hence they tended to be small. Larger barracks required longer beams, which generally were unavailable at short notice and within easy reach.[26]

Until the late eighteenth century, the design of the barrack generally followed the prescription for the temporary and somewhat flimsy structure provided by

25 Bastier, "Les tentes de guerre de Louis XV," 58–65.
26 See, for example, "Baraken," *Deutsche Encyclopädie oder allgemeines Real-Wörterbuch aller Künste und Wissenschaften*, ed. Heinrich Martin Gottfried Köster and Johann Friedrich Roos, 23 vols. (Frankfurt am Main: Varrentrapp, 1778–1807), 2:822.

de Solemne. None of these descriptions were accompanied by illustrations. Only in the nineteenth century did manuals for military engineers routinely include engravings of barracks to guide construction in the field. Exceptions to this were two designs that were part of the curriculum of the engineering program at the French Royal Army's military academy, the Ecole Spéciale Militaire, which was based on the doctrine of Louis de Cormontaigne, an eighteenth-century military engineer and architect who had transformed the lore of military engineering into a system of scientific, standardized procedures, and whose teachings survived in handwritten notes. One of these manuscripts, addressing the way to attack fortified places, presented rules on where and how to dig trenches, create and fortify works closest to enemy lines, and accommodate the soldiers of the attacking army, and provided an extremely detailed manual on how to cost, assemble the materials for, and construct *baraques*. Both of the two designs offered in the curriculum, which was not printed until the early nineteenth century, show a plan and elevation; the first was a barrack for soldiers, and the second was for officers.

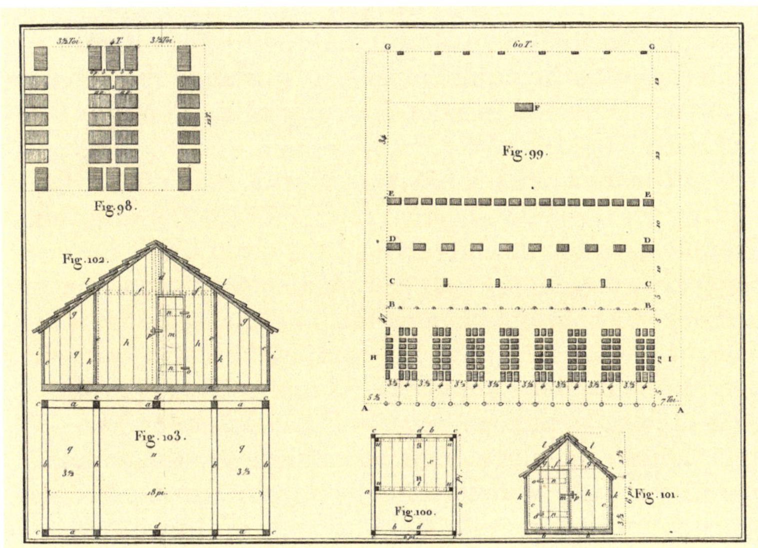

Fig. 11
Louis de Cormontaigne, Two designs for barracks and their arrangement in a camp, from Henri Jean-Baptiste de Bousmard, *Memorial de Cormontaigne pour l'attaque des places*, 1803. Collection: author.

As works of architecture, these designs were extremely simple: small, one-room structures with a single entrance that had to provide access and light. But if the two buildings looked like vernacular huts, as officially prescribed barracks they were the object of careful consideration and regulation.[27]

27 The secret curriculum was published between 1797 and 1803 by Henri Jean-Baptiste de Bousmard. Educated at Mezières, the aristocratic Bousmard had almost been guillotined during the Great Terror. In exile in Germany, the penniless refugee decided to cash in on his education and published the curriculum in four volumes. It earned him a commission in the Prussian army. The instruction on how to build barracks appears in Henri Jean-Baptiste de Bousmard, *Memorial de Cormontaigne pour l'attaque des places* (Berlin: George Decker, 1803), 285–97.

The French Revolution changed the character of war in Europe. The War of the First Coalition (1792–97) began conventionally enough, with the French government declaring war on Austria to obtain some territory from what had been the Spanish Netherlands between 1598 and 1714 and, after a transfer to the Vienna-based branch of the Habsburg family, had been known as the Austrian Netherlands since. Prussia joined Austria, and within months the war spun out of control, with France, now ruled by revolutionary radicals who also faced a civil unrest, declaring war also on Britain, Spain, and the Republic of the Seven United Netherlands, with the aim to bring thorough political and social change in the rest of the continent. As the French regular army and the large revolutionary militia were not up to fight so many enemies at once, the National Convention introduced a *levée en masse* (mass levy), a national conscription that decreed that, "until the enemies have been driven from the territory of the republic, the French people are in permanent requisition for army service. The young men shall go to battle; the married men shall forge arms and transport provision; the women shall make tents and clothes, and shall serve in the hospitals; the children shall turn old linen into lint; the old men shall repair to the public places, to stimulate the courage of the warriors and preach the unity of the Republic and hatred of kings."[28]

The idea of national conscription was not new. Twenty years earlier, twenty-year-old Jacques Antoine Hippolyte, comte de Guibert had observed in his *Essai général de la tactique* that European states and societies had become soft and degenerate, and that, as a result, nations had lost the power to compel their will on their neighbors. Ancient Rome offered many lessons to eighteenth-century Europe: wars should be undertaken only if they aimed at a decisive victory over the enemy, and they should be fought not by military professionals recruited from everywhere, who were indifferent to the national issues that were at stake in the conflict, but by conscripted citizens. "Let us suppose," Guibert exhorted, "that a vigorous people, of genius, of means, and of government, arises in Europe—a people that joins austere virtues with a national militia, a fixed plan of conquest that is not abandoned, an ability to wage war cheaply, a willingness to subsist on the basis of its victories, and a determination not to be forced to lay down arms because money has run out. Such a people will subjugate its neighbors and overthrow the weak constitutions, like the northwest storm snaps frail reeds."[29]

28 John Hall Stewart, *A Documentary Survey of the French Revolution* (New York: Macmillan, 1951), 472–74.

29 Jacques Antoine Hippolyte de Guibert, *Essai général de tactique, précédé d'un discours sur l'état actuel de la politique & de la science militaire en Europe*, 2 vols. (London: Librairies Associés, 1772), 1:xvii–xviii.

From 1792 onward, the revolutionary governments in Paris continuously invoked the ideal, the authority, and the forms of Rome as a reference point for their decisions. When the convention instituted the *levée en masse* in the summer of 1793, it did so not only with the pragmatic aim to almost instantaneously triple the size of the army to over 800,000 men. The new conscript army was also to embody the ideal of a nation-at-arms and to be a school of patriotism. The government's aims were fulfilled: the new army won decisive victories in the War of the First Coalition and the War of the Second Coalition (1798–1802). The success of the French conscript army was remarkable because it lacked almost everything. While the decree that established the *levée en masse* stipulated that married men were to forge arms and women uniforms and tents, it proved impossible to turn the nation into a large armament workshop overnight. Thus, many soldiers marched to battle in rags and were forced to bivouac in the open air. When the nights became cold, they were told to create temporary barracks with whatever materials they could find.

Fig. 12
The French camp at Weinhof, outside Altdorf, near Nuremberg, 1796. Collection: Bibliothèque Nationale de France, Paris.

The inability to equip the conscript army with tents quickly acquired a tactical justification. In his memoirs written in Saint Helena, Napoleon Bonaparte, who, incidentally, had established his career in the conscript army and considered Guibert his main guide, noted that in most situations bivouacs constructed from a few boards and bundles of straw allowed soldiers to be perfectly comfortable. Also, the army could not spare the horses needed to carry tents. Most importantly, he insisted, tents betrayed an army's presence: "Tents can be observed by enemy spies and staff officers, providing them with information about your number and position; this inconvenience occurs every day, and every instant in the day. An army that is arranged in two or three lines of bivouac can only be seen at a distance by the smoke, which the enemy may mistake for the clouds of the atmosphere. It is impossible to count the number of fires; it is very easy to count the number of tents, and to establish the position that they occupy."[30] The presence of tents violated the key element that defined Napoleon's tactical genius: his ability to create surprise. "Where is Bonaparte?" the Austrian generals often asked the evening before battle during Napoleon's Italian campaign. "Where is the French army? Above all, where will it be tomorrow?" The great scholar of Napoleon's tactical genius, Jean Lambert Alphonse Colin, noted that "it is on these questions that night draws her veil."

> At sunrise, here is Bonaparte! And while the divisions seen the day before return to the fight, suddenly cannons thunder at the rear of the Imperial Army, and they are of troops that one believed to be ten leagues away; it is Fiorella who has hastened from Marcaria to Solferino; Masséna, from Rivoli to Mantua. It is, in a word, systematic surprise, obtained by the extension of the front and by night marches, made terrifying by the cannons that one suddenly hears behind one's back in the morning mist. Soon a torrent will descend on one of the flanks of the disempowered enemy, and once a breach is made, will carry everything away.[31]

During the Napoleonic Wars (1803–15), soldiers of European armies often lived in bivouacs when on campaign, though when tents were available, they were of course used. Even the French Imperial Army returned to the frequent use of tents during campaigns. But during armistices, when the belligerent parties negotiated a peace settlement, an army needed a somewhat more permanent base. In his memoirs of his time in Napoleon's army, Elzéar Blaze observed that quartering the soldiers in nearby villages and towns not only prevented a quick mobilization if and when hostilities resumed but also led to a decline in discipline: "As soon as a suspension of arms existed between the two armies, we formed camps by divisions. The hostilities being able to recommence each moment, it was necessary to be ready to meet and walk as one man." Blaze described a camp as "a town of wood and straw, sometimes of canvas, well aligned,

30 Damas Hinard, *Dictionnaire-Napoléon, ou Recueil alphabétique des opinions et jugements de L'Empereur Napoléon Ier*, 2nd ed. (Paris: Plon Fréres, 1854), 514–15.
31 Jean Lambert Alphonse Colin, *L'Education militaire de Napoléon* (Paris: Chapelot, 1901), 366.

with its streets large and small, long and short; everything is kept in excessive cleanliness." As in the case of the French occupation of Altdorf, despoliation of the surrounding villages and countryside continued to provide building materials. "In general, to make our camps," Blaze disclosed, "we demolished the villages; at Tilsit each regiment had about thirty villages to cut up; one or two were assigned to each company. We had a large quantity of carts and found horses used to transport the materials. With such means, it is easy to believe that our camps were superb; those who have not seen them cannot get an idea."[32] No image of the Tilsit camp survives, but an aquatint engraving that shows a French camp near Flensburg in Schleswig provides a good sense of the typical appearance of any such camp during the Napoleonic era.

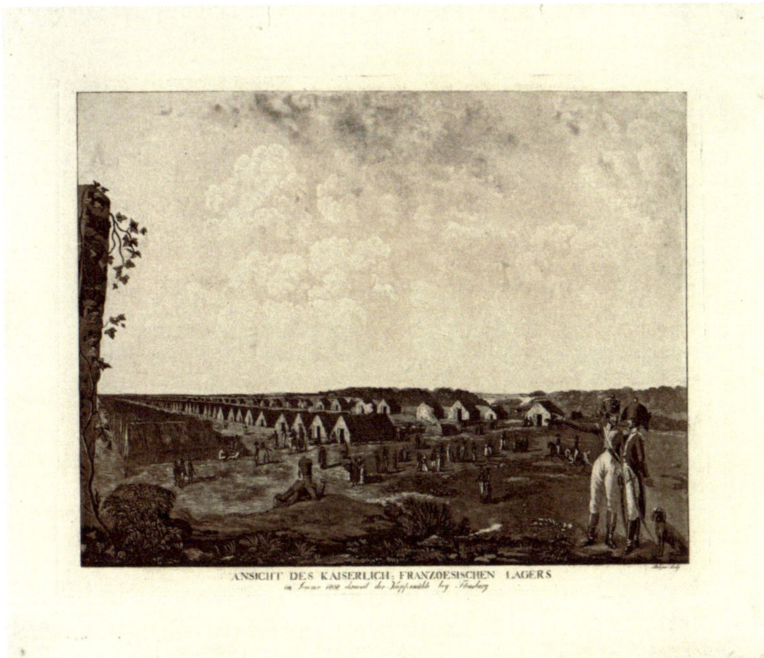

Fig. 13
Carl Gottlieb Stelzner, View of the French imperial camp in the summer of 1808, not far from the village of Kupfermühle, near Flensburg, Schleswig, 1808. Collection: Anne S. K. Brown Military Collection, Brown University, Providence, Rhode Island.

The barrack, which had saved the Army of Flanders during the siege of Haarlem and had become a key component of the Dutch Republic's army, had returned to military life. Its renewed importance can be seen by comparing the first and second editions of the *Guide de l'officier particulier en campagne* (The guide for subaltern officers in the field), by Jean-Gérard Lacuée, comte de Cessac. In 1785, at age thirty-three, the captain in the French Royal Army first published his two-volume, thirty-three-chapter manual on an army officer's daily duties during military campaigns. The book discussed tents as the exclusive form of shelter during campaigns and did not mention *baraques*. In 1806, after service as

32 Elzéar Blaze, *La Vie militaire sous l'Empire, ou Moeurs de la garnison, du bivouac et de la caserne*, 2 vols. (Paris: Bureau de l'Album des Théatres, 1837), 2:5–7.

a brigadier general in the French Revolutionary Army and having held high military and administrative posts under the Directoire and the Consulate, Cessac published a second edition of his *Guide*, which would remain in print for more than four decades, with an Italian edition appearing as late as 1852—a clear indication of the relative lack of innovation in the operation of an army in the field in the first half of the nineteenth century. The main difference from the first edition was the addition of a new concluding chapter that described in detail the layout of hutted camps and the construction of barracks, with separate models for soldiers and officers, as well as a half-buried barrack suited to dry soil.[33]

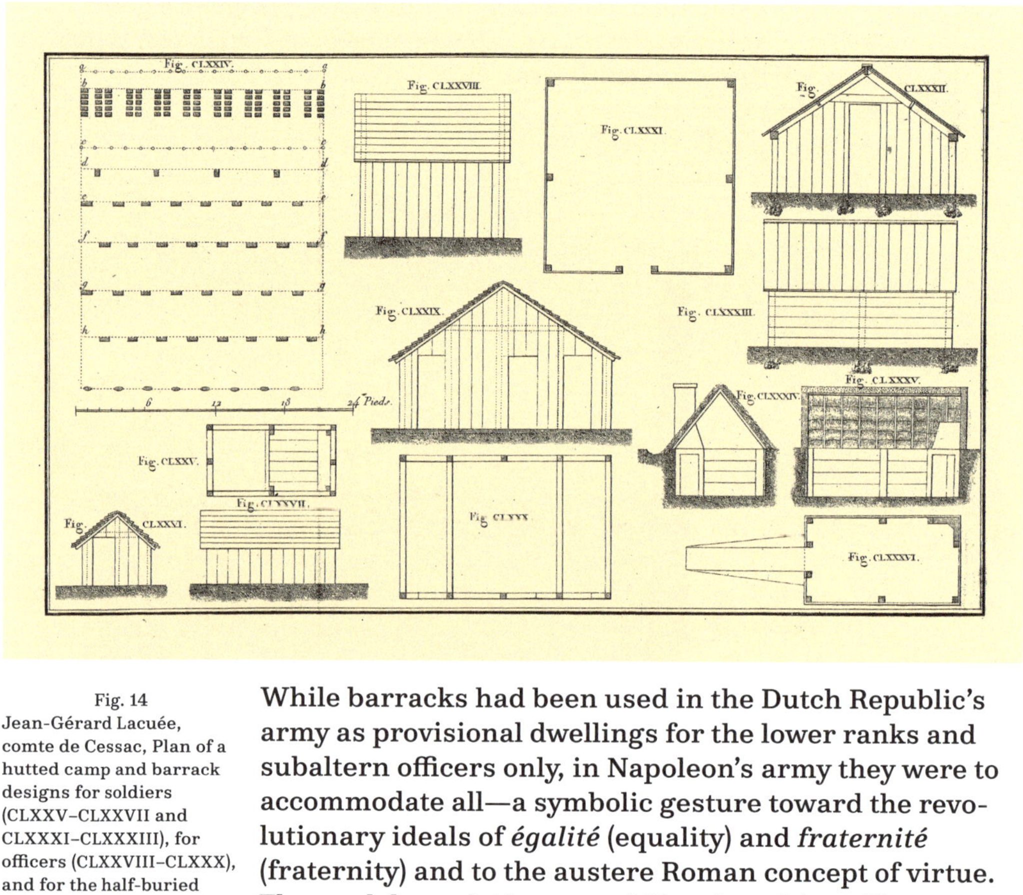

Fig. 14
Jean-Gérard Lacuée, comte de Cessac, Plan of a hutted camp and barrack designs for soldiers (CLXXV–CLXXVII and CLXXXI–CLXXXIII), for officers (CLXXVIII–CLXXX), and for the half-buried version to be created in appropriate terrain (CLXXXIV–CLXXXVI), from his *Guide de l'officier particulier en campagne*, 3rd ed., 1816. Collection: author.

While barracks had been used in the Dutch Republic's army as provisional dwellings for the lower ranks and subaltern officers only, in Napoleon's army they were to accommodate all—a symbolic gesture toward the revolutionary ideals of *égalité* (equality) and *fraternité* (fraternity) and to the austere Roman concept of virtue. The model regulations—and Napoleon himself—were strict about the fact that senior officers should not requisition houses for themselves. Pierre Antoine Savart, who taught fortification and camp construction at the Ecole Spéciale Militaire de Saint-Cyr, the premier military academy in France, established in 1802 by Napoleon, did allow officers to make the barracks as comfortable as circumstances allowed: "Officers may design and execute their *baraques* more or less according to their desires and according to their needs. They will subdivide

33 Jean-Gérard Lacuée, comte de Cessac, *Guide de l'officier particulier en campagne*, 3rd augmented ed., 2 vols. (Paris: Barrois, 1816), 2:336–55.

it in parts to house their servants and horses."[34] The principle that officers were to lodge in barracks was maintained; yet, in practice, during an armistice, general officers would normally requisition a nearby castle or manor house to serve as their quarters, and senior officers often sought lodgings in a nearby village. "The colonel's *baraque* exists, but ordinarily it is not occupied," Elzéar Blaze noted in his memoirs. "These gentlemen prefer to live in the nearest village—only of course when the enemy is far away, or when peace is negotiated; in wartime, they are with the soldiers night and day."[35]

An ability to think outside the box, which had been the basis of France's military supremacy since the mid-1790s, also applies to the French deployment of the barrack. Savart noted that, while a typical barrack might cover an area as small as 2 by 5 meters, with heights of 1.5 meters at the sides and 2 meters at the center, it made sense for the quartermaster to be opportunistic: "In the same camp it may be necessary to allow different forms of construction, including work in light masonry; but as any military formation is a gathering of men from very different countries with different customs, one will not lack either resources or experience, and one will be able to easily overcome local difficulties."[36] Confirmation of the adaptable character of barrack construction can be found in the writings of one of Napoleon's military engineers, Guillaume Henri Dufour. "There is nothing predetermined about this way of building," Dufour noted, "and therefore one cannot establish any rules about it, and each must move forward in accordance with the means at hand." Recounting his experiences in the Grande Armée, Dufour recalled that he and his compatriots had relied on local knowledge. Sometimes they had made "*barraques*" covered with tiles, filling the spaces between the structural parts with brickwork, and sometimes the roof and walls consisted of leafy branches. "We made *barraques* that could accommodate an entire company, and others that could hold only a squad."[37] This flexibility became enshrined after the fall of Napoleon in the curriculum for future general-staff officers: "The manner of construction of *baraques* varies according to the country, the climate, the season, and circumstance. In general one ought to adopt the quickest and most economical method of construction in use in the country where one finds oneself."[38]

While the barracks constructed in hutted camps erected during campaigns were most often the result of improvisation, when local labor and building materials were available and the camp was to be occupied

34 Nicolas Pierre Antoine Savart, *Cours élémentaire de fortification à l'usage de MM. les élèves de l'Ecole spéciale impériale militaire* (Paris: Valade, 1812), 62.
35 Blaze, *La Vie militaire sous l'Empire*, 2:14–16.
36 Savart, *Cours élémentaire de fortification*, 61–62.
37 Guillaume Henri Dufour, *Mémorial pour les travaux de guerre* (Geneva: Paschoud, 1820), 275.
38 L'Ecole d'Application du Corps Royal d'Etat-Major, *Instruction sur les campemens avec tentes ou baraques*, 2nd ed. (Paris: Anselin, 1830), 68.

for a longer time, the military engineer in charge could aspire to a higher level of standardization. After the decisive defeat of the Prussian army in the Battle of Jena-Auerstedt (1806) and the subsequent surrender, the French imposed a military occupation on the country. General Honoré Théodore Maxime Gazan de la Peyrière was given responsibility for the Prussian province of Silesia (located today in Poland), and he ordered Captain Charles Marie Etienne Prétet, the divisional engineer, to design and construct a semipermanent camp near Brieg (today Brzeg). Prétet designed a spacious barrack for twenty-four soldiers that measured 7 meters in length, 5 meters in width, 2.5 meters in height on the long sides, and 5 meters in height at the ridge. The entrance was on one of the short sides. The walls consisted of pieces of timber at the corners, poles driven into the soil at 0.5-meter distances, and wattle stretching between the poles. A mixture of mud, straw, and cut hay covered the pole-and-wattle structure. The roof consisted of wooden boards with battens covering the joints. In the interior, an L-shaped wooden sleeping platform ran along the side and back. Typically, the army allowed 40 centimeters per soldier. Then Prétet laid out the camp and ordered his sappers to construct one model barrack for each of the regiments, leaving the regimental officers to organize and oversee the construction of the remainder.[39]

General Gazan and Captain Prétet's ambition to create a camp with uniform barracks reflected their shared experience in the largest hutted camp created under Napoleon's reign: the 60,000-soldier camp of the Armée des Côtes de l'Océan (Army of the Ocean Coasts) in Boulogne-sur-Mer, France. In the fall of 1803, the coffers of the French government were full, thanks to the sale of a large part of North America to the fledgling United States. France and Britain were, once again, at war. Napoleon decided to use the sudden windfall to create a new army of 200,000 men that was to invade Great Britain. The training of the army happened at various camps, the largest of which were at Boulogne, the anticipated point of embarkation. These two camps were meant to serve for at least a year, and their planning and construction were the result of careful consideration in Paris.

Both camps consisted of standardized barracks, 3 meters wide and 4 meters deep, constructed with wattle-and-pole walls covered with daub. The entrance was on one of the long sides and sleeping platforms for twelve men were on the other. A small window above the sleeping platform provided light. A rack for weapons

39 Ibid., 71–72.

occupied the short wall left of the entrance, and shelves the right walls. The roof was thatched. In the camp constructed near the lighthouse, the barracks were constructed on grade; in the camp located on the left bank of the Liane River, they were lowered a meter into the ground. The latter barracks were more popular, as they proved warmer in winter.[40]

With the construction of the semipermanent hutted camps in Boulogne, the design of the barrack was of sufficient importance to warrant the compilation of a detailed design guide. Colonel Antoine-François Lomet des Foucaux, who had been trained as a civil engineer and had taught architecture at the Ecole Polytechnique—France's premier school of civil engineering, established in 1794—began work in 1803 on a treatise on military camps, "Traité sur le baraquement des troupes." He never published it in book form, but as he was working on it, the manuscript acquired a reputation and was considered to be the final word on the issue. Only one design survives. It concerns a model based on a wooden barrack Lomet had constructed in 1793 at a military base at the French-Spanish border at Hendaye. Measuring 5 meters wide, 9 meters deep, and 3 meters high at the ridge, it offered an entrance on the short side. The interior consisted of a narrow path flanked by two sleeping platforms, each offering space to twenty men. With a capacity of forty soldiers, each soldier had 1 square meter of floor space and 3.5 cubic meters of interior space. For the record, the minimum amount of space deemed acceptable for English soldiers a century later was 4.5 square meters of floor area and 13.5 cubic meters of interior space.[41]

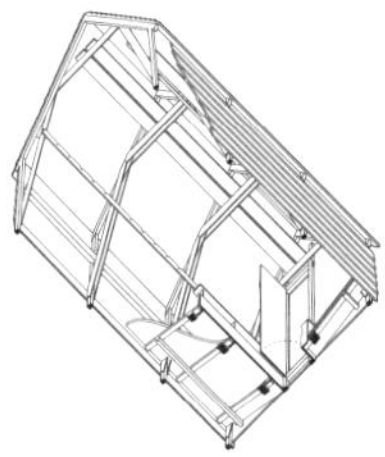

Lomet des Foucaux's Barrack
→ p. 508

Lomet's design survived because the well-known architect Jean-Charles Krafft included it in his *Plans, coupes et élévations de diverses productions de l'art de la charpente* (Plans, sections and elevations of various examples of the art of carpentry), published in 1805. It appears to be the first instance of a barrack being the object of both discussion and illustration in a general treatise of architecture. To be sure, the Austrian-born Krafft had a military background; he had moved to Paris in the mid-1780s to serve in the Gardes Suisses (Swiss Guards) that protected the royal family at Versailles, and after the dissolution of these regiments, he had served in the French Revolutionary Army before undertaking his training as an architect. As a practitioner, Krafft had an unusual appreciation of the broad scope of the profession, from the most formal work to the most vernacular. Nevertheless, the appearance of the design

40 Ibid., 70–71.
41 Lomet never published his treatise. The barrack design appears in Jean-Charles Krafft, *Plans, coupes et élévations de diverses productions de l'art de la charpente exécutées tant en France que dans les pays étrangers* (Paris and Strasbourg: Levrault, 1805), 27, plate 78.

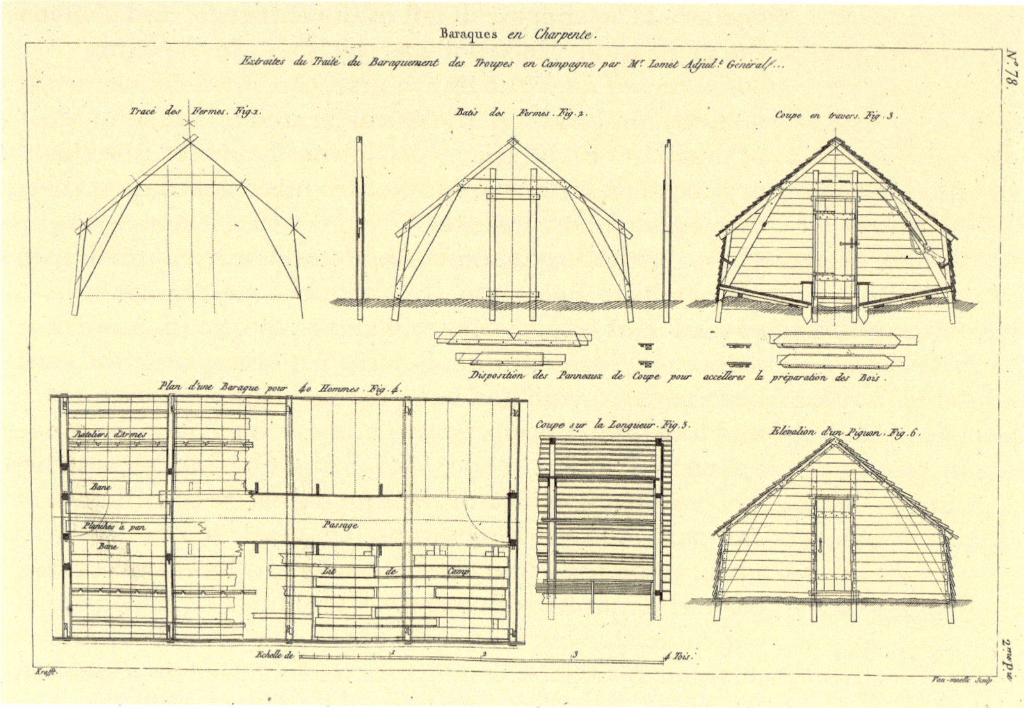

Fig. 15
Antoine-François Lomet des Foucaux, Barrack constructed in Hendaye, France, 1793, from Jean-Charles Krafft, *Plans, coupes et élévations de diverses productions de l'art de la charpente*, 1805. Collection: Bibliothèque Nationale de France, Paris.

of a barrack in a more general book on architecture is noteworthy; it would take until the end of the nineteenth century before the barrack would make a reappearance in books written by architects for architects.[42]

In the Napoleonic era, barracks were the principal building blocks of military camps expected to last for a relatively short time: during sieges or during armistices that separated the end of a military campaign and a peace treaty. Yet the two camps at Boulogne, originally intended as a temporary shelter for an invasion force to be sent to England, remained in operation for two years. They turned out to provide ideal conditions for conscripts to be initiated into the art of war, for veterans to improve their skills, and for all soldiers, noncommissioned officers, and officers to live a life that approached conditions in the field. This utilization suggested a new kind of military installation: the permanent *camp d'instruction militaire* (camp of military instruction), where regiments that were based all over the country were assembled in divisions for periods of three months of collective training.

In 1805 Napoleon decided to establish such a training camp in the Regno d'Italia (Kingdom of Italy), a state proclaimed in 1805 that centered on Savoy, Lombardy, and the Veneto. This kingdom had evolved from the revolutionary Repubblica Cisalpina (Cisalpine Republic), established as a French protectorate in 1797,

42 See Heinrich Wagner, Paul Wallot, and Friedrich Richter, *Gebäude für Verwaltung, Rechtspflege und Gesetzgebung*; Militärbauten, vol. 2, *Parlamentshäuser und Standehäuser, Gebäude für militärische Zwecke* (Darmstadt: Arnold Bergsträsser, 1887); Oswald Kuhn, *Gebäude fur Heil- und sonstige Wohlfahrts-Anstalten*, vol. 1, *Krankenhäuser* (Stuttgart: Arnold Bergsträsser, 1897). Both Richter's discussion of barracks used by the military and Kuhn's presentation of the architectural type of the barrack as an essential component of the more general typology of hospitals appeared as part of the famous multivolume *Handbuch der Architektur*, which appeared in 143 parts between 1880 and 1943.

and its successor, the Repubblica Italiana (Italian Republic), led by Napoleon as president. When he elevated his own status in France to that of emperor of the French, Napoleon declared the Italian Republic a kingdom, and accepted the invitation to be crowned king of Italy. Born in Corsica one year after the island's incorporation in France, Napoleon was raised speaking Italian, and the regal dignity he received in the Duomo in Milan gave him as great a satisfaction as the imperial one taken in the Notre-Dame in Paris. Yet he was to govern his kingdom from the French capital, dispatching to Milan his stepson, Eugène de Beauharnais, as his personal representative.

Three months after his coronation, Napoleon wrote to his chief of staff, Marshal Louis-Alexandre Berthier, that the Italian soldiers needed better training. "I would like to form in the plains of Montechiaro a camp of barracks, arranged in a square. These barracks would be made of brick or wood, depending on what would be healthy." The arrangement was to house twelve battalions, and everyone, from general officers to privates, was to camp together. Troops would rotate through the camp on a three-month cycle. "By this means one would have trained troops. It is known that the system of permanent barracks does not succeed, that the maneuvers are bad, and that the soldier does not acquire the habit of service that he obtains in a camp."[43] Nothing much happened in the year that followed—except that Beauharnais somehow internalized the idea of a large training camp for 25,000 men consisting of barracks. In June 1806 he wrote to his stepfather proposing such a training camp, to be created either east of Venice or south of Lake Garda.[44] Napoleon responded tersely, repeating his earlier instruction that a camp should be constructed at Montechiaro (near the present-day city of Montechiari, Lombardy), this time specifying that the barracks should be either brick or dry-stone construction, "so that it may last for a long time."[45]

Beauharnais drew the parti of the camp; it was to be an enormous square, measuring one kilometer on each side, which was to consist of three concentric square boxes. A large area for drills, exercises, and parades located at the center was surrounded by six rows of acacia and plane trees to provide shade, and beyond their perimeter arose the quarters for sixteen battalions, each consisting of nine companies, with barrack dwellings for generals, the minister of defense, and the king—that is, Napoleon—occupying sites within the acacia and plane groves. This original project was only partially

43 Napoleon I, letter to Marshal Louis-Alexandre Berthier, June 7, 1805, *Correspondence de Napoléon Ier*, 30 vols. (Paris: Henri Plon and J. Dumaine, 1858–69), 10:491.
44 Eugène de Beauharnais, letter to Napoleon I, June 4, 1806, *Mémoires et Correspondence Politique et Militaire du Prince Eugène*, ed. Albert du Casse, 2 vols. (Paris: Michel Lévy Frères, 1858), 2:424.
45 Napoleon I, letter to Eugène de Beauharnais, June 10, 1806, in *Mémoires et Correspondence*, 2:435.

realized; in the final version the battalions occupied only three of the four sides of the square, while the barrack dwellings for the generals and the royal residence were grouped on the fourth side. As a camp of military instruction, Montechiaro was an innovation that was ahead of its time; in the 1830s this type of establishment was revived in the context of the Herculean task of establishing a Belgian army, and it was not until the 1850s and 1860s that such places become an integral component of the military landscape (see Chapter Four).[46]

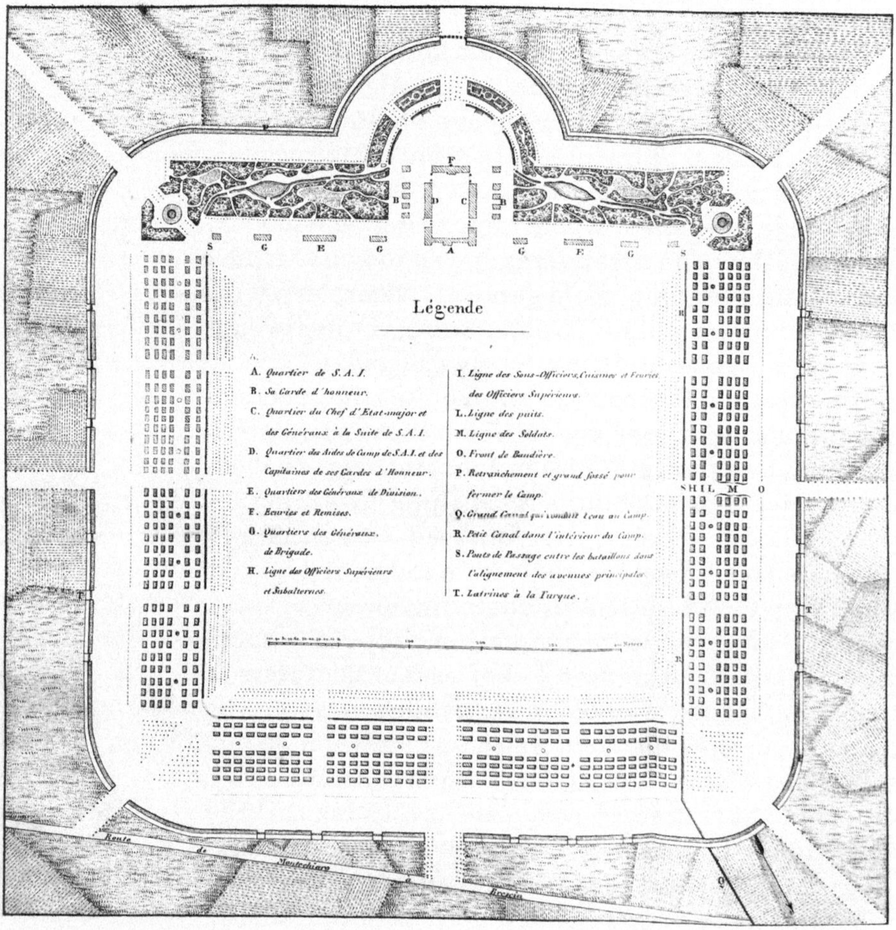

Fig. 16
Plan of the camp at Montechiaro, Italy, as executed, c. 1812, from Maurice Joseph Didier Ravicchio de Peretsdorf, *Notice sur le camp d'instruction des troupes Sardes etabli a Cirié en 1838*, 1839. Collection: Nationaal Militair Museum, Soesterberg, the Netherlands.

46 On Montechiaro, see Alfredo Ardenghi, *Gli accampamenti Napoleonici del Regno Italico* (Montechiari: Zanetti Editore, 2007).

If Napoleon's genius and determination were key to his ascent to power and greatness, his highly developed sense of theater helped smooth out some of the social friction that his career generated and proved decisive at key moments, such as during the bloodless coup d'état of November 9, 1799 (18 Brumaire of year VIII of the French republican calendar), that brought him to power as First Consul of France. In September 1803, he decided it was good for the morale of the Army of the Ocean Coasts if he lodged with the troops in Boulogne, and he would need, therefore, a simple *baraque* for his own use and a few for his aides. Pierre-François-Léonard Fontaine, who had been introduced to Napoleon in 1799, and Charles Percier quickly became his go-to architects and set designers for official ceremonies—Napoleon liked to work with them because both men shared his understanding of the importance of spectacle, and they were able to deliver lots of pomp and circumstance at a discount. The imperial barrack, which propaganda was to call *La Baraque de Napoléon*, was to be a considerably more substantial building than the soldiers' barracks, measuring about 40 meters long and 9 meters wide and made of more luxurious building materials. Yet construction of such a building using conventional building technologies would have taken weeks, if not months, spoiling the theatrical effect of Napoleon's gesture of camaraderie. The obvious solution was to create *baraques* that were to be prefabricated off-site and assembled on-site in a couple of days on prepared brick foundations. It was to be a remarkable coup de théâtre. "We have made two small models of different shape and distribution," Fontaine wrote in his diary on September 15. "One has an octagonal layout accompanied by a square part, the other is a long square divided into five rooms. They were presented to the First Consul, who approved them both and ordered their construction."[47]

In twelve days Fontaine oversaw the construction of six portable barracks to be erected in the army's camps in Boulogne, Ambleteuse, and Etaples. "The First Consul wanted to see them mounted in the garden of St. Cloud. They were sent there for this purpose, but we only erected the octagonal one. He also wanted to see a square one, so I told him that when he woke up the next day he would find it in place, and by 9 a.m. the next day this was the case." On October 3, 1803, the parts of the barracks were loaded on carts and driven to Boulogne. Installation, however, proved difficult. On January 5, 1804, Fontaine expressed his frustration in his diary: "The wooden barracks were mounted with endless

47 Pierre François Léonard Fontaine, *Journal 1799–1853*, 2 vols. (Paris: Ecole Nationale Supérieure des Beaux Arts, 1987), 1:64.

Fig. 17
Henri-Toussaint Gobert, *La Baraque de Napoléon*, 1805. Collection: Musée de Boulogne-sur-Mer, copyright Monsieur Devos.

punishments."[48] Fontaine had not counted on the coastal winds that buffeted the dramatic but exposed construction site. Neither the roof nor the anchoring of the barrack to the foundation had been designed with strong winds in mind. *La Baraque de Napoléon* was finished only in the beginning of January 1804. However, it did not matter: many people will believe what they want to believe, and the ten-week-long struggle to erect the structure was quickly forgotten, and soon the tall tale circulated that *La Baraque* could be both assembled and disassembled in a single hour.[49]

Louis Constant Wairy, Napoleon's valet, provided a lengthy description of *La Baraque*, which appears in a painting by Henri-Toussaint Gobert.

> The Emperor's barrack was built of plank, like the booths of a country fair; with this difference, that the planks were neatly planed, and painted a grayish white. In form it was a long square, having at each end two pavilions of semicircular shape. A fence formed of wooden lattice enclosed this barrack, which was lighted on the outside by lamps placed four feet apart, and the windows were placed laterally. The pavilion next to the sea consisted of three rooms and a hall, the principal room, used as a council-chamber, being decorated with silver-gray paper. On the ceiling were painted golden clouds, in the midst of which appeared, upon the blue vault of the sky, an eagle holding the lightning, and guided towards England by a star, the guardian star of the Emperor.[50]

← Fig. 17

Adjacent were Napoleon's bedroom, equipped with a simple iron bed; a room that housed Napoleon's campaign wardrobe and telescope; a salon; a vestibule; and a dining room. Two smaller barrack huts, located at a distance, housed the kitchen and laundry.

Napoleon did not make it to Britain in 1805. Ten years later, upon his defeat at the Battle of Waterloo, Napoleon was exiled to the British dependency of Saint Helena in the South Atlantic. There he was given Longwood House, a small and badly maintained country house located in the center of the island. It was meant to be a temporary solution; in 1816 the British Board of Ordnance in Woolwich initiated the design and production of a prefabricated mansion that was to be shipped in crates to the island and erected as a more worthy abode for the ex-emperor. Napoleon witnessed the arrival of

48 Ibid., 66, 69.
49 Emile Marco de Saint-Hilaire, *Souvenirs intimes du temps de L'Empire*, 2nd ser., 2 vols. (Paris: Dumont, 1839), 1:99.
50 Louis Constant Wairy, *Recollections of the Private Life of Napoleon*, 3 vols., trans. Walter Clark (Akron, OH: Saalfield, 1902), 1:224–25.

the parts in 1819 but was at that time already ill and had little interest in its assembly. In many ways, the rather wretched condition of Longwood House served him well, as it framed an evolving narrative of martyrdom. New Longwood projected bourgeois comfort, which did not fit the need of the day: New Longwood did not have the potential of La Baraque fourteen years earlier. In addition, Napoleon sensed he would die before its completion. And so he did, in 1821, at age fifty-one.[51]

In 1854, fifty years after his uncle had concentrated 200,000 soldiers in Boulogne to prepare for the invasion of England, Napoleon III, emperor of the French, brought 100,000 soldiers together in the same area, this time to prepare for a joint French-British expedition to the Crimean Peninsula. Captain Hugues Charles Antoine Vertray recorded a moment in the construction of the Ambleteuse camp in a watercolor sketch. Soldiers are busy erecting two structures that, a few hours later, will be their home; nearby are the camp kitchen, with a tile roof, and many other wattle-and-daub-walled and straw-covered barracks—the standard self-made housing in French military camps.

→ Fig. 18

Chapter One, Fig. 8
→ p. 51

If the Dutch engraver Hendrik Hondius, who had made the charming illustration for David de Solemnc's *La Charge du mareschal des logis* that shows two soldiers constructing a barrack, had been alive and present at Ambleteuse, he would not have been surprised at the way the French soldiers went about their task—at first sight, not much had changed in 220 years.

But, of course, there were major differences. The most important was that, beginning with the Napoleonic Wars, the construction of barracks by soldiers using local materials had developed in a very well-regulated practice, as shown in military manuals issued not only to sappers or combat engineers but, more importantly, to subaltern infantry officers, who were expected to lead their men, when necessary, in the construction of bivouacs. The range of options described included the simplest of shelters, consisting of a roof made of rods or poles covered with straw or turf, erected to protect soldiers from the wind; a somewhat more substantial barrack with a roof made of posts and covered with boards; a winterized dugout version that included a wooden floor and a roof covered not only by boards but also a layer of sod to provide better insulation; and various hybrid forms. And in some armies, these officers were even supposed to know how to construct more permanent

51 E. L. Jackson, *St. Helena: The Historic Island, from Its Discovery to the Present Date* (New York: Thomas Whitakker, 1905), 223–25.

Fig. 18
Hugues Charles Antoine Vertray, Construction of barracks at Ambleteuse, France, 1854. Collection: Archives Départementales Pas-de-Calais, Dainville, France.

barracks with post-and-plank walls—a practice that, of course, necessitated a steady supply of prescribed building materials.

As the military manuals issued by the Danish, Austrian, and German armies show, the leadership of most European armies considered such knowledge to be part and parcel of a junior officer's education. However, British officers were not educated in this field. A specialized corps, known initially as the Corps of Royal Military Artificers and from 1812 onward as the Corps of Royal Sappers and Miners, was supposed to do construction work for the army under leadership of the Corps of Royal Engineers, a body consisting of officers only, all of whom were trained in construction.[52] While these specialized units ensured a high quality of whatever construction work might be done, their establishment also led to a process of atrophy in whatever basic construction knowledge existed among the officers and men of the fighting regiments—an ignorance that was to have dire consequences during the Crimean War, when the sappers were fully engaged in the siege of Sevastopol and could not be spared to construct winterized shelters for the army in the late fall of 1854.

52 See T. W. J. Connolly, *History of the Royal Sappers and Miners*, 2 vols. (London: Longman, Brown, Green, Longmans, and Roberts, 1857).

→ p. 97

Two

Each Hut Weighs More Than Two Tons

Both European and Ottoman elites had feared Russia since the early eighteenth century, when the country steadily began to increase its territory toward the west and the south. The formal annexation in 1831 of the Congress Kingdom of Poland, established in 1815 by the Congress of Vienna as a sovereign Polish national state connected through a personal union to Russia, and the subsequent abolition of all Polish national institutions, confirmed a perception of Saint Petersburg's appetite for conquest in Europe. And the slow but certain Russian advance in the Caucasus toward both Persia and Anatolia, and Russian support for Greek independence from Ottoman rule, were seen as deadly threats to the future of the Ottoman Empire. By the early 1850s, there was agreement in London, Paris, Turin, and Constantinople that something had to be done to stop Russian expansion. The Ottoman government, known as the Sublime Porte, decided it could eliminate a Russian threat by creating a conflict in the Ottoman-ruled Balkans. In October 1853 the Sublime Porte declared war on Russia, which had occupied the Danubian principalities of Moldavia and Walachia, self-ruling territories within the Ottoman Empire. When a month later ships of the Russian Navy's Black Sea Fleet destroyed a Turkish naval squadron, London and Paris, fearing that Moscow would project its power into the Mediterranean, joined the Russo-Ottoman conflict. This decision was made under pressure by that new force in politics, daily newspapers, which, thanks to steam-driven rotary printing presses and cheap newsprint made of wood pulp, had become, in the late 1840s, a major player in shaping and mobilizing public opinion. Any sober reflection on long-term British or French interests counseled against intervention.

In preparation for the war in the East, the French army created two enormous camps near Boulogne-sur-Mer to assemble an expeditionary force that was to conduct operations in alliance with the British Army. The barracks, which were constructed by the soldiers themselves, following practices that went back fifty years, proved of special interest to British journalists. In 1804 they had not been welcome to describe the housing of the Army of the Ocean Coasts at the very same place—after all, that force was to invade Britain. Now they were given ample opportunity to inspect the barracks and tell the British public about them. "The mud huts are, of course, not very luxurious habitations to dwell in, but soldiers in all time have been obliged to fare hard, and these structures show an amount of ingenuity in the cheap use of materials for making them which is highly instructive," *The Times* (London) reported.

> The side walls are of clay, held together by a rough lathing of wood internally, and a thick coating of white-wash on the external surfaces. The frame of the roof, roughly put together, is well thatched with straw. The tie beams of the rafters form a convenient open loft on which to stow away arms, other equipment, and odds and ends. From the entrance a passage way is kept clear to the opposite wall of the hut, thus bisecting it into two equal halves, and on each of these a sloping platform of planks, supported from the ground by a very simple staging, gives room for six men to lie down. The hut therefore accommodates 12 men, six on one side and six on the other, with their feet towards the centre, and their heads towards the walls. An aperture above the door, and another directly opposite, afford ample facilities for ventilation in summer, and may be more or less entirely closed in winter. The cost of the whole structure must be very trifling, and if any part gives way it can be readily repaired.[1]

In 1857 the *Illustrated Times Weekly Newspaper* (London) belatedly published a few wood engravings of the Boulogne camp. At this time the popular press did not yet have the technology to print the remarkable set of photos taken by British photographer Charles Thurston Thompson in the Boulogne camp.

→ Fig. 1

1 "The French Emperor's Visit to Boulogne," *The Times* (London), Sept. 12, 1854, 7.

OCTOBER 10, 1857. ILLUSTRATED TIMES. 245

A FRENCH MILITARY CAMP.

INTERIOR OF SOLDIERS' HUT.

Fig. 1
Overview of the French army's camp at Boulogne-sur-Mer and the interior of one of the camp's barracks, *Illustrated Times Weekly Newspaper*, 1857. Collection: author.

That same year, London and Paris dispatched a fleet of 360 ships to secure the Dardanelles and Constantinople and destroy the Black Sea Fleet and its home, the heavily fortified port of Sevastopol on the Crimean Peninsula. For that purpose, the fleet carried 50,000 British and French soldiers. The Russians scuttled the ships of the Black Sea Fleet in the Sevastopol harbor, but this did not pacify the allies: Sevastopol had to be surrendered. The Russians refused to do so. The result was an eleven-month siege.

Accompanying the expeditionary force was war correspondent William Howard Russell. Thanks to a telegraph connection between Britain and Bulgaria, Russell's dispatches were printed in *The Times* shortly after they were written; for the first time in history, the folks back home got a frontline seat in the theater of war. And the news was not pretty. On September 15, Russell reported on the first night ashore: "Seldom were 27,000 Englishmen more miserable," he noted. "No tents were sent on shore, partly because there had been no time to land them, partly because there was no certainty of our being able to find carriage for them." Rain poured and, he reported, the bivouacs did not offer protection. Russell systematically described the incompetence of the army command and the corruption and inefficiency of the Commissariat, which was responsible for supplies. On September 19, he reported that the army had begun to move inland, there encountering a territory "perfectly destitute of tree or shrub";[2] all buildings had been burned down by retreating Russians. In October, the expeditionary forces realized that Sevastopol would not fall quickly, and that the besieging armies would have to spend the winter in the field.

By early November, the prospects of the British Army in the Crimea became increasingly dire, and in order to get boards and posts that would allow for the construction of barracks, the quartermaster general of the expeditionary force, Major General Richard Airey, dispatched, on November 7, Lieutenant Francis Horatio de Vere of the Royal Engineers with one of the newest steamships to the northern coast of Anatolia. His mission was to obtain, in quantity, sturdy beams, long planks, and poles, siding, and lathing of all sizes. Within a week de Vere reported back from the port of Sinop that no stocks were kept in the city and that supplies from the villages in the mountains would take at least two months to reach the port. Hearing there was a supply of planks in two coastal villages some 80 kilometers west of Sinop, he ordered the ship to set course to there, where he

2 [William Howard Russell], "The British Expedition," *The Times* (London), Oct. 2, 1854, 6; "The Battle of the Alma," *The Times* (London), Oct. 10, 1854, 7.

obtained 12,500 planks and also picked up samples of short scantlings, which did not fit the army's specifications but were cheap, in abundant supply, and might be useful. In general, the prospects seemed bleak: not only was timber in short supply, there was no way to have it delivered. The weather was bad, the waters were treacherous, the locals had no vessels large enough to transport the lumber to Sinop, and the steamship that was to bring the lumber to the Crimea could not find safe anchorage where supply was to be found. De Vere wrote to Captain John William Gordon of the Royal Engineers, who was in charge of the sappers of the expeditionary force, despite his relatively junior rank, as a result of the high number of casualties suffered before Sevastopol: "Supposing, then, that timber could not be embarked at these places, it would be necessary to convey all supplies to Sinope by land, a tedious and difficult operation where the roads are very bad and the only means of conveyance used being the backs of ponies."[3] When de Vere returned to the Crimean port of Balaklava, there was considerable irritation that he had not taken the initiative to purchase the scantlings. The army was desperate for anything it could get. Major General Airey dropped any specific requirements for lumber to be obtained, writing: "I request that you will be good enough to instruct officers going upon this service, that they are authorized to purchase wood of any description whatever which they may consider calculated to meet the object in view, viz., the hutting of this army."[4]

De Vere's assessment of the difficulties in embarking whatever timber could be found on the ship was certainly informed by the terrible weather all around the Black Sea but particularly in the north. On November 13, a powerful hurricane ravaged the Crimea. It destroyed many of the tents that had been pitched and sank eight ships loaded with supplies. Five days later, Colonel George Bell, commander of the famous Royal Scots, wrote in his diary that his men "go down to the trenches wet, come back wet, go into the hospital tents wet, die the same night, and are buried in their blankets next morning!"[5]

Crimea had a reputation for offering a semi-Mediterranean climate, but the area also experiences incredible fluctuations of temperature over short distances. Having to besiege a well-defended city without adequate supplies and in a horrible climate, the allied armies quickly faced an impossible situation. "Day after day passed in severe bodily exertion and anxious watching—one moment digging laboriously in extending

3 Francis Horatio de Vere, letter to John William Gordon, Nov. 14, 1854, in Howard Craufurd Elphinstone, *Journal of the Operations Conducted by the Corps of Royal Engineers*, 2 vols. (London: Eyre and Spottiswoode, 1859), 1:130.

4 Richard Airey, letter to [probably] Commissary General William Filder, Nov. 22, 1854, in Elphinstone, *Journal of the Operations*, 1:132.

5 George Bell, *Rough Notes by an Old Soldier*, 2 vols. (London: Day and Son, 1867), 2:227.

the approaches, and the next with arms in hand repelling the assaulting enemy; almost always wet; exposed without cover to the drenching rain and soaking snow, the keen frost and biting wind; standing for days in wet mud," staff surgeon George Husband Baird MacLeod reported after his return to Britain. The conditions in the British camps were awful: uniforms quickly turned into rags, lice were everywhere, and everyone was cold, as there was a lack of firewood. The freezing soldiers "dug beneath the snow-covered sod for wet roots wherewith to kindle a feeble and tantalizing blaze; without food till, after hours of persevering exertion, they managed to half cook their unpalatable ration over their winking fire; huddled into a crowded tent to pass the night in a close noisome atmosphere, on the oozy ground, covered by the same blanket which protected them in the wet and muddy trenches."[6]

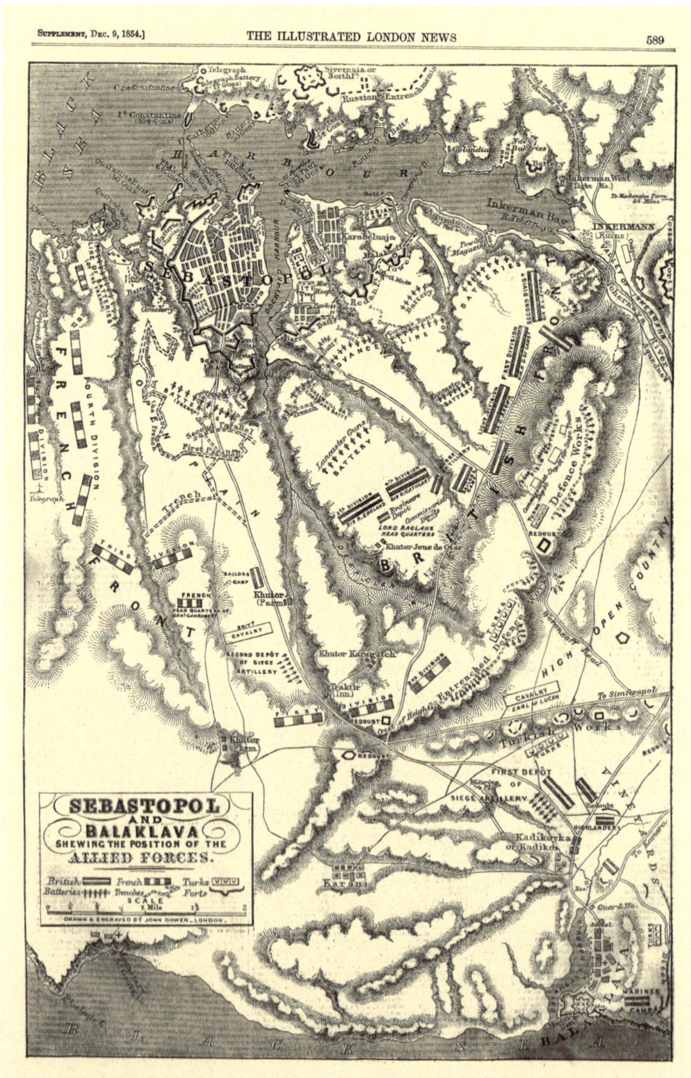

Fig. 2
Map showing the position of the allied forces at Balaklava and Sevastopol, Crimea, *The Illustrated London News*, 1854. Collection: author.

6 George H. B. MacLeod, *Notes on the Surgery of the War in the Crimea* (London: John Churchill, 1858), 13–15, 34–35.

The French proved well prepared to make the best of a bad situation. Since the War of the First Coalition (1792–97), French soldiers had been trained to create barracks with whatever materials were at hand, which in practice meant structures with wattle-and-daub walls and straw roofs. The French understood that the barracks that had served them well in Boulogne-sur-Mer, in both 1803–04 and 1854, could be used in the Crimea. "The huts [*huttes*], which our soldiers called *mole-hills* [*taupinières*], were dug a yard, at least, below the surface, and were about seven yards long by three wide and two and a half high," French military surgeon Lucien Baudens reported after the war. "The floor and sides were covered with stone when they could be had. The walls were raised above the surface by brush woven together, and covered with a thick coat of clayey earth, and upon these was placed a roof, with double slope, made of the same materials. One or two openings in the roof admitted light, but these were closed with a sod when it rained."[7] A willingness to make do with whatever was at hand applied to both the ranks and the officers.

There was no tradition in the British Army to create such wattle-and-daub barracks or, for that matter, any kind of improvised shelter, and officers lacked instructions, and the men experience. The problem becomes clear when one consults the handbook that informed army operations at the time—the second, updated edition of the *Aide-Mémoire to the Military Sciences* (1853). In its entry on castrametation, the art of making a camp, the text provided little guidance: "For Winter or other standing Cantonments, when towns or villages are not to be had,—Huts should be made. These have every shape, size, and quality; from the open screen of the Hottentot,—the roof-shaped Gypsey straw shed,—or the lowest Irish turf sheeling,—to the cottage built of stone set in clay,—of raw brick,—of cob,—or of 'wattle-and-dab.'"[8] While it made sense to provide the greatest flexibility, as the British Army had to be ready to operate both in Canada and South Africa, in India and Afghanistan, the lack of a few standard options and procedures meant that quartermasters in the field would always have to begin from scratch when building a camp. The twenty-six-page entry "Hut" hence provided almost full courses on how to construct various huts, in each case taking as its point of departure an available civilian prototype—in the case of Canada, the settler's log cabin. In countries where houses were made of bricks, the military huts were also to be made with bricks, and thus the *Aide-Mémoire* provided a six-page course on the

7 Lucien Baudens, *On Military and Camp Hospitals and the Health of Troops in the Field*, trans. Franklin B. Hough (New York: Baillière Brothers, 1862), 46; for the exact use of terminology see the original French-language edition, *La Guerre de Crimée: Les Campements, les abris, les ambulances, les hôpitaux, etc., etc.* (Paris: Michel Lévy Frères, 1858), 63–64.

8 Great Britain, Royal Engineers, *Aide-Mémoire to the Military Sciences*, 3 vols. (London: John Weale, 1853), 1:221.

art of brickmaking. Obviously, these instructions were of little help when an army found itself in an emergency. Underlying the whole approach to hutting was a basic assumption articulated right at the beginning of the relevant section: "the Officer is considered to have mechanics to assist him, either as Artificers of the Line or as Sappers and Miners, and that materials are near at hand."[9] Without a limited number of standard options to consider, and with an assumed reliance on the specialist corps of Royal Sappers and Miners, which was fully absorbed with the digging of trenches that would allow combat troops to approach Sevastopol, the British Army was caught wholly unprepared in November 1854.

The failure of British soldiers to create improvised shelters on the Crimean Peninsula was noted in London, and it elicited much critical commentary. In a speech given in the House of Commons on January 26, 1855, Secretary of State Sidney Herbert of the War Office placed blame not on his own lack of foresight, or that of the British Army establishment for having ignored proven practices of European continental armies, but on industrial civilization as such. "In England you have the highest degree of civilisation to be found in the world," he proclaimed. "As a matter of course, therefore, you have the minutest subdivision of labour; and, from the smallness of the country and the close proximity of different places, you have the most rapid communication between your cities and towns and the country." In a remarkable instance of psychological projection, the politician, a son of the 11th Earl of Pembroke who had spent his youth in Wilton House, one of the most impressive stately piles in the whole of the British Isles, concluded that, as a result of the division of labor brought about by industrialization, "the English peasant never does anything for himself, as is the case in less advanced states of society. Everything, in consequence of the great division of labour, and the great proximity of supply of all kinds, is done for him." The Crimean disaster showed the result: "A man does not know how to turn if he is thrown upon his own resources and left to shift for himself, in the same way as the inhabitants of other countries can do."[10] If he had been confronted with the option of imitating his French comrades, the ordinary British soldier in the Crimea might have happily taken a spade to dig a hole and collect mud, and a knife to cut branches and weave a wattle. Yet the British officers, who had grown up in country houses with ready-supplied comforts, certainly thought that it ought be possible to find an off-the-shelf solution. Thus the commander of the British Army

9 Ibid., 2:256.
10 *Hansard Parliamentary Debates*, 3rd ser., vol. 136, H.C., Jan. 26, 1855, cols. 985–86.

in the Crimea, General FitzRoy James Henry Somerset, 1st Baron Raglan, decided to order prefabricated barracks.[11]

Great Britain had entered the war without having calculated whether it had a vital interest in the question as to which country was the dominant power in the Black Sea, and it had sent an army to the Crimea without giving much thought to the fact that it might spend the winter there. Its thoughtlessness fitted an old pattern. "We seem, as it were, to have conquered and peopled half the world in a fit of absence of mind," British historian Sir John Robert Seeley famously observed at the beginning of *The Expansion of England*, published in 1883.[12] Without direction from London, religious dissidents looking for places where they could worship freely, businesspeople seeking profit, and jailers looking for places to dump the unwanted had first brought the British flag to North America, the West Indies, southern Africa, India, Australia, and New Zealand. Inattentive settlement and conquest meant that the British government did not really ask itself if and how its growing empire served the interests of a midsize island nation located at the periphery of the European continent—and political and moral indifference shaped the British attitude to the destruction of native and aboriginal lives and cultures due to disease, the expansion of white settlement, and colonial policies of divide and rule. The British trusted that the so-called invisible hand, postulated in the mid-eighteenth century by Adam Smith as the unintentional but beneficial effects of a *laissez-faire* ("allow to do") competition of countless instances of economic self-interest, would produce a moral order, the achievement of which was beyond the abilities of any individual or group.

In the early nineteenth century, whole industries developed to serve the needs of those leaving for new lives overseas. While the bulk of construction in the colonies depended on local labor using local materials, there are reports that, as early as 1804, one-off prefabricated structures were erected in the Australian colony of New South Wales, and in 1820, precut timber frames were dispatched from England to South Africa to help British settlers make a new beginning in the Eastern Cape.[13] A carpenter and builder in London with the family name Manning (first name either Henry, John, or Henry John) conceived in the late 1820s fully prefabricated cottages using modular parts produced on an industrial scale in England for use in colonies overseas. In 1830, he sent

11 *Report of the Commission of Inquiry into the Supplies of the British Army in the Crimea, Presented to both Houses of Parliament by Command of Her Majesty* (London: Harrison and Sons, 1856), 33.
12 John Robert Seeley, *The Expansion of England: Two Courses of Lectures* (London: Macmillan, 1883), 8.
13 Gilbert Herbert, "The Portable Colonial Cottage," *Journal of the Society of Architectural Historians* 31, no. 4 (1972), 261–63.

prospective settlers who were preparing to leave Britain to settle the Swan River area in Western Australia a pamphlet suggesting that they purchase, before departure, "a comfortable Dwelling that can be erected in a few hours after landing, with windows, glazed doors, and locks, bolts, and the whole painted in a good and secure manner, carefully packed and delivered at the Docks, consisting of two, three, four, or more roomed Houses, made to any plan that may be proposed."[14]

The Manning Portable Colonial Cottage for Emigrants, as the structure came to be known, marked a technological breakthrough. First, it was designed with an eye to the ease of transportation, both between England and Australia and also overland between the shore and the site of construction. In addition, the Manning cottage could be easily erected: one did not need any carpentry skills. The famous horticulturalist John Claudius Loudon judged Manning's cottage to be "one of the most perfect things of the kind that we have seen," and in 1834 published a full description with a set of drawings of the cottage in his best-selling *Encyclopaedia of Cottage, Farm and Villa Architecture*.

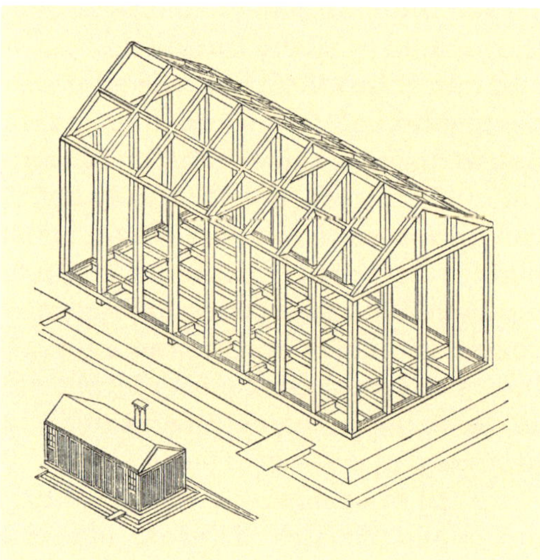

Fig. 3
Henry, John, or Henry John Manning, Two isometric views of the Manning Portable Colonial Cottage for Emigrants, from John Claudius Loudon, *Encyclopaedia of Cottage, Farm and Villa Architecture*, 1834. Collection: author.

Loudon understood well that the key to the success of prefabrication was a standardization of the various elements, which made it unnecessary to cut pieces to size at the building site. "Every part of it being made exactly to the same dimensions; that is, all the panels, posts, and plates, being respectively of exactly the same length, breadth, and thickness, no mistake or loss of time can occur in putting them together."[15]

Within a few years, many builders had entered the market for prefabricated dwellings in Australia. However, the cottages did not prove popular as perma-

14 Quoted in Gilbert Herbert, *Pioneers of Prefabrication: The British Contribution in the Nineteenth Century* (Baltimore and London: Johns Hopkins University Press, 1978), 4.

15 John Claudius Loudon, *Encyclopaedia of Cottage, Farm and Villa Architecture* (London: Longman, Brown, Green, and Longmans, 1834), 256.

nent dwellings in subtropical conditions. They had no thermal insulation; the low ceiling height did not allow for heat dissipation; and, constructed out of timber only, the prefabricated cottages proved a fire hazard. In addition, the hollow walls were popular with vermin. A custom-built house made of rammed loam was cooler, sturdier, and considerably cheaper. Manning and most of the other builders who had hoped to serve the Australian market with prefabricated cottages turned to other sources of revenue.[16]

The prefabricated-dwelling industry in England had a bit of a revival when, in 1851, prospector Edward Hargraves found gold near Orange, New South Wales. His discovery triggered a gold rush that brought many immigrants to Australia and also led to a revival in the design and production of prefabricated and dismountable shelter. If, in the 1830s, the focus of builders like Manning had been on providing emigrant families with permanent dwellings that aspired to some level of decorum, in the early 1850s the ambitions of the English builders involved were more modest: they knew that the mostly single prospectors moved around and that a simple barrack would do.

William Eassie, a Gloucester contractor who owned a large sawmill and timber yard, became an important supplier of prefabricated and dismountable wooden barracks for use by gold prospectors in Australia. Eassie's main lumber supplier was Price & Co., a major importer of Canadian and Baltic timber. In early November 1854, the company's managing partner, Richard Potter, heard about the British Army's troubles in the Crimea and saw an opportunity. He asked Eassie if he could set up a production line for prefabricated barracks to be used by the expeditionary force. Eassie responded enthusiastically and developed a sketch based on the prospector's hut, a set of specifications, and a budget. Potter then approached government officials and the military leadership in London. When it looked as if the process would become protracted, however, he decided to act boldly, putting pressure on his chief contact, Major General Sir John Mark Frederick Smith, commanding Royal Engineer of the Southern District: "I told him that it seemed to be a case of great emergency," he informed a committee of the House of Commons a few months later. "I thought we could produce a building, perhaps, in some respects better adapted for the facilities of carriage and lightness than his plan, but based on his ideas, and if he could give me an order to commence the next day, I would go down to Gloucester, and return and bring him

16 Herbert, "The Portable Colonial Cottage," 272–73.

17 Great Britain, Parliament, House of Commons, *Accounts and Papers*, 21 vols. (London: Her Majesty's Stationery Office, 1864), Army; Navy; Ordnance, session Apr. 30–Aug. 28, 1857, vol. 28, 214.

18 Hugh Conway Jones, "William Eassie: A Notable Victorian Contractor," *Gloucestershire Society for Industrial Archeology Journal* 34 (2004), 53–54.

a plan."[17] After some hesitation, Potter was told to go ahead. He returned home and consulted his foremen; in response to some suggestions from Major General Smith, they modified the proposed roof to make the barracks both lighter and easier to transport. The resulting structure, which was to shelter twenty men, was 8.5 meters long and 5 meters wide, offering a door with a window above it in one gable and two windows in the other. The parts of the barrack were to be numbered, bound together in thirty-four packages, and, along with a box containing hardware, tools, and a lithograph image of the hut, sent to the Crimea.[18]

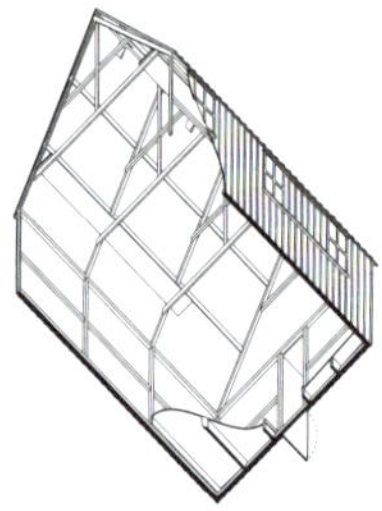

Drawings, Gloucester Soldiers' Hut
→ p. 509

That same day, production began for a batch of 500 barracks made of yellow pine and spruce. The next day, a government inspector arrived at the Eassie establishment and ordered the halt of production; he disagreed with the modifications suggested by the foremen. After some negotiations, a compromise was reached: 300 barracks were to be made using the roof design developed by the Eassie men, which became known as the Gloucester hut.

Fig. 4
William Eassie, Description, parts list, plan, elevations, and sections of the Gloucester soldiers' hut, 1856. Collection: National Archives, Kew, England.

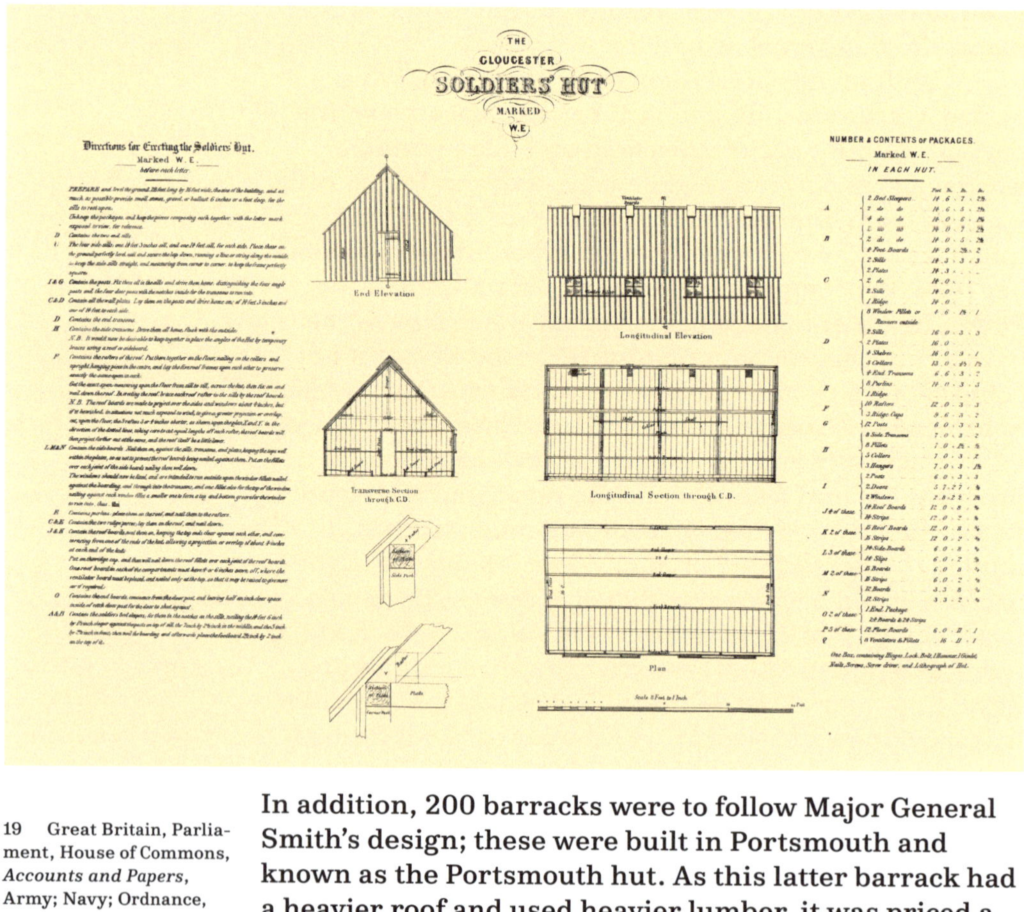

In addition, 200 barracks were to follow Major General Smith's design; these were built in Portsmouth and known as the Portsmouth hut. As this latter barrack had a heavier roof and used heavier lumber, it was priced a bit higher.[19]

19 Great Britain, Parliament, House of Commons, *Accounts and Papers*, Army; Navy; Ordnance, session Apr. 30–Aug. 28, 1857, vol. 28, 214.

Having impressed the British government, Potter was introduced to Jean-François Mocquard, the private secretary to Napoleon III.[20] The French emperor, a nephew of the "Great" Napoleon, had been elected president of the Second French Republic in 1848 and been elevated to the status of *empereur des Français* (emperor of the French) in 1851. He was very interested in architectural matters; a year earlier, he had set in motion the massive project to transform Paris into a modern city. He was also interested in military matters, and the barracks were the meeting point between his two passions. Finally, he was an Anglophile and believed that France and Britain were natural allies. As a result, Potter found a warm welcome when he arrived at Château de Saint-Cloud. The emperor had studied the design of the Gloucester hut. According to an article that appeared two months after the men's meeting, in the January 6, 1855, issue of *The Illustrated London News*, Napoleon III "suggested many alterations; lowered the height of the walls, to give 'solidity' to the building against the storms of Crimea; introduced two doors into the Barracks, one at each end; simplified the framework of the roof, to save space and weight in carriage, and raised the height of the bed-boards above the ground." The emperor ordered Potter to construct an original Gloucester hut in the Tuileries Garden alongside a barrack of the modified design. Then, the article reported, "both Barracks were subjected to a minute and thorough examination, and a guard of twenty-six men were made to lie down on the bed-boards, and were accommodated without pressure."[21] Of course, Napoleon's version was deemed to be superior, and Potter walked away with an order for 1,850 units to be produced in Eassie's factory; another 1,050 units were to be produced under license in Toulon and Marseille.[22]

20 Ibid., 216.
21 "Wooden Barracks for the French Army in the Crimea," *The Illustrated London News*, Jan. 6, 1855, 14.
22 "Rapport du Maréchal Vaillant sur l'expedition de Crimée," *Archives Belges de Médicine Militaire* 18 (1856), 320.

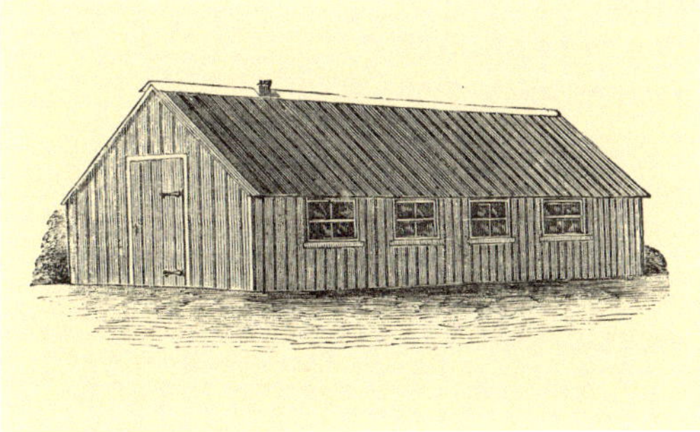

Fig. 5
Exterior of a French officers' barrack, following Napoleon III's design modifications, *The Illustrated London News*, 1855. Collection: author.

Fig. 6
Interior of a hut to shelter common soldiers, following Napoleon III's design modifications, *The Illustrated London News*, 1855. Collection: author.

To ensure quality and to teach his engineers how to assemble the barracks, Napoleon sent a team to Gloucester. On December 19, 1854, the first of a fleet of French clippers left Southampton with 300 barracks.

Both the British and the French expeditionary armies were to use the barracks conceived and developed by Potter and Eassie. They deployed them differently, however. The barracks shipped to the British forces were primarily to house soldiers in the field; those sent to the French were to be used as sick wards. Each French regiment was to get two barracks to serve as infirmaries, while larger field hospitals to be constructed along the shores of the Dardanelles were to use the bulk of the barracks ordered.[23]

On December 9, *The Illustrated London News* carried a report on the Portsmouth barrack, which measured 8.5 by 5 meters, designed to "comfortably lodge twenty or thirty men." The article predicted that these dwellings would be "very acceptable to our brave soldiers against the inclemency of the weather." Of particular note was the facility of the product. "The whole are carefully fitted up, taken down, packed into easy, portable packages for the convenience of stowage in the ship's hold, and easy removal afterward, hooped together with iron, and systematically lettered. The letters and numbers on each package will agree with that on a lithographed plan, which is to accompany each house. A box will also be sent with each house, containing two hammers, two gimlets, two pair of pincers, and 14 lb. [6.4 kilograms] of nails, in case the Sappers and Miners, who are to erect them, have not sufficient at their disposal."[24]

The loading of the huts onto ships was sufficiently newsworthy to be described in illustrated reports. Yet time was running out. The first shipment arrived in Balaklava on November 25, 1854, but the second and third shipments were delayed until January.[25] And there was chaos in Balaklava: in his memoir, American journalist Richard Cunningham McCormick recalled, "Confusion worse confounded stamped every thing. Men, horses, wagons and carts crowded the slimy beach, where all sorts of stores were carelessly scattered."[26] On December 21, the issue was raised in the British House of Commons. The secretary at war announced that barrack construction was well underway, and that "a portion of them is at sea." Efforts were in progress to gather building materials for barracks in Turkey, and he also noted that some barracks obtained in Austria had been loaded onto a steamer.[27] On December 25, the

23 See Baudens, *On Military and Camp Hospitals*, 58, 63, 67, 168.
24 "Portable Barracks for the Crimea," *The Illustrated London News*, Dec. 9, 1854, 575.
25 *Report of the Commission of Inquiry*, 33.
26 Richard C. McCormick, *Visit to the Camp before Sevastopol* (New York: Appleton, 1855), 28.
27 *Hansard Parliamentary Debates*, 3rd ser., vol. 136, H.C., Dec. 21, 1854, col. 787.

first shipment of more than 3,500 prefabricated barracks arrived in Balaklava, and eight more shipments shortly followed.

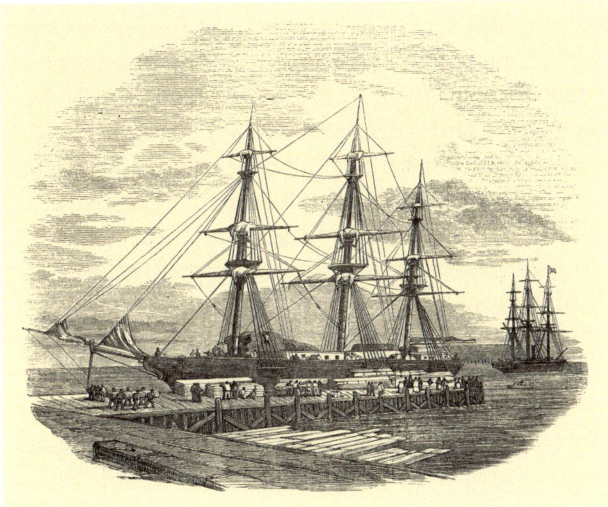

Fig. 7
Loading of wooden barracks on board the merchantman *White Falcon*, moored at Southampton, for the French army in the Crimea, *The Illustrated London News*, 1855. Collection: author.

On January 2, 1855, however, Russell, the war correspondent, reported that it might be too little too late:

> While our friends at home are disputing about the exact mean degree of cold of the Crimean winter, and are preparing all kinds of warm clothing, which at some good time or other will come out to the men, our army is rapidly melting away. [...] Think what a tent must be, pitched, as it were, at the bottom of a marsh, into which some twelve or fourteen miserable creatures, drenched to the skin, have to creep for shelter after twelve hours of vigil in a trench like a canal, and then reflect what state these poor fellows must be in at the end of a night and day spent in such *shelter*, huddled together without any change of clothing, and lying packed up as close as they can stow in saturated blankets.

And then he asked the obvious question:

> But why are they in tents? Where are the huts which have been sent out to them? The huts are on board ships in the harbour of Balaklava, and are likely to stay there. Some of these huts, of which we have heard so much, I have seen floating about the beach; others have been landed, and now and then I have met a wretched pony, knee-deep in mud, struggling on beneath the weight of two thin deal planks, a small portion of one of these huts,

> which would be most probably converted into firewood after lying for some time in the camp, or be turned into stabling for officers' horses.

Later that day, Russell wrote another dispatch, showing his despair. "We have no means of getting up the huts—all our army can do is to feed itself. Captain Keen, R. E., is here in charge of 4,000 tons of wood for hutting, but he cannot get anyone to take charge of it, or unload it out of the ships. Each hut weighs more than two tons, and, somehow or other, I fear it will so happen that no effort will be used to get them up till men are found frozen to death in their tents."[28]

A few months later, Colonel Alexander Murray Tulloch and surgeon Sir John McNeill, sent from Britain to Crimea to investigate the catastrophic supply problems, wrote down their conclusions. By the end of December, when the first ship with barracks arrived, soldiers had been employed for weeks carrying provisions to the front, "and so much had their strength been reduced by their sufferings, and such was the state of the roads, that a weight of from 20 lb. to 25 lb. [9–11.3 kilograms] was as much as a man could bring up from Balaklava." Balaklava was surrounded by steep hills. "It consequently required from 250 to 300 men to carry up a single hut sufficient to accommodate, at the utmost 25 men; and as, at this rate, it was impossible to spare a sufficient number from their other duties, the attempt had to be abandoned."[29] The investigators also discovered that two shipments of boards that had arrived in January had done little good, because a shipment of rafters only reached the Crimea in February.

While the ill-coordinated parts of the prefabricated barracks languished in the harbor, *The Illustrated London News* carried a long article on the barracks that portrayed Potter, Eassie, and Price & Co. as the saviors of both the British and French armies.[30] But when Russell's reports reached the British public on January 24, panic ensued. The next day, *The Times* carried a grim editorial stating that the army in Crimea suffered "all that Englishmen have read of before, when they could afford to amuse themselves with the horrible in the narrative of Napoleon's Russian campaign. Vast piles of wooden huts were at Balaklava, but the army was in tents, and it was certain must remain in tents as long as it lasted, for there was not the least chance of transport sufficient to bring up the huts." There was no prospect of things improving quickly—hence, the editorial concluded, "the finest army that ever left these shores will

28 [William Howard Russell], "The British Expedition," *The Times* (London), Jan. 24, 1855, 7.
29 *Report of the Commission of Inquiry*, 34–36.
30 "Wooden Barracks for the French Army in the Crimea," 14.

soon cease to exist as a force."[31] A few days later the government fell.

The new British government finally began a concerted effort to ensure that supplies reached not only the harbor of Balaklava but also the army surrounding Sevastopol. Yet it took a long time before soldiers noticed any change. As of February 6, 1855, Colonel Bell noted, the men were "looking miserable in their clay-cold death beds; no fuel, extremely cold, nothing joyful. People at home are led to suppose we are all living in huts, *i.e.* little wooden houses. We are existing in ragged tents full of slimy mud."[32] To the American journalist McCormick, the barracks were another symbol of the "inexplicable want of forethought" and "astounding negligence" of the whole campaign: "It required sixty horses, or one hundred and fifty men, to convey the materials of a single hut from the harbor to the camp. A man could scarcely manage to make any progress through the deep mud even with one plank on his shoulder."[33]

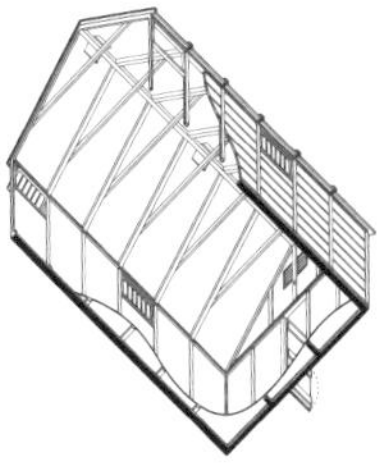

Wooden Hut for Fifty Men
→ p. 509

In the summer of 1855, Britain's Board of Ordnance began to consider the possibility that the army might have to spend the winter of 1855–56 in the Crimea. There is no indication that it considered sending extra sappers to the peninsula to create simple wattle-and-daub shelters for the soldiers. Instead, it commissioned from Eassie a somewhat modified version of the Gloucester hut, which had proven to be more successful than the Portsmouth hut, and in addition developed designs for four different barracks, which included one that was twice the size and others that came with a double thickness of boarding.[34] The first of these barracks began arriving while the physician Dr. John Sutherland and civil engineer Robert Rawlinson were still in the Crimea. They had been sent in March to Constantinople to investigate the allegedly catastrophic sanitary situation in the large military hospital the British had created in an Ottoman military building located on the southern shore of the Bosporus, and after they had written their report, they had traveled to the Crimea, where they had inspected the existing barracks. Sutherland and Rawlinson liked the modified huts:

> So far as concerned the health of the troops, the huts were well adapted for their purpose. They were spacious and had ample means of ventilation. Their defects were the want of eaves to turn the rain from the foundations, and the liability of the roofs to leak, which, however, was readily

31 "There Is a Season for All Things," *The Times* (London), Jan. 25, 1855, 6.
32 Bell, *Rough Notes of an Old Soldier*, 2:240.
33 McCormick, *Visit to the Camp before Sevastopol*, 154–55.
34 "Huts for the Crimea," *Civil Engineer and Architect's Journal* 18 (1855), 335–36.

overcome by covering the joinings with tarred felt or canvas. The number of men accommodated varied with the size of the hut, the space for each man being about 165 cubic feet [5 cubic meters]. It was small; but, on the other hand, the means of ventilation were ample, and the free use of these is the only way of supplementing the limited space at the disposal of armies in the field.[35]

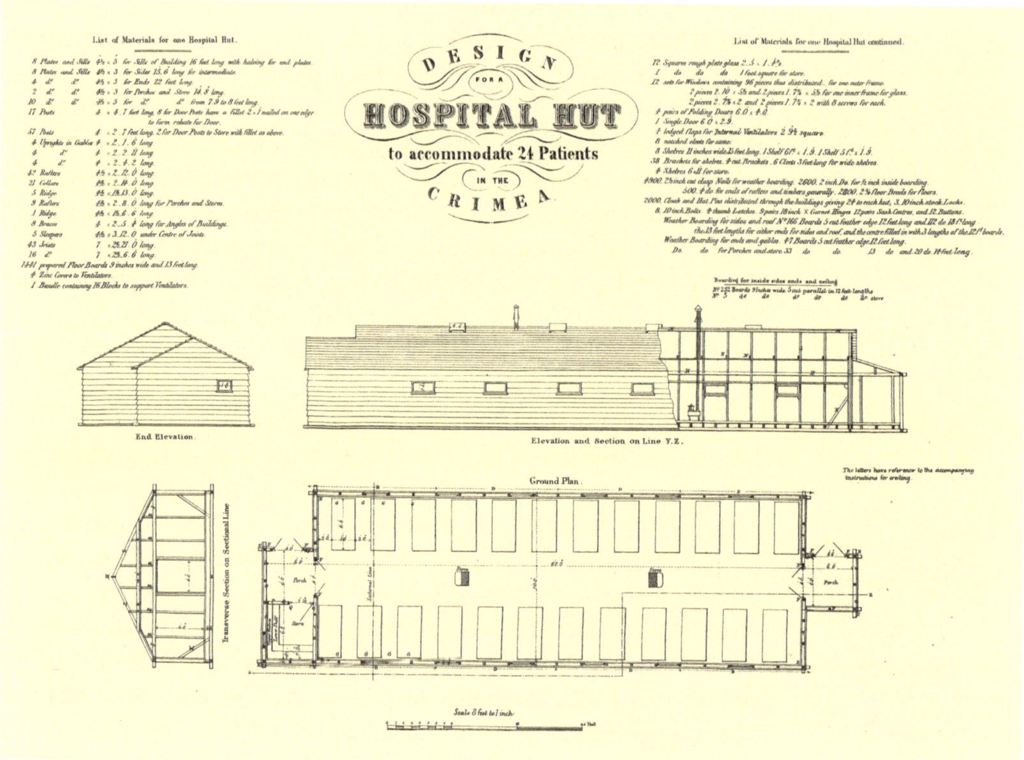

Their praise meant something, as Sutherland and Rawlinson had been generally very critical of the performance of the first generation of Portsmouth huts. In the case of those housing the 79th Highland Regiment of Foot, they blamed the site. "We found the floors of the infected huts very damp; and on removing the boarding, the surface of the ground beneath was found covered with threads of fungi, and the atmosphere in the huts had the peculiar odour and dampness usually experienced on going into an underground cellar," they reported. "So wet was the subsoil, that water was found under one of the angles of a hut. The men slept on the boarding, hardly raised above the ground, and breathed the damp malarial atmosphere arising from it. [...] The ventilation was insufficient; and under all the circumstances, the huts were overcrowded." Sutherland and Rawlinson expressed the opinion that "even the healthiest men would succumb quickly when lodged in those huts."

Fig. 8
List of materials, plan, elevations, and sections of a hospital barrack designed for twenty-four patients in the Crimea, 1856. Collection: National Archives, Kew, England.

35 Great Britain, Sanitary Commission, *Report to the Right Hon. Lord Panmure, G. C. B., &c., Minister at War, of the Proceedings of the Sanitary Commission Dispatched to the Seat of War in the East, 1855–56* (London: Harrison & Sons, 1857), 163.

The men of the 79th had banked earth against the sides of the barracks, one of the reasons for the dampness, Sutherland and Rawlinson concluded, and they recommended "that the ground occupied should be drained, the huts isolated by digging the earth away from the sides, and the site of each barrack separately drained by a trench cut round the cleared space, and about a foot below the level of the floor; that the huts should be thoroughly ventilated by ridge and floor ventilation, and the number of men reduced in each."[36] Drawings made on the spot and published in the printed version of the report illustrated the situation in a before-and-after manner.

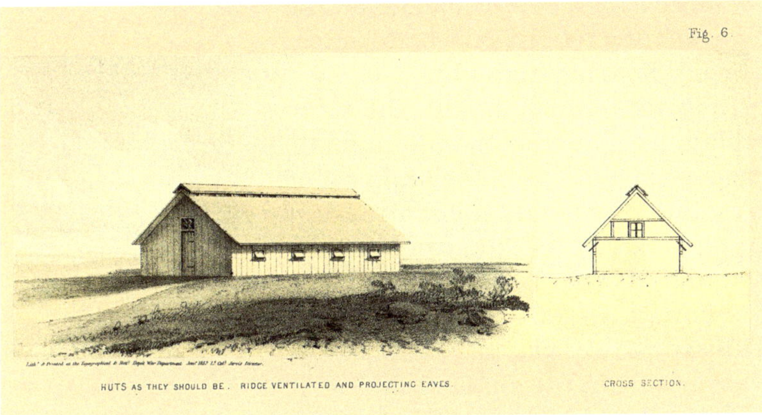

Fig. 9
Final improved version of the Portsmouth barrack, from *Report to the Right Hon. Lord Panmure, G. C. B., &c., Minister at War, of the Proceedings of the Sanitary Commission Dispatched to the Seat of War in the East, 1855–56.* Collection: Wellcome Library, London.

As Sutherland and Rawlinson inspected many other camps, they discovered that the key issue determining the morbidity of the soldiers was the site—men living in barracks built on wet and badly drained sites became ill, while those living in barracks built on dry and well-drained sites remained healthy. Everywhere, they initiated small modifications to increase ventilation by means of creating openings in the walls and a ridge ventilation in the roof, ending up with what they considered to be the final improved version of the Portsmouth barrack. They went beyond modifying the barracks that had been shipped from England when they visited the sick of the naval brigade, who were kept on the main deck of HMS *Diamond*, which was moored in the harbor of Balaklava. Considering this a bad situation, they suggested that the sick be moved ashore and housed in barracks. The commanding officer agreed, but as there was no supply of barracks, the commission had no choice but to begin from scratch. Rawlinson collaborated with the ship's carpenters to create a new barrack design that allowed for superior ventilation and could be constructed with the prefabricated building materials sent from Britain. Sutherland and Rawlinson reported:

36 Ibid., 110–11.

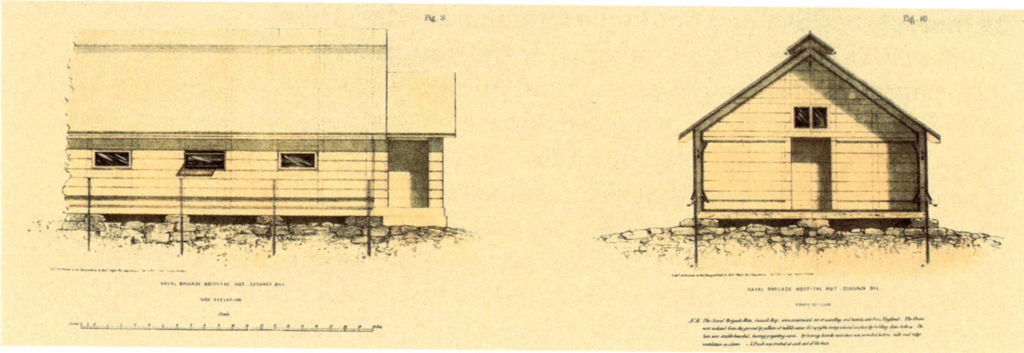

> The ground was cleared, leveled, and drained. A foundation of large rough stones picked off the adjacent surface, about a foot high, was formed, and the timbers and flooring of the hut laid on these stones. [...] By this simple means, the air was allowed to circulate freely under the hut, and all risk of damp was removed. The sides and roof of each hut were double, and a current of air was allowed to pass upwards in the space between the outer boarding and the inner lining, in the manner already mentioned. As the result of this arrangement the temperature was the same inside the hut as it was outside in the shade.[37]

Fig. 10
Side elevation and section of the barrack designed in collaboration by Robert Rawlinson and unnamed Royal Navy carpenters to house the naval brigade hospital, from *Report to the Right Hon. Lord Panmure, G. C. B., &c., Minister at War, of the Proceedings of the Sanitary Commission Dispatched to the Seat of War in the East, 1855–56*. Collection: Wellcome Library, London.

While Sutherland and Rawlinson focused on the performance of the barracks from a health perspective, a committee of military engineers considered them from a construction and transportation angle: "The large-sized panel double huts are roomy and warm, and having felt on the roofs, between the boards, are waterproof, excepting at the joints, where, if they be not very accurately fitted, the wet and wind penetrates," their report, authored by Captain Charles R. Binney, stated. "They are easily put up when the different parts are on the ground, and, being fastened with screws and nuts, are intended, if required, to be taken to pieces and removed to other positions." Yet these barracks also had problems:

> They are heavy, and the different pieces cannot be carried conveniently on pack-horses, and unless very carefully packed and numbered, much delay takes place in sorting and in erecting the huts. In many cases, owing to their [being] badly fitted, it has been necessary to use nails in erecting these huts, which was never intended. Their great length frequently causes considerable straining at the joints, and there is generally more difficulty with the ground, as to secure a good foundation.

37 Ibid., 142.

> From what they have seen of these huts, the members of the Board are of opinion that many of those now in use in this army would not stand being taken down, trans-shipped, and re-erected.[38]

In fact, the original Gloucester hut developed in the fall of 1854 had proven to be the best model, as it was both simple and relatively easy to transport. In an appendix to the committee's report, Captain Binney of the Royal Engineers suggested that the experience of the British Army in Crimea provided an important lesson: soldiers should become less dependent on supplies and be more inventive in ways of making shelter in a variety of conditions.[39]

While the actual impact of prefabricated barracks on the comfort, health, and the survival of the British Army in Crimea in the winter of 1854–55 had been limited, their erection marked a psychological turning point that was to linger in the British collective memory of the war. In his illustrated book on the campaign, published after the first winter, author George Brackenbury used one image to represent a sea change in the fate of the British expeditionary force—not an image of a breach held or a battle won but a lithograph entitled *Huts and Warm Clothing for the Army*. Based on a drawing by war artist William Simpson, the image shows the arrival of a train with supplies at a camp site in the peninsula's interior. Everywhere, barracks are being constructed. "Slowly, partially, and scantily indeed are the first supplies

Fig. 11
William Simpson, *Huts and Warm Clothing for the Army*, 1855. Collection: author.

38 Charles R. Binney, "Reports on Hutting Made by the Board of Officers Assembled in the Crimea, and Observations and Suggestions on the Subject," British Army, *Papers on Subjects Connected with the Duties of the Corps of Royal Engineers*, n.s., 7 (1858), 53.
39 Charles R. Binney, "Observations and Suggestions on Hutting," British Army, *Papers on Subjects Connected with the Duties of the Corps of Royal Engineers*, n.s., 7 (1858), 62–63.

distributed," Brackenbury observed, while "the hardships of winter must drag on a lingering existence ere they vanish for ever in the genial presence of spring." He also declared that "the worst is over."[40] For Brackenbury, the fact that the barracks got erected at all—if with great delay—marked a return to somewhat civil conditions. In the second volume of his book, which covered the spring and early summer of 1855, he emphasized how much the situation had improved. Commenting on Simpson's depiction of a camp of the Fourth Division, Brackenbury found evidence of "comfort and plenty" that contrasted sharply with the "scene of desolation and misery" in the winter. "Huts are now thickly interspersed with the tents, and the men have reassumed the distinctive military characteristics of the British soldier."[41] That winter the British artist John Dalbiac Luard traveled to the Crimea to visit his brother, who served as an infantry captain, and to make sketches of the siege. While at the front he also visited the regiment in which he had served for some time, and there he experienced the delight when a few of his onetime comrades opened and unpacked a box of provisions from home in the comfortable setting of their hut, decorated with cutouts from *The Illustrated London News*. Upon his return to England, Luard produced a painting of the occasion, exhibited at the Royal Academy in 1857, which created, like Simpson's image of the construction of the huts, good feeling all around. Perhaps it is right to give the final word in this matter to William Howard Russell. On December 7, 1855, he noted in his diary that, while the British soldiers besieging Sevastopol were now amply

Fig. 12
John Dalbiac Luard,
A Welcome Arrival, c. 1855.
Collection: National Army Museum, London.

40 George Brackenbury, *The Campaign in the Crimea: An Historical Study*, 2 vols. (London: Colnaghi and Longman, Brown, Green and Longmans, 1855), 1:81–82.
41 Ibid., 2:94.

supplied with huts, the structures seemed unable to keep them dry. "It is considered that if the Government had sent out hammers, nails, planks, and felt, the men would have done much better."[42]

In 1855 the Kingdom of Sardinia also joined the allies. Turin needed the support of Paris to realize its ambition to unify Italy, and by making a well-trained expeditionary force available, it would not only put France into its debt but also gain a place at the table in any peace conference. In May an expeditionary corps of 18,000 soldiers led by the very capable General Alfonso Ferrero La Marmora disembarked in Balaklava.[43] The core of the Sardinian army in the Crimea was the Bersaglieri (sharpshooters) infantry corps, a highly mobile and trained shock troop that had to compensate for the fact that the Sardinian state was too poor to afford many cavalry brigades. Like today's commandos, Bersaglieri were supposed to take care of themselves in rough terrain and, if necessary, live off the land.

La Marmora immediately began to plan how to shelter his soldiers in the upcoming winter. On July 17 he submitted a lengthy report to Turin in which he reviewed the British and French experience in the previous winter. His provisional conclusion was that the British prefabricated huts were easy to assemble but not strong enough, while the French huts shipped from Marseille were stronger but required more work. "For the troops, I am studying whether I can shelter them partly in underground huts," La Marmora noted.[44] By early September he had appointed a commission led by Major General Manfredo Fanti. After two weeks of work, the commission reported back to La Marmora. The daily journal of the Sardinian headquarters reported the results on September 17: "The Commander-in-Chief, following the project of the specially appointed commission, orders the construction of the barracks and huts for the winter to be carried out with materials from the country. On the basis of discussions that took place within the commission, and taking into account experiences made, it appears that the main condition that must be taken into account in determining the form of such shelters is that of the materials available." The main issue was the size of available timber. While in theory it was preferable to construct large barracks which might shelter up to 200 men, the reality was that large timbers were difficult to obtain and located far away, and that the Sardinian army had little transport capacity. The report continues:

42 William Howard Russell, *The War: From the Death of Lord Raglan to the Evacuation of the Crimea* (London: Routledge, 1856), 373.
43 See Cristoforo Manfredi, *La Spedizione Sarda in Crimea nel 1855–56* (Rome: Voghera Enrico, 1896).
44 As quoted in ibid., 221.

> The commission therefore adopted the plan presented by Major Ferrero, commander of the 17th infantry battalion; which is only an improvement of the system of huts, which the soldiers of some battalions, and especially those of the 5th Bersaglieri battalion, built themselves, guided by instinct and adapting to the available possibilities. These rectangular huts measure 4.30 meters by 2.20 meters wide and have a capacity of 6 men. They are dug up to 0.80 meters below the ground level and covered with a roof. [...] The ridge of the roof arises 1.30 meters above grade. It is covered with a layer of 5 cm of mortar composed of earth and dung, and is then covered with a 10 cm layer of earth.[45]

The Sardinian command issued the general principles to be followed, allowing every battalion or even company to make changes as necessary. During his stay at Crimea, La Marmora had established excellent relations with the Ottoman army, and obtained permission to pull down unused huts in an Ottoman camp for parts.

The half-buried barracks used by the Sardinian army provided good shelter without causing much of a fuss and earned the praise of British officers serving in the Corps of Royal Engineers. Many French soldiers followed the example of the Sardinians, realizing that the same attitude to providing shelter had served the soldiers of the first Napoleon very well. William Howard Russell admired the ability of the Italian and French soldiers to take care of their own housing. "The French camp here is built like that of their neighbours the Sardinians, very much on the Tartar or Russian plan, and the huts are semi-subterranean. They present in appearance a strong contrast to the regular rows of high wooden huts belonging to the Highland Division opposite, at Kamara, but the money saved to France and Sardinia by the ingenuity and exertions of their soldiers in hutting themselves must have been very considerable in amount." Russell was especially impressed by the practice of the French to plant young firs and evergreens in their camps. "They have also made gardens, which promise to bear fruit, flowers, and vegetables for Tartars and Muscovites, and they have turned a large portion of ground by the banks of the Tchernaya, and close to the Traktir Bridge, into a succession of gardens, each appropriated to different companies of the regiments encamped in the neighbourhood."[46] Another British journalist who reported on the preparations made in the fall of 1855

45 Ibid., 222–23.

noted that French and Sardinians were well prepared for the winter: "An immense city has grown up as if by enchantment." Not understanding their highly opportunistic practice of barrack construction, he assumed that the locally made huts adapted "the experience of the natives to their own purposes—a square space dug out, about six feet deep, and a roof of osier work, plastered over with mud and then covered with earth. It would seem to the uninitiated that the heavy rain would soak through the plaster, but the natives in the Crimea and the villagers in many parts of the East know better."[47] The prefabricated barracks used to house the French sick and wounded were judged wanting. "While some of the barracks (*baraques*) were chinked up and very close, others were open to the day, the joints between the boards admitted the rain, and although the stoves were always burning the cold was intense," Baudens noted in his report on the health of the French army in the Crimea. "The corps of engineers was blamed, as if it could do everything. It had built the barracks, and closed the joints with battens, and if the dryness had drawn the wood apart, the inmates should have repaired it."[48] Of course, the French spirit of self-help in matters relating to barracks was deeply ingrained—but should it also apply to the sick and the wounded?

The important lesson was that in a winter campaign soldiers ought to be capable of creating their own shelter—prefabricated barracks to house a whole army in the field was not to have a future in Western warfare. Major Richard Delafield of the Military Commission to the Theater of War in Europe, dispatched by the US Secretary of War, Jefferson Davis, to observe the Crimean War, provided a clear judgment in his *Report on the Art of War in Europe in 1854, 1855, and 1856* (1860). "The Sardinian army, in preparing for the winter of 1855–56, without incurring any expense, was enabled to hut itself in apparently very comfortable, warm, dry, and durable huts, while their allies have, at great cost, imported materials for their huts from England and France, and bestowed much workmanship of carpentry, as well as iron work, to form and put up temporary huts that do not possess the warmth of the Sardinian's, although more dry in damp, wet weather, and at such times more healthy." Delafield did go through the effort to describe the prefabricated barracks shipped from Britain and France, but did not find any need to recommend them. One observation, which in fact had become a common refrain in those days, implied enough of a judgment: "They weighed two and a half tons each."[49]

46 Russell, *The War*, 444.
47 "The Winter Quarters of the Allies," *Bentley's Miscelany* 38 (1855), 578.
48 Baudens, *On Military and Camp Hospitals*, 63.

Both the French and British armies needed military hospitals not only on the Crimean Peninsula but also in the rear, far from the battlefields, in or close to major urban centers like Constantinople. *Médecin inspecteur* (medical inspector) Michel Lévy was charged with organizing the medical service of the French expeditionary force. The author of a famous treatise on hygiene, Lévy had been a physician at the military hospital of Val-de-Grâce, located in a monumental five-story former Benedictine abbey. There, he had witnessed an interesting experiment: in 1841, a colleague erected three barracks in the adjacent gardens. The mortality of the patients lodged in those barracks was dramatically lower than those in the main building, and Lévy had become convinced that in hospitals, "unhealthiness increases in direct proportion to their height." For Lévy, the size of a hospital was the single most important factor determining its salubrity: "The history of epidemics, and that of armies at all periods, testifies with the authority of the greatest names and under the terror of the most painful recollections, to the toxic power created in the accumulations of sick people."[50]

When Lévy was asked to establish a large facility in Constantinople to treat the wounded and sick of the French expeditionary army, he decided to create fourteen smaller hospitals, many made up of barracks. Having been raised in the French military tradition, which had taken a very opportunistic approach to design and materials, Lévy approached the task of building the barracks without preconceived ideas. He discovered that Turkish domestic architecture served his purpose:

> The production of *baraques* is one of the few industries that is indigenous in the East: the majority of the houses in Gallipoli, in Varna, and even in Constantinople, are merely *baraques*, not even excepting the palace and the villas that stretch along the two banks of the Bosporus. A hospital made of *baraques* could be quickly constructed: it offered us the multiple advantages of allowing us to choose the location and determine the capacity of each *baraque*, which, limited to a ground floor only, represents a single room with two rows of beds, and with an easy ventilation lengthwise by means of the doors at the two ends, and transversely by means of the windows placed in the two façades.[51]

49 Richard Delafield, *Report on the Art of War in Europe in 1854, 1855, and 1856* (Washington, DC: Bowman, 1860), 86–88.
50 Michel Lévy, *Sur la salubrité des hopitaux en temps de paix et en temps de guerre* (Paris: Baillière et Fils, 1862), 10, 13.
51 Ibid., 16–17.

Fig. 13
Alexandre-Gabriel Decamps, *A Turkish Guard House*, 1834. Collection: Metropolitan Museum of Art, New York.

Mortality rates in these improvised field hospitals were within what was considered at that time an acceptable range.

The British took a different approach. When the Sublime Porte offered the monumental Selimiye Barracks, located in the town of Scutari, on the southern shore of the Bosporus, the British accepted it. The enormous three-story stone building had been created in 1826 as part of Ottoman military reforms. At the time of its construction, the Selimiye Barracks were the largest military quarters in the world. Given the century of opinion suggesting that sick and wounded soldiers should not be concentrated in large permanent buildings, it is stunning that the British Army was willing to use the Selimiye Barracks as a military hospital. Thirty years earlier, Robert Jackson, an experienced military surgeon who was at that time inspector general of army hospitals, had strongly counseled against using large buildings as military hospitals in the second edition of his *A View of the Formation, Discipline and Economy of Armies*—a treatise that continued to be an authoritative source of practical information during the Crimean War. “The chief property of a military Hospital consists in ventilation and the means of assuring warmth in winter, or coolness in summer, or in hot climates.” Of these two preconditions, ventilation was the more important. “For, the air being contaminated by the breathings of a crowd of people in confined space, the disease is aggravated, and mortality is multiplied to an extraordinary extent."[52]

On October 12, 1854, *The Times* of London printed a dispatch from Constantinople. "It is with feelings of surprise and anger that the public will learn that no sufficient preparations have been made for the proper care of the wounded," wrote Thomas Chenery—a rookie reporter stationed in Constantinople. The hospital in Scutari was filling up with wounded soldiers, but there were hardly any surgeons and no nurses or bandages. The men were "left to expire in agony."[53] A few days later, the editors of *The Times* weighed in. They agreed the situation in Scutari was very difficult but, clearly unwilling to hold the government to account, argued the place could be made to work: "The edifice which has been placed at our disposal by the Turkish Government is as admirably adapted to the purposes of a military hospital as can possibly be conceived. It is airy, well situated, and capacious, nor is anything but organization wanted to render it one of the most perfect establishments of its kind." Sufficient medical staff and supplies were lacking, but if those were to arrive, it was clear that "the hospital at Scutari will be one of the best in the world."[54]

It took another couple of days for everyone to realize that, despite these assurances, a catastrophe was unfolding. A week after the first article appeared, *The Times* reported that "Mrs. Nightingale, who has been for some time acting as superintendent of the Ladies' Hospital, at No. 1, Upper Harley-street, has undertaken to organize a staff of female nurses, who will at once proceed with her to Scutari at the cost of the Government."[55] Self-educated, well-traveled, and driven by a desire to improve the lot of humankind, Florence Nightingale had found her calling in 1850, when she had visited a Lutheran religious community in Germany where deaconesses attended to the sick. Impressed with their work, she had submitted to four months of medical training at the community and then had published her findings in an anonymous pamphlet in which she praised the deaconesses as providing a model for British women interested in becoming engaged as professional nurses.[56]

Nightingale left for Scutari with thirty-nine nurses. She arrived on November 4 to find a filthy place filled with 1,500 patients. That month, more than 300 of them died. Mortality increased in December and peaked in January, when 1,473 perished.

52 Robert Jackson, *A View of the Formation, Discipline and Economy of Armies; with an Appendix, Containing Hints for Medical Arrangement in Actual War* (Stockton: William Robinson, 1824), 541–42.
53 "The Crimea," *The Times* (London), Oct. 12, 1854, 7.
54 "The Descriptions Recently Given of the Condition," *The Times* (London), Oct. 16, 1854, 6.
55 "We Are Authorized to State That Mrs. Nightingale," *The Times* (London), Oct. 19, 1854, 6.
56 [Florence Nightingale], *The Institution of Kaiserswerth on the Rhine, for the Practical Training of Deaconesses, under the Direction of the Rev. Pastor Fliedner, Embracing the Support and Care of a Hospital, Infant and Industrial Schools and a Female Penitentiary* (London: Printed by the inmates of the London Ragged Colonial Training School, 1851).

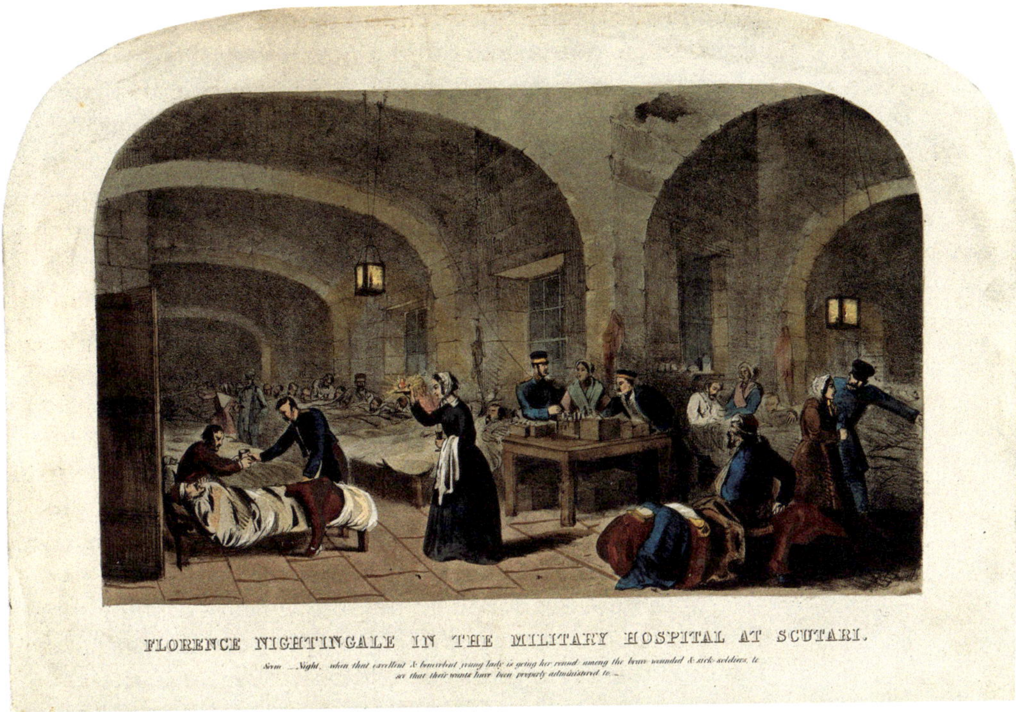
FLORENCE NIGHTINGALE IN THE MILITARY HOSPITAL AT SCUTARI.

Fig. 14
Joseph Austin Benwell, *Florence Nightingale in the Military Hospital at Scutari*, 1856. Collection: Wellcome Library, London.

Nightingale became convinced that the Selimiye Barracks had been a bad choice for a hospital: “The sanitary conditions of the hospitals of Scutari were inferior in point of crowding, ventilation, drainage, and cleanliness, up to the middle of March, 1855, to any civil hospital, or to the poorest home in the worst parts of the civil population of any large town that I have seen.” Crowding and cleanliness could be addressed relatively easily, but improving drainage and ventilation proved more difficult. “It is impossible to describe the state of the atmosphere in the Barrack hospital at night,” she declared upon her return to Britain. Noting the high mortality rate, she observed that “there is only cause for wonder that the mortality in Scutari was not more, as such an atmosphere as there prevailed was, perhaps, worse than that known to produce cholera and typhus among healthy persons.”[57] Nightingale blamed bad air for the devastation. Significantly, she did not mention the French field hospitals once.

Back in Britain, in the wake of the fall of the government led by George Hamilton-Gordon, 4th Earl of Aberdeen, on January 29, 1855, it was abundantly clear to Sir Benjamin Hawes, the senior civil servant in charge of the day-to-day operations of the War Office, that in addition to establishing its sanitary commission, the army needed to do something more dramatic to overcome the catastrophe in Scutari. In February 1855, Hawes did the hitherto unthinkable and decided to follow the example of the French—except he refused to go the

57 Florence Nightingale, “Answer to written questions addressed to Miss Nightingale by the commissioners appointed to inquire into the Regulations affecting the Sanitary Condition of the Army,” in Florence Nightingale, *Notes on Hospitals: Being Two Papers Read before the National Association for the Promotion of Social Science, at Liverpool, in October, 1858. With Evidence Given to the Royal Commissioners on the State of the Army in 1857* (London: Parker, 1859), 38–39.

whole way. He did not want the British Army to use Turkish carpenters to build a new hospital consisting of multiple barracks in the Turkish vernacular. Instead, the sick and wounded soldiers in the East were to be treated in a state-of-the-art field hospital that showed British building technology at its best. Hawes entrusted the project to the brilliant engineer Isambard Kingdom Brunel, who happened to be his brother-in-law. Three years earlier, Brunel had designed the SS *Great Eastern*, an all-iron steamship that was six times larger than the largest vessel ever built before it. By entrusting the design and construction of the hospital to him, Hawes ensured the British Army would not get a simple solution to the problem, as devised by the pragmatic Lévy for the French soldiers, but a barrack hospital that would surpass any field hospital either created or imagined up to that time.[58]

Brunel proposed a portable version of the most famous and, in terms of design, advanced hospitals of his day: the Lariboisière Hospital in Paris. Financed by a large bequest from Elisa Roy, comtesse de Lariboisière, it provided two series of parallel sick wards that had been designed with an eye to cross ventilation.

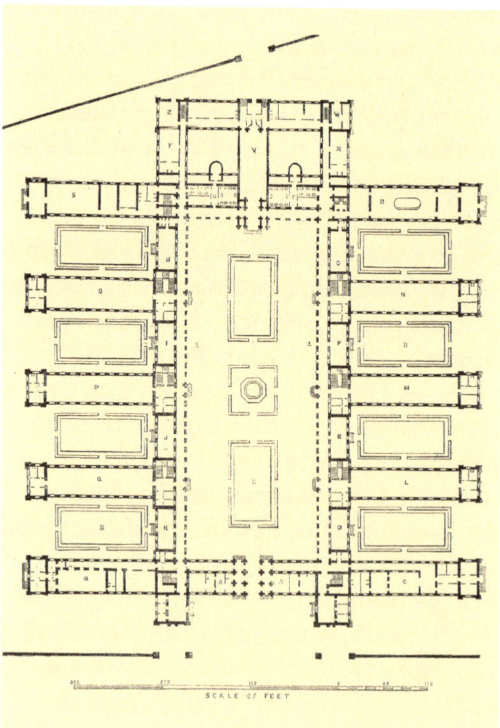

Fig. 15
Martin-Pierre Gauthier, Plan of the Lariboisière Hospital, Paris, from Florence Nightingale, *Notes on Hospitals*, 1859. Collection: Wellcome Library, London.

Within days, Brunel had drawn up plans, and within weeks, a prototype of a two-ward hospital barrack, measuring 27.5 by 12 meters and rising 7.5 meters high at the ridge, had been built for inspection.

58 Christopher Silver, *Renkioi: Brunel's Forgotten Crimean War Hospital* (Sevenoaks: Valonia Press, 2007).

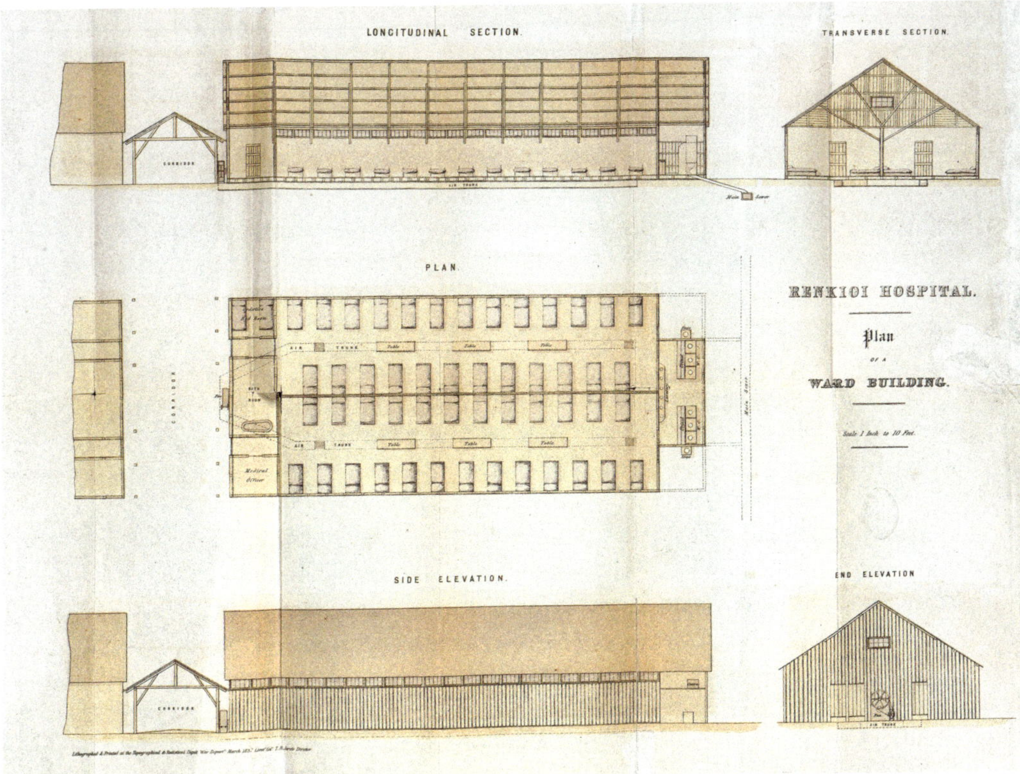

Fig. 16
Isambard Kingdom Brunel, Plan, sections, and elevations of a ward building, Renkioi Hospital, Turkey, 1857. Collection: Wellcome Library, London.

Brunel paid a lot of attention to the problem of air movement:

> To secure ventilation in a hot climate with low buildings extending over a large area, and therefore incapable of being connected with any general system of ventilation, it was considered that forcing in fresh air by a small mechanical apparatus attached to each building would be the only effective means. Each ward-room is therefore furnished with a small fan, or rotatory pump. [...] Besides this mechanical supply of air, opening windows are provided along the whole area of the eaves, and spaces left immediately beneath the roof at the two gables, amply sufficient together to ventilate the rooms thoroughly if any breezes are stirring, without the help of the fan.[59]

When production was underway, Dr. Edmund Alexander Parkes, a professor of clinical medicine at University College Hospital, London, accepted the offer to become director of the new hospital. He immediately set out to Constantinople to identify a site. With the help of John Brunton, an engineer of the Army Works Corps, Parkes identified a good candidate near Renkioi (Erenköy), overlooking the Sea of Marmara.

59 Isambard Brunel, "Memorandum by Mr. Brunel: Hospital Buildings in the East," in Edmund Alexander Parkes, *Report on the Formation and General Management of Renkioi Hospital, on the Dardanelles, Turkey. Addressed to the Right Honourable the Secretary of State for War* (London: War Department, 1857), 40–41. See also Isambard Brunel, *The Life of Isambard Kingdom Brunel, Civil Engineer* (London: Longmans, Green, and Co., 1870), 463–65.

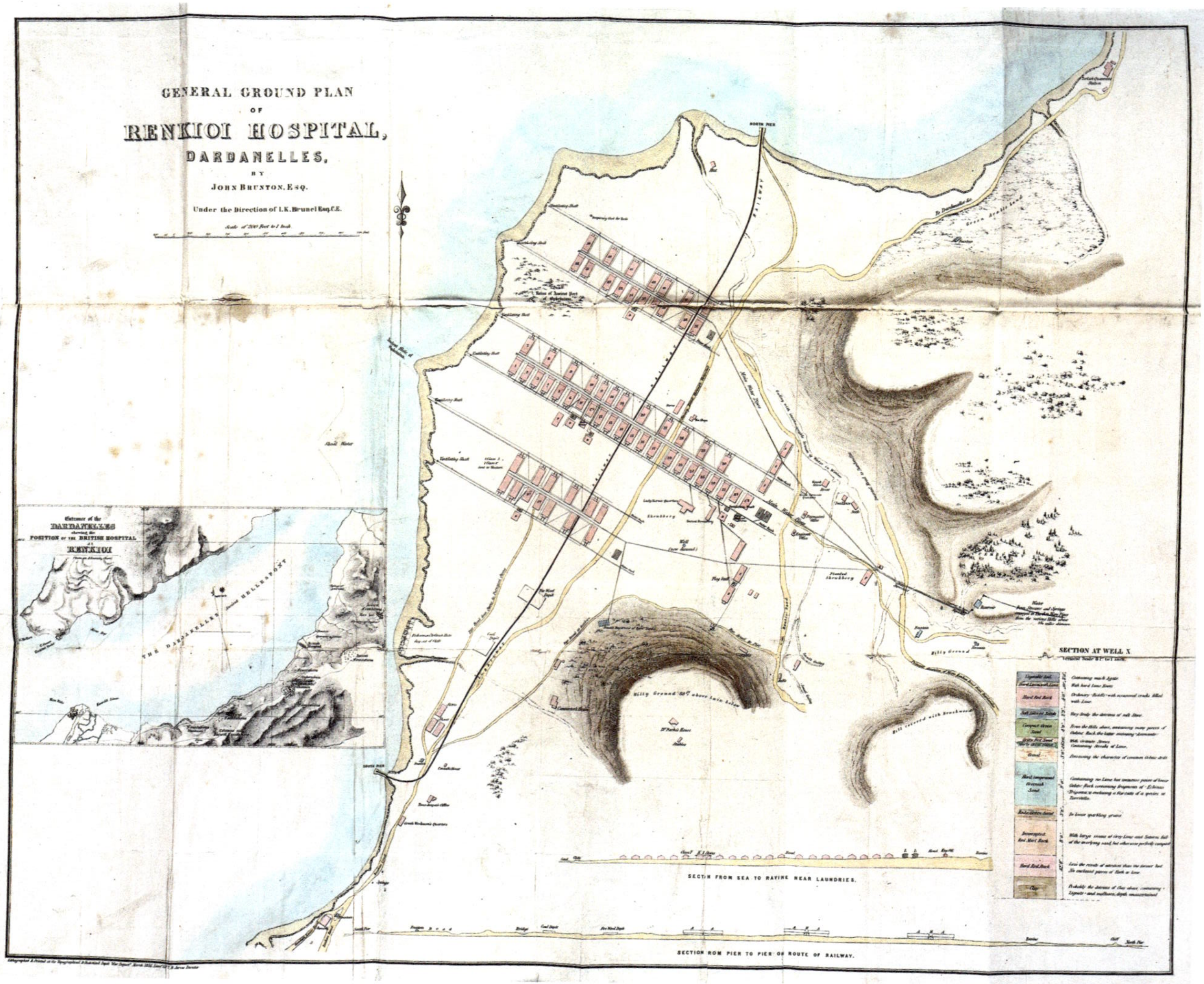

Fig. 17
John Brunton, General ground plan of Renkioi Hospital, 1857. Collection: Wellcome Library, London.

Things moved fast: in May 1855, construction began on the first of the thirty-two barracks that, connected to two covered walkways, were to be the core of the hospital. Construction was not yet finished when hostilities ceased in April 1856, and a month later, patients who had been lodged in the completed barracks were discharged. In July, the hospital officially closed. Brunton was given the job to sell it.

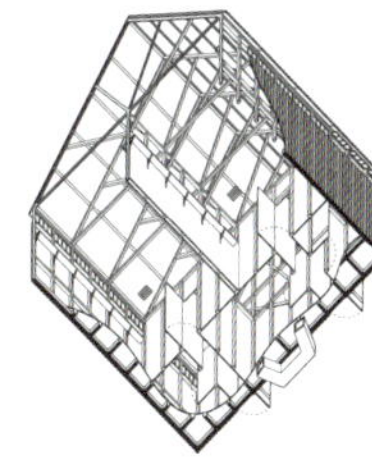

Drawings, Renkioi Hospital Barrack
→ p. 510

Fig. 18
John Kirk, Interior of a ward at Renkioi Hospital, 1855–56. Collection: J. Paul Getty Museum, Los Angeles, California.

"I took the steamer up to Constantinople, went to the Grand Viziar and tried my best to persuade the Turkish Government to purchase the whole of the Buildings and appliances as they stood, showing what a splendid military school might be established there." Yet the Sublime Porte was not interested, and so Brunton decided on an auction. "A short time previously a great fire at Salonica had rendered some thousands of the inhabitants houseless—so a deputation came over to purchase some of the wards of the Hospital, which were of timber, for housing the houseless ones. When the Tallal or Auctioneer commenced his labours the bidding for these wards was brisk, and they realised good prices."[60] The barracks were dismantled and shipped to Salonika (Thessaloniki), which at that time was the most important city in the Balkans. It was also home to the largest Sephardic Jewish community in the world—a community that was to be murdered in the crematoria and barracks of Auschwitz.

60 John Brunton, *John Brunton's Book: Being the Memories of John Brunton, Engineer, from a Manuscript in His Own Hand Written for His Grandchildren and Now First Printed*, ed. John Harold Clapham (Cambridge: Cambridge University Press, 1939), 70–71.

As to its place in the history of prefabricated architecture, Renkioi Hospital would not receive recognition until the 1970s, when modular "prefabs" moved from the periphery to the center of architectural discourse. In his seminal study of Brunel's hospital, British architectural educator David Toppin summarized its importance in the brilliance of Brunel's organization of the enterprise as a whole. "This was not just a collection of huts and other components modified from a manufacturer's catalogue, but a highly organized plan of action, right down to the last detail of assembly and transportation, yet with built-in latitude, so that at no point could the plan become too highly stressed and shatter."[61]

Unlike architects of the time, physicians immediately recognized Brunel's achievement. In his report to the secretary of state for war, Parkes noted: "Nothing could exceed the simplicity of the whole arrangement; it was a repetition of similar parts throughout; and experience enables me to say, that nothing could be better adapted for a hospital than this system of buildings, between every one of which was a large body of moving air, rendering ventilation easy, and communication of disease from ward to ward impossible."[62] In 1857, the *British and Foreign Medico-Chirurgical Review* added its voice. "The Renkioi Hospital, in which appear to have been united all the requirements of sanatory and sanitary science, was a thing of a day, and the necessities which called it into existence having ceased, it was—we would almost say ruthlessly—scattered to the winds."[63] A sad epitaph to be sure—and one that applies to almost all the achievements in barrack construction discussed in this book.

61 David Toppin, "The British Hospital at Renkioi 1855," *Arup Journal* 16, no. 2 (July 1981), 18.
62 Parkes, *Report on the Formation and General Management of Renkioi Hospital*, 16.
63 Review of Parkes, *Report on the Formation and General Management of Renkioi Hospital*, in *British and Foreign Medico-Chirurgical Review* 20 (July–Oct. 1857), 445.

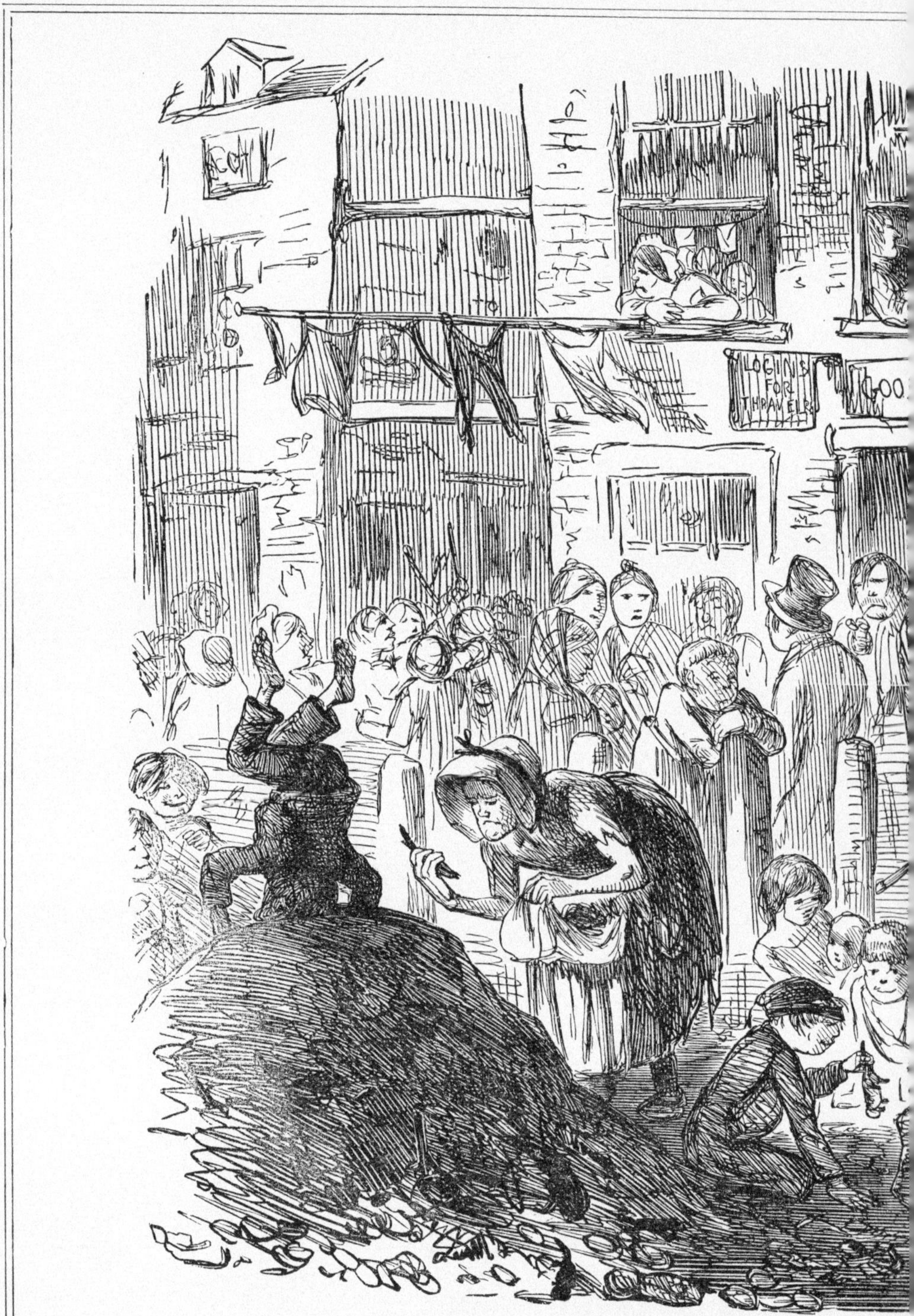

A COURT FOR

→ p. 135

NG CHOLERA.

Three

A Simple, Inexpensive Hut

"It was often proved, in the history of the late war, that more human life was destroyed by accumulating sick men in low and ill ventilated apartments, than in leaving them exposed in severe and inclement weather at the side of a hedge or common dyke," British inspector general of army hospitals Robert Jackson noted in the second edition of his *A View of the Formation, Discipline and Economy of Armies* (1824), adding that a military officer ought to consider the implications: "Churches and palaces are less proper receptacles of military sick than barns, hovels, and open sheds."[1] Jackson's observation reflected an almost universally shared understanding, in the eighteenth century and most of the nineteenth century, of the importance of supplying great amounts of fresh air in sick wards—a discourse that led Isambard Kingdom Brunel to pay particular attention to the problem of ventilation when he designed the Renkioi Hospital in Turkey. All windows could be opened to provide cross ventilation, and in addition, he provided each building with a double mechanical ventilation system that supplied fresh air through a duct located below the floorboards of each ward. Brunel explained: "By forcing the air into the room, instead of drawing it out, the entrance of bad air from the closets, drains, or any surrounding nuisances is prevented. The fan is placed at the opposite end to the closets and drains."[2]

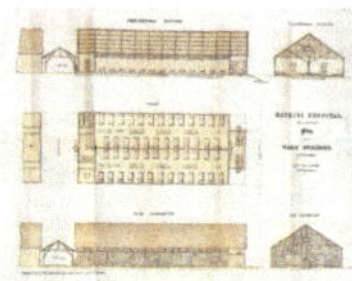

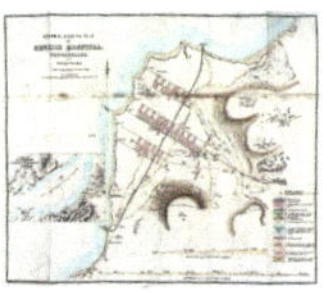

Chapter Two, Figs. 16–18 → p. 107

The "bad air" to which Brunel referred was not a loosely defined term that might mean different things to different people. Instead, it denoted a precise concept that had its roots in common-sense medical notions going back to the ancients and revived in the Renaissance, which speculated on the effect of what was sometimes defined as "unwholesome" or "intemperate" air on human health. In general, these ideas had little theoretical underpinning beyond the common experience that a clear and fresh atmosphere seems healthful, and a hazy and smelly environment seems harmful. The Scientific Revolution generated a new ambition to formulate explanation of physical phenomena that both looked beyond the writings of the Greeks and Romans and provided a comprehensive explanation of the phenomena studied.

1 Robert Jackson, *A View of the Formation, Discipline and Economy of Armies; with an Appendix, Containing Hints for Medical Arrangement in Actual War* (Stockton: William Robinson, 1824), 542.

2 Isambard Brunel, "Memorandum by Mr. Brunel: Hospital Buildings in the East," in Edmund Alexander Parkes, *Report on the Formation and General Management of Renkioi Hospital, on the Dardanelles, Turkey. Addressed to the Right Honourable the Secretary of State for War* (London: War Department, 1857), 41.

In the nature and behavior of air, the go-to authority in the early eighteenth century was the Italian physician Giovanni Maria Lancisi.

Professor of anatomy at the Sapienza University in Rome, Lancisi was especially interested in the causes of malaria, which was prevalent in the Pontine Marshes southwest of Rome. In his landmark study *De noxiis paludum effluviis* (On the noxious effluvia of marshes), published in 1717, Lancisi recommended drainage of these marshes to prevent malaria. While he correctly understood that the bite of mosquitoes living in the marshes caused malaria in humans, he did not know that this happened only when they were infected with parasitical microorganisms after consuming the blood of a human being suffering from malaria, in a vicious cycle. Instead, he believed the mosquitoes that transferred malaria to humans had been poisoned by bad air arising from the putrid soil of the marsh.

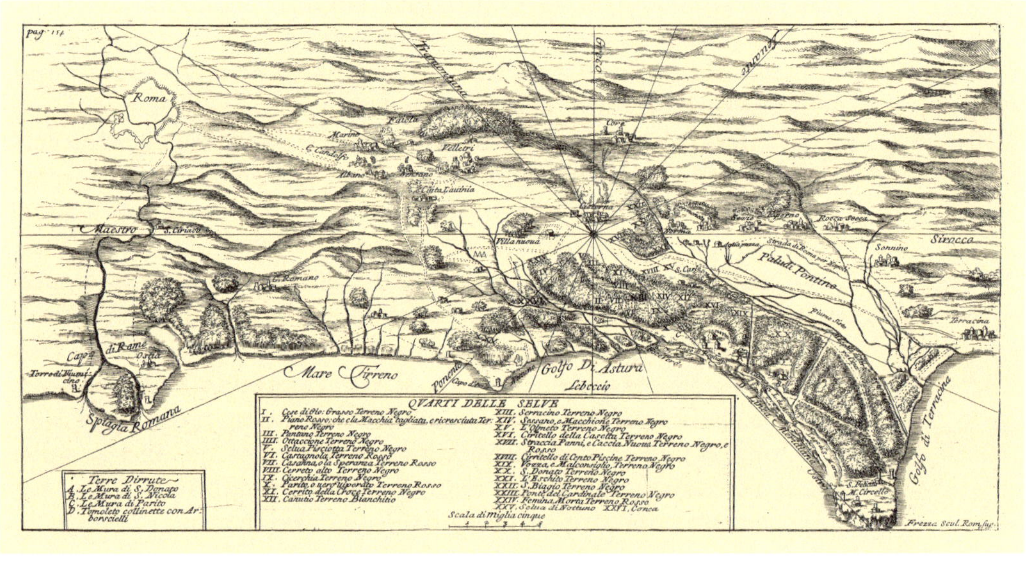

Fig. 1
Map of the southern Lazio region of Italy indicating the nature of the soil at different localities, mapping by implication the cause and character of particular miasmas, from Giovanni Maria Lancisi, *De noxiis paludum effluviis*, 1717. Collection: Wellcome Library, London.

While we understand air as a mixture of a variety of nitrogen, oxygen, carbon dioxide, water vapor, and small amounts of other elements, Lancisi considered air more as a spongelike substance made up of denser air particles with holes in between them: “Among experimental philosophers, it is no longer a matter of doubt that the surrounding air which we call the atmosphere is a fluid, thin, and porous body, not so specifically heavy as the earth, and naturally moveable, exceedingly compressible and elastic.” Air separated the celestial and terrestrial spheres, and Lancisi believed that it absorbed from the former ether, which moved between the air particles to the lungs of humans and animals, providing them with energy. However, the free flow of this vital ether could be jeopardized by organic particles arising from the soil that filled up the pores of the atmosphere, slowing down the free movement of ether from the sky to the lungs. A gentle breeze could prevent those vapors from clogging up the air, he asserted: "A proper degree of mobility, agitation and circulation [...] renders the air free and clear. This agitation principally depends upon the openness of places, the aspects of the heavens, and the intensity of light, giving the aerial fluid an opportunity to move with little impediment."[3] The pore-clogging vapor was commonly known as "miasma," from the Greek μίασμα (pollution). Environmental in origin, miasma could be avoided by moving from, for example, a forest-lined swamp to some breezy highland. It could be permanently eliminated by cutting trees or draining marshes. And it could be temporarily combated by sweeping, washing, scraping down, fumigating, and airing one's dwellings.[4]

Lancisi provided an apparently robust (but later proven to be wrong) scientific understanding of the nature of air and the need to keep it clear of miasmas by means of "mobility, agitation and circulation"—that is, ventilation. He was not interested in just understanding the etiology of disease but hoped also to find a cure for it—in the case of the Pontine Marshes through drainage. In that sense he was a typical representative of an age in which (natural) philosophers competed to find ways to set things right based on insights achieved by means of reason and confirmed by experimentation. The so-called Enlightenment was the Age of the How. And in that Age of the How, the avant-garde of innovation—both in general and in the case of combating the presence of miasmas within enclosed spaces—was certainly not the Sapienza University where Lancisi taught (which explains why the reclamation of the Pontine Marshes had to wait another two hundred years) but the British Royal Navy.

Throughout history, naval architecture and land-based architecture have influenced each other. The Roman warships carried a fighting bridge shaped like a triumphal arch; the sterns of early modern men-of-war looked like the façades of the town houses of the aristocracy; and the clean lines of the great villas of early modernism resembled the upper decks of the ocean liners that, between 1900 and 1940, represented the zenith of technological advancement and cosmopolitan sophistication. The impact of maritime history on the history of the barrack is not well known, yet it was significant. British naval officers faced the greatest sense of urgency

3 Giovanni Maria Lancisi, "Of Marshes and Their Effluvia," trans. Samuel L. Mitchell, *Medical Repository* 13 (1810), 12, 14–15.

4 A classic account of all the various methods of purification of bad air can be found in Gilbert Blane, *Observations on the Diseases Incident to Seamen* (London: Joseph Cooper, 1785), 252–81.

to solve the problem of disease caused by miasmas. They were entrusted with the task to hold together an ever-expanding empire of trade with heavily armed ships of the line and fast, independently operating frigates that required very large crews, which were housed in cramped and overcrowded conditions in the lower decks.

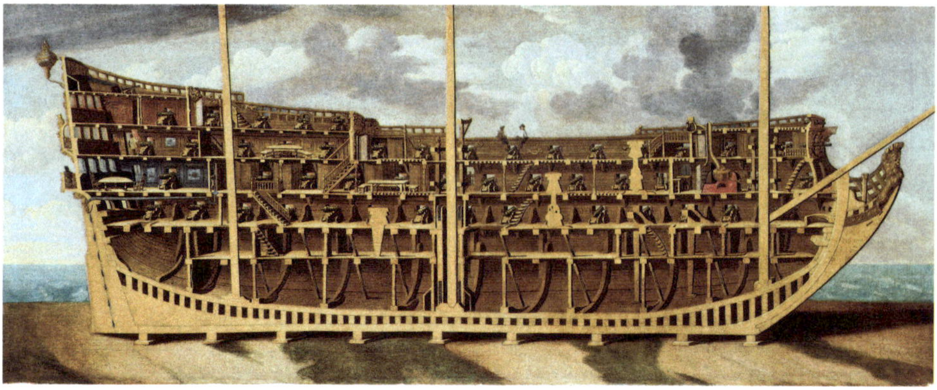

Fig. 2
Thomas Phillips, Section of a first-rate ship of the line, 1701. Collection: National Maritime Museum, Greenwich, London.

The foul air belowdecks was not caused only by overcrowding. Brackish water always gathered at the bottom of the hull, and equipment, supplies, cargo, and the personal possessions of the sailors could easily get wet, causing widespread rot. Morbidity and mortality were terrible on ships, and a solution to the problem was not straightforward. The portholes and hatches that were available had to remain closed when the ship was under sail in open sea. Radically reducing the size of the crew reduced the effectiveness of the ship as vessel and fighting machine. Moving the men higher up in well-aired quarters destroyed the stability and seaworthiness of the ship.

Around 1740, clergyman and amateur scientist Stephen Hales became interested in improving the health on ships. Two decades earlier, he had begun experiments to understand the conditions under which air, which ought to be "elastic" to provide life to animals and plants, became "fixed," with particles.[5] "We have from the foregoing Experiments evident proof, that its elasticity is easily, and in great abundance destroyed," he wrote in his *Vegetable Staticks* (1727), which is recognized as the first scientific thesis on pneumatic chemistry. "Elasticity is not an essential immutable property of air particles; but they are, we see, easily changed from an elastic to a fixed state, by the strong attraction of the acid, sulphureous and saline particles which abound in the air."[6] Hales also considered the adverse health effects of the thick air, clogged with "fuliginous vapours, arising from innumerable coal fires, and stenches from filthy lay-stalls and sewers," that characterized towns

5 See Archibald Edmund Clark-Kennedy, *Stephen Hales, D.D., F.R.S.: An Eighteenth Century Biography* (Cambridge: Cambridge University Press, 1929).
6 Stephen Hales, *Vegetable Staticks: Or, an Account of Some Statical Experiments on the Sap in Vegetables* (London: W. and J. Innys and T. Woodward, 1727), 315.

and cities and which introduced "pestilential, and other noxious epidemical infections"[7] into the blood.

When these words appeared in print, in 1727, miasmas were for Hales, who lived a comfortable life in a rural rectory, a largely theoretical issue. This changed two years later, when his younger brother William died in Newgate Prison from typhus, commonly known as "gaol-fever." This disease was a scourge among prisoners and was, of course, believed to be the result of the presence of miasmas in the dungeons. But jail keepers were not that interested in improving conditions. In 1739, when Hales heard that an America-bound fleet anchored outside of Spithead, England, could not sail because of the morbidity of the crew, he interested navy officials in his proposal to install ventilators using large, manually operated bellows to introduce fresh air belowdecks.

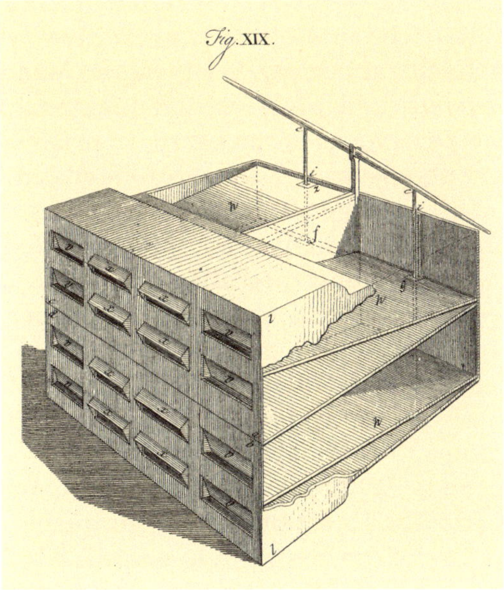

Fig. 3
Stephen Hales, Ship ventilator, from his *A Description of Ventilators*, 1743. Collection: Wellcome Library, London.

In 1743 Hales published *A Description of Ventilators*, making broad claims about both the general significance and broad application of his invention in ships, mines, jails, prisons, workhouses, and hospitals: "It ought in reason to convince us of the great Importance that plenty of fresh Air is to our Welfare, when we consider that the great Author of Nature has allotted near one half of the Trunk of our body for the Office of Respiration, or Breathing only."[8]

Hales's publication appeared at a time when, in fact, his ventilator faced a formidable competitor in Samuel Sutton's "fire pipes" or "air pipes"—a method of ventilation based on two facts: (1) a chimney can serve as a ventilation channel; and (2) a fire burning in fireplaces consumes a lot of air—up to 8.5 cubic meters per

7 Ibid., 257–58.
8 Stephen Hales, *A Description of Ventilators: Whereby Great Quantities of Fresh Air May with Ease Be Conveyed into Mines, Goals, Hospitals, Work-Houses and Ships, in Exchange for Their Noxious Air* (London: W. Innys, R. Manby and T. Woodward, 1743), 39.

minute—which in the mostly drafty houses of the eighteenth century was replaced with fresh air coming from the outside. After reading about the problems at Spithead, Sutton, a London brewer and coffeehouse keeper, began a series of experiments that took its point of departure from the natural draft created by a chimney, which was reinforced when a fire burned at its bottom. "I at length found, that by stopping the air out of a room that had three fire-places, and making two large fires in two of them, I could bring the air to draw down the third chimney, with such force as to put out a candle," he wrote in the account of his invention.[9] Sutton now devised a ventilation system that was to use a series of pipes, heated by the fire in the ship's cookhouse, to both provide fresh air to the lower decks and draw "bad air" out of them.

Sutton approached the personal physician of King George II, Richard Mead, who immediately presented Sutton's invention to the Royal Society. In his paper, Mead first summarized the conditions under which miasmas arise—"in deep wells and caverns of the earth, in prisons or close houses, where people are shut up with heat and nastiness: but most of all in large ships, in which, with the stench of water in the hold, many men being crouded up in close-quarters, all the mentioned circumstances concur in producing greater mischief than would follow from any of them single"—and then described how they reduced the "elasticity" or "springiness" of the air. Heat reversed this process. It only required a minimal investment of some pipes to connect the hold to the ship's galley, he proposed: "Whereas in every ship of any bulk there is already provided a copper or boiling-place proportionable to the size of the vessel, it is proposed to clear the bad air by means of the fire already used under the said coppers or boiling-places, for the necessary uses of the ship."[10]

Mead's advocacy convinced the Admiralty to make a hulk (a ship that had its rigging removed) moored in Deptford available for tests. A crowd of officials and scientists observed the experiments, and one of them, physician and scientist William Watson, reported the results to the Royal Society in December 1741. After discussing the general theory of miasmas, Watson turned to Sutton's solution, which he described in great detail. "Mr Sutton's machine, which being put in execution on board the hulk at Deptford, before the lords of the admiralty, commissioners of the navy, our very learned and ingenious president, M. Folkes, Esq; Dr. Mead, &c. performed to their satisfaction, in bringing air from the

9 Samuel Sutton, *An Historical Account of a New Method For Extracting the Foul Air out of Ships, etc. with the Description and Draught of the Machines, by which It Is Performed: In Two Letters to a Friend*, 2nd ed. (London: J. Brindley, 1749), 2.

10 Richard Mead, "An account of Mr. Sutton's invention and method of changing the air in the hold, and other close parts of a ship; communicated to the royal society by Richard Mead, M.D., physician to his majesty, fellow of the royal society, and of the royal college of physicians, London. Read Feb. 11, 1741," in Richard Mead, *The Medical Works (London: Hitch and Hawes*, 1762), 415–17.

bread-room, horlop [lowest deck] and well of the ship at the same time, in such quantity that large lighted candles being put to the end of tubes, the flame was immediately sucked out as fast as applied, though the end of one of the tubes was above twenty yards distant from the fire."[11] Despite the endorsement of the scientists, the officers running the ships did not adopt Sutton's technology. Because it used heat, it violated a basic principle of ship management, which was based on the need to reduce fire risk. Hence, they resisted the introduction of Sutton's air pipes and grudgingly accepted, if fresh air had to be provided belowdecks, Hales's bulky and labor-intensive ventilators.[12] Sutton was not paid for his expenses at Deptford, and this undoubtedly fueled his increasing rage against the Admiralty and Hales. In a book he published, he not only demanded a substantial payment for his invention but also engaged in a sharp polemic against Hales and his contraption. "His ventilators are cumbersome machines, taking up more room than can conveniently be spared, and require many hands to work them; my pipes take up no room, but what may be very well spared, and stand in need of no manual labour at all. His ventilators have only a casual and uncertain, but my pipes a certain and uninterrupted, effect."[13]

Both Hales and Sutton claimed that their inventions could also be used to improve air circulation in buildings. In 1749 Hales convinced the authorities to allow him to install a ventilator in the county jail in Winchester, a town where he had senior standing as a cleric. The secretary of state for war, Henry Fox, heard of this and remembered Hales's earlier publication. Fox maintained a military jail and a recruiting center in the rambling, medieval precinct known as Savoy Palace, and was disturbed that many of those housed in the building—jailed deserters and men pressed into service—caught typhus. Hales's ventilator proved to make a difference: morbidity and mortality dropped dramatically.[14] Combative as ever, Sutton was not impressed and responded with his usual hyperbole: "His ventilators, he tells us, will keep a prison sweet; but my pipes will even sweeten a bog-house [outhouse or latrine], and may be conveyed miles under ground into the deepest mines and subterraneous cavities, with the same success."[15]

The problem of miasmas acquired a very high profile when, in the spring of 1750, forty-five people, including the lord mayor, two senior judges, and several lawyers, succumbed to typhus after a sitting in the Old Bailey, London's criminal court. A committee quickly concluded that air emanating from a holding cell crowded

11 William Watson, "Some observations upon Mr. Sutton's invention to extract the foul and stinking air from the well and other parts of ships, with critical remarks upon the use of wind-sails, by William Watson, F.R.S.," in Mead, *The Medical Works*, 424.

12 Arnold Zuckerman, "Scurvy and the Ventilation of Ships of the Royal Navy: Samuel Sutton's Contribution," *Eighteenth-Century Studies* 10, no. 2 (Winter 1976–77), 222–34.

13 Sutton, *An Historical Account*, 38.

14 Clark-Kennedy, *Stephen Hales*, 189–91.

15 Sutton, *An Historical Account*, 39.

with defendants had been the cause. Advised by Hales, the committee decided to introduce artificial ventilation in the adjacent Newgate Prison. Hales welcomed the opportunity to ventilate such a high-profile building and constructed a ventilation system using a windmill as its source of power. The results were mixed, and by the end of the 1750s, there was a general agreement that even with ventilators the building was beyond redemption. In 1767 Parliament decided to pull the prison down.[16] Despite the various problems, the idea that good ventilation was key to the health of those forced to live in crowded conditions had taken root.

The search for better means of ventilation began in Britain but soon caught on in France. Henri Louis Duhamel du Monceau, inspector-general of the French navy, proposed that the air in hospitals could be improved by creating windows close to the ceiling and by introducing an artificial ventilation system in the attic that consisted of large vents connected to massive extraction hoods, each supplied with a small stove, in which the heat generated by the stove was to create an upward movement of the air in the hood that, in turn, would extrude the bad air from the ward.[17]

Ventilators were one way to deal with the problem of miasmas, and in the case of ships or prisons, in which many people were crowded together in confined spaces as a matter of course, they seemed to offer an obvious if cumbersome and technically complicated solution. The air pipes had potential, but it was only to be realized a century later. With solutions such as those proposed by Hales and Sutton at hand, the presence of miasmas in a building could not be accepted anymore as an unavoidable fact of life. It did not take long for an alternative solution to become a topic of reflection and action: the dispersal of a large group of people in many smaller buildings that, equipped with sufficient windows and located at some distance from each other, did not need any mechanical contraptions to disperse miasmas.

In 1742 the British Royal Navy had initiated the experimental method based on ventilation to combat miasmas; soon thereafter, the British Army picked up the baton. In his groundbreaking *Observations on the Diseases of the Army* (1752), John Pringle analyzed the morbidity in the British Army. Having served as the physician-general to the British forces dispatched during the War of Austrian Succession to the Habsburg Netherlands, Pringle noted that, in selecting places to lodge sick and wounded soldiers during a campaign,

16 Ibid., 193–207. Also, John Pringle, "An Account of Several Persons Seized with the Gaol-Fever, Working in Newgate; and of the Manner, in which the Infection Was Communicated to One Intire Family," *Philosophical Transactions of the Royal Society of London* 48 (1753), 42–55.

17 Henri Louis Duhamel du Monceau, "Differens moyens pour renouveller l'air des infirmeries, & généralement de tout endroit ou le mauvais air peut incommoder la respiration," *Histoire de l'Academie Royal des Sciences, année MDCCXLVIII, avec les mémoires de mathématique & de physique pour la meme année, tirés des registres de cette académie* (Paris: L'Imprimerie Royale, 1752), 5–8.

"spacious and airy" structures like "barns, granaries and the like places" were better than peasant cottages. When he had set up a field hospital in the major church of the Dutch city of Maastricht in 1747, no one had died of typhus. "Wherefore we may lay it down as a rule, that the more fresh air we let into hospitals, the less danger there is of breeding this distemper," he proposed in his *Observations*. One of the ways to ensure that all patients would have access to fresh air was "to have the regimental hospitals scattered, and not crowded into one village." And Pringle drove the point home once more: "The greatest danger is from foul air, which can never be compensated by diet or medicine."[18]

Pringle's concept of what was to be known as "dispersal" gave rise to a new concept of hospital design. As late as 1750, hospitals were typically monumental buildings. Embodying the Christian idea that the sick and the poor were "especially" blessed by God and that, in taking care of them, those who founded and maintained hospitals gave to the Lord, the well-off were happy to commit large bequests to hospital foundations, on condition that the institution would represent in its architecture the munificence of its patrons.

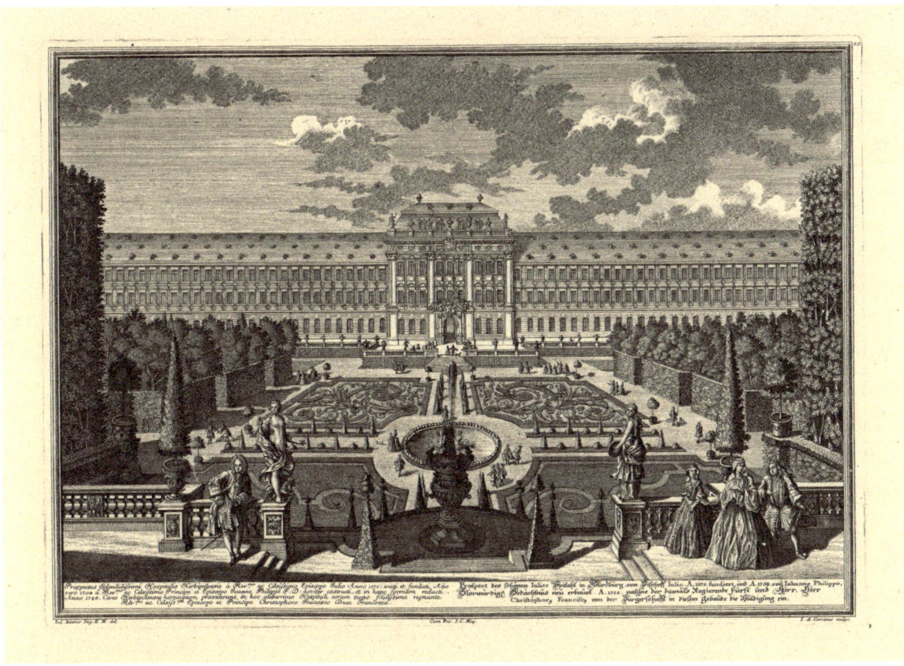

Fig. 4
Johann August Corvinus, Juliusspital, Würzburg, Germany, from his *Ducalis et Episcopalis Residentia Wurzburgum seu Herbipolis in Franconia*, 1740. The Juliusspital (Julius's Hospital) was founded in 1576. By 1700 it had acquired a truly palatial size and appearance. Collection: Rijksmuseum, Amsterdam.

18 John Pringle, *Observations on the Diseases of the Army* (London: Millar a.o., 1752), 126–28.

19 On the history of the pavilion hospital, see John D. Thompson and Grace Goldin, *The Hospital: A Social and Architectural History* (New Haven, CT, and London: Yale University Press, 1975), 118–203; Jeremy Taylor, *The Architect and the Pavilion Hospital: Dialogue and Design Creativity in England 1850–1914* (London and New York: Leicester University Press, 1997); Philip Steadman, *Building Types and Built Forms* (Kibworth Beauchamp, UK: Matador, 2014), 52–92.

A hospital consisting of a collection of individual pavilions did not resemble a palace but a village—and this offered little of the architectural glory that patrons expected.[19] In 1745, when the British Admiralty decided to construct a hospital in Portsmouth, it supported a palatial design that stressed the dignity of the Royal Navy as one of the most important institutions in the British Isles. Yet, while the Naval Lords were anxious that any naval buildings would proclaim their status, they also were proud to run the most innovative organization in the eighteenth century. Hence, when they commissioned the construction of the Royal Naval Hospital in Stonehouse, near Plymouth, in 1758, they insisted that it reflect Pringle's findings, published in 1752. The Plymouth hospital, designed by master mason Alexander Rouchead (in some sources Rovehead or Rowehead) and completed in 1762, was the first facility to reflect the new ideas.

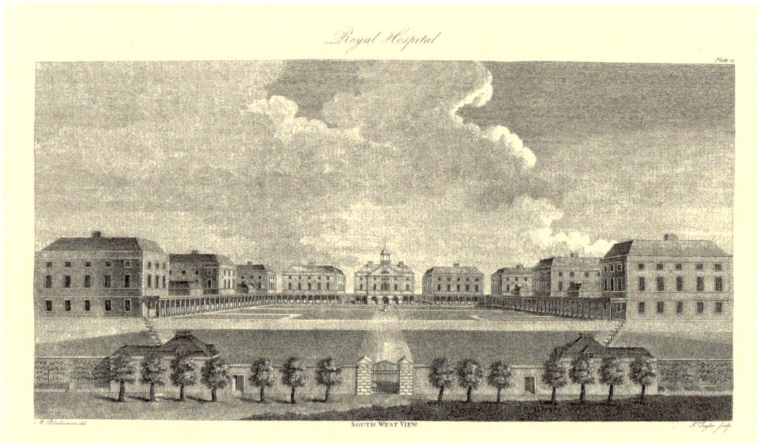

Fig. 5
The Royal Naval Hospital, Stonehouse, Plymouth, from John Howard, *The State of the Prisons in England and Wales*, 1792. Collection: Wellcome Library, London.

It offered a spacious courtyard surrounded on three sides by an open colonnade. Attached to this armature were fifteen three-story pavilions, ten of which consisted of two rooms per floor with windows at two sides.[20]

The idea to combat miasmas through the breaking up of a large, heavily constructed and badly ventilated hospital into a collection of smaller, well-ventilated wards was justified by evidence gained in the difficulties arising from the use of mechanical ventilators and by the success of a particular form of housing provided to British soldiers who had come down with contagious diseases. In his 1764 *Oeconomical and Medical Observations*, Richard Brocklesby, surgeon general of the British Army, recalled how, in 1758, naval ships were forced to unload many sick soldiers at the Isle of Wight. As there were too many to accommodate in the local hospital, "some Gentleman of the hospital proposed to erect a temporary shed with deal [pine] boards, upon the open

20 Christine Stevenson, *Medicine and Magnificence: British Hospital and Asylum Architecture 1660–1815* (New Haven, CT, and London: Yale University Press, 2000), 182–84; Christine Stephenson, "From Palace to Hut: The Architecture of Military and Naval Medicine," in Geoffrey L. Hudson, *British Military and Naval Medicine, 1600–1830* (Amsterdam and Atlanta, GA: Rodopi, 2007), 238–40.

forest, and to have it thatched over with a coat of new straw, thick enough to keep out the wind and rain, and capacious enough to hold one hundred and twenty patients, or upwards."[21] The structure was badly put together, and conditions were cold. Remarkably, the patients housed in the shed did much better than those in the hospital: fewer died, and the survivors recovered faster. Significantly, a century later, Brocklesby's account was to become a commonplace reference in the exploding literature on barrack design and use, justifying the deployment of what many concerned citizens initially condemned as substandard accommodation.

Two years after his first use of crude sheds as sick wards, Brocklesby was faced with an outbreak of endemic typhus among soldiers in Guildford. He ordered the construction of a shed in an airy location, describing the process in his *Observations*: "I drove perpendicular stakes, about six feet high from the surface of the earth, and placed wattles between them, well coated on the side next the weather, with fresh straw; rafters were laid over in a workman-like manner, and coated thick, like the sides; this made it spacious and airy over head, and yet abundantly warm and dry, for the intended purpose." A brick chimney was constructed, and the result was "an exceedingly comfortable, spacious, and sufficiently occasional habitation." Every few days a layer of the sand that provided the floor was removed, and the inner surface of the shed, "which might be suspected to imbibe and retain any infectious matter proceeding from the patients," was scraped off. Only a couple of the soldiers died. "I candidly ascribe their fortunate escape, more to the benefit of a pure keen air they breathed therein every moment, than to all the medicines they took every six hours, or oftner."[22]

The experiment was repeated in the years that followed, and Brocklesby came to the conclusion that barracks might be used to house the sick at all military installations: "And in all future expeditions to the West Indies, or to any Tropical Climates, I hope to see due provision, in time, be previously appointed, to have a large ship or two from North America, or elsewhere, with lumber and boards always attending the fleet, that whenever a landing is once made good, in any warm climate, occasional huts, such as I have here described, may be constructed at proper distances from the fleet and army."[23] Brocklesby's advocacy of barracks as sick wards was certainly informed by the fact that they were technologically simple. Hales's ventilation technology, while providing useful results in lowering morbidity

21 Richard Brocklesby, *Oeconomical and Medical Observations* (London: Becket and De Hondt, 1764), 66.
22 Ibid., 72–74.
23 Ibid., 80–81.

from typhus and other contagious diseases in regular hospitals, did not work in the ad hoc conditions faced by military surgeons.

A second consideration also supported the idea to use simple barracks: the fact that they were made of free or cheap materials that could be discarded on a very regular basis. Brocklesby was convinced that the floors and walls of permanent hospitals became impregnated with contagious agents excreted from the bodies of the ill, and cleansing the surfaces with vinegar and smoking the wards with burning brimstone or gunpowder could do only so much. “The seeds of infection once sown, continue, in some instances, to spread contagious diseases, and to contaminate the house,” he wrote.[24]

In 1772, eight years after the publication of Brocklesby’s book, a fire damaged a significant part of the main hospital of Paris, the Hôtel-Dieu. Established in the seventh century and, 1,100 years later the biggest hospital in the world, it was a den of disease and death, consisting of ill-ventilated interconnected wards that occupied two sides of the Seine.

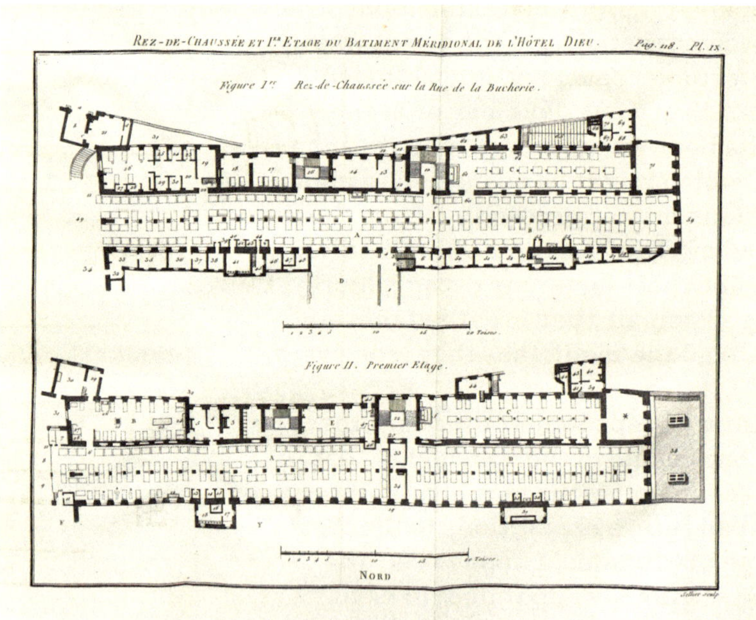

Fig. 6
Plan of the ground floor and first floor of the southern wing of the old Hôtel-Dieu, Paris, from Jacques-René Tenon, *Mémoires sur les hôpitaux de Paris*, 1788. Collection: Cornell University Library, Ithaca, New York.

Immediately after the fire, physicians, scientists, and architects began to consider what kind of building should replace it. In 1773, the Académie des Sciences (Academy of Sciences) organized a *charrette*, in which various proposals for rebuilding were considered—all of them suggested dividing the hospital into a number of smaller buildings. In 1776, Jean-Baptiste Le Roy, a member of the Academy of Sciences who had participated in the

24 Ibid., 59.

charrette, approached architect Charles-François Viel, and the pair began collaborating on the plan for a new hospital that was to take advantage of natural ventilation. Theirs was a revolutionary design, arranging two dozen one-story, gallery-like wards or pavilions in two rows, spaced 15 meters apart. "As the result of this arrangement, each hall, like an island within air, is surrounded by a considerable volume of this fluid, which the winds can easily blow away and renew because of the free access offered to them all around," wrote Le Roy.[25] Ventilation was also to be aided by a unique ceiling design that combined a series of domes with openings at their apex designed to extract the foul air from the sick rooms.

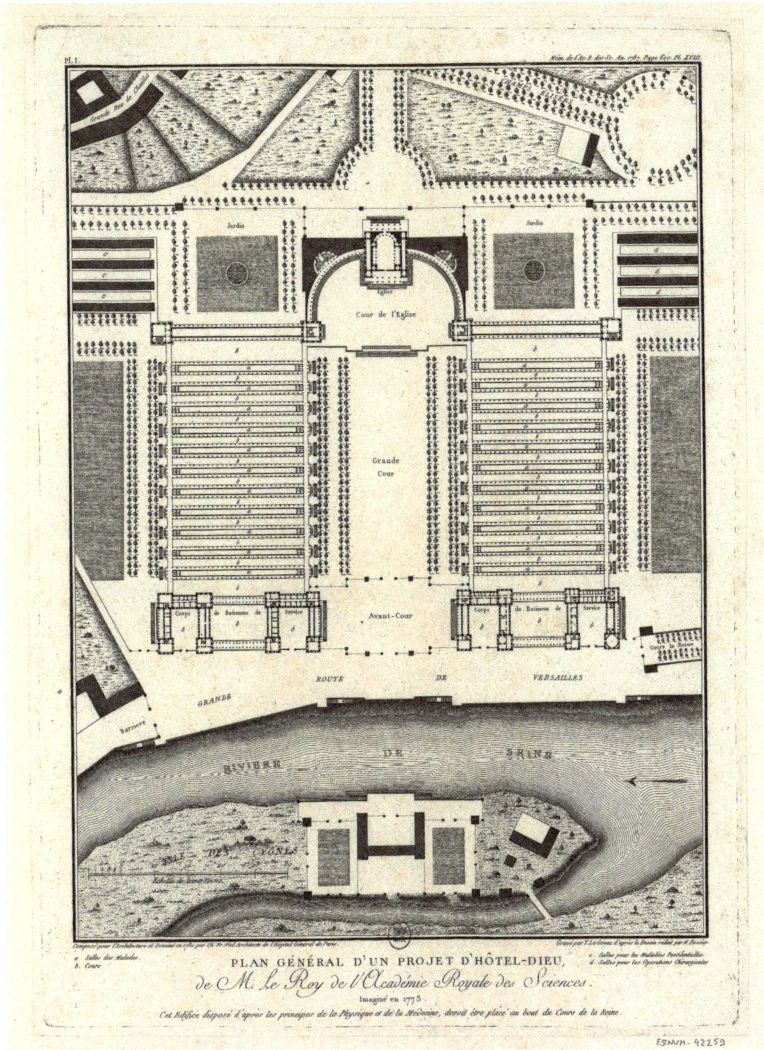

Fig. 7
Jean-Baptiste Le Roy and Charles-François Viel, Plan of the new Hôtel-Dieu, Paris, 1787. Collection: Bibliothèque Nationale de France, Paris.

25 Jean-Baptiste Le Roy, "Précis d'un ouvrage sur les hôpitaux, dans lequel on expose les principes résultant des observations de physique & de médecine qu'on doit avoir en vue dans la construction de ces edifices; avec un projet d'hôpital disposé d'après ces principes," *Histoire de l'Academie Royal des Sciences, année MDCCLXXXIX, avec les mémoires de mathématique & de physique pour la même année, tirés des registres de cette académie* (Paris: L'Imprimerie Royale, 1789), 594.

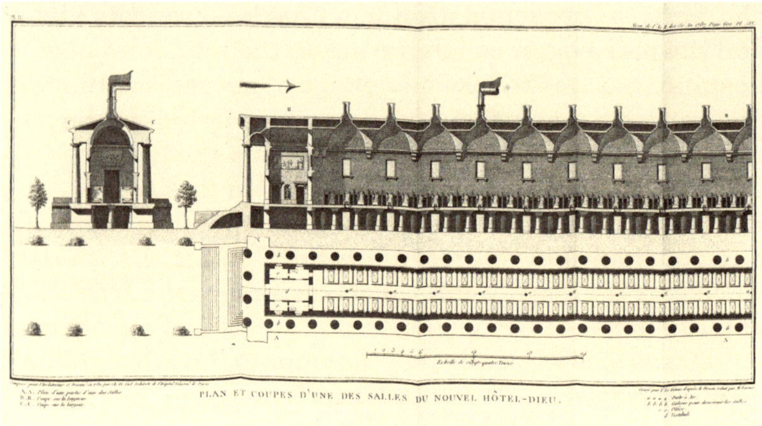

Fig. 8
Jean-Baptiste Le Roy and Charles-François Viel, Plan and section of a sick ward of the new Hôtel-Dieu, 1787. Collection: Cornell University Library, Ithaca, New York.

In the meantime, the French physician Jacques-René Tenon labored on an extensive and exhaustive review of both existing hospital environments in Paris and past proposals to ameliorate poor conditions—including the design made by Le Roy and Viel. A conscientious researcher, Tenon traveled to Plymouth, England, to see the Royal Naval Hospital. Tenon's work, which he originally submitted in five separate parts to the Académie des Sciences, was published in a single volume, *Mémoires sur les hôpitaux de Paris*, in 1788. The last part contains detailed design proposals. A key principle to be observed was the need for continuous ventilation. Tenon also included various plans that had been developed by French architect Bernard Poyet. Sick wards were to come in only one form: as a long, narrow hall with windows placed opposite each other to ensure excellent cross ventilation. France erupted in revolution a year after the publication of Tenon's book, and with chaos enveloping the country, construction of large-scale projects like a new Hôtel-Dieu became impossible. A new building was not to be constructed until eighty years later.

Until the wars that were triggered by the French Revolution, there was little medical evidence that provided more detailed understanding of the etiology of infectious disease and its implication for the design of civilian and military hospitals. However, in 1794, Sebald Justinus Brugmans, professor of medicine at the University of Leiden, began what became a two-decade-long investigation that ended up with an important, evidence-based endorsement of the vital importance of the barrack as a field hospital. In 1793 a 200,000-soldier French force, made possible by the *levée en masse* conscription effort, invaded the Habsburg Netherlands. Its ruler, Franz II, Holy Roman emperor, Archduke of Austria, and so on, was the principal leader of the anti-French alliance in the War of the First Coalition, and he convinced the governments in The Hague, London, Hanover, Darmstadt, and Berlin to have Dutch, British-Hanoverian, Hessian, and Prussian troops join the Austrian garrison that protected his domain in the Low Countries. However, the allies were no match for the French, and by the summer of 1794 the British-Hanoverian and Dutch armies had abandoned the Habsburg Netherlands and retreated north of the Rhine. The allies made camp near the Dutch city of Leiden. Over 1,200 of them were wounded or sick. Discussions between Hanoverian army surgeons, Professor Brugmans, and the Leiden city authorities led to the establishment of an emergency hospital in the Pesthuis (Plague House), a large, handsome, moated hospital built in the 1660s outside the city to allow for the concentration, isolation, and treatment of victims of plague.[26]

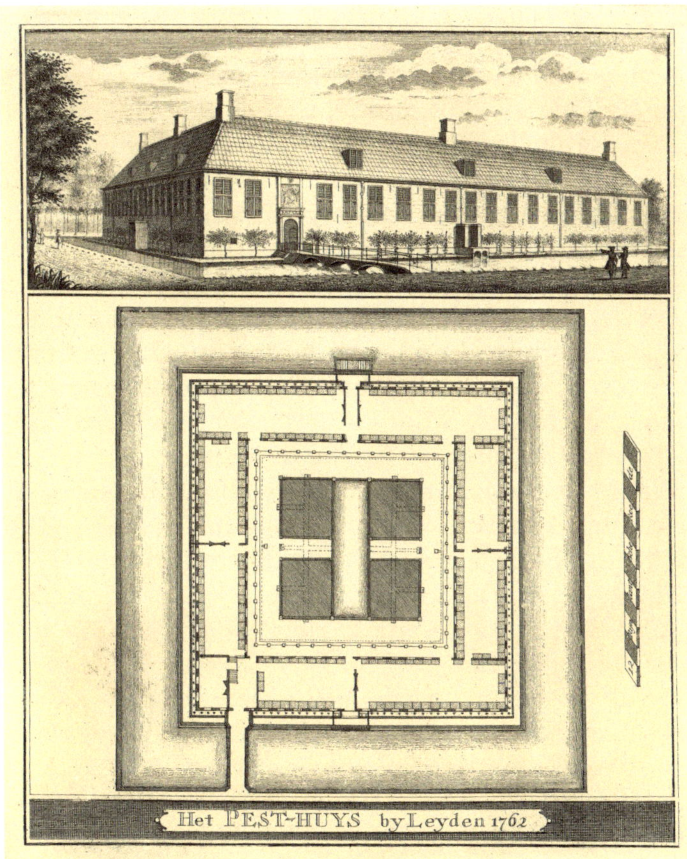

Fig. 9
Plan and view of the Pesthuis, Leiden, the Netherlands, 1762. Collection: Rijksmuseum, Amsterdam.

For six months the Pesthuis functioned as a military hospital, and Brugmans and his students attended to the sick every day. However, in January 1795 the French army resumed its offensive and crossed the now frozen Rhine. The soldiers were hungry, and the Dutch granaries were full. The advance to the north was triggered not

26 *Rapport wegens den finantiëlen staat der gesubsidieerde stigtingen of godshuizen binnen Leiden, met andere stukken, daartoe betrekkelijk* (Leiden: Gemeente van Leiden, 1795), 67–69.

only by these pragmatic needs; Dutch revolutionaries who had tried to overthrow the Republic of the Seven United Netherlands in the 1780s, and who had lived in exile in Paris ever since, had convinced the general commanding the French forces to help them "liberate" their country. As the French moved toward The Hague, Leiden, Haarlem, and Amsterdam, the English and Hanoverians retreated to Hanover, and the Dutch forces laid down their arms. The two-centuries-old Dutch Republic collapsed, and in its ruins arose a new, unitary state: De Bataafsche Republiek (the Batavian Republic)—named after the Germanic tribe that had inhabited the area 1,800 years earlier and had been an important ally of the Romans.

The Leiden Pesthuis now became a French military hospital. Brugmans attended to the French patients as he had to the English and Hanoverians. It was during this time that he became interested in the prevention of hospital gangrene, a bacterial disease that kills living tissue and begins in amputated stumps and other war wounds.[27] Before the development of modern hygiene, hospital gangrene had been the scourge of crowded military hospitals. Brugmans noted that when a young and otherwise healthy man received a small wound, he normally healed quickly when left on his own. But if he were conveyed into a crowded sick ward, often the condition of the wound and the general health of the patient quickly worsened, leading to death. The infected patient produced a very peculiar smell, which normally overtook the ward. Quickly other patients would begin to decline in a similar manner as the first one.

When the Batavian Republic established a new army, Brugmans became head of its medical service, and as such he also became the de facto physician in chief of the 25,000-man French garrison that was to "protect" the alignment of the Dutch and French republics. He observed that when hospital gangrene broke out in one of the wards on the ground floor, the military surgeon in charge decided to cut holes in the ceiling to allow the foul air to vent through the airy garret to the outside. Three soldiers who had been lightly wounded were resting in that attic. "Thirty hours afterwards," Brugmans reported, "the three wounded men who lay in the garret, nearest the aperture, were attacked with gangrene, which soon spread throughout the whole room."[28] He concluded the "foul air" from the ward below had transported the hospital gangrene. Now Brugmans began a series of experiments to analyze the composition of the various gases in the air of the sick wards of military

27 See Teun van Heiningen, "Sebald Justinus Brugmans' strijd tegen de hospitaalversterving," *Gewina* 26 (2003), 216–33.

28 Sebald Justinus Brugmans, "Memoir on the State and Composition of the Atmosphere, Considered as the Cause of the Hospital Gangrene, or Putrescence, among the Wounded," pt. 1, *London Medical and Physical Journal* 34 (Nov. 1815), 402.

hospitals, following the methods pioneered a decade earlier by the French scientist Antoine-Laurent de Lavoisier.

In 1806, when Emperor Napoleon abolished the Batavian Republic and established the Koningrijk Holland (Kingdom of Holland), a puppet state nominally ruled by Napoleon's younger brother Louis Bonaparte, Brugmans accepted a commission from King Louis; and in 1810, when Napoleon gave up all pretense, deposed his brother as king, and incorporated Holland as a province within the French Empire, Brugmans became, as *inspecteur-général* (inspector general) the nominal head of all the military hospitals of the French Grande Armée. In that role, he continued to seek ways to understand and prevent hospital gangrene through the analysis of the chemical composition of the air in places where this disease occurred. Convinced that miasmas caused hospital gangrene, and accepting received opinion that the only way to deal with this problem was through ventilation, he decided that the common practice to use ill-ventilated churches (or other large permanent buildings such as the Leiden Pesthuis) as field hospitals was to be abandoned and that, instead, breezy tents and barracks should be used to accommodate the sick and wounded.

In 1813 Napoleon was defeated in Leipzig, and the Dutch reestablished their independence as the Soeverein Vorstendom der Verenigde Nederlanden (Sovereign Principality of the United Netherlands). Brugmans was not offered a position in the new Dutch army due to his strong affiliation with the French. Having time on his hands, he decided to enter an essay competition organized by the Hollandsche Maatschappij der Wetenschappen (Dutch Society of Sciences) in Haarlem. The topic was hospital gangrene and how to mitigate and, if possible, prevent it.[29] Brugmans's submission won the gold medal and was published in the society's proceedings.[30] It received international attention a year later, when the *London Medical and Physical Journal* published an English translation of the work.

Brugmans presented his analysis of the problem, a record of his measurements and experiments done over many years, and what appeared to him the obvious solution to the problem: well-ventilated wards were key to the prevention of hospital gangrene. Brugmans recommended that every patient should have at least 14 cubic meters of air: "The renewal of this air is not less indispensable. Ventilators ought to be open as much as possible over the beds and placed opposite to each other:

29 Ibid., 394.
30 Sebald Justinus Brugmans, "Verhandeling over de Gesteldheid en Zamenstelling van den Dampkring in welke de zoogenaamde Hospitaal-Versterving by Gewonden plaats heeft," *Natuurkundige Verhandelingen van de Hollandsche Maatschappij der Wetenschappen te Haarlem* 7, pt. 2 (1814), 1–68.

the breadth of the whole taken together ought to be nearly equal to the half of the length of the ward. Besides these, it is absolutely necessary that on a level with the floor there should be air-holes, about a foot square [0.1 square meter], and which may be shut at pleasure by sliding doors." By keeping the air flowing, even in winter, he argued, "I dare venture to say that the air of the hospital will never be infected so as to occasion the slightest apprehension of this dreadful disease."[31]

Now the Dutch government realized it needed Brugmans's services, despite its misgivings about his career in the French army, and he received an invitation to take control of the medical services of the fledgling Royal Netherlands Army. In that capacity, he organized the relief for 27,000 wounded soldiers during and after the Battle of Waterloo by means of tents and barracks erected in and around Brussels. The 72,000-man French army had almost won the battle against the combined armed forces of Great Britain (31,000 men), the Netherlands (17,000), Hanover (11,000), Brunswick (6,000), and Nassau (3,000), when, at the last moment, the 50,000-man Royal Prussian Army arrived to turn the tide. As a result, Brugmans met the Prussian military surgeon Dietrich Georg Kieser, who had seen the ravages of hospital gangrene in field hospitals. Kieser offered to translate Brugmans's essay on the subject into German and publish it, together with a second study on hospital gangrene undertaken by French surgeon Jacques Delpech, adding to this a fifty-one-page afterword that expanded on the conclusions of both Brugmans and Delpech through an analysis of the relationship between the mortality statistics and the location and the physical arrangement of a range of civilian and military hospitals—including, of course, the Hôtel-Dieu in Paris.

In addition to his afterword, Kieser also contributed a seventeen-page memoir that considered the practical implications for field hospital design. It confirmed Brugmans's assertion that any confined space, whether small rooms in houses or even large churches, should not be used as field hospitals. If enclosed spaces were the only choice available, it was better to keep the patients outside: "Rain and snow, the cold of night and the burning sun of the day will not harm them as much as such a stay [in churches converted into field hospitals], because under the open sky they can enjoy at least the first necessity of life, clear atmospheric air."[32] Field hospitals consisting of tents would offer acceptable conditions in summer, while barracks were the preferred option in winter.

31 Brugmans, "Memoir on the State and Composition of the Atmosphere, Considered as the Cause of the Hospital Gangrene, or Putrescence, among the Wounded," pt. 2, *London Medical and Physical Journal* 35 (Jan. 1816), 21.

32 Dietrich Georg Kieser, "Über die Errichtung von Zelten und Baracken bei durch Anstecking mit Lazarethfieber und anderen epidemischen Lazarethkrankheiten unbrauchbar gewordenen Lazarethgebäden, und bei vorhandener, in den Lazarethgebäuden nicht zu fassender groser Anzahl von Verwundeten," in Sebald Justinus Brugmans and Jacques Delpech, *Über den Hospitalbrand* (Jena: Maute und Sohn, 1816), 267.

The publication of Brugmans, Delpech, and Kieser's book coincided with a renewed interest in hospital design. Ironically, lodging wounded soldiers in three unfinished slaughterhouses during the War of the Sixth Coalition (1813–14) provided a crucial experience. In 1810 Emperor Napoleon had appointed a commission to review the hygiene of French slaughter practices, and later that year it decided on a program of construction of a standardized type of abattoir that could be more easily managed and cleaned. The result was a new architectural type that consisted of walled and fully paved compounds that held two rows of sheds where the slaughtering took place, with parallel rows of sheds where cattle, sheep, and calves were consigned after their arrival from the markets.[33] The city of Paris initiated the construction of five of these places.

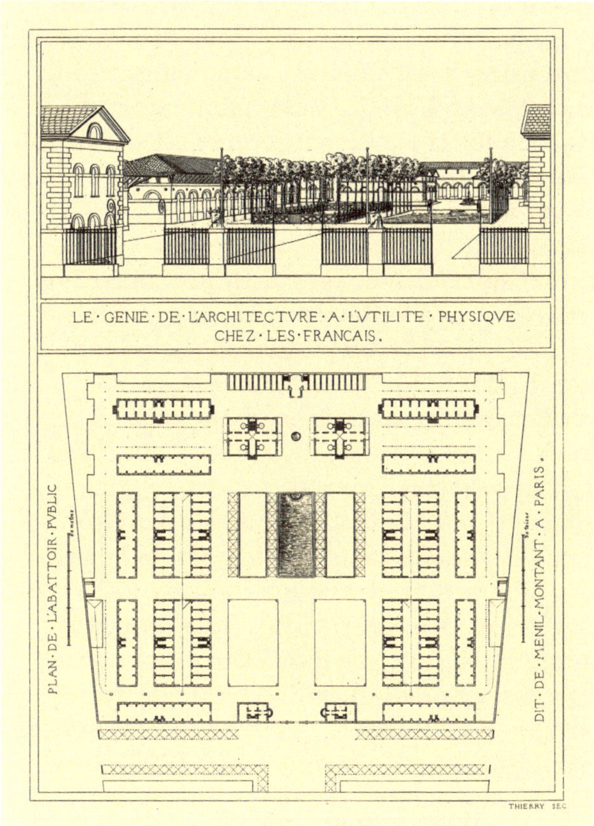

Fig. 10
View and plan of the abattoir at Ménilmontant, from Jean-Antoine Coussin, *Modèles d'architecture*, 1849. Collection: author.

In early 1814, when Austrian, Prussian, Russian, and other German armies advanced to Paris, many wounded soldiers were brought into the city, and with hospitals full, the municipality decided to lodge them in the sheds at the Montmartre, Ménilmontant, and Du Roule abattoirs. "None of these slaughterhouses was completed," a report written a year later observed. "Several of the buildings that compose them were without doors and

33 Richard Boxall Grantham, *Description of the Abattoirs of Paris* (London: Clowes and Sons, 1849).

without windows; they were not surrounded by any fence; the courtyards were encumbered with stones, wood, materials of all kinds. In six days the courtyards were cleaned; most of the windows were finished, the rooms tiled or planked; a provisional fence was made around the enclosure of each of these slaughterhouses. In eight days, counting from that of the circular from Monsieur le Préfet, the slaughterhouses were made fit to receive 6,000 patients." Remarkably, these patients did much better than those housed in the regular hospitals, and the fact that the men had been housed in a collection of separate, well-ventilated buildings was seen as key to their success. "The use made of these buildings for the service of the sick has made their distribution recognized as much cleaner for this new destination than any of the hospitals that exist today; experience has thus sanctioned the correctness of the views of Mr. Tenon and Mr. Bailly in their reports on the Hôtel-Dieu and the usefulness of dividing hospitals into separate pavilions, first proposed by Mr. Le Roy. This idea, henceforth, ought to be adopted for the construction of all the hospitals in which we want to meet desirable conditions of health and convenience."[34]

The various unexecuted plans for a new Hôtel-Dieu in Paris all assumed that well-ventilated pavilions would make healthy wards. There was also agreement that such hospitals would be considerably more expensive than conventional models: a pavilion hospital required a greater amount of land, and because of the smaller volume-to-surface ratio, its square-foot price was at least double when compared to more traditional designs. It took until 1825 before ground was broken for the first large pavilion hospital to be realized in France: the Saint-André Hospital in Bordeaux. A large gift made in 1821 by Prime Minister Armand-Emmanuel du Plessis, duc de Richelieu, provided the means to both run a large design competition, which was won by Bordeaux architect Jean Burguet, and pay the 1.5 million francs in construction costs. Completed in 1829, the Saint-André Hospital became known for its low mortality rate. Nevertheless, cost issues remained, and so it was not until 1846 that construction began in Paris of a second pavilion medical center: the Lariboisière Hospital—the building that had inspired Brunel when he set out to design the Renkioi Hospital.

The Lariboisière Hospital was designed to minimize the presence of miasmas in the sick wards. It is, however, important to note that by the middle of the nineteenth

34 Conseil Général des Hôpitaux et Hospices Civils de Paris, *Compte rendu par le conseil général des hôpitaux et hospices civils de Paris, du service de ses établissements pendant le premier semestre 1814 et jusqu'au 1er janvier 1815, et de l'emploi des dons faits par les habitans de Paris* (Paris: Huzard, 1815).

century, the understanding of the condition under which miasmas existed and what they were had changed since Lancisi's time. No one believed anymore that air was a spongelike body or that miasmas caused disease by clogging up the pores of the atmosphere. However, the term "miasma" persisted, assuming different, if not fully defined meanings. For example, German physician, biologist, and climatologist Adolf Mühry posited that most miasmas were microscopically small fungi and dustlike fungal spores that were generated by certain soils, could become abundant in the air in certain temperatures, and caused a variety of endemic and epidemic diseases, including the dreaded cholera.[35] French physician Jean-Baptiste Nacquart maintained that the term "miasma" should apply only to the evaporations of ill people and not to those that emerged from the decay of organic matter and so on. As far as the general public was concerned, miasmas were the result of overcrowding and the resulting filth and stench that characterized the poorest districts of quickly growing industrial cities.

Fig. 11
John Leech, "A Court for King Cholera," *Punch*, 1852. This cartoon illustrates the common nineteenth-century understanding of the cause of epidemic disease as one that could be both directly observed and, as architects, planners, and utopian thinkers believed, ameliorated through design. The key role of microorganisms in the etiology of many diseases was only to be understood many decades later. Collection: Wellcome Library, London.

A good guide to both the medical understanding (and lack of understanding) of the nature of miasmas in the 1850s and 1860s is the *Lehrbuch der Allgemeinen Aetiologie und Hygieine* (Textbook of general etiology and hygiene), written in 1858 by the young, ambitious, and brilliant physician Eduard Maria Anton Johann Reich. Born in Bohemia and educated at the University of Jena in the German Grand Duchy of Saxe-Weimar-Eisenach, the recently graduated Reich aimed to provide a comprehensive account of the causes of diseases.

35 Adolf Mühry, *Die geographischen Verhaeltnisse der Krankheiten, oder Grundzuege der Noso-Geographie, in ihrer Gesammtheit und Ordnung und mit einer Sammlung der Thatsachen Dargelegt* (Leipzig and Heidelberg: Winter'sche Verlagshandlung, 1856), 122.

Having neither practiced nor taught medicine yet, he was not invested in a particular medical paradigm, which allowed him to review them with equitable criticism. The introduction to the section "Contagions and Miasmas," which followed one on medications and poisons, makes this abundantly clear.

> If one wants to speak of dark spots on the terrain of medical knowledge, then those things must be designated as such, first and foremost, whose names form the heading of this main section. If one has full reason to complain about the darkness that envelops the field of pharmacology and toxicology, if one is therefore justified in speaking of an immense distance from the goal that the researching person is striving for, then these are only infinitesimal discrepancies in comparison to the teaching of contagions and miasmas. It is an essential advance and advantage of the pharmacological-toxicological, as well as of the bromatological [concerning the study of food] doctrines over our present subject matter, that in these disciplines the acting bodies are known wholly or for the most part, that there one has, if not a clear idea, at least an inkling of the processes which arise in the concurrence of the individual organism with the corpuscular objects of that doctrine: Here, the nature of the contagions and miasmas is only conjectured, fictions are built; one is hardly justified in making a hypothesis here or there.[36]

While much was unknown, that did not prevent Reich from skillfully summarizing the prevalent understandings.

> Let us first ask what is meant by the word contagion and what is meant by the word miasma. Contagions as well as miasmas are external influences which, if they concur with the organism endowed with the right "disposition," make it ill; but other external influences, such as poisons, medicines, food, etc., also do the same, but are not designated as either contagions nor miasmas. Therefore we must attempt to understand the matter more exactly. If something harmful is to deserve the name of a contagion, it must satisfy the following premises: (1) it must be the product of such a disease as we shall later call "contagious," (2) when it interacts with the organism of

36 Eduard Reich, *Lehrbuch der Allgemeinen Aetiologie und Hygieine* (Erlangen: Ferdinand Enke, 1858), 282.

> which it is a part, it must produce the same disease of which it is the product; if a substance does not satisfy these two points, then we do not call it a contagion under any condition. With regard to a miasma, it must be said that it is generally a product of the decomposition of organic and inorganic substances, and when it acts on the organism it puts it into a certain pathological state.[37]

Reich admitted that, at the current state of knowledge, the exact boundary between contagions and miasmas was not clear. They were, in his view, a part of a single continuum. "Only the extremes of the series, which begins with the most clearly pronounced contagion, and which closes with just such a miasma, are precisely characterized, if we are permitted to speak so according to the present standpoint of science." And to make matters even more confusing, it wasn't clear where the boundaries were between contagions and miasmas on the one hand and poisons on the other. What was clear, however, was that contagions are the products of a disease that reproduce in another organism, while poisons are not. But while poisons could be chemically known, contagions could not, nor could miasmas. What was assumed about the contagions was that they arose from the putrefaction of the substances of birds and mammals, while miasmas resulted from the decomposition of plants, invertebrates, fish, and reptiles. As to the nature and speed of the decay of the organic material, this was dependent on the nature of the soil, temperature, light, and atmosphere, with the soil being the most important factor, ranging from that underlying swamps and meadows to clayey soils, alluvial soils that are dry and sandy at the top but with lot of groundwater in deeper layers, heaps of rubble that result from earthquakes or war, land recently cleared as the result of deforestation, and so on. But, in the end, Reich admitted the world's ignorance about miasma: "Everything that is trumpeted to the world about the nature of miasmas must be received very carefully and subjected to very strict criticism, because otherwise one runs the risk of constructing an edifice without foundations, a fiction that is not only shaken in its foundations by the first strong gust of wind but often is completely destroyed."[38]

Reich's skepticism about the nature and effect of miasmas might suggest that the concept of a hospital as an amalgamate of well-ventilated wards might have lost currency in the late 1850s. In fact, the opposite happened.

37 Ibid. 282–83.
38 Ibid., 309–10.

Despite its short existence, Brunel's Renkioi Hospital had introduced a radical new way to think about hospital architecture. Thanks to Florence Nightingale, the lessons embodied in that building were not forgotten. While in Scutari, Nightingale had become a celebrity, and after returning to Britain she had begun a crusade to ensure reform in hospital management and design. She was particularly vocal about the proposal to build a large hospital at Netley, near Southampton; conceived in the first months of 1855, when the suffering of the army in the Crimea held center stage in British politics and public opinion, it was to receive sick and wounded veterans, who until that time had been accommodated in the miserable and unhealthy casemates of Saint Mary's Barracks in Chatham. The secretary of state for war, Fox Maule-Ramsay, 2nd Baron Panmure, insisted that this new hospital would follow the pavilion structure that had been experimented with in France. Yet the director general of the Army Medical Department, Dr. Andrew Smith, opposed this plan and proposed one large and magnificent building. Lord Panmure acquiesced, and on May 19, 1856, Queen Victoria laid the first stone of what would be known as the Royal Victoria Hospital, Netley.

When Nightingale returned to Britain in September, she met Lord Panmure, who asked her for her opinion of the plans. It did not help that Nightingale detested Smith; she believed that he, more than anyone else, had been responsible for the disaster in the Crimea.[39] Nightingale replied that the project reminded her of the hospital in Scutari, and in many ways the arrangement at Scutari had been better.[40] She then decided to politicize the issue, and approached the prime minister, Henry John Temple, 3rd Viscount Palmerston, presenting him with the plans for Netley and with plans of hospitals of which she approved. On January 17, 1857, Lord Palmerston wrote to Lord Panmure: "I had the other day a long conversation with Miss Nightingale about the proposed arrangements of the Military Hospital now building at Netley, and I am bound to say that she has left on my mind at present a conviction that the plan is fundamentally wrong, and that it would be better to pull down and rebuild all that has been built there than to finish it upon the present plan."[41]

Nightingale had been able to convince Lord Palmerston that Netley was a catastrophe in the making. The main issue was the lack of cross ventilation, attributable to the fact that the sick wards were arranged along a lengthy corridor.

39 Florence Nightingale, letter to Sidney Herbert, Dec. 30, 1857, in *Collected Works of Florence Nightingale*, ed. Lynn McDonald, 16 vols. (Waterloo, ON: Wilfrid Laurier University Press, 2001–12) 14:551.
40 Florence Nightingale, "Confidential Report on the Plans of the Royal Victoria Hospital, Southampton," in McDonald, *Collected Works of Florence Nightingale*, 16:241.
41 Lord Palmerston, letter to Lord Panmure, Jan. 17, 1856, in *The Panmure Papers: Being a Selection from the Correspondence of Fox Maule, Second Baron Panmure, Afterwards Eleventh Earl of Dalhousie*, ed. George Brisbane Douglas and George Dalhousie Ramsay, 2 vols. (London: Hodder and Stoughton, 1908), 2:332.

Fig. 12
Royal Victoria Hospital, Netley, England, *The Illustrated London News*, 1859. Collection: author.

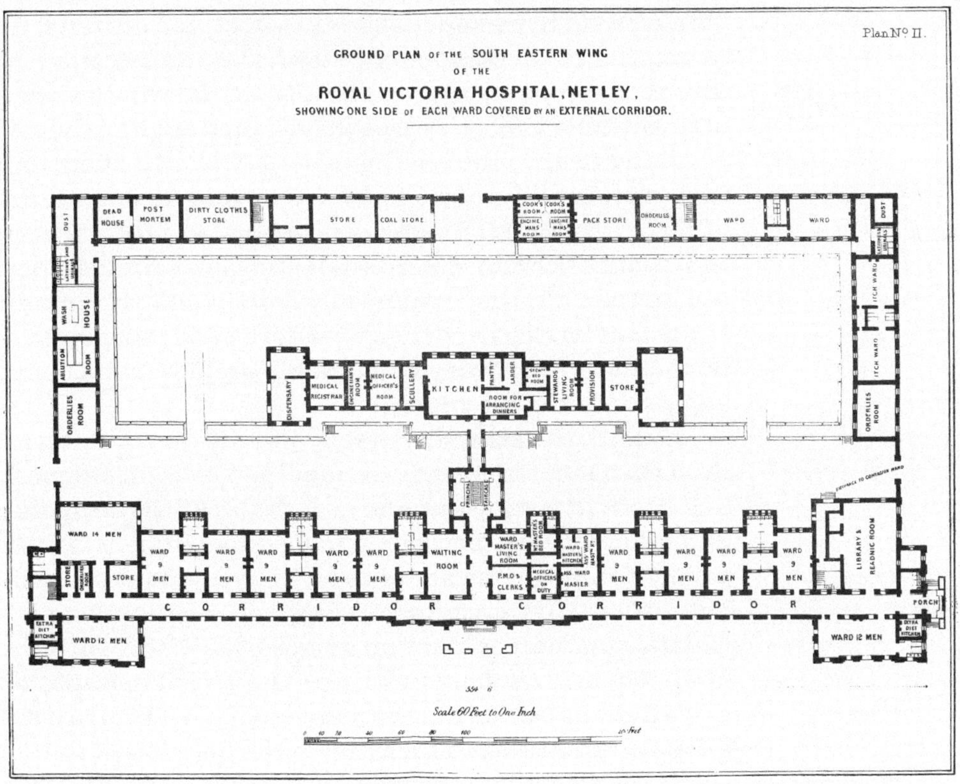

Fig. 13
R. O. Mennie, Plan of a wing and its adjacent structures of the Royal Victoria Hospital, from Florence Nightingale, *Notes on Hospitals*, 1859. Collection: Wellcome Library, London.

"This matter seems to me to be one of the greatest importance, and the lives of thousands of our soldiers may depend upon the nature of the arrangements we are now making," Lord Palmerston wrote. "As this building is to last for a century, and is to be filled by hundreds at a time, any sacrifice of money in correcting errors in its intended construction would be better than a deliberate perseverance in arrangements demonstrated to be bad. Pray, therefore, for the present stop all further progress in the work till the matter can be duly considered."[42]

Construction of the hospital did not halt, however, and Nightingale became increasingly vocal about the expensive catastrophe she saw arising at Netley. She was not alone: in March 1856, the Manchester physician John Roberton had presented a paper: "On the defects, with regard to the plan of construction and ventilation of most of our hospitals for the reception of the sick and wounded." Roberton praised the Saint-André Hospital in Bordeaux and the Lariboisière Hospital in Paris as examples to be followed. Ventilation of the wards was key to preventing high mortality, and Roberton rejected mechanical or "scientific" ventilation, "whether the downward mode, the upward mode, or the circuitous mode." Instead, he favored the ventilation created in a long, narrow ward with open windows on the long sides: "If a ward is to be kept perfectly sweet, *the air must flow through it in correspondence with the natural movements of the atmosphere without.* Let the windows of the opposite side walls—tall windows, they ought to be tall, reaching near to the cieling [*sic*]—be thrown open, and instantly, the air enters on one side, and escapes at the other."[43] In July 1856, the most important medical serial in Britain, *The Lancet*, enthusiastically endorsed Roberton's paper, quoting extensively from it and recommending that it be read by "the governors of all our public hospitals, and of every respectable architect and civil engineer in the kingdom."[44]

Both the size, the status, and the fact that it was a project that could have been modified or even stopped had brought Netley into the crosshairs of Nightingale and others. Yet its perceived flaws immediately led to a concern in the army about the 243 permanent barracks and 167 military hospitals in England, Scotland, and Ireland. In October 1857, on advice of Dr. John Sutherland, who with Robert Rawlinson had tried to improve hygienic conditions in the Crimea, Lord Panmure established a committee to investigate the housing of the army and to make improvements where possible, if their cost did not exceed 100 pounds per building, and to recommend more expensive ones. A general principle to be observed was that soldiers should have at least 17 cubic meters per person when lodged in permanent barracks, and patients in military hospitals should have double that amount of space.

In 1861 the Commission Appointed for Improving the Sanitary Condition of Barracks and Hospitals

42 Ibid., 2:333.
43 John Roberton, "On the defects, with regard to the plan of construction and ventilation of most of our hospitals for the reception of the sick and wounded," in "Reviews and Notices of Books: 'On the Defects . . .,'" *Lancet* 2 (1856), 50.
44 Ibid.

issued its report. "The barrack hospitals in the United Kingdom present almost every variety of plan except the right one," the report noted. Their design mimicked those of the permanent stone or brick barracks used at garrisons and offered too little or no ventilation. In addition, there was chronic overcrowding. The care of ailing soldiers faced an emergency, and the commission had a simple solution: give the existing hospitals a new function, and initiate the construction of new hospitals based on principles of ventilation. As it would take time for these buildings to be completed, the army should use detached barracks as a temporary measure to house the sick. "These huts insure subdivision of the sick, and facility of ventilation on account of their previous structure." While wooden barracks were preferable from a ventilation point of view, they were expensive to maintain and also prone to be "infested with vermin and saturated with organic matter."[45] Hence, a brick version of barracks might be preferable, as long as the space per inmate was doubled, from 17 to 34 cubic meters.

The influential editor of *The Builder*, architect George Godwin, also became a champion of hospital reform, publishing three articles on the subject in August and September 1858. The pieces appeared anonymously but were republished a year later as an appendix in Nightingale's book *Notes on Hospitals*, which led many people to believe that Nightingale had written them. In the opening lines of the first article, the author put the case clearly: "The sanitary history of hospitals may be summed up in very few words. There are hospitals on very bad sites: there are hospitals on comparatively good sites; but there is hardly an instance, in this country at least, of both hospital and site fully embodying those sanitary principles which are essentially necessary for a rapid recovery of the sick and maimed. The one paramount sanitary condition which ought to be observed in all hospitals is that of having *pure and dry air* both within and without the walls of the buildings." The author had worked hard to find historical evidence to back up this thesis. Particular attention was paid to the horrific mortality in the Hôtel-Dieu of Paris, which was compared to the situation in Scutari: "In the case of the Hôtel Dieu, it resulted eventually in the introduction into France of the greatest improvements in hospital construction and management which have taken place up to the present time. [...] From the Scutari case it is also hoped, that great permanent improvements will arise in military hospitals; and it will be well, if the experience of our own civil

45 Great Britain, Commission Appointed for Improving the Sanitary Condition of Barracks and Hospitals, *General Report of the Commission Appointed for Improving the Sanitary Condition of Barracks and Hospitals* (London: Eyre and Spottiswoode, 1861), 123, 149, 173.

hospitals should lead to similar results." The end of the article addressed those who did not believe that air, and air only, mattered, and took a rhetorical swipe at the theory of contagion which, it argued, "may be said to rest on no stronger foundation than the observation of facts in badly-constructed and ill-ventilated hospitals, where emanations from the sick play a corresponding part to the emanations from cesspools and other nuisances, in producing fevers out of hospitals."[46]

The second article reviewed the principles of hospital planning and included a lengthy and detailed discussion on hospital design. A key mistake was to believe that sick wards adjacent to courtyards would enjoy decent ventilation: "The air must be 'moving air' in mass. [...] There must be no 'stagnation.'" It recommended an arrangement of separate wards, reviewing wards placed in a straight line, in U and H shapes, and finally in one or two parallel rows, located at some distance from each other and connected by an armature. The author defined this as "the only plan which allows as much extension as can be necessary in any single hospital up to (say) 1000 sick (beyond which hospital management becomes very difficult), is the plan adopted in the hospital at Bordeaux; or still better, that of the Lariboisière at Paris."[47]

The third article focused on the individual ward. It did not miss opportunities to mock the Royal Victoria Hospital in Netley, which, as most readers would have known, was the focus of Nightingale's contempt: "A great mistake and a lamentable misfortune is Netley Hospital. But let us hope we have seen the last of such fatal blunders in hospital building." The author first considered the ideal size of a ward from a management point of view. "It is highly important that patients, who must necessarily be in various stages of sickness or convalescence, should feel that they are continually under the eye of the head nurse. It is, of course, most economical to have one ward to each head nurse. The ward, therefore, should be large enough to occupy her whole attention; but not too large to render its ventilation difficult. [...] If we are to be guided by the results of recent experience in hospital building, we should say that a ward with thirty sick, or thereabouts, is, upon the whole, the best for sanitary reasons." Taking the wards of the Lariboisière Hospital as guidance, the article postulated that such a ward might be 10 meters wide, between 34 and 39 meters long, and 5 meters high, with windows on both sides, one for every two beds.

46 "Sites and Construction of Hospitals," *The Builder*, Aug. 28, 1858, as printed in Florence Nightingale, *Notes on Hospitals: Being Two Papers Read before the National Association for the Promotion of Social Science, at Liverpool, in October, 1858. With Evidence Given to the Royal Commissioners on the State of the Army in 1857* (London: Parker, 1859), 89, 92–93.

47 "Construction of Hospitals—The Ground Plan," *The Builder*, Sept. 11, 1858, as printed in Nightingale, *Notes on Hospitals*, 93, 96, 98.

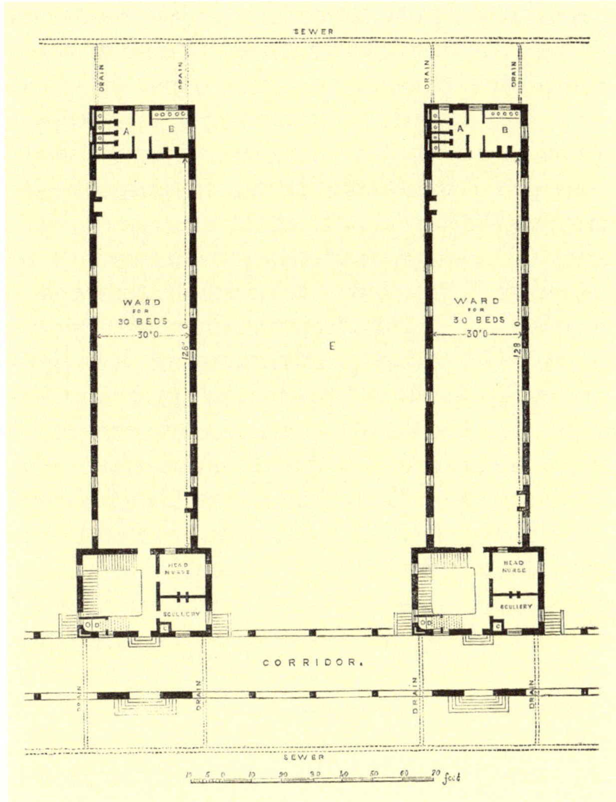

Fig. 14
Plan for an ideal sick ward and its arrangement, "Hospital Construction—Wards," *The Builder*, 1858. Collection: author.

"The ward construction, now described, is that which, up to the present time, experience has shown to be best suited for fulfilling all the requirements of ventilation, light, cheerfulness, recovery of health, and economy, in this country."[48]

Nightingale's 1859 book *Notes on Hospitals* also contained a paper she had given a year earlier at a meeting of the National Association for the Promotion of Social Science in Liverpool, alongside the articles from *The Builder* as well as testimony she had given in an 1857 public inquiry into the health of the British Army during the Crimean War. Her book was to have an enormous impact on the history of hospital design—and the history of barracks. In her introduction, Nightingale felt obliged to strike out against those who opposed the miasmatism, mocking the "very modern invention" of contagion, which she defined as an absurdity. Drawing a comparison between the very high mortality in the hospital in Scutari, with its almost nonexistent ventilation, and the standard level of mortality in the hutted hospital created by the sanitary commission for the British naval brigade at Balaklava, Nightingale noted: "All experience tells the same tale, both among sick and well. Men will have a high rate of mortality in large barracks, a low one in separate huts, even with a much less amount of cubic

48 "Hospital Construction—Wards," *The Builder*, Sept. 25, 1858, as printed in Nightingale, *Notes on Hospitals*, 101–02, 106.

space." The way forward in hospital design was clear: the sick wards of hospitals were to be distinct pavilions, "containing generally not more than 100 sick each."[49]

Nightingale presented much material on pavilion design and provided particularly rigid prescriptions on the width of the wards. "It does not appear as if the air could be thoroughly changed, if a distance of more than thirty feet intervenes between the opposite windows," she wrote. By limiting the width of the ward to 10 meters, one also avoided the temptation of having "double wards," with more than two rows of beds between the windows, as existed in Guy's Hospital and King's College Hospital in London. Nightingale observed, "These double wards are from twelve to nearly twenty feet [3.5 to 6 meters] wider than they ought to be between the opposite windows for thorough ventilation. The partition down the middle with apertures makes matters rather worse." She made one exception: four rows of beds might be made to work in "a one-storied hut hospital, ventilated through the ceiling, like that of Dr. Parkes, at Renkioi. But his were magnificent huts, and the partition was little more than a bulkhead."[50] The impact of all of this was a clear understanding that the future of hospital design was not to be found in large permanent buildings but in the flexible arrangements of well-ventilated, smaller, one-story pavilions.

So far, so good. An important question that remained was whether sick pavilions ought to be of permanent construction or temporary barracks. Ninety years earlier, Brocklesby, the British Army surgeon general, had clearly argued against permanent sick wards when he observed that "infirmaries, or hospitals, in all countries, are for the most part unclean and infectious places," and that "a perfectly safe purification, in some cases, can never be fully effected, unless after a great length of time; the seeds of infection once sown, continue, in some instances, to spread contagious diseases, and to contaminate the house."[51] He did not have at that time scientific evidence to support his assertion.

In 1858 Sir John Simon, chief medical officer of the Privy Council and, as such, the most senior public health official in Great Britain, heard of a remarkable reduction in the occurrence of a debilitating skin disease among patients of a floating naval hospital in the Thames when an old wooden hospital ship had been replaced by a new one. Launched in 1801 as a ninety-eight-gun ship of the line, HMS *Dreadnought* had seen action in the Battle of Trafalgar and then served as a

49 Nightingale, *Notes on Hospitals*, 7–8.
50 Ibid., 13–14.
51 Richard Brocklesby, *Oeconomical and Medical Observations*, 58–59.

quarantine ship and, from 1827 to 1857, as a hospital ship. "The old hospital ship 'Dreadnought' had acquired a very evil reputation for the prevalence of these infections," Simon observed in an account that invoked the mortality in the old Hôtel-Dieu in Paris and the British military hospital in Scutari. Simon blamed "organic contamination still lingering in the wooden walls of the wards. Early last year another more commodious ship was substituted for the 'Dreadnought'; and Mr. Tudor, the resident surgeon, informs me that, 'whereas in the two years preceding that change 9 out of 22 amputations had terminated fatally, only one amputation had proved fatal out of 16 performed in the year following the change.'"[52] Hospital gangrene, common on the older ship, also had completely disappeared. The drop in mortality after the replacement of the old hospital ship with a new one suggested a similar course of action for hospitals.

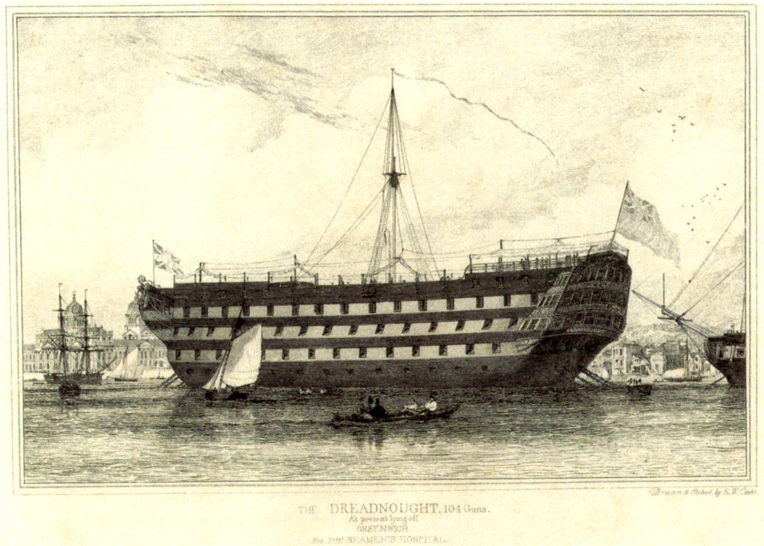

Fig. 15
Edward William Cooke, HMS *Dreadnought* at Greenwich, London, 1831. Collection: National Maritime Museum, Greenwich, London.

One year later, Sir Douglas Strutt Galton, who as assistant inspector general of fortifications had overseen the design and construction of a large military hospital in Woolwich, and who had authored various works on hospital construction, addressed a meeting of the British Medical Association in Leeds. In his lecture, he noted that, in the case of infectious diseases, mortality "is high in special hospitals, it is low in shed buildings, and even in no buildings at all. If, therefore, it be necessary to make special provision for epidemic disease cases, would it not be better to make such special provision in small hut wards, attached to ordinary hospitals, but separate from each other, and from the hospital proper? A simple, inexpensive hut for a few beds, capable of perfect

52 John Simon, "Introductory Report by the Medical Officer of the Board," in Edward Headlam Greenbow, *Papers Relating to the Sanitary State of the People of England* (London: George Eyre and William Spottiswoode, 1858), xl.

ventilation, and admitting of being occasionally pulled down and rebuilt with fresh materials at no great expense, would in all probability afford more recoveries from fever and wounds than the most costly special hospital wards." If this principle applied to hospitals for infectious diseases, why not to all hospitals? "Do not build for a long futurity. Buildings used for the reception of sick become permeated with organic impurities, and it is a real sanitary advantage that they should be pulled down and entirely rebuilt on a fresh site periodically."[53]

Galton was not alone. In France the up-and-coming surgeon Charles Sarazin loudly pleaded for what he considered a "radical" solution to hospital design: "No more permanent hospitals; they must be replaced by *barrack hospitals*. The permanent hospital is the *sepulchre hospital*, which nothing can keep wholesome, and which entails fabulous expenditure. The barrack hospital, renewed in nearly all its parts every ten or fifteen years, alone presents the hygienic conditions necessary for hospitals, and admits of the realization of appreciable economies."[54]

Galton and Sarazin made their proposals at an important cusp in the history of medicine: by 1860, the doctrine of miasmas began to give way—albeit very, very slowly at first—to a new theory that focused on the key role of microorganisms like bacteria, viruses, and fungi in the development and transmission of disease. This ought to have forced both hospital patrons and architects to, once again, reconsider the principles of hospital design. But having finally embraced the architectural implications that came with the idea that miasmas cause disease, they were not ready to abandon the miasma paradigm so easily. Ventilation was a concept they could translate in spatial and architectural terms. But antimicrobial and antiseptic protocols seemed to have little relevance except where it applied to the porousness of surfaces. And so, in the decades that followed, hospital patrons and architects were to remain wedded to what turned out to be increasingly outmoded concepts.

53 Douglas Galton, *An Address on the General Principles Which Should Be Observed in the Construction of Hospitals: Delivered to the British Medical Association at Leeds, July 29, 1869, with the Discussion Which Took Place Thereon* (London: Macmillan and Co., 1869), 22, 55.

54 Charles Sarazin, "Hôpital: des établissements hospitaliers en temps de paix et en temps de guerre," in *Nouveau Dictionnaire de Médicine et de Chirurgie Pratique*, 40 vols. (Paris: Baillière et fils, 1864–86), 17:698.

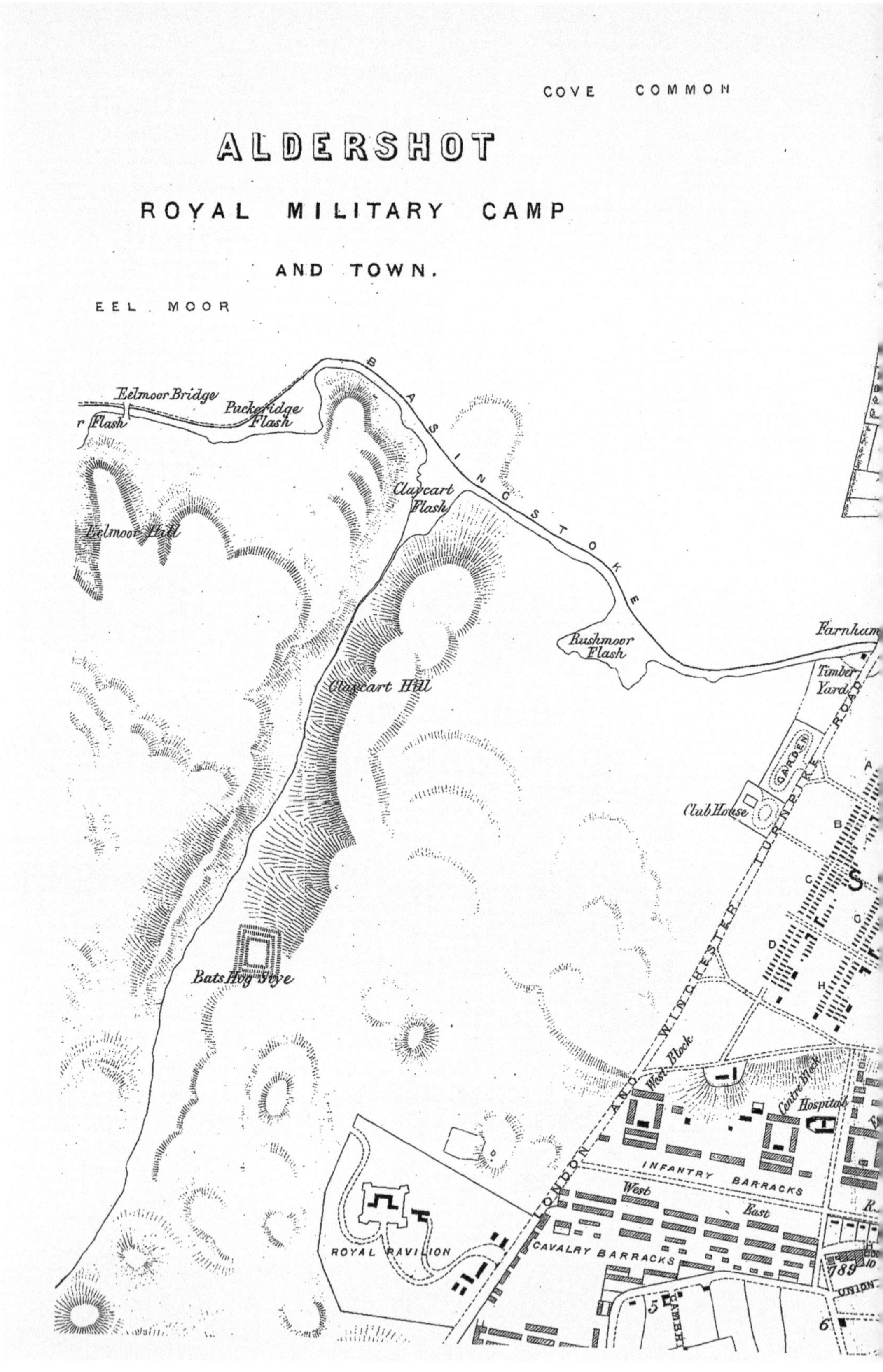
COVE COMMON
ALDERSHOT
ROYAL MILITARY CAMP
AND TOWN.
EEL MOOR
Eelmoor Bridge
Packeridge Flash
BASINGSTOKE
Claycart Flash
Eelmoor Hall
Rushmoor Flash
Farnham
Claycart Hill
Timber Yard
GARDEN
Club House
TURNPIKE ROAD
WINCHESTER
LONDON AND
Bats Hog Stye
West Block
Centre Block
Hospital
INFANTRY BARRACKS
West
East
ROYAL PAVILION
CAVALRY BARRACKS
UNION

→ p. 169

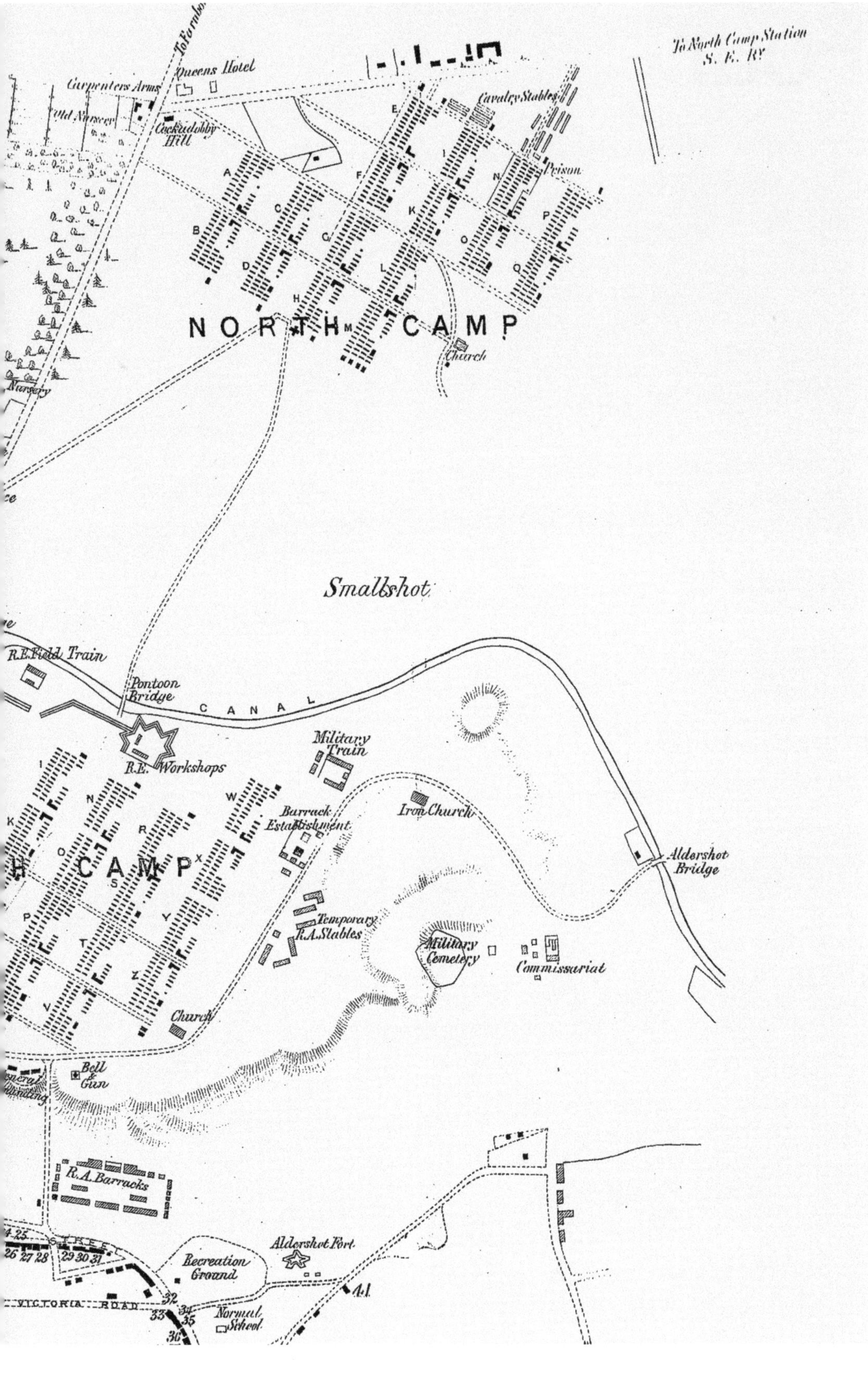

Queens Hotel
Carpenters Arms
Old Nursery
Cockadobby Hill
Cavalry Stables
Prison
To North Camp Station S. E. Ry
NORTH CAMP
Church
Nursery
Smallshot
R.E. Field Train
Pontoon Bridge
CANAL
Military Train
R.E. Workshops
Barrack Establishment
Iron Church
Aldershot Bridge
CAMP
Temporary R.A. Stables
Military Cemetery
Commissariat
Church
Bell & Gun
R.A. Barracks
Recreation Ground
Aldershot Fort
VICTORIA ROAD
Normal School

Four

Shabby, Low, Draughty, Ill-Contrived, and Unsightly

The barrack is the child of war, and for most of history, war marked the breakdown of politics, bringing hatred, hunger, poverty, pillage, disease, destruction, injury, and death. The simple if not primitive architecture of the barrack carries the signature of life reduced to its most basic level, a condition typically brought about by war, and one that most civilians dread. Throughout history, however, conflict has not been perceived only in a negative way. William Shakespeare touched on the glory of war in King Henry V's speech on the eve of the Battle of Agincourt, in which he rallies his men, reminding them that the experience of shared battle ennobled the soldier. Two centuries later, a new spirit of nationalism understood war—fought for the sake of some national ideal and not to realize some dynastic ambition, as in the case of the Hundred Years' War—as the crucible of national identity and national solidarity. For example, the First Schleswig War may have begun in some dynastic muddle, but for the great majority of Danes, it quickly became a way to symbolically overcome the disasters and humiliations Denmark had faced in the Napoleonic era: the destruction of Copenhagen, the loss of Norway, and national bankruptcy. While the outcome of that conflict was mixed, the fact that Danish resolve and feats of arms had successfully resisted the creation of a Danish-German boundary in Jutland augmented Danish pride. Otto Bache's painting of the triumphant entry of units of the Danish army into Copenhagen, painted four decades after the war, evokes that sense of shared joy, pride, and patriotism forged in the crucible of wars interpreted as tests of the nation. The scene depicts a particular moment at a particular place, but the theme was universal in the so-called long nineteenth century, which began in 1789 with the French Revolution and ended in 1914 with the outbreak of World War I: the departure of national armies for the front and the return of the veterans from battle were events that both shaped and confirmed—and continue to do so today—national identities in almost every European country.

→ Fig. 1

The nineteenth century is often identified as the Age of Nationalism. Indeed, one might define the concept of the nation as the primary vehicle of historical destiny as the most important invention of that period—more impactful than the steam engine, the electromagnetic telegraph, photography, the telephone, the electrical grid, the internal combustion engine, and so on. In a famous lecture given in 1882, French scholar and public intellectual Ernest Renan characterized a nation as "a soul, a spiritual principle" that consists of both "the possession in common of a rich legacy of memories" and "present-day consent, the desire to live together, the will to perpetuate the value of the heritage that one has received in an undivided form. [...] To have common glories in the past and to have a common will in the present; to have performed great deeds together, to wish to perform still more—these are the essential conditions for being a people."[1]

Renan articulated an idea, commonplace in the nineteenth century, that nations, and not individuals, classes, or dynasties, were the vehicles of historical destiny, that nations enacted their allotted roles in history, and that, as a result, each nation created and preserved a unique moral inheritance that was shared by all citizens, rich and poor, city dwellers and country-folk. This patrimony, which was to be the foundation of a program to forge national solidarity, could be found in the stories of heroic deeds by ancestors told in history books; in the art collected in public museums; in the great works of literature; in cathedrals and other monuments of architecture; in contemporary scientific, technological, and economic achievements; in the defense and development of what was believed to be one's ancestral land; in the "liberation" of territories that had once belonged to the fatherland but had been severed at some past date; and in the acquisition, "pacification," and exploitation of overseas colonies.[2]

Methods to allow the masses to comprehend the significance of their national inheritance almost always involved comparisons with the achievements of neighboring nations or those that were similar in size and character. Thus, the idea of a nation implied the reality of competition, which in the most extreme case meant

1 Ernest Renan, "What Is a Nation?," trans. Martin Thom, in *Nation and Narration*, ed. Homi K. Bhabha (London and New York: Routledge, 1990), 19.
2 See Francis Delaise, *Political Myths and Economic Realities* (New York: Viking, 1927), 216–17.

Fig. 1
Otto Bache, *Danish Soldiers Return to Copenhagen*, 1849. Collection: Frederiksborg Nationalhistorisk Museum, Hillerød, Denmark.

war. Of course, many nations remembered battles that had been lost, cities that had been surrendered, and wars that had ended with capitulation. But that did not really matter. As Renan observed, the memory of shared suffering united a nation more than that of shared achievement: "Where national memories are concerned, griefs are of more value than triumphs, for they impose duties, and require a common effort. A nation is therefore a large-scale solidarity, constituted by the feeling of sacrifices that one has made in the past and of those that one is prepared to make in the future."[3]

As a result, a nation's military forces, above all the army, in which, in principle, every able-bodied young man had to serve, comprised the most important institution of the nation conceived as a community of both shared moral patrimony and shared sacrifice. Before the French Revolution, European armies composed of professionals had been tools of government policies; they served the state. Beginning with the French *levée en masse*, the army had become the core of the nation understood as the "nation-at-arms"—a dedicated community in which every member was impelled to transcend one's material interests for the sake of what could turn out to be the supreme sacrifice, death, for a superior end, the nation. The French historian Jules Michelet graphically articulated the lesson in patriotism conveyed by the sight of marching soldiers. When a boy "is just beginning to be a man," Michelet urged his readers, "let his father take him" to a great public festival in Paris. "From some roof or terrace he shows him the people, the army passing by with its bayonets flashing and glittering, and the tricolored flag." And, in the solemn moment just before the parade begins, when the crowd turns silent in the expectation of the spectacle to unfold, the father will tell the son: "Look, my son, look: there is France; there is your native land! All this is like one man—with one soul and one heart. They would all die for a single man, and each one ought also to live and to die for all. Those men passing by, who are armed and now departing, they are going away to fight for us. They are leaving their father and their aged mother who will need them. You will do the same, for you will never forget that your mother is France."[4]

If the troops on parade provided one view of the nation-at-arms, soldiers caught in the middle of the slaughter deepened the understanding of what this means—at least to the perceptive observer. When Count Lev Nikolayevich Tolstoy found himself in the besieged city of Sevastopol in 1854, he wrote three reports on his

3 Renan, "What Is a Nation?," 19.
4 Jules Michelet, *The People*, trans. John P. Mackay (Urbana: University of Illinois Press, 1973), 204.

experiences. What was the source of the soldiers' composure under fire, their loyalty, and their patience under the most difficult of conditions? "Men cannot accept these frightful conditions for the sake of a cross or a title, nor because of threats," Tolstoy observed. "There must be another, a lofty incentive, as the cause. And this cause is the feeling which rarely appears, of which a Russian is ashamed, that which lies at the bottom of each man's soul—love for his country."[5] Many of these men came from the region closest to the Crimea, known as the Ukraine. Today their descendants, professionally trained soldiers and volunteers, young and old, men and women, demonstrate in Mariupol, Kharkiv, and countless other cities, towns, and villages the continuing truth of Tolstoy's observation.

The barrack got caught up in this heady mix of identity, purpose, fitness, and readiness to both kill and die. It did so during war, at the front, and also during peace, in the heartland, in the form of large permanent training camps for the new national armies.

In the summer of 1830, the citizens of the United Kingdom of the Netherlands, the unitary state that had been created fifteen years earlier in the Congress of Vienna, rose up against the government in The Hague. The raison d'être of this state was the need to control France. In 1792, when the War of the First Coalition broke out, eleven sovereign or semi-sovereign territories, many of which were fragmented in smaller parts, faced France between Switzerland and the Channel.[6] Hence it was no surprise that the French army, large as the result of national conscription and driven by patriotism, had done so well. When the leaders of Austria, Russia, Prussia, and Great Britain met in Vienna in 1815 to reorganize Europe, they agreed that a stable Europe required that the border with France that stretched between Basel and Dunkirk should be guarded by four well-armed states.[7] One of these was the United Kingdom of the Netherlands, an amalgam of the territories of the largely Protestant Dutch Republic (also known as the Republic of the Seven United Netherlands), and the Roman Catholic Southern Netherlands and the Principality of Liège.

The United Kingdom of the Netherlands was a state; it never became a nation. The strict Calvinist mentality of the inhabitants of the north and the easygoing attitude of the mainly Roman Catholic south clashed against the background of a badly designed political arrangement. In August 1830, the revolution in France triggered a rebellion that resulted in the secession of

5 Leo Tolstoy, "Sevastopol in December," in *The Cossacks, Sevastopol, the Invaders, and Other Stories*, [trans. Isabel F. Hapgood] (New York: Charles Scribner's Sons, 1925), 221.

6 The eleven territories were: (1) the Margraviate of Baden, (2) a Habsburg-ruled territory commonly known as Further Austria, (3) the Principality of Fürstenberg, (4) the Electorate of the Palatinate, (5) the Landgraviate of Hessen-Darmstadt, (6) the Principality of Palatine-Zweibrücken, (7) the County of Nassau-Saarbrücken, (8) the Electorate of Trier, (9) the Governorate of the Austrian Netherlands, (10) the County of Bouillon, and (11) the Principality of Liège.

7 The four states were: (1) the Grand Duchy of Baden, (2) the Kingdom of Bavaria, (3) the Kingdom of Prussia, and (4) the United Kingdom of the Netherlands (of which the Grand Duchy of Luxembourg, though formally independent, was practically a part).

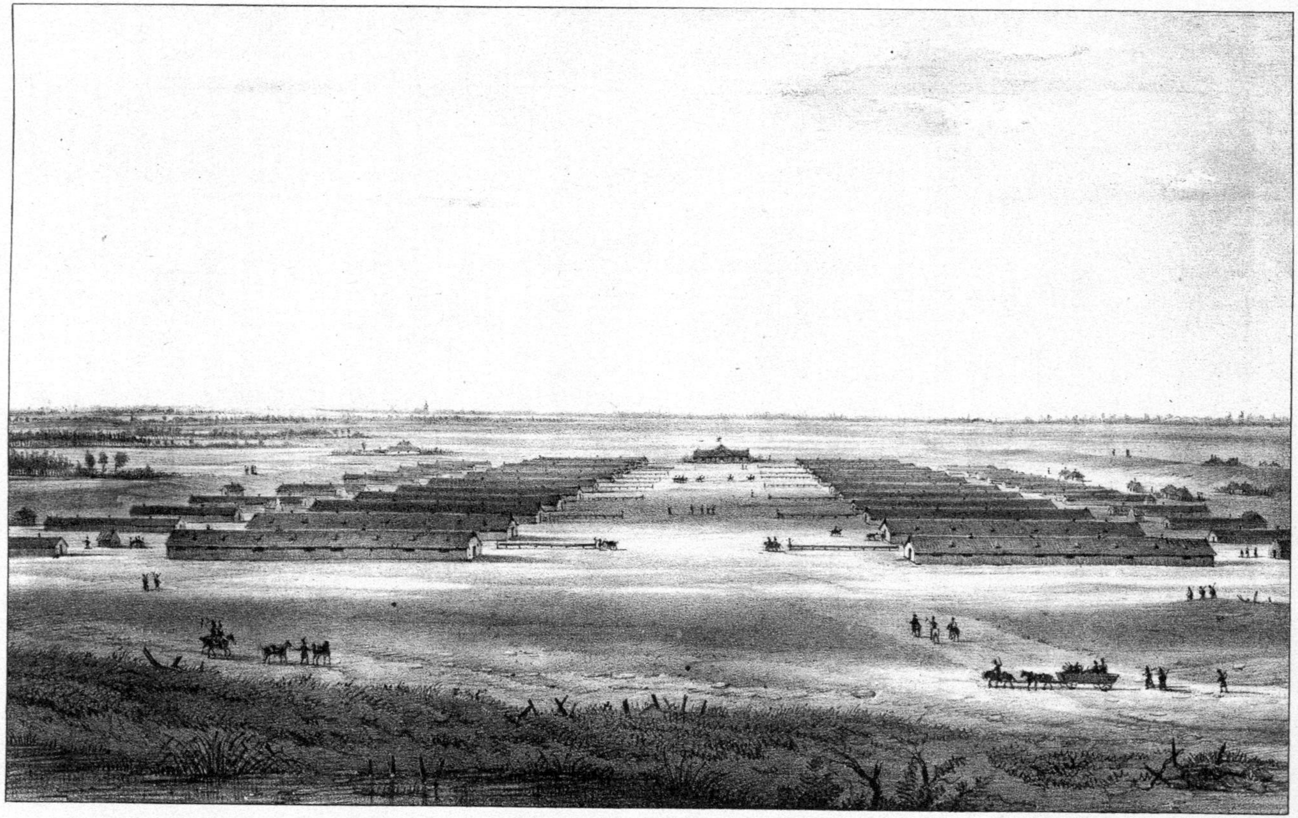

Fig. 2
Jean-Baptiste Gratry, The camp at Beverloo, Belgium, from his *Vues du camp de Beverloo*, 1843. Collection: Erfgoedbibliotheek Hendrik Conscience, Antwerp.

most of the southern half of the United Kingdom of the Netherlands and the establishment of the Kingdom of Belgium; the north subsequently dropped the adjective "United" from the name of its kingdom. In July 1831, Prince Leopold of Saxe-Coburg and Gotha became *roi des Belges* (king of the Belgians). The Dutch did not accept these developments and in August launched an invasion of the breakaway territory, defeating a quickly formed Belgian force, only to be pushed back to the old border of the former Dutch Republic by a French army that intervened in the conflict on the side of the Belgians. There followed an eight-year armistice, during which the Dutch continued to object to Belgian sovereignty.

Anticipating the possibility of another Dutch invasion, King Leopold set out to organize a modern, efficient, and well-trained force to defend Belgian sovereignty and help forge nationhood. A large, permanent camp close to the Dutch border was to provide campaign-like conditions allowing for the kind of large maneuvers in which soldiers from all over Belgium might merge into a single army. A combination of twenty-four infantry battalions, twenty cavalry squadrons, and four artillery batteries would engage simultaneously in large exercises that simulated battlefield conditions in scale and setting. The extensive heaths in the sparsely populated province of Limburg fit the bill, and in 1835, Captain Bruno Rénard and a unit of military engineers began construction of a camp near the hamlet of Beverloo.[8] The result was what a travel guide to Belgium defined as "one of the most curious, as well as one of the most gratifying sights in the country." The soldiers' dwellings consisted of tents, straw huts, and large wooden barracks.

← Fig. 2

Both the huts and the barracks were constructed by the soldiers themselves. "They are their own builders, carpenters, joiners, brickmakers, bricklayers, and locksmiths," the travel guide noted. "The result of their labours prove them to be, not only good workmen, but workmen of excellent taste."[9] Beverloo also provided a barrack-like pavilion for King Leopold, who often stayed there with his nephew, Prince Albert of Saxe-Coburg and Gotha.

In providing 500 square kilometers of heath that allowed for realistic maneuvers, Beverloo offered a kind of halfway house between the permanent garrisons that housed the army and the conditions in the field the

8 Bruno Renard, *Considérations sur l'infanterie légère* (Tournai: Hennebert, 1840); *L'Histoire politique et militaire de la Belgique* (Brussels: Stienon, 1847); *Considérations sur la tactique de l'infanterie en Europe* (Paris: Librairie Militaire/Dumaine, 1857); *Histoire militaire: Cours abrégé de tactique générale* (Brussels: Librarie Européenne de Muquardt, 1879).

9 Henry Robert Addison, *Belgium as She Is* (Brussels and Leipzig: Muquardt, 1843), 295–96.

Chapter Two, Fig. 1
→ p. 79

Chapter One, Fig. 16
→ p. 66

army would face during actual military operations against an enemy. While it had antecedents in the camps at Boulogne-sur-Mer, created in 1803 to house the French Army of the Ocean Coasts, and the camp of instruction at Montechiaro, constructed four years later to provide training facilities for Napoleon's Italian army, Beverloo was seen in the 1830s as a radical innovation in army training and management, and military magazines raved about the camp. In fact, King Leopold consciously used Beverloo as an instrument of propaganda, and although the Belgian army was very young and relatively small, the camp allowed its generals to acquire a place at the table of the established powers. Charles Albert, King of Sardinia (which encompassed Sardinia, Liguria, and Savoy) adopted the idea of Beverloo for his own purposes. An Italian nationalist, King Charles Albert aimed to end Austrian rule over Lombardy and the Veneto, possibly annex those territories into his own kingdom, and perhaps, down the road, even create an Italian federative state under his leadership. In order to achieve this, the Royal Sardinian Army needed to be modernized, and a large training camp, constructed on a 1,300-hectare proving ground some 20 kilometers from Turin, was to offer ample training facilities.[10] The camp at Cirié consisted of seventy large stable-like barracks of 24 meters by 12 meters, each offering space to 130 soldiers.

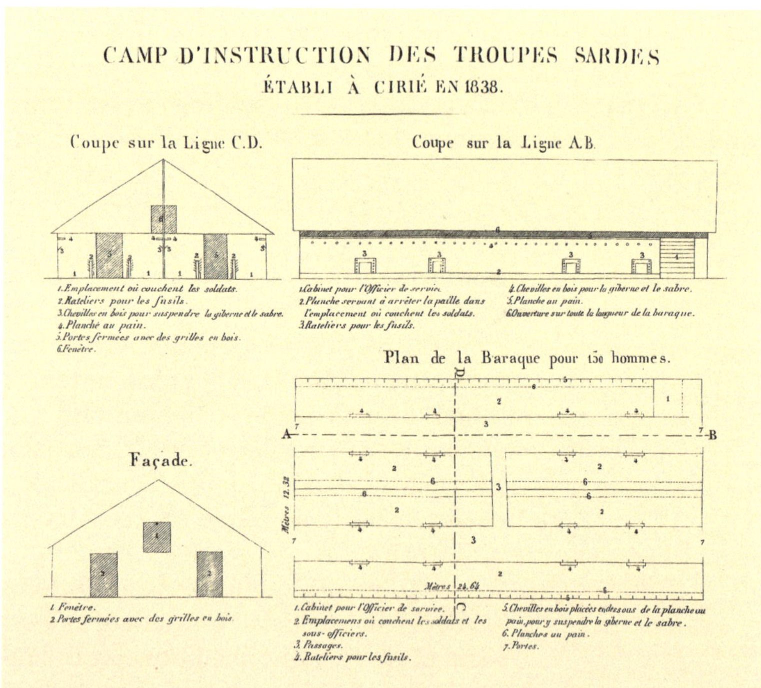

Fig. 3
Plan, elevations, and section of a typical barrack constructed for the Royal Sardinian Army at Cirié, Italy, from Maurice Joseph Didier Ravichio de Peretsdorf, *Notice sur le camp d'instruction des troupes Sardes établi a Cirié en 1838*, 1839. Collection: Nationaal Militair Museum, Soesterberg, Netherlands.

10 Maurice Joseph Didier Ravichio de Peretsdorf, *Notice sur le camp d'instruction des troupes Sardes établi a Cirié en 1838* (Paris: Leneveu, 1839).
11 "A Sketch of the Belgian Army," *United Service Journal and Naval and Military Magazine*, Dec. 1836, 475–78.

In France in the 1830s, there was no need to look at Beverloo as a model. Since the French invasion of Algeria in 1830, the establishment of a French colonial administration, and the beginning of settlement of French peasants in the North African territory, indigenous populations had been engaged in a continuous series of revolts that invited French military responses. Making a virtue out of necessity, the French military command decided that Algeria was to be a training ground for the regular army and continuously rotated regiments from Metropolitan France through the region—a practice made possible because of the short distance.

Beverloo did not inspire only King Charles Albert and Sardinian military officials. In 1836, shortly after the establishment of the camp, the British Army's *United Service Journal* published a report by an unnamed British officer. He marveled at the Beverloo camp and its maneuvers and returned from a visit with great admiration for the Belgian army, "so perfectly equipped, so well disciplined, and, above all, so admirably steady under arms." The editors of the magazine added a postscript in which they asked when it would please "our Rulers, or rather the false 'Economists' who control them, to grant the British Army at home such opportunity of combination [of different arms] and instruction as that recorded in the foregoing Sketch by our gallant Correspondent?"[11] In Great Britain in the 1830s, the relatively small professional army resided in dispersed garrisons or billeted in cities and towns. Only two of these locations offered training facilities. But the commander in chief of the British Army, Field Marshal Arthur Wellesley, 1st Duke of Wellington, was not interested: Beverloo had nothing to teach the victor of Waterloo.

The Belgian military spirit arrived in Great Britain in the form of King Leopold's nephew Albert, who had been educated in Brussels and trained at Beverloo. In 1840, Leopold arranged for the marriage of Albert to his first cousin Victoria, queen of the United Kingdom of Great Britain and Ireland. Albert had many ideas about how to reform the British Army; his stays in Beverloo had convinced him of the need to provide soldiers with realistic training opportunities, and those did not exist in Britain. His cause received a major theoretical justification when, in 1845, one of Napoleon's most successful generals, Auguste Frédéric Louis Viesse de Marmont, Duke of Ragusa, published *De l'esprit des institutions militaires* (*The Spirit of Military Institutions*, 1862)—a major theoretical work that sought to define the conditions that made an army into an instrument of victory and conquest—a fact that, after a very distinguished military career, still was a marvel to him. "The assemblage of 100,000 men, in the same place, far from their families, from their property, [...] their ease of combined movement (*mobilité*) and their preservation; in short, the spirit which animates them, and—at a signal given by one man only—impels them to precipitate themselves with pleasure into imminent danger, where many of them will find death;—all these surely constitute one of the most extraordinary spectacles which can be presented by men in society; a phenomenon the cause and principle of which are to be found in the mysteries of the human heart."[12] Yet, apart from this mystery, there were pragmatic aspects to the question raised. Projecting backward the radical innovations in military training represented by Beverloo and Cirié to the camps created in 1803 by Napoleon at Boulogne-sur-Mer, Marmont believed that large camps of instruction were an essential tool in the transformation of an agglomeration of men into an effective army.

> These alone, during peace, can give to troops the habits and instruction which they need. Military spirit is only developed in the midst of the dangers of war, and such union of troops as present its image. Life in camp, the movements incident to it, the mingling of arms, that peculiar life from which civil society is so far removed, and which is the prime element of success and of glory, can only be created by assemblages of troops of some permanence and surrounded by comforts. [. . .] I would suggest that permanent establishments be formed in provinces which have but poor agricultural resources, like Champagne; and that durable barracks be arranged to receive 30,000 men. The same troops should occupy them for three months at least. Three such establishments would suffice to give and preserve to the French army a military spirit and an instruction which would keep it constantly ready for war. But there is just now a vaster field for such exercises,—Algeria, which, if it makes us pay dear for its benefits, endows the army most richly in the matter of which I have spoken.[13]

Unlike France, Great Britain in the 1830s and early 1840s did not have a colony in continuous revolt at its doorstep that could serve as a training ground for its soldiers—Ireland was easily controlled by the quasi-

12 Auguste Frédéric Louis Viesse de Marmont, Duke of Ragusa, *The Spirit of Military Institutions; or, Essential Principles of the Art of War*, trans. Henry Coppée (Philadelphia: J. B. Lippincott, 1862), 243.
13 Ibid., 235–36.

military police force of the Royal Irish Constabulary. But the Duke of Wellington blocked any attempt to modernize the army through the creation of camps like Beverloo, and having defeated Napoleon at Waterloo, Wellington always had the last word in military matters. Albert decided to bide his time, and focused his energies on organizing the Great Exhibition of 1851, the first of the world's fairs and, in the eyes of many, the beginning of the modern age. Luck had it that the Duke of Wellington died shortly after the Great Exhibition closed. His successor as commander in chief of the British Army, Lieutenant General Henry Hardinge, 1st Viscount Hardinge, was not only a capable soldier but also a well-known politician and a friend of Prince Albert. Lord Hardinge set out to modernize the army and began by setting up a training camp at Chobham Common in Surrey. In the summer of 1853, some 8,000 men, 1,500 horses, and twenty-four guns mustered on the heathland for drills, field operations, and parades, attracting large crowds of spectators, including Queen Victoria and Prince Albert.

Fig. 4
Edward Matthew Ward, *Chobham Camp*, 1853. Collection: National Army Museum, London.

The soldiers were housed in tents and huts. Each day, *The Illustrated London News* reported on the goings-on. Given the well-publicized success of this experiment, Lord Hardinge pushed for the establishment of more permanent facilities.

In 1853, Lord Hardinge advised the government to establish a training center for two divisions on a heath near the village of Aldershot, Hampshire. Some

25,000 soldiers trained there that summer, and the area was deemed ideal. With the support of Prince Albert, Lord Hardinge actively pushed for the purchase of the land, and in January 1854, the owners of the heath agreed to sell 10,000 hectares. Four months later, Lord Hardinge considered the nature of accommodations to be constructed. Noting that other garrisons could accommodate only a maximum of 21,197 soldiers, he argued that Aldershot should allow for a massive increase in the number of soldiers in the region closest to the continent—the only direction from which an invasion might come—by providing year-round housing for many thousands of troops: "The construction of the Buildings therefore on the score of the health of the troops should be such as to ensure their warmth in the severest winter. On this account it would be inexpedient to attempt the hutting system which can only be advantageously resorted to on any great and sudden emergency. Low wooden sheds on weak foundations are damp and unhealthy and can only be occupied in the Summer season—and their construction although cheap at the outset is found in the end to be very expensive by the frequency of the repair required." In other words, building wooden barracks was not the way to go. Lord Hardinge noted the example of Beverloo: while that camp had originally consisted of temporary barracks, most of these had been replaced by somewhat more permanent structures. He suggested that a British officer visit Beverloo to inspect the grounds, and that the Belgian minister in London should arrange for Lord Hardinge to be "favoured with the sight of the Printed Plans and Printed Estimates and Reports" of the Beverloo camp.[14]

In 1854 the question of training the army in realistic field conditions had ceased to be a theoretical question: Britain, allied with France and the Ottoman Empire, was at war with Russia. None of the armies of the belligerent states were prepared for war in the Crimea, but the British Army was probably the worst equipped in terms of training and gear. During the debate in the House of Commons held on January 26, 1855, Sidney Herbert did not just deplore the British soldiers' lack of initiative in making themselves shelters when the tents failed (see Chapter Two). In addition, he observed that a basic reason for the bad performance of the British Army was the fact that there had *been* no British Army since the Battle of Waterloo. "We have, indeed, maintained a certain number of men in a state of high discipline up to a certain extent of organisation, but not beyond it. [...]

14 In Howard N. Cole, *The Story of Aldershot: A History and Guide to Town and Camp* (Aldershot, UK: Gale & Polden, 1951), 29f.

I ask, what is your English army? It is only a collection of regiments or rather a number of regiments not collected." Noting that many of the field officers in the Crimea had never seen a brigade, he exclaimed, "Can you expect men who have not only never seen an army in the field, but who have never seen two regiments brigaded together, to exhibit an acquaintance with the organisation of an army? Can you expect men who are utterly unacquainted with the movements of such a force, and with the regulations required for its sustenance and movements—can you expect such persons to be Heaven-born administrators, who can do not only what they have never practised, but what they never even saw done?"[15]

In early 1854, when Lord Hardinge pushed for the purchase of the Aldershot heath, he assumed the area would be used to train the professional soldiers who were garrisoned all over Great Britain and Ireland. But in January 1855, the site acquired a second purpose, which would become even more important: together with a second camp located in Ireland, it would be the training ground of a new reserve army created on the basis of militia regiments. Since Anglo-Saxon times, there had been an understanding that all able-bodied men could be mustered into military bodies in case of invasion; yet in the early modern age, militia regiments, which were typically made up of family men who worked as tradesmen or skilled laborers and who came together for military training for a maximum of four weeks a year, were no more than token forces—especially because they could be deployed only in the local county.[16] A conscript army that represented the nationalist ideal of a nation-at-arms was unthinkable in nineteenth-century Britain, but a new reserve army made up by the militias at least approximated the military spirit of the age. After Great Britain's entry into the Russian-Ottoman war, the militia became the focus of government action. In May 1854, Parliament increased annual militia training from four to eight weeks and decided that each militia regiment could be deployed anywhere in the British Isles. Another act, passed in December 1854, established the legal basis for the transformation of the militia into a viable reserve force; now militia regiments could be sent to render garrison duty overseas—a decision that allowed the units of the standing army deployed overseas to be sent to the Crimea.[17]

In January 1855, while the expeditionary force in the Crimea faced disaster, the British government decided to build permanent training camps to transform the militia into an effective reserve army. One of these

15 *Hansard Parliamentary Debates*, 3rd ser., vol. 136, H.C., Jan. 26, 1855, cols. 984–95.

16 "State of the Militia," *Blackwood's Edinburgh Magazine* 77 (Jan.–June 1855), 475.

17 See the remarks of Lord Palmerston, *Hansard Parliamentary Debates*, 3rd ser., vol. 163, H.C., June 25, 1861, col. 1601.

was to accommodate the militia regiments raised in Ireland, and Lieutenant General Sir John Burgoyne, inspector general of fortifications, decided that the Curragh, a plain near Kildare, 60 kilometers southwest of Dublin, would be the location for a hutted cantonment for 10,000 militiamen.

Fig. 5
Robert French, General view of the British Army's camp in the Curragh, Ireland, c. 1870. The photo was taken from the water tower. The large building in the front is one of the two garrison churches. Collection: National Library of Ireland, Dublin.

Lieutenant Colonel Henry Williamson Lugard, a military engineer based in Dublin, laid out the camp and designed the barracks, establishing that such accommodations would house everyone, including the general officers.[18] As such, the Curragh camp embodied a decisive revolution that was taking place in the British Army. Before 1855, the officers were everything, and the men, in the eyes of their superiors, were just rabble.[19] But as dispatches from the Crimea had brought to light the total incompetence of officers and the suffering of ordinary soldiers, a new attitude had emerged, in which the

18 On the history of the Curragh camp, see Con Costello, *A Most Delightful Station: The British Army on the Curragh of Kildare, Ireland, 1855–1922* (Cork: Collins Press, 1996); on the construction of the camp see Henry W. Lugard, *Narrative of Operations in the Arrangement and Formation of a Camp for 10,000 Infantry on the Curragh of Kildare* (Dublin: Alex. Thom and Sons, 1858).

19 William Denison, "Observations on Barracks, and on the Moral Condition of the Soldier," *Corps Papers and Memoirs on Military Subjects; Compiled from Contributions of the Officers of the Royal Engineers and the East India Company's Engineers*, vol. 1 (London: John Weale, 1849–50), 256–57.

soldier became the hero and the officer the villain. In addition, unlike professional soldiers, who were typically recruited from the lower classes, militia soldiers came from the lower-middle classes, and this also meant that the rigid class distinction between officers and men lost some of its edge. The fact that militia officers and soldiers shared the same form of accommodation—barracks—in the Curragh reflected the new idea that the unity of the reserve army as a whole was more important than the social distinctions within.

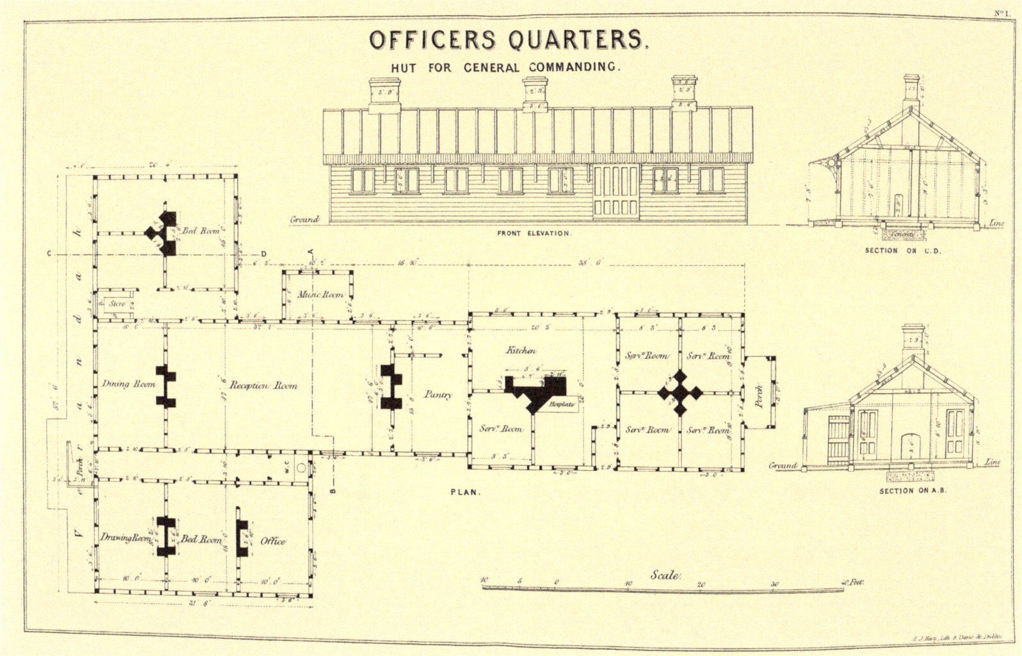

On May 5, 1855, the Irish *Leinster Express* noted, "the works are now fast progressing." Some 2,000 men were at work on the Curragh site. "The trenches for the foundations having been all marked out, we easily trace the plan of the entire camp. It will consist of three squares of houses, or huts, each of which squares will enclose a spacious barrack yard or parade ground, having entrance at each angle only—the sides being defended by a ditch and breastwork of sods firmly pegged. Each square will have its own cooking house, kitchen, and other offices. The buildings, when complete, will have a frontage extending a mile and a half [2.5 kilometers] in length, with a depth of 750 feet [230 meters]." Worthy of special note was the speed of construction and the enormous amount of building material brought to the site. The cut nails, which made all of this possible, deserved special mention; some fourteen tons had been brought in, and five tons had already been used. "These nails themselves are a curiosity," the paper observed. "They have been cut by

Fig. 6
Henry W. Lugard, Plan, elevation, and sections of the barrack of the commanding general at the Curragh camp, from his *Narrative of Operations in the Arrangement and Formation of a Camp for 10,000 Infantry on the Curragh of Kildare*, 1858. The design provided a generous suite of rooms that allowed for entertainment, but the height of the rooms was the same as those in the quarters of the ranks. Collection: National Library of Ireland, Dublin.

machinery out of cold wrought iron, and moulded into shape and headed by hydraulic pressure without heat."[20] Because of the accelerated construction schedule, much of the work was done in England and then transported from the railway station to the building site by means of two narrow-gage tracks. The paper praised the conditions of work. The workmen were paid well, and on time, and did not need to travel to obtain food and items for personal use; everything was made available at their camp, at ordinary prices.

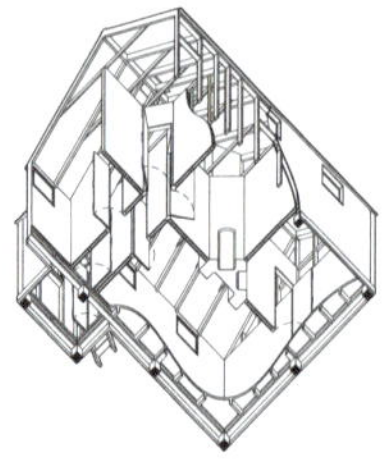

Drawings, Curragh Officers' Quarters → p. 511

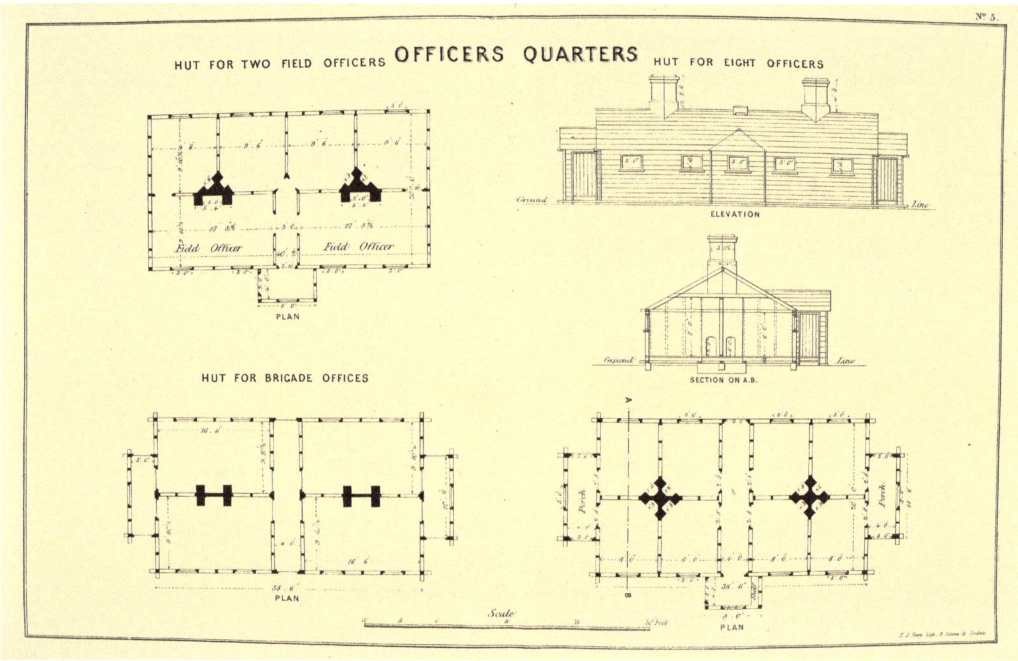

Fig. 7
Henry W. Lugard, Officers' quarters at the Curragh camp, from his *Narrative of Operations in the Arrangement and Formation of a Camp*, 1858. The barracks for junior officers were almost identical to those constructed at the same time in Aldershot, England. None of these quarters provided what was considered at that time the bare minimum for such officer housing in permanent barracks. Collection: National Library of Ireland, Dublin.

Unlike the cut nails, galvanized corrugated iron, another new building material used on the site, did not make it into the article. The first patent to corrugate iron sheets for building purposes had been issued in Britain in 1829. At that time, corrugated iron promised to be a strong, durable, lightweight, stackable material, but it was prone to corrosion. The solution was to coat the sheets with a thin layer of zinc. By the mid-1840s, improved ways of both corrugating and galvanizing the iron sheets had made corrugated iron into a viable building material, and by the mid-1850s it had become the building material of choice for prefabricated buildings shipped from Britain to Australia.[21] At that time, corrugated iron buildings were still very rare in the

20 "The Camp at the Curragh," *Leinster (Ireland) Express*, May 5, 1855.
21 See Adam Mornement and Simon Holloway, *Corrugated Iron: Building on the Frontier* (New York: Norton, 2007), 1–20, 28–38; also Nick Thomson, *Corrugated Iron Buildings* (Botley, UK: Shire Publications, 2011), 7–13.

British Isles, but Lieutenant Colonel Lugard saw a use for the material: in order to improve the fire resistance of the camp, he decided to create, at carefully calculated intervals, lines of barracks that were sheeted with corrugated iron walls and roofs.

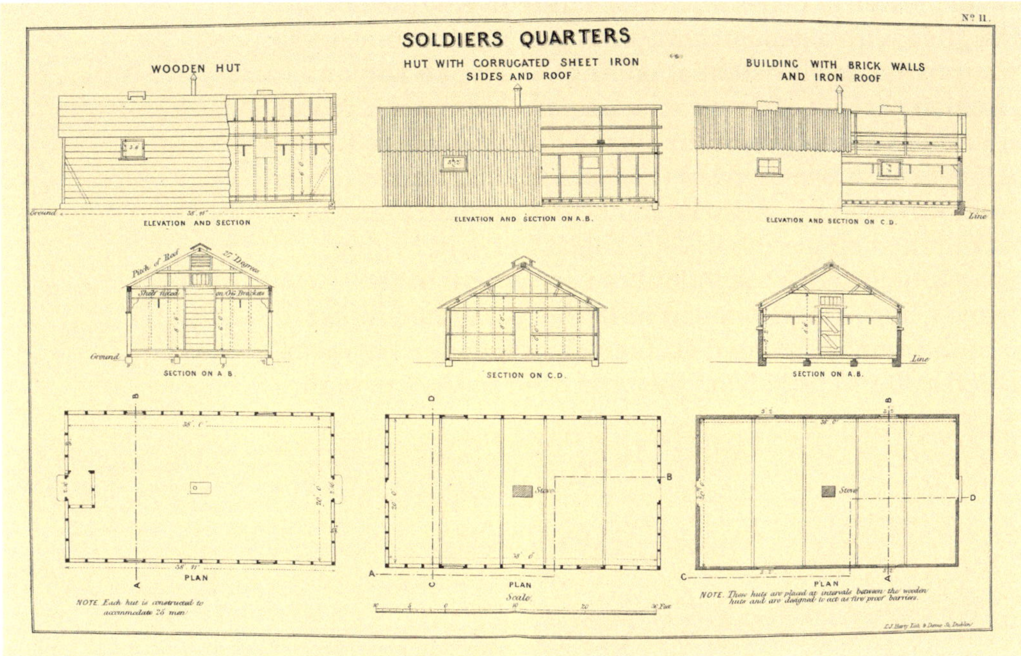

As the first phase of construction at the Curragh came to an end, Lieutenant Colonel Lugard decided to create a permanent record of what had been achieved, in which the plans, elevations, and sections of every barrack and more permanent structure designed for and built on the Curragh would be documented. He explained his motivation in a letter to Lieutenant General Burgoyne. When charged with creating the camp, he had tried to locate records of an earlier camp that had been pitched on the Curragh during the Napoleonic Wars and had found nothing. "To guard against the recurrence of a similar inconvenience and the absence of information at some future day respecting our recent operations, and to place on record the results of our proceedings, and with a view, also, of affording some professional information and assistance to officers who may have similar establishments to design and execute without having had the advantage of gaining practical experience at either of the camps in the United Kingdom, I employed a short period of relaxation from my ordinary duties in drawing up the following Narrative," Lugard wrote.[22] But he did not get to finish the book. In 1856, England and France came into conflict with China, and Lugard assumed command of the military engineers going east. He died

Fig. 8
Henry W. Lugard, Soldiers' quarters at the Curragh camp, from his *Narrative of Operations in the Arrangement and Formation of a Camp*, 1858. The barracks for the soldiers included buildings with corrugated iron siding. Collection: National Library of Ireland, Dublin.

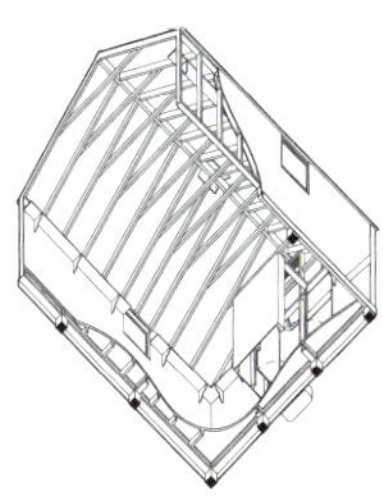

Drawings, Curragh Soldiers' Quarters
→ p. 511

22 Lugard, *Narrative of Operations*, 7.

in November 1857 in Hong Kong. Captain George A. Leach brought both the camp and the book to completion.

The construction of the camp at the Curragh was a relatively straightforward business. Two smaller camps of instruction were also constructed in England, in Colchester in Essex and Shorncliffe in Kent. Each designed with a capacity of 5,000 men, both camps were to serve the newly established Anglo-German Legion, a British version of the French *Légion étrangère*. Created in 1831 by King Louis-Philippe, the French Foreign Legion had become a backbone of the French counterinsurgency operation in Algeria and also played an important part in the Crimean War. The Anglo-German Legion never amounted to much, did not see action in the Crimea, and was disbanded in 1856.[23] Accommodation in both camps consisted exclusively of wooden barracks, which differed little from the type used in the Curragh.

Fig. 9
Construction of the camp for the Anglo-German Legion at Shorncliffe, England, *The Illustrated London News*, 1855. Collection: author.

The construction of the camps for the Irish militiamen and the German volunteers proceeded quickly and without much fuss. The situation at Aldershot, which was to house the largest of the four camps, proved much more complicated. This was partly because Aldershot had not been intended as a hutted camp, and the change of plans drew critics. In January 1855, the British Board of Ordnance had decided to reallocate a portion of the funds set aside to create permanent soldiers' accommodations at Aldershot, using this capital to erect 1,260 barracks for 20,000 militiamen. On January 22, the board issued a tender. As the British Army faced catastrophe in the Crimea and needed reinforcements immediately, the camp needed to be built by March 15. Lord Hardinge, who had very much opposed the use of barracks a few months

23 Charles Calvert Bayley, *Mercenaries for the Crimea: The German, Swiss, and Italian Legions in British Service*, 1854–1856 (Montreal: McGill-Queen's University Press, 1977).

earlier, had no choice but to concede. On February 24, he went down to Aldershot, where he met Major General Sir Frederick Smith, who had been instrumental in activating barrack production for the Crimea. They laid out a rough plan that was executed as planned: one section for 12,000 men, known as the South Camp, was to be created south of the Basingstoke Canal, and one section for 8,000 men, the North Camp, north of that waterway.

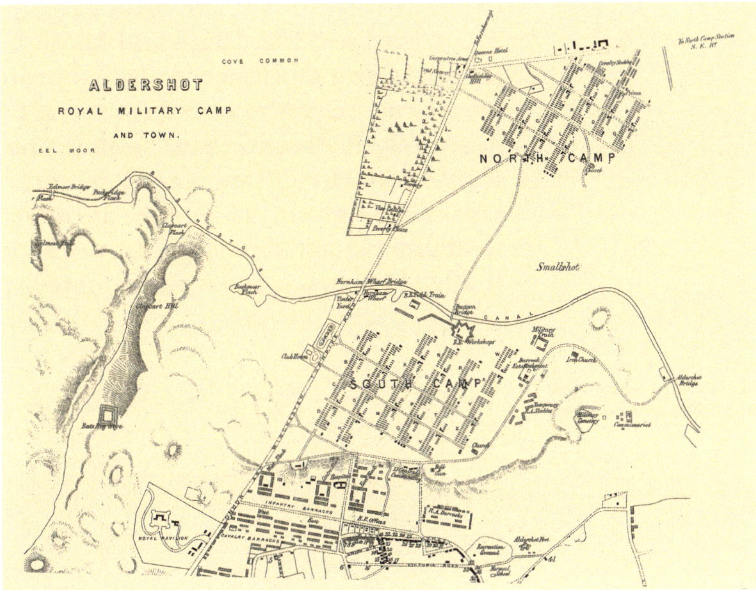

Fig. 10
Detail of a map of both the town of Aldershot, England, and the military facilities, showing the North and South Camps, from William Sheldrake, *A Guide to Aldershot and Its Neighbourhood*, 1859. Collection: author.

Both sections were subdivided into subsections that housed a regiment of 1,000 men each. As a regiment consisted of two battalions, each subsection consisted of two parts, laid out in four rows of barracks, with two rows housing the common soldiers, and two rows the officers and a miscellany of workshops, a laundry, a common washroom, stables, and so on. Each regiment had one schoolroom, one canteen, and two detention barracks connected by a courtyard; the quarters of staff sergeants, who served in the administration of the regiment, were scattered throughout the two parts.

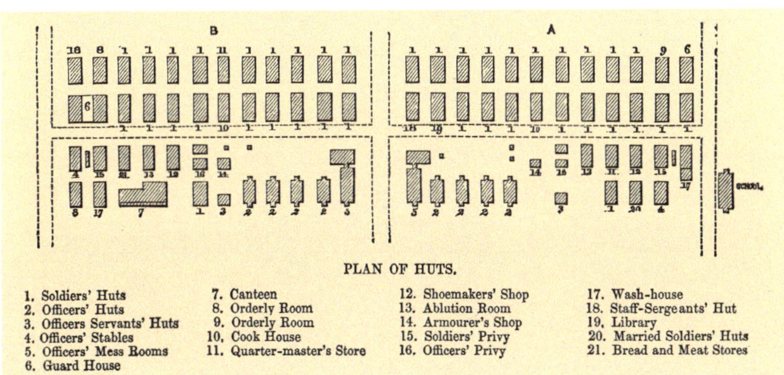

Fig. 11
Subsection, housing a regiment, of the British Army camp at Aldershot, from William Sheldrake, *A Guide to Aldershot and Its Neighbourhood*, 1859. Collection: author.

Within one of the battalions, two corrugated iron buildings, located perpendicular to the second row of barracks that housed the common soldiers, served as storehouse and as the regimental kitchen. “These large huts, being of iron, and much higher than the rest, would prevent the spread of fire, should any of the ordinary ones by any accident become ignited,” noted a guide to Aldershot published in the late 1850s.[24] A space around 30 meters wide, located between each regiment, was to ensure additional fire protection.

As Lord Hardinge and Major General Smith laid out the camp at Aldershot, a few prototype barracks were erected in the social center of London, the Willis’s Assembly Rooms in Saint James. The standard barrack was to measure 12 meters by 6 meters, and it was to rise to a height of 3.5 meters at the ridge. Intended to house twenty-five soldiers, each given an iron bed, it offered a space of 9.5 cubic meters per person.

Fig. 12
Exterior of soldiers’ huts at Aldershot camp, *The Illustrated London News*, 1855. Collection: author.

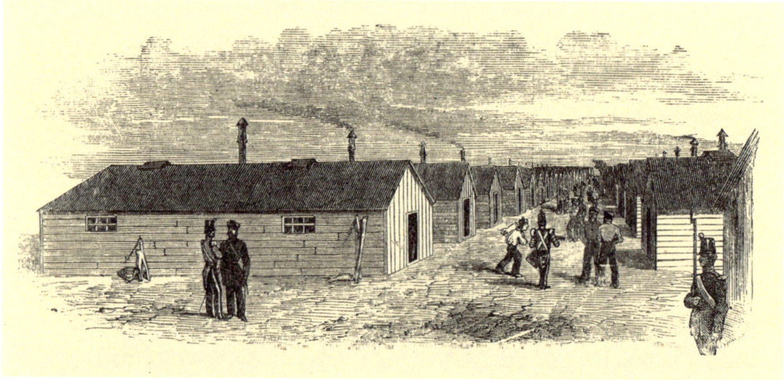

Fig. 13
Interior of a soldiers’ hut at Aldershot camp, *The Illustrated London News*, 1855. Collection: author.

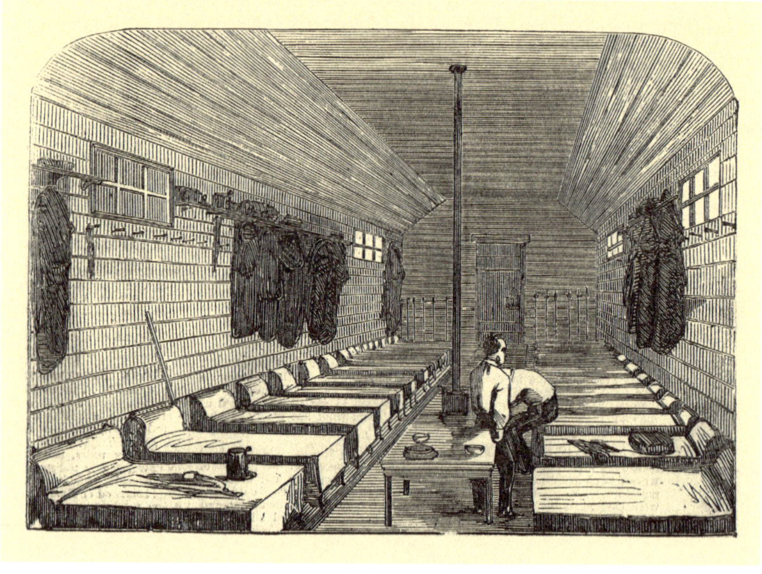

24 William Sheldrake, *A Guide to Aldershot and Its Neighbourhood* (Aldershot, UK: W. Sheldrake, 1859), 19.

Its structure was to be simple: a wooden frame, resting upon dwarf walls of brick, was to be roofed with boards that, in turn, were to be covered with tarred felt. The sides were to be painted wooden weatherboarding, while the interior lining was to be, in the case of a soldiers' barrack, plain boarding. Officers were lodged in barracks that provided four small private rooms. "On lifting the latch of the small wooden door of an officer's hut, we are confronted by a second wooden door, opening for the benefit of the room adjoining; by which means an almost constant draught is produced through the connecting corridor, which is lighted by a small window, and furnished with a coal-box," the aforementioned travel guide reported. "There is a grate in each room, and the furniture consists, in addition to that barely necessary portion furnished by the Barrack department, of such articles as the taste of the occupant may lead him to supply; and as this of course varies with each individual, so the appearance and accommodation of each room presents a somewhat different aspect, although in shape and size the same; some of them being extremely neat and comfortable-looking, and others possessing very little pretensions to luxury or refinement."[25] Each room offered, as a cartoon published in the satirical magazine *Punch* pointed out, very little space for the kind of entertainment expected from members of the gentry. Small windows provided light during the day, and oil lamps did so at night. Small stoves burning coal provided heat.[26]

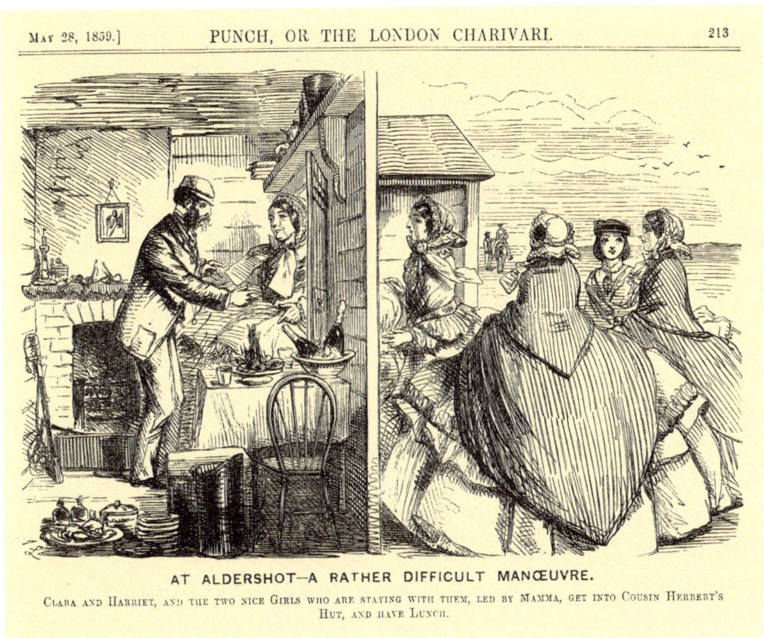

Fig. 14
John Leech, "At Aldershot—A Rather Difficult Manoeuvre," *Punch*, 1859. Collection: author.

25 Ibid., 18–21.
26 Great Britain, Commission Appointed for Improving the Sanitary Condition of Barracks and Hospitals, *General Report of the Commission Appointed for Improving the Sanitary Condition of Barracks and Hospitals* (London: Edward Eyre and William Spottiswoode, 1861), 29; George Kenneth Scott-Moncrieff, "Training Camps, Military," *The Encyclopædia Britannica*, 12th ed., 32 vols. (London: Encyclopædia Britannica, 1922), 32:756.

The camp at the Curragh had been built far away from Westminster; politicians simply did not know what was happening there, which gave Lieutenant Colonel Lugard the space to move boldly forward without interference. Things were very different in Aldershot: the heath was just a train ride away from London. On March 5, 1855, Sir Joseph Paxton, who had acquired fame as the designer of the Crystal Palace—the revolutionary prefabricated iron and glass exhibition venue of the 1851 Great Exhibition—announced in a committee meeting of the House of Commons that the Board of Ordnance was utterly incompetent if it thought it could begin construction in six weeks. The total store in Great Britain of the main building materials specified would allow for the construction of only 600 barracks. And then there was the issue of the foundations, which had been tendered only in February. The minutes note that Paxton declared it next to impossible to finish the buildings by March 15; if they were, in fact, finished, "he would willingly admit that it would be one of the most wonderful things ever accomplished in this country."[27]

A few days later, William Monsell, member of Parliament and clerk of the Board of Ordnance, responded in the House of Commons. "Many of the builders who offered themselves for the work said there would be no difficulty in obtaining the quantity of timber of the description specified, but they doubted whether the sawing could be performed. It was considered that the best timber would be the most economical for permanence, and the inside lining might be of an inferior quality." There was much doubt as to the life span of the barracks, and Monsell tried to address those concerns. "It was supposed that with care those wooden barracks would last for many years, and the engineer of the Ordnance had stated that by the adoption of an inexpensive process they might probably last twenty years."[28] Monsell then addressed the great hurry with which the Board of Ordnance had moved ahead. "The ordinary mode, when a great work had to be executed, was to provide plans, specifications, and bills of quantities. Some sort of plans, indeed, there had been, but there had been no bills of quantities—the contracts having been let on a schedule of prices."[29]

Yet Paxton returned to the issue. On March 30, he noted that only 400 barracks—or one third of the number to be built—had been completed, and that they were inferior. "About double the quantity of boards that were necessary were put upon these huts; and the roofing was badly designed, because it was flat, and

27 *Hansard Parliamentary Debates*, 3rd ser., vol. 137, H. C., Mar. 5, 1855, cols. 127–28.
28 Ibid., Mar. 9, 1855, cols. 354–55.
29 Ibid., 361–62, 365.

the water would certainly penetrate through. The boards were what were called feather-edged, and, consequently, as soon as the dry weather set in and the sun's power was felt, they would all start [to crack]. [...] Another defective part of the hut was the provision for lighting and ventilation. The windows were placed in such a position that any man above 4 feet 6 inches [1.4 meters] high would be breathing an impure atmosphere." He also criticized the foundations. On March 9 he had called for sturdy foundations, and now he noted the contractors had made them too solid, "as if they were going to build a house, although a little concrete and a few bricks would have answered every purpose. If continued in this style, the huts would not be finished for two or three months." Paxton argued that the design of the remaining 800 barracks should be reconsidered; an even better solution would be to radically reduce the number of barracks to be built and accommodate 5,000 of the 20,000 men in tents, "where they would be much more likely to learn the real business of campaigning, the pitching of tents, and moving from place to place, than if domiciled in these semi-barracks."[30]

Everybody had an opinion about Aldershot. And everyone had an opinion about the role of the militia in the British Army. There was universal agreement that the creation of training facilities for the militia was of the greatest urgency. In April, *Blackwood's Edinburgh Magazine* carried a long overview of the new status and function of the militia, and suggested that the greatest problem with the idea of the reserve army supporting the army in its war abroad was the fact that the militia either had no training or had training that occurred within the context of skeleton regiments: "Training shall as nearly as possible resemble that of the regular army, so that the militia may be made effective as a valuable military force. This is necessary for the sake of the militiamen themselves; for although we have no doubt that they would be ready to volunteer upon any duty, and to embark at once for Sebastopol, it is the business of the authorities to take care that they are not allowed to undertake any duty for which they are not thoroughly qualified."[31] *The Illustrated London News* added its voice a couple of months later:

> The war has already done us one good service—it has for ever put an end to the notion that a great nation, even with the security of an insular position, can afford to neglect her army. A very few years ago it was the opinion of many people that

30 Ibid., Mar. 30, 1855, cols. 1423–24.
31 "State of the Militia," *Blackwood's Edinburgh Magazine*, 475–77.

> pageantry—the finding sentinels for the Royal palaces and providing a nice little review in Windsor-park for the amusement of any foreign potentate who happened to be passing that way—was the sole use of our army while at home, and that its other more active employment might be safely handed over to the police or the yeomanry.

That illusion had died in the Crimea.

> We all know that we must henceforth keep up a large army; and we have also learnt that, in order to make that force thoroughly efficient, we must give it a sort of training different from that which it would get from regimental drilling in barrack-yards. In many ways the Camp at Aldershott may exercise a most beneficial influence on the future of the British Army. A thousand things will be easily learnt there, which it would be almost impossible to acquire on the restricted space of a drilling ground, and with the restricted numbers of a regiment, or even of a brigade. Twenty thousand men are an army; and the mere assembling of such numbers, and the manoeuvres they will go through, must teach many a useful lesson both to men and officers. Without going through the hard ordeal of actual warfare, the former will become more self-reliant; they will learn how to hut themselves, to build ovens or fireplaces, to cook; in short, to do for themselves more comfortably and completely: while the latter will become accustomed to all the intricate arrangements necessary in moving large bodies of men, and the system of keeping those men well fed, well clothed, and well tended in case of wounds or sickness.[32]

Self-reliant soldiers, competent officers—a new army indeed, and one that had the potential to become the core of a nation-at-arms.

If there was agreement on the ends, there were doubts about the means. On April 18, *The Times* (London) ran a critical article on the construction of the camp at Aldershot, stating: "The arrangement of the huts is not good. In fact, we should not be honest if we did not say that it seems to us to be very bad. A flat ceiling is formed with boarding at the level of the underside of the tie-beams; and the windows, hinged at the top to make the matter worse, are placed low on the sides of the hut, not more than 4 feet 6 inches [1.4 meters] from the hinges

32 "Notes of the Week," *The Illustrated London News*, June 2, 1855, 534.

to the floor. The room has the aspect of a large eggbox; with a quarter of a hundred men sleeping in it, the atmosphere will become poisonous."[33]

The article had an effect. Two months later, *The Times* reported that in the new barracks the flat ceiling had been removed and the boarding now followed the line of the rafters, creating a more generous sense of space. The windows had also been raised closer to the eaves. But now the paper wondered whether providing hundreds of identical barracks, built by contractors, had been a good idea to begin with: after all, during a campaign it was unlikely that contractors would be available to provide instant barrack accommodations in the field.[34] Five months later, when rain and cold had arrived, another report: the barracks were dry but not very warm. A major concern was the problem of maintenance. *The Times* speculated that "the felting, which covers every portion of the huts [...] will have, probably, to be renewed every year. Already it has received two coatings of tar, and a third will shortly be requisite. It is the only protection which the wood has against the weather, and its want of durability points strongly to the temporary character of the huts, while its inflammable properties suggest grave anxieties as to the risk from fire." Ultimately, *The Times* believed that at Aldershot the wooden barracks would be replaced by brick buildings. "In fact it can no longer be disguised that Aldershott is a military town, improvised with public money for a population of 20,000 soldiers, built in the first instance like a Californian city of very flimsy materials, but destined when occasion serves to assume a more fixed and solid form."[35] It took over thirty years for such occasion to come along—but by 1890 all the wooden barracks had indeed been replaced by brick buildings.

Aldershot loomed large not only in Westminster; it also acquired an important place in the British imagination. "Whatever Aldershott may have been in the former history of its country, it is now a place which the British soldier has thoroughly taken by storm." Thus began an article published on August 20, 1859, in Charles Dickens's weekly *All the Year Round*, which, alongside serializations of his novels, contained tales of exploration in distant continents and journalistic pieces on current affairs. One of the latter was a long, somewhat skeptical report on the four-year-old military town and camp on Aldershot heath. The anonymous writer—who some believe to have been Dickens himself—had traveled the 65 kilometers from London to see the camp, and had not been impressed with the way the British soldier

33 "The Camp at Aldershott," *The Times* (London), Apr. 18, 1855, 12.
34 "The Camp at Aldershott," *The Times* (London), June 11, 1855, 12.
35 "The Camp at Aldershott," *The Times* (London), Nov. 21, 1855, 8.

"squatted (in obedience to superior orders) upon its peat and sandy common; he has pitched his white tents in groups upon the scanty patches of grass, until they look, in the distance, like conjurors' cups arranged upon a green baize table; he has had planted his long black rows of dwarfed wooden huts down the gravelly slopes, like streets in the early days of some colonial settlement; and he has had built a long and lofty range of clean, new yellow-brick barracks which overshadow the little mushroom town that has risen up hurriedly to meet and trade with them."[36]

Of chief interest to the writer were the 1,200 barracks. He noted how the same hut was repeated over and over again, serving all kinds of different functions. "There is a bread-hut, a meat-hut, and a library-hut; a men's school-hut, a children's school-hut, which latter looks like the national schools in many small villages. There are a number of officers' sleeping-huts, placed back to back, and also a number of men's sleeping huts, in the same position."[37] The list went on and on: orderly huts, guard huts, wash huts, laundry huts, family huts, hospital huts, messroom huts, and more. The writer obviously did not think much of the seriality of identical barracks, and he certainly did not think much about the subaltern officers' barrack in which he stayed, comparing the six-room building to a coal shed and his small room, heated by a fireplace and illuminated by a small window, to a cupboard.

During the construction of the hutted compound at Aldershot, debate about the virtues and vices of the buildings had raged in the House of Commons. After its completion, discussion continued, both in Parliament and among the public. In the debate on the budget for the army, held in the House of Commons on June 25, 1861, Ralph Bernal Osborne mocked the barracks as a prime example of the government's blundering, judging them to be both "bad in design" and "infamous in construction," as they "were neither watertight nor airtight." He continued: "The Government then entered into a contract to cover the huts with patent felt at an expense of £14,000; but then even they were found not to be watertight, and another contract was entered into to tar them over. Certainly those who had constructed them ought not only to be tarred, but feathered; at any rate, they had feathered their nests well. The whole expense of erecting these huts for Aldershot and other stations had been £796,100."[38] William Monsell, who had overseen the construction, tried to remind Bernal Osborne that the barracks at Aldershot "were erected under great pressure,

36 Anonymous, "Aldershott Town and Camp," *All the Year Round* 1 (1859), 401.
37 Ibid., 405.
38 *Hansard Parliamentary Debates*, 3rd ser., vol. 163, H. C., June 25, 1861, col. 1587.

and it was absolutely necessary to erect them quickly," and that huts in subsequent camps had shown great improvements.[39] Paxton could not resist the temptation to weigh in on the matter. The barracks were "most miserable erections," he argued. "They were totally unfit for soldiers or any other persons to live in, as the ventilation was two or three feet [0.6–0.9 meter] below the heads of the occupants, consequently they had to breathe a deleterious atmosphere. The great mistake that was made at Aldershot was the omission to construct the camp on a permanent and comprehensive plan."[40]

Bernal Osborne's diatribe inspired Julia Clara Byrne, a sharp-tongued writer of anonymous tracts and an admirer of all things continental. In her book on the French military, Byrne compared the barracks at Aldershot with those at the Châlons camp, created on the initiative of Emperor Napoleon III and located east of Paris in the Champagne region. "Our readers are perhaps aware that the 'huts' at Aldershott are really what they are called, and nothing more—i.e., small, low, clumsy structures of rough timber, roof and walls being alike smeared over with a uniform coat of pitch, and therefore as utterly deficient in attractiveness of colour, as disappointing in form, proportion, solidity, or any of the resources of architecture." She was particularly surprised by the fact that officers lived in barracks that did not stand out from those of the men. "It is curious to see an officer and his family domesticated in one of these baby-houses, and one is forcibly reminded of a gipsying party temporarily accommodating itself to the privations of nomad existence for the sake of change—only there is this difference, that there is no fun in the discomfort, and no charm in the novelty, for the inconvenience is permanent."[41]

The situation in Châlons was different, Byrne wrote.

> Now, the "*Baraque*" of the French camp is no carpenter's shed, clumsily designed, flimsily constructed, caulked in the seams, and bedaubed with tar to remedy the want of durability of the material employed—it is *not* the failure of a bungling journey-man—it is *not* the experiment of an interested contractor who actually receives from the country £150 for each temporary, trumpery cabin—a disgrace to his taste, if not to his skill, and reflecting most certainly no credit on the facile acquiescence or deplorable inexperience of those who, by their assent to such a bargain, indicate

39 Ibid., 1592.
40 Ibid., 1593.
41 [Julia Clara Byrne], *Red, White, and Blue: Sketches of Military Life*, 3 vols. (London: Hurst and Blackett, 1862), 2:201–2.

> their unfitness to be trusted with the administration of public money. It is *not* all this.[42]

Singing the praises of the "commodious, spacious, airy, solid, and even picturesque *baraque*" that lodged fifty men at an expense of £240, she shamed the British army's "shabby, low, draughty, ill-contrived, and unsightly constructions, holding only 20 men," which were built at an expense of £150–200. "The imposition, or jobbery, or mismanagement, is so gross, it fills one with indignation to hear that this sum has been actually *paid* to *somebody*, for every one of these kennels."[43]

In early 1856, Emperor Napoleon III had decided that the French army needed a camp that would allow four divisions (two infantry, one cavalry, and one artillery) to undertake large maneuvers, and thereby allow him to strengthen his military credentials by assuming command in the field. The camps he had created two years earlier in Boulogne had increased his taste for playing soldier, but in that densely inhabited area of the Pas-de-Calais, there was no room for larger operations. The thinly populated area between the cities of Reims and Châlons-en-Champagne offered a large space that potentially could be used for military maneuvers. It was an infertile region where land was cheap and villages stood far apart—an area not much different from the surroundings of Beverloo or Aldershot. Purchasing large tracts in the region would be relatively cheap, and it afforded easy access to Paris.[44] This proximity was important, as the camp was to be a stage set for an annual propaganda spectacle designed to convince both France and the rest of the world that the Second Empire did not stand in the shadow of the First, and that Emperor Napoleon III did not stand in the shadow of his uncle.

Like the British Army, the French Army in the 1850s was not a unified force but a conglomerate of almost independent regiments. But if in Britain Prince Albert and some younger officers had come to the realization that things had to change, in France the general staff and the senior officers, all products of the elite Ecole Spéciale Militaire de Saint-Cyr (Special Military School of Saint-Cyr) did not question the status quo, which certainly projected a splendid appearance. Napoleon III agreed; a very insecure man, he never lost the sense that he needed to produce a constant pageant—the *Fête Impérial*—to both astound and seduce the nation. Like the new Paris that arose under his patronage, the camp at Châlons supported the image politics that presented Paris, worldwide, as the Capital of the Nineteenth Century.[45]

42 Ibid., 2:203.
43 Ibid., 2:207–8.
44 On the Châlons camp, see: Jean Darius Philippe Riolacci, *Le Camp de Châlons, précédé, 1° D'un aperçu historique sur la Champagne, etc. 2° Considérations philosophiques, historiques et militaires sur les camps, et sur les camps d'instruction en France, etc.* (Paris: J. Dumaine, 1865); Georges-Frédéric Espitallier, "Les Origines de Camp de Chalons," *Revue du Génie* 8, pt. 2 (Mar.–Apr. 1894), 353–428; Georges-Frédéric Espitallier, *Les Origines de camp de Chalons* (Paris and Nancy: Berger-Levrault, 1898).
45 Matthew Truesdell, *Spectacular Politics: Louis-Napoleon Bonaparte and the Fête Impérial, 1849–1870* (New York: Oxford University Press, 1997).

By the summer of 1856, the French government began to expropriate land, assembling an area of 9,200 hectares, and in November, Napoleon III officially ordered the creation of the Châlons camp. A year later, in the summer of 1857, it was inaugurated.

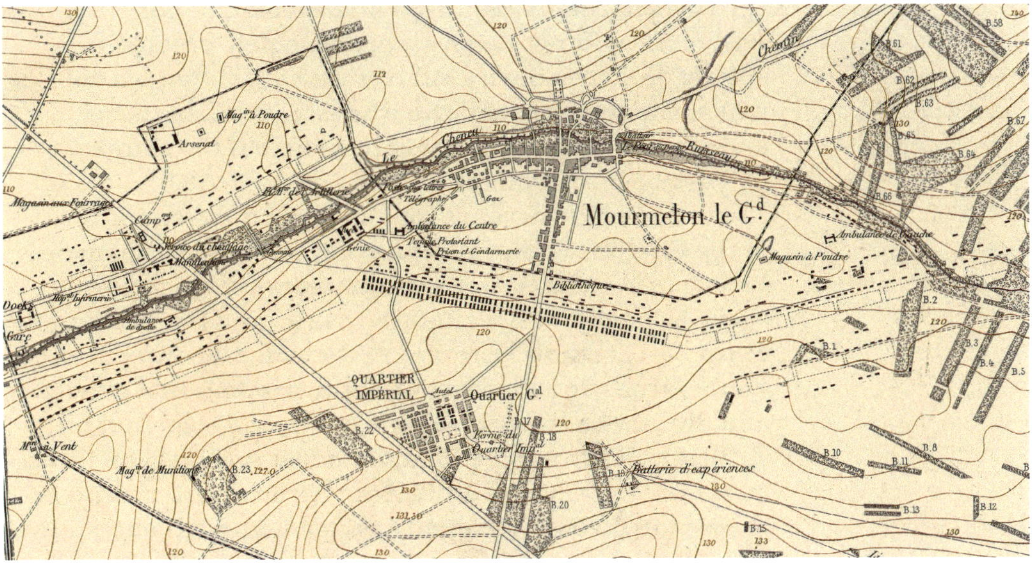

A hastily constructed spur connecting the site to the main line allowed the imperial party to reach the camp in great comfort. They disembarked to find an imperial compound of barracks and tents centered around a blue-and-white-striped structure that looked like a cross between a large garden pavilion and a tent; officially known as the *Baraque de l'Empereur*, it was a somewhat gaudy reinterpretation of the plain *Baraque de Napoleon* that, more than fifty years earlier, had served Napoleon III's uncle at Boulogne.

Fig. 15
Erhard Schieble (engraver), *Plan du Camp de Châlons* (detail), scale 1:20,000, as surveyed by the French Officiers du Génie, 1869. This detail of the map shows the arrangement of the village of Mourmelon, France (top), the main section of the Châlons camp completed by the late 1860s (center), and the imperial quarter (bottom). Collection: Bibliothèque Nationale de France, Paris.

Fig. 16
Jules Gaildrau, General view of the camp of Châlons, with the *Baraque de l'Empereur* to the right, *L'Illustration*, 1861. Collection: Bibliothèque Nationale de France, Paris.

A few days before the official inauguration, the emperor visited the camp in a more private capacity, and spoke to the men: "Soldiers! I have brought you here together under my command because it is useful that the military draws from the common life of the camps a shared spirit, a shared discipline, a shared instruction. [...] This camp will not be an empty spectacle created to satisfy public curiosity but a stern school that we will make valuable through the work undertaken there, and of which the results will be visible if the country will ever have to call on you."[46]

In the three years that separated the opening of the Châlons camp from the outbreak of the Franco-Prussian War in 1870, Parisian papers reported on every celebrity who visited the camp, and many civilians toured its grounds. Parades of the magnificently dressed Cent-Gardes squadron, the emperor's personal guard, and dramatically enacted charges by the colorful and sufficiently savage *tirailleurs algériens* (Algerian skirmishers), the cavalry units from Africa, were meant to provide the Parisian bourgeoisie with both entertainment and a sense of the glory and reach of the French Empire. The maneuvers looked magnificent, but they were meaningless from a military point of view. Choreographed to the last detail, they represented the great battles conducted by the first Napoleon but did not take into account modern developments in weaponry, logistics, and communication. Only during the French Third Republic, which was established in 1870 after the surrender of Emperor Napoleon III to the Prussian king in Sedan, was Châlons to become the site of serious combat training.

The military engineer who designed and oversaw the construction of the structures in the Châlons camp, Captain Pierre Weynand, had a solid sense of the raison d'être of the site. As the camp was a showcase for the new empire, Weynand was not to fill it with the crude daub-and-wattle barracks that had provided soldiers with shelter at Boulogne-sur-Mer and in the Crimea. And he was certainly not to emulate the accommodations provided across the Pas-de-Calais in Aldershot. Instead, he was to build something that had more in common with the Hameau de la Reine (Queen's Hamlet), built for Marie-Antoinette in the park of Versailles, than with a genuine military camp. Significantly, Weynand planned the camp site itself as a large park, with flower gardens, arbors, and even statues. The half-timbered barracks with brick masonry infill he designed also showed aesthetic considerations that transcended the mundane

46 Charles-Louis Bonaparte, Emperor Napoleon III, *Discours, messages, lettres et proclamations de S.M. Napoléon III, Empereur des Francais: 1849–1861, 1er série* (Paris: Humbert, 1866), 139.

function of providing a shelter to the troops. Measuring about 30 by 9 meters, they typically consisted of a large room (26.5 by 6 meters) that housed fifty soldiers, and a second room, taking up the rest of the building, designed to house six noncommissioned officers.

Fig. 17
Jean-Pierre Désiré Delaplace, The camp at Châlons, c. 1870. Collection: author.

While the barracks were permanent structures, they projected the appearance of a provisional camp, as this was considered more proper for a camp of instruction. Captain Ben Hay Martindale, director of the Barrack Department in the War Office in London, visited the new French camp in 1862 and published a detailed description of it. He was surprised by this contradiction and discussed it with Weynand: "Everywhere the object has been kept in view of making a marked distinction between a camp and a permanent barrack. It is on this ground, Monsieur Weynand informed me, that the huts are not made two stories high."[47] Appearance counted in the Châlons camp, which dazzled civilian observers, such as an anonymous German journalist who visited the camp in 1863 and published his account in the popular illustrated family magazine *Die Gartenlaube* (The garden arbor). The camp, he asserted, was "a magnificent school of war without a parallel anywhere."

> Assembled at Châlons are normally between 40,000 and 50,000 soldiers. There they are trained and hardened and made ready to be employed at a moment's notice for political and military purposes without the need to waste precious time in collecting and preparing them. While the camp is an excellent school for soldiers, noncommissioned officers, and officers, it is even more useful for the generals. Even the largest garrisons do not allow for the assembly of such large masses.

47 Ben Hay Martindale, "Notes on the Camp of Châlons-sur-Marne," *Papers on Subjects Connected with the Duties of the Corps of Royal Engineers*, 33 vols. (Woolwich, UK: Jackson, 1839–76), n.s., 11:133–34.

> Here they are all together in a single space, unhindered and uninfluenced by the kind of bourgeois amenities that can never be entirely avoided in cities.[48]

The article described the camp as a large city, organized in a radial pattern, suggesting a spider's web connected to the rest of France. The journalist praised the way many barracks were equipped with pleasant *Trinkstuben* (watering holes), "where the soldier kills his free time with games, smoking, singing, and comradely discussions."[49] Yet behind the pleasantries represented by those *Trinkstuben* was a potentially sinister purpose. "The future will reveal to what extent a threatening war cloud, that seeks to achieve the somewhat absurd idea of natural boundaries, will emerge from this camp," the journalist observed. "In any case, the German rulers might do well to counterbalance the weight of this camp and create similar facilities." *Die Gartenlaube*'s publisher, Ernst Keil, believed this appeal needed reinforcement and added a footnote: "In response to this article we cannot suppress the wish that authoritative circles in Germany will seriously consider the camp at Châlons. No one can deny that the German soldier completely lacks what the Frenchman is offered here as the most perfect and realistic military training. Let's hope that we will not be reminded 'too late' that, once again, we failed to imitate such an example: the lack of such investment today might turn out to be extraordinarily expensive tomorrow."[50]

Until this point, the generals of the Prussian and other German armies had not felt the need to copy the examples set in Beverloo, Cirié, the Curragh, Aldershot, and Châlons. But recent developments in artillery design changed their minds. New rifled, breech-loading field guns allowed for much greater range and accuracy than their smoothbore predecessors, and also made possible a more curved trajectory that enabled an artillery to fire over its own infantry lines. These new guns forced artillerists to relearn their trade from the bottom up. In addition, due to the greater reach of the rifled guns, the forces needed much larger exercise areas. Thus, in 1864, the Bavarian Army decided to incorporate a site measuring 6.4 by 3.2 kilometers that would allow for infantry training exercises adjacent to a small artillery school at Lechfeld near Augsburg—the place where in 955 a united force of Saxons, Franks, Swabians, and Bavarians defeated the Hungarians, in a decisive battle for the course of European history.

48 Anonymous, "Im Lager von Chalons," *Die Gartenlaube* 5 (1863), 636.
49 Ibid., 638.
50 Ibid., 636.

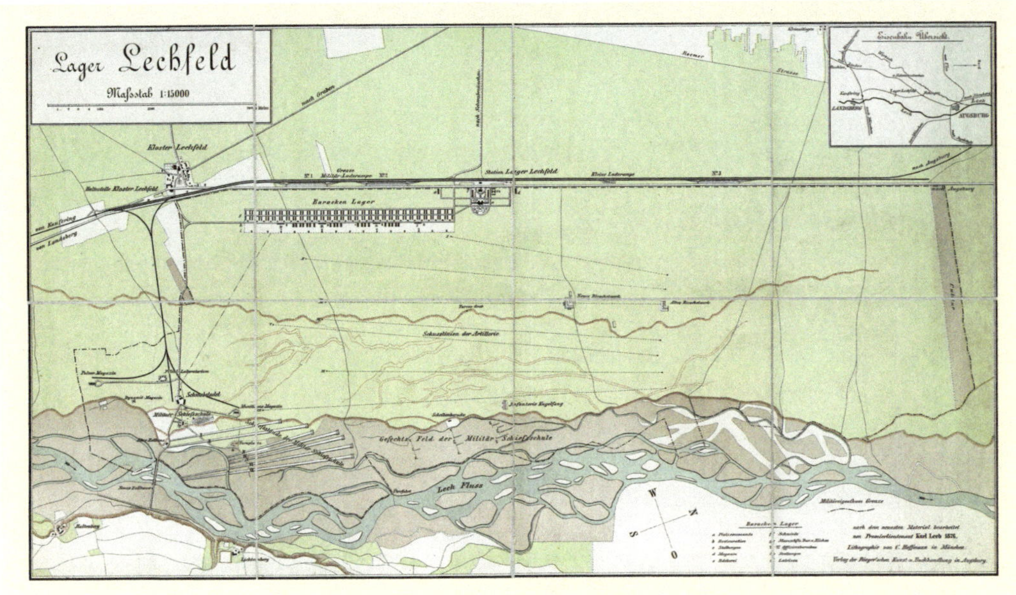

Fig. 18
Karl Leeb, Map of the Lechfeld camp, Germany, 1876. Collection: Bayerische Staatsbibliothek, Munich.

Initially, the artillerists were accommodated in tents, but the quartermasters quickly decided to provide straw barracks that could house up to forty soldiers.[51] These were replaced after a few years by 120 wooden barracks, with brick walls at each end, each measuring 40 by 6 meters and offering space to sixty soldiers and four sergeants in two large dormitories and two semi-private rooms.[52]

→ Fig. 19

In Great Britain, France, and Germany, the form and the construction of the barrack differed from the urban and rural vernacular. In Northern Europe vernacular architecture was typically constructed in wood, which meant that the obvious distinction between wooden barracks as prescribed in army manuals or constructed at training grounds and either house, stable, or barn construction, which was explicit in western and central Europe, did not necessarily exist.

In the seventeenth and early eighteenth centuries, Sweden had been a military superpower, and select parts of its constructed landscape represented that ambition, including the Landskrona Citadel and the supersize barracks constructed by father Hector Loffman in Malmö and son Jacob Loffman in Halmstad. Between 1700 and 1809, four ill-advised wars with Russia diminished Sweden's imperial status. By the early nineteenth century the army was antiquated. It comprised regiments of around 1,200 men that were raised by and located in a particular province, with each soldier being supported by a so-called *rote* (military ward) that

Note on the Word "Barrack," Fig. 1
→ p. 30

51 "Das Lager auf dem Lechfelde," *Bayerische Volksblatt*, no. 226 (Aug. 1867), 902–3; Karl Glonner, *Blattern-Erkrankungen im Lager Lechfeld 1870/71* (Würzburg: Bonitas-Bauer, 1871), 7.
52 "Einige Tage auf dem Lechfelde," *Allgemeine Militär-Zeitung* 47, no. 32 (Aug, 10, 1872), 253.

Fig. 19
Plan, elevation, and section of a barrack at the Lechfeld camp, from Prussia, Royal Prussian Ministry of War, *Der Sanitätsdienst bei den deutschen Heeren im Kriege gegen Frankreich 1870/71*, 1884. Collection: Staatsbibliothek zu Berlin.

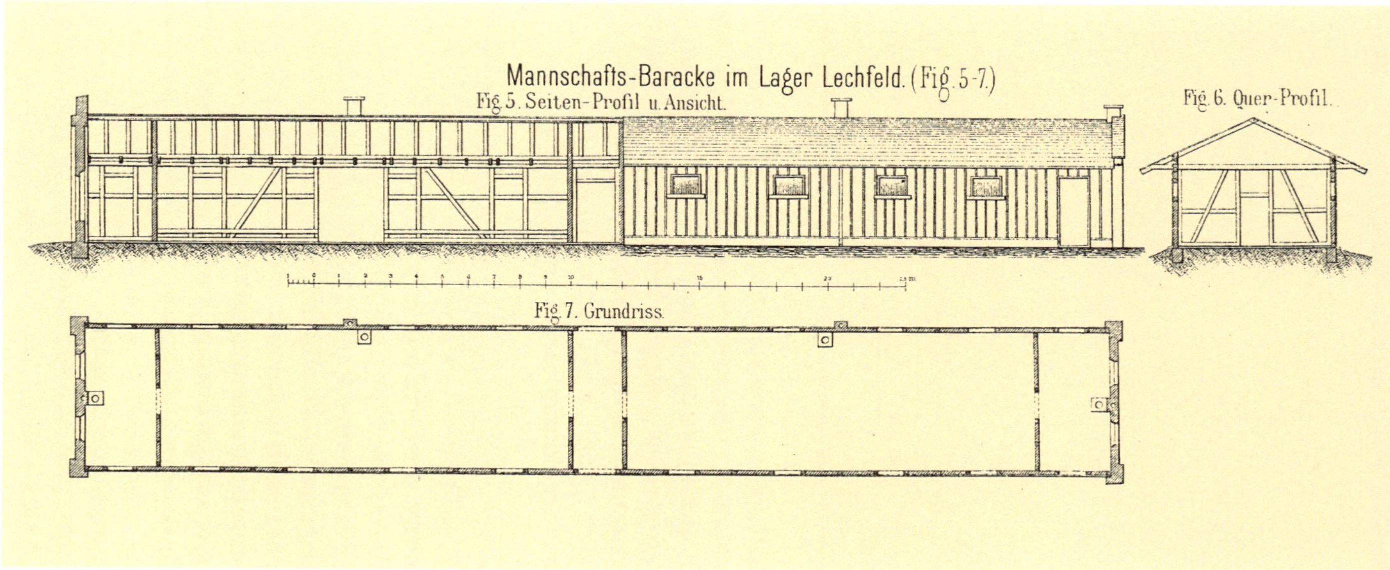

consisted of either a larger more prosperous farm or a few smaller farms. The soldier and his family typically lived within the *rote* in a modest *soldattorp* (soldier's croft), maintained by the farmers, which the soldier had to vacate when his service ended.

Fig. 20
Deputy Corporal Carl Oscar Lundin and his wife outside soldier's croft no. 89, Second Norra Vedbo company of the Jönköping regiment of the Swedish army. Collection: Riksarkivet, Täby, Sweden.

In the summer months, all the soldiers would leave their rotar for a two-week period to join in regimental training exercises held at a fixed location in the province. There they would live under canvas.

At best a glorified militia, the Swedish army was no match for any of the European armies that had participated in the Napoleonic Wars—which included the most likely opponent, the Russian army. In 1810, when Napoleon was at the apex of power, the Swedish parliament elected Marshal of France Jean-Baptiste Bernadotte, who was the brother-in-law to Joseph Bonaparte, as heir-presumptive to King Karl XIII, who was childless. When Bernadotte ascended the throne in 1818 as King Karl XIV Johan, he began to apply his French military experience in a series of reforms of the Swedish army, which began by grafting on top of the existing *rote*-based military structure a universal conscription system that, in theory, forced all able-bodied men to undergo a minimum military training and be available for five years. Service time for the conscripts was twelve days a year. On a more practical level, King Karl XIV Johan, in 1833, abolished tents as shelter, both in the regimental training camps and, if war were to break out, during campaigns. Instead, Swedish soldiers were to be housed in their training camps in barracks. The result was a uniquely Swedish tradition of barrack design that led to various hybrid forms, all of which tended to be significantly larger than those in use elsewhere—a practice that, perhaps, was rooted in the oversize *Baraquen* constructed in the seventeenth century by father and son Loffman in Scania.[53] In 1839 the army issued a series of designs for wooden barracks to guide construction in the field. One design, drawn by C. N. Frisch, featured a shed-like structure, 57.3 meters long and 6.6 meters wide, offering place to 150 men and a dozen or so noncommissioned officers. It had the look and architecture of a barrack but the size of a small casern.

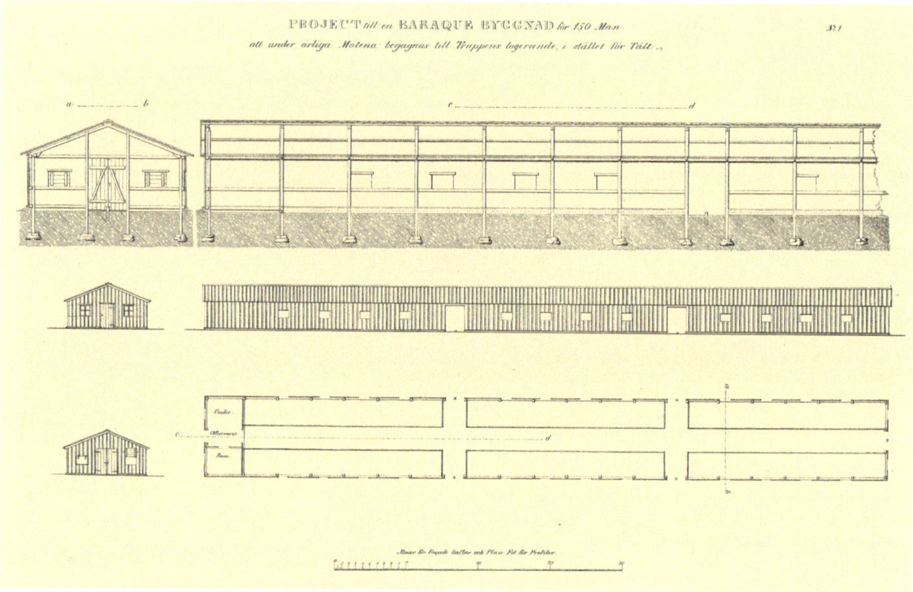

Indeed, throughout the remainder of the nineteenth century, Swedish barracks were typically an order of magnitude larger than those found elsewhere. Around 1870 the Swedish army introduced colossal barracks that combined the typology of the soldier's croft, the barrack, and the barn, reinterpreted on a heroic scale. The standard design for these large barracks to be constructed at regimental training camps in the provinces provided space for 336 men and twenty noncommissioned officers. Conditions were tight, but this didn't matter much, as each soldier's obligation of actual involvement in military maneuvers was limited to four weeks every two years. Many variations of these often handsome buildings, some of which designed by prominent architects like Erik Josephson, still adorn the Swedish landscape.

Fig. 21
C. N. Frisch, Plan, sections, and elevations of a barrack type issued by the Swedish army, 1839. Collection: Riksarkivet, Täby, Sweden.

53 See Ejnar Berg, *Kaserner, barracker och hyddor: Svenska soldatboningar under fyra århundraden* (Stockholm: Almqvist & Wiksell International, 1981).

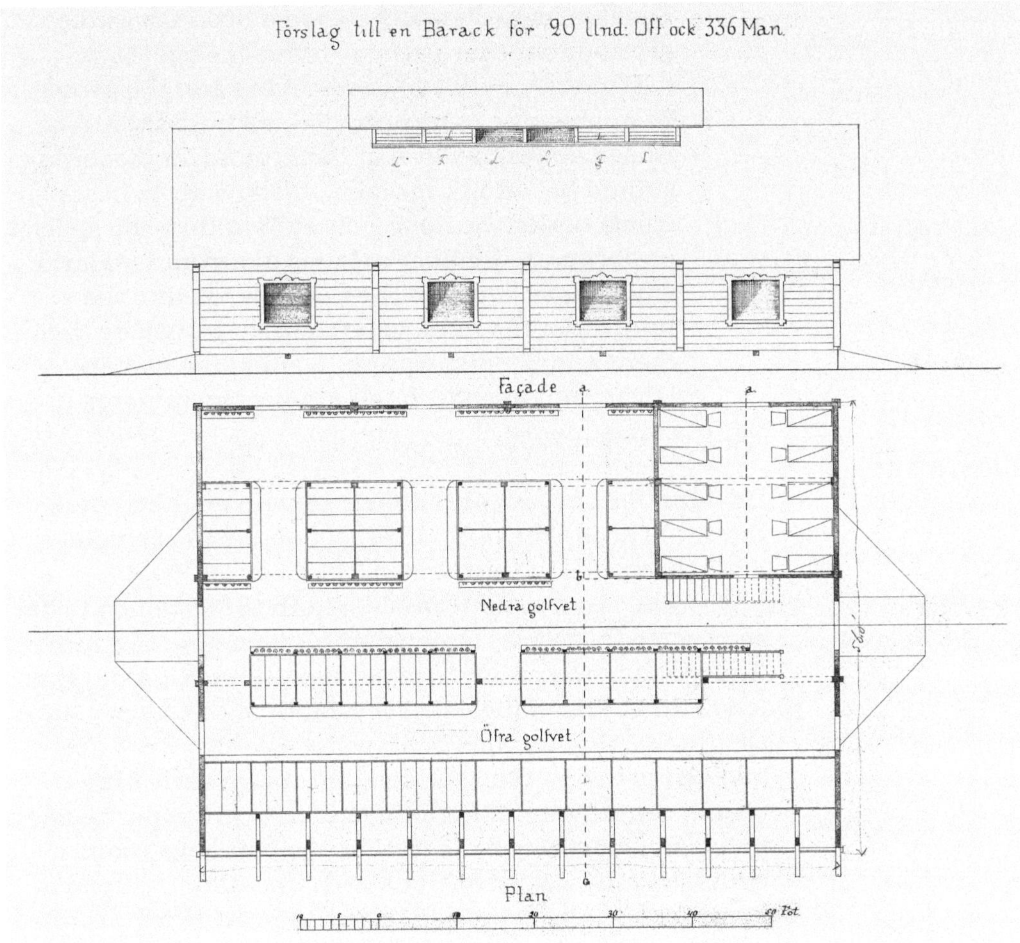

Fig. 22
Plan and side elevation of a standard barrack to be constructed at Swedish army training camps in the provinces, 1873. A total of forty of this type were constructed. Collection: Riksarkivet, Täby, Sweden.

The large Swedish barracks approached civilian standards of construction. As such these buildings responded to the worries of military surgeons all over Europe, who believed that hutted camps were inherently unhealthy. These medical professionals found ample evidence in data provided by the two commissions charged with inspecting the sanitary conditions of British garrisons and camps. A first commission, established in 1857, noted that while the concept of hutted camps was good, practice in the Aldershot camp showed that there were many problems. "None of these wooden barracks, although much more healthy than permanent barracks, are in so good a sanitary condition as they ought to be," a report issued in 1861 noted. In order to stop drafts, soldiers had filled the space between the two wooden walls with earth. "This proceeding at once deprives the interior of the advantages of percolation of air through the walls, and converts it into a kind of permanent barrack, in which several important sanitary advantages of that construction are lost." Worse was the lack of ventilation below the barracks.

> The flooring is usually raised a little above the ground, but there are no sufficient openings to admit air between the flooring and the ground. To enable this to be provided, all huts should be raised above the level of the ground, and openings should be left in the walls, to allow air to pass freely under the floor. For want of this, the space underneath the floor exhales damp and malaria, which pass between the floorboards into the interior of the huts, to be there breathed by the men, and predisposition to epidemic disease is very apt to show itself among the inmates in consequence.[54]

Dr. John Sutherland and Robert Rawlinson had noted the same problems in their report on the performance of the barracks in the Crimea (see Chapter Two).

The observations published in 1861 seemed to be confirmed four years later, when an epidemic of scarlet fever among the children of soldiers living in Aldershot led to an epidemiological assessment of the camp's huts. Originally, the families of married soldiers were not allowed to live in the garrison, but in the early nineteenth century, a few of them had been given permission to live in a curtained-off section of a barracks room, which usually led to tensions with the other occupants. By the 1850s, the army had begun to provide for a limited number of separate rooms to accommodate army wives and children; in Aldershot, a standard barrack, divided by wooden partitions into 16-square-meter compartments, each with its own door, window, and fireplace, served as married quarters for enlisted men. The investigators focused on the barracks in which scarlet fever had been rampant. "We had the floors of several affected huts taken up for the purpose of examining the subsoil. The timbers were sound, but as they were laid on the earth without ventilation beneath them, there was no means of getting rid of the damp air. In one hut (near the new hospital) in which several fatal cases had occurred, the ground beneath was very damp and hollowed out below the level of the ground outside." The commission was "inclined to attribute much of the higher intensity of the disease in certain huts and lines to this condition of the subsoil."

54 Great Britain, *General Report of the Commission Appointed for Improving the Sanitary Condition of Barracks and Hospitals*, 29–30.

> The huts are all old and decaying, and the cubic space and means of ventilation were very deficient at the time we inspected them. Wooden huts if well ventilated and otherwise in a good sanitary

> condition may be safely occupied if the present regulation space of 400 cubic feet [11 cubic meters] per occupant be given. But, as already stated, the amount of space per man falls far short of this allowance. The crowding both in the huts of single men and in married huts was excessive. In some of the divided huts the space per adult and child was scarcely 200 feet [5.5 cubic meters]. The huts were originally constructed with overlapping boards, which afford a ready means of renewing air when combined with ridge ventilation. Ridge ventilators are provided throughout, but in many cases they had been to a great extent closed up. The hut walls have besides been rendered impervious to air by tarring them, and the huts we examined, where scarlet fever had appeared, were most carefully lined inside with paper purposely to exclude the outer air.[55]

All in all, the barracks stood condemned. In the wake of the report, the Lancet Sanitary Commission visited Aldershot and "uncompromisingly" denounced the barracks. "We doubt very much whether, if a hurricane were to carry the whole body of them away, anyone but the War Department would grieve over their fall."[56]

Yet the Aldershot barracks, built in 1855 with an intended life span of thirteen years, continued to serve into the 1880s. By the time they were pulled down, they had become objects of sentiment. No one articulated a romantic understanding of the barrack better than Juliana Horatia Ewing, a pioneering author of children's books in Victorian England. Born in 1841, she married Major Alexander Ewing at the age of twenty-five and began the life of an officer's wife, which included many years in the simple conditions offered at the frontier in Canada and others in a wooden barrack at Aldershot. To Ewing, the simplicity of life in small quarters marked a golden age in her life, and she believed that it was the perfect environment for children to grow up in, as she summarized in a poem in 1879. "Our home used to be in a hut in the dear old Camp, with lots of bands and trumpets and bugles and Dead Marches, and three times a day there was a gun, / But now we live in View Villa at the top of the village, and it isn't nearly such fun."[57] Ewing's poem goes on to extol the happy life of soldiers' children raised in a military camp, reflecting implicitly on the mixed blessings that come with growing up, with advancement in civil society, and with increase of comfort.

55 Great Britain, Army Sanitary Commission, *Report on the Late Epidemic of Scarlet Fever among Children in Aldershot Camp* (London: Edward Eyre and William Spottiswoode, 1866), 16, 18–19, 22.
56 "The Hygienic Condition of Aldershot Camp," *Lancet*, n.s., 88, no. 2256 (1866), 591.
57 Juliana Horatia Ewing, *A Soldier's Children* (London: Society for Promoting Christian Knowledge, 1883), 5.

Fig. 23
Richard André, Children playing soldier in a hutted camp, from Juliana Horatia Ewing, *A Soldier's Children*, 1883. Collection: author.

Shortly before her death, at age forty-three, Ewing completed *The Story of a Short Life*, which concerns Leonard, a single, spoiled, and sensitive child of rich aristocratic parents, who grows up near the camp of Asholt—a fictionalized Aldershot. Leonard establishes friendships with the soldiers and begins to dream of becoming one himself. Asholt is superbly drawn right at the beginning of the book, and it reflects not only Ewing's poetic abilities but also a remarkable—and, in the history of the barrack, unique—meditation on many contradictory aspects of such buildings, "little wooden huts, which were painted a neat and useful black."

> The huts for married men and officers were of varying degrees of comfort and homeliness, but those for single men were like toy-boxes of wooden soldiers; it was only by doing it very tidily that you could (so to speak) put your pretty soldiers away, at night when you had done playing with them, and get the lid to shut down.
>
> But then tidiness is a virtue which like Patience is its own reward. And nineteen men who keep themselves clean and their belongings cleaner; who have made their nineteen beds into easy chairs before most people have got out of bed at all; whose tin pails are kept as bright as average teaspoons (to the envy of housewives and the

shame of housemaids!); who establish a common and a holiday side to the reversible top of their one long table, and scrupulously scrub both; who have a place for everything and a discipline which obliges everybody to put everything in its place; nineteen men, I say, with such habits, find more comfort and elbow-room in a hut than an outsider might believe possible, and hang up a photograph or two into the bargain.

> But it may be at once conceded to the credit of the camp, that those who lived there thought better of it than those who did not, and that those who lived there longest were apt to like it best of all.[58]

Ewing made clear that many inhabitants hated the camp and its barracks, declaring it ugly, crude, and crowded, its layout both monotonous and confusing, and complaining that its accommodations were hot in summer, cold in winter, in every season both stuffy and drafty, and that the low roofs, which seemed to weigh on one's head, always leaked. At the same time, life in the camp had its defenders, and the compact quarters allowed for a life without social formalities, as Ewing explains:

> In truth, the Camp's best defence in the hearts of its defenders was that it was a camp, military life in epitome, with all its defects and all its charm; not the least of which, to some whimsical minds, is, that it represents, as no other phase of society represents, the human pilgrimage in brief. Here be sudden partings, but frequent re-unions; the charities and courtesies of an uncertain life lived largely in common; the hospitality of passing hosts to guests who tarry but a day. [...] Bare and dusty are the Parade Grounds, but they are thick with memories.[59]

And thus, in the few decades of its existence, Aldershot had begun to take a hold in the identity of a relatively small island nation ruling the largest empire the world had ever seen—a common identity that at least in the British collective imagination transcended the divisions of class that continued to plague day-to-day encounters in civilian society.

Châlons never earned a similar place in the French imagination; the chasm between the apparent glory this camp had projected to the outside world, including the domestic comforts it had provided to the

58 Juliana Horatia Ewing, *The Story of a Short Life* (New York: Thomas Y. Crowell, 1893), 34–35.
59 Ibid., 41–42.

military elites, and the ignominious performance of the French army during the Franco-Prussian War could not be overcome. At the beginning of war, Emperor Napoleon III had been at Châlons, and he left there with much fanfare to take command of his army, only to surrender, two weeks later, at Sedan. This military, political, and personal humiliation marked the end of the Second Empire.

Despite its promising and internationally noted beginnings, the camp at Beverloo likewise never achieved a place in the Belgian national imagination. In 1830, the revolt against the Dutch-dominated state had temporarily united the Flemish- and French-speaking inhabitants of the southern part of the United Kingdom of the Netherlands, but after achieving independence, the new Belgian state struggled—and continues to struggle almost two centuries later—to create a unified Belgian nation. From its inception, the Belgian army was supposed to be the crucible of that new nation.[60] By implication, the major training ground of the army, Beverloo, was to be the key location for the emergence of the Belgian nation. However, an ill-advised language policy, enforced with arrogance, destroyed the nation-building potential of the armed forces. French was to be the language of the army, and the result was that the great majority of commissioned officers and noncommissioned officers were monolingual Walloons, and the minority of officers who were Flemish refused to speak their mother tongue because it carried lower-class associations in the new state, while the majority of enlisted men were mostly poor monolingual Flemish speakers. For a century, neither King Leopold nor his successors, nor the various Belgian governments, nor the military leadership ever made a serious attempt to address this debilitating rupture in the middle of the most important nation-building institution.[61]

60 Louis de Vos, "De smeltkroes: De Belgische Krijgsmacht als natievormende factor, 1830–1885," *Belgisch Tijdschrift voor Nieuwste Geschiedenis* 15, nos. 3–4 (1984), 421–60.

61 Richard Boijen, "Het leger als smeltkroes van de natie?," *Bijdragen tot de Eigentijdse Geschiedenis* 1997, no. 3, 55–70.

Entered according to Act of Congress A.D. 18

LINCOLN HOSPITA

Published by Chas. Magnus, 12 Fran

2508

→ p. 225

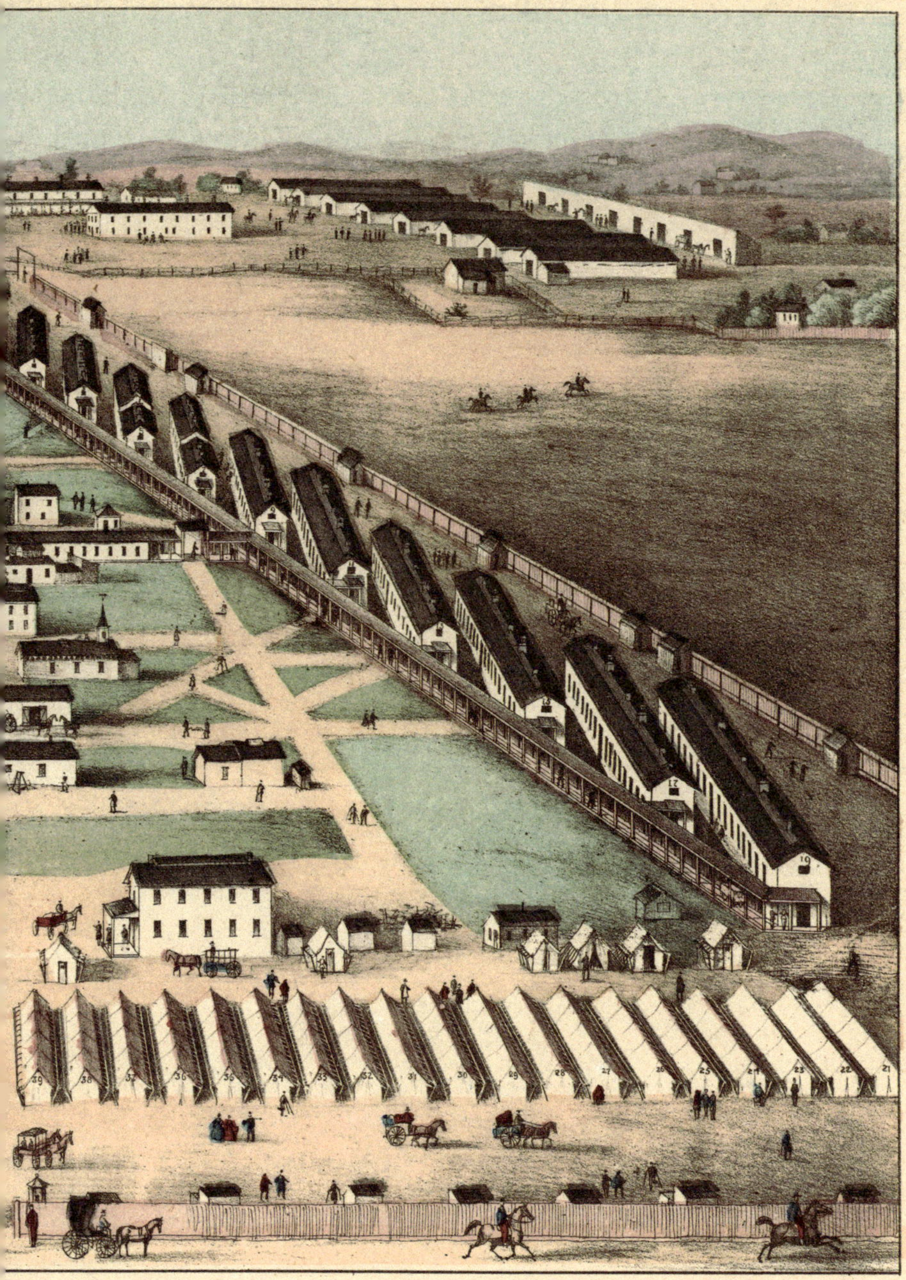

n the Clerks Office of the S. Distr. of N.Y.

Lith. & Printed by Chas. Magnus 12 Frankfort St. N.Y.

ASHINGTON, D.C.

Seventh Street, Washington D.C.

Ca 17 X 10 1/2 in

Five

A Great Show in the Landscape

On February 26, 1863, *The New York Times* carried a lengthy article entitled "The Great Army of the Sick," written by poet and essayist Walt Whitman. A couple of months earlier, he had traveled to Washington, DC, to help his brother, a soldier in the Union Army, who had been injured in battle. Realizing there was a great need to be filled, Whitman had stayed to help wounded and sick soldiers who crowded the many military hospitals. In his article, he tried to give a face to one of the 50,000 taken care of in and around the capital. "Take this case in Ward 6, Campbell Hospital 4—a young man from Plymouth Country, Massachusetts; a farmer's son, aged about 20 or 21, a soldierly American young fellow, but with sensitive and tender feelings." After participating in the Battle of Fredericksburg, Virginia, in December, Private John Holmes had fallen ill and been brought to an emergency hospital in the capital.

> Poor boy! the long train of exhaustion, deprivation, rudeness, no food, no friendly word or deed, but all kinds of upstart airs, and impudent, unfeeling speeches and deeds, from all kinds of small officials, (and some big ones,) cutting like razors into that sensitive heart, had at last done the job. He now lay, at times out of his head, but quite silent, asking nothing of anyone, for some days, with death getting a closer and surer grip upon him—he cared not, or rather he welcomed death. His heart was broken. He felt the struggle to keep up any longer to be useless. God, the world, humanity—all had abandoned him. It would feel so good to shut his eyes forever on the cruel things around him and toward him.
>
> As luck would have it, at this time, I found him. I was passing down Ward No. 6 one day, about dusk (4th of January, I think,) and noticed his glassy eyes with a look of despair and hopelessness, sunk low in his thin pallid-brown young

face. One learns to divine quickly in the hospital, and as I stopped by him and spoke some commonplace remark, (to which he made no reply,) I saw as I looked that it was a case for ministering to the affections first, and other nourishment and medicines afterward. I sat down by him without any fuss—talked a little—soon saw that it did him good—led him to talk a little himself—got him somewhat interested—wrote a letter for him to his folks in Massachusetts, (to L. H. CAMPBELL, Plymouth County,)—soothed him down as I saw he was getting a little too much agitated, and tears in his eyes—gave him some small gifts, and told him I should come again soon. (He has told me since that this little visit, at that hour, just saved him—a day more, and it would have been perhaps too late.)[1]

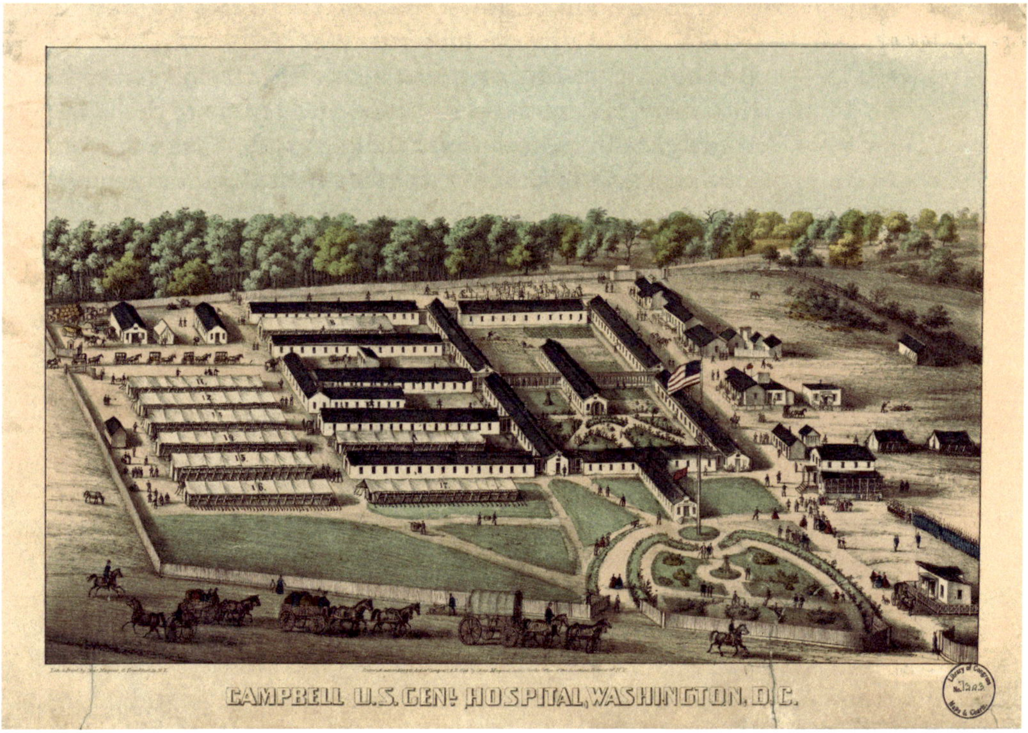

Whitman's portrait of one of the thousands of casualties of the bitter Civil War between the North and the South was accompanied by a description of a new, large-scale initiative by the federal authorities to provide better facilities for them.

Fig. 1
The United States (Union) Army's Campbell General Hospital, Washington, DC, 1864. Collection: Library of Congress, Washington, DC.

The Government, (which really tries, I think, to do the best and quickest it can for these sad necessities,) is gradually settling down to adopt the plan of placing the hospitals in clusters of one-story wooden barracks, with their accompanying tents

1 Walt Whitman, "The Great Army of the Sick," *The New York Times*, Feb. 26, 1863, 2.

> and sheds for cooking and all needed purposes. Taking all things into consideration, no doubt these are best adapted to the purpose; better than using churches and large public buildings like the Patent Office. These sheds now adopted are long, one-story edifices, sometimes ranged along in a row, with their heads to the street, and numbered either alphabetically, Wards A, or B, C, D and so on; or Wards 1, 2, 3, &c. The middle one will be marked by a flagstaff, and is the office of the establishment, with rooms for the Ward Surgeons, &c. One of these sheds or wards, will contain sixty cots—sometimes, on an emergency, they move them close together, and crowd in more.[2]

While most of these places were purposefully designed as hospitals, Campbell General Hospital, where Private John Holmes was recovering from his wounds, had been constructed as the home of a cavalry regiment. The original barracks, designed to be dormitories for healthy soldiers who spent most of the day outside, were rather primitive: a postwar report on medical care during the Civil War described them as "long, low, narrow buildings of rough boards."[3] In order to transform them into sick wards, the army introduced ridge ventilation and added covered walkways to connect the buildings.

Fig. 2
View from the main courtyard of the Campbell General Hospital, 1861. Collection: Library of Congress, Washington, DC.

More than twenty-one months later, Whitman contributed another article to *The New York Times*, in which he updated his initial report on the care of the sick and wounded in the capital. By that time, he had made many hundreds of visits to the military hospitals in the District of Columbia, Maryland, and northern Virginia.

2 Ibid.
3 Charles Smart, *The Medical and Surgical History of the War of the Rebellion*, pt. 3, vol. 1, *Medical History* (Washington, DC: Government Printing Office, 1888), 912.

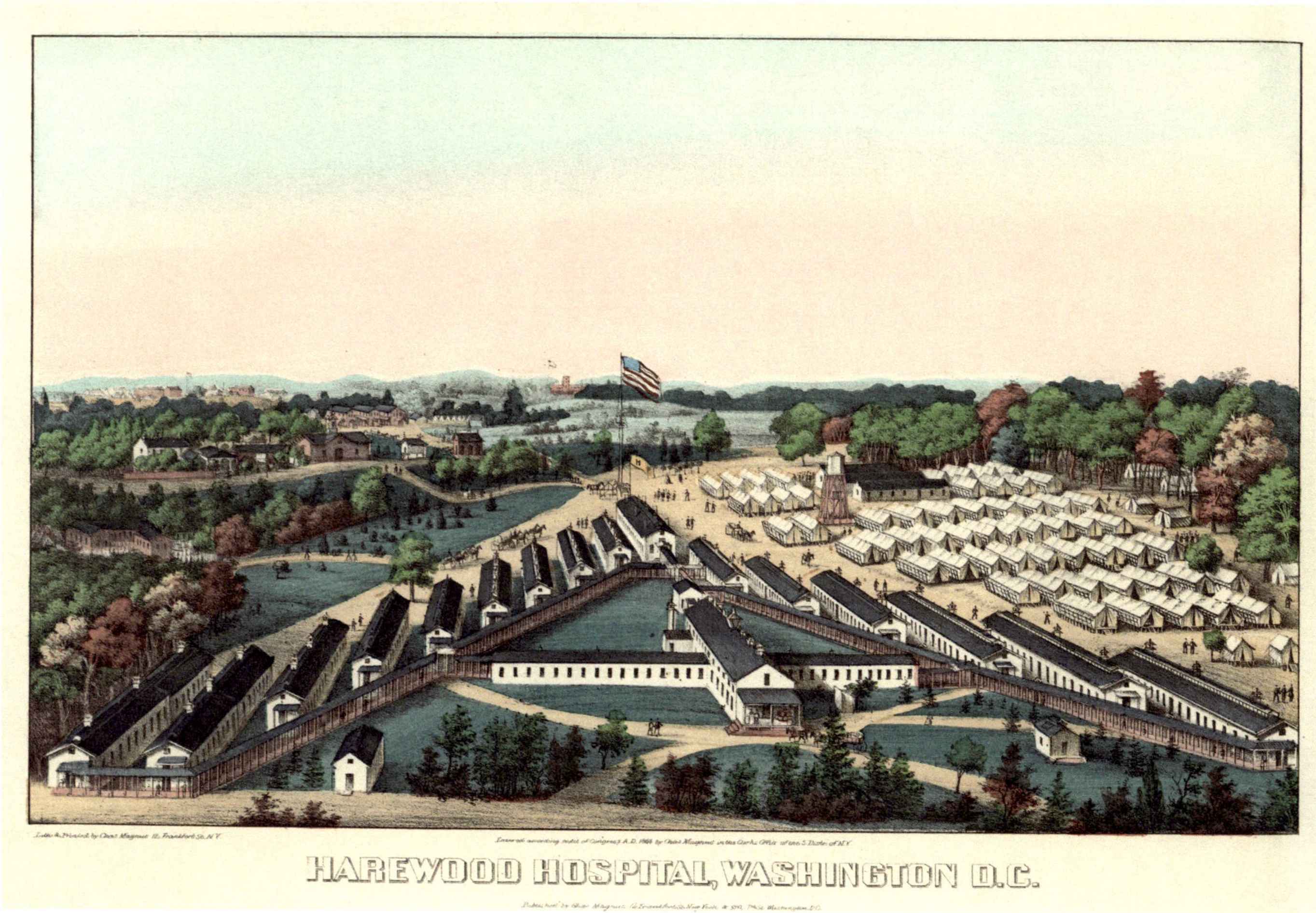

Fig. 3
General view of the US (Union) Army's Harewood General Hospital, near Washington, DC, 1864. Collection: Library Company of Philadelphia, Pennsylvania.

> Of the army hospitals now in and around Washington, there are thirty or forty. I am in the habit of going to all, and to Fairfax seminary, Alexandria, and over Long Bridge to the convalescent camp, etc. As a specimen of almost any one of these hospitals, fancy to yourself a space of three to twenty acres [1 to 8 hectares] of ground, on which are grouped ten or twelve very large wooden barracks, with, perhaps, a dozen or twenty, and sometimes more than that number, of small buildings, capable all together of accommodating from five hundred to a thousand or fifteen hundred persons. Sometimes these large wooden barracks, or wards, each of them, perhaps, from a hundred to a hundred and fifty feet long [30 to 45 meters], are arranged in a straight row, evenly fronting the street; others are planned so as to form an immense V; and others again arranged around a hollow square. They make all together a huge cluster, with the additional tents, extra wards for contagious diseases, guard-houses, sutler's stores, chaplain's house, etc. In the middle will probably be an edifice devoted to the offices of the surgeon in charge and the ward surgeons, principal attachés, clerks, etc. Then around this centre radiate or are gathered the wards for the wounded and sick.[4]

After a more detailed description of the numbering system of the wards, Whitman provided a more general impression of the contribution of these radically new architectural forms to the urban landscape. "A wanderer like me about Washington pauses on some high land which commands the sweep of the city (one never tires of the noble and ample views presented here, in the generally fine, soft, peculiar air and light), and has his eyes attracted by these white clusters of barracks in almost every direction. They make a great show in the landscape, and I often use them as landmarks."[5]

← Fig. 3

The American Civil War led to many important innovations in warfare and also allowed earlier inventions to be applied and tested in real-world conditions. The telegraph, used during the Crimean War to send news dispatches to London, now became a primary tool of military communication; the railways were the backbone of military logistics; aerial reconnaissance by means of hot-air balloons allowed for better-informed

4 Walt Whitman, "Visits among Army Hospitals," *The New York Times*, Dec. 11, 1864, 2.
5 Ibid.

tactical planning, while rifled muskets, which tripled the range and lethal effectiveness of an infantry soldier, and the rapid-fire Gatling gun made the ensuing battles ever more deadly. Battlefield photography helped to record the terrible cost of war. These innovations are well known, as are those used in naval warfare, including ironclad steam-propelled warships, naval mines, and torpedoes. The widespread use of mostly standardized barracks in military hospitals and camps created by the Union Army, which struck informed contemporaries as a significant development, tends to be ignored. It deserves, however, an honorable mention in the history of human invention.

Fig. 4
Group of patients outside of Ward B of Harewood General Hospital, 1864. Collection: Library of Congress, Washington, DC.

Chapter One, Fig. 8
→ p. 51

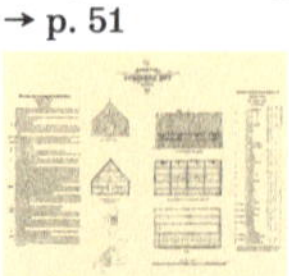

Chapter Two, Fig. 4
→ p. 88

The history of the barrack originates at the periphery of societies that took pride in the aesthetics and permanence of both their public architecture and the traditions and solidity of their private buildings. The army huts described in David de Solemne's *La Charge du mareschal des logis* had little relation to seventeenth-century Dutch monumental and vernacular architectures, and while the portable barracks developed and marketed by British entrepreneurs William Eassie and Richard Potter for use in the Crimea had some relation to prefabricated shelters made for export to Australia, they had little relation to anything being constructed in the British Isles at that time.

In the United States the situation was different. First of all, since the arrival of European settlers, wooden buildings had been the dominant vernacular in the English, French, Dutch, and Swedish colonies, in the territories of the original thirteen colonies, officially ceded by Great Britain in 1783, and in the territory of the Louisiana Purchase of 1805. Timber framing, log construction, plank framing, and corner-post construction defined the structure and appearance of the great majority of buildings, which were usually erected by "housewrights" or "mechanics" who, in general, had not enjoyed much of an apprenticeship in the building trade. When settler Mary Cleavers and her family found a spot to settle in Michigan, she noticed how, out of nowhere, carpenters showed up to offer their services. She quickly discovered that none of them had much experience: "A plane, a chisel, and two dollars a day make a carpenter in Michigan," she wrote.[6] There were, of course, skilled builders who knew the rudiments of design and would draw rough plans. But before the 1850s, few of these men and few of their clients had any concern in building beyond the most basic vernacular.

A revolutionary lightweight framing technology invented in 1830 that became known as "balloon framing" reinforced the dominance of unskilled "mechanics" in the building trade, as it allowed them to assemble very sturdy buildings very quickly, using masses of cheap, industrially produced nails and pine studs.[7] Visiting "the village" of Chicago in 1833, the Englishman Charles Joseph Latrobe, who was to acquire fame later as an effective colonizer of Australia, noted, "frame and clapboard houses were springing up daily under the active axes and hammers of the speculators, and piles of lumber announced the preparation for yet other edifices of an equally light character."[8] By 1845 balloon-frame technology dominated the American West, but carpenters in the developed areas of the United States spurned it: balloon framing made their joining skills irrelevant, and clients did not trust it. The few professional architects working on the East Coast ignored the revolutionary lightweight technology; public commissions called for more durable construction. An influential opinion maker at that time, Solon Robinson, became the technology's principal advocate: "To erect a balloon-building requires about as much mechanical skill as it does to build a board fence," he observed in 1858. "If it had not been for the knowledge of balloon-framers, Chicago and San Francisco could never have arisen, as they did, from little villages to great cities in a single year."[9] Two years later, architect George Evertson Woodward broadcast the advantages of the new technology in a series of articles. "So general is its use West

6 Mary Cleavers, *Our New Home in the West* (New York: James Miller, 1872), 75.
7 William E. Bell, *Carpentry Made Easy; or, The Science and Art of Framing, on a New and Improved System* (Philadelphia: Howard Challen, 1857), 46–54; also Paul E. Sprague, "The Origin of Balloon Framing," *Journal of the Society of Architectural Historians*, vol. 40 (1981), 311–19.
8 Charles Joseph Latrobe, *The Rambler in North America: 1832–1833*, 2 vols. (London: Seeley and Burnside, 1835), 2:209.
9 As quoted in Gervase Wheeler, *Homes for the People in Suburb and Country: The Villa, the Mansion, and the Cottage, Adapted to American Climate and Wants* (New York: Scribner, 1858), 412.

of Lake Michigan and throughout California, that a builder of the old style of timber frame would be regarded with the same sympathy as a man who prefers travel by stage instead of by rail."[10] The balloon frame had been tested at the frontier, "and found to stand the test."[11] It allowed anyone who needed an almost instant roof over one's head to build a cheap, strong, and easy-to-repair building, be it a home, shop, school, shed, shack—or, of course, barrack.

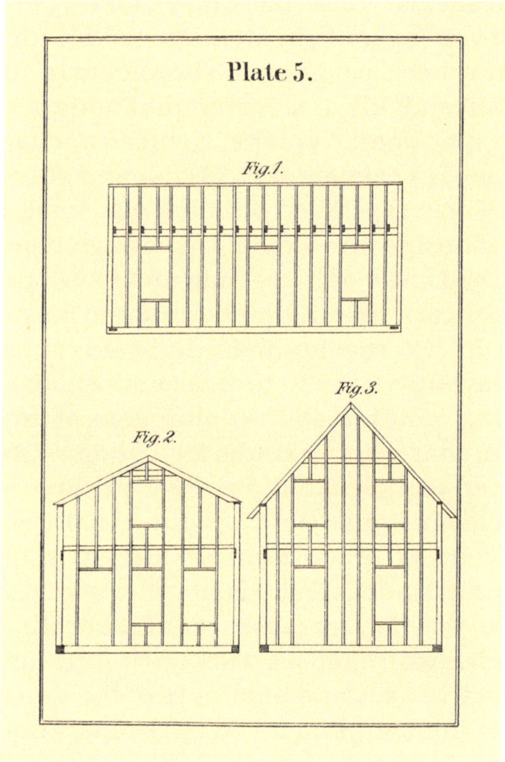

Fig. 5
Balloon-frame construction. William E. Bell, *Carpentry Made Easy; or, the Science and Art of Framing*, 1857. Collection: author.

Americans quickly became used to the cheapness of balloon-frame construction—one that allowed working-class people to aspire to ownership of a single-family home. Immigrants continued, and continue, to be amazed by the economics of American house construction. After his arrival in America in 1882, Swedish builder Henry Ericsson made his first balloon-frame house in the Chicago suburb of Moreland. As a youth, he had enjoyed watching the log construction of his family house in Bokeholm—measuring 11 by 8.5 meters—over two years. A balloon-frame version of that house would have been available to people who could never have owned a house in Sweden: "Here at Moreland, four men built a house in as many weeks as years were required to build Bokeholm." For Ericsson, the balloon frame was "a miracle hardly less dramatic than the feeding of the multitudes with the loaves and fishes."[12]

10 George E. Woodward, "Balloon Frames," *Cultivator* 8, no. 1 (Jan. 1860), 20.
11 George E. Woodward, "Balloon Frames III," *Cultivator* 8, no. 5 (May 1860), 147.
12 Henry Ericsson with Lewis E. Myers, *Sixty Years a Builder: The Autobiography of Henry Ericsson* (Chicago: Kroch and Son, 1942), 53, 163.

While from a European perspective most Americans in the nineteenth century lived a culturally narrow existence, they also were recognized for their inventiveness and dynamism. Of particular interest was the way they did not wait for the government to organize their lives but organized themselves, within the boundaries of duly established laws. "Americans of all ages, all conditions, and all dispositions, constantly form associations," French political philosopher Alexis de Tocqueville observed in the 1830s. "They have not only commercial and manufacturing companies, in which all take part, but associations of a thousand other kinds—religious, moral, serious, futile, extensive, or restricted, enormous or diminutive."[13] Among these associations, state militias were unique, as they were authorized by Congress. These voluntary and essentially egalitarian units were conceived during the American Revolution as counterweights to the regular army. In the American colonies, the British Army had become a tool of London to maintain civil control, and the resulting loathing of the colonists for the soldiers spilled over in a distrustful attitude toward any standing army—including their own Union Army, which was maintained with minimal expense. By the mid-nineteenth century the state militias, backed up by the Second Amendment of the United States Constitution, had come to embody the originally French concept of the nation-at-arms adjusted to North American circumstances.

In 1861, following the secession of Southern states from the Union, these militias became key in helping to recruit volunteers to augment the paltry Union Army—although they initially imposed on it their haphazard, disorganized character. Shortly after the secession of the Southern states, François-Ferdinand d'Orléans, Prince de Joinville, traveled to the United States to observe the Union Army in the field. He was a professional military man and was both impressed and dismayed by what he saw. "The North went seriously to work to create an army—a grand army," he noted. "Seconded by public opinion, Congress resolved upon the raising of five hundred thousand men, with the funds necessary for the purpose. Unfortunately, it could not command the traditions, the training and the experience requisite to form and manage such a military force." Yet the French aristocrat did acknowledge that, despite its obvious shortcomings, the Union Army was a great credit to the motivating and organizing power of democracy. "Never, we believe, has any nation created, of herself, by her own will, by her single resources, without coercion of

13 Alexis de Tocqueville, *Democracy in America*, trans. Henry Reeve, 2 vols. (New York: Langley, 1840), 2:106.

any kind, without government pressure, and in such a short space of time, so considerable an armament. Free governments, whatever may be their faults and the excesses to which they may give rise, always preserve an elasticity and creative power which nothing can equal."[14]

In 1861, the governments of the Northern states quickly established camps to allow the state militias to recruit and train volunteers. Many consisted of tents only, but a number were formed of rows upon rows of quickly constructed balloon-frame barracks. In Ohio, for example, Governor William Dennison responded to the secession of the Southern states by asking the commander of the state militia, George Brinton McClellan, to create such a camp for the intake of volunteers. McClellan, in collaboration with fellow militia officers and a professional engineer, Captain William S. Rosecrans, selected a site near Cincinnati for the hutted camp that was to be named Camp Dennison. "It seemed an excellent place for our work," former Union Army general Jacob Dolson Cox noted in his 1900 book *Military Reminiscences of the Civil War*.

> Captain Rosecrans met us [...] coming from Cincinnati with a train-load of lumber. He had with him his compass and chain, and by the help of a small detail of men soon laid off the ground for the two regimental camps, and the general lines of the whole encampment for a dozen regiments. [...] A general plan was given to the company officers by which the huts should be made uniform in size and shape. The huts of each company faced each other, three or four on each side, making the street between, in which the company assembled before marching to its place on the regimental color line. At the head of each street were the quarters of the company officers, and those of the "field and staff" still further in rear. The Regulations were followed in this plan as closely as the style of barracks and nature of the ground would permit. Vigorous work housed all the men before night.[15]

14 François-Ferdinand d'Orléans, Prince de Joinville, *The Army of the Potomac: Its Organization, Its Commander, and Its Campaign*, trans. William Henry Hurlbert (New York: Anson Randolph, 1863), 11–13, 16–17.
15 Jacob Dolson Cox, *Military Reminiscences of the Civil War*, 2 vols. (New York: Scribner, 1900), 1:21–22.

→ Fig. 6

The next day, work continued. "The huts which were half finished yesterday were now put in good order, and in building the new ones the men profited by the experience of their comrades," Cox wrote, adding, "we were however suddenly thrown into one of those small tempests which it is so easy to get up in a new camp."

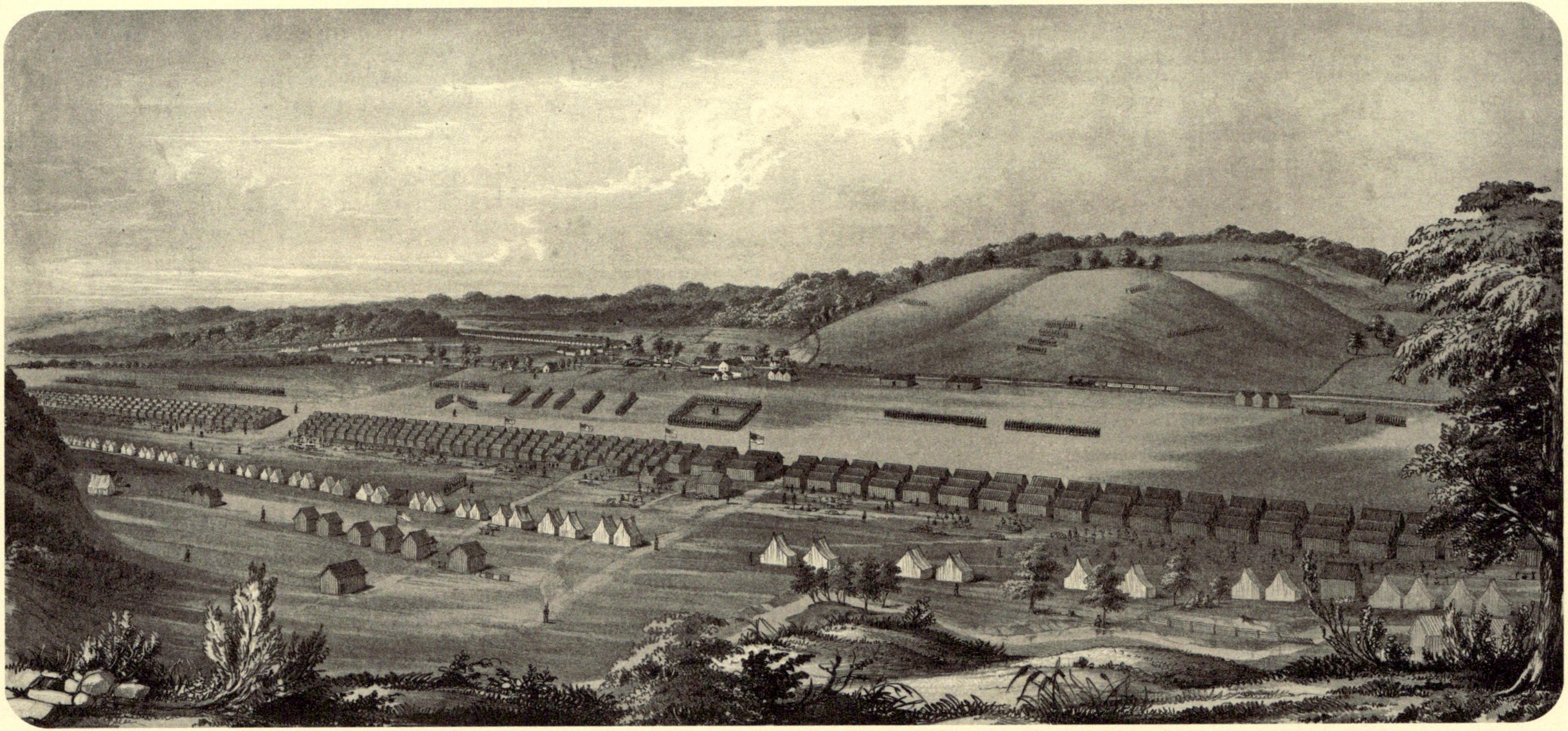

Fig. 6
The US (Union) Army's Camp Dennison, near Cincinnati, Ohio, 1863. Collection: Library of Congress, Washington, DC.

> Captain Rosecrans, as engineer, was superintending the work of building, and finding that the companies were putting floors and bunks in their huts, he peremptorily ordered that these should be taken out, insisting that the huts were only intended to take the place of tents and give such shelter as tents could give. The company and regimental officers loudly protested, and the men were swelling with indignation and wrath. [...]
> I said I would examine the matter and submit it to General McClellan, and meanwhile the floors already built might remain, though no new ones should be made till the question was decided.
> I reported to the general that, in my judgment, the huts should have floors and bunks, because the ground was wet when they were built,—they could not be struck like tents to dry and air the earth, and they were meant to be permanent quarters for the rendezvous of troops for an indefinite time. The decision of McClellan was in accordance with the report.[16]

All over the Northern states, amateur soldiers like Cox and professionals like Rosecrans collaborated to create, almost overnight, American versions of the European camps at Beverloo, Cirié, Aldershot, or Châlons. When a camp was located close to a town, a local contractor might be involved. Creatively modifying the local architectural vernacular of crudely and quickly built shacks, sheds, bunkhouses, and homes, these builders produced many different models. The designs for barracks built in the Crimean Peninsula and the Curragh in Ireland had been published by 1861, but there is no evidence that Rosecrans or any of the other mechanics or engineers knew of these precedents. They improvised as they went along.

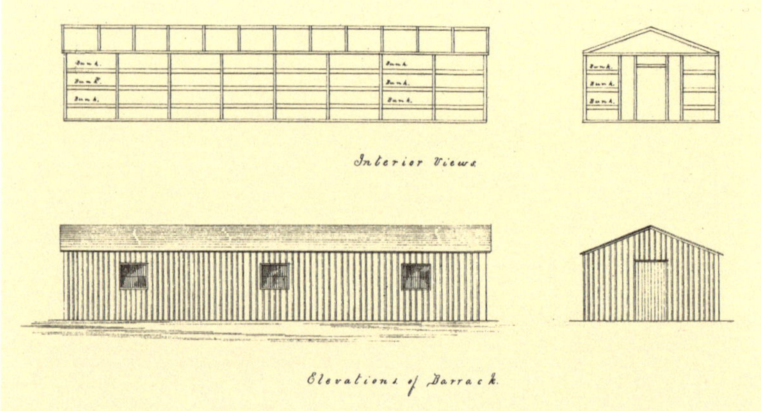

Fig. 7
Elevations and sections of the barracks constructed in the US (Union) Army's Camp Perrine, Trenton, New Jersey, 1861. Collection: US National Archives, College Park, Maryland.

16 Ibid., 1:24–25.

Some saw a significant business opportunity. David N. Skillings and David B. Flint, who both owned large lumberyards in New York and New England, realized that they could not only sell the posts and boards for barrack construction but also design and produce a line of portable structures that included prefabricated soldiers' accommodations. In late 1861, they patented a system based on a modular frame, using posts 10 centimeters square, spaced at intervals of 1.2 meters, and filled with interchangeable panels.[17] Using this system, Skillings and Flint designed two soldiers' huts: one measuring 5 by 7.5 meters and claimed to house fifty-six men, and a smaller one measuring 3.5 by 5 meters for thirty-two men. A key design feature was collapsible bunks.

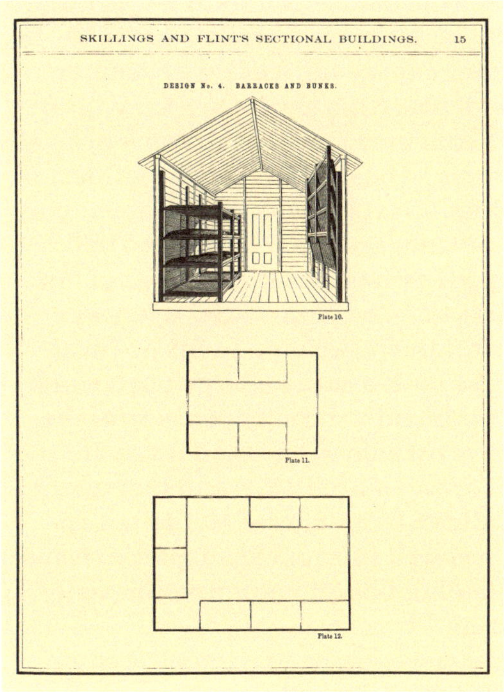

Fig. 8
David N. Skillings and David B. Flint, Barracks with collapsible bunks, from their *Illustrated Catalogue of Portable Sectional Buildings*, 1861. Collection: Canadian Centre for Architecture, Montreal.

"They are superior to any bunks now in use; for, while they afford a comfortable bed for the night, they can be folded up by day, rendering the sleeping apartment available as a sitting-room or hall," the quickly produced sales catalogue proclaimed. As to the hut itself, it "is easily warmed, perfectly ventilated, and can be taken down, removed, and rebuilt without difficulty or additional material."[18]

It is not a surprise to learn that the officers in the Quartermaster Department of the Union Army, who were trained to adopt the simplest solution to any problem, did not adopt the Skillings and Flint barrack: why move prefabricated posts and panels all the way

17 Margaretta Jean Darnall, "Innovations in American Prefabricated Housing: 1860–1890," *Journal of the Society of Architectural Historians* 31 (1972), 51–52.
18 David N. Skillings and David B. Flint, *Illustrated Catalogue of Portable Sectional Buildings* (Boston and New York: Skillings and Flint & Hall, 1862), 14.

from the North when both carpenters and abundant supplies of lumber were locally available? As for any accommodation for soldiers in the field, if the army-supplied tents ceased to be suitable at the end of the fall of 1861, soldiers were on their own. There were no prescribed solutions of how to construct winterized shelters and with what kind of materials. If the winter camps were located close to a major city like Washington, DC, the winter camp might show a formality of design and a quality of construction that seemed appropriate given the civic context. A splendid example is the Carver Barracks, which housed a brigade consisting of the 104th Pennsylvania, the 52nd Pennsylvania, the 56th New York, and the 11th Maine volunteer infantry regiments in the winter of 1861–62 in the nation's capital. The commander of the brigade was Colonel William Watts Hart Davis, a veteran of the Mexican-American War (1846–48). Davis's men lived under canvas until early December, when he decided that it was time to prepare for winter: "A simple calculation convinced me that it was more economical to put troops in board huts for the winter, than keep them in tents." Davis contacted his divisional commander, Brigadier General Silas Casey, who told him to prepare plans, an estimate of the amount of lumber needed, and a budget. "The plan I fixed upon was that of a Mexican town," Davis recalled in his postwar memoir, "the huts to be built around a large open court yard, or plaza, each regiment to occupy one side of the square. In the matter of estimates I availed myself of the experience of major Gries, an architect, and lieutenant Carver, a practical builder. [...] General McClellan approved the plan and ordered the quartermaster to issue the requisite amount of lumber and other materials upon proper requisition."[19]

Having obtained permission to create the camp on the grounds of Columbian College (now George Washington University), around two miles from the US Capitol, Davis charged Lieutenant James M. Carver with the task to construct the barracks. "They were built around a court yard seven hundred feet [210 meters] square," Davis recollected. "Each company hut was eighty feet [25.5 meters] long, sixteen [5 meters] wide and twelve [3.5 meters] high, with the end to the square."

> The roof had the ordinary pitch, was covered with felt and pitched, with projecting gable and eaves, to improve the finish. In front was a room partitioned off for the commissioned, and a similar one in the rear for the non-commissioned, officers.

19 William Watts Hart Davis, *History of the 104th Pennsylvania Regiment: From August 22nd, 1861, to September 30th, 1864* (Philadelphia: Jas. B. Rodgers, 1866), 30.

> Bunks were put up and windows and doors enough for light and ventilation. In the rear of each hut was a convenient cook-house. Each regiment occupied ten company huts, one for the field and staff, and another for the non-commissioned staff and band. A hut of equal size was erected on the north side for the accommodation of brigade head quarters. One row of huts was on the east side of Fourteenth street which ran through the barrack yard. Before the work was commenced each regiment was assigned its side of the square, and carpenters detailed to build the huts. Guard houses were erected at the north-west and south-east angles. The barracks consumed a million feet of lumber.[20]

→ Fig. 9

All the huts were painted white, which increased their domestic appearance. Davis was quite pleased by the decorating initiatives taken by both officers and men to make the hut interiors more comfortable: "The quarters of the officers were generally papered with wall-paper, while those of the men were covered with *Harper's Weekly* and other pictorials, which presented them with an illustrated history of the rebellion as far as it had progressed." Meticulous in giving credit where credit was due—a key quality for an officer who had raised a volunteer regiment and commanded a volunteer brigade—Davis went out of his way to praise Lieutenant Carver for the speedy execution of the camp, and ordered that it was to be officially known as "Carver Barracks." In his memoir, Davis noted, "When we vacated [the barracks] in the spring the government fitted them up for a general hospital, for which they were well adapted, with a slight alteration. They were then called 'Carver General Hospital.' How easily was the name of an unknown lieutenant made historic!"[21]

Lieutenant Carver had been given the means to create an exemplary winter camp that was meant to showcase the Union's appreciation for the volunteers' loyalty and sense of duty. In the field, winter quarters were very primitive, as soldiers were given neither materials nor money to create a winter camp. The primary source of building material was the forest, and log cabins were the default. Vernacular traditions maintained themselves: when the soldiers had a Scandinavian background, they typically constructed huts with vertical logs; when German, the logs were laid horizontally.

20 Ibid., 30–31.
21 Ibid., 31–33.

Fig. 9
The US (Union) Army's Carver Barracks, Washington, DC, 1862. Collection: Library of Congress, Washington, DC.

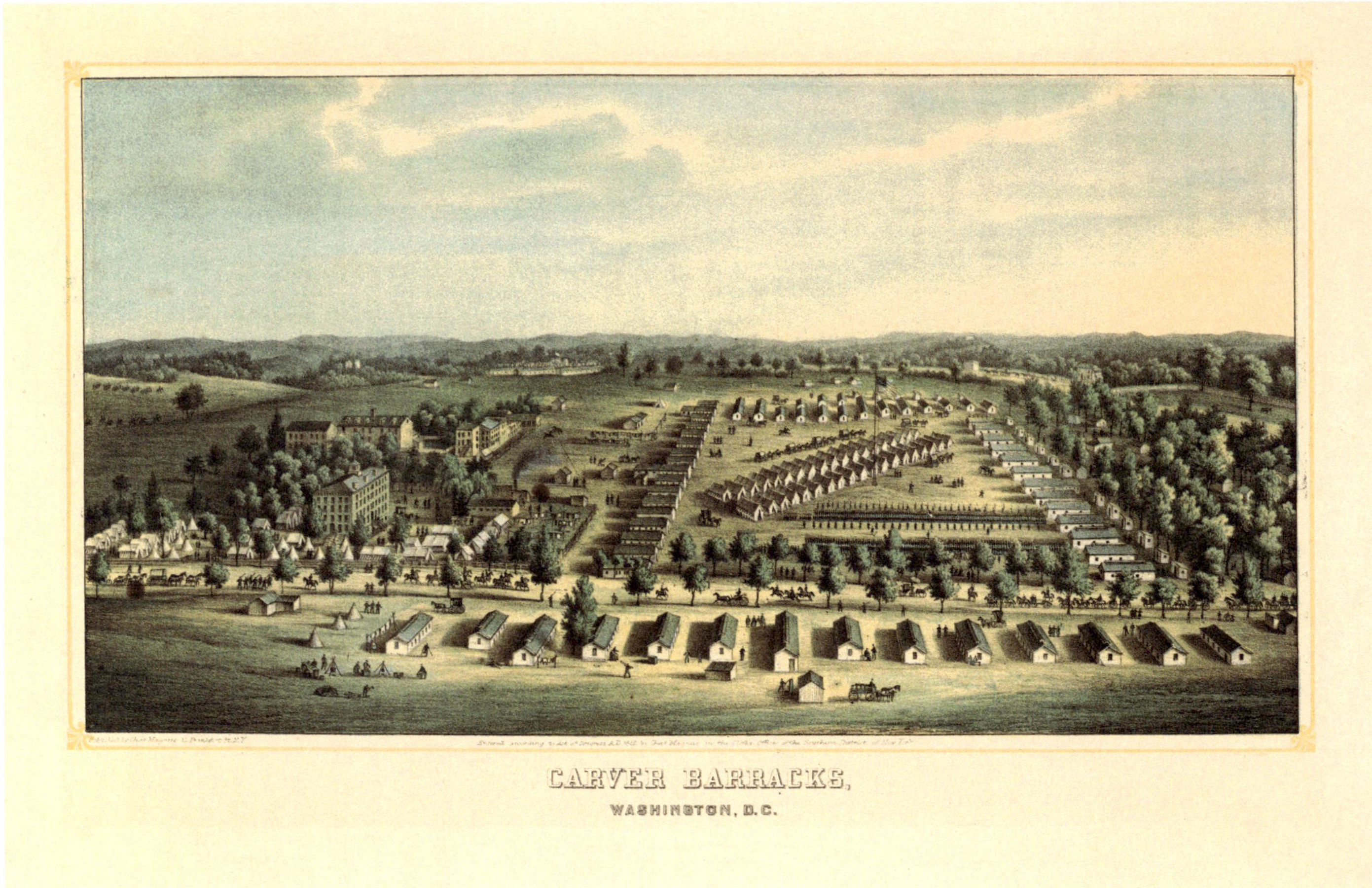

Fig. 10
Mathew B. Brady, "Pine Cottage," unidentified US (Union) Army winter encampment, c. 1862. Collection: Library of Congress, Washington, DC.

Roger Hannaford of the 2nd Ohio Volunteers described in his diary the construction of a log cabin near Winchester in northern Virginia in the winter of 1864–65. "Dec. 28. Rumors were rife that we were going to move into winter quarters & that an opportunity would be given for men to build log huts for protection. It was a dreary dark day with snow 3 in. [8 centimeters] deep." The next day the officers identified a site at the edge of a forest, and laid out the camp in a rough fashion. "Friday, Dec. 30. Every company was busy chopping down trees; the sound of the axe & the crash of falling trees was heard all over the camp. [...] There were but two axes in our Company; very few Companies were any better off, so building winter quarters [...] was very slow work." It was over a week before Roger and two friends got to construct their own hut, "which was to be of larger size than any other (in our company); the inside dimensions were 8 by 10½ ft. [2.4 by 3.2 meters] high. Our huts were all of the same general pattern, with logs on [the] east & west sides & north end, while the south end was open for the chimney & door." Roger decided to scout for nails and lumber; ruined barns, stables, and fences yielded some boards to serve as rafters. "It was no small trouble to build these huts, lacking as we did every necessary to work with. [...] Now came topping out our chimney, chinking & daubing, fixing our door, then the putting up [of] our bunks." It was an imperfect shelter to be sure, especially as the chimney was without draft. Yet Roger remembered it fondly. "Our hut being much the largest, was the great place for the boys to congregate, to tell tales & yarns, fight our battles o'er again, but most of all, talk of home, a theme the dullest became eloquent on."[22]

22 Stephen Z. Starr, "Winter Quarters near Winchester, 1864–1865: Reminiscences of Roger Hannaford, Second Ohio Volunteer Cavalry," *Virginia Magazine of History and Biography* 86, no. 3 (July 1978), 32–228.

The military surgeons of the Union Army did their best to ensure that these camps did not become death traps. Most of them had been civilians before the beginning of the hostilities, with no experience with military medicine, and now had to oversee the preservation of health in a rapidly expanding army in which the great majority of soldiers were volunteers. “In the volunteers, almost all who offer are received,” Charles Stuart Tripler observed in his hastily assembled *Hand-Book for the Military Surgeon*, which aimed to provide the physicians—who were themselves volunteers—with some basic information. Many of these volunteers were in bad health and, “exposed to the fatigues and labors of the camp,” they were “almost sure to become sick.”[23]

In the fall of 1861, it became clear that the Union Army would have to spend the winter in the field. The British experience in the Crimea suggested the possibility of catastrophe, but the soldiers of the Union Army used their proverbial “Yankee inventiveness” to take care of themselves. Daniel McRuer, a surgeon serving in the Army of the Potomac, had studied the Crimean War and learned of a contraption to heat tents. Building on this design, he developed the so-called Crimean oven, which consisted of “A trench 1 foot [30 centimeters] wide and 20 inches [50 centimeters] deep to be dug through the center and length of each tent, to be continued for 3 or 4 feet [1–1.2 meters] farther, terminating at one end in a covered oven fire-place and at the other in a chimney.” McRuer went on:

> By this arrangement the fire-place and chimney are both on the outside of the tent; the fire-place is made about 2 feet [60 centimeters] wide and arching; its area gradually lessening until it terminates in a throat at the commencement of the straight trench. This part is covered with brick or stone, laid in mortar or cement; the long trench to be covered with sheet-iron in the same manner. The opposite end to the fire-place terminates in a chimney 6 or 8 feet [1.8–2.4 meters] high: the front of the fire-place to be fitted with a tight movable sheet-iron cover, in which an opening is to be made, with a sliding cover to act as a blower. By this contrivance a perfect draught may be obtained, and no more cold air admitted within the furnace than just sufficient to consume the wood and generate the amount of heat required, which not only radiates from the exposed surface of the iron plates, but is conducted throughout the

23 Charles Stuart Tripler, *Hand-Book for the Military Surgeon* (Cincinnati: Robert Clarke, 1861), 10.

> ground floor of the tent so as to keep it both warm and dry, making a board floor entirely unnecessary, thereby avoiding the dampness and filth, which unavoidably accumulates in such places.[24]

Tripler, who served as medical director of the Army of the Potomac, feared that the onset of the cold would lead to an outbreak of typhus and typhoid fever, and sought a way to modify the tents so that they offered a tolerable ventilation. The Crimean oven provided the answer. Tripler endorsed McRuer's simple, cheap, and practicable design, and ensured it became the standard way of heating the tents. In a letter to his mother, written in February 1864, Walt Whitman described the arrangement: "I suppose you know that what we call hospital here in the field, is nothing but a collection of tents on the bare ground for a floor, rather hard accommodation for a sick man—they heat them there by digging a long trough in the ground under them, covering it over with old railroad iron & earth, & then building a fire at one end & letting it draw through & go out at the other, as both ends are open—this heats the ground through the middle of the hospital quite hot."[25]

The military surgeons faced great difficulties, but they could rely on the support of the United States Sanitary Commission. When the war erupted in 1861, it did so at the beginning of the age of mass media. The first global celebrity was Florence Nightingale. "The wounded from the battle-plain, / In dreary hospitals of pain, / The cheerless corridors, / The cold and stony floors. / Lo! in that house of misery / A lady with a lamp I see / Pass through the glimmering gloom / And flit from room to room."[26] Thus the American poet Henry Wadsworth Longfellow had fixed the Nightingale brand in his poem "Santa Filomena," written four years before the Southern states seceded from the Union. Many women in the North, inspired by the lady with a lamp, decided to establish local relief associations to teach nurses how to help the wounded. As these initiatives mushroomed, a number of prominent New York City leaders (all male) intervened to ensure the experience of the British Army in the Crimea would not be repeated. By rousing public opinion, they forced the federal government and the Union Army to adopt precautionary measures to protect the lives and safety of the men in the field, and they also created the United States Sanitary Commission.[27] A private agency organized in local chapters—by 1863 there were more than 7,000—and supported by

24 Charles Stuart Tripler, letter to Randolph Barnes Marcy, Nov. 25, 1861, as quoted in *The War of the Rebellion: A Compilation of the Official Records of the Union and Confederate Armies*, ed. Robert N. Scott, 4 ser. (Washington, DC: Government Printing Office, 1880–1901), ser. 1, vol. 5, 664–65.
25 Walt Whitman, letter to Louisa Whitman, Feb. 12, 1864, in "Walt Whitman in Wartime: Familiar Letters from the Capital," *Century Illustrated Monthly Magazine*, n. s., 24 (May–Oct. 1893), 846.
26 Henry Wadsworth Longfellow, "Santa Filomena," *Atlantic Monthly* 1, no. 1 (Nov. 1857), 22–23.
27 Charles J. Stillé, *History of the United States Sanitary Commission* (Philadelphia: Lippincott, 1866), 27, 29.

donations, the US Sanitary Commission was authorized by the federal government in June 1861. Men were to be in charge, but tens of thousands of women, most of them volunteers, provided the muscle by raising funds, running kitchens, and working as nurses. They included the well-known author Louisa May Alcott, philanthropist Almira Fales, and educational reformer Eliza Emily Chappell Porter.

At once a committee went to work to create a series of guidelines for the design and construction of Union Army military hospitals. It looked to debates that had taken place in Britain in the past couple of years, in which Nightingale had played a dominant role. The resulting discussions and insights included Nightingale's observation that "All experience tells the same tale, both among sick and well. Men will have a high rate of mortality in large barracks, a low one in separate huts, even with a much less amount of cubic space. The example which France and Belgium have lately set us of separating their hospitals in a number of distinct pavilions, containing generally not more than 100 sick each, should be everywhere imitated."[28] It took the committee only a month to issue a first set of recommendations to the US government: "Hereafter instead of hiring old buildings for General Hospitals they should order the erection of a sufficient number of wooden shanties or pavilions of appropriate construction, and fully provided with water for bathing, washing, and water-closets, and ample arrangements for ventilation and for securing warmth in winter, to accommodate from thirty to sixty each, and to be sufficiently distant not to poison each other." The committee also suggested the creation of "two cheap temporary model hospitals at Washington."[29] One of these was to be built in Judiciary Square, the other at Mount Pleasant.

The buildings that arose followed the principles established by Nightingale, but their initial execution was poor. The Judiciary Square Hospital consisted of ten single-room wards attached to a central spine; although these wards were cross-ventilated, the walls separating them from the corridor did not go to the peak of the roof, allowing air to circulate from one ward to the next. The Armory Square Hospital, designed by assistant surgeon

28 Florence Nightingale, *Notes on Hospitals: Being Two Papers Read before the National Association for the Promotion of Social Science, at Liverpool, in October 1858. With Evidence Given to the Royal Commissioners on the State of the Army in 1857* (London: Parker, 1859), 7–8.
29 "Sanitary Commission No. 23," *Documents of the U.S. Sanitary Commission*, vol. 1, nos. 1–60 (New York: Sanitary Commission, 1866), 8, 21.

Fig. 11
Exterior of Armory Square Hospital, 1863. Collection: Library of Congress, Washington, DC.

Joseph Janvier Woodward and constructed in Mount Pleasant, near the Smithsonian Institution, was a clear improvement. Its design reflected a general agreement on the basic principles informing the design of the hospitals: single-story barracks connected by covered walkways.[30] Those buildings that were used as sick wards were equipped with ridge ventilation, air shafts, and floor inlets. But too many issues were unresolved. What was the ideal length, width, and height of a pavilion? How far should pavilions be spaced from one another? In the case of the Armory Square Hospital, the width separating the wards was deemed to be too narrow. And, of course, there was the all-important question concerning the location of the toilets. It took many tries before these issues were sorted out.

Fig. 12
Interior of a ward of Armory Square Hospital, 1863. Collection: Metropolitan Museum of Art, New York.

30 Smart, *The Medical and Surgical History of the War of the Rebellion*, pt. 3, vol. 1, *Medical History*, 936–37.

William A. Hammond, who had served for a decade as an army surgeon before being given a professorship at the University of Maryland, proved instrumental in establishing strict standards of hospital design. When the Civil War broke out, Hammond left his professorship to accept a new commission. An excellent scientist, Hammond had read up on the latest theories of hospital design. He knew of Jean-Baptiste Le Roy and Charles-François Viel's plan, drawn in the 1770s, for a new Hôtel-Dieu in Paris, had studied the experiences of the British and the French in the Crimea, and was familiar with Nightingale's ideas. Yet he was also a very practical man, shaped by life on the frontier, and believed that key issues in the design of barrack hospitals were to be resolved not by elite architects and engineers but through the collaboration of military surgeons and local craftsmen.

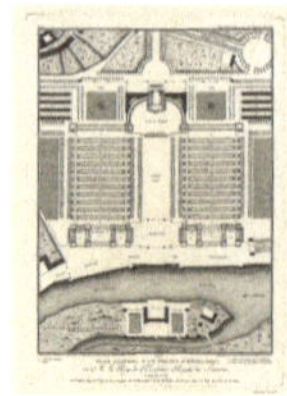

Chapter Three, Fig. 7
→ p. 127

In the fall of 1861, Hammond found himself on duty in the wilds of West Virginia, where he met assistant army surgeon Edward Swift Dunster, who had been charged with setting up a small military hospital. He counseled Dunster to use two wooden pavilions, as in Nightingale's design, but to improve air circulation by including the ridge ventilation the British sanitary commission had introduced in the barracks built in the Crimea. The result was a hospital consisting of two pavilions that were 40 meters long, 7.5 meters wide, and 4.3 meters high.[31] In early 1862, serving as a military surgeon on the front, Hammond gladly took a break from his daily duties to inspect two field hospitals on behalf of the US Sanitary Commission. One was located in requisitioned buildings in Cumberland, Maryland, and Hammond was appalled by its "sanitary evils." He suggested that it move into thirteen specially built barracks, with ten accommodating fifty patients each, and three for offices and kitchens. "These huts should be each 150 × 30 feet [45 × 9 meters], ten feet [3 meters] high at the eaves, and unceiled. Each would, therefore, have over 70,000 cubic feet [2,000 cubic meters], if the roof, which it should be, is sufficiently high pitched. They should be ventilated at the sides and ends by windows, and at the top by ridge ventilation. [...] These huts should be so placed that the wind, no matter from what quarter it should blow, would circulate freely around them."[32] The barracks Hammond proposed reflected, by and large, the design of those built by men like Rosecrans and the ideas about sick pavilions propagated by Nightingale. While they were to have the simple construction of the barracks in the recruitment

31 Samuel Dunster, *Henry Dunster and His Descendants* (Attleborough, MA, and Central Falls, RI: Freeman & Co., 1876), 319–20; William A. Hammond, *A Treatise on Hygiene with Special Reference to the Military Science* (Philadelphia: Lippincott, 1863), 361; Smart, *The Medical and Surgical History of the War of the Rebellion*, pt. 3, vol. 1, *Medical History*, 908.

32 United States Sanitary Commission, *Two Reports on the Condition of Military Hospitals at Grafton, Va., and Cumberland, Md.* (New York: Bryant & Co., 1862), 37–38.

training camps, they were to show in their dimensions an affinity with Nightingale's pavilions: the width, which was of key importance in terms of cross ventilation, was to be identical, but they were to be 30 percent longer, and the number of beds was to be 50 percent greater, leading to a 15 percent higher density of occupation.

After receiving Hammond's report, the lead physician of the Sanitary Commission believed he had found the perfect man to take on the role of surgeon general of the Union Army. Secretary of War Edwin McMasters Stanton initially resisted Hammond's appointment, as Hammond had very low seniority. But the commission convinced President Lincoln, who appointed Hammond as surgeon general, despite Stanton's objections, in April 1862. Hammond lost no time reforming the army's medical service, beginning by appointing new department heads and cutting red tape. He centralized the military hospital authority and initiated, in collaboration with the army's Quartermaster Department in Philadelphia, a large program of hospital construction that reflected all he had learned from the European debates. His most important collaborator was the well-known Philadelphia architect John McArthur Jr., best known as the designer of Philadelphia City Hall.[33] McArthur joined the Quartermaster Department on July 1, 1862, and became responsible for the construction of military hospitals, including the largest one built during the Civil War, the Satterlee General Hospital in the western outskirts of Philadelphia. Constructed in forty days (a number with biblical resonance) it consisted of two parallel galleries that were connected halfway by an administration building and thirty barracks, of which twenty-eight functioned as sick wards and two as kitchens and laundries. In addition, the hospital grounds contained barracks that housed a barbershop, a dispensary, a library and reading room, various smoking rooms, a post office, a carpenter shop, a printing office, and dormitories for guards. The official capacity was 1,960 patients in summer and around 1,400 in winter.

→ Fig. 13

33 Lawrence Wodehouse, "John McArthur, Jr. (1823–1890)," *Journal of the Society of Architectural Historians* 28 (1969), 277.

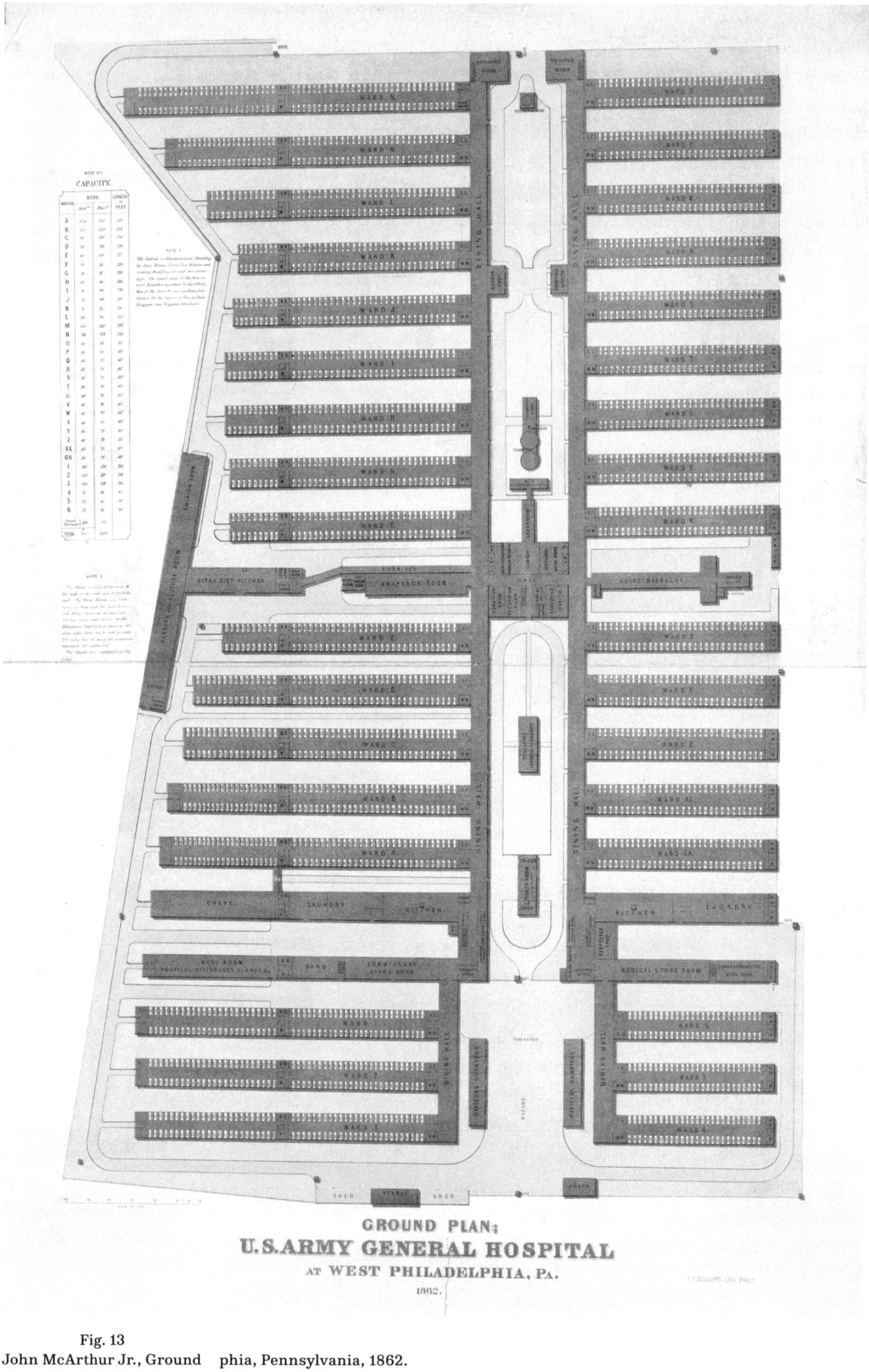

Fig. 13
John McArthur Jr., Ground plan of the US (Union) Army's Satterlee General Hospital in West Philadelphia, Pennsylvania, 1862. Collection: Library Company of Philadelphia, Pennsylvania.

At the end of October 1862, a few months after Satterlee's completion, Dr. Isaac Israel Hayes, the physician in charge, expressed his satisfaction with the general arrangement and the preparations undertaken for the coming winter.

> In relation to the fitness of the building for hospital purposes and the advantages and disadvantages of the plan, I am not able to speak with the accuracy which is desirable, the hospital only having been in use during the summer; but thus far it has borne the test very well, and I entertain no doubt that as a winter hospital it will prove to be both comfortable and healthy. The parallelism and closeness of the wards to each other I have not found to be practically objectionable. The circulation of air has been good and the wards were reasonably cool during the hot weather. The wards have been always free from odor and the air fresh. The long corridors give great facilities for atmospheric circulation. The ventilation, however, is imperfect and must be changed for winter use. The ventilators of the first twenty wards are too open and too large, and of the eight other wards the ventilator roof is four inches [10 centimeters] too high; it should, besides, project one foot [30 centimeters] farther. The plan is in most respects admirably arranged for administration, the chief fault being in the division of the kitchens and their distance from the offices; its principal merit is its compactness, and it is recommended by the ease with which every part of the building may be reached. If it did not involve two kitchens I should prefer it to any other which I have seen. The disadvantages anticipated from the parallelism of the wards is found to be trifling in practice. The building is now being plastered and will be rendered tight and comfortable. It will be heated by means of coal-stoves, of which 200 are now being put up.[34]

It is very likely that McArthur also wrote the specifications for the pavilions Hammond summarized in his 1863 book *A Treatise on Hygiene with Special Reference to the Military Service*. The plan for the pavilion of the Crittenden General Hospital in Louisville, Kentucky, reflected the guidelines established by Dr. Hammond.

34 Smart, *The Medical and Surgical History of the War of Rebellion*, pt. 3, vol. 1, *Medical History*, 930.

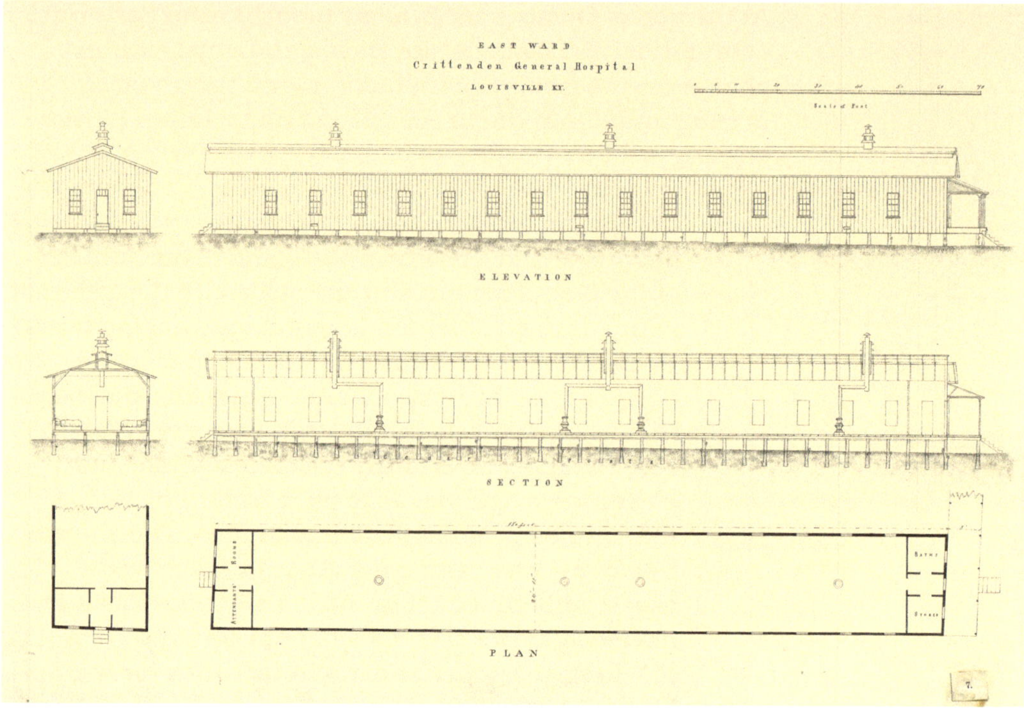

Fig. 14
Elevation, section, and plan of a pavilion of the US (Union) Army's Crittenden General Hospital in Louisville, Kentucky, c. 1863. Collection: US National Archives, College Park, Maryland.

Hospitals, he advised, both permanent and temporary, ought to consist of independent wards arranged in an oblong shape, "the form which is best adapted for the arrangement of beds, and supplying the patients with sufficient light and fresh air without wasting space. The width should not exceed twenty-five feet [7.5 meters], a space which will allow seven feet six inches [2.3 meters] for the length of each bed, with a passage of ten feet [3 meters] between the rows. If the width is greater than this, the distance between the windows is such as to prevent free ventilation; if less, sufficient room is not afforded." The bed, he decreed, should be 1 meter wide, and there should be 1.2 meters of space between beds. "Every patient in such institutions," Hammond insisted, "should receive, as a *minimum allowance*, 1200 cubic feet [34 cubic meters] of space, about 87 [2.5 cubic meters] of which should be superficial. If less than this is allotted to him, an offense is committed against the laws of human health, which can only be excused on the ground of absolute necessity." Hammond noted that "in temporary hospitals, ventilated at the ridge and furnished with a sufficient number of windows, less than this will suffice"; in such wards, the allowance should be at least 27 cubic meters. As to the arrangement of the wards, Hammond was explicit: "No other arrangement than that which entirely separates the wards from each other is worthy of consideration, except to receive condemnation."[35]

35 Hammond, *A Treatise on Hygiene*, 324–25, 331.

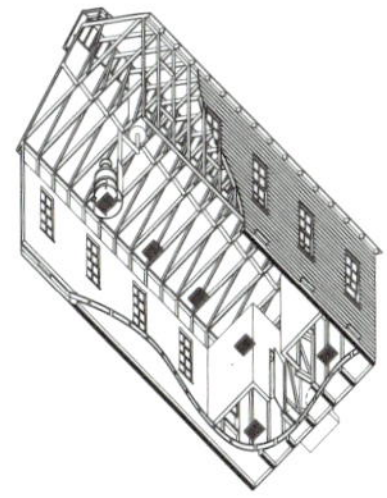

Drawings,
Hammond's Pavilion
→ p. 512

These principles structured the official guidelines Secretary of War Stanton issued to the Union Army in July 1864 and were to be universally applied and "deviated from only in cases of imperative necessity." The illustrated guidelines stipulated, "General hospitals will be constructed on the principle of detached pavilions, each ward being a separate building. [...] Each ward will be a ridge-ventilated pavilion one hundred and eighty-seven by twenty-four (187 × 24) feet [57 × 7.3 meters]." They also specified that "the wards will be fourteen (14) feet [4.3 meters] high from floor to eaves—the pitch of the roof to vary in accordance to the materials composing it. The floor to be elevated at least eighteen (18) inches [46 centimeters] from the soil, with free ventilation beneath it. A ward thus constructed will accommodate sixty (60) patients, allowing more than one thousand (1000) cubic feet [28 cubic meters] of air-space to each." The ventilation system was a key component of the design: "During warm and mild weather the wards will be ventilated by the ridge (*Figure 7*), but during winter the ridge will be closed (*Figure 8*), and ventilation by shafts substituted. Four stoves will be allowed to a ward, each partly surrounded by a jacket of zinc or sheet-iron, with an air-box beneath it to furnish the supply of fresh air. At eight (8) feet [2.4 meters] from the stove will be a shaft, properly capped, through which the stove-pipe will ascend. *Figure 8* gives a section and *Figure 9* a side view of the arrangement."[36]

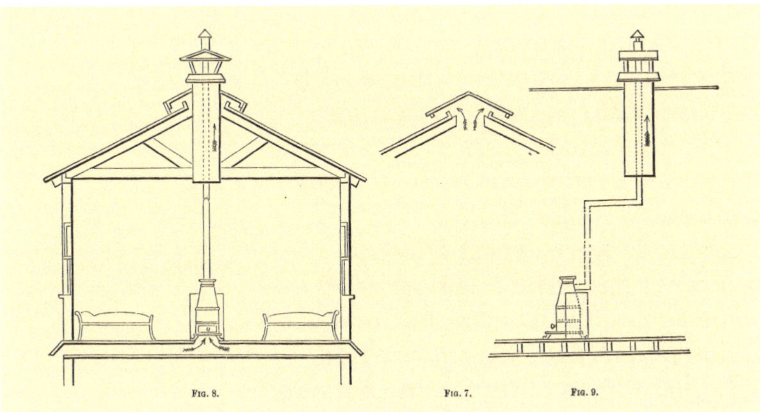

Fig. 15
Sections showing the ventilation options in summer and winter for a standard ward of a general hospital as prescribed in Secretary of War Edwin Stanton's guidelines of July 1864, from US War Department, Surgeon General's Office, *Circular No. 6: Reports on the Extent and Nature of the Materials Available for the Preparation of a Medical and Surgical History of the Rebellion*, 1865. Collection: author.

The official guidelines of 1864 only confirmed what had been more or less standard practice for two years. Since the beginning of 1862, every week, the Union Army built another large hospital consisting of a collection of single-story wooden pavilions, usually attached to a covered walkway. In their plan, these hospitals were both similar and different: one or two spines, consisting of a covered walkway, connected the sick wards and

36 US War Department, Surgeon General's Office, *Circular No. 6: Reports on the Extent and Nature of the Materials Available for the Preparation of a Medical and Surgical History of the Rebellion* (Philadelphia: Lippincolt & Co., 1865), 153–55.

the other buildings. The hospital's spine might be a straight line, or two parallel lines, a half-circle, a full circle, or an oval; the form and arrangement chosen depended either on the fancy of the surgeon in charge, who was able to arrange the barracks along this system of circulation as he saw fit, or on the shape and condition of the site available—or both.

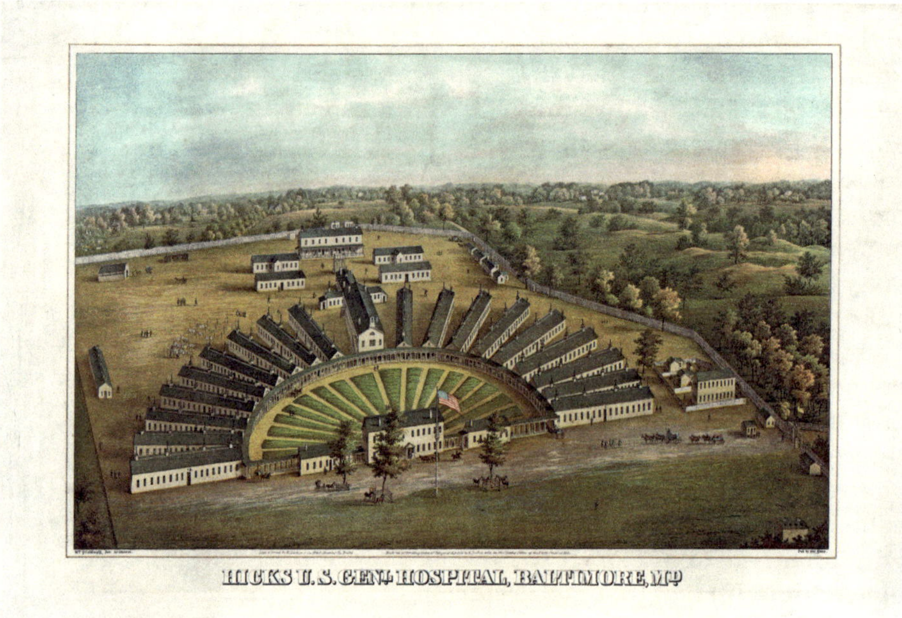

Fig. 16
The US (Union) Army's Hicks General Hospital, Baltimore, Maryland, 1865. Collection: Library of Congress, Washington, DC.

But the general shape of the plan did not matter. What *did* matter was that each hospital was conceived as part of a network. The value was not in individual units or hospitals but in their standardization and proliferation, which allowed military surgeons not only to move with ease from one hospital to another but also to compare the effectiveness of procedures and treatments. The pavilions were also part of an open system: once the designs had been issued, anyone could make them.

Some hospital pavilions were established in former assembly or winter camps. The adaptation of the Carver Barracks was deemed a success, but in most cases, the transformation of barracks hastily erected for use by soldiers, who spent most of their time outside, into wards for sick and wounded soldiers, who spent most if not all of their time inside, was difficult. "The essential change involved the adaptation of the former company dormitories for use as hospital wards," noted a lengthy official report on the medical history of the Civil War, published twenty-three years after the conflict's end. "These dormitories were generally long, low and narrow one-story frame buildings, roughly constructed, imperfectly lighted, frequently with windows only on one side, unventilated save by the doors, windows and unauthorized crevices, and fitted up with single or double bunks in two or three tiers." Too narrow to allow for beds positioned perpendicular to each of the sides, and too low to provide adequate ventilation, most of these barracks also lacked an air space below the floors, while many of them had earth embanked against the lower part of the walls to prevent drafts. "To adapt these to hospital purposes," the report explained, "the earth was cleared away from the walls and provision, if possible, made for some air-movement beneath the buildings. The floors were repaired; additional windows were inserted. The ridge was laid open for ventilation in summer and louvered exits were provided for winter use, with inlet openings near the stoves. Ventilating apertures were made in the walls, and the unauthorized crevices closed by laths and plaster in the interior and weather-boarding on the exterior."[37] One of those adaptive-reuse projects was the Campbell General Hospital, where Whitman had attended to Private John Holmes. Another hospital arose at Camp Dennison. In 1862, onehalf of the camp was cleared of 300 or so barracks built under the supervision of Rosecrans, as they did not fit the minimum hygienic standards articulated by Surgeon General Hammond. They were replaced by a long row of sixty-seven regulation barracks that were to serve as the hospital.

Most hospitals arose, however, on greenfield sites. The most famous of these was Lincoln Hospital, located on Capitol Hill in Washington, DC. It consisted of two walkways forming two sides of a triangle.

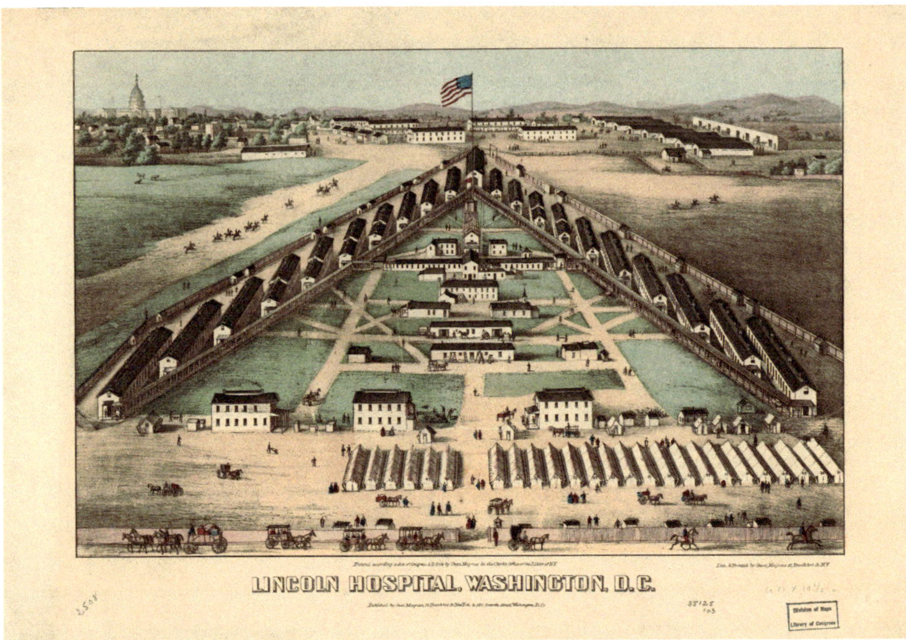

Fig. 17
The US (Union) Army's Lincoln Hospital, Washington, DC, 1865. Collection: Library of Congress, Washington, DC.

37 Smart, *The Medical and Surgical History of the War of Rebellion*, pt. 3, vol. 1, *Medical History*, 909.

Ten wards connected to each walkway. The surgeon in charge described them as follows: “The *Wards* are pavilion barracks, built of rough boards, white-washed, with roofs of boards covered with tarred paper; they are twenty (20) in number, ten on each wing. Each ward is 187 feet by 24 [57 by 7.3 meters], 16 feet [5 meters] to the eaves and 20 [6 meters] to the ridge, at which there is the usual ridge-ventilation the whole length of the ward. They are plastered on the inside for about eight feet [2.4 meters] above the floor.” He continued,

> Each ward contains thirty-four windows and four doors, one at each end and two in the middle, opposite each other. Four ventilating gratings, at regular distances in the floor of the ward, communicate by wooden flues under the floor with the air outside, thus giving a full supply of fresh air whenever the weather requires the doors and windows to be closed. With sixty-two patients, there are 72 square feet [6.7 square meters] of floor and 1447 cubic feet [41 cubic meters] of air-space for each. Thirty-one beds are arranged on each side, with a chair and bedside table between each pair. An avenue of eleven feet [3.4 meters] is left between the two rows of beds.[38]

Fig. 18
Interior of one of the wards of Lincoln Hospital, 1865. Collection: US National Library of Medicine, Bethesda, Maryland.

38 In Joseph Janvier Woodward, “Hospital Organization and Construction,” in War Department, Surgeon General’s Office, *Circular No. 6*, 155.

One of the most remarkable innovations in the design of the Lincoln Hospital was the way the wards were supplied. A Surgeon General's Office report explains: "On the inner side of the two wings of the hospital, and running the whole length of each, is a raised covered walk or corridor, on which is laid a railway track two feet [60 centimeters] wide and 2156 feet [657 meters] long. Box-cars convey the food from the main and extra kitchens to each ward."[39] This covered walkway was an effective countermeasure against the most important nuisance that resulted, and still results, from the rapid erection of temporary accommodations on sites that are not properly prepared for drainage: the slimy and slippery presence of mud.

In the twenty months of its existence, the Lincoln Hospital admitted a total of 21,379 sick and wounded. Of those, 1,221 died—a mortality rate of 6 percent. Such statistics impressed at the time and still do today. But they do not mean that these hospitals were gentle places. "The Government [...] is anxious and liberal in its practice toward its sick," Whitman observed, adding that many of the officials working in the hospitals acted like petty tyrants. "Some of the ward doctors are careless, rude, capricious, needlessly strict. One I found who prohibited the men from all enlivening amusements; I found him sending men to the guard-house for the most trifling offence. In general, perhaps, the officials—especially the new ones, with their straps or badges—put on too many airs. Of all places in the world, the hospitals of American young men and soldiers, wounded in the volunteer service of their country, ought to be exempt from mere conventional military airs and etiquette of shoulder-straps. But they are not exempt."[40] And yet the results obtained stood out: over the whole military hospital system, which admitted more than a million casualties, the average mortality was 8 percent. This compared favorably with the record of military hospitals during the Crimean War, when the Koulali and the Scutari general hospitals showed mortality rates of 26 and 12 percent, respectively.

Dr. Hammond's pavilions not only served to provide accommodation to sick and wounded soldiers in general hospitals. They also were used in hospitals constructed in the convalescent camps created by the US Sanitation Commission, providing the first of two levels of halfway house between establishments such as the Lincoln Hospital and the regiments at the front. The most famous of these was located near Fairfax, Virginia, not far from Washington, DC.

39 Ibid.

40 Walt Whitman, *The Wound Dresser: A Series of Letters Written from the Hospitals in Washington during the War of the Rebellion*, ed. Richard Maurice Burke (Boston: Small, Maynard & Company, 1898), 9–10.

A lithographed map, printed for fundraising purposes, shows the general arrangement.

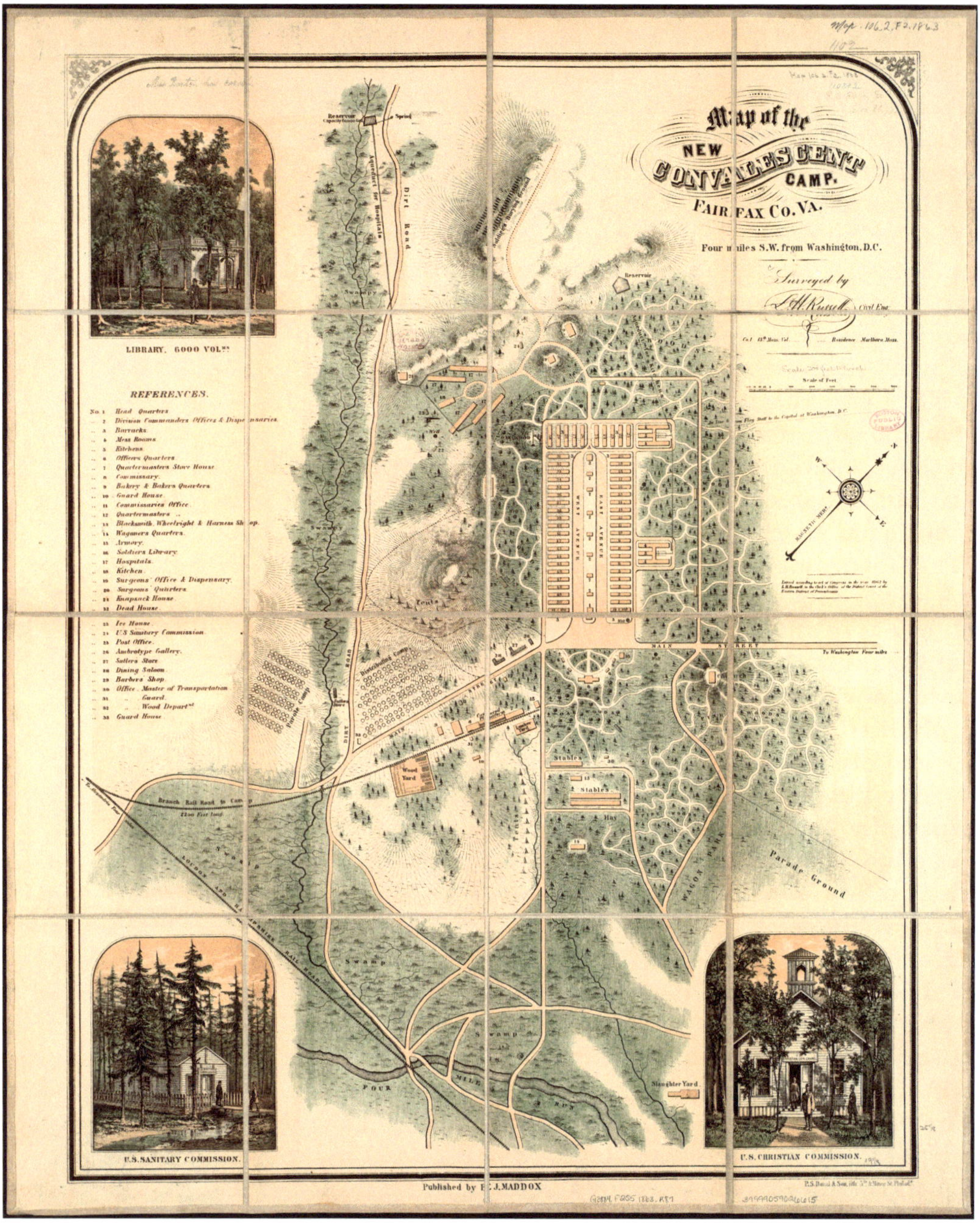

Fig. 19
Lauriman H. Russell, Map of a US (Union) Army convalescent camp, Fairfax County, Virginia, 1863. Collection: Norman B. Leventhal Map Center, Boston Public Library, Boston.

The U-shaped camp, designed and constructed under the guidance of Captain Joshua Norton, consisted of fifty dormitory barracks measuring 23 by 6 meters that accommodated 100 convalescing soldiers each. In addition, the camp contained two kitchens connected to four messrooms, a post office, a library, a chapel, a bakery, a blacksmith shop, an armory, offices, stables, and a variety of other buildings to support life in the camp. These are located in what appears—at least on paper—

to be an almost park-like setting. A hospital consisting of four pavilions took care of those who had been discharged a bit too hastily from the general hospital or had fallen ill in the camp. An area of the map labeled "Distributing Camp," made up of conical Sibley tents, constitutes the second halfway house. There soldiers discharged from the convalescent camp to go back into regular military service were housed until transport to the front was available.

To be sure, the number of soldiers of the Union Army who died as the result of dysentery, typhoid, pneumonia, measles, tuberculosis, malaria, and other diseases—caused by the overcrowded and unhygienic conditions in which they had to live during campaigns, often without access to potable water—far exceeded the number of soldiers who died as the result of gunshots, accidents, and suicide. Yet most of these men succumbed to these diseases in the field or during transport, before they reached a hospital. However, the quick creation of 202 general hospitals with 136,894 beds, and the system of aftercare represented by the convalescent camps, combined with the relatively low mortality of the patients admitted to these places, were sufficient causes for self-congratulation, in which assistant surgeon Woodward—the de facto architect of Armory Square Hospital—engaged during an overview of the achievement of the US Sanitary Commission, Surgeon General Hammond, his colleagues, and himself: "Never before, in the history of the world, was so vast a system of hospitals brought into existence in so short a time. Never before were such establishments, in time of war, so little crowded or so liberally supplied." Until the Civil War, army hospitals had been more lethal than the battlefield. Supported by enlightened political and military administrations, American army surgeons had been able to dramatically reverse this proportion. "Never before, in the history of the world, has the mortality in military hospitals been so small, and never have such establishments so completely escaped from diseases generated within their walls," Woodward proclaimed.[41]

Undoubtedly, the fact that the Confederate States Army had little to show in terms of innovative military hospital design played a role in the way those who believed in the righteousness of the Union celebrated the achievement that centered on Surgeon General Hammond's pavilion. The Confederate military hospital created on Chimborazo Hill on the outskirts of Richmond, Virginia, by the eminent local physician Dr. James Brown McCaw applied the most important lesson from

41 Woodward, "Hospital Organization and Construction," 152.

the Crimean War by dispersing the wounded and sick in many smaller buildings. By the end of 1862, the Chimborazo Hospital complex consisted of ninety-eight barracks, each designed to hold thirty-two patients. Yet neither the design of the ward—which, equipped with few small windows and lacking ridge ventilation, appeared to be a mere shack compared to Surgeon General Hammond's pavilion—nor that of the Chimborazo Hospital as a whole, which lacked the functional articulation of the hospitals constructed by the Union Army, was ever made the object of much reflection or representation.[42]

Fig. 20
Distant view of the Confederate States Army's Chimborazo Hospital, Richmond, Virginia, 1865. Collection: Library of Congress, Washington, DC.

In 1865 and 1866, many took Woodward's self-congratulation at face value, and this helps explain the incredible impact the Civil War hospitals constructed by the Union Army would have on the theory of hospital design during the next seven years. But a sober reassessment of the performance of Dr. Hammond's barracks, undertaken twenty years later, provided a useful footnote to this story of undoubted achievement. "The experience of the war was decidedly in favor of the pavilion system, each pavilion constituting a single ward isolated from adjacent buildings by somewhat more than its own width, and connected by a covered walk with the other buildings of the hospital," observed Major Charles Smart in his authoritative study on the medical history of the Civil War, published in 1888. Smart had served in the Civil War as acting medical inspector in the Army of the Potomac and in 1883 had become the official in the Surgeon General's Office responsible for the Sanitary Division. "In their aggregation," he continued, "this separation was effected, without removing any of the wards to an inconvenient distance from the administrative and executive buildings,

42 See Carol C. Green, Chimborazo: *The Confederacy's Largest Hospital* (Knoxville: University of Tennesee Press, 2004).

by radiating them around some central point in a form to be determined by the configuration of the ground available for building." So far, so good. Yet experience showed that these hospitals were not perfect. "The length of the pavilion as usually constructed was less than that recommended by the official circular. The latter assigned a length of 165 feet [50 meters] for 60 beds, but the advantage of this over 115 feet [30 meters] for 40 beds, as planned and carried out at the SEDGWICK HOSPITAL, may readily be questioned. The reports of our medical officers show a decided preference for a ward containing not over 50 beds. The experience of the British in the Crimea with similar pavilions was in favor of a ward containing only from 20 to 36 patients, as giving better ventilation and greater comfort and economy of labor than one of larger capacity."[43] Smart added that Dr. Hammond's barracks provided less floor space per bed than the British model: 19.5 square meters instead of 26.5 square meters. Another issue was the location of the toilets, which provided an unpleasant environment for patients located nearby.

Smart provided a lengthy account of the pragmatic way the management of these hospitals continued to make modifications, especially in the ventilation system.

> During the first summer of their use the wooden pavilions, open at the ridge, were conceived to fulfil all the requirements of a hospital-ward. The free communication with the external atmosphere furnished by the open ridge seemed to guarantee a purity of the air within, which, however, was not always found. The obvious explanation of this led immediately to the introduction of counter-openings along the wall near the level of the floor. These were provided with sliding-panels for closure in breezy or chilly weather, when the open ridge alone sufficed to give a free ventilation. But it frequently happened during the calm hot days of summer that, with all these provisions for the inlet and outflow of air, its stagnation in the wards was not overcome, and hospital gangrene occasionally appeared in pavilions crowded with wounded men. [...] Apertures do not create a movement; they merely permit it to take place when forces naturally or artificially directed have called it into existence. When no aspiratory force operated as an exhaust at the ridge, and no material difference between the external and internal temperatures developed an inward current, the open ridge and

43 Smart, *The Medical and Surgical History of the War of Rebellion*, pt. 3, vol. 1, *Medical History*, 950–51.

> floor apertures became for the time being valueless. In one of the Washington hospitals an effort was made to work fans by hand-power over any or all of the beds of a ward; but this was intended more for the comfort of the patients in sultry weather than as a method of artificial ventilation.[44]

At the onset of winter, the ridge ventilation had to be closed, as it caused the ward to become too cold. This necessitated the introduction of a ventilation system that consisted of air shafts and that used the draft created by the stoves. Yet, by and large, "this system of ventilation gave satisfactory results."

Smart noted that overall the hospitals had worked well enough, but he also admitted that the Union had been very, very lucky in that none of the hospitals had burned down.

> In the early period of the history of these hospitals no efficient provision was made against danger from fire. [...] The means of guarding against this danger became a subject of special inquiry by inspectors, and in a short time each hospital endeavored to rival the others in the efficiency of its fire department. Had a fire attained any headway among pavilions covered with tarred paper and massed together as were those of the SATTERLEE and many other hospitals, it is hardly to be supposed that the engine and hose would have preserved the establishment; but the fire-drill and the fire-buckets and axes in every ward, by keeping constantly before the inmates the imminence of the danger, led to such precautions and vigilance that fire was either prevented or detected and suppressed in its incipiency.[45]

Yes, these hospitals had been conceived under a lucky star. The question was, of course, whether the expectation of luck is an acceptable element in future planning.

None of the hospitals was lost by fire—but all were pulled down within years after the end of the Civil War, mostly to make place for residential development. A lithographed plan of the site of Satterlee General Hospital, now to be occupied by one-family houses, provides a somewhat melancholic coda to one of the most interesting episodes in the architectural history of the Americas—and the first one that gave Europeans a sense that the New World might teach them a lesson or two about construction.

44 Ibid., 952.
45 Ibid., 955.

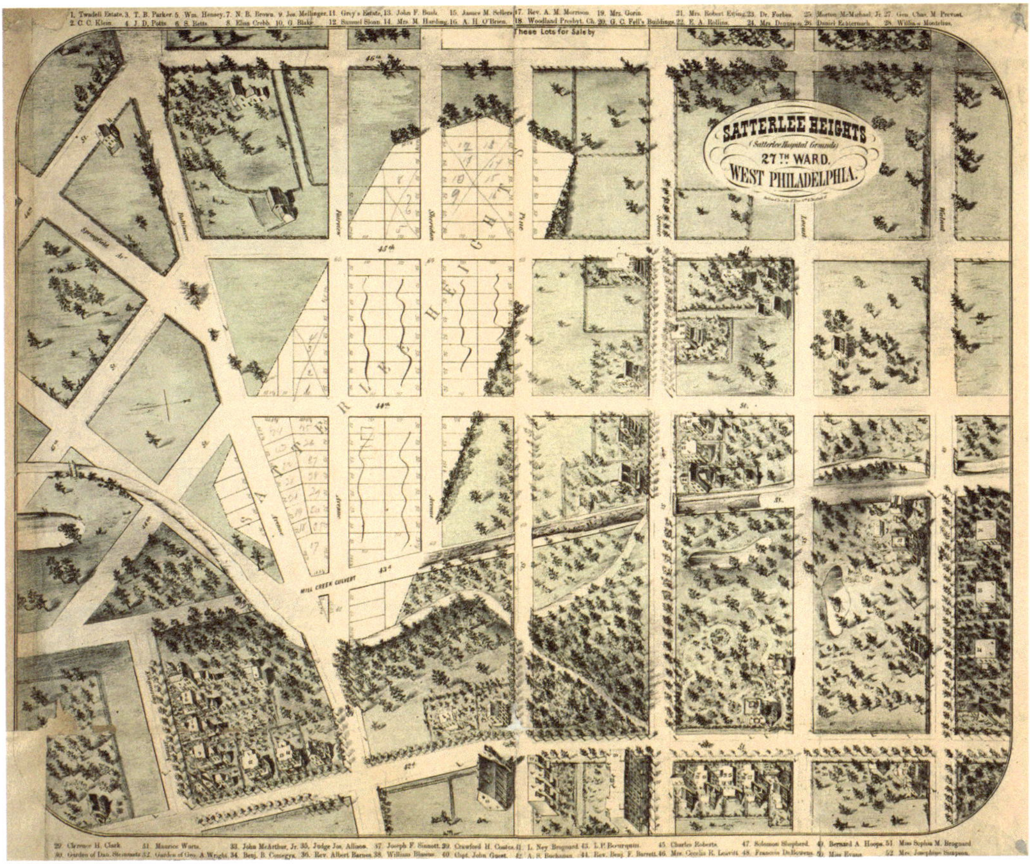

Fig. 21
Satterlee Heights. Satterlee Hospital Grounds, 27th Ward. West Philadelphia, 1870. Collection: Library Company of Philadelphia, Pennsylvania.

Einstöckiger hölzerner Pav

Giebelansicht.

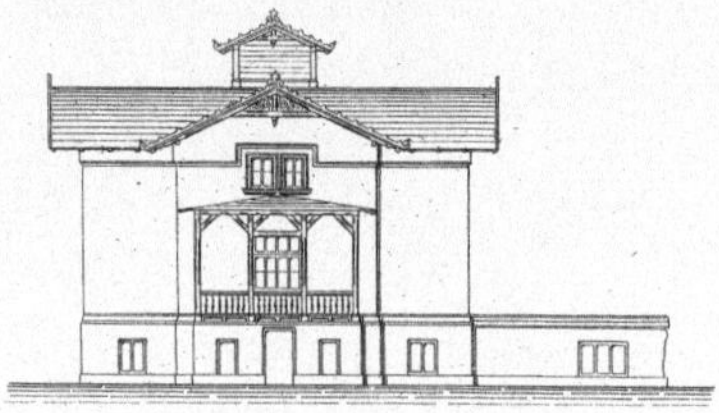

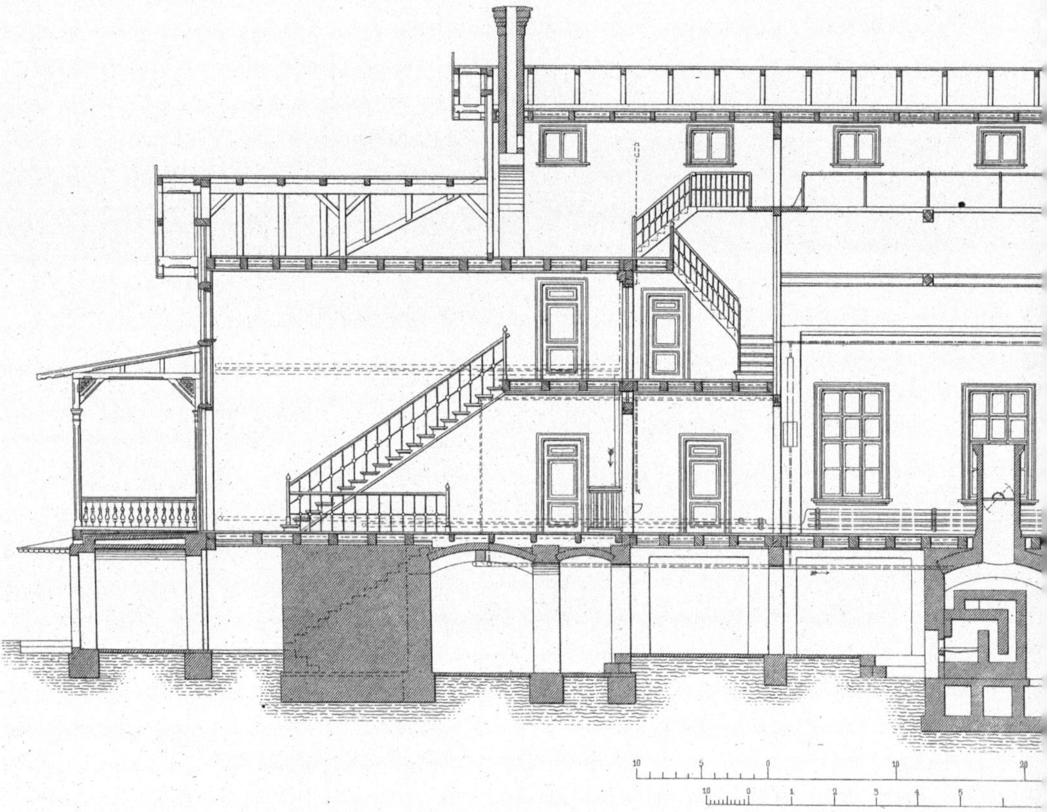

→ p. 263

t.

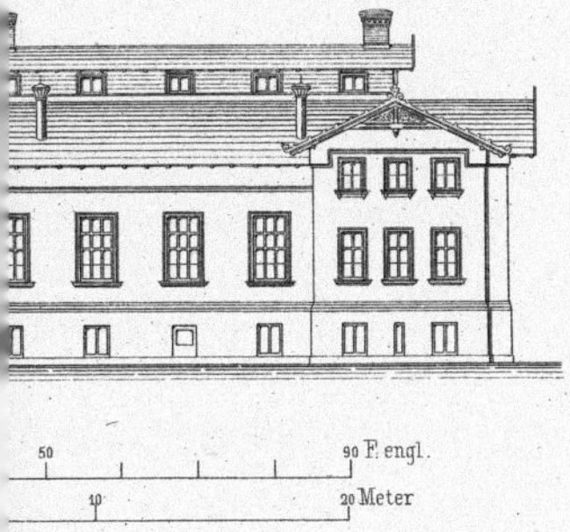

Giebelansicht.

schnitt.

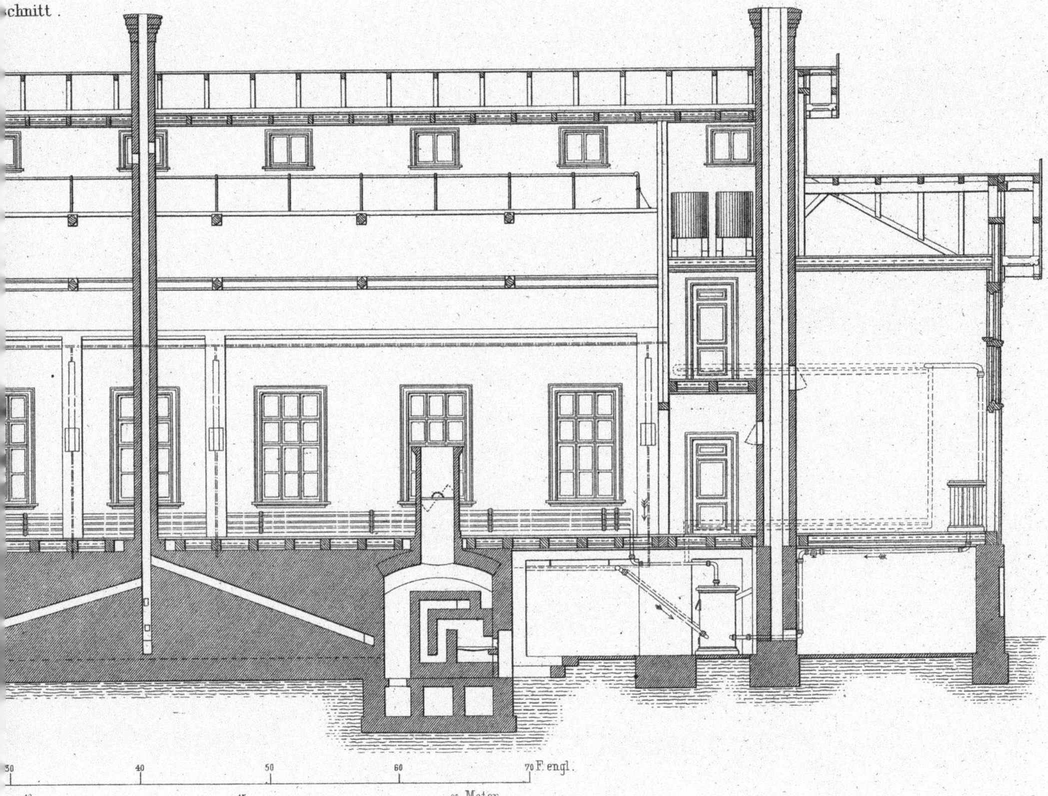

& Korn. Berlin.

gest.

Six

Learning From America

On August 31, 1867, *The Illustrated London News* carried a half-page illustration showing a plan, elevation, two sections, and a chimney detail of a building identified in the caption as a "hospital pavilion of the construction adopted by the United States government," inviting readers to look for a description on the next page.

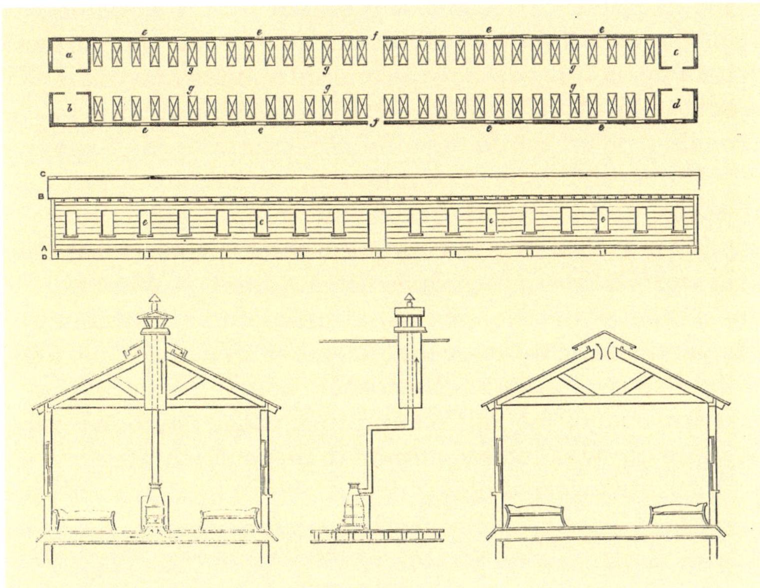

Fig. 1
Plan, elevation, and sections for the hospital pavilion adopted by the United States Army on recommendation by Surgeon General William A. Hammond, *The Illustrated London News*, 1867. Collection: author.

Because of its technical nature, the diagram was a rather odd choice for a popular magazine and very different from the normal pictorial fare found on the pages of this publication, and few of its readers would have been able to understand its conventions. The article on the next page was a lengthy extract from a report on a display of new developments in the design of barracks and hutted military hospitals, written by a veteran of the Crimean War, Major Arthur Leahy of the Royal Engineers. He noted that since the Crimean War, "great attention has been directed to the construction, equipment, and administration of military hospitals and barracks; valuable statistics have been collected, important principles of construction have been enunciated and carried out, the system of hospital administration has been improved, and greater importance has been attached to sanitary science in all its branches."[1] Leahy noted that the 1867 Exposition Universelle (Universal Exhibition) in Paris, which had been opened early in the year by Emperor Napoleon III, contained many exhibits dealing with hospital and barrack construction, including

1 Arthur Leahy, "Military Hospital and Barrack Buildings," *The Illustrated London News*, Aug. 31, 1867, 250.

an exhibition of American military hospitals constructed during the Civil War. Leahy was generous in his praise for these hospitals, which consisted of an accumulation of separate wards, all provided with excellent cross ventilation and a heating system that pulled fresh air into the building, heating it before it dispensed the air into the ward itself.

The Exposition Universelle in Paris, occupying 70 hectares, was the fourth and greatest international exhibition yet held, covering an area seven times that of Prince Albert's Great Exhibition of 1851 in London. France and Britain were allies but also fierce competitors, driven by an increasingly passionate sense of what it meant to be French and not British, or British and not French. And so, while the official purpose of the Exposition Universelle was to promote universal peace by stressing the essential unity of all humankind, it also tried to clearly articulate national differences. It was the first world's fair to introduce the national pavilion as the symbol of the idea of the nation-state as a community of a particular character that is rooted in a deep past and embodied in a unique inheritance. Located around the gigantic oval of the Palais Omnibus, these pavilions were designed in what was assumed to be each country's architectural vernacular.

Fig. 2
Exposition Universelle, Paris, 1867. The Palais Omnibus, which held the core exhibitions, is located at the center of the Champ de Mars. The pavilions were placed in the gardens to the northwest and southeast. Collection: Bibliothèque Nationale de France, Paris.

Their adjacency suggested that these nations were engaged in the kind of peaceful rivalry that, according to classical liberal doctrine, was to produce progress and wealth. Thus nationalism and globalism were just different sides of, indeed, the same coin.

National rivalry applied to all fields of human endeavor—especially that of war. The 1867 exhibition gave much attention to recent military developments, and visitors browsed exhibitions not only on the latest rifle, field-gun, and battleship technologies, but also on contemporary insights on soldiers' training, which included presentations on the Aldershot and Châlons camps and detailed descriptions of the form and construction of barracks. The presentation of the rapidly increasing capacity for destruction was justified by an extract from a sermon defending armed nationalism given earlier that year in Notre-Dame Cathedral by the famous Roman Catholic preacher Charles Jean Marie Loyson, better known as Père Hyacinthe. While the submission to a greater force may be acceptable in the case of an individual who is willing to become a martyr, it was unacceptable to a nation. "For a nation to turn the other cheek is not an act of moral heroism," Père Hyacinthe asserted, "but both a mistake and a dishonorable act."[2] However, the organizing committee of the military section of the Exposition Universelle did also recognize that the weapons exhibits did not show the whole picture.

> What emerges in a striking way from the examination of so many and so ingenious materials of war, presented at the *Exposition Universelle* of 1867, is the struggle that [...] occurs in the human spirit between two ideas, two opposing tendencies: on the one hand, the keen desire manifested by each nation to make itself formidable, by applying all modern inventions to the improvement of weapons; on the other hand, the also clear desire to soften, as much as possible, the horrors and fatal consequences of the war. It is thus that beside revolvers, needle rifles, Gatling machine guns, torpedoes, and central-battery ironclads, we have seen that all governments have made zealous preparations to fight epidemics, cure the sick, and relieve the wounded; we have witnessed the ceaseless efforts, driven by charitable and humanitarian sentiments of nations, of relief societies in the Old and New Worlds.[3]

2 France, Ministry of War, *Exposition Universelle de 1867 à Paris: Rapport de la Haute Commission Militaire* (Paris: Paul Dumont, 1869), 1244.
3 Ibid. 1239–40.

The humanitarian idea was embodied not only in the models of American military hospitals that had been of interest to Major Leahy but also in a special exhibition created by the Société de Secours aux Blessés Militaires (Society for the Care of Wounded Soldiers), a French relief organization formed three years earlier. This exhibition featured displays by eighteen countries that had signed the Geneva Convention for the Amelioration of the Condition of the Wounded in Armies in the Field (1864), and one that had not yet signed the convention—the United States. Significantly, the society's exhibition buildings were wooden barrack-like pavilions marked with a red cross.

Fig. 3
Pavilions of the Société de Secours aux Blessés Militaires, Exposition Universelle, Paris, 1867, *The Illustrated London News*, 1867. Collection: author.

Thirteen years earlier, when Florence Nightingale and her nurses had left for Scutari, Turkey, they had gone under the auspices of the British government to take care of British soldiers of the Crimean War and had worked in a hospital marked by the Union Jack. But since then, a dramatic change had taken place in civilians' understanding of their moral responsibility for the suffering of soldiers—all soldiers—and their place in international law. This change had been triggered by the Battle of Solferino, on June 24, 1859, the key engagement in the Second Italian War of Independence. (Solferino was the largest battle fought in Europe since the Battle of Leipzig in 1813, which had led to the abdication of Emperor Napoleon I and his exile to Elba—from which he escaped, in 1815, in the failed attempt to regain his empire that led to his second and permanent exile in Saint Helena.) In this particular battle in northern Italy, the combined forces of over 82,000 French and 37,000 Sardinian soldiers defeated the 120,000-man-strong Imperial Austrian Army, which had been the pillar of Habsburg rule in Lombardy and Venetia. In the wake of the battle, thousands of wounded Austrian soldiers were brought to the Lombardian town of Castiglione delle Stiviere, where efforts to organize a volunteer force to help them came to little. The town became an image of hell.

A Swiss businessman, Henri Dunant, found himself in Castiglione, where he encountered thousands of dying soldiers.

Fig. 4
Jean-Louis Barrault as Henri Dunant in the emergency hospital of the church of Castiglione, Italy. Still from the movie *D'Homme à hommes (Man to Men)*, 1948. Collection: International Committee of the Red Cross, Geneva.

"Oh, the agony during those days," he later wrote. "Wounds were infected by the heat and dust, by shortage of water and lack of proper care, and grew more and more painful. Foul exhalations contaminated the air, in spite of the praiseworthy attempts of the authorities to keep hospital areas in a sanitary condition." He recorded with brutal honesty the suffering, filth, and anarchy that marked the aftermath of battle: "With faces black with the flies that swarmed about their wounds, men gazed around them, wild-eyed and helpless. Others were no more than a worm-ridden, inextricable compound of coat and shirt and flesh and blood. Many were shuddering at the thought of being devoured by their worms, which they thought they could see coming out of their bodies."[4]

The Italian townspeople had a profound hatred for the Austrians, but Dunant was able to organize a small group of local volunteers by impressing on them the need to attend to all the wounded without regard for nationality. The group worked in that spirit, repeating what became their mantra: *Tutti fratelli* (All are brothers). Dunant was aware of the moral dilemmas of the situation. "It is," he wrote, "excessively distressing to realize that you can never do more than help those who are just before you." Yet he also was energized by the endeavor. "The moral sense of the importance of human life; the humane desire to lighten a little the torments of all these poor wretches, or restore their shattered courage; the furious and relentless activity which a man summons up

4 Henry Dunant, *A Memory of Solferino* (Geneva: International Committee of the Red Cross, 1986), 60–62.

at such moments: all these combine to create a kind of energy which gives one a positive craving to relieve as many as one can."[5]

Long after his return to Geneva, Dunant remained driven by the suffering he had seen in Castiglione, the result of both the destructive violence of modern weapons and the military medical services' complete inability to deal with their consequences. Dunant realized that war was not only the business of soldiers; civilians too had a responsibility to provide relief. "Would it not be possible," he asked himself, "in time of peace and quiet, to form relief societies for the purpose of having care given to the wounded in wartime by zealous, devoted and thoroughly qualified volunteers?" In 1862, three years after the Battle of Solferino, Dunant published a French-language account of the episode, in which he posed a question to the nations of the world: "In an age when we hear so much of progress and civilization, is it not a matter of urgency, since unhappily we cannot always avoid wars, to press forward in a human and truly civilized spirit the attempt to prevent, or at least alleviate, the horrors of war?"[6]

The book was an instant success, and German, English, Italian, and Swedish editions appeared in quick succession. Charles Dickens provided a long paraphrase-cum-endorsement in his weekly *All the Year Round*, praising Dunant's proposal to establish relief committees that were prepared to care for wounded soldiers. "In time of war, every one will contribute his mite in answer to appeals from the committee," Dickens concluded.[7] By the time Dickens's review appeared, Dunant had been able to obtain the support of the Societé Genévoise d'Utilité Publique (Geneva Society of Public Welfare). Four members of the organization were inspired by his proposal and invited him to join an ad hoc committee that would study the steps and obstacles involved in realizing his ideas.

The committee soon became convinced of its global and world-historical mission and established itself first as the Comité International de Secours aux Blessés (International Committee for the Relief of the Wounded) and then as the Comité International de la Croix-Rouge (International Committee of the Red Cross). Its members worked to prepare a proposal that would be presented at a conference to be held later that year. In the meantime, Dunant traveled to Berlin and other European capitals seeking official endorsements. Prussia's minister of war, Albrecht Theodor Emil, Count von Roon, in the presence of an aide-de-camp of King Wilhelm I, endorsed

5 Ibid., 72–73.
6 Ibid., 115, 127.
7 [Charles Dickens], "A Souvenir of Solferino," *All the Year Round* 9 (1863), 288.

Dunant's ideas, and the aide-de-camp reported that the king was very interested. Roon and the Prussian king were both military men, and they sensed that Dunant's ideas could help limit chaos on the battlefield and support what they conceived as an "orderly conduct" of war. The conversation between Dunant, Roon, and the king's aide also generated an idea: to give neutral status to both army medics and volunteers who helped the wounded.

Excited by the support, Dunant moved boldly ahead. Without consulting the other members of the International Committee of the Red Cross, he drafted a proposal for a conference to be held at short notice in Geneva, recommending that status under international law be given to relief societies that organize medical help on the battlefield, transport the wounded to safety, and manage hospitals.[8] In the days following, Dunant won the support of King Johann of Saxony and Emperor Napoleon III, and these monarchs' willingness to send delegates to Geneva inspired others to follow suit.

In October 1863, twenty-six delegates from seventeen nations met in Geneva to discuss the options. They understood that in an age of nation-states, the only way forward was to organize the effort on a national basis: each country was to establish a national relief organization, which would prepare in peacetime for the care of the wounded in war. This had to be done with the sanction of, and in collaboration with, national governments, as the initiative could be successful only within the context of existing power structures. Yet it was desirable that each of these national organizations should be recognizable by a common sign, and hence those involved were to wear a white armlet with a red cross—an inverted version of the Swiss flag, which carries a white cross on a red background. The meeting also broached the idea that had been born in Prussia: neutrality. With little discussion, the conference recommended that "in time of war the belligerent nations should proclaim the neutrality of ambulances and military hospitals, and that neutrality should likewise be recognized, fully and absolutely, in respect of official medical personnel, voluntary medical personnel, inhabitants of the country who go to the relief of the wounded, and the wounded themselves."[9]

In the wake of the conference, relief organizations were set up in many countries, but a diplomatic effort was needed to get governments to ensure their neutrality. In June 1864, the Swiss government issued an official invitation to the governments of "all civilized powers"—twenty-five in total—to attend another conference in

8 See Martin Gumpert, *Dunant: The Story of the Red Cross* (New York: Oxford University Press, 1938), 87–92, 110–132; Caroline Moorehead, *Dunant's Dream: War, Switzerland and the History of the Red Cross* (New York: Carroll and Graf, 1999), 67.

9 Dietrich Schindler and Jiří Toman, eds., "Resolutions of the Geneva International Conference," in *The Laws of Armed Conflicts: A Collection of Conventions, Resolutions, and Other Documents* (Dordrecht: Martinus Nijhoff, 1988), 276.

Geneva, this time to discuss and, if possible, agree on granting immunity to relief associations in times of war. Sixteen governments arranged to send representatives. The British delegates were Dr. William Rutherford and Dr. Thomas Longmore, who sought Nightingale's opinion of the endeavor. She initially responded to Dunant's ideas with harsh criticism. She believed that governments ought to remain responsible for the care of the sick and wounded, and that only governments had the financial means to bring real relief. In addition, it did not make sense to her that a major international relief organization could be effective when based in a third-tier power like Switzerland. But during the Geneva meeting, Longmore sent Nightingale some ideas that had been tabled for the convention, and she decided it would be "quite harmless for our government to sign the convention as it now stands. It amounts to nothing more than the declaration that humanity to the wounded is a good thing."[10]

At the time of the conference, the United States was engaged in its Civil War and was also weary of Europe. President Lincoln decided not to send an official representative but asked Charles S. P. Bowles of the United States Sanitary Commission, a voluntary association that had been instrumental in organizing the care of wounded soldiers, to attend the meeting. Bowles traveled to Geneva with a trunkful of reports on the work of the US Sanitary Commission and photographs of its ambulances and military hospitals, which he shared with the official delegates. "These life-pictures, books, and practical proofs, produced an effect as great as it was valuable," Bowles noted in his report. "It was to many of them—earnest men, seeking for light, with their whole hearts in the interest of a long suffering humanity,—like the sight of the promised land."[11]

At the opening of the conference, its chairman, Swiss general Guillaume-Henri Dufour, addressed the fears of many governments. Promising "no interference with the consecrated military code of nations" he asserted: "We have in view but one object, and that is: *the neutrality of ambulances and Sanitary personnel of belligerent armies*. This is all. We ask nothing more than this."[12] The organizers got what they wanted: delegates agreed on the text of a treaty that stipulated, in its first article, "The Ambulances and the Military Hospitals shall be recognized as Neutral, and as such, so long as they shall contain Wounded or Invalid Soldiers, shall be protected and respected by Belligerents. Neutrality shall cease in case the Ambulances or Hospitals shall

10 Florence Nightingale, letters to Thomas Longmore, July 23 and Aug. 31, 1864, in *Woman Theorists on Society and Politics*, ed. Lynn MacDonald (Waterloo: Wilfrid Laurier University Press, 1998), 188–89.

11 European Branch of the United States Sanitary Commission, *Report of Charles S. P. Bowles, Foreign Agent of the United States Sanitary Commission, upon the International Congress of Geneva, for the Amelioration of the Condition of the Sick and Wounded Soldiers of Armies in the Field, Convened at Geneva, 8th August, 1864* (London: Clay and Taylor, 1864), 11.

12 Opening speech by Guillaume-Henri Dufour at the First Geneva Convention, Aug. 8, 1864, as quoted in European Branch of the United States Sanitary Commission, *Report of Charles S. P. Bowles*, 33–34.

be guarded by a Military force."[13] The governments of Baden, Belgium, Denmark, France, Great Britain, Hesse, Italy (which had become a unified state after Solferino), the Netherlands, Portugal, Prussia, Spain, Sweden, Switzerland, and Württemberg ratified within a year what became known as the Geneva Convention and, after the adoption of three subsequent treaties expanding its scope, is usually referred to as the First Geneva Convention.

In 1866 the French Societé de Secours decided that the 1867 Exposition Universelle in Paris would provide a great opportunity to present the initiative to the public, and it agreed to build and equip an exhibition pavilion. But what to show? A prominent American expatriate living in Paris, Thomas Wiltberger Evans, had an idea. The court dentist of Emperor Napoleon III since 1853, Evans had been instrumental in changing the perception of his profession and was very interested in the idea of civilians assisting wounded soldiers. In 1864, Evans traveled to the United States, which was in the third year of its bitter Civil War, with a double mission. His imperial patient had charged him with the task of evaluating the Union's chance of victory, and Evans had wanted to get a sense of the nature and scope of the work of the US Sanitary Commission. In fact, Empress Eugénie of France, who was quite fond of Evans, had asked him about the care of the wounded in the Civil War and especially about the role of volunteers.[14]

Upon his return to France, Evans had announced he was convinced the Union would win the war and, in response to Empress Eugénie's request, published a book about the medical achievements of the American military. He did not hide his enthusiasm: "The establishment of the United States Sanitary Commission marks the beginning of a new era in the history of the world. That act of philanthropy is the largest humanity ever conceived and accomplished."[15] The publication paid particular attention to the design of the American military hospitals and provided illustrations of the large wooden barracks that were their basic building blocks. Evans also brought back the first batch of what would become a large collection of documents and artifacts that illustrated the work of the US Sanitary Commission. In the following years, Evans continued to amass medical books, documents, photographs, apparatuses, and equipment; his stockpile included not only an actual hospital tent but also models and drawings of hospitals in Pennsylvania, Virginia, and Washington, DC. Thus, when the Société de Secours was given the opportunity

13 "Treaty for the Amelioration of the Condition of Wounded Soldiers of Armies in the Field," in Schindler and Toman, *The Laws of Armed Conflict*, 280.
14 Thomas Wiltberger Evans, *The Second French Empire*, ed. Edward A. Crane (New York: Appleton, 1902), 141–42.
15 Thomas Wiltberger Evans, *La Commission Sanitaire des Etats-Unis, son origine, son organisation et ses résultats, avec une notice sur les hôpitaux militaires aux Etats-Unis et sur la réforme sanitaire dans les armées européennes* (Paris: Dent, 1865), xi.

to impress the importance of its work on the world—but found itself without objects to show—its members realized that a selection of Evans's collection might provide a good idea of how to assist the sick and wounded in future wars. Thus the material he had collected ended up in both the official American exhibit in the main building and the special exhibition organized by the Societé de Secours.[16]

The Exposition Universelle celebrated a new American building type: the pavilion, or as the French called it, the *baraque*. In his own report about the exhibition submitted to the United States government, Evans found ample opportunity to note the superiority of the American exhibits: "The pavilion system of barrack hospitals so extensively and successfully used during our war, is well illustrated in the several models and plans exhibited," he wrote. "As to the superiority of this system over all others for the special purpose for which it was intended, there is at present but one opinion among military surgeons."[17]

From the moment the first Civil War military hospitals created by the Union—nothing even remotely comparable existed within the Confederacy—began operation, Europeans were both fascinated by them and happy to take credit. The Medical Department of the British Army reported in detail on the American achievement in its sanitary report for 1862, referring to the field hospitals advocated by William A. Hammond, surgeon general of the Union Army. "Dr. Hammond, in his work on Hygiene, enters at great length into the principles of hospital construction, and describes some of the American hospitals constructed during the war," it read. "He adopts *in toto* Miss Nightingale's opinions, and endorses them by his own weighty experience." The report paid much attention to the ventilation of the pavilions and provided descriptions of six hospitals. The Satterlee General Hospital in West Philadelphia was judged to be "very similar to that designed by the late Mr. Brunel in the Crimean War, and erected at Renkioi." And before quoting Hammond's paean to the salubrious environment of the pavilion hospitals, it stressed for a last time the British precedent: "The Crimean naval hut with double walls and openings above and below, and with projecting eaves and ridge ventilation, was used as a model for many of the wooden huts."[18]

The French were also anxious to take credit for the American inventions. In 1866 the prominent military surgeon Venant Antoine Léon Legouest published an

16 Gerald Carson, *The Dentist and the Empress* (Boston: Houghton Mifflin, 1983), 92–100.
17 Thomas Wiltberger Evans, *Report on Instruments and Apparatus of Medicine, Surgery and Hygiene* (Washington: Government Printing Office, 1868), 35–36.
18 Great Britain, British Army Medical Department, "Statistical, Sanitary, and Medical Reports of the Army Medical Department, For the year 1862," in Great Britain, Parliament, House of Commons, *Accounts and Papers*, 36 vols. (London: Her Majesty's Stationery Office, 1864), session Feb. 4–July 29, 1864, vol. 36, 345–47.

overview of the American experience in which he praised the hospitals built as a serial agglomeration of a standardized *pavillon-baraque*. Yet Legouest shared the deeply rooted anti-American prejudices of the French elites, who were unwilling to credit Americans with any true civilizing potential, and he worked hard to find French precedents for whatever had succeeded.[19] Praising the barrack hospitals as a "salutary revolution," he stated, "It is fair to claim priority to the former director of health of our army in the East, *Monsieur* Michel Lévy, who, in 1854 in Varna as well as in Crimea, in Constantinople as well as at Gallipoli, urged for and suggested barrack hospitals in the form of parallel pavilions. [...] The Americans knew these examples well, and appreciated them."[20] And so it continued: the Americans had simply applied ideas and principles developed in Europe in general, and France and Britain in particular.

But if European military health professionals were happy to take credit, those visiting and judging the 1867 Exposition Universelle were equally happy to recognize American achievements. Henry Morford, an American journalist and travel writer, attended the exhibition and reported that, "at Paris, and measurably over Europe, this year, Americans have gratified nearly as much curiosity as they have manifested. Never before, so much as since the rebellion, have America, American events, and the American people, been so much in the whole world's mouths and minds." Morford marveled at the fact that "America (the United States absolutely claiming and filling the name) has won more solid honors per cent, in the Great Exposition, than any other country on the globe." According to Morford, the credit for the United States' excellent performance at the fair was due to "American inventions being of that practical order which compels recognition under every disadvantage—to the energy of a few moved by public spirit, and a few more by that rational commercial spirit which recognizes great opportunities—and to a combination of the sacred and profane adages: 'The last shall be first,' and 'A fool for luck!'" It was not surprising that the US Sanitary Commission received the grand prize for its presentation on the Union Army's medical services. Morford thought it "an honor well deserved, as the collection reflected credit upon every American, and awoke much national pride."[21]

Yet, while French military surgeons were generally interested in the American experience, the inflexible administration of the French Ministry of War and the French army opposed any revisions to its existing

19 See Philippe Roger, *The American Enemy: The History of French Anti-Americanism*, trans. Sharon Bowman (Chicago: University of Chicago Press, 2005).
20 Venant Antoine Léon Legouest, *Le Service de santé des armées américaines pendant la guerre des Etats-Unis, 1861–1865* (Paris: Baillière, 1866), 13.
21 Henry Morford, *Paris in '67; or, The Great Exposition, Its Side-Shows and Excursions* (New York: Carleton & Co., 1867), 63, 211, 213, 225.

procedures. Many French people were aware of this, and the more enlightened among them lamented the power of the bureaucrats and the generals to obstruct change. In his review of the material submitted by the European relief associations and the US Sanitary Commission to the Exposition Universelle, Charles Sarazin, a professor of surgery at the University of Strasbourg, praised the American achievement without any qualification: "How is it possible that most inexperienced people, who seemed the most ignorant of things of war, have achieved this superiority? The real reason for our inferiority vis-à-vis America can be found in the activity, energy, initiative, but also the freedom and independence of the medical corps, which here finds itself paralyzed by an omnipotent bureaucracy."[22]

Until the end of the 1850s, the attitude of senior military leaders in Germany toward providing medical services in the midst of battle was one of skepticism: they believed that the arrival of ambulances and the erection of field hospitals slowed down the army. The experience of the war of 1859 that had routed Austria from Lombardy and initiated the final act of Italian unification changed attitudes: for the first time, both politicians and military theorists began to consider the army a collective body whose health needed constant attention. In Prussia, King Wilhelm I, who had ascended the throne in 1861, began to push for a general draft of all able-bodied men of military age. He believed military service was a civic duty; if this were to become the nation's view, the government needed to organize professional care of wounded and sick soldiers. In addition, advances in medical science seemed to offer the tools to create an effective medical service, and there was a new spirit of volunteerism among upper-class and upper-middle-class women, who strove to care for the wounded.[23] As a result, the views of military surgeons came to be respected by the military establishment of the Prussian, Austrian, and other German armies—and this meant that the German military establishment began to consider what had unfolded in terms of military medicine on the other side of the Atlantic. While they certainly considered North America to be a continent-size *Provinz* in terms of its cultural level, the military experience gained during its Civil War was not to be discarded.

In the nineteenth century, the nation-state, embodied in a most perfect form by France, had become the political ideal, and in no place did this ideal seem further from reality than in the German lands. Since the

22 Charles Sarazin, "Matériel d'ambulances," *Annales d'Hygiène Publique et de Médicine Légale*, 2nd ser., 29 (1868), 240.
23 M. Schmidt-Ernsthausen, *Studien über das Feld-Sanitätswesen* (Berlin: Mittler & Sohn, 1873).

French occupation of the first decade of the century, Germans had seen themselves as a single nation rooted in a shared past, and they celebrated a common national inheritance embodied in a shared language, a national literature, an architecture, the visual arts, and above all music. But their sense of a shared nationhood did not match the political reality. In the Middle Ages the feudal *Heiliges Römisches Reich* (Holy Roman Empire, also known as the First Reich) had been the key European power because it was the only power that shared in the universality of the Holy Roman Church. "It is under the emblem of soul and body that the relation of the papal and imperial power is represented to us throughout the Middle Ages," medieval historian James Bryce (later Viscount Bryce) observed in his classic history of the Holy Roman Empire. "Thus the Holy Roman Church and the Holy Roman Empire are one and the same thing, seen from different sides. [...] As divine and eternal, its head is the Pope, to whom souls have been entrusted; as human and temporal, the Emperor, commissioned to rule men's bodies and acts."[24]

The empire had been torn apart both ideologically and politically in the European religious wars that, between 1524 and 1648, pitted Roman Catholics against Protestants. After the Peace of Westphalia, the Holy Roman Empire survived only as a very loose confederation of effectively independent domains, territories, and cities, to finally collapse when Napoleon I began to rearrange the map of Europe, which included an addition of another empire—his own. After Napoleon's final defeat, the representatives of the Germans states gathered in Vienna had created a shadow of the First Reich: the Deutscher Bund (German Confederation). Its purpose was to provide some framework of cooperation between the now thirty-five sovereign German states—which included two major German powers (the Austrian Empire and the Kingdom of Prussia), four second-tier German states (the Kingdoms of Bavaria, Württemberg, Saxony, and Hanover), and twenty-nine third-tier German states (including the Danish-ruled Duchy of Holstein)—and four independent cities (Bremen, Frankfurt, Hamburg, and Lübeck). This arrangement worked for the many German sovereigns, a powerful few, such as the Austrian emperor and the king of Prussia, and many petty. But the confederation was anathema to German nationalists, who dreamed of unifying the thirty-nine entities into a single nation-state.

Between 1815 and 1848, the conservative governments in Vienna and Berlin had been allied against

24 James Bryce, *The Holy Roman Empire*, rev. ed. (London: Macmillan, 1941), 103–05.

the nationalists, who also happened to be in favor of political, social, and economic modernization. But after 1848, Austria and Prussia had become first competitors, then rivals, and by the early 1860s had become adversaries. While remaining conservative in its outlook, Berlin had allied itself with German nationalists in all German states but Prussia. It was an odd alliance between a state that stood for Machiavellian power politics and a romantic ideal, but Prussian prime minister Otto von Bismarck was quite willing to consider a unification of Germany under Prussian leadership. This could be achieved only if Austria were eliminated as a force within German politics.

Austria and Prussia were formally allies against Denmark in the Second Schleswig War (1864), which ended with the Danish-ruled Duchy of Schleswig becoming a Prussian territory and Danish-ruled Holstein becoming a part of Austria. But the war against Denmark had been a lopsided effort in which the Austrian military had been as inept as the Prussian had been efficient. A war for hegemony over the German lands was now only a matter of time. On paper, Austria seemed stronger, as it counted all second-tier German states as allies, while Prussia could count only on the support of third-tier German states. Yet the Prussian army was to prove infinitely superior to the combined forces of Austria, Bavaria, Hanover, Saxony, Baden, Württemberg, and Hesse. And one of the reasons was the willingness of the Prussian military to learn from America.

In early 1866, planners in the Prussian Ministry of War established guidelines on the construction of barracks for use as military hospitals—the first governmental rules on barrack construction to be issued in Europe.

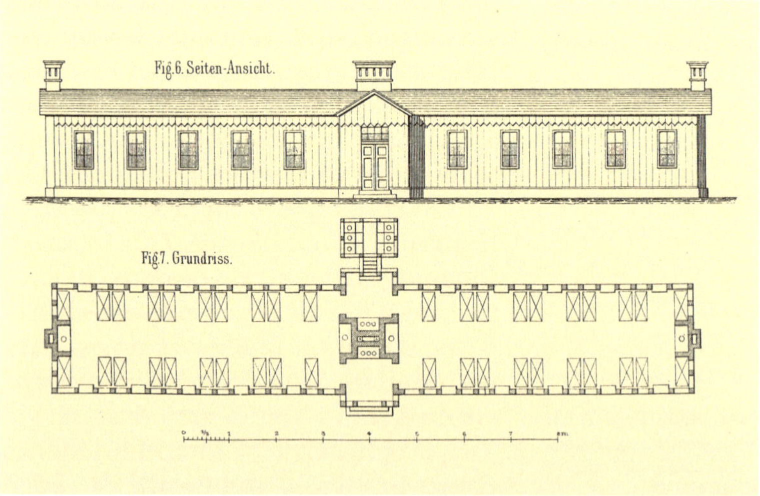

Fig. 5
Plan and elevation of the barrack as prescribed by the Prussian Ministry of War, 1866, from Prussia, Royal Prussian Ministry of War, *Der Sanitätsdienst bei den deutschen Heeren im Kriege gegen Frankreich 1870/71*, 1884. Collection: Staatsbibliothek zu Berlin.

They decided to modify the American model by shortening the barrack from 57 to 42 meters and subdividing the enlongate single ward into two shorter ones, providing space for twenty patients each. These wards were to be separated by a vestibule and cooking and toilet facilities. The design proposed by the ministry also included masonry fireplaces at both ends of each ward, suggesting not only the more permanent nature of the building but also what became and remained a key issue in the German adoption of the barrack: the question of the building's performance during winter. As the open-ridge ventilation of the American original seemed too crude, the Prussian copy was to provide a version of the ventilation concept developed a century earlier in England by Samuel Sutton: a complex system of ventilation ducts that were to be connected to the metal chimneys of the stoves. When warmed by the fire, the chimneys would transfer their heat to the ventilation ducts. The air within would be heated and seek to escape through chimneys in the roof, creating a vacuum that would attract the foul air from the wards.[25]

It appears that only five of the new regulation barracks were ever built. The Austro-Prussian War, which erupted on June 14, 1866, generated new experiences to be considered, while a more detailed review of the design revealed many flaws. Hermann Eberhard Fischer, a prominent physician and military surgeon, compared the Prussian barrack to the American original, and judged the Prussian version to be totally inadequate, and not only because the amount of space per person had been reduced from 41 to 28 cubic meters. "This model is considerably worse than the American. First and foremost it lacks the ridge ventilation that is so effective in the summer. In addition two stoves will not suffice to create ventilation in the winter, the amount of air allocated to each patient is also too meager, and finally [...] the toilets are at the center of the barrack, and they're not water closets. [...] Also, the wards in this barrack are too low, and the number and size of the windows too little. For these reasons, one will have to totally refrain from using this model of barrack."[26]

Unlike the barrack developed by the Royal Prussian War Ministry, a few so-called *Zeltbaracken* (tent-barracks) conceived by Dr. Georg Friedrich Louis Stromeyer saw service in the war of 1866. The author of a famous textbook on military surgery, Dr. Stromeyer was chief of the medical service of the Kingdom of Hanover's army during the Austro-Prussian War. The Battle of Langensalza, on June 27, 1866, sealed the fate

25 Hermann Eberhard Fischer, *Lehrbuch der allgemeinen Kriegs-Chirurgie* (Erlangen: Ferdinand Enke, 1868), 321–32; Prussia, Royal Prussian Ministry of War, *Der Sanitätsdienst bei den deutschen Heeren im Kriege gegen Frankreich 1870/71* (Berlin: Mittler & Sohn, 1884), 314.
26 Fischer, *Lehrbuch der allgemeinen Kriegs-Chirurgie*, 322.

of Hanover, ending with the surrender of its army and the destruction of its independence—the state became part of Prussia. The battle was also the first military engagement in which the Red Cross flag and insignia, agreed upon in the First Geneva Convention, marked hospitals, ambulances, and medical personnel.

In the wake of the battle, Dr. Stromeyer set up a field hospital in Langensalza, in what is now central Germany. Having studied the medical history of the Crimean War, he commissioned a local master carpenter to design and build *Zeltbaracken* for an emergency field hospital.

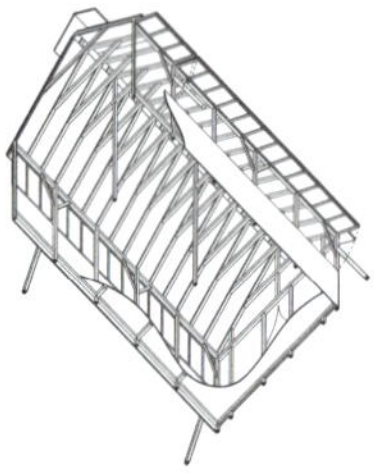

Drawings, Stromeyer's Tent-Barrack
→ p. 517

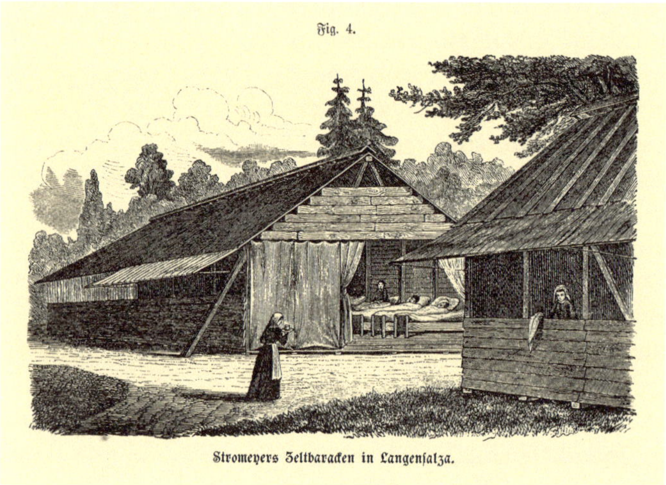

Fig. 6
Tent-barracks (*Zeltbaracken*) commissioned by Dr. Louis Stromeyer at Langensalza, Prussia, 1866, from Johann Friedrich August von Esmarch, *Ueber den Kampf der Humanität gegen die Schrecken des Krieges*, 1869. Collection: Wellcome Library, London.

"In the urgency of the moment I was thrown back on my own imagination, and only knew the barracks built by the English in the Crimea as described in the interesting blue book *Report of the Proceedings of the Sanitary Commission Dispatched to the Seat of the War in the East, 1855–1856*," Dr. Stromeyer wrote in a postwar report on gunshot wounds. "It contains very instructive pictures of barracks, which were, however, largely designed for the cold season and were constructed more like houses. Expecting a use of two or three months in July, August, and September, I believed that more tentlike barracks were appropriate for the needs in Langensalza."[27] These tent-barracks measured 26.5 by 6 meters and provided room for thirty beds. The design was simple, consisting of a light frame held up by posts, which carried the frame of the roof. Boards covered the lower half of the long walls, while the upper half was hung with canvas that could be lifted up by iron rods to create an opening protected by an awning. One of the short sides was covered with boards while the other had no boards but canvas panels that could be opened and closed. Tarred cardboard provided the roof covering, and ridge

27 Georg Friedrich Louis Stromeyer, *Erfahrungen über Schusswunden im Jahre 1866* (Hanover: Hahn'sche Hofbuchhandlung, 1867), 33. The blue book Stromeyer refers to is: Great Britain, Sanitary Commission, *Report to the Right Hon. Lord Panmure, G. C. B., &c., Minister at War, of the Proceedings of the Sanitary Commission Dispatched to the Seat of War in the East, 1855–56* (London: Harrison & Sons, 1857).

ventilation ran the whole length. Below the wooden floor was a bed of slag. It was a very simple structure, and only a few examples were built.[28]

A few months after the battle, Dr. Stromeyer reported on his achievement in his book on gun wounds, marveling at how well patients had done in these airy tent-barracks: "It almost appeared to me as if people are not meant to live in the summer in solid houses. Wounded of all categories were lodged in the barracks, and it became clear that there was not a single category that was not appropriate for this."[29] He admitted there was no comparison between the Union Army's general hospitals and the few tent-barracks he had designed and built, yet he took pride in his initiative as an example that might trigger a change in the generally negative attitude of military surgeons toward the use of provisional shelters as field hospitals.

The key event in the Austro-Prussian War, which would result in the dissolution of the Deutscher Bund and the establishment of the Prussian-dominated Norddeutscher Bund (North German Confederation), was the Battle of Königgrätz (or Sadowa). It proved a military catastrophe for the Austrian army and a humanitarian catastrophe for the many wounded. While Prussia had signed the Geneva Convention, Austria had not, and this meant that when the Austrian army withdrew from the battlefield, its medical personnel chose to join in the retreat, as they were not covered by the protection of the Red Cross. It fell to Prussian military surgeons, such as Bernhard von Langenbeck, who was to assume a very important role in the history of the barrack in the mid-1880s (see Chapter Eleven), to take care of all the wounded, and they did so to the best of their abilities and without prejudice to the Austrians.

In the wake of the Battle of Königgrätz, Austrian military surgeon Johann Freiherr Dumreicher von Österreicher praised the Prussian medical service but also criticized some of its practices, and reflected on the purpose and use of military hospitals in the aftermath of a war in which citizen armies had fought and suffered. "In our time, we cannot postpone raising the question about field-hospital care," Dumreicher proclaimed, arguing that the care of wounded soldiers had become a primary obligation of the modern state. "Every man who risks his life, his health, his limbs for the Fatherland has indeed the right, when he is wounded in the service of his country, to claim as victim of war the best possible care." To achieve this goal, Dumreicher looked to the United States for guidance: "In their recent, gigantic

28 Stromeyer, *Erfahrungen über Schusswunden im Jahre 1866*, 33–35; for a plan, section, and elevation and additional technical information about Dr. Stromeyer's barrack-tents, see Johann Friedrich August von Esmarch, *Verbandplatz und Feldlazareth: Vorlesungen für angehende Militairärzte* (Berlin: August Hirschwald, 1868), 103–04.

29 Louis Stromeyer, *Erfahrungen über Schusswunden im Jahre 1866*, 36.

battles the North Americans have achieved exemplary results in this field. Along with other preparations for war one should also set up in the rear, close to railway lines, military hospitals that follow North American examples. They should be equipped with all materials and with cadres of capable physicians who are ready for the wounded."[30]

Dumreicher articulated the principles of what ought to be done, and with his improvised *Zeltbaracke*, Dr. Stromeyer had set a practical example of what was possible. Dr. Stromeyer's son-in-law, Johann Friedrich August von Esmarch, then became the most important advocate in Germany of adopting barracks as the standard shelter for field hospitals. Known today as the father of emergency medicine, Esmarch was the most prominent military surgeon in 1860s Germany. He had studied the US Civil War and reported on what he considered to be the astonishing progress represented by the army hospitals. In a course on military medicine presented in the winter of 1866–67 at the University of Kiel in Holstein (which had been ruled by Denmark until 1864, by Austria from 1864 to 1866, and became part of Prussia in 1866), Esmarch identified the *Holzbaracken* (wooden barracks) of the American hospitals as key to their success.

Fig. 7
A standard ward for use in the US (Union) Army's general hospitals as prescribed by Surgeon General William A. Hammond, from Johann Friedrich August von Esmarch, *Ueber den Kampf der Humanität gegen die Schrecken des Krieges*, 1869. The caption reads: "Model of an American hospital-barrack. A fifth of its length is cut off in order to show its interior arrangement and a stove." Collection: Wellcome Library, London.

Reflecting ideas on hospital hygiene developed in the Crimea by Florence Nightingale, whose work had just been translated into German, Esmarch saw these quickly built barrack hospitals as an embodiment of the practical sense of the Americans. In an illustrated twenty-six-page appendix to the published version of his lectures, he presented a wealth of information about those barracks and how they had been serially assembled into exemplary hospitals.[31]

→ Fig. 8

30 Johann Freiherr Dumreicher von Österreicher, *Zur Lazarethfrage, Erwiderung von Prof. von Dumreicher an Prof. von Langenbeck* (Vienna: Moritz Gans, 1867), 42.
31 Esmarch, *Verbandplatz und Feldlazareth*, 100–01, 107–33.

Fig. 8
Jefferson General Hospital, Jeffersonville, Indiana, United States, from Johann Friedrich August von Esmarch, *Verbandplatz und Feldlazareth*, 1868. Collection: Wellcome Library, London.

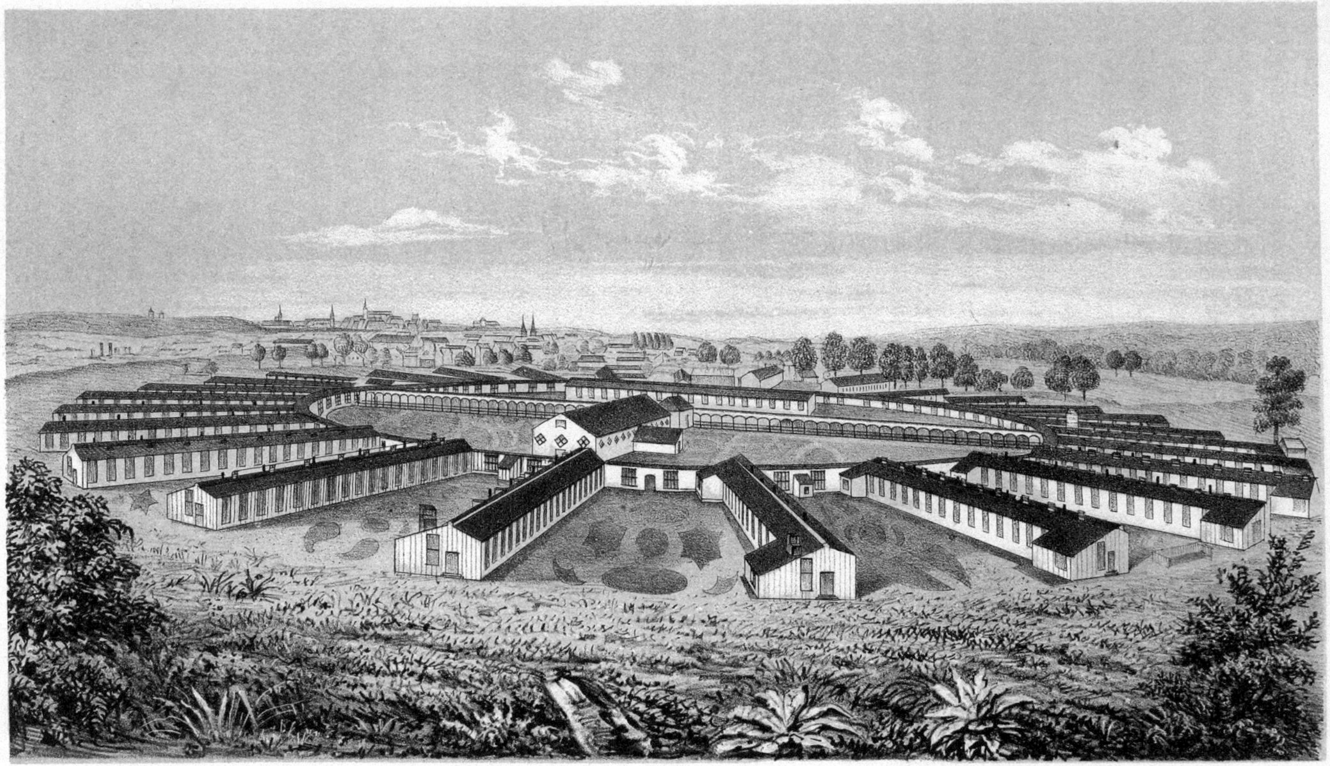

A. Schütze Lith. Inst. Berlin.

Jefferson General-Hospital bei Jeffersonville in Jndiana.

Taf. IV.

Military surgeons were not the only doctors interested in Dr. Hammond's pavilions. Dr. Rudolf Virchow, one of the most prominent German physicians of the nineteenth century, also admired Hammond's pavilion and believed that it ought to have a future within a civilian context. He lamented that the great revolution in hospital design, which had begun in France with the construction of the pathbreaking Saint-André and Lariboisière Hospitals, had not been emulated in Germany.[32] In December 1866, Virchow gave a lecture in Berlin in which he reflected on the American achievement in hospital design. "The American Republic has amply demonstrated what level of sick-care a people is able to achieve in a joint effort," he stated. He also praised what he saw as a revolutionary approach to hospital design. "In relation to hospitals, the Crimean War, and even more the American War, have shattered boundaries that had been maintained as the result of a certain timidity, an often scarcely believable unwillingness to spend money that physicians had maintained against their better judgment. [...] The Americans have tried it for the first time, boldly, not to expand hospitals but to reduce their size by fragmenting them into a much larger number of separated departments (*Baracken*)." He summed up the success of this tactic: "The barrack-system and the dispersal of the sick has achieved a sudden victory over practices that merely concern themselves with ventilation and disinfection."[33] Virchow certainly did not believe that the Americans had solved the problem of hospital design once and for all, yet he knew that the Civil War hospitals created by the Union Army marked a major achievement, and that no progress was possible without learning the lessons provided.

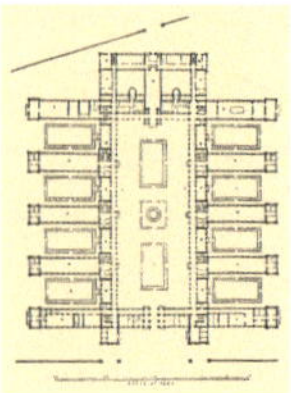

Chapter Two, Fig. 15
→ p. 106

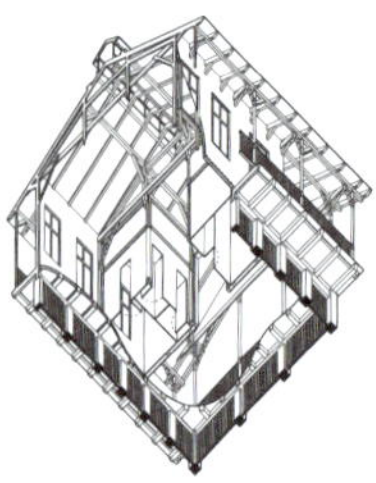

Drawings, Charité Hospital Barrack
→ p. 513

By the time Virchow gave his lecture, he had begun to test a specially built barrack. Virchow ran a laboratory of pathology on the grounds of the Charité Hospital in central Berlin, and he had a close working relationship with its director, Carl Heinrich Julius Esse. In early 1866, Virchow asked Esse if he could build a substantial version of a barrack at the Charité and monitor its conditions and mortality rate over an extended period of time. Esse agreed to the construction of this *Versuchsbaracke* (experimental barrack) on the north side of the hospital compound, and commissioned Hermann Blankenstein with its design. Because of the site's restrictions, the barrack was only 25.6 meters long and 8.8 meters wide. In essence, it followed the design developed by Nightingale and used in the United States, but around its perimeter ran a gallery that could be

32 Dankiwart Leistikow, "Das deutsche Krankenhaus in der erste Hälfte des 19. Jahrhunderts," in *Studien zur Krankenhausgeschichte im 19. Jahrhundert im Hinblick auf die Entwicklung in Deutschland*, ed.Hans Schadewaldt (Göttingen: Vandenhoeck & Rupprecht, 1976), 11–37.
33 Rudolf Ludwig Karl Virchow, "Ueber Hospitäler und Lazarette," in *Sammlung gemeinverständlicher wissenschaftlicher Vorträge*, ed. Rudolf Ludwig Karl Virchow and Franz von Holtzendorf, 3rd ser., nos. 49–72 (Berlin: Lüderitz'sche Verlagsbuchhandlung, 1868–69), 20, 25.

closed by means of canvas panels, creating semi-tent conditions. Erected atop 1.2-meter-high pillars, the walls were 4 meters high, while the ridge reached a height of 5.8 meters. The barrack had space for twenty patients and two nurses and offered a generous 50 cubic meters of space per person. Twelve windows on each side and an elaborately designed ridge-ventilation system ensured good air circulation in the summer.[34]

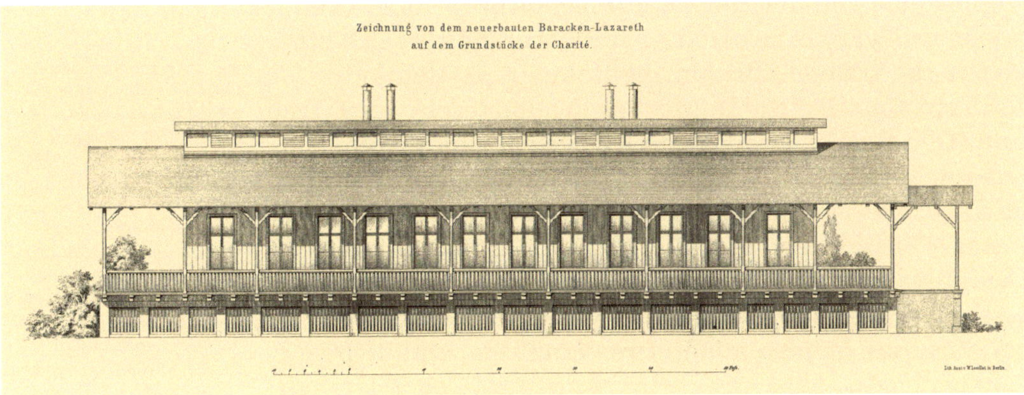

Fig. 9
Hermann Blankenstein, Elevation of the *Versuchsbaracke* at the Charité Hospital, from Carl Heinrich Julius Esse, *Das Baracken-Lazareth der Königlichen Charité zu Berlin in seinen Einrichtungen dargestellt*, 1868. Collection: ZB Med: Informationszentrum Lebenswissenschaften, Bonn and Cologne.

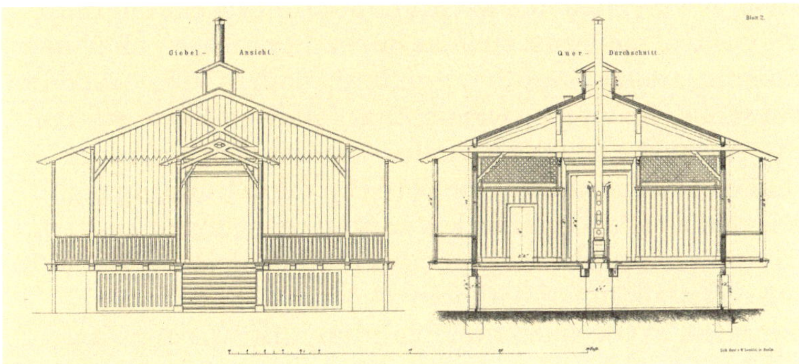

One of the main issues to be researched was the performance of barracks in the German winter, as the barracks used in the United States had been designed for generally milder winter conditions. The Charité barrack had a triple-layer wall made of boards. The space between the first and the second walls was filled with brick fragments, which were believed to provide good insulation. Between the second and third walls was an air space, which was connected to an air chamber located in a double floor. Ventilation holes led from this below-floor air chamber to the main room, which was equipped with two stoves, and flue pipes adjacent to the stove flues linked to the exterior. An intricate system allowed these stoves to heat the below-floor air chamber, creating an updraft of hot air into the flues and lowering the pressure in the air chamber. As the air pressure in the ward was higher, the vitiated air would move from the ward into the below-floor air chamber, creating artificial ventilation.

Fig. 10
Hermann Blankenstein, Sections of the *Versuchsbaracke* at the Charité Hospital, from Carl Heinrich Julius Esse, *Das Baracken-Lazareth der Königlichen Charité zu Berlin in seinen Einrichtungen dargestellt*, 1868. Collection: ZB Med: Informationszentrum Lebenswissenschaften, Bonn and Cologne.

34 See Carl Heinrich Julius Esse, *Das Baracken-Lazareth der Königlichen Charité zu Berlin in seinen Einrichtungen dargestellt* (Berlin: Enslin, 1868); also Arnold Körte, *Martin Gropius: Leben und Werk eines Berliner Architekten 1824–1880* (Berlin: Lukas Verlag, 2010), 283.

In addition to providing the vacuum that allowed for the extraction of the foul air from the ward, the warm air in the air chamber also heated the walls and floors, providing a comfortable environment.

The reputation of the Charité barrack brought Blankenstein the commission to build a small hospital sponsored by Queen Augusta of Prussia. The wife of King Wilhelm I was a great admirer of Florence Nightingale and met her on numerous occasions. The queen was very interested not only in public health but also in the state of military medicine in particular. In 1866 she founded the Deutscher Frauenverein zur Pflege und Hilfe für Verwundete im Kriege (German Women's League for the Care and Aid of the Wounded in War) and also was very active as the patron of the German Red Cross. The hospital named after her was immediately recognized by the architecture profession as a *Musteranstalt* (model institution) and was to influence the construction of hospitals in Dresden, Riga, and Leipzig.[35] A hybrid between a conventional hospital and a barrack style, it consisted of a permanent building that housed the central facilities, such as operating theater, pharmacy, meeting rooms, laundry, and bathroom, and two wooden barracks, serving as wards, that followed the design of the one at the nearby Charité. The wooden corridors that connected the barracks to the main building could be used as additional sick wards in the warmer season. In times of war, extra capacity could be created through the construction of both extra barracks and tent-barracks in the spacious Invalidenpark surrounding the hospital.[36]

35 "Architekten-Verein zu Berlin: Fünfte Exkursion, Sonnabend den 9. Juli 1870," *Deutsche Bauzeitung* 4 (1870), 228.

36 Carl Heinrich Julius Esse, *Das Augusta-Hospital und das mit demselben verbundene Asyl für Krankenpflegerinnen zu Berlin* (Berlin: Enslin, 1873); Ludwig Klasen, *Grundrissvorbilder von Gebäuden für Gesundheitspflege und Heilanstalten* (Leipzig: Baumgärtner, 1884), 359–60.

Fig. 11
Hermann Blankenstein, Elevation of the Augusta Hospital, from Carl Heinrich Julius Esse, *Das Augusta-Hospital und das mit demselben verbundene Asyl für Krankenpflegerinnen zu Berlin*, 1873. Collection: ZB Med: Informationszentrum Lebenswissenschaften, Bonn and Cologne.

Inspired by the Charité barrack, the director of the university hospital in the northern Prussian city of Greifswald organized the construction of a much simpler version, in which Karl Friedrich Mosler, a professor of medicine, treated patients with infectious diseases. Mosler initially opposed the barrack approach, but his views changed in 1867, when a typhus epidemic hit Greifswald. Mosler decided to admit typhus patients to the barrack and noted that none succumbed to the disease—a fact he credited to the superb ventilation in the ward.[37]

When Berlin city officials began to plan the construction of a large municipal hospital in the Friedrichshain (Frederick's Grove) park in 1866, many insisted that they ought to follow the precedent set by the Americans and use the wooden barrack as a basic building element. One of the arguments was that the barrack was cheap to make and could be easily burned down if it became infected. Architects Martin Carl Gropius and Heino Schmieden looked carefully at Blankenstein's barrack at the Charité and then created a brick version. Significantly, they preserved in the brick pavilions one of the most important characteristics of the barrack: ridge ventilation. Yet the pavilions created at Friedrichshain were not barracks; with their brick construction and a full basement, they had assumed a sense of permanency that went against the provisional character of the barrack.[38]

37 Karl Friedrich Mosler, *Erfahrungen über die Behandlung des Typhus exanthematicus: mit Berücksichtigung dabei erforderlicher prophylaktischer Maassregeln* (Greifswald: Akademische Buchhandlung, 1868), 83.

38 Rudolf Virchow, *Ueber Lazarette und Baracken: Vortrag gehalten vor der Berliner medicinischen Gesellschaft am 8. Februar 1871* (Berlin: August Hirschwald, 1871), 14; Körte, *Martin Gropius*, 281.

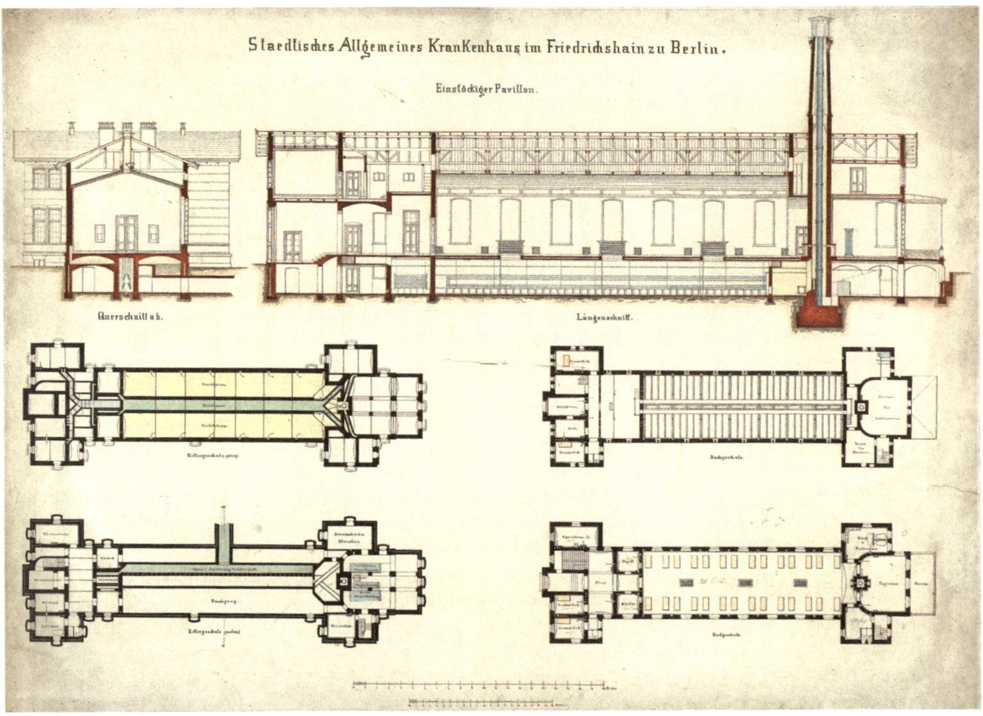

Fig. 12
Martin Carl Gropius and Heino Schmieden, Plans and sections of a pavilion at the Friedrichshain hospital, c. 1870. Collection: Architekturmuseum, Technische Universität München.

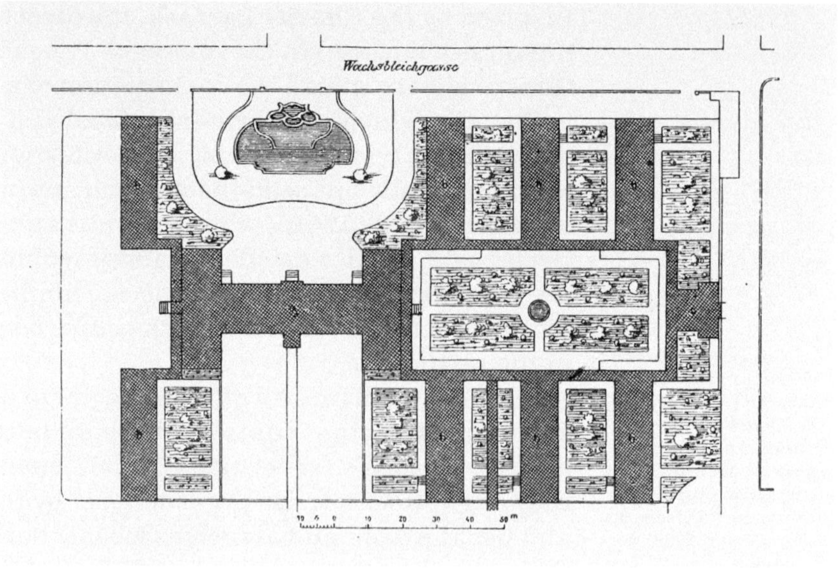

Fig. 13
Theodor Friedrich, Plan of the satellite buildings of the Dresden municipal hospital, 1870, from Sächsischer Ingenieur- und Architekten-Verein und dem Dresdener Architekten-Verein, *Die Bauten, Technischen und Industriellen Anlagen von Dresden*, 1878. Collection: Bayerische Staatsbibliothek, Munich.

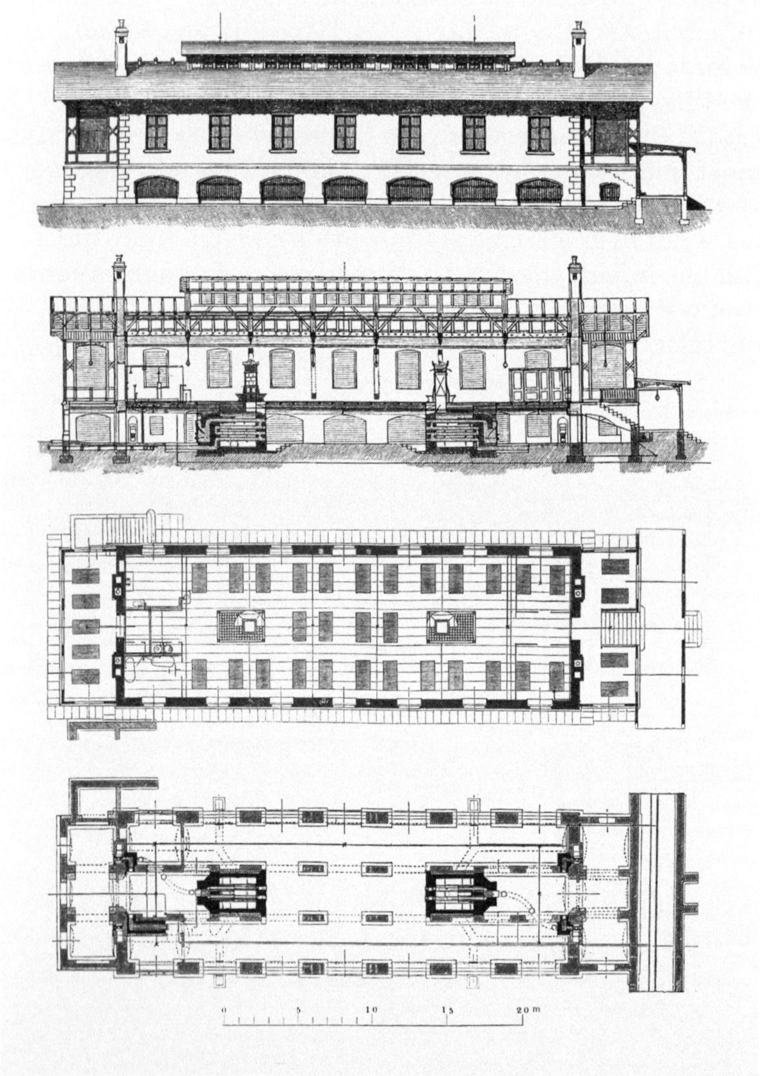

Fig. 14
Theodor Friedrich, Plan, sections, and elevation of a pavilion of the Dresden municipal hospital, 1870, from Sächsischer Ingenieur- und Architekten-Verein und dem Dresdener Architekten-Verein, *Die Bauten, Technischen und Industriellen Anlagen von Dresden*, 1878. Collection: Bayerische Staatsbibliothek, Munich.

In Dresden, the extension of the *Stadtkrankenhaus* (municipal hospital), designed in 1870 by city architect Theodor Friedrich, likewise incorporated pavilions that were inspired by barracks but were constructed as permanent buildings. In 1845 the Dresden municipality had purchased the eighteenth-century Palais Brühl-Marcolini and converted it into a hospital. The palace garden offered ample space for new construction, and Friedrich designed a satellite hospital that consisted of a three-story building with a capacity of 124 patients housed in wards that ranged from single-occupancy rooms for private patients to rooms holding seven people. On the west side of the core building stretched a cloister-like garden enclosed by a covered walkway that gave access to six large pavilions, each with a large stone basement containing two forced-air furnaces, and a main floor, constructed from brick, that consisted of a single ward holding twenty-eight patients.

← Figs. 13, 14

An intricate system of pipes connected to the furnaces, the sick room, and the outside, allowing for heating and ventilation. In the summer, windows and a monitor allowed for the entrance of fresh air and the evacuation of foul air without the need to fire the furnaces. While the simultaneous construction of traditional patient wards in the main building and those inspired by barrack design in the pavilions gave an opportunity for a comparative study on the mortality and recovery rates in the different buildings, no such research was conducted. The only differentiation undertaken at the time concerned the capital and operational cost per bed, with the pavilion proving on both counts to be substantially more economical than the core building. However, the calculation did not take into account the capital cost of the land, as the site had been in possession of the hospital for a quarter century. If this had been considered, the cost per bed of both parts of Friedrich's design might well have been equal.[39]

The pavilions at the Friedrichshain hospital in Berlin and the municipal hospital in Dresden were architectural examples of what biologists define as "speciation," in the case of the barrack, showing unique characteristics that created a new building type. The sick wards of a new hospital built in Riga were an example of the very cusp where the classic barrack type and the expanded and more solid version employed in Berlin and Dresden meet. Today in Latvia, Riga was the historic capital of a territory that had been ruled by the Teutonic

39 Theodor Friedrich, "Die Pavillonbauten im Stadtkrankenhause zu Dresden," *Deutsche Bauzeitung* 6 (1872), 363–65, 367; Robert Wimmer and Hermann August Richter, "Die Hochbauten des 19. Jahrhunderts," in Sächsischer Ingenieur- und Architekten-Verein und dem Dresdener Architekten-Verein, *Die Bauten, Technischen und Industriellen Anlagen von Dresden* (Dresden: Meinhold, 1878), 230–38.

Order in the Middle Ages and then of the Livonian province of the Russian Empire. Until the empire's dissolution in 1917, ethnic German aristocrats and gentry ruled the Livonian countryside, and German merchants, professionals, and tradesmen ran the cities and towns. Initially, Riga aimed to build a traditional, palatial hospital building, but by 1868 reports about the success of Virchow's barrack and the debates around the new hospital at Friedrichshain convinced the city fathers to change course. They commissioned city architect Johann Daniel Felsko to design a barrack/pavilion hospital that combined some key ideas of the Charité barrack and the Friedrichshain pavilion and adapted these to the more extreme climatological conditions that prevailed in Riga.

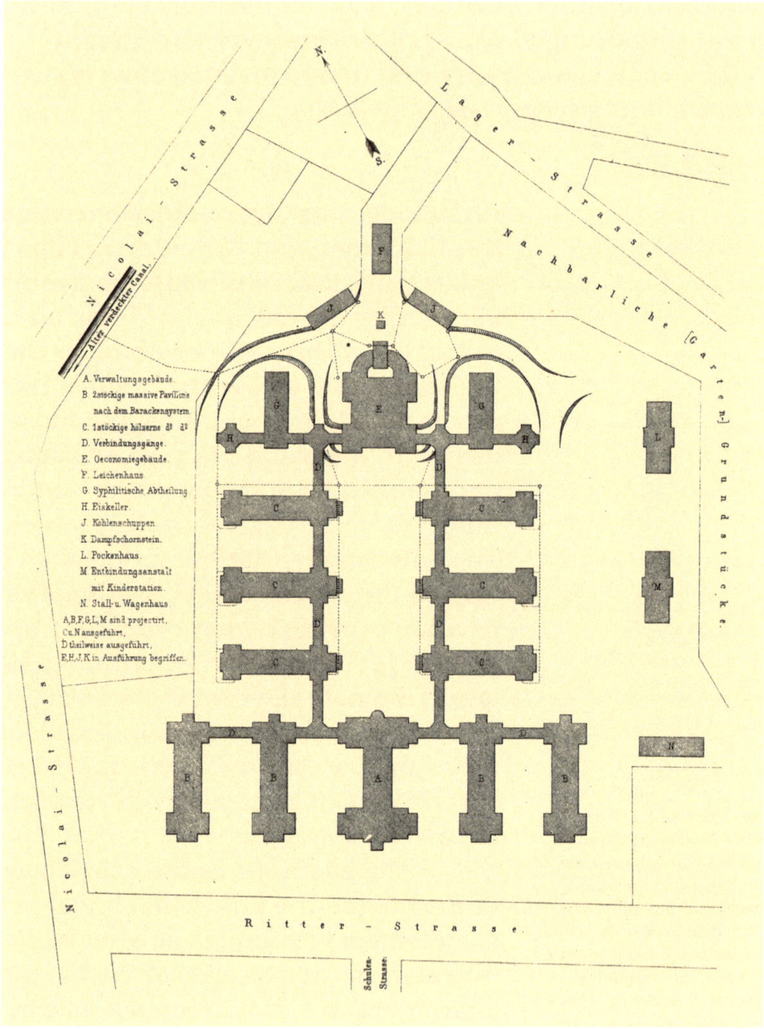

Fig. 15
Johann Daniel Felsko, Plan of the Riga hospital, Livonia, *Zeitschrift für Bauwesen*, 1873. Collection: author.

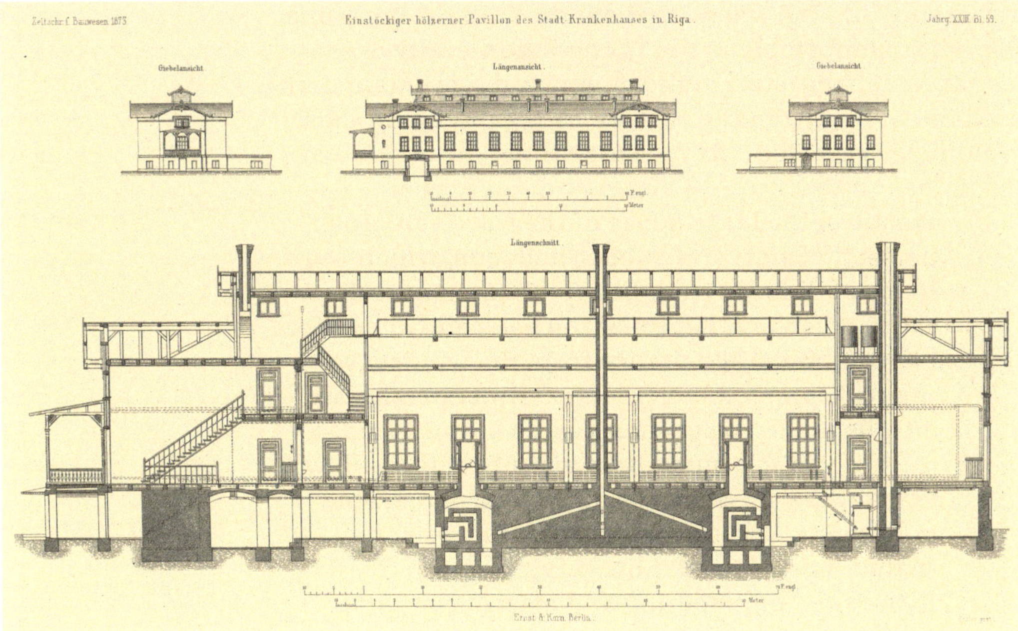

Fig. 16
Johann Daniel Felsko, Section and elevation of a ward at the Riga hospital, *Zeitschrift für Bauwesen*, 1873. Collection: author.

Each of the Riga barracks, constructed from wood, was placed on a full basement. A heated corridor connected the basements of these barracks to one another, while a generous stairwell connected the corridor to the barrack itself. This underground corridor was a perfect compromise: it comfortably connected the barracks in severe winter conditions but also allowed them to be exposed to the greatest amount of air. The ward was a post-and-beam construction with walls made of a layer of vertically placed boards covered with a layer of lime plaster, which gave the building a more solid appearance. The frame and the roof were conceived as permanent parts of the building, but the walls, floors, and insulation material could be replaced.[40]

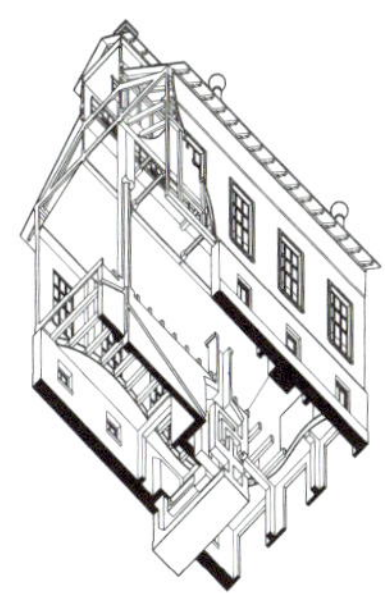

Drawings, Riga Barrack
→ p. 514

The Riga hospital was not only a synthesis of a provisional and permanent structure, it was also a highly advanced building in terms of heating and ventilation. Each barrack contained two heating systems: one based on hot water circulated through an elaborate structure of iron pipes that served as radiators, and a second system that used hot air. The building also had a complicated method of ventilation that relied on both a ridge-ventilation structure that could be opened or closed and a system of eight ventilation tubes that could be warmed by the hot-water heating system, improving the draft. The system was tested when the outside temperature was a bit below freezing. Inside, the ward was heated to a temperature of 50° Celsius. Then the ridge-ventilation structure and the eight ventilation tubes were opened. Fresh air, warmed to a temperature of 17.5° C, began

40 Carl Waldhauer, "Stadt-Krankenhaus zu Riga," *Zeitschrift für Bauwesen* 23 (1873), 505.

streaming into the ward. "Amidst the tropical heat, one felt quite comfortable in the immediate vicinity of the entrance duct because of the downward movement of the cool air coming from the outside," Riga physician Carl Waldhauer reported. "At the same time," he continued,

> the air in the large space of the ward remained perfectly quiet, and rubber balloons, which were let up at different heights of the room as well as the location and height of the beds and at two feet [60 centimeters] distance from the window remained completely motionless and upright, and only began to sway when people began to move. [...] Only in the immediate vicinity of the inflow and outflow passages was there demonstrable movement, while everywhere else was at rest—that is, a gentle and quiet mixing, not noticeable to the skin, of incoming and existing air, and a gentle outflow.[41]

When, shortly thereafter, the first patients moved into the ward, immediate improvement in their health could be seen: "It was remarkable how, within a few weeks, they acquired a healthy and thriving appearance," Waldhauer noted. The Riga barrack, he believed, marked a decisive advance, and he maintained it should be the model for not only hospitals but also other building types. "I do not pretend that the arrangement [of the Riga barracks] cannot be improved, and I am certain that many deficiencies will arise, but anyone who is concerned with this issue and who has studied the results will be convinced that this building system should be nurtured and developed," he wrote.[42]

In designing the Riga barrack, Felsko had been inspired by both Blankenstein's design for the barrack at the Charité and Gropius and Schmieden's design for the Friedrichshain hospital pavilion. Blankenstein's building was typologically a barrack, as it still carried the signature of the provisional, but the Friedrichshain pavilion, while inspired by the barrack, was permanent. Felsko's design occupied an uneasy position between the two. The Riga building was most often referred to as a *Baracke*—even if at times it was also called a "pavilion"—and the use of wood as its primary material and the single core ward with ridge ventilation reflected the typology of the post–Crimean War barrack.[43] The fact that the Riga building was partly provisional, with floor, ceiling, and walls that could be dismantled in case of serious contagion, also reflected an essential character-

41 Ibid., 509.
42 Ibid., 512.
43 At Riga, the ridge ventilation had morphed into what American English refers to as a "monitor"—that is, a superstructure gable roof that is extended for most of the length of the main roof and that, equipped with openings for light and ventilation, resembles the clerestory of an early Christian basilica. See Betsy H. Bradley, *The Works: The Industrial Architecture of the United States* (New York: Oxford University Press, 1999), 188–91.

istic of the barrack. Yet the presence of a full and permanent basement, the large scale of the building, the proliferation of secondary spaces, and the state-of-the-art heating and ventilation technology suggest that the Riga structure was in fact a permanent building.

Felsko's building revealed the extent to which the ridge-ventilated barrack had become a focus of sophisticated design and the object of speciation. But architects tried not only to push the limits of the type but also to get its basics right. In 1867 the Prussian physician Wilhelm Emil Brinkmann approached the architecture partnership of Gustav Knoblauch and Friedrich Hollin and in collaboration with them developed a barrack design for use in army hospitals that included ridge ventilation, centrally placed stoves, a much greater amount of air per patient, toilets moved to the periphery, high-ceilinged wards, and large windows. Brinkmann, Knoblauch, and Hollin did not aim to create an absolute standard. "We merely sought to imagine something that is concrete, to make a precise proposition that can be the departure for further research and design," they noted.[44]

Knoblauch continued to think about the barrack. In July 1867, the Architekten-Verein zu Berlin (Berlin Society of Architects) ran a competition for a military hospital barrack that would house thirty-two men. "The installation is intended not for stationary use but for provisional use, possibly as an auxiliary installation for an existing hospital," the announcement read. "The barrack should be executable in the shortest time, with relatively little cost, in case of a large war that will have an effect that exceeds a summer."[45] Each patient ought to have at least 28 cubic meters of air, and special attention ought to be given to the problem of ventilation. In September, the society met, and Blankenstein, who had designed the Charité barrack, gave a lecture on the concept and history of the barrack. He also argued that year-round use of barracks was problematic in the German situation because excellent ventilation might be easily achieved in summer but was difficult to obtain in winter, when there was also a need to keep the place warm, and he doubted that this contradiction could be overcome. He noted that there had been only two submissions in the competition, and that he judged both to be failures in their approach to the question of ventilation in winter.[46]

The two entries survive in the collection of the Architekturmuseum (architecture museum) of the Technische Universität Berlin. One rejected design shows a half-timbered building with a steep roof that harks back

44 Wilhelm Emil Brinkmann, *Die freiwillige Krankenpflege im Kriege* (Berlin: Enslin, 1867), 122.
45 "Konkurrenzen im Architekten-Verein zu Berlin," *Wochenblatt herausgegeben von Mitgliedern des Architekten-Vereins zu Berlin* 1 (1867), 215.
46 "Mittheilungen aus Vereinen," *Wochenblatt herausgegeben von Mitgliedern des Architekten-Vereins zu Berlin* 1 (1867), 360–61; "Haupt-Versammlung am 7. September 1867," *Zeitschrift für Bauwesen* 18 (1868), 308.

to medieval precedents. The second one, submitted with the annotation "July 3, 1866"—the date of the Battle of Königgrätz—was quite sophisticated, which is not surprising, as it was designed by Knoblauch. An evolution of the model endorsed by the Prussian Ministry of War in 1866, it provided not only ridge ventilation and shutters above each of the windows and doors, and a much greater amount of cubic space per patient, but also a greater distance between the toilets and the wards. In addition, access had been dramatically amplified: instead of one point of entry in the middle of the barrack, Knoblauch offered six entrances: one at each of the ends and four at the sides. Obviously, the patients were to be rotated between the interior of the building and the outside at an unusually high frequency.[47]

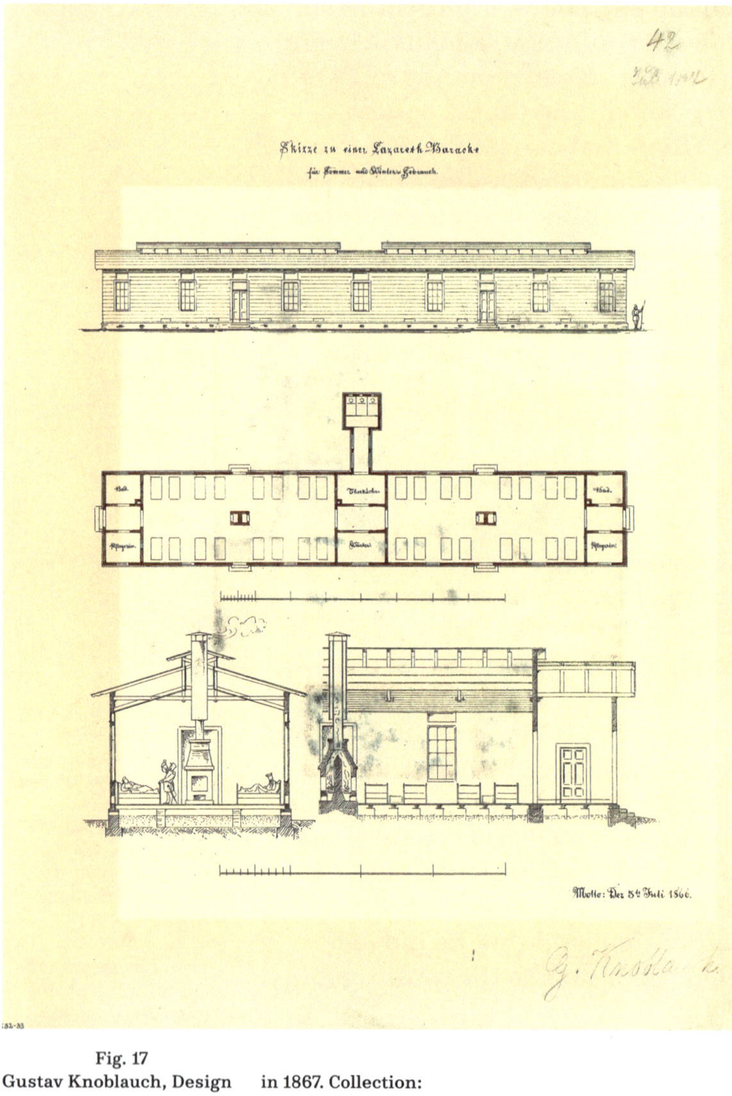

Fig. 17
Gustav Knoblauch, Design submitted in the barrack competition held by the Berlin Society of Architects in 1867. Collection: Architekturmuseum, Technische Universität Berlin.

47 Anonymous, "Lazarettbaracke, Monatskonkurrenz July 1867," Architekturmuseum, Technische Universität Berlin, inv. no. MK 32-034; Gustav Knoblauch, "Lazarettbaracke, Monatskonkurrenz July 1867," Architekturmuseum, Technische Universität Berlin, inv. no. MK 32-033.

In the last years leading up to the Franco-Prussian War (1870–71), Esmarch assumed leadership in the movement to adopt prefabricated barracks as sick wards in military hospitals. After publishing *Verbandplatz und Feldlazareth: Vorlesungen für angehende Militairärzte* (Dressing station and field hospital: Lectures for prospective military doctors), his overview of the hospitals created by the US Sanitary Commission, in 1868, he began to explore the practical implications of creating such hospitals in Germany, if and when another war were to break out. He counseled the Zentralkomitee der deutschen Vereine zur Pflege im Felde verwundeter und erkrankter Krieger (Central Committee of the German Societies for the Care in the Field of Wounded and Sick Soldiers), the coordinating organ of German Red Cross societies, to stimulate such preparations in its local associations, and in Kiel organized an association himself. As a teacher of surgery, Esmarch believed that examples and illustrations were key to effective communication. In 1867, he had visited the Red Cross pavilion at the Exposition Universelle and had marveled at the display of the work of the US Sanitary Commission. Back in Kiel, in order to generate local enthusiasm, he commissioned a cabinetmaker to make a large model of Hammond's pavilion and asked a medical illustrator to produce paintings of hospitals and tent-barracks. When, finally, he held a public lecture to generate interest in the project, he hung the pictures on the wall and placed the models on large tables. He explained that every local association devoted to the care of the wounded should commission or purchase such visual materials to generate and maintain enthusiasm during peacetime. In addition, it should have examples of all the equipment to be used in the field. "If such a collection were installed in an appropriate place, it would serve the instruction for members of all aid societies across the province," he said, adding, "A special wish is that the Central Committee in Berlin establishes a complete museum that displays all that relates to voluntary aid. The 1867 exhibition in Paris has shown that such a museum can be extremely interesting and instructive."[48]

Once the Kiel organization had been established, Esmarch began to lay the groundwork for the construction of a 500-bed hospital that, if war were to break out, could quickly be built on the grounds of the existing navy hospital. He commissioned a builder from Kiel to produce a design and received a concept that include a nice perspective of the interior—the first attempt

48 Johann Friedrich August von Esmarch, *Ueber den Kampf der Humanität gegen die Schrecken des Krieges: Mit 5 Holzschnitten nach Zeichnungen von J. Wittmaack* (Kiel: Schwers, 1869), 51–52.

to depict the interior of a lowly barrack as if it were a serious architectural proposition.

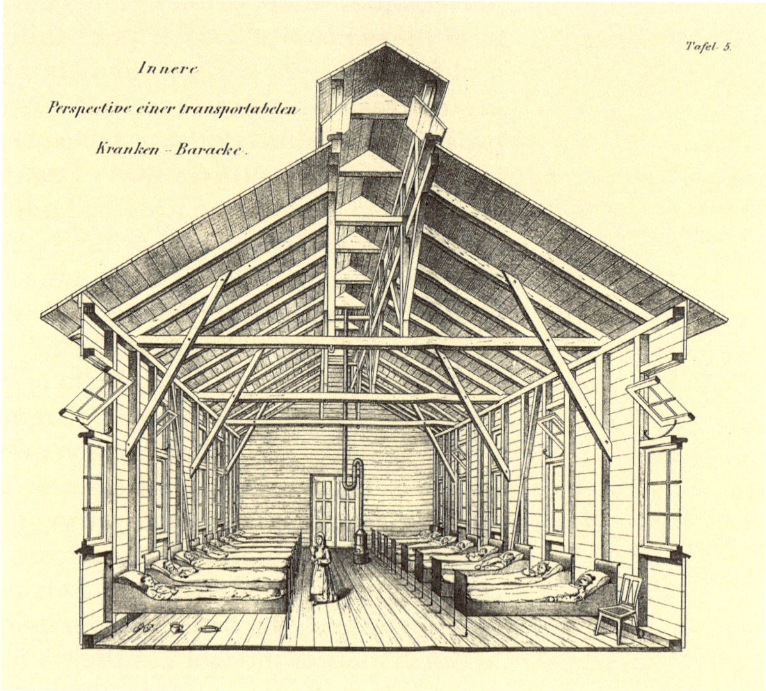

Fig. 18
J. A. Lauer, Interior perspective of a barrack design commissioned by Johann Friedrich August von Esmarch, from Esmarch's *Ueber Vorbereitung von Reserve-Lazaretten*, 1870. Collection: Staatsbibliothek zu Berlin.

But the proposal did not convince. In the fall of 1869, Esmarch traveled to Interlaken, Switzerland, where he visited the mill of Weyermann, Seiler, and Indermühle. Originally established as a manufacturer of parquet floors, the firm had expanded into the production of prefabricated Swiss chalets. Esmarch noticed that all the parts were prepared at the factory and assembled into the final product in the mill yard, then taken apart again and shipped to actual building sites. He approached the mill's chief engineer, Paul Risold, and commissioned him to study the American pavilions and design a prefabricated hospital barrack that could be quickly assembled and disassembled. In January 1870, Risold submitted a design and detailed specifications for a barrack that closely resembled the American prototype; it was 57 meters long, 7.5 meters wide, and 5 meters at its highest point and was to have ridge ventilation and offer 27 cubic meters of air space per inmate.[49]

The technology of Risold's barrack was very different from the crude construction of the American prototype. Its frame consisted of posts, beams, rafters, and a ridge beam that were clipped and bolted together by means of iron hooks and bolts. Prefabricated wood panels provided walls and were fastened into place by means of iron hardware. Prefabricated roof panels were covered with a mixture of jute, canvas, and asphalt.

49 Johann Friedrich August von Esmarch, *Ueber Vorbereitung von Reserve-Lazaretten: Drittes Beiheft Kriegerheil, Organ der Deutschen Vereine zur Pflege im Felde verwundeter und erkrankter Krieger* (Berlin: Central-Comite des Preussischen Vereins zur Pflege im Felde verwundeter und erkrankter Krieger, 1870), 93–111.

The foundation was a series of stone piles supporting the beams. Construction of one barrack necessitated fifty men and could be completed in two to three days. Risold's barrack never went into production: by the time Esmarch and his colleagues had compared the advantages and disadvantages of this and other schemes, the third—and what proved to be the decisive—war of German unification, the Franco-Prussian War, had broken out.

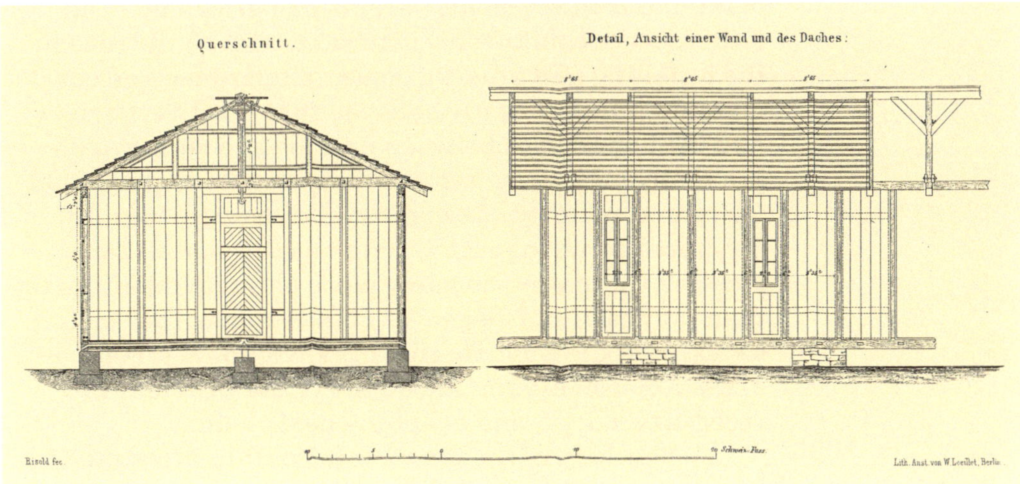

Fig. 19
Paul Risold, Section and partial elevation of the barrack design commissioned by Johann Friedrich August von Esmarch, from Esmarch's *Ueber Vorbereitung von Reserve-Lazaretten*, 1870. Collection: Staatsbibliothek zu Berlin.

Esmarch had studied Hammond's pavilion because he believed it to be a crucial element in the medical care of soldiers. And, like Virchow, he had become convinced that, even though the barrack represented a relatively primitive building type, it might be a good building block for civilian hospitals. In the lecture he gave in Kiel to motivate interest in the local aid organization, Esmarch addressed the criticism that his advocacy for the American barrack hospitals had generated. "Often enough I have to hear the objections that American barrack hospitals neither fit European conditions nor our climate, that claims about them probably contained a lot of American Humbug, and that the next wars in Europe would be of such short duration, that it would not be worthwhile to build such hospitals," he said. "Let's be clear: this is not a case of aping some American Humbug but of *understanding* and *complying* with an *incredible progress* in medical and nursing care during war, of no less importance than the move from the muzzle-loading to the breech-loading gun. I am convinced that the American system will become increasingly popular, also for civilian hospitals."[50]

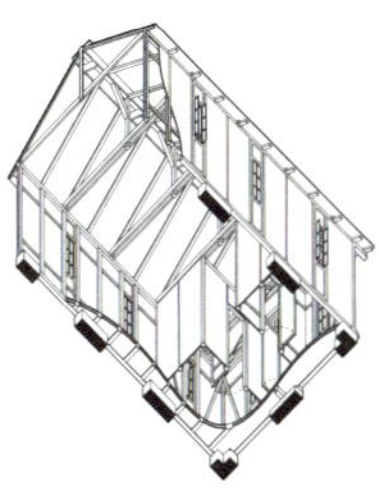

Drawings,
Risold's Barrack
→ p. 516

50 Esmarch, *Ueber den Kampf der Humanität gegen die Schrecken des Krieges*, 41–42.

The long nineteenth century was marked by an unparalleled spirit of social, scientific, and technological invention and a remarkable trust in the beneficial effects of innovation. "In its liberal idealism, the nineteenth century was honestly convinced that it was on the straight and unfailing path toward being the best of all possible worlds," the Austrian-Jewish writer Stefan Zweig observed in 1939, reflecting back on the Europe of the 1860s in which his parents had grown up. "Our fathers were comfortably saturated with confidence in the unfailing and binding power of tolerance and conciliation. They honestly believed that the divergencies and the boundaries between nations and sects would gradually melt away into a common humanity, and that peace and security, the highest of treasures, would be shared by all mankind."[51] And as the world's fairs showed, there were so many more national talents to tap than the "ease and elegance" of the French, the "technical skill" of the English, the "organizational talent" of the Americans, and the ability of the Germans to recognize, adopt, and adapt the best on offer.

Thinkers of the nineteenth century attempted to understand the laws of change, both in nature and in society. The French philosopher Auguste Comte postulated his consecutive "theological," "metaphysical," and "positive" stages of intellectual and social development, while British philosopher Herbert Spencer proclaimed that everything develops from a simple, undifferentiated homogeneity to a complex, differentiated heterogeneity. In the case of society, the state of homogeneity is represented by a hierarchical and vertically organized "militant" form, while the second state is the complex and horizontally organized "industrial" form, which is structured by negotiated obligations. Comte, Spencer, and most others who tried to identify the principles of change—that is, "progress"—focused on the kind of change that took many generations.

In the 1870s, the French sociologist and criminologist Gabriel Tarde developed a fine-grained understanding of change that centered on the practice of imitation happening at both the individual and a broader societal level, and hence he believed that he was able to describe both short-term and long-term change. Imitation typically moved in one direction: classes, persons, practices, and things recognized as superior are imitated, while classes, persons, practices, and things judged as inferior are not. Where was the superior model to be found? There were two options. The first assumed it was found in the past, and generated *imitation-coutume*

51 Stefan Zweig, *The World of Yesterday: An Autobiography* (London: Cassell, 1943), 14–15.

(imitation as custom), shaping and supporting tradition. The second located it in the experiences and inventions by contemporaries, and led to *imitation-mode* (imitation as fashion). The latter led to explicit change in which the new model found in the present either replaces the one from the past, or is found to be wanting and is discarded, or is somehow integrated into the older one, effecting a change that appears as continuity. History was both at the macro and the micro scale a series of parallel but not necessarily coordinated alternations between stable conditions—in which customs and habits, understood as vital common inheritance, predominate—and dynamic periods of fashion, which, after it has succeeded in overcoming and destroying tradition, was destined to become in its turn a social inheritance through the formation of a new tradition (which might, in fact, be a revitalized form of the older one).[52]

In the history of the barrack, the year 1854 marked the cusp where a long period shaped by a conservative attitude of *imitation-coutume* met a vital, three-decade-long stretch of *imitation-mode* shaped by an explicit desire and opportunity to learn about developments elsewhere, by a readiness to debate fundamentals, by a willingness to try anything, and by a commitment to apply the results of that research, debate, experiment, and application at home. If we consider the barrack as a work of architecture, and look at it within the context of architectural history, not only it but every other building type as well has gone through periods marked by a spirit of *imitation-coutume* and those of *imitation-mode*. Tarde suggested that his understanding of these two different models of imitation had major implications for the nature and scope of production.

> It is clear that in an age when custom imposed different kinds of food and clothing and furniture and houses in different localities, in localities where they remained fixed for several generations, machine production on a large scale would be, even if it were known, without a market. The artisan of such an epoch is bent on making only a small number of very solid and durable articles, whereas, later on, in periods when the same fashion holds sway over more than one country, although it changes from year to year, the quantity and not the stability of the product is the aim of industry. [...] In ages of custom the producer seeks the narrow and long drawn-out market of the

52 See Gabriel Tarde, *The Laws of Imitation*, trans. Elsie Clews Parsons (New York: Henry Holt, 1903).

> future, in ages of fashion he seeks the vast ephemeral market of the outside world.[53]

Tarde concluded that works of architecture, which are expensive to produce and demand *firmitas* (durability), if only to protect their users from physical harm, prospered in times of *imitation-coutume*, while the production of consumer goods languished during such epochs. "Inversely, if the fickleness of taste in times of fashion hinders the development of such arts as architecture and statuary, things that must look to the future, a uniformity of taste over a vast territory highly favours, in spite of their instability, the progress of all manufacture which is essentially ephemeral, such as paper-making, journalism, weaving, landscape gardening, etc."[54]

Tarde's analysis touches on what has been, indeed, one of the major problems of architecture since the beginning of the industrial revolution: as an easily purchased and readily dispensable consumer good it does not work. Today both commercial and residential buildings using modular shipping containers carry a promise to resolve the contradiction between the essential durability of architecture and the transitory nature of a consumer society driven by the cycles of fashion. In the second half of the nineteenth century, both the immense and temporary exhibition halls created for the world's fairs and the modest barrack carried such a reconciliatory potential. As a result, together with Joseph Paxton's 1851 Crystal Palace and Léopold Hardy and Jean-Baptiste Krantz's 1867 Palais Omnibus, we must identify William Eassie's 1854 Gloucester hut, William Hammond's Union Army pavilions, and Rudolf Virchow and Hermann Blankenstein's 1866 *Versuchsbaracke* as key buildings in an age of rapid change.

53 Ibid., 334.
54 Ibid., 335.

GRANDES AMBULANCES

Mr. Michel-Lévy — Inspecteur des armées. (Médecin en chef.)

Fig. 4. Élévation — Coupe.

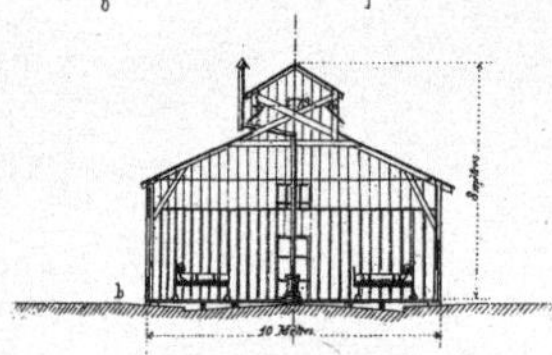

Fig. 5. Plan (Coupe)

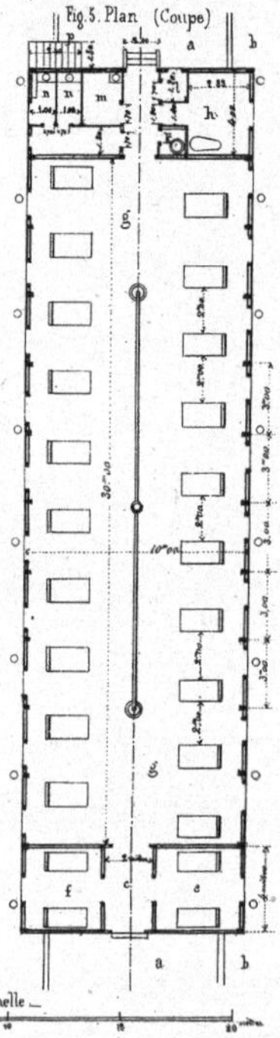

Fig. 6. Coupe longitudinale.

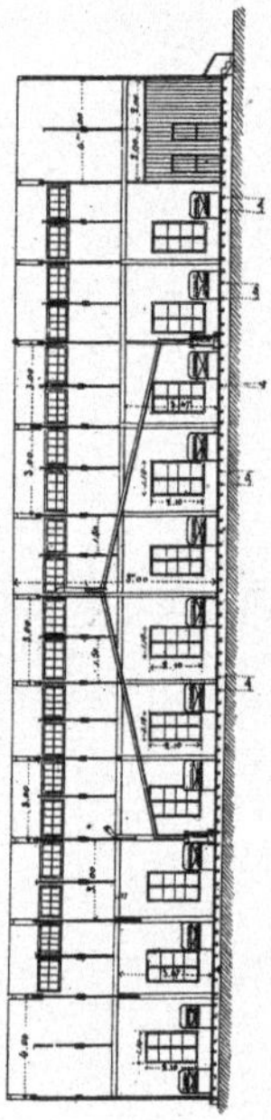

Fig. 1.

Fig. 2.

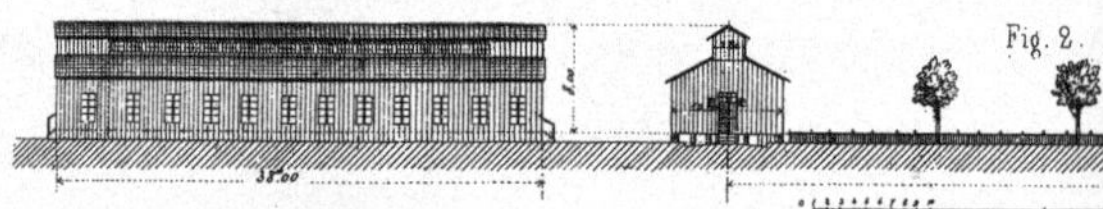

a. Chaussée bitumée.
b. Trottoir.
c. Vestibule.
ef. Salles des sœurs et infirmiers.
g. Salle des malades.
h. Salle de bain.
k. Appareil de chauffage.
l. Linge sale.

Fig. 3. Pl

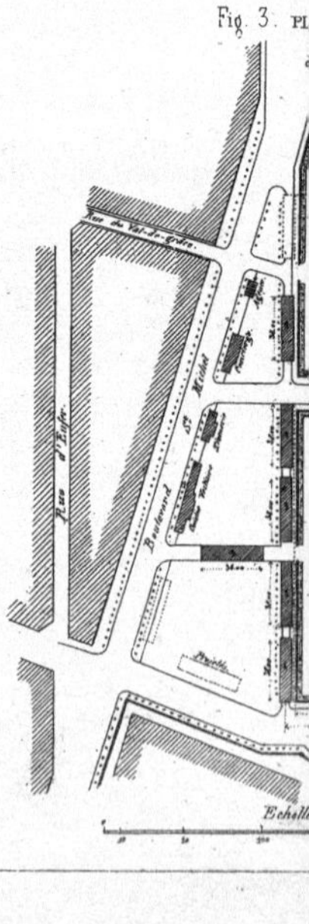

Fig. 10. Travée extrême (Entrée)

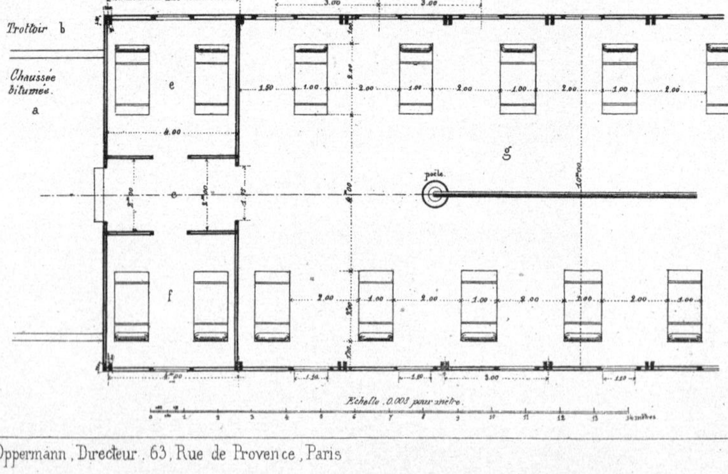

C. A. Oppermann, Directeur. 63, Rue de Provence, Paris

→ p. 293

ES du LUXEMBOURG, (Paris).

Mr Simonet Entrepreneur général.

Fig. 7. Elévation

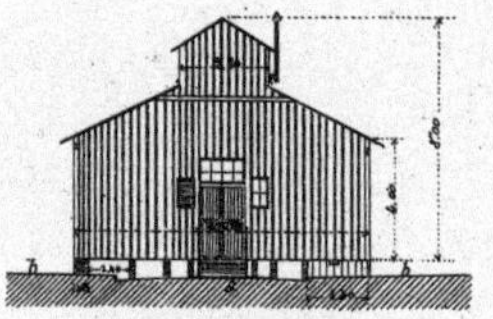

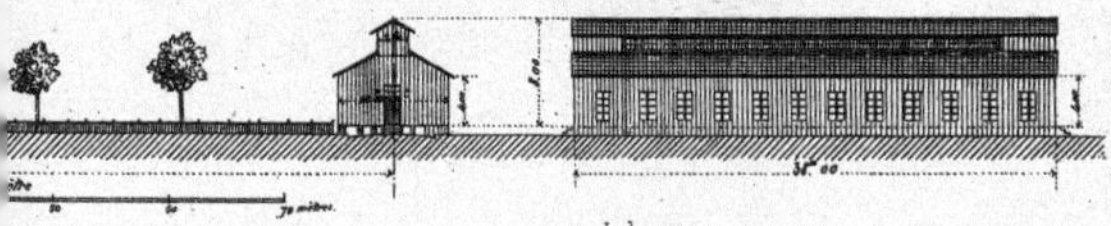

Fig. 8. Plan.

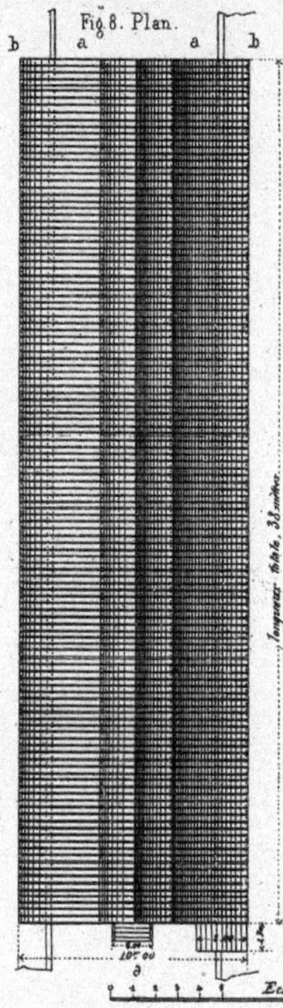

Fig. 9. Elévation longitudinale.

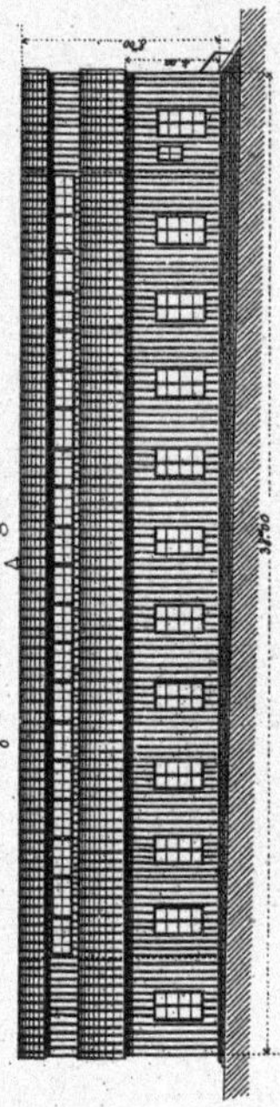

m Laboratoire.
n Water closet.
p Fosse des lunettes.
q Robinets d'eau chaude et froide.
r Evier.
s Tuyaux de vidange.
t Tuyaux d'eau chaude et froide.
v Tuyaux d'eau froide.

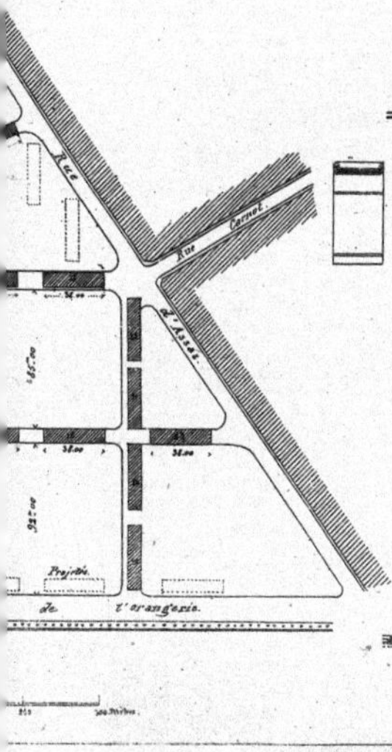

Fig. 11. Travée extrême (Sortie)

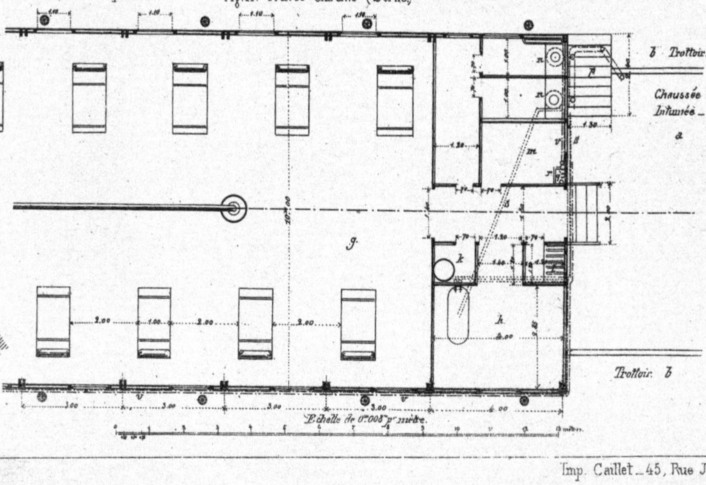

Imp. Caillet _ 45, Rue Jacob

C - 454.

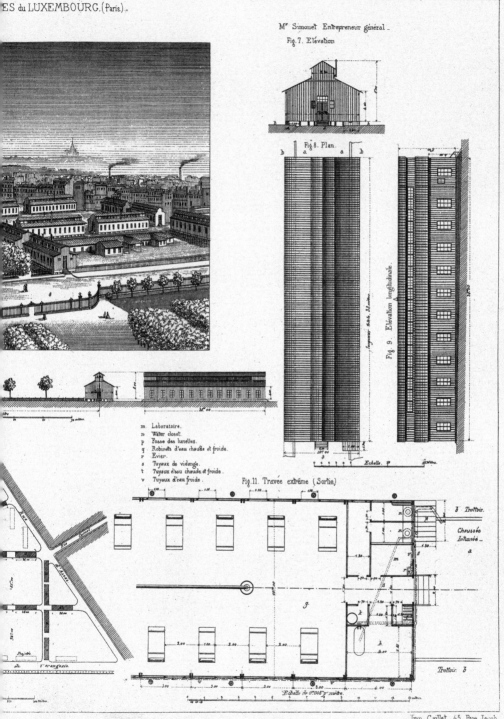

Seven

Germany, Germany Above All

The Franco-Prussian War (1870–71) is remembered as a watershed in the history of Europe that ended the hegemony of France and established the newly constituted and popularly backed German Reich as the dominant power on the European continent. "The German Reich was an empire built on war," German author Sebastian Haffner wrote in his concise but masterly history of this state, which lasted for a mere seventy-four years. And, as Haffner observed, the German Reich was destined to cause war because, when that state was established, it quickly came to be seen by all too many Germans "as the springboard for a never clearly defined expansion."[1] This, then, ties the Franco-Prussian War to World War I, which led to the National Socialist party's ambition for vast territorial expansion in the east, the Third Reich, World War II, and the Holocaust.

→ Fig. 1

Because the German Reich was both the child and parent of war, its history has a special relationship to the history of the barrack, likewise a product of war. In the history of the barrack, the war fought in 1870–71 denotes a divide. The Crimean War brought the barrack to prominence as a building type that could provide emergency shelter, and the US Civil War showed its potential to dramatically ameliorate the survival rates of sick and wounded, when it was deployed as part of a comprehensive strategy of hospital construction. Yet, in both wars, the barrack arrived on the stage as a character without much baggage. In the case of the Crimea, the initiative to produce the barracks and dispatch them to what was called the Seat of War in the East primarily rested with a couple of businessmen; and in the case of the US Civil War, when Surgeon General William A. Hammond adopted this building type as a key element of field hospitals constructed in the rear, the extent of precedent on which he relied was small.

In the five years between the end of the US Civil War and the beginning of the Franco-Prussian War, the barrack had been a topic of much consideration and

1 Sebastian Haffner, *The Ailing Empire: Germany from Bismarck to Hitler*, trans. Jean Steinberg (New York: Fromm, 1989), 2, 8.

Fig. 1
Charles de Mazade, Map of the German invasion of France, 1875. Collection: Bibliothèque Nationale de France, Paris.

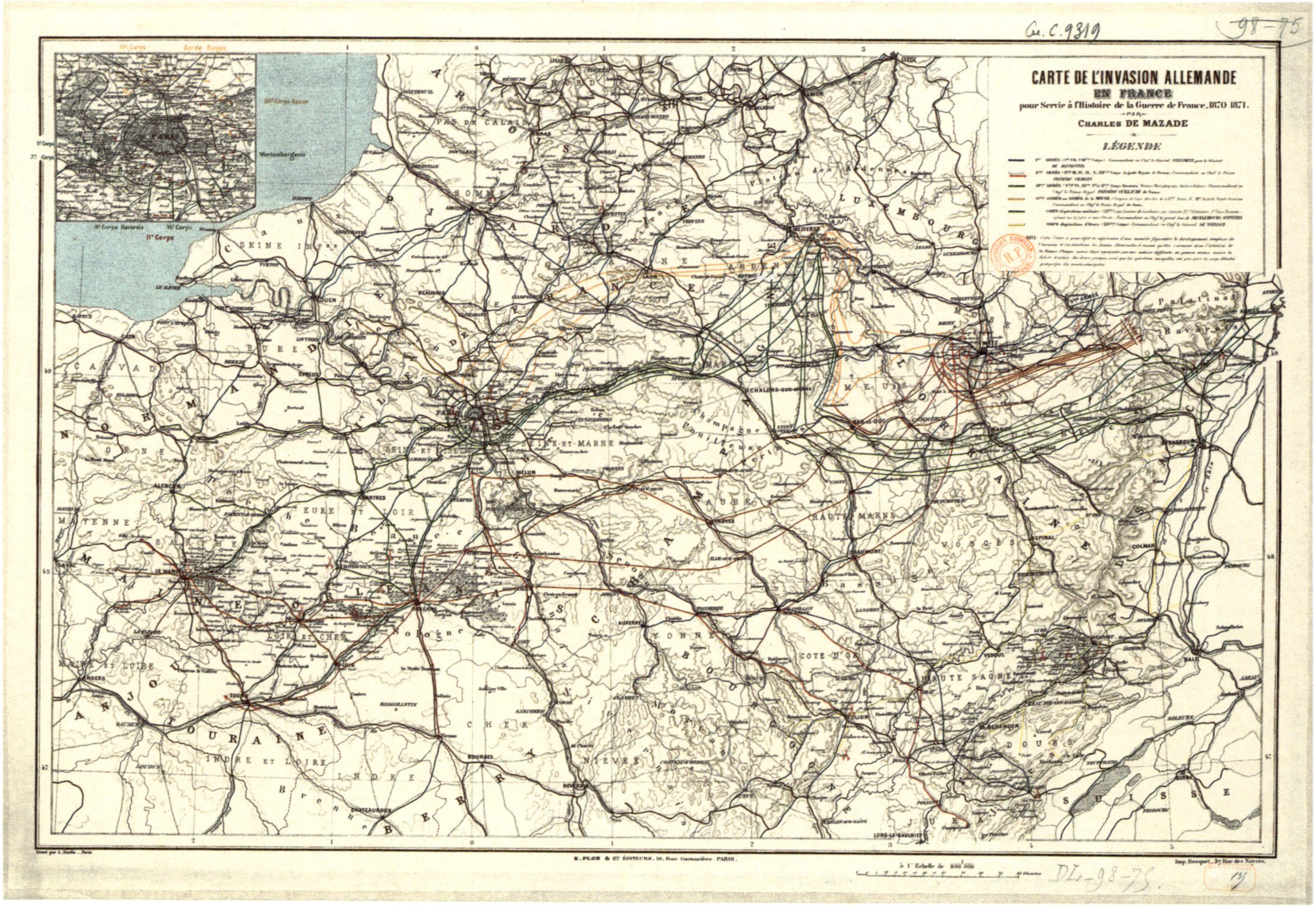

experimentation. With the outbreak of the Franco-Prussian War, when civilian authorities, military leaders, and members of the Red Cross and other volunteer societies in both France and Germany considered the capacity of hospitals in the rear to accommodate sick and wounded soldiers, they immediately considered the construction of barracks wherever there appeared to be a shortage of room in permanent buildings deemed suitable for the purpose of patient care. The developments in the 1860s had created high expectations about the beneficial potential of the barrack in both military and civilian contexts and, in addition, a plethora of architectural options. The six months that separated the outbreak of the war on July 19, 1870, and the armistice of January 28, 1871, produced a surfeit of different solutions, which at first sight suggest that within the history of the barrack, the German contributions in 1870–71 established the Reich as a barrack power.

In a concise review of the state of the art of barrack construction, published in 1873 as part of a report on his own effort to provide relief during the Franco-Prussian War by means of a small, tented hospital erected in Paris, Thomas Wiltberger Evans praised the successes of the deployment of barracks in Germany during the war. Evans knew what "state of the art" meant; after all, since the end of the US Civil War, he had been the most eager advocate of Hammond's pavilions in France, and he had organized the display of these structures at the 1867 Exposition Universelle. "If any advance has recently been made in the theory and practice of barrack hospital construction, we are certainly indebted to the Germans for it," he wrote. "In constructing the German barracks, means have never been neglected to secure a constant ventilation in summer, and also in winter, when a winter use may have been anticipated."[2] But the last clause was the catch: most of the barracks designed and constructed in Germany in the summer of 1870 were not intended for winter use, as German military planners assumed the war would be over by October. Hastily adapted for winter conditions, many of the German barracks failed the test, resulting in doubts about the general efficacy of the barrack as a building type.

The war that is commonly designated in English as the Franco-Prussian War is known in French as the *Guerre franco-allemande de 1870* (Franco-German War of 1870) and in German as the *Deutsch-Französischer Krieg* (German-French War). None of the three labels precisely describes the political conditions of the conflict. The

2 Thomas Wiltberger Evans, *History of the American Ambulance Established in Paris during the Siege of 1870–71* (London: Chiswick Press, 1873), 217–18.

English name Franco-Prussian War recognizes that within the alliance of German states, the Kingdom of Prussia was the dominant power. With four-fifths of the territory and population of the North German Confederation—a federal state that consisted of two kingdoms, five grand duchies, five duchies, seven principalities, and three so-called Free and Hanseatic Cities—Prussia controlled the confederation, which, in turn, dominated the four independent southern German states that joined in the war against France. The French and German names emphasize a different aspect of the war—the fact that it became, in the hearts of the people who fought in it, a struggle between two nations: the French nation, assembled in a single state, and a German nation that, in January 1870, comprised many different states.

German nationalism, which aspired to unite all Germans into a German nation-state, and Prussian statecraft had had a rocky relationship since the first decade of the nineteenth century, when German armies had been defeated in four Coalition Wars, which brought Prussia under French occupation and made other German states into clients of Napoleon.[3] Between 1807 and 1813, the Prussians appealed to the German nation as a whole to join in its resistance against the French. However, after the Battle of Leipzig (1813), which brought an end to French rule over the continent, the royal, ducal and grand ducal, and princely rulers and governments of Prussia and the other thirty-eight states that made up the newly established Deutscher Bund (German Confederation) joined forces to suppress German nationalism, because it demanded a unified, democratic national state, which implied the retirement of all but one of the many ruling houses within Germany.

But when Otto von Bismarck became prime minister of Prussia in 1862, he decided to harness the emotional force of German nationalism to the chariot of Prussian policy in Germany, an alliance between opposites that led to the intended result of a German Reich that centered on Prussia and was led by Bismarck—and the unintended consequence of the dissolution of Prussia within the new nation-state. The unification of Germany required three Prussian-led wars. The Second Schleswig War (1864), against Denmark, brought the hitherto Danish-ruled duchy of Schleswig under Prussian control and the duchy of Holstein under Austrian administration. The Austro-Prussian War (1866) separated Austria from the other German states and led to a provisional and incomplete unification of Germany north of the Main River within the North German Confederation.

3 Friedrich von Schiller, "Deutsche Grösse," in *Schiller: Ausgewählte Werke*, ed. Kläre Buchmann and Hermann Missnharter, 6 vols. (Stuttgart: J. G. Cottasche Buchhandlung Nachfolger, 1944–50), 5:366–67.

The Franco-Prussian War (1870–71) was necessary to complete the unification.

The Kingdoms of Bavaria and Württemberg and the Grand Duchies of Baden and Hesse-Darmstadt, which had been allied with Austria against Prussia in 1866, had not joined the North German Confederation, and the mostly Roman Catholic and easygoing populations of these four states were weary of the mostly Protestant and heavy-handed Germans from the north—and in particular they were antagonistic to Prussia, the dominant power. Overestimating the power of anti-Prussian sentiment, French emperor Napoleon III believed that these southern German states could become a French protectorate. Napoleon did not know that, in fact, the state governments in Munich, Stuttgart, Karlsruhe, and Darmstadt had concluded secret treaties with the government in Berlin, agreeing to mutual military assistance in case of war, after they heard that Napoleon III insisted on French territorial gains east of the Rhine as a reward for having remained neutral during the Austro-Prussian War. It was an ambition that was sure to mobilize German national feeling in all the German states, as the Rhine had become, in the nineteenth century, a symbol of Germany itself, celebrated in patriotic paintings, sculptures, and songs. Bismarck realized that a common defense of the Rhine frontier was to be the most effective means to politically unify the north and the south. Once southern German armies were fighting shoulder to shoulder with those of the north, Munich, Stuttgart, Karlsruhe, and Darmstadt would be under great popular pressure to negotiate admission to the North German Confederation, transforming it into the (almost) united Germany that, without Austria, would be dominated by Prussia.

The secret treaties of mutual military assistance applied only if one of the contracting parties was attacked. Bismarck skillfully used the candidacy of a German, Prince Leopold of Hohenzollern-Sigmaringen, for the throne of Spain, vacant since the deposition of Queen Isabella II in 1868, to suggest the possibility of a hostile encirclement of France. And he first edited and then leaked a report about a tense meeting between Prussia's King Wilhelm I and the French ambassador to Berlin—did the ambassador insult the king? did the king insult the ambassador? Both the Spanish business and the report provoked Napoleon III, who still fretted about Bismarck's refusal to grant some territories to France at the expense of Baden and perhaps even Württemberg. In addition, the emperor could have used a quick military success to draw attention away from domestic political troubles. Napoleon's generals had convinced him that victory would be easy—like everyone else in France, even military professionals were dazzled by the staging of the French Imperial Army at Châlons. A war would offer a quick demonstration of the superiority of French arms.

Chapter Four, Fig. 16
→ p. 179

On July 19, 1870, France declared war on Prussia. The French Imperial Army, made up largely of professional soldiers, proved wholly unprepared, while the German armies, made up largely of conscripts, were ready for war. Trained to operate in small units, covered by superior artillery produced by the Krupp steelworks in Essen, and supported by excellent logistics, the Germans quickly forced the French Armée du Rhin (Army of the Rhine), commanded by Marshal Achille Bazaine, into hasty retreat to the city of Metz, the strongest fortress in France.

One week after the declaration of war, the mayor of Metz, Philippe Félix Maréchal, instructed city architect Antoine Demoget to construct on a field located north of the old city a military hospital to accommodate up to 2,000 wounded that were expected to come from the battles the Army of the Rhine was supposed to fight on German territory—at this time no one in Metz expected that the city itself would be besieged. For inspiration, Demoget turned to the description of the American hospitals published by the Surgeon General's Office of the US War Department in 1865 and to his copy of Friedrich von Esmarch's *Verbandplatz und Feldlazareth* (Dressing station and field hospital).[4] If he had desired to use some French prototypes, he would not have come far. Unlike the Germans, the French (nor for that matter the English) had not used the five years that separated the end of the US Civil War from the beginning of the Franco-Prussian War to experiment with barrack technology. The only significant advance made on the issue of emergency shelter in France during the 1860s concerned the design and use of tent-barracks, a hybrid between a tent and a barrack that provided the capacity of the latter with the technology of the former.[5] The most prominent advocate for the use of tents was Léon Clément Le Fort, a surgeon who convinced the management of the Cochin Hospital in Paris to create extra patient capacity by pitching three tent-barracks of his design. Because Le Fort had not been able to solve the problem of how to safely heat tents in the winter, they were to be used from the early spring to the late fall.

4 United States War Department, memo, July 20, 1864, in War Department, Surgeon General's Office, *Circular No. 6: Reports on the Extent and Nature of the Materials Available for the Preparation of a Medical and Surgical History of the Rebellion* (Philadelphia: Lippincott & Co., 1865); Johann Friedrich August von Esmarch, *Verbandplatz und Feldlazareth: Vorlesungen für angehende Militairärzte* (Berlin: August Hirschwald, 1868).

5 See, among others, Armand Husson, *Note sur les tentes et baraques appliquées au traitement des blessés* (Paris: Paul Dupont, 1869); Isaac Schatz, *Étude sur les hôpitaux sous tentes* (Paris: A. Parent, 1869).

Demoget either did not know of the tent-barracks at the Cochin Hospital, or he did know of them but chose to ignore them. Instead, he turned to the design of the Lincoln Hospital in Washington, DC, which was to inform the parti of the Metz hospital: the plan was based on an isosceles triangle, with barracks aligned along the two legs and various common facilities, such as the administration, the kitchen, bathhouses, operating rooms, and the pharmacy in the center. Demoget made a few modifications; in Washington, DC, the pavilions were located parallel to the axis of the arrangement, while at Metz the barracks were rotated some fifteen degrees. This was supposed to improve ventilation.

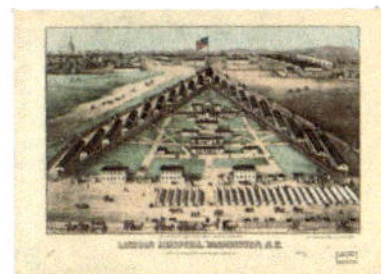

Chapter Five, Fig. 17
→ p. 225

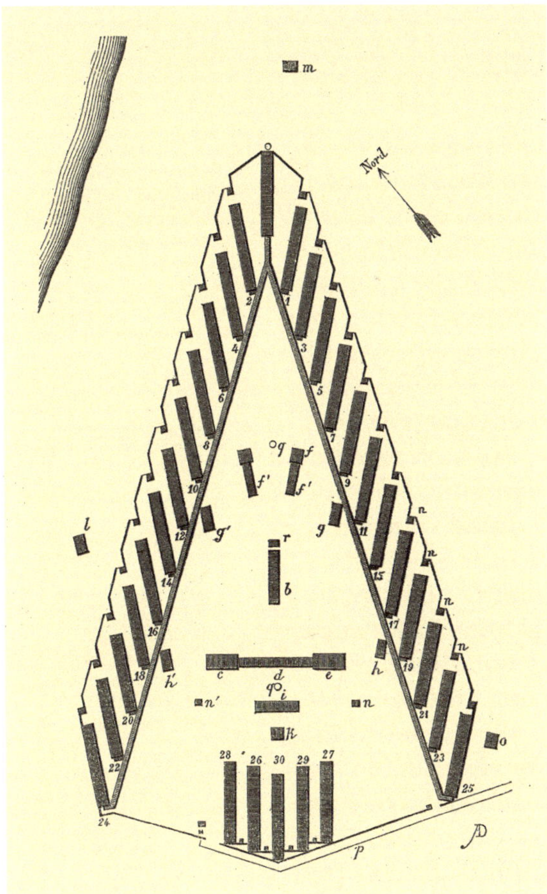

Fig. 2
Antoine Demoget, Plan of the emergency hospital in Metz, France, 1870, from Antoine Demoget and Ludovic Brossard, *Etude sur la construction des ambulance temporaires*, 1871. Collection: author.

Originally Demoget intended to copy the design of Surgeon General Hammond's pavilions, but it quickly became clear that he could not obtain the required windows at short notice, and so he dropped them and settled for one long window and ventilation strip located just below the eaves. With a height of 46 centimeters and stretching the whole length of the building, it featured alternating fixed glass panes and movable wooden flaps. These Metz barracks were a bit smaller than the

American model, and because of the limited supply of lumber and boards and the great haste of construction, the buildings were uneven and crude.

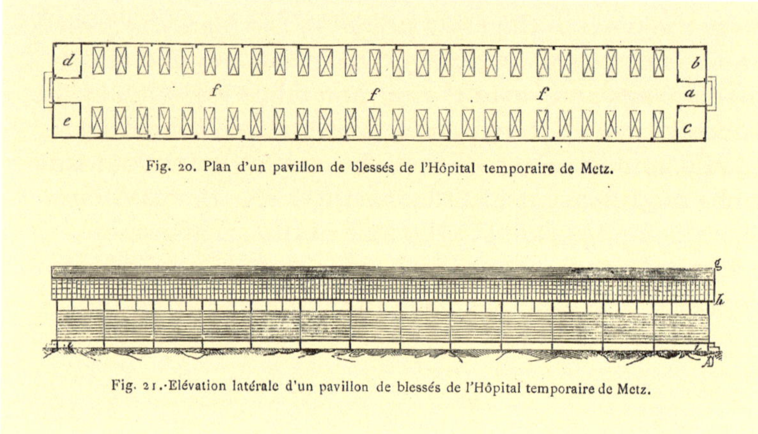

Fig. 20. Plan d'un pavillon de blessés de l'Hôpital temporaire de Metz.

Fig. 21. Elévation latérale d'un pavillon de blessés de l'Hôpital temporaire de Metz.

Fig. 3
Antoine Demoget, Plan and elevation of the Metz barrack, 1870, from Antoine Demoget and Ludovic Brossard, *Etude sur la construction des ambulance temporaires*, 1871. Collection: author.

In his report on his hospital, published a year after its construction, Demoget was happy to note that the ventilation had been perfect. "At all times, even when the population under treatment reached the highest number, of 2,270 sick, one did not smell in the wards that obnoxious, persistent, and characteristic odor that denoted danger for both the sick and those who attend to them."[6]

Eugène Grellois, the chief medical surgeon in Metz, expressed a very different view: the barracks had been the product of *un certain engouement* (a certain craze). While they certainly offered a quick solution to the problem of shelter, there were few other benefits. "In summer, the barracks are unpleasant to live in; in winter, they are not livable. The single board that separates the inside from the outside does not offer sufficient protection against the effects of thermal conductivity; in cold weather, the stoves are hardly able to maintain a bearable temperature, even for those who are close to them. The fir lumber that was almost exclusively used in these constructions was wet, and as the result of it the interior of the barrack was very humid. And as the lumber dried it contracted, resulting in openings between the joints of the boards."[7] He concluded that, all in all, barracks like those erected at Metz should not be used for longer than two months and never in the cold seasons.

The retreat of the Army of the Rhine to Metz in August was followed by the Battle of Sedan (September 1–2, 1870), which caused the collapse of French military resistance in the northeast and the humiliating surrender of Napoleon III to King Wilhelm I and Bismarck.

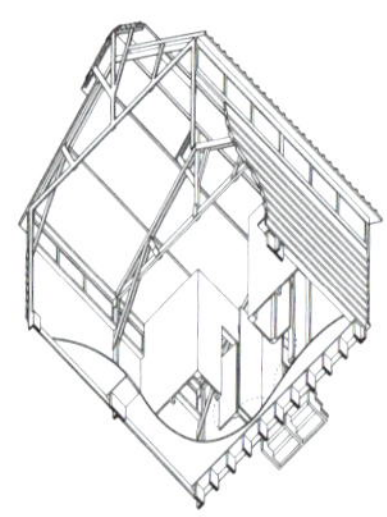

Drawings, Metz Hospital Barrack
→ p. 517

6 Antoine Demoget and Ludovic Brossard, *Etude sur la construction des ambulances temporaires suivie d'un essai sur l'application des baraquements a la construction des hopitaux civils permanents* (Paris: Cerf, 1871), 109.
7 Eugène Grellois, *Histoire médicale du blocus de Metz* (Paris and Metz: Baillière and Alcan, 1872), 197–98.

In Paris, the politician Léon Gambetta proclaimed France a republic again and participated in the formation of the provisional Government of National Defense, led by General Louis-Jules Trochu, the newly appointed commander in chief of the Paris military district. The provisional government had little opportunity to organize itself: within two weeks the German armies arrived at the gates of Paris, and on September 19 they had encircled the city and begun a siege. Gambetta left Paris by hot-air balloon and established a second headquarters for the provisional government in the city of Tours. From there he made a valiant effort to raise new armies to drive back the Germans and relieve Paris. On November 26, 1870, the German philosopher Friedrich Engels noted, in an article published in the London *Pall Mall Gazette*, that despite very low expectations, the effort seemed to pay off. "We all know the immense difficulties under which the new army had to be formed: the want of officers, of arms, of horses, of all kinds of Matériel, and especially the want of time," he observed. Acknowledging that the French were motivated by patriotism and hatred for the Germans, Engels predicted that, within a month, the provisional government might succeed in raising significant new armies. "There are more men than are wanted; thanks to the resources of modern industry and the rapidity of modern communications, arms are forthcoming in unexpectedly large quantities; 400,000 rifles have arrived from America alone; artillery is manufactured in France with a rapidity hitherto quite unknown. Even officers are found, or trained, somehow. Altogether, the efforts which France has made since Sedan to reorganize her national defence are unexampled in history, and require but one element for almost certain success—time."[8] Time was needed to train the new soldiers, and for that purpose, eleven large camps of instruction were to be constructed in a matter of weeks.

One of those training sites was the Camp des Alpines, located south of Avignon, adjacent to the small town of Graveson. Its stated purpose was to house up to 60,000 conscripts from Provence. Colonel Jacques Quiquandon, who commanded a battalion of sappers located in Marseille, was charged with both the construction and, after its completion, the operation of the camp. The contract to construct barracks went to the Marseille-based builder Pierre Gémy, who had developed a system of construction based on prefabricated trestles that supported the central purlin carrying the rafters. These trestles were hinged to prefabricated

8 Friedrich Engels, "Notes on the War," in Karl Marx and Frederick Engels, *Collected Works*, 50 vols. (London: Lawrence & Wishart, 2010), 22:183.

foundation beams that also contained at the outer end a wall post, which in turn carried the lowest purlin. With the trestles spaced at intervals of 3.5 meters, Gémy's system allowed for the erection of a barrack on uneven terrain, even on a slope, at a very modest cost.

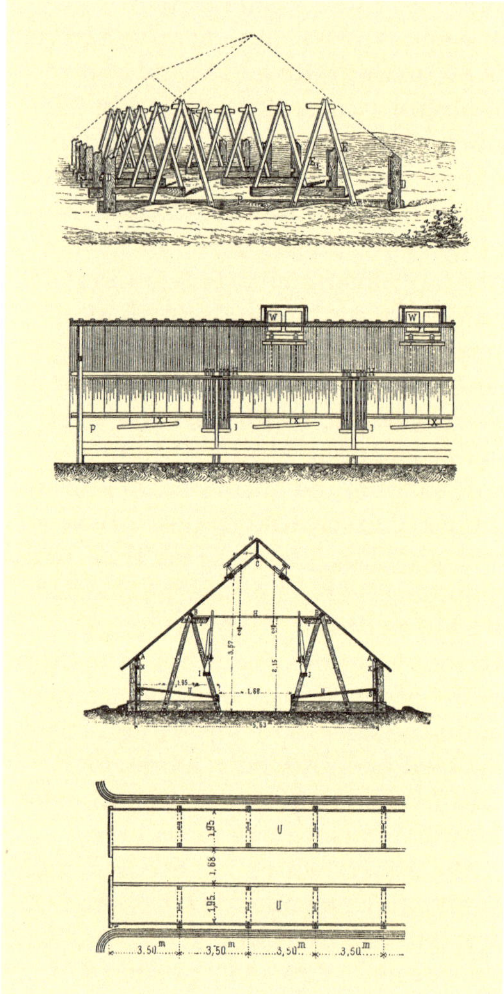

Fig. 4
Pierre Gémy, Perspective view of the trestles during construction, two sections, and a plan of a section of a barrack for the Camp des Alpines, France, 1870, from Friedrich Richter, *Gebäude für militärische Zwecke*, 1900. Collection: author.

A crew of one foreman and ten laborers was to construct 60 linear meters per day, which provided shelter for a typical company consisting of 120 men.[9] Construction indeed proved to be easy, and Gémy applied for a patent, which was issued on December 14, 1870. However, these buildings were incapable of keeping out the rain and cold, and the camp at Graveson became known among the wet and cold recruits as Camp de Crevaison ("camp of punctures," presumably a reference to leaky roofs) or as the Camp de Crèves-Hommes ("camp of shattered men"), and various locations of these buildings were marked with graffiti directing arrivals to one side to catch a cold and the other to pick up a throat infection or diarrhea.[10]

9 D. A. Least, "Baraques de Campement," *Gazette des architects et du bâtiment*, 2nd ser., 6 (1877), 280–82.
10 Anonymous, *Camp des Alpines: République en baraques; Carnet d'un officier* (Marseille: Chespin, 1873), 11–12.

While training camps like the Camp des Alpines were constructed in great haste, the eyes of the world were focused on Paris. Considering the capability of the French to prevent a German victory, Engels noted, in his article of November 26: "For the present everything of course hinges upon Paris. If Paris hold out another month—and the reports on the state of provisions inside do not at all exclude that chance—France may possibly have an army in the field large enough, with the aid of popular resistance, to raise the investment by a successful attack upon the Prussian communications."[11] By that date, Paris had been encircled for ten weeks, but it was still holding out.

→ Fig. 5

In 1870, Paris was the only strongly fortified capital city in the world. Thirty years earlier, then Prime Minister Adolphe Thiers had initiated a massive construction project of fortification that became popularly known as the Enceinte de Thiers (Thiers's Wall). It consisted of a 32-kilometer-long rampart with ninety-four bastions, a ditch, a 300-meter-wide glacis, and forty-nine separate forts and batteries located outside the Enceinte. In case of war, the forts and batteries would be garrisoned by units of the regular army, but volunteer soldiers of the Garde Nationale (National Guard), a militia drawn from the citizenry of Paris, was to patrol the Enceinte de Thiers.

When it became clear in the second week of September that the Germans aimed to launch an assault on Paris, the government proved able to strengthen the garrison with regulars who had escaped from Sedan and the Garde Mobile (Mobile Guard), militias of part-time soldiers from the provinces, also known as Moblots or Mobiles. Although badly trained, many Moblots were peasants and, unlike the members of the Garde Nationale, used to life outside. The Moblots provided a backup for the defense of the city's ramparts. "When the town was first invested the greatest disorder existed," English politician and journalist Henry Labouchère wrote in his diary on September 27. "For a few days officers, even generals, were shot at by regiments outside the fortifications; the National Guards performed their service on the ramparts very reluctantly, and, when possible, shirked it. The Mobiles were little better than an armed mob of peasants. The troops of the line were utterly demoralised. The streets were filled with troopers staggering about half drunk, and groups of armed Mobiles wandering in ignorance of the whereabouts of their

11 Engels, "Notes on the War," 183.

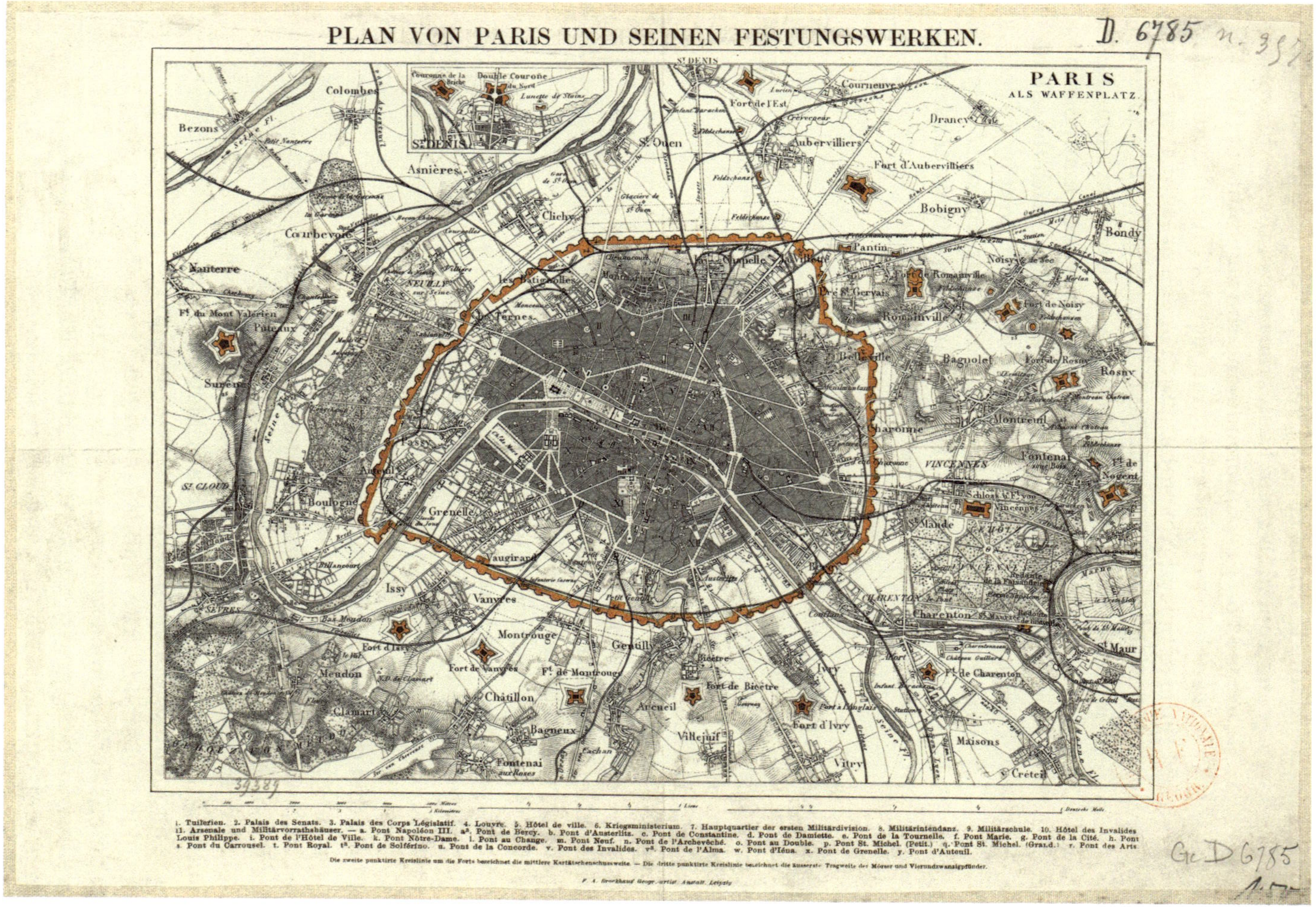

Fig. 5
This plan of Paris and its fortifications, published by the Leipzig encyclopedia publisher F. A. Brockhaus during the Franco-Prussian War, allowed Germans to record the progress of the siege of Paris at home, 1870. Collection: Bibliothèque Nationale de France, Paris.

quarters and of their regiments." Yet the commander of the city, General Trochu, quickly established some order. "The National Guard, although it still grumbles a little, does its duty on the ramparts," Labouchère continued. "The soldiers of the line are kept outside the town. The Mobiles have passed many hours in drill during the last ten days; they are orderly and well conducted, and if not soldiers already, are a far more formidable force than they were at the commencement of the siege." Labouchère believed that Paris might hold out, at least until December: "If, then, the capital does not hold out for two months, she will deserve the contempt of the world—if she does hold out for this period, she will at least have saved her honour, and, to a certain extent, the military reputation of France."[12] In fact, Paris held out for four months.

The Enceinte de Thiers was not equipped with dormitories for the Garde Nationale and Moblots, and the city initiated the construction of hundreds of barracks all along the interior of the ramparts. The barracks of the Garde Nationale took the basic design developed seventy years earlier for the army of Napoleon I. Around 4.5 meters wide, they offered a sleeping platform on each side. But whereas the original model had a length of 9 meters, accommodating forty soldiers, the 1870 version was 40 meters long, accommodating a whole company of 120 men. Unlike the original version, the Garde Nationale barrack was equipped with nine small windows on each side.

12 Henry Labouchère, *Diary of the Besieged Resident in Paris* (London: Hurst and Blackett, 1871), 41–43.

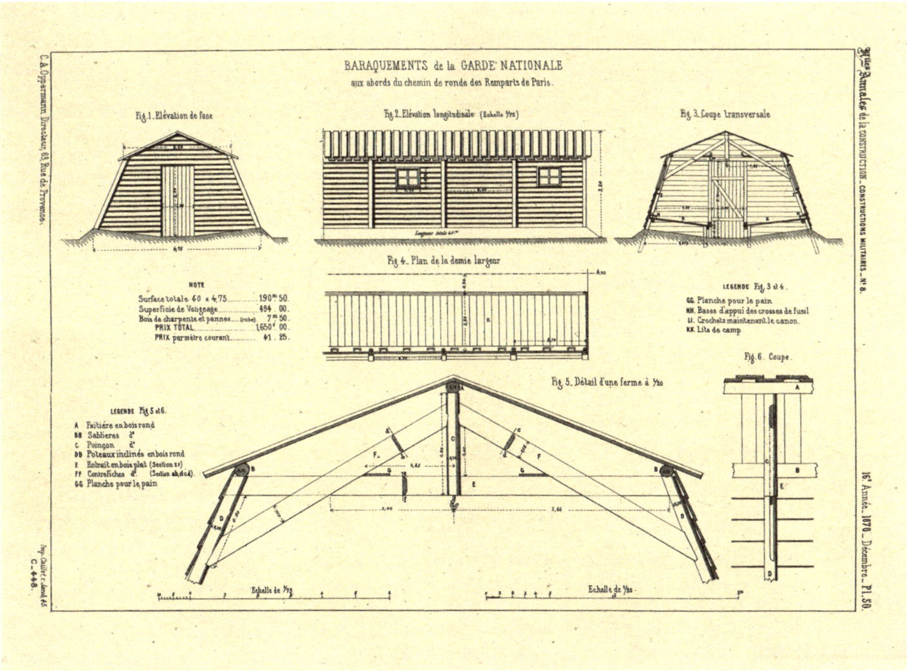

Fig. 6
Partial plan, elevations, section, and construction details of a French Garde Nationale barrack, Paris, *Nouvelles Annales de la Construction*, 1870. Collection: author.

The barracks that housed the Moblots were somewhat wider and longer, at 5 by 50 meters. They were dark spaces, with only two windows on each of the long sides and two small windows adjacent to the door on each of the gables. Like the accommodations for the Garde Nationale, those for the Moblots were simple, with a central pathway flanked by two sleeping platforms along each of the long walls. Typically, the roof was covered with cardboard impregnated with asphalt. Both barrack types were wet and drafty, and many of their occupants fell ill during their sojourn.[13]

A good-humored description of them survives in the anonymous memoir of a member of the Garde Nationale who published a journal covering a twenty-four-hour day of service on the ramparts.

> The barracks are made of white wood, like the big lodges where street entertainers spend their nights. At first sight, this dwelling is not very comfortable; but one finds there true luxury if one compares it with the situation in the first days of the siege, when the grass of the embankments served as mattresses, and the sky was the canopy above one's bed. Today our home is closed and covered: a tarpaulin stretches over the roof, and paper is glued on the walls inside. A sleeping platform stretches on each side along the whole length of the barrack. This bed is padded with a thin layer of straw that is covered with canvas. Finally, there is a shelf to store both bags and trinkets. In short, if it weren't for the humidity, the wind, the lack of any heat, the most spoiled of hedonists would find nothing to complain about. Everyone has chosen his place and is getting ready to have lunch. The comrades settle down and empty their bags on the blanket that serves as a tablecloth. The life of the camps has this privilege to tighten the friendly bonds with an equality and a fraternity that compete with the most developed, democratic and indivisible.[14]

As the account proceeds, it clearly invokes the romance of friendship, if not comradely love, between the occupants of the barrack as prefigured in the literature of classical antiquity by warrior pairs such as Castor and Pollux, Orestes and Pylades, and Nisus and Euryalus. An object of sentiment for some of those who lived in them, those barracks were also an object of interest to the architectural community: the prestigious architectural

13 "Baraquements de la Garde Mobile sur les boulevards extèrieurs de Paris," and "Baraquements de la Garde Nationale aux abords des remparts de Paris," *Nouvelles Annales de la Construction* 16, no. 192 (Dec. 1870), 106–07.
14 *Vingt-quatre heures de garde aux remparts par un fusilier du 19e bataillon* (Paris: Adrien le Clère, n. d.), 14–15.

journal *Nouvelles Annales de Construction* published a full documentation of both types in its December 1870 issue. Humble buildings to be sure, they were seen as belonging to architectural discourse—at least while Paris was under siege.

Expecting many ill and wounded soldiers, General Trochu requisitioned many buildings for use as emergency hospitals. The largest of these establishments was set up in the Grand Hôtel du Louvre, constructed on the occasion of the first Exposition Universelle (1855). Located at the Place du Palais-Royal, it was at the time of its erection the largest, most modern, and most luxurious hotel in France. Famous for its culinary excellence, the Grand Hôtel had been one of the social centers of the Second Empire. Transformed into an emergency hospital, it did not take long for this establishment to become a French version of the Scutari hospital in the Crimean War. "Ventilation cannot be said to be imperfect, for there is none; and the dead, as many as fifty at a time, are placed, 'packed like biscuits,' in the center of a gallery into which the rooms open," American journalist Thomas Gibson Bowles observed. Filled with soldiers, the place had become a slum. "The stench is something so terrible, and only last night a French gentleman said to me, 'To be taken there is death.'"[15]

Michel Lévy, director of the Ecole Impériale d'Application de la Médecine et de la Pharmacie Militaires au Val-de-Grâce (Imperial School of Military Medicine and Pharmacy at Val-de-Grâce), had overseen the creation of military hospitals during the Crimean War and in the 1860s had pleaded with the bureaucrats of the Ministry of War to stop using convents, permanent barracks, churches, and other old buildings as emergency hospitals. They were not suited, he informed them, and it would pay off to prepare designs for temporary barrack hospitals in advance, in case a war were to break out. The ministry was not interested. In July 1870, when war seemed imminent, Lévy made another attempt, invoking the experience of the American Civil War.[16] Again his proposal was met with refusal. After the Battle of Sedan, however, Lévy received permission to proceed as he saw fit. He approached Colonel Alfred Bernard de Courville, the military engineer responsible for construction on the Left Bank of Paris. They quickly decided that the gardens of the Luxembourg Palace, located within Bernard de Courville's jurisdiction, would offer a good location, and then commissioned Swiss-born architect Joseph-Frédéric Jaeger to design the hospital.[17]

15 Thomas Gibson Bowles, *The Defence of Paris: Narrated as It Was Seen* (London: Sambson Low, Son and Marston, 1871), 278–79.
16 Michel Lévy, "Note sur les hopitaux-baraques du Luxembourg et du Jardin des Plantes," *Annales d'Hygiene Publique et de Médicine Légale*, 2nd ser., 35 (1871), 117.
17 Ibid., 119–21. See also Charles-Alfred Oppermann, "Ambulance hygiéniques de Luxembourg (Siége de Paris)," *Nouvelles Annales de la Construction* 17, no. 195 (Mar. 1871), 25–28.

Chapter Six, Fig. 9
→ p. 257

Jaeger had become interested in barracks a couple of years earlier, and he had made the effort to visit the Charité Hospital *Versuchsbaracke* (experimental barrack) in Berlin. Now he quickly read up on the hospitals created by the US Sanitary Commission and set out to design a hospital of thirty-two barracks, which he labeled *chalets-hôpitaux* (hospital-chalets). While inspired by Surgeon General Hammond's pavilions, Jaeger also felt the need to reflect the dignified setting of the palace garden in the architecture of the barracks, and he designed wards that had a more explicit aesthetic ambition than any temporary barracks constructed before; one-third shorter, one-quarter wider, and one-third higher than the American model, the Luxembourg barracks had a formal presence. "Everything pertaining to them was on a larger scale, the doors were larger, the windows were larger, the walls higher," Thomas Wiltberger Evans noted in his 1873 book on barrack construction. Yet he also observed that their ventilation system was considerably inferior to that provided in Hammond's pavilions: "The barracks were unprovided with ventilating shafts,"[18] and ridge ventilation occurred only at the center. Yet no one else noted that Jaeger had not addressed the problem of ventilation adequately. But in the case of the Luxembourg barracks, first appearances and aesthetic satisfaction were indeed more important than actual performance. Unlike Demoget, who had created in Metz a temporary and crudely constructed hospital that was clearly meant as a very temporary solution, Jaeger had designed an ensemble that was meant to be shown to the public. Lévy believed that the hospital of the future was to be temporary in nature. "I want our *baraques* to become the hospitals of the future, with a duration of ten years, to be destroyed at the end of this period and replaced elsewhere by new constructions that show improvements derived from experience."[19] Thus Lévy exploited the crisis created by war to provide a lesson for peace. His ambition was confirmed when the *Nouvelles Annales de Construction* included a spread showing a general view of the hospital, a plan, and a full documentation of the Luxembourg barrack in its March 1871 issue. The journal did not address Jaeger's lack of attention to the problem of ventilation.

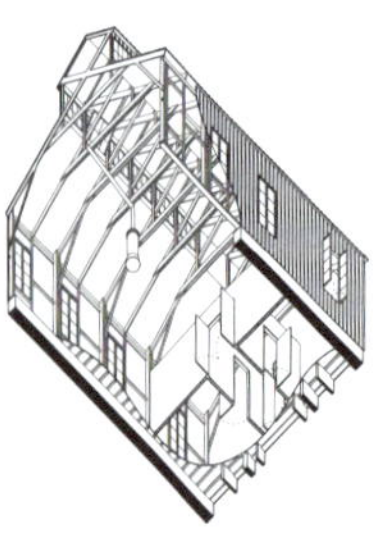

Drawings,
Luxembourg Barrack
→ p. 518

→ Figs. 7, 8

18 Evans, *History of the American Ambulance*, 215.
19 Lévy, "Note sur les hopitaux-baraques du Luxembourg et du Jardin des Plantes," 133.

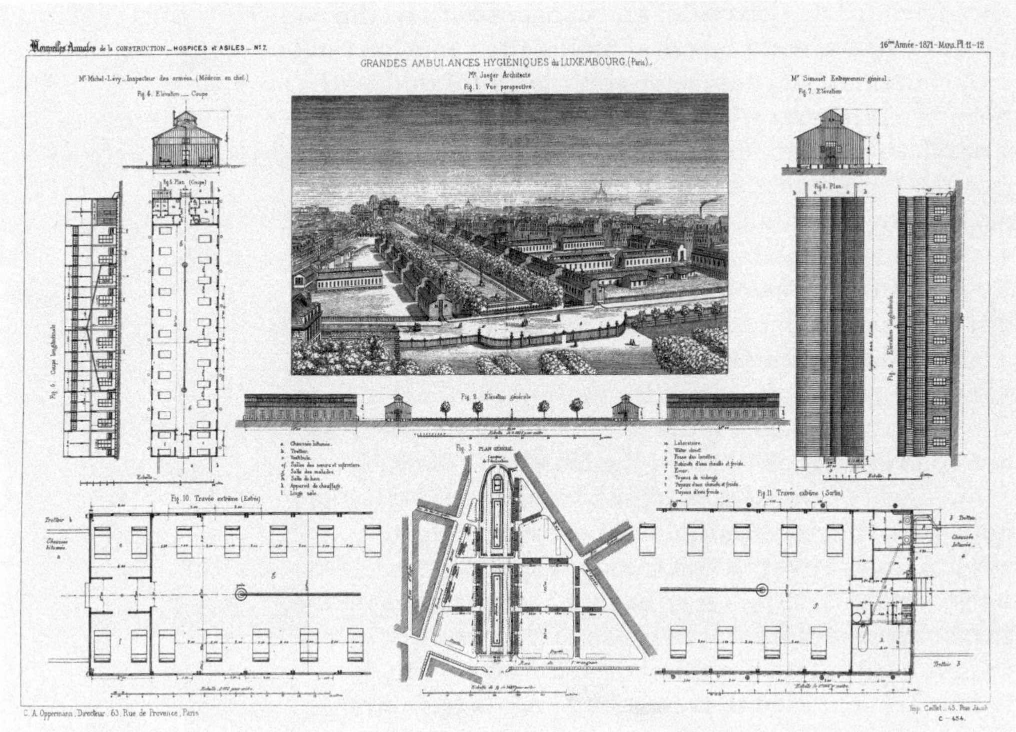

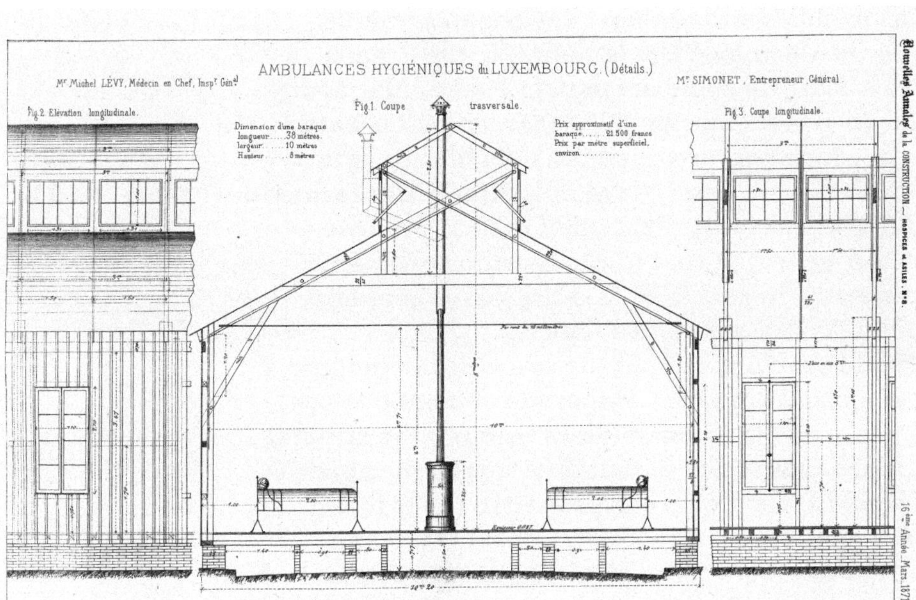

Fig. 7
Joseph-Frédéric Jaeger, Site plan and general view of the Luxembourg barrack hospital and plans, elevations, and sections of the barrack, *Nouvelles Annales de la Construction*, 1871. Collection: author. → p. 274

Fig. 8
Joseph-Frédéric Jaeger, Partial elevation and two sections of a Luxembourg barrack. *Nouvelles Annales de la Construction*, 1871. Collection: author.

Lévy, Bernard de Courville, and Jaeger oversaw the construction of a second hospital, using the same barracks, in the botanical garden, again on the Left Bank. With these two interpretations of the American paradigm at hand, the Société de Secours—the French Red Cross organization—could not stay behind, and at its headquarters in the Palais de l'Industrie, the site of the 1855 world's fair located between the Seine and the Champs-Elysées, it finally established its own barrack hospital, following the model set by the US Sanitary Commission.

By January, Paris was starving and under constant bombardment. In addition, General Trochu began to lose control of the populace. On January 22, a large demonstration took place at the Hôtel de Ville (City Hall), in which workers backed by the Garde Nationale demanded the establishment of a directly elected revolutionary government that would take control of the garrison. A battalion of Breton Moblots, loyal to the Government of National Defense in Bordeaux, was assigned to protect the Hôtel de Ville, and when the demonstrators tried to enter, the Moblots opened fire. Six demonstrators died. The government realized that Paris was in chaos and the next day began armistice talks with the Germans. On January 26, the French agreed to a cease-fire and armistice. The regular army was to be disarmed, but the 300,000 men of the Garde Nationale, which had provided the bulk of the city's garrison during the siege, were not. Either ill-informed about the political radicalization of the Paris Garde Nationale or believing that it was harmless, the provisional government assumed that the guard could be relied on to maintain order in the city.

Food began arriving in the starving city immediately, and apart from a victory parade of 30,000 Prussian, Saxon, and Bavarian soldiers through the streets, Paris did not endure the indignity of foreign occupation. German troops were to be garrisoned in the existing fortresses and camps immediately east of the capital until the agreed-on indemnity of 200 million francs had been paid to Berlin. In the subsequent peace negotiations, France was forced to surrender the Alsace and Lorraine regions, creating a revanchism that was to be one of the factors leading to the outbreak of another war in 1914.

Throughout February, tensions had been growing in Paris between the increasingly radicalized Garde Nationale and the provisional government. On March 18 the conflict escalated when members of the Garde Nationale captured their recently retired commander,

General Jacques Léon Clément-Thomas, while he was taking a stroll through the city and murdered him. Outnumbered and outgunned, the regular army left the city; the Garde Nationale took control and established a revolutionary government that became known as the Commune. In response to the revolt, a new provisional government was established in Versailles and elected as its head the same Adolphe Thiers who had overseen the construction of the fortifications of Paris three decades earlier. In open collaboration with the German garrisons located to the east of Paris, Thiers organized a new siege of Paris, which he pursued with a ruthless determination. Marshal Patrice de MacMahon organized a new national army created from regular army regiments from the provinces, Moblots, and French prisoners of war released by the Germans for that purpose. To the north, west, and south of the city, at Saint-Maur, Meudon, Rocquencourt, Villeneuve-l'Etang, Satory, and Saint-Germain, camps arose to house the army, and barracks provided the accommodations. The buildings were very simple; there was neither time, budget, nor inclination for luxury or innovation.[20]

As the siege began in earnest, the Société de Secours, which now operated within the area controlled by the Thiers government, established a field hospital close to the new camp of Villeneuve-l'Etang in the park of Saint-Cloud. It comprised eight barracks that served as sick wards and seventeen that served auxiliary purposes. The man in charge of what became known as the Ambulance de la Grande Gerbe (Field Hospital of the Large Bouquet) was the Moravian-born physician Jaromír Freiherr von Mundy, who in 1859, as a captain in the Austrian army, had taken care of the wounded at the Battle of Solferino. There he had met Henri Dunant, and as a result he had become involved with the Red Cross. He developed a special interest in improving ambulance services to move the wounded from battlefields to hospitals. In the fall of 1870, Mundy found himself in Paris. He organized an emergency hospital in the Austro-Hungarian embassy, and after the armistice offered his services to the Versailles government.

Chapter Six, Fig. 6
→ p. 252

Mundy was responsible for the design of the eight sick wards, which were a hybrid between a barrack and a tent and in that sense continued a design approach pioneered five years earlier during the Austro-Prussian War by Louis Stromeyer at Langensalza. Measuring almost 40 meters in length, 5 meters in width, and 6 meters in height at the first of the long sides and 4 meters at the second, Mundy's barracks had shed roofs covered

20 Angel Marvaud, "Étude sur les casernes et les camps permanents," *Annales d'Hygiene Publique et de Médicine Légale*, 2nd ser., 39 (Jan. 1873), 124–34, 241–83.

with a double layer of waterproof cloth. They had walls with windows on each of the ends and the lower of the long sides but were open on the higher of the long sides, creating a gallery-like space. Twelve posts located at 4-meter intervals supported the roof at the open side. The open side could be closed with a length of sailcloth that could serve as an awning when the weather allowed. Twenty-four beds were aligned along the lower long wall.

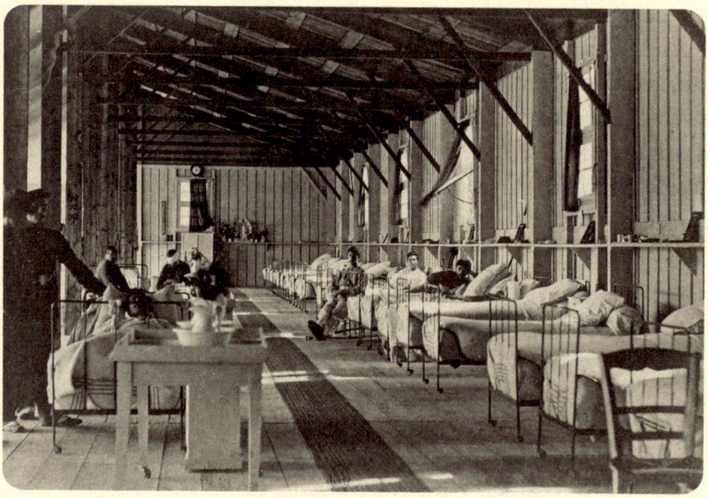

Fig. 9
Barrack of the Ambulance de la Grande Gerbe in the park of Saint-Cloud, near Villeneuve-l'Etang, France, 1871. Collection: Bibliothèque Nationale de France, Paris.

Because it should be possible to move the beds quickly into the open air and then back into the buildings, the floor was only 15 centimeters above grade. The philosophy of design went back to British Army surgeon general Richard Brocklesby's discovery a century earlier that sick and wounded soldiers did best when they were lodged under roofs only (see Chapter Three). Mundy's structures could be used only during the late spring, summer, and early fall.[21] By the end of May, the new army had conquered Paris. Between 6,000 and 7,000 Communards were killed. Almost 16,000 were tried in military tribunals, and 13,500 were convicted, of whom ninety-five were sentenced to death and the rest to prison, forced labor, and deportation to New Caledonia in the southwest Pacific.

The double catastrophe of the seven-month-long Franco-Prussian War and three-month *guerre civile* shook the French and France to their foundations. Yet individuals and the country both recovered quickly. The loss of Alsace-Lorraine brought Metz under German rule, and city architect Antoine Demoget decided that, despite the deep roots of his family in Lorraine, his loyalty to France was more important. He moved to Angers,

21 Anton von Fillenbaum, Julius Netolitzky, and Franz Danek, *Bericht über das französische Baracken-Lazareth für Verwundete im Parke von St. Cloud im Jahre 1871* (Vienna: K.-K. Hof- und Staatsdruckerei, 1872).

located along the Loire River, and there took up the position of city architect. Demoget published a substantial book on the construction of temporary military hospitals, drawing from both his study of American prototypes and his experience in Metz, providing two different projects based on an arrangement of barracks in the now customary triangular arrangement. Significantly, Demoget also proposed that civilian hospitals should adopt the barrack as the basic element of all future construction: it made sense from both a financial and a health perspective. Invoking the precedent created at the Charité Hospital in Berlin and the parti of the Metz hospital, he proposed a large civilian hospital of 1,200 beds, divided over twenty-four barrack wards, arranged, of course, in an isosceles triangle in which shared facilities—administration, chapel, kitchen, pharmacy, operating theaters, and so on—were located along the central axis.

As individuals like Demoget recovered their careers and lives, France quickly recovered its proverbial *joie de vivre* and its appetite for grandeur. In 1878 Paris hosted a third Exposition Universelle that was even larger than the one held eleven years earlier, covering not only the Champs-de-Mars, as had the 1867 fair, but also the opposite shore of the Seine. After some very difficult years, the French were determined to show the world at large not only that the Third Republic was superior to Napoleon III's Second Empire, destroyed at Sedan, but also that, once again, their country had become the center of civilization. While the German states had been very much present at the 1867 exposition—a gigantic fifty-ton Krupp cannon had been a major exhibit—in 1878 neither the German Reich nor individual German states or institutions were offered a place in the Exposition Universelle. The not-so-subtle point of the organizers of the event was that their neighbors to the east had nothing to contribute to *la civilisation humaine*. The Germans, of course, did not care that much in 1878; they had by then claimed *Kultur* as their bailiwick.

In 1867 the Société de Secours had contributed a small pavilion equipped with materials provided by imperial dentist Thomas Evans that showed the work of the US Sanitary Commission during the American Civil War. Eleven years later, the society provided a much more substantial exhibition on a quarter-hectare compound adjacent to one of the main entries to the site. The prominence of the society reflected its official position within the French state: a presidential decree issued in March 1878 had granted the society a monopoly to provide medical care in field hospitals during war and a budget to make it possible to do so. Given the new position of the society, it made sense that the exhibition did not look back to the Franco-Prussian War, when its role had been unclear and its achievements not that impressive, but forward to the future.

The site hosted an operating theater, a railway-station medical post, a hospital tent, eight special railway wagons designed for transporting the sick and the wounded, and ten different horse-drawn ambulances. These carriages were displayed in a building that was meant to evoke the architecture of the barracks constructed in the park of Saint-Cloud at Villeneuve-l'Etang and give a sense of the advantages they offered as an accommodation for the wounded and the sick. They provided "life in fresh air, amidst the trees, the flowers, and the beautiful lanes of the Park of Saint-Cloud, which offer convalescents opportunities for healthy walks," as a richly illustrated, 188-page guide to the Société de Secours exhibit explained. "What a contrast between these largely open pavilions, the summer, pure air, light, everywhere surrounded by greenery, amidst the quiet of the countryside, and the hospitals and emergency hospitals of the large cities, and especially of Paris in 1870! One understands easily how morale was always high, and that the rate of healing was much higher, in this blessed emergency hospital, the happy creation of the *Société française de secours* for wounded soldiers."[22]

At the center of the compound stood a fully equipped barrack of a more conventional type. Complete with ridge ventilation, it contained a large ward with fourteen beds, a bathroom, two toilets, a room for an attendant, and a linen storeroom. This barrack was intended to be a model of the standard building block for field hospitals that were to be designed following patterns that went back to those constructed during the US Civil War. The society made considerable claims about the building: "The barrack can be set up very quickly: six to ten days suffice for this operation. When we recall the time it took during the last war (several months) to prepare plans, to look for models to follow, we understand the advantage of having a type available that has been decided in advance and put together with care, if not necessarily absolutely perfectly. The hut can be dismantled very easily, thanks to the construction method we have indicated. [...] Transport of the materials to build the barrack will take five or six carriages."[23]

22 Aimé Riant, *Le Matériel de secours de la Société à l'exposition de 1878: Manuel pratique* (Paris: Société Française de Secours, 1878), 97.
23 Ibid., 94.

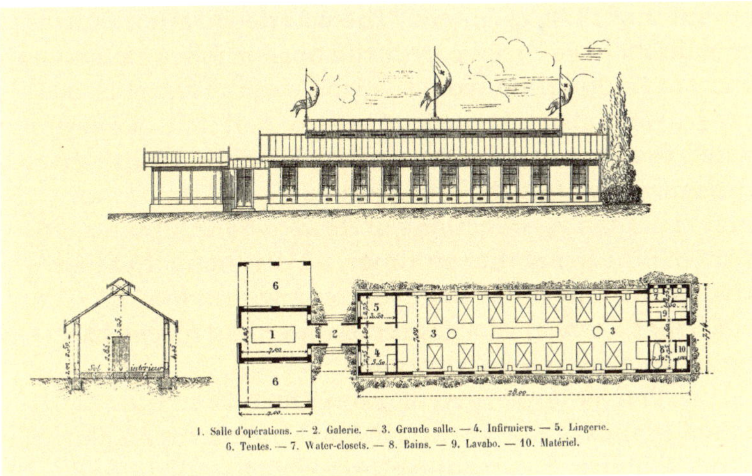

Fig. 10
Plan, elevation, and section of the barrack of the French Société de Secours at the 1878 Exposition Universelle, from Aimé Riant, *Le Matérial de secours*, 1878. Collection: author.

However, it appears that these claims were largely aspirational; in the considerable literature on what came to be known a few years later as "portable knockdown" barracks, the model displayed at the 1878 Exposition Universelle is never mentioned, and no record exists about what would have been at the time a remarkable technology, if it had worked. Seven years later, in 1885, at the Exposition Internationale d'Anvers, or Wereldtentoonstelling van Antwerpen (the world exposition in Antwerp, Belgium), the situation was radically different; many prototypes of such prefabricated barracks were on display, and the principles and technical details concerning what made these structures easy to construct, take down, transport, and reconstruct somewhere else were fully accounted for. Mere aspiration had turned into a demonstration of actual capabilities (see Chapter Eleven).

Incidentally, the driving force behind the 1885 exhibition was a group of senior German military surgeons whose careers had been shaped by the Second Schleswig War, the Austro-Prussian War, and above all the Franco-Prussian War. Not invited to show the remarkable advances made by the Germans in the care of wounded in 1870–71, in 1885 the victors of that third war gave the French a polite but decisive comeuppance by showing what a systematic consideration of the problem of prefabricated barrack design entails.

In France, the barrack hospitals in Metz, Paris, and in the park of Saint-Cloud arose in the midst of the chaos of hasty retreats, great demoralization, and confusion. In the German lands, the context was radically different; from the moment France declared war on the North German Confederation, enthusiasm was absolute. A book published in 1896, celebrating the twenty-fifth anniversary of a volunteer aid society created in Baden in the summer of 1870, recalled: "The war declaration that seemed to have thrown over the border fence caused not a cry of indignation from the whole of the German people [...] and also triggered cheers of patriotic exaltation when the command of general mobilization followed immediately after the declaration of war." And if we may trust the recollections of those who volunteered to support the army that summer, all divisions that had riven Germany had been overcome within hours: "The centripetal power of a shared danger had forced the heterogeneous parts together."[24]

The national revival intensified when the coordinated armies of the North German Confederation, Bavaria, Württemberg, Baden, and Hesse-Darmstadt gained victory after victory on French soil, in the battles of Spicheren (August 5), Gravelott (August 18), and Sedan (September 1–2) and in the sieges of Metz (surrender October 26) and Paris (surrender January 28, 1871). Obviously Germans delighted to return the humiliations suffered during the era of Napoléon le Grand to his nephew Napoléon le Petit, and they gloried in the imperial dignity bestowed on King Wilhelm I of Prussia in the Hall of Mirrors of the palace at Versailles—the enduring symbol of French royal ambition. But beyond that, there was an elevated spiritual dimension rooted in a profound sense of patriotism that colored the German people's experience of the war. The enthusiasm of ordinary Germans would wane in the years that followed the Franco-Prussian War—a severe economic depression that began in 1873 forced common folk to focus on economic survival—while German officialdom and a host of patriotic societies preserved the memory of 1870 as a glorious apex of German history and the experience of battle as the highest vocation for a German man. It was to prove a toxic legacy that shaped the career of the German Reich from its beginning in January 1871 to its end in May 1945.

Unlike the French, the Germans were well prepared for the evacuation, reception, and treatment of the wounded and the burial of the dead. They had learned from the experience of 1866, when the medical services of the Prussian army had been overwhelmed by the number of casualties. In April 1869 the medical corps of the army of the North German Confederation had issued guidelines for the creation of field hospitals in case of war. They stipulated, among other things, that any building selected to serve the treatment of the wounded ought to have sufficient space around it for the erection of either tents or barracks.[25] In 1870 the confederation augmented

24 Thomas Cathiau, *Der Karlsruher Männerhilfsverein und sein Wirken während des Feldzugs 1870/71* (Karlsruhe: Reiff, 1896), 7, 9.

25 Prussia, Royal Prussian Ministry of War, *Der Sanitätsdienst bei den deutschen Heeren im Kriege gegen Frankreich 1870/71* (Berlin: Mittler & Sohn, 1884), 42, 315.

these instructions with a standard design for a barrack, measuring 27 by 6.4 meters, that was ventilated through the ridge and provided space for thirty beds.

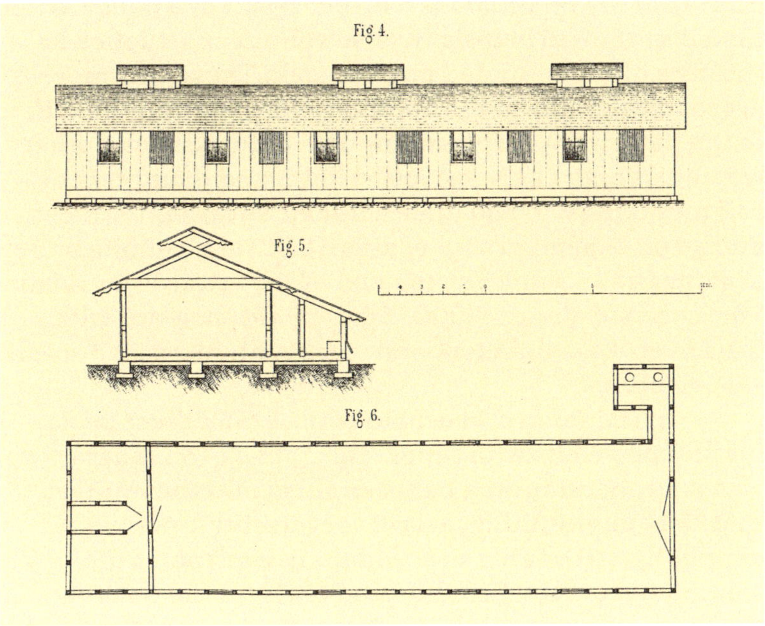

Fig. 11
Plan, section, and elevation of the design of a regulation barrack issued by the North German Confederation in 1870, from Prussia, Royal Prussian Ministry of War, *Der Sanitätsdienst bei den deutschen Heeren im Kriege gegen Frankreich 1870/71*, 1884. Collection: Staatsbibliothek zu Berlin.

This regulation barrack was conceived as a framework to be covered with a light removable shell that sufficed in summer, to which could be added a heavy second shell in the fall, while in winter the space between the two shells could be filled with whatever insulation material was at hand.[26] Intended to provide a model for the reserve hospitals to be built in Germany by the Army Medical Service, seventy-one examples of the prescribed design were constructed and another 192 of a modified design that provided a continuous ventilation ridge.[27] So far, so good: German contingency planning at its best.

However, in addition, at least another 300 barracks of thirty different designs were constructed to house over 100 third-line military hospitals.[28] At first sight, the plethora of different barrack designs adopted in Germany surprises, especially when compared to the almost total standardization of the building type in the United States during the Civil War; one circular issued by the

26 Appendix 96, “Beschreibung einer in Anschluss zu Reservelazarethe zu erbauende Baracke für 30 Kranke,” in ibid., 253*–56*.

27 The original design was used in the reserve hospitals in Halle, Hanover, Kassel, Meiningen, and Lübeck; the modified one in Berlin, Hamburg-Altona, Wezel, Karlsruhe, Heidelberg, Giessen, and Weimar. See Prussia, Royal Prussian Ministry of War, *Der Sanitätsdienst bei den deutschen Heeren im Kriege gegen Frankreich*, 336–58.

28 In Germany, the most popular barrack type followed the design principles of the regulation barrack and had the toilet located adjacent to the barrack. A variation model provided space for the toilet inside the barrack itself (e.g., those constructed in Frankfurt). In general, the German barracks were smaller than the American version; while the latter provided space for sixty beds, the German barrack typically accommodated twenty beds only. Some twenty-two barracks followed the design of the Berlin Charité Hospital experimental barrack, approaching civilian standards of comfort, with bathrooms, gaslight, and a veranda (e.g., those constructed in Bremen). Another group of barracks were of a more primitive sort; intended for use in summer and early fall, they did have ridge ventilation but were directly built on grade and not supplied with a floor (e.g., those constructed in Ludwigsburg, Gmünd, and Darmstadt). Another group did not carry ridge ventilation but used ventilation pipes (Neu Ulm). A final group did not offer any special ventilation options except by means of opening windows. In terms of barrack design, Germany in the fall of 1870 experienced an explosion of ideas and inventions, some good and some not so good, and this generated a blossoming of opinions, some informed by experience, some by prejudice, and some by theory.

US secretary of war on behalf of the surgeon general had been sufficient to enforce conformity in barrack design. But with a closer look at the variety of options, it becomes clear that the plenitude is a direct result of a policy articulated in 1869 to heavily involve volunteer societies in the care of the wounded and the sick. These societies arose in the wake of the Second Schleswig War. Thanks to the patronage of Queen Augusta of Prussia and other women of high rank—wives, sisters, and daughters of reigning kings, grand dukes, dukes, sovereign princes, and so on—membership of almost all such volunteer organizations, which by the end of the Franco-Prussian War counted almost 2,000 different aid societies with a little over 320,000 members, came with increased social respectability.[29]

In the Austro-Prussian War of 1866 these societies had played little practical role, but by 1869 there was an understanding between them and the military that they might fulfill several very useful functions: supplying attendants to accompany transports of wounded from the field hospitals behind the front to the rear; creating posts at railway stations to offer food, refreshments, and if necessary shelter for soldiers in transit; convincing civilian doctors to volunteer as military surgeons in field hospitals; providing an information service about missing persons; organizing the creation and distribution of care packages and medical supplies; arranging spa treatments for the wounded; and attending to the long-term needs of disabled veterans and the widows and orphans of those who died in war. In addition, these aid societies were to manage, when called upon, medical care for soldiers in the rear, beyond the hospitals run by the Army Medical Service, either by negotiating the establishment of special wards in existing civilian hospitals; by leasing hotels; by coordinating care in private palaces, manor houses, or homes; or by creating extra capacity through the construction of barracks either adjacent to existing hospitals or in newly established barrack hospitals. In 1869 it was not clear whether this service, or how much of it, would be needed during wartime.[30]

From 1869 onward, all these societies were coordinated by the Central Committee of the German Societies for the Care in the Field of Wounded and Sick Soldiers and overseen by a *königliche Kommissar und Militär-Inspekteur* (royal commissioner and military inspector), but in 1869 this position remained vacant. One day after the declaration of war, King Wilhelm I hastily appointed a senior aristocrat, Prince Hans Heinrich XI of Pless,

29 Central-Comités der deutschen Vereine zur Pflege im Felde Verwundeter und Erkrankter Krieger, *Bericht des Central-Comités der deutschen Vereine zur Pflege im Felde Verwundeter und Erkrankter Krieger über seine Thätigkeit un die Wirksamkeit der mit ihm verbundenen Vereine während des Krieges von 1870–1871* (Berlin: Starcke, 1872), 1–4.

30 Prussia, Royal Prussian Ministry of War, *Der Sanitätsdienst bei den deutschen Heeren im Kriege gegen Frankreich*, 405–15.

as royal commissioner. While fielding the many responsibilities that came to him in the first days on the job—establishing lines of communication with the Ministry of War and with the many aid organizations all over Germany, gathering information about who was doing what, investigating the nature and quantity of the greatest needs, and so on—Prince Hans Heinrich did not prioritize making a standard design for barracks to be paid for and constructed by these otherwise independent societies. The result was that volunteer architects in different local aid organizations considered the problem from scratch, designing barracks that reflected their insights into the state of knowledge on the topic, the amount of money the local aid organization had been able to raise, and—if both financial and material resources and the nature of the site allowed—their architectural ambition and that of the major patron.

Sharing a border with France along the Upper Rhine, the Grand Duchy of Baden was most exposed to the impact of the war. The center of its capital, Karlsruhe, was only 8 kilometers from the frontier. As a result, the Badische Frauenverein (Baden Women's Society), chaired by Louise, Grand Duchess of Baden and Princess of Prussia—the only daughter of King Wilhelm I and Queen Augusta—was particularly well organized. Immediately after the declaration of war, it called into being the parallel Badische Männer-Hilfsverein (Baden Men's Aid Society), which resulted in a quick and effective mobilization of a significant part of the civilian population for the purpose of providing aid. In the meantime the Baden War Ministry began to set up emergency hospitals in the large engine-maintenance shop at the railway station in Karlsruhe and also in school and university buildings and sports halls all over the state, which stood empty because of the summer holidays. Architect Jakob Hochstetter, who already had a career behind him as professor of architecture and director of the Karlsruher Polytechnikum (Karlsruhe Technical University), enthusiastically accepted the commission to add two barrack wards to expand the patient capacity of the Karlsruhe sports hall. His reputation tarnished because one of his major works, a prison located in Durlach, had been constructed so poorly that after only twenty-four years of service it had had to be closed and pulled down, he happily volunteered his time to join the national effort. Erected in August, these barracks were designed to be easily adaptable for winter use. In a somewhat self-congratulatory manner, Hochstetter described their appearance as "domestic, cozy, and friendly."[31]

31 Jakob Hochstetter, *Friedrichs-Baracken-Lazareth zu Carlsruhe* (Karlsruhe: n.p., 1871), 1.

On the strength of his work at the sports hall, Hochstetter received the commission to build a second and larger hospital erected under patronage of Grand Duke Friedrich I. Both as the sovereign ruler of Baden and as the son-in-law of King Wilhelm I of Prussia, Friedrich had a great prestige, and the Friedrichs-Baracken-Lazareth (Friedrich Barrack Lazaretto, or Friedrich Barrack Military Hospital) was to express the latest insights on barrack design and the ventilation and heating technologies that were key to their success as sick wards. "As to the external architectural form of such charitable institutions, the focus must remain on the main purpose," Hochstetter wrote in his 1871 publication about the project. "Therefore, a certain sense of measure and modesty symbolizes in a most dignified manner the idea of the whole, which serves as a memorial to noble humanitarian action and creation."[32] The result was a barrack hospital that matched its sponsor's and its architect's ambitions, and the arrangement of both the six sick wards and the supporting buildings, such as the central kitchen, workshop, and morgue, reflected a clear sense of spatial order.

Fig. 12
Jakob Hochstetter, Site plan of the Friedrich Barrack Military Hospital, Karlsruhe, Germany, 1870, from his *Friedrichs-Baracken-Lazareth zu Carlsruhe*, 1871. Collection: Bayerische Staatsbibliothek, Munich.

32 Ibid., 2.

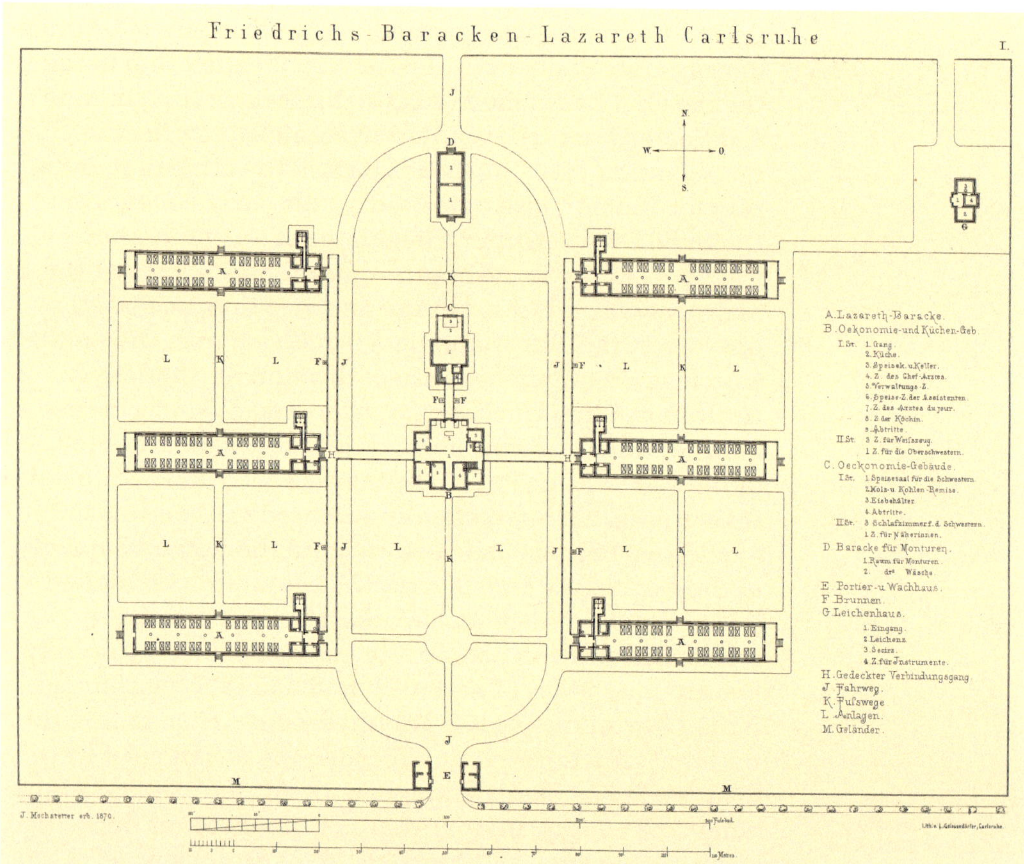

The design and technology of each of the barrack wards embodied a good compromise between the most advanced barrack design realized in peacetime, such as shown in the *Versuchsbaracke* at the Charité Hospital in Berlin, and the need to create, in the shortest possible time and in a situation of many other competing demands on financial and other resources, the greatest capacity. The wards were spacious but simply built with, in addition to windows in the walls and a monitor that could be opened and closed, many small ventilation openings in the walls that could be individually controlled. To the great satisfaction of the inmates, the doctors and attendants, and of course the architect, the wards performed very well in the winter.

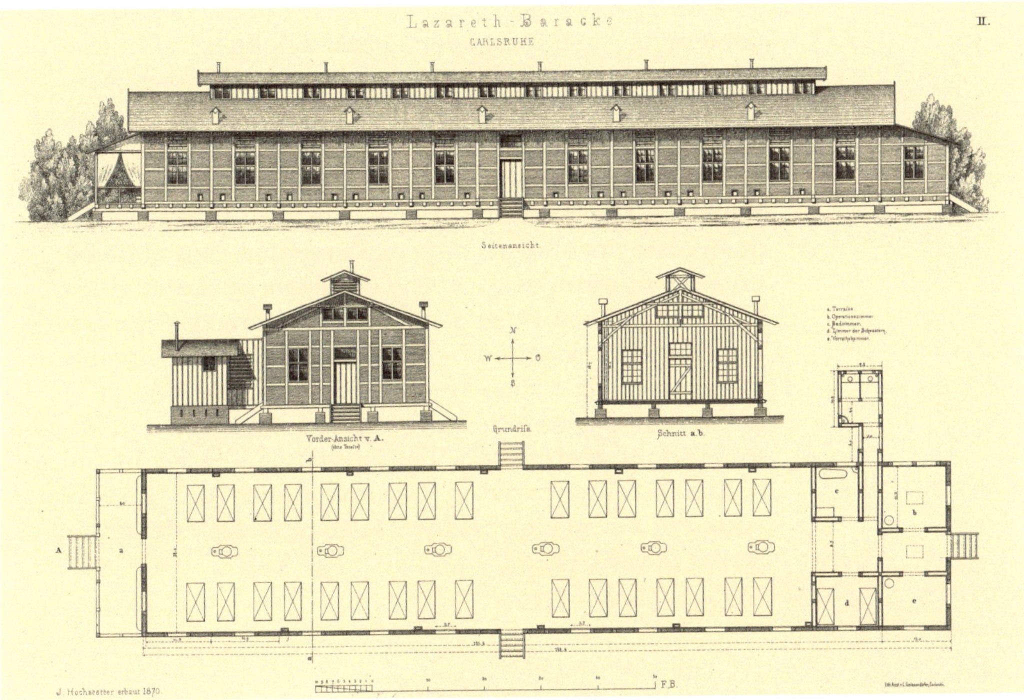

Fig. 13
Jakob Hochstetter, Plan, elevations, and section of a barrack from the *Friedrich Barrack Military Hospital, 1870, from his Friedrichs-Baracken-Lazareth zu Carlsruhe*, 1871. Collection: Bayerische Staatsbibliothek, Munich.

Fig. 14
Interior of the Friedrich Barrack Military Hospital, 1871. Collection: Landesarchiv Baden-Württemberg, Karlsruhe.

Thanks to a relatively simple heat-exchange system, Hochstetter had been able to square the circle in barrack design, obtaining in cold weather a simultaneously well-ventilated and well-heated building. It is no surprise that in 1871, after the Franco-Prussian War had ended, Hochstetter chose to publish the project in a well-illustrated monograph—redeeming an otherwise somewhat damaged reputation.

The only complaint about the wards of the Friedrich Barrack Military Hospital was the somewhat complicated manner in which the windows of the monitor could be controlled. When the incidence of typhus and dysentery increased as a result of the war, the German physician Nikolaus Friedreich, professor of pathology at the University of Heidelberg, decided to push for a special barrack hospital in that city for those suffering from epidemic diseases. As Heidelberg was located in Baden, it made sense to copy Hochstetter's design, and two copies of the barracks created in Karlsruhe were constructed in Heidelberg. However, the local municipal architect, Wilhelm Waag, desired to develop an improved version that allowed for easy manipulation of the windows in the monitor, by means of a narrow passage just below the clerestory that could be reached by a ladder placed in a side room. Eager to claim a role, albeit modest, in the history of barrack development, Friedreich took great pride in this unique feature in a small illustrated book he published in 1871, stressing its convenience and the way it added to a superior performance of Waag's design in terms of ventilation.[33]

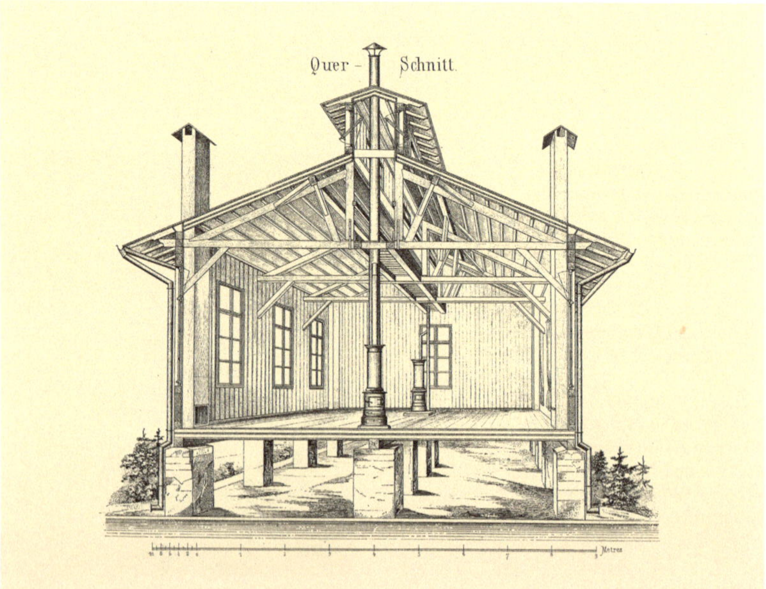

Fig. 15
Wilhelm Waag, Interior perspective of a barrack of the Heidelberg hospital for epidemic diseases, 1870, from Nikolaus Friedreich, *Die Heidelberger Baracken für Kriegsepidemieen während des Feldzuges 1870–1871*, 1871. Collection: author.

33 Nikolaus Friedreich, *Die Heidelberger Baracken für Kriegsepidemieen während des Feldzuges 1870–1871* (Heidelberg: Basserman, 1871).

In the Kingdom of Saxony, which was part of the North German Confederation, a large, temporary hospital consisting of twelve wooden barracks with a capacity of fifty-five patients each, constructed at the outskirts of Leipzig, established a high standard of quality. The wards matched the sizes specified by US surgeon general William A. Hammond six years earlier, but they were fully winterized. These barracks were arranged on both sides of a gallery that connected to the existing military hospital that was to house the administration, kitchens, operating theater, and so on. (Thus the Leipzig military hospital followed the design principles developed a year earlier for the city's Saint Jacob's Hospital, a building still under construction when the war broke out; see Chapter Eight for a discussion of this hospital.) It proved a successful formula—the military hospital functioned without any problems for over a year.

Fig. 16
Leipzig Barrack Military Hospital, Leipzig, Germany, *Illustrirte Zeitung*, 1870. Collection: author.

In 1866 Prussia annexed the internationally famous spa town of Bad Homburg vor der Höhe, and with it came a substantial castle that quickly became a favorite summer residence of Queen Augusta's daughter-in-law, the British-born Princess Victoria, daughter of Queen Victoria and Prince Albert, and her family, including her son Wilhelm, who as German Kaiser was to carry a major responsibility for the outbreak of World War I. In the summer of 1870, Princess Victoria helped establish and launch a large military hospital in Bad Homburg's garrison building, to be run by Florence Nightingale protégée Florence Sarah Lees. As part of this effort, Princess Victoria commissioned architect Louis Jacobi, who had worked and lived for five years in the United

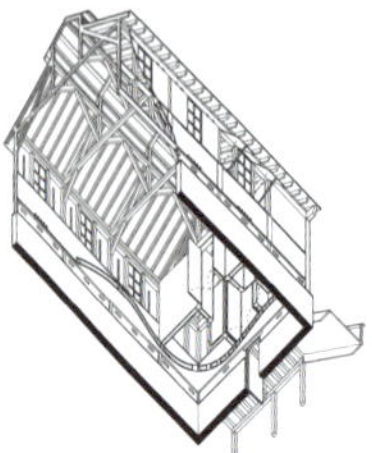

Drawings,
Bad Homburg Barrack
→ p. 519

States, to construct a twenty-bed barrack with ridge ventilation that was not only to function as a hospital ward but also be a model building that embodied the most advanced medical and sanitary concepts. One of the distinguishing elements of this building, which was officially known as the *Baracke Ihrer Königlichen Hoheit der Frau Kronprinzessin von Preussen* (Barrack of Her Royal Highness the Madam Crown Princess of Prussia) was the alternation of fixed windows and movable ventilation flaps, which reinterpreted the movable canvas panels of Georg Friedrich Louis Stromeyer's Langensalza tent-barrack of 1866 in a more permanent form. In addition, it had many other ventilation openings close to the floor and a central heating system, which during the cold winter of 1870–71 maintained an even temperature of 15° C while allowing for constant ventilation. With 40 cubic meters of space per patient, it matched the exact specifications of Surgeon General Hammond's pavilions. Much admired at the time for its technological sophistication, Jacobi's design received a gold medal at the 1873 world's fair in Vienna.[34]

Fig. 17
The barrack at Bad Homburg, 1870, from Ludwig Ziemssen, *Friedrich: Deutscher Kaiser und König von Preussen*, 1888. Collection: author.

If the barracks erected in Karlsruhe and Bad Homburg represented rather accomplished designs that reflected the dignity of their royal patrons, and those at Leipzig measured up to standards of construction expected within a major city, a great many barracks occupied the lower end of the spectrum. Among those are the twelve erected on the grounds of a boys' school in the Salon forest near Ludwigsburg, though they were praised at the time for a beautiful location with great views and excellent air.

34 Alfred Biallas, *Louis Jacobi, 1836–1910: Baumeister und Bürger Homburgs* (Homburg: Magistrat der Stadt Homburg, 1986), 13; Oswald Kuhn, *Handbuch der Architektur: Gebäude fur Heil- und sonstige Wohlfahrts-Anstalten: Heft 1: Krankenhäuser* (Stuttgart: Bergstrasser, 1897), 610.

Fig. 18
The barrack hospital at Ludwigsburg, Germany, *Vom Kriegschauplatz: Illustrierte Zeitung für Volk und Heer*, 1870. Collection: author.

They belonged to a hospital dedicated to the care of wounded French officers who had been captured and paroled. The Ludwigsburg barracks were very simple structures that lacked foundations and floors; the structural posts were placed in holes, and the floor consisted of a layer of sand. These barracks were not supplied with stoves, as they were not intended for use during the winter. They relied for ventilation on windows that opened and a permanently open ridge. In the fall of 1870, when these barracks were still in use, they were given a stove each, and the ridge ventilation was supplied with wooden flaps. However, despite these interventions, temperatures sank to 4° C overnight, rising only to 13° C by afternoon, and on November 8, 1870, the French officers were moved to a building in Ludwigsburg, and the barracks were taken down.[35]

In the middle range between the relative luxuries offered in Karlsruhe, Leipzig, and Bad Homburg and the austere conditions in Ludwigsburg are the barracks paid for by the Berlin municipality and erected as part of the large hospital built at the outskirts of Berlin on Tempelhof field—so called because it had been owned in the Middle Ages by the Knights Templar. During the war of 1866, Berlin had been able to provide adequate space for 3,500 wounded soldiers. Expecting the need to accommodate some 5,000 wounded at any given time, the Prussian Ministry of War began planning in the spring of 1870 for the creation of extra facilities with a capacity of 1,500 men. The Berlin municipality was ready to sponsor 600 beds, and a local aid organization, the Berliner Hilfsverein für die Deutschen Armeen im Felde (Berlin Aid Society for the German Armies in the

35 Prussia, Royal Prussian Ministry of War, *Der Sanitätsdienst bei den deutschen Heeren im Kriege gegen Frankreich*, 369–70.

Field), undertook to take care of 450, which left the War Ministry with the responsibility for the final 450 beds. Tempelhof, which was a training field for the Berlin garrison, was a plateau of well-drained sandy soil, exposed to the winds, and as such was considered the healthiest site near Berlin. In addition, it was only 2 kilometers from a water main, very close to a brewery that was the terminus of the municipal gas line (important because gas lighting was the main source of illumination), and adjacent to a major railway line.

Physician Rudolf Virchow, a consistent champion for the use of barrack hospitals since the mid-1860s, and architect James Hobrecht, in charge of Berlin's urban development since 1862, established the Tempelhof layout within days after the declaration of war. They divided the site into western and eastern halves, separated by a broad central avenue with a railway spur that connected to existing railway lines leading to Berlin, Frankfurt-am-Main, and Munich. The northwestern side was to be occupied by the 450-bed *Gruppe* (group) operated by the War Ministry, the southwestern side by the 450-bed *Gruppe* operated by the Berlin Aid Society, and the central-eastern by the 600-bed municipal *Gruppe*. The layout of each group was inspired by the triangular shape of the most famous of the Civil War hospitals: Lincoln Hospital in Washington, DC. At Tempelhof, the barracks aligned in a perfect east–west direction along four lines—two that ran northeast to southwest, and two that ran southeast to northwest. Unlike the American model, the Tempelhof barracks were not connected by means of covered walkways.[36]

Fig. 19
Bird's-eye view of the Tempelhof Barrack Military Hospital, Germany, 1870, from Johann Friedrich August von Esmarch, *Verbandplatz und Feld-lazareth*, 2nd ed., 1871. Collection: author.

36 Ibid., 341–45.

Two different barrack types, both offering room to thirty beds, were to serve as sick wards. The War Ministry and Berlin Aid Society groups, which encompassed fifteen wards each, used a modified version of the 1870 regulation barracks. Austere in appearance and stripped to essentials, these barracks clearly reflected the emergency character of the Tempelhof hospital. They offered 17 cubic meters of space per patient. The twenty wards of the municipal group, with an average space of 23 cubic meters per person, were roomier inside, and in addition their exterior posture was more urban. Designed by Hobrecht, they were inspired by Hermann Blankenstein's experimental barrack at the Charité Hospital but were technologically simplified. Like the model constructed at the Charité, these barracks offered galleries on each of the long sides, and unlike the regulation barracks, which were sitting close to grade, the municipal barracks were elevated 1.5 meters above grade. Initially intended to serve only in summer and early fall, Hobrecht's original design did not include glass windows, which he considered to be inappropriate for a barrack, but large openings covered with screens or, if necessary, by canvas.[37] However, Virchow convinced him to include proper windows.

Fig. 20
James Hobrecht, Site plan of the Tempelhof Barrack Military Hospital and plans and elevations of the two barrack types constructed there, 1870, from Prussia, Royal Prussian Ministry of War, *Der Sanitätsdienst bei den deutschen Heeren im Kriege gegen Frankreich 1870/71*, 1884. Collection: Staatsbibliothek zu Berlin.

37 James Hobrecht, "Das Barackenlazareth auf dem Tempelhofer Felde bei Berlin," *Deutsche Vierteljahsschrift für öffentliche Gesundheitspflege* 2 (1870), 502.

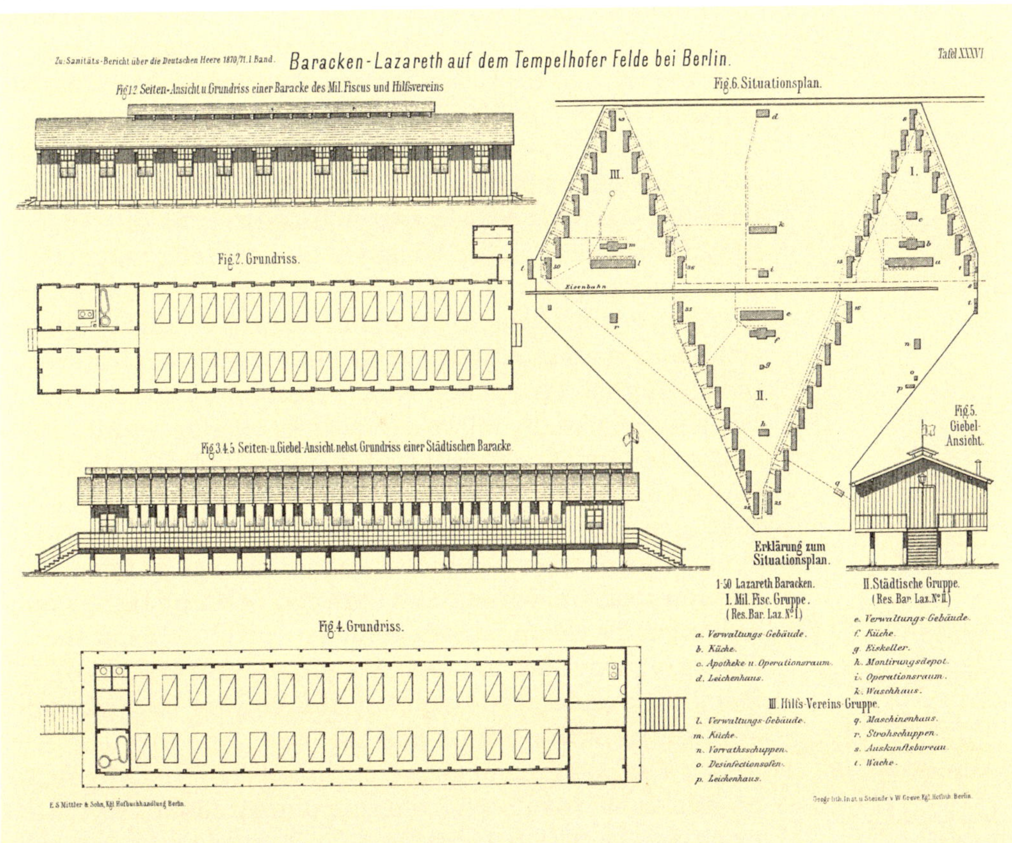

The continuation of the war into the late fall and winter, which produced a regular supply of casualties brought in by train from France, made it necessary to retrofit the buildings with insulation. Using different approaches and materials created an ideal situation to obtain data on the comparative thermal performance of the modified barracks. The temperature measurements taken in the wards confirmed the experience of the physicians, attendants, and patients—the barracks were too cold to be comfortable. The senior naval surgeon of the Imperial German Navy, August Friedrich Adolph Steinberg, provided high-level testimony. In the winter of 1870–71, Steinberg attended patients at Tempelhof, and he kept a record of the temperature inside. Even when all the stoves were worked day and night, during December and January the temperature in some barracks reached only 5° C, and on average it did not rise above 9° C. Steinberg's conclusion, published in his report on Berlin's wartime hospitals, was clear: the use of such wooden barracks in the German climate could be justified only in conditions of war, and in conditions of peace only during the outbreak of epidemics. "This judgment does not apply to barracks in general, but only to the use of wooden barracks in winter."[38]

Steinberg's report appeared in 1872, at a time when many had begun to doubt the efficacy of wooden barracks as sick wards, and even the *Versuchsbaracke* at the Charité Hospital, such a promising achievement only five years earlier, had began to slip into irrelevancy as a model for future hospital construction. It was the same year Eugène Grellois, who had served two years earlier as the chief medical surgeon in the besieged city of Metz, had articulated the view that the discourse on barracks represented *un certain engouement* (a certain craze). At this very time, a new noun of lowly origin had begun to circulate in the English language: "fad," referring to an activity or pastime, usually followed, with an outsize enthusiasm, widely but briefly. At times a fad denotes a craze that causes investors to put all their assets in enterprises that turn out to be bubbles, easily burst. Such fads are symptoms of all-too-rapid change in an age of mass communication, when the tried ways of doing things may no longer be the most efficacious or profitable but the emerging ways are too new to yield measurements of feasibility, understanding of accompanying hazards, and a weighing of the risks involved.

The design and construction of buildings tends to be somewhat insulated from this phenomenon. Stylistic preferences, which are at times influenced by a current

38 August Friedrich Adolph Steinberg, *Die Kriegslazarethe und Baracken von Berlin nebst einem Vorschlage zur reform des Hospitalwesens* (Berlin: August Hirschwald, 1872), 41.

fancy, come and go, but even those tend to have a longer life span than the typical fad, craze, or bubble. Buildings typically require financial resources that far exceed any individual's or organization's cash flow or savings, leading to significant oversight by a lender. Building codes add to the system of checks and balances that tend to reinforce a cautious and conservative approach to construction. Hence, architectural fads are limited mostly to small structures: garden follies, single-family geodesic domes, office sheds, tiny houses.

As a relatively cheap building type, the wooden barrack had, from the moment it began to be employed within a society shaped by consumerism and founded on mass production, the potential to become a fad. This potential was activated the moment the deployment of this building type was considered as an immediate and effective response to a catastrophe. The huts shipped to the Crimea in 1855 were to save the British Army and by implication the empire; the Renkioi Hospital was to save not only sick and wounded soldiers but also the reputation of British medicine; in the US Civil War, Dr. Hammond's pavilions were to keep up the spirit of both the Union Army and the home front during four interminable years; and in the three wars that heralded German unification, the barracks were to demonstrate the unity of German civil and military society. In most of these cases, the expectations projected on the use of barracks carried the signature of a craze, albeit of a minor variety. Because of the broad claims made that the well-ventilated barrack was all but a miracle tool in health care in both war and peace, it was inevitable that it was to be charged with expectations it could not fulfill, leading to an unfolding sequence of attitudes that began with disappointment, turned into coolness, and ended with mockery.

A final note. In August 1870, the 24-year-old German philosopher, Friedrich Nietzsche, who had a year earlier obtained a professorial appointment at the University of Basel, applied to his employer for leave to join the German armies in their advance to Paris. The university authorities worried that Nietzsche might violate the principles and practice of Swiss neutrality if he were to serve in a combat unit. Yet they did not object to give him a leave-of-absence if he was to provide help to the sick and wounded. Having agreed to those terms, Nietzsche underwent a two-week training as a medic, after which he received orders to travel to the front, where he visited various field hospitals. Finally he was put in charge of six wounded soldiers who were to be evacuated to the military hospital in Karlsruhe. Nietzsche spent three days with them in a freight wagon, cleaning their wounds, providing them with food, and disposing of their excrements. By the time the group arrived in Karlsruhe, Nietzsche had been infected with dysentery and diphtheria. After his recovery, Nietzsche was released from his duties, and he returned to Basel to pick up his academic life, following the progress of German arms from afar.

The violence of the Franco-Prussian war shook Nietzsche deeply. Remarkably, it did not turn him into a pacifist. Instead he became deeply convinced that the pleasure many people take in violence, and the universal capacity for wanton cruelty, were part-and-parcel of the human condition. These brute facts should not be suppressed, but acknowledged and, if possible, transposed unto a spiritual level. The Greeks had been able to achieve this through the practice of competition. Violence, in other words, was the basis of progress. From now on Nietzsche considered the stated aim of European governments and civil societies to overcome war to be not only a pious lie, but also an obstacle that barred the way to a higher age in which humanity would be able to get most out of life through the medium of wars fought for ideological reasons.

In a now classic statement, first published twelve years after his very short service as a medic, Nietzsche welcomed the first signs announcing the arrival of a "more virile, warlike age."

> To this end we now need many preparatory brave human beings who surely cannot spring from nothingness any more than from the sand and slime of present-day civilization and urbanization: human beings who know how to be silent, lonely, determined, and satisfied and steadfast in invisible activities; human beings profoundly predisposed to look in all things, for what must be *overcome*; [. . .] For—believe me—the secret for harvesting from existence the greatest fruitfulness and the greatest enjoyment is—*to live dangerously*![39]

As to the dwelling places of such preparatory human beings Nietzsche had a concise advice as to their location: "Build your cities on the slopes of the Vesuvius!" He did not mention their form. But we may assume that the barrack more than adequately served both the physical requirements of this new avant-garde of humanity, one that had rediscovered the happiness that comes with danger.

39 Friedrich Nietzsche, *The Gay Science: With a Prelude in German Rhymes and an Appendix of Songs*, trans. Josefine Nauckhoff and Adrian del Caro (Cambridge: Cambridge University Press, 2001), 160–61.

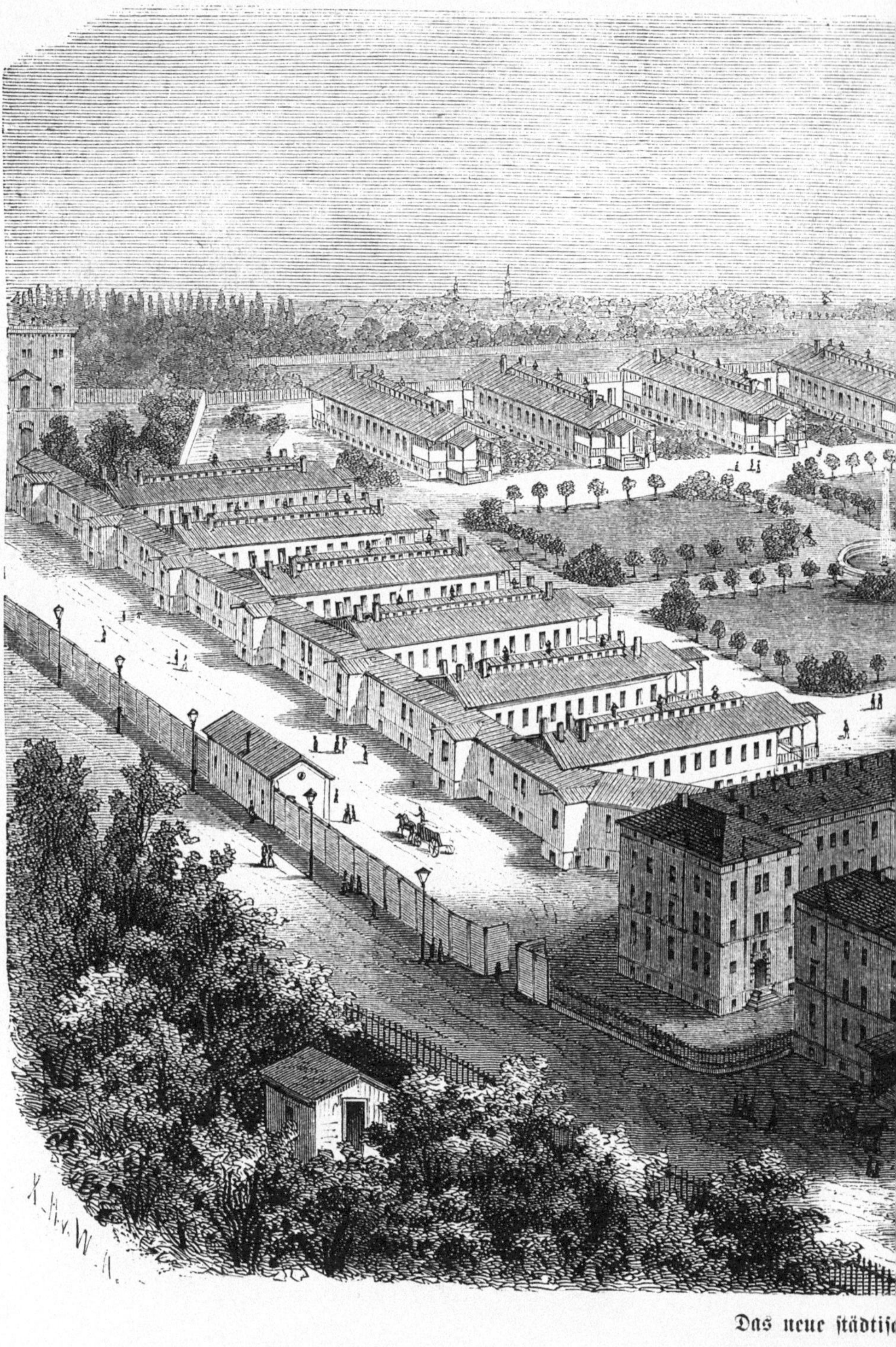

Das neue städtis

→ p. 321

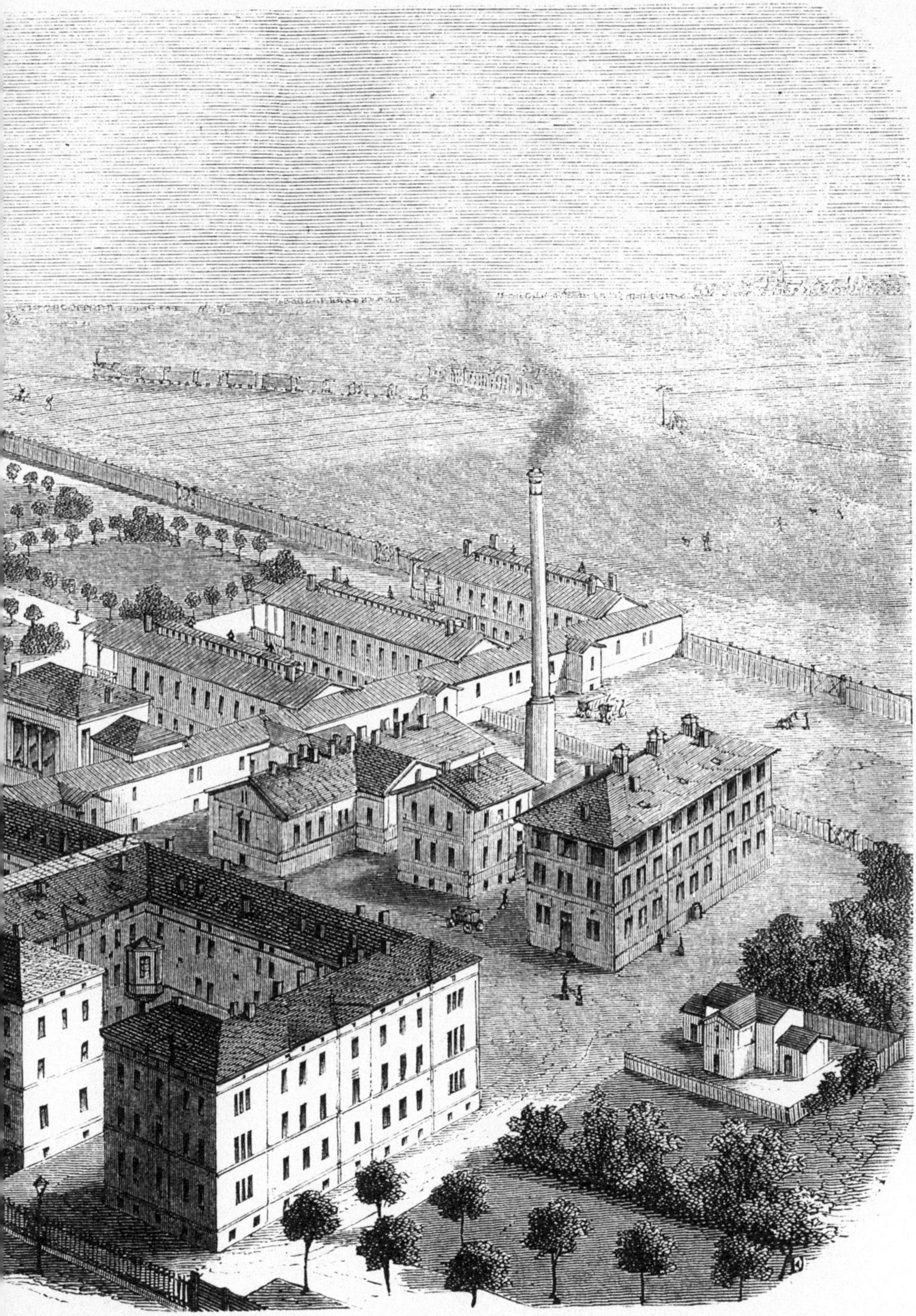

haus zu Leipzig.

Eight

Germany Pays Its Debt

In early April 1871, less than three months after the proclamation of the German Reich in Versailles, a new hospital opened in the German city of Leipzig. At that time, it was praised as an example of the most advanced ideas in hospital design. Its origin went back some eight years, when two professors of medicine at the University of Leipzig, Carl Reinhold August Wunderlich and Carl Thiersch, learned about the barrack hospitals created during the American Civil War. They faced an urgent situation, as the ancient and admittedly picturesque Saint Jacob's Hospital, which functioned as a teaching hospital, was both much too small and too ramshackle to meet even the most minimum standards of accommodation. Wunderlich and Thiersch convinced the university to purchase the newly constructed city orphanage, which came with a large garden, and to use it as the service core for a hospital that included thirteen wooden barracks, each holding twenty-four patients, connected by covered galleries. Municipal architect Ferdinand Dost was to be in charge of the project. In consultation with Wunderlich and Thiersch, Dost adopted the *Versuchsbaracke* (experimental barrack) designed for the Charité Hospital in Berlin as a general model for those to be constructed in Leipzig.

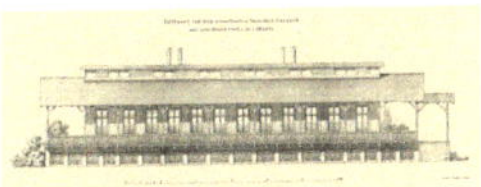

Chapter Six, Fig. 9
→ p. 257

Fig. 1
Exterior of sick wards at Saint Jacob's Hospital, Leipzig, Germany, c. 1911.

Collection: Stadtgeschichtliches Museum Leipzig.

Carl Reclam, a physician employed by Leipzig's police department, reviewed the project at the time the ground was being prepared for the barracks. He first provided a short history of the accommodation of the sick that culminated in the enlightened form of the pavilion system invented by the French and embodied in the construction of the Lariboisière Hospital in Paris. He also noted that the French pavilion system, with its three floors, had been only moderately successful in suppressing patient mortality, and this led him to the next logical step in hospital design: the single-story, ridge-ventilated barrack. "What the pavilion system intended, the 'barrack-system' realizes: it supplies the sick with large quantities of pure, oxygen-rich air, which is one of the three main factors of metabolism and thus is a necessary condition of recovery," he wrote. Reclam provided a full account of the construction guidelines drafted by Surgeon General William Hammond of the Union Army of the United States, and ignoring the precedent of the Augusta Hospital in Berlin, he somewhat erroneously described the design of Saint Jacob's Hospital as the first instance in which revolutionary principles in hospital design developed for the military had been applied in a civilian context. "In this case Germany, which so often received with gratitude examples of progress from abroad, pays its debt by reversing the situation," he wrote.[1]

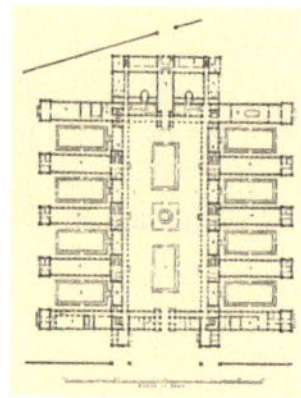

Chapter Two, Fig. 15
→ p. 106

Chapter Six, Fig. 11
→ p. 258

Reclam wrote his review before the outbreak of the Franco-Prussian War, when "Germany" was still a loose notion, encompassing the North German Confederation, established in 1866; the independent German states of Bavaria, Baden, Württemberg, and Hesse-Darmstadt, tied to the North German Confederation by means of a customs union and secret treaties of military assistance; and the Austrian lands, which were politically separated from the rest but culturally still part of Germany. By the time Leipzig's Saint Jacob's Hospital opened in April 1871, "Germany" was identified with the newly established German Reich, which was a major European power, equal to Great Britain, France, and Russia. The Saint Jacob's Hospital seemed to validate Germany's standing in terms of hospital design: the popular press hailed it as a health-care institution without rival. But the hospital also confirmed a shift in the relations between Germans and other peoples. "We Germans are so accustomed to be in major reforms the imitators of foreign countries that we only gradually gain the energy necessary for the elimination of obsolete abuses," Leipzig physician Livius Fürst wrote in the

1 Carl Reclam, "Das erste städtische Baracken-Krankenhaus in Leipzig," *Deutsche Vierteljahrsschrift für öffentliche Gesundheitspflege* 1 (1869), 147, 165.

weekly *Die Gartenlaube* a month after the opening of the hospital. “It can be argued that this achievement, which necessitates not only scientific and theoretical rigor, but also initiative and an opportunistic practical sense, only came to the foreground with the advance of our national consciousness.” With this he alluded, of course, to the creation of the German Reich. “We seek to combine the ease and elegance of the Frenchman with the technical skill of the Englishman and the practical administrative and organizational talent of the North American. Pride in our national position, which gives us an influential voice in the realm of politics, has aroused to a high degree the quest to surpass all the other nations in all facilities and improvements.”[2]

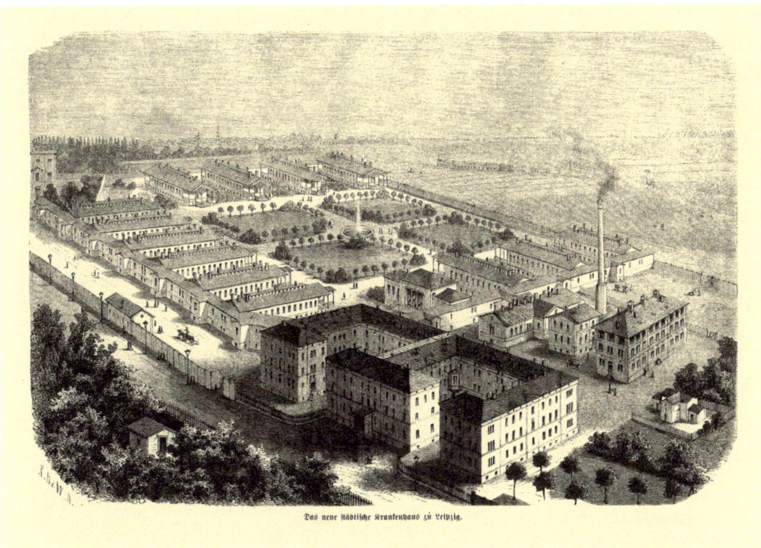

Fig. 2
Saint Jacob’s Hospital, *Die Gartenlaube*, 1871. Collection: author.

Ironically, at the very time that the Leipzig hospital seemed to provide both Germany and the world at large with a lesson in hospital design, leading German physicians were expressing doubts as to the viability and appropriateness of wooden barracks as sick wards in civilian hospitals. The first was Christian Albert Theodor Billroth. Born, raised, and educated in Prussia, Billroth was the chair of surgery at the University of Vienna. During the Franco-Prussian War, Austria stood on the sidelines, but Billroth, knowing that the conflict would lead to major advances in military surgery, took a leave from his position when the war broke out and traveled to the Grand Duchy of Baden to volunteer his services as a surgeon. Upon his arrival, he decided to write a letter-diary, and starting on October 24, 1870, the *Berliner Klinische Wochenschrift* (Berlin Clinical Weekly) published two of his *chirurgische Briefe* (surgical letters) in each issue.

2 Livius Fürst, “Ein Musterkrankenhaus,” *Die Gartenlaube* 18, no. 21 (1871), 344–47.

Billroth's eighth surgical letter, written two months earlier in the city of Mannheim, was published on November 28. It dealt with the form and arrangement of the field hospitals created in the first months of the war. Close to France, Mannheim was a major reception center for wounded brought in from the front—both German and French—and hosted various hospitals set up in existing buildings. Billroth described them quickly before turning to the main focus of his letter, which he identified as "the pride of Mannheim: the *Baracken-Lazareth* on the Exercierplatz." He described this hospital as "a totally new creation based on the American model." Comparing the complex of wooden structures to a small village, he listed the accessory buildings—kitchen, dormitories for the physicians, surgery rooms, storehouses, clothing storage, offices, gatekeeper's lodge, isolation ward, morgue, and an icehouse—and then focused on the nine wooden barracks that served as sick wards. He judged these simple structures to signify a revolution in the care of wounded and sick soldiers, and hence they deserved a detailed description:

Fig. 3
Exterior of barrack in Mannheim, 1871. Collection: Landesarchiv Baden-Württemberg, Karlsruhe.

The length of these barracks was about 60 feet [18.5 meters], their width 22 feet [6.5 meters], the height at the sides 12 feet [3.5 meters], up to the gable 18 feet [5.5 meters]. The board wall reached only about 7 feet [2 meters] high on both sides, and 12 feet [3.5 meters] high on the gable ends; thus 5 feet [1.5 meters] remained open at the top of the side walls, as did the entire gable triangles on the narrow sides; these openings were closed by strong canvas; the curtains of the long sides could be drawn up and were usually open during the

> day. Each *Baracke* was divided lengthwise in the middle by a 7-foot-high [2-meter-high] wooden wall; the beds stood with their heads against this partition, the corridors were thus on each side of the long outer walls; correspondingly, there were 2 doors in each gable wall, which, however, often had to be adjusted with screens on the inside in order to keep out the continuous drafts from the next bed.[3]

At first Billroth was doubtful that these very well-ventilated barracks would provide enough protection from the elements, especially during inclement weather.

> The very wet conditions that prevailed in August and several thunderstorms in September provided an opportunity to test this; the barracks were pretty much sufficient in this respect. [...] Another concern I had was that these barracks had no wooden floor. The floor was covered with gravel about two inches [5 centimeters] high, over which were laid planks in the corridors and along the beds. I noticed no particular inconveniences of this arrangement. [...] I no longer have any reservations about the lack of a floor in open barracks intended only for the summer. The matter is of importance, because a floor in a barrack occupied by wounded must be of solid construction, which substantially increases the cost. The roofs of asphalt-covered cardboard proved to be waterproof after the addition of two coats of tar.[4]

All in all, Billroth judged the barracks to be an excellent tool to house the sick and wounded soldiers. Yet, as the winter set in, his enthusiasm began to wane. In order to keep the temperature in the barrack at an acceptable level, the management closed the ridge ventilation, and even technologically more complicated solutions to provide ventilation during the cold season, such as the one installed in the barracks of the Friedrich Barrack Military Hospital in Karlsruhe, did not function as promised. Somewhat self-conscious about his lengthy discussion of the technicalities of barrack design, he acknowledged this to his readership in his ninth letter:

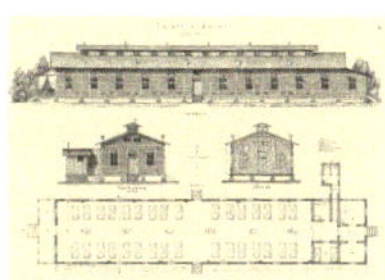

Chapter Seven, Fig. 13
→ p. 305

> I have heard you sigh for a long time about the breadth with which I treat this *Baracken- und Zeltangelegenheit* [matter of barracks and tents], but I am adamant in this and return from the

3 Theodor Billroth, “Chirurgische Briefe aus den Feld-Lazarethen von Weissenburg und Mannheim: VIII,” *Berliner Klinische Wochenschrift* 7, no. 48 (1870), 574.
4 Ibid., 574–75.

> theater of war with the conviction that a precise knowledge of these things is more necessary in the field than the decision as to whether a circular incision or a flap incision should be made in the case of an amputation. Surgeons who are destined to be at the head of a hospital should never look at these things with indifference for the sake of the cause, because otherwise there is a danger that technicians who cannot know what is essential and unessential will take charge of these things.[5]

As he continued to work in these barracks, Billroth discovered not only that they failed to provide much comfort to the patients but also that they did not meet the high expectations about the beneficial qualities of this building type generated in the years 1865–70. His thirteenth surgical letter, which appeared in January 1871, included a long reflection on the unexpectedly high (in his view), and hence unacceptable, mortality caused by pyemia, blood poisoning initiated by pus-forming bacteria released in the bloodstream as the result of an abscess. Before his arrival in Mannheim, Billroth had assumed that pyemia, like gangrene, had a miasmatic origin and that the treatment of the sick in clean, well-ventilated barracks located at considerable distance from each other would lower or even eliminate the instances of pyemia. But his experiences in Mannheim had taught him differently. "The bold hopes for exceptionally favorable results, which I had in the first weeks, were unfortunately fulfilled only to a limited extent." While the accommodation had been ideal, many had died from the disease. Billroth's conclusion was simple: "We prevent pyemia neither by means of the complete isolation of the sick nor by the greatest cleanliness, the best food, or the cleanest air." This led to a more general reflection on the sudden popularity among physicians of the barrack as a sick ward. "I have watched with some concern the enormous proliferation of *Barackenbau* [barrack construction] in Germany in recent years. A setback is inevitable. It was thought for a time that ventilation could prevent pyemia, and if that was not the case, one explained that the ventilation system was insufficient. Then came the idolization of the treatment in tents, but that craze quickly passed! Now it is the turn of the barracks!" Billroth admitted that rough, quickly constructed barracks had a use as military hospitals: they certainly were better than requisitioned buildings. Yet this did not mean that barracks were appropriate for civilian hospitals. Billroth explained:

5 Theodor Billroth, "Chirurgische Briefe aus den Feld-Lazarethen von Weissenburg und Mannheim: IX," *Berliner Klinische Wochenschrift* 7, no. 49 (1870), 587.

> To build in our climate as a matter of principle small wooden houses instead of small brick buildings, as has been done and as has been proposed, is certainly very inappropriate. In time of war one builds barracks of wood because it allows for quick construction and because it is relatively cheap. For civilian hospitals this flammable building type makes no sense: the ventilation mechanism, the oil-paint coat, the isolation, and all the other advantages that the more refined barracks offer, can also be enjoyed in brick buildings of stone, which are, after all, more solid and easier to heat in our climate.

Barracks, Billroth argued, would remain a staple of the architecture of temporary military hospitals constructed during war, but they had no role in peacetime. "For us, physicians, it is salutary to realize that the treatment of the wounded in *Baracken* only improves the terrain for treatment, but that the often mentioned dreaded pyemia is not eliminated."[6]

Returning to Vienna, Billroth resumed his teaching and his practice and issued a new edition of the handbook on surgery that had made him famous. The experience in Mannheim had given him food for thought, and he now articulated a crucial qualification to his support of the miasmatic origin of pyemia. "I can entirely agree to the miasmatic origin of pyæmia, if by miasma is understood what I understand by it in the present and some other cases, namely dust-like, dried constituents of pus, and possibly also accompanying minute, living, very small organisms."[7] Under the cloak of providing merely an expansion or perhaps revision of the theory of miasma, which still shaped the discourse of the time, Billroth in fact planted in his textbook, which is an inherently conservative kind of publication, the seeds for a new paradigm: that of the bacterial etiology of pyemia and many other diseases. Having posited the thesis that microbes forming a "dust-like" miasma caused pyemia, he immediately attacked the classic theory of miasma. "The old doctrine of the gaseous form of miasmata has always led us into deep water; many shrewd persons have exhausted their brains on this point, without advancing it much."[8] And Billroth delivered on the revolution implied in these words: in 1874 he provided a breakthrough in the science of the microbial cause of disease—sounding the death knell for explanations that relied on miasma—with a thoroughly researched book on coccus bacteria as the main cause of wound fever.[9]

6 Theodor Billroth, "Chirurgische Briefe aus den Feld-Lazarethen von Weissenburg und Mannheim: XIII," *Berliner Klinische Wochenschrift* 8, no. 1 (1871), 3–4.

7 Theodor Billroth, *General Surgical Pathology and Therapeutics, in Fifty Lectures*, trans. Charles E. Hackley (New York: Appleton & Company, 1874), 358.

8 Ibid., 359.

9 Billroth is remembered as a superb surgeon and medical researcher—and also, sadly, as an antisemite. In 1876 he published a treatise on the state of German medical schools, in which he identified Jews as people who could not, and ought not, be integrated into Austrian and German society. Theodor Billroth, *Über das Lehren und Lernen der medicinischen Wissenschaften an den Universitäten der deutschen Nation nebst allgemeinen Bemerkungen über Universitäten: Eine culturhistorische Studie* (Vienna: Carl Gerold's Sohn, 1876), 152–54.

Billroth's thirteenth surgical letter did not help to create confidence in the barrack, especially as a sick ward in a civilian hospital. But as its author had at that time no significant standing in matters of hospital design, it did not have a great impact. The situation was different when the prominent German physician Rudolf Virchow added his voice to the issue a month later, in a lecture given to the Berliner medicinischen Gesellschaft (Berlin Medical Society). Four years earlier, Virchow had been the first to propose the use of wooden barracks for civilian hospitals (see Chapter Six). Now it was time to assess the results that had been obtained in third-line military hospitals. Virchow noted that there were many success stories to be told. For example, the construction of the large hospital on the Tempelhof field had been undertaken without preparation in very difficult circumstances, yet it had happened quickly and cheaply. Virchow noted that, on the face of it, this experience might suggest the viability of the wooden barrack as a building block of future hospitals. Yet one should resist the lure of the barrack, Virchow told the gathering; he had changed his mind about the barrack as a hospital ward in peacetime. "For considerable time I have considered the future not without apprehension," he confessed. His main worry was fire risk. The Germans had been lucky: no barrack hospital had yet burned down, but it was only a question of time before this would happen. "For my part I would not assume responsibility for a large hospital of this type." He listed all the precautions that had been taken, including the establishment of a fire station on hospital sites, and also summed up the continuous fire drills that had characterized life in the American Civil War hospitals. "But you certainly cannot consider this for a normal arrangement if one is compelled to resort to such exceptional precautions. If the distress of war or an epidemic forces us to build such buildings, it does not follow that one should choose them as the basis of the permanent hospitals."[10]

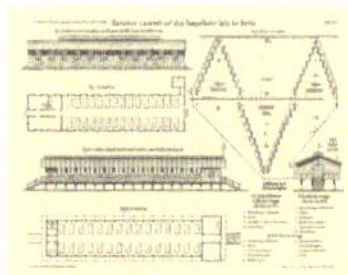

Chapter Seven, Fig. 20
→ p. 311

On February 27, nineteen days after Virchow gave his lecture, a fire erupted in one of the barracks that served as a hospital for French prisoners of war interned in the fortress of Minden, in northern Germany. Five of the thirteen barracks completely burned down. All 362 patients were saved, but the fire shook many who believed that the civilian barrack hospital embodied the future. We have no account about what went through the minds of Drs. Wunderlich and Thiersch when they opened the *Leipziger Zeitung* on February 28. But looking forward to the opening of their state-of-the-art hospital,

10 Rudolf Virchow, "Ueber Lazarette und Baracken," *Berliner klinische Wochenschrift* 8, no. 11 (1871), 123.

equipped with wooden barracks, they must have been overtaken by a wave of anxiety, panic, and perhaps also regret.

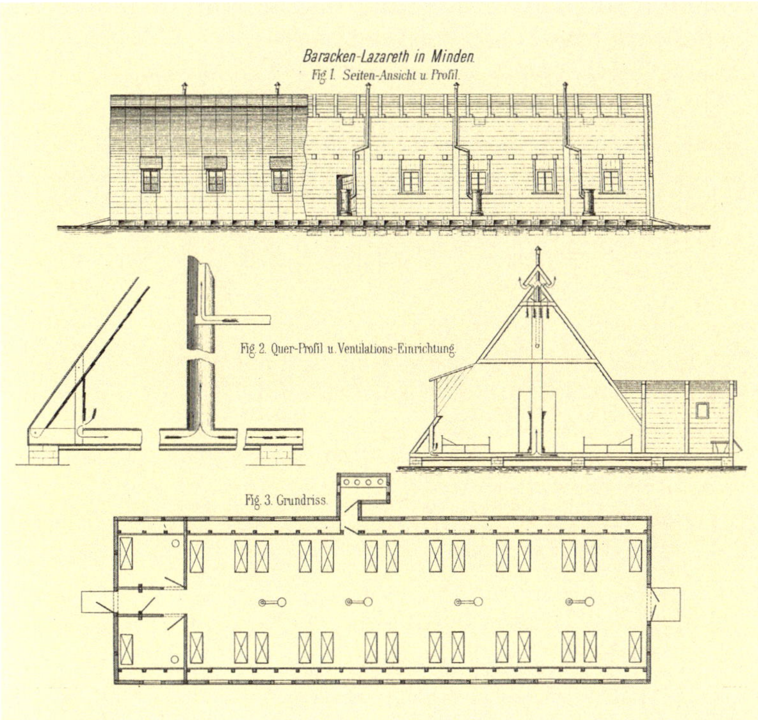

Fig. 4
Plan, elevation, and sections of a barrack at Minden, Germany, 1870, from Prussia, Royal Prussian Ministry of War, *Der Sanitätsdienst bei den deutschen Heeren im Kriege gegen Frankreich 1870/71*, 1884. Collection: Staatsbibliothek zu Berlin.

From 1871 onward, German physicians allowed one exception to the rule that civilian hospitals were to be housed in permanent structures; hospitals for infectious diseases might be well served with barracks. After the capitulation of Paris on January 28, 1871, the design and planning of such a hospital became an object of careful consideration when French prisoners of war triggered a smallpox epidemic that killed 5,216 of Berlin's 825,000 inhabitants and 3,647 of Hamburg's 235,000. At that time the Tempelhof hospital stood largely empty, and its relatively isolated location at the periphery of the city allowed for a quick transformation into an epidemic hospital. But it was only a temporary solution, as the Berlin military authorities demanded the return of the hospital grounds to the garrison. Infectious diseases such as typhus, typhoid fever, cholera, and smallpox had become common in European cities as a result of easy travel afforded by steamships and railways and the creation of massive metropolitan areas. Virchow pushed for an infectious-disease hospital that would use fireproof barracks, which could be constructed cheaply, that would have a ten-year life span. The Berlin municipality set aside a large site in the Berlin suburb of Moabit, and architect Carl Adolf Ferdinand Gerstenberg filled it with two dozen barracks, an administration building, kitchen and laundry buildings, a central heating plant, a morgue, and a gatehouse. The barrack structure consisted of wooden frames filled in with brick, and on the inside the wards were lined with grooved boards.[11]

Fig. 5
Carl Adolf Ferdinand Gerstenberg, Site plan, and plans, elevations, and sections of a barrack and the kitchen building, at the Moabit Hospital, Berlin, 1872, from Frederic J. Mouat and Henry Saxon Snell, *Hospital Construction and Management*, 1883. Collection: author.

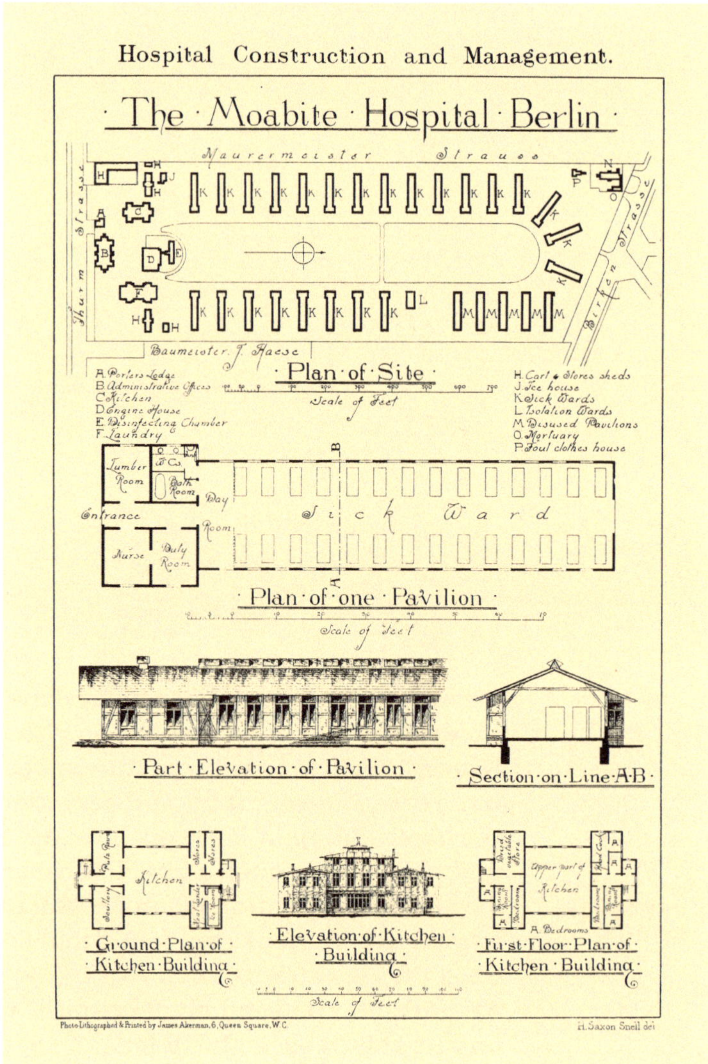

Moabit Hospital opened in May 1872, just at the time the smallpox epidemic began to subside. By 1874 the capacity of Moabit was considered to be redundant, especially in view of the opening of the general hospital in Friedrichshain. Moabit was closed—only to be reopened a year later as a general hospital for the destitute and the working poor. Architect Hermann Blankenstein, who had designed Virchow and Carl Esse's *Versuchsbaracke*

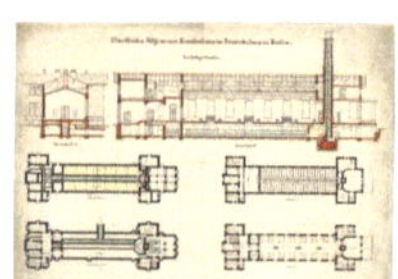

Chapter Six, Fig. 12
→ p. 259

11 Rudolf Virchow and Albert Guttstadt, eds., *Die Anstalten der Stadt Berlin für die öffentliche Gesundheitspflege und für den naturwissenschaftlichen Unterricht* (Berlin: Stuhr, 1886), 107–08; Frederic J. Mouat and Henry Saxon Snell, *Hospital Construction and Management* (London: J. & A. Churchill & Co., 1883), 205–09.

at the Charité Hospital in the 1860s, oversaw a decade-long program that replaced Moabit's original barracks, one-by-one, with permanent pavilions that were connected to a central heating plant.

Despite its checkered history, Moabit Hospital received much praise. The well-known English hospital architect Henry Saxon Snell considered the Friedrichshain Hospital with its permanent pavilions to be the model for future hospital construction, but the Moabit Hospital, constructed at a third of the cost of the former, allowed for a comparative study that would have to account for the costs of repairs, maintenance, heating, capitalization of interest paid, and so on. Snell believed that taking all such considerations into account, Moabit might be superior to Friedrichshain. And he added a final thought: "It has been suggested by high authorities that during the course of twenty or thirty years advances made in the science of medicine and surgery may result in the treatment of patients under altered conditions, and therefore it is not unreasonable to anticipate in the future as great a difference of opinion existing as to what should be the construction of a hospital as has been found to be the case in the past."[12] Ahead of his time, Snell determined that the relative low cost of a modular barrack hospital allowed for the kind of adaptive reuse necessitated by evolving medical knowledge, emerging technologies, and changing care practices and staffing models—all issues that guide hospital design today.

Most of the discussion in the West on the advantages of barrack hospitals had focused on military hospitals, which needed to be created in times of war, and large urban hospitals. However, this did not exhaust the possible use of barracks. In 1873 German physician Heinrich-Christoph Niese proposed barrack hospitals as a means to bring professional medical care to German rural areas. A resident of the city of Altona, located near Hamburg in the Duchy of Holstein, Niese had overseen the medical services of the volunteer army formed in 1848 by German nationalists from the Danish-ruled Duchies of Schleswig and Holstein, who aimed to create an independent state of Schleswig-Holstein within the German Confederation. In the 1850s and 1860s Niese remained interested in the advances of military medicine while making a living as a general practitioner. He read about the role of huts in the Crimean War and the pavilions of the American hospitals. And in the early 1870s he studied the plans of barracks designed and built during

12 Mouat and Snell, *Hospital Construction and Management*, 206.

the Franco-Prussian War. Niese also read up on the British cottage hospital, invented in 1859, which by the early 1870s had become an increasingly important tool in providing professional medical care outside of large cities.[13]

In early 1873 Niese published a proposal to create a German version of the British cottage hospital system. It began with a paean on the importance of fresh air as the key to life and healing. "The first thing a human being needs once born is that without which he cannot do for a minute without dying: that is *air*. Hence a human being takes for his whole life *fresh air* in massive quantities. A grown man (and similarly already a ten-year-old boy) breathes in 24 hours *9000 liters* or *8100 quarts* of *air*, while the solid and fluid materials, which he consumes and excretes in 24 hours, only take the space of three liters." None of the German vernacular building types offered the generous ventilation necessary for a hospital, but the barrack did. Niese proposed that the village hospitals to be built all over the German Reich should have as their basic building block the *Pavillon* and the *Baracke*. The former he defined as a ward that had a ceiling but lacked ridge ventilation, while the latter was a ward that lacked a ceiling but included ridge ventilation; the pavilion was easier to heat, and the barrack easier to ventilate. These civilian pavilions and barracks were very small versions of the military original. Niese proposed for a village hospital an arrangement of two two-bed pavilions and two two-bed barracks, arranged in a cross and connected to a nurse's room in the middle. They were to be constructed on a large site at the edge of each village. "There, free and isolated, these pavilions and barracks stand. Fresh air has unimpeded access not only from all sides but also from below, as they stand on pillar foundations, which create an air space below the floor; and by the barracks the air also has access from above."[14] For small towns, he proposed hospitals that were just a larger version of the village hospitals, with two pavilion and two barrack wards that accommodated eight patients each.

13 See Albert Napper, *On the Advantages Derivable to the Medical Profession and the Public from the Establishment of Village Hospitals: With General Instructions Concerning Costs, Plans, Rules, &c. and an Appropriate Dietary* (London: Lewis, 1864); Edward John Waring, Cottage Hospitals: *Their Objects, Advantages, and Management* (London: John Churchill & Sons, 1867); Henry Burdett, *Cottage Hospitals: General, Fever, and Convalescent; Their Progress, Management, and Work in Great Britain and Ireland, and the United States of America*, 3rd ed. (London: Scientific Press, 1896).

14 Heinrich-Christoph Niese, *Das combinirte Pavillon- und Baracken-System beim Baue von Krankenhäusern in Dörfern, kleinen und großen Städten* (Altona: Schlüter, 1873), 5, 8.

→ Fig. 6

Niese's view of a healthy Germany, embodied in smaller and larger pavilion and barrack hospitals at the edge of each community, was not realized. The ground-up approach in health care embodied in the cottage hospital—an easy fit in the idealized English traditional village life, centered on the manor, the rectory, the pub, and the village common—had no future in Germany, with its

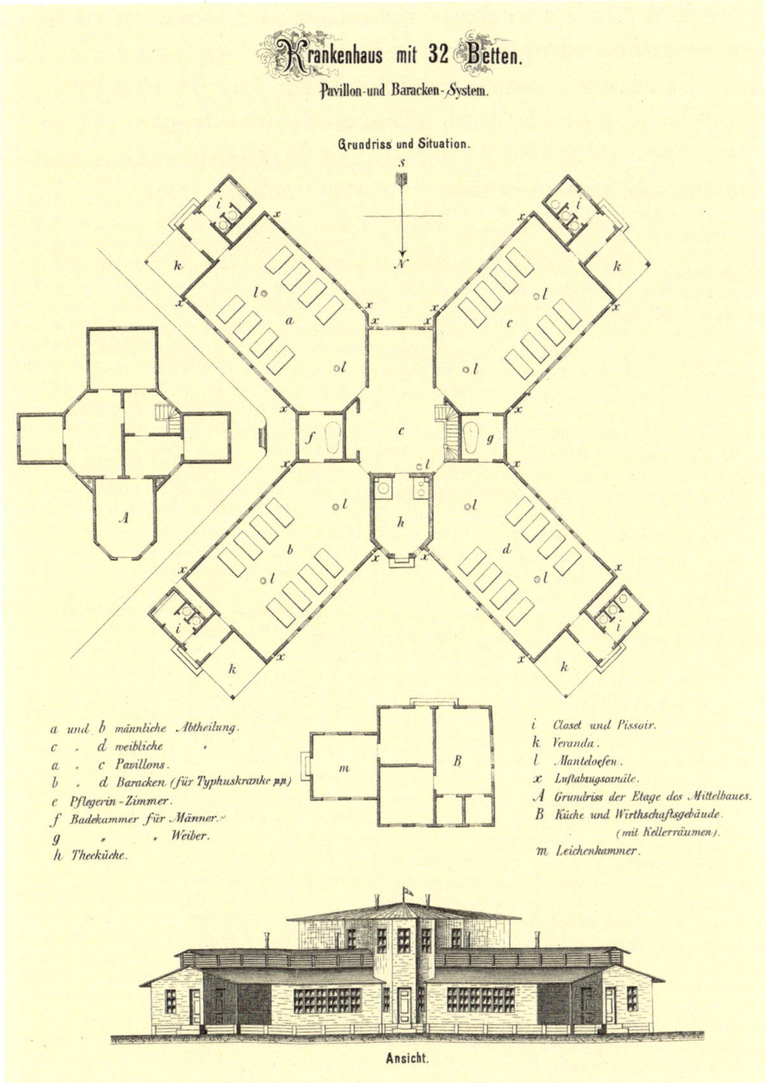

Fig. 6
Heinrich-Christoph Niese, Plan and elevation for a small-town cottage hospital, from his *Das combinirte Pavillon- und Baracken-System beim Baue von Krankenhäusern in Dörfern, kleinen und großen Städten*, 1873. Collection: Bayerische Staatsbibliothek, Munich.

top-down, professionalizing and centralizing approach to everything. Finally, there were the stricter social boundaries that characterized life in the *Dorf*.

Published in early 1873, Niese's book made its way to the Netherlands, where it inspired the regents of the Amalia Foundation, which was closely tied to the Dutch Red Cross, to propose the construction of a modified version in the city of Utrecht. The building was to provide a training hospital for volunteer nurses who could be called up in times of war to attend to sick and wounded soldiers. Instead of offering four wings emanating from a central core made up by two pavilions and two barracks, the Dutch version was to attach to the core building four identical barrack wards, each with eight beds. The whole offered a somewhat more domestic appearance than the German original. In the end, the Amalia Foundation did not erect a cruciform hospital based on Niese's design—probably because of the difficulty of expanding it. Instead, it provided, on a reduced scale, a reinterpretation of the Saint Jacob's Hospital in Leipzig: a brick, central services building that faced the street, with two freestanding barracks, each accommodating sixteen patients, in the back garden.

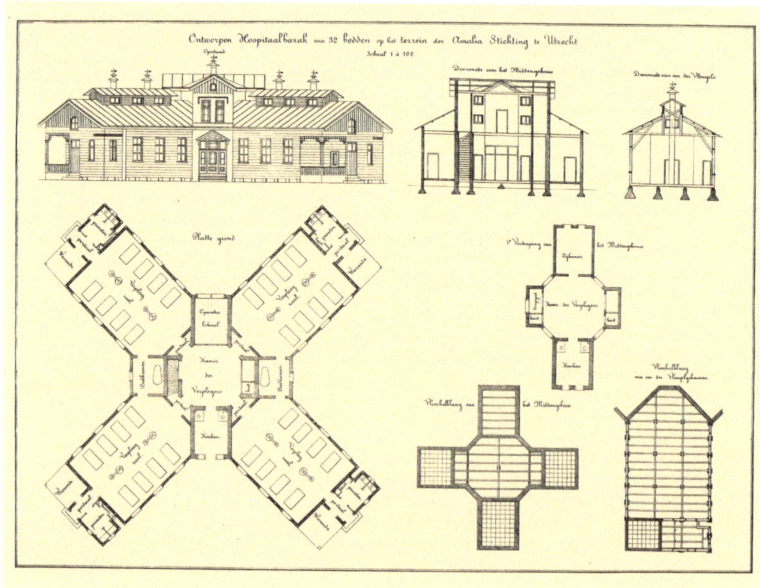

Fig. 7
Egbertus Gerhardus Wentink, Plans, elevation and sections of a barrack hospital for thirty-two patients to be constructed in Utrecht, 1873. Collection: Het Utrechts Archief, Netherlands.

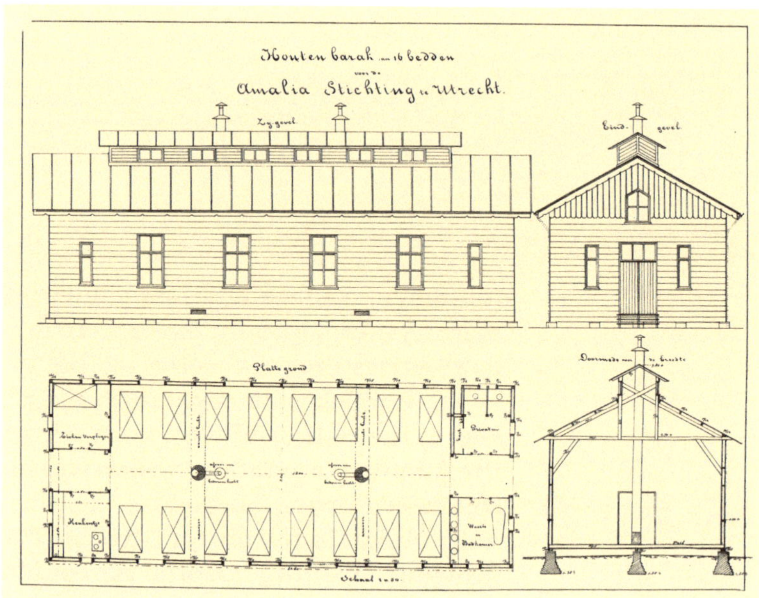

Fig. 8
Egbertus Gerhardus Wentink, Plans, elevation and sections of a barrack for sixteen patients constructed for the hospital of the Amalia Foundation in Utrecht, 1873. Collection: Het Utrechts Archief, Netherlands.

Until the 1870s, the Netherlands seemed out of pace with its neighbors Germany, France, Belgium, and Great Britain. While these other western European countries industrialized and modernized, each in its own way, time had stagnated in the Netherlands. Then, as in the seventeenth century, remembered as the Golden Age, the Dutch economy was based on trade, a strong agricultural sector, and the wealth generated by a vast colonial empire. Ever closer economic relations with the newly established German Reich were based on the rapid expansion of the Ruhr industries, which depended on imports of raw materials from other countries through the port of Rotterdam and a continuous traffic of Rhine barges. And those working in the Ruhr factories were fed with sandwiches made with bread made from Dutch wheat, filled with a thick layer of Dutch butter and heavy slices of Dutch cheese and Dutch bacon. And German innovation floated down the Rhine towards the cities in the river's estuary: Amsterdam, Rotterdam, and in the case of hospital design, the oldest of them: Dordrecht.

That city's only hospital, the Sacramentsgasthuis (Sacrament Hospital), which dated back to the early fourteenth century, had become an embarrassment, rife with awful hygienic conditions. A series of cholera epidemics convinced the Dordrecht authorities to take action, and in 1871 it charged municipal architect Hendrik Linse to design and construct a new hospital on the grounds used in earlier times by the city's militia as an exercise area and shooting range.[15] Linse's proposal, a traditional building, was rejected by a commission of physicians because it did not reflect any knowledge of the latest in hospital design, which was the barrack hospital. Subsequently, one of the physicians, Martin Fredrik Onnen; the medical supervisor of the Dordrecht mental asylum, Nicolaas Bernhard Donkersloot; and Linse collaborated on an illustrated study entitled *De Waarde der Barakken, als Tijdelijke of Duurzame Verblijfplaats ter Verpleging van Zieken* (The value of barracks as temporary or permanent dwelling places for the care of patients). Published in 1872 it provided a summary of the use of barracks in the Crimea and of subsequent American and German developments, and endorsed the barrack hospital as the model to be followed.[16] This report also mentioned the remarkable mortality statistics of a twenty-four-bed barrack that served as an emergency hospital during the 1870 typhus epidemic in the Dutch coastal village of Egmond aan Zee. Commissioned by the Dutch Red Cross and designed and manufactured as a semi-prefabricated building in The Hague by master carpenter Pieter Mouton Jr. and his son, architect Pieter Frederik Willem Mouton, this barrack was credited for the relatively low mortality of a mere 6 percent of all typhus patients taken care of in it.[17]

Despite his willingness to embrace the barrack as a sick ward, Linse did not get another opportunity to design the Dordrecht hospital; a continuing conflict with

15 On Linse, see Gerrit van Diesen, "Hendrik Linse, 18 Maart 1825–5 September 1905," *De Ingenieur: Orgaan van het Koninklijk Instituut van Ingenieurs* 21 (1906), 565–68.

16 Hendrik Linse, Martin Fredrik Onnen, and Nicolaas Bernhard Donkersloot, *De Waarde der Barakken, als Tijdelijke of Duurzame Verblijfplaats ter Verpleging van Zieken* (Dordrecht: H. R. van Elk, 1872).

17 Ibid., 12.

both the municipal council and his own collaborators led to his resignation from the project in 1873. His successor, the twenty-seven-year-old Jacobus van der Kloes, was charged to design and construct the barrack hospital recommended in the 1872 report. An ambitious architect who was to become a dominant force in Dutch architectural production through his standard-setting six-volume handbook on building materials and his long career as a professor of building science at the precursor of Delft University, van der Kloes began his work with an extensive literature review; he found two recently published articles, written by a certain Emil Plage, in the prestigious German architectural magazine *Zeitschrift für Bauwesen* (Magazine for the building industry).[18] Plage ran an architectural practice in the famous spa town of Wiesbaden, located on the right bank of the Rhine some 15 kilometers west of Frankfurt.[19] In 1871, he received the commission to design the city's hospital. Plage had an appetite for learning and approached the job in an unusually thorough manner that produced a comprehensive study on theories of hospital design. Giving much attention to the American developments and Florence Nightingale's theories on the design of patient wards, Plage concluded that a hospital consisting of both double-story permanent pavilions and single-story wooden barracks that were equipped with ridge ventilation was the preferred option, if space was available. Plage believed that patients should be housed in wards containing those with similar reason for admission, distinguishing twelve categories in total. Those belonging to four groupings were to be housed in barracks that were to provide one-third of the total capacity of the hospital. These included patients who had undergone surgery and those suffering from diseases that were believed to have a completely miasmatic cause: typhus, cholera, and smallpox. As syphilis and scabies were believed to have an only partially miasmatic origin, patients admitted with those illnesses could be housed in the pavilions. Because each barrack provided half the patient room of a pavilion, a hospital would have as many pavilions as barracks. Plage then proceeded to sketch a conceptual design for a barrack hospital to be built in Wiesbaden. Sadly for Plage, the municipality hired both military surgeon and barrack advocate Friedrich von Esmarch and Rudolf Virchow as consultants to review the proposal, and they rejected it, proposing instead an architectural competition that, quickly organized, was won by the Berlin architects of the Friedrichshain hospital, Martin Carl Gropius and Heino

18 Emil Plage, "Studien über Krankenhäuser," *Zeitschrift für Bauwesen* 23 (1873), 305–42, 438–92.
19 "Todtenschau: Emil Plage," *Deutsche Bauzeitung* 24 (1890), 12.

Schmieden. Yet Plage's effort was not completely in vain: it generated the two articles in the *Zeitschrift für Bauwesen* that inspired van der Kloes.

Based on a close analysis of Plage's research, van der Kloes proceeded to draw a building that was inspired by the design of the Saint Jacob's Hospital in Leipzig, combining a permanent structure housing the administration, doctors' offices, pharmacy, laboratory, laundry, kitchen, operating theater, and recovery room; and barracks as patient wards, each housing thirteen patients. The regular wards were constructed of brick, supplied with a monitor to ensure superior ventilation, and connected to the main building by closed galleries.

Fig. 9
Jacobus van der Kloes, Plan of the Dordrecht hospital, *Bouwkundige Bijdragen*, 1878. Collection: Regionaal Archief Dordrecht, the Netherlands.

Fig. 10
Jacobus van der Kloes, Elevations of the Dordrecht hospital, 1885. *Bouwkundige Bijdragen*, 1878. Collection: Regionaal Archief Dordrecht, the Netherlands.

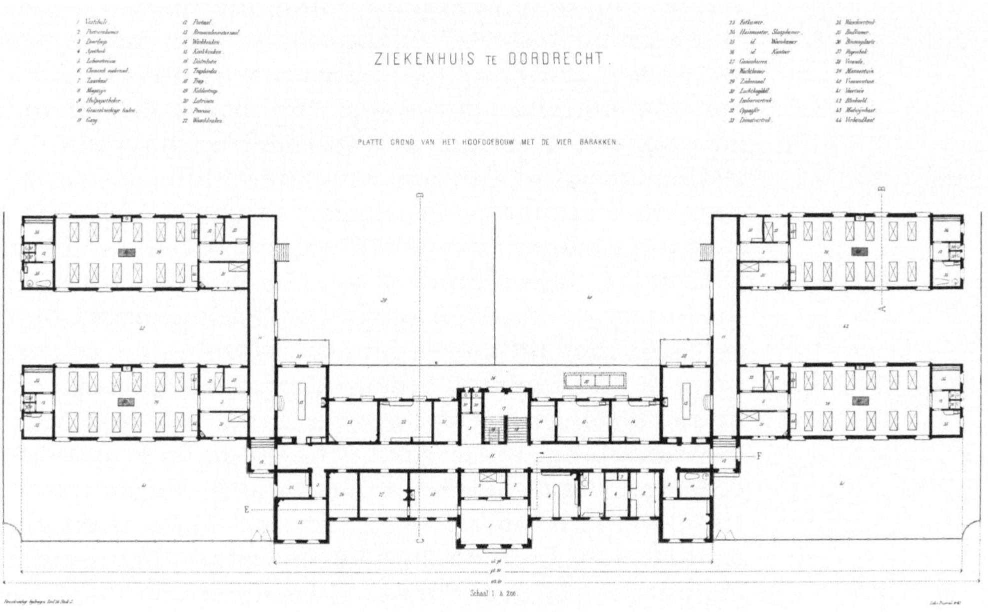

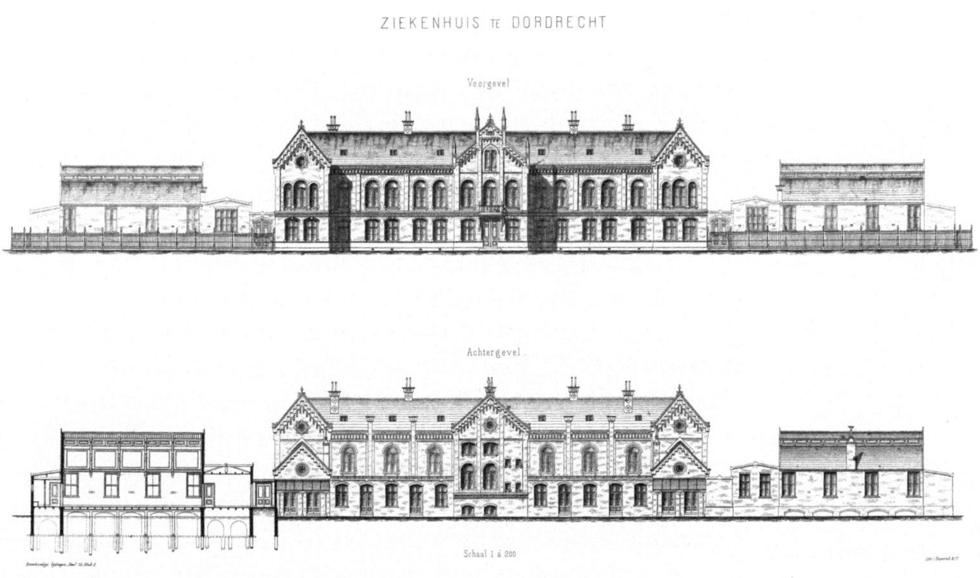

A separate building, consisting of a central brick structure to which were attached two wooden barracks, one on each end, served to house patients suffering from infectious diseases.[20] It was the first hospital constructed in the Netherlands that attracted international attention. Yet it was never completed as planned—only four of the ten barracks were constructed. The Dordrecht hospital remained a torso. And thus a building that was seen by many as proof that Dutch hospital architecture was finally catching up with European developments was, at the same time, a symbol of the decline in the status of the barrack hospital in Europe in the 1870s.

While information about the military hospitals created by the Union Army during the US Civil War had inspired Virchow to undertake the experiment with the *Versuchsbaracke*, American physicians were slow to call for an adoption of the barrack as a standard ward type in civilian hospitals. Captain John Shaw Billings, an army surgeon, was the first to consider a transfer of the barrack technology from the military to the civilian sphere. In the early days of the Civil War, Billings had overseen the transformation of a hastily constructed army camp set up on the Cliffbourne estate in Washington, DC, into the well-functioning Cliffbourne Hospital. Subsequently, he had taken charge of the Satterlee General Hospital in Philadelphia, the largest in the Union. In 1870 Billings observed, in *Circular No. 4: Report on Barracks and Hospitals with Descriptions of Military Posts*, that for all the defects of the military hospitals attached to army installations all over the North American continent, they had the "decided advantage" that, without exception, they were housed in temporary buildings. "I believe that no hospital should be constructed with a view to its being used as such for more than fifteen years," he wrote, noting that the moneys poured into standard brick-and-mortar municipal hospitals could be reallocated, allowing for construction of new temporary barrack hospitals every twelve years.[21]

Three years later, now former French imperial dentist Tom Evans, who had been such an effective propagandist in Europe for the medical achievements of the American Civil War, and who had also run an ambulance during the siege of Paris of 1870–71, published his views. In hospital design, as in the design of all public buildings, "the idea of permanency is commonly brought very prominently forward," Evans noted. The only way to convince potential benefactors to fund the construction of public buildings was to ensure them that the buildings

20 Jacob A. van der Kloes, "De Gemeentewerken van Dordrecht: II. Het Ziekenhuis," *Bouwkundige Bijdragen* 25 (1878), 209–38.

21 United States, War Department, Surgeon General's Office, *Circular No. 4: Report on Barracks and Hospitals with Descriptions of Military Posts* (Washington, DC: Government Printing Office, 1870), xxii–xxiii.

would also become lasting memorials of their beneficence and, of course, taste. While a desire to create monuments that would impress future generations was perfectly legitimate when designing churches, town halls, or museums, Evans believed it made no sense in hospital design: "No architect ever yet constructed a permanent hospital which did not prove to be a monstrous failure, and the few redeeming merits which may be found within his piles of stone and brick are but the shattered fragments of systems, which from some cause he was unable to completely crush." The ideal hospitals were those "designed only for a temporary use" and "erected almost solely with reference to furnishing a shelter for the sick." In such shelters,

> an abundant aëration can thus be obtained by the simplest and cheapest mechanical devices; outlets and inlets for the air can be placed wherever they may be needed, in order to obtain the largest and most constant interchange between the interior and exterior atmospheres; while the very rudeness and imperfection of the construction often serve to fit it, all the more completely, to be used as a shelter for a large number of sick; and it is not a little remarkable that the very earliest wise and practical conclusions, concerning the relative fitness of buildings to serve as hospitals, were the results of the accidental use of constructions generally supposed to be wholly unfit for such a service.[22]

Of course, both Billings and Evans were out of step with an evolving consensus in central and western Europe. Yet their suggestions resonated in the memory of Baltimore businessman and philanthropist Francis T. King when, a few years later, he was entrusted with the project to construct a new hospital in the city of his birth.[23] Funded by the largest bequest in United States history at the time, the Johns Hopkins Hospital was to embody in its design and operation the latest insights and provide a model to be copied elsewhere. As president of the board, King wrote to five experts inviting them to provide their views on hospital design.

> It will readily occur to you that the subject most prominent this day, in the professional consideration of the Hospital question as applicable to cities, is the choice between the *pavilion* system, which admits buildings of two or more stories

22 Thomas Wiltberger Evans, *History of the American Ambulance Established in Paris during the Siege of 1870–71* (London: Chiswick Press, 1873), 198–201.
23 Gert H. Brieger, "The Original Plans for the Johns Hopkins Hospital and Their Historical Significance," *Bulletin of the History of Medicine* 39 (1965), 518–28.

> in height, permanently constructed, of which the Herbert Hospital in England and several in this country may be considered good modern types; and the *barrack* system of one story structures, destructible in whole or in parts, which were so successfully used in the late war, but of which no extensive and prominent example is now in operation. In determining the claims of these systems respectively, as applicable to us, careful regard should be had to the character of patients intended to be the subjects of our nursing, so as to avoid the error of building an institution which shall prove not to meet the requirements demanded in the care and cure of women and children, and the generally enfeebled inhabitants of the sheltered lanes and alleys of a city, however much such a structure may have been a success when applied to the uses of hardy men in the field.[24]

King loaded the dice when he appointed Billings, who had been such a strong advocate for barrack wards only five years earlier, as one of the experts. Therefore, he must have been surprised that all consultants unanimously rejected the provisional hospital. Billings noted in his response to King that, indeed, in 1870 he had been an advocate for temporary hospitals because, at that time, there was a generally shared concern that "any building continuously occupied by sick and wounded men will become contaminated, that its walls and floors will themselves become sources of infection, that it will be better to destroy or abandon them when this occurs, and therefore, for economic reasons, that they should be built cheaply with reference to such destruction." Yet he had changed his mind. "The statement that this temporary character should be adopted for all hospitals, and especially all parts of hospitals, was, I am now satisfied, too sweeping." Barrack hospitals were still the ideal solution of military hospitals, or for isolation hospitals, but for civilian hospitals, such as the one to be built in Baltimore, they were inappropriate. "The objections to such hospitals are their inflammability, the large space and increased number of nurses, attendants, and laborers they require, the amount of fuel necessary, and the difficulty of enforcing proper discipline among and supervision of the employees and the patients."[25]

Norton Folsom, who had served as a military surgeon in the Civil War, dealt with the issue in a few lines. "I do not consider destructible barracks, which are so excellent for military hospitals, at all suitable for

24 Francis T. King, "Letter Addressed to the Authors of the Essays," in Trustees of the Johns Hopkins Hospital, *Hospital Plans: Five Essays Relating to the Construction, Organization & Management of Hospitals* (New York: William Wood & Co., 1875), x–xi.

25 John S. Billings, "Hospital Construction and Organization," in Trustees of the Johns Hopkins Hospital, *Hospital Plans*, 15–18.

a private, civil institution. I believe that careful administration will make permanent structures at least equally healthful with them, and, in a temperate climate, physical comfort is greater in a building with comparatively thick walls. I should consider the moral effect of barracks in a civil hospital, unless for temporary and exceptional use, positively prejudicial."[26]

Philadelphia physician Caspar Morris offered the longest and most devastating critique of the idea that temporary hospitals were more healthful.

> It must not be assumed that all the peril of what is termed *hospitalism* rests lurking in old buildings; much less can it be admitted that it is found only there, and can be escaped or annihilated by adopting barrack buildings of one-story and of cheap construction, easily erected and quickly destroyed. Hospital gangrene, the most formidable malady supposed to originate peculiarly in old, illy ventilated, and over-crowded wards, was found in one-story newly constructed barracks during our late war. Cheapness of construction and facility of removal may lead to a want of vigilance, both in original construction and subsequent administration, which will be productive of the worst consequences. In truth, cheapness of construction *involves* the use of inferior materials, and less care and skill in building. Such a barrack after three or four years' use, may have more cracks in illy plastered walls, more open seams and fissures in badly laid floors of inferior wood, more pockets for the accumulation of fomites, and be more saturated with poisonous influences, than a solid structure which has resisted the storms of centuries and been kept in proper repair, and has afforded relief to the sick and wounded of successive generations.[27]

To support his argument Morris referred to the mortality statistics in the Pennsylvania Hospital in Philadelphia, founded in 1751 by Benjamin Franklin and Thomas Bond, which was supported in a permanent, elegant, monumental building that today is a National Historic Landmark.

Having settled the issue that permanent hospitals designed with an eye to the future are not necessarily death traps, Morris turned to practical issues. As a temporary structure, the barrack fitted the demands

26 Norton Folsom, "Hospital Construction and Organization," in Trustees of the Johns Hopkins Hospital, *Hospital Plans*, 59.
27 Caspar Morris, "Hospital Construction and Organization," in Trustees of the Johns Hopkins Hospital, *Hospital Plans*, 186.

of an army in the field operating within the context of the limited duration of a war. A civic hospital should be designed with a view to provide continuing service over decades in a dynamically growing urban environment. And where would the patients go while a temporary hospital was being reconstructed, either as a whole, or bit by bit? Permanent structures, Morris believed, would function well if properly maintained. "Solid walls, and good roofs raised on substantial foundations, permit the entire renewal of floors and plastering and other interior parts of the structures, whenever age has caused dilapidation, or other influences call for renovation; and thus all the practical advantage of new structures is actually obtained."[28]

The fear that barrack hospitals might easily burn, were difficult to heat, and required many more personnel; the new insight that the basic assumption of hospitalism was wrong; and the logistical problems connected with the rebuilding of the buildings at regular intervals seem to have carried the day. Baltimore architect John R. Niernsée was commissioned to distill, in collaboration with Billings, a general parti of the hospital that reflected the convergence of opinion in the report, and the result was a plan that centered on a long, U-shaped corridor that connected at the bottom to an administration building and on each of the long sides to five permanent single-story wards to the south of the corridor, balanced by five service buildings on the north side, with an isolation ward at each end. Buildings containing operating theaters, dispensaries, kitchens, laundry, and so on were located on edges of the site.

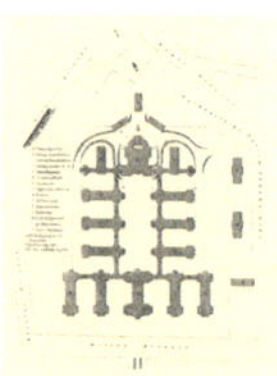

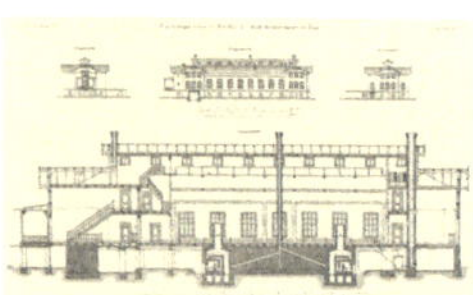

Chapter Six, Figs. 15 and 16
→ p. 262

Chapter Eight, Figs. 1 and 2
→ p. 319

The discussion generated by King and the Johns Hopkins Hospital that was constructed as a result ensured that, at least for the design of civilian hospitals, the precedent set by the hospitals in Riga and, more perfectly, Leipzig was not followed in either Baltimore or, in the wake of the construction of the Johns Hopkins Hospital, anywhere else in North America or western and central Europe. The multi-flue ventilation system that brought fresh air into the wards of the Baltimore hospital and that extracted the foul air via a ventilation shaft in the ceiling was considered state of the art and initiated the decline of ridge ventilation as the preferred way of ensuring proper aeration of sick wards. The problem was, however, that in making the ventilation system invisible, the perfect achievement between form and function expressed in the ridge ventilation was lost. Only in the two isolation wards did the exterior of the building continue to express a sense of the centrality of

28 Ibid., 188–190.

air movement through two rows of fourteen chimneys and a monitor boldly expressing the purpose of the building.

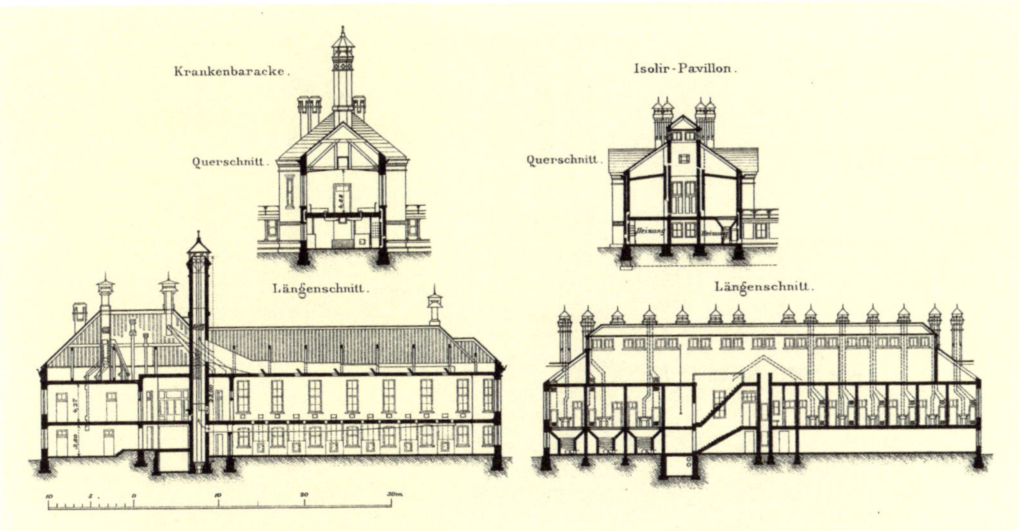

Fig. 11
John R. Niernsée and John Shaw Billings, Sections of a standard ward and the isolation ward of the Johns Hopkins Hospital, Baltimore, Maryland, United States, 1876, *Zeitschrift für Bauwesen*, 1895. Interestingly, in this German construction journal, the standard ward is identified as a barrack (*Krankenbaracke*), while the isolation ward is identified as a pavilion (*Isolir-Pavillon*); the reason for this distinction in terminology is not clear. Collection: author.

In military circles, the achievement in hospital construction of the US Sanitary Commission during the Civil War remained the paradigm to be followed. In 1876 the Surgeon General's Office of the US Army contributed a special exhibition on these hospitals to the Centennial International Exhibition in Philadelphia—the first world's fair to be held outside of Europe. Scale models of the most important hospitals created between 1862 and 1865 filled the display cases located in a full-size replica of a standard two-ward post hospital used in garrisons all over the United States and its territories. A large scale model of one of Dr. Hammond's Union Army pavilions took pride of place. Its roof could be flipped open to show the interior of the ward and the roof construction with the still all-important—for temporary buildings—ridge ventilation.

→ Fig. 12

While Dr. Billroth at the University of Vienna had played an important role in sowing doubt about the validity of the miasmatic origin of infectious diseases, Robert Koch's 1876 discovery of the anthrax bacillus, followed by his 1882 discovery of the tuberculosis bacillus and, one year later, the discovery of the cholera bacillus, proved to be decisive blows to the legacy of eighteenth-century Italian physician Giovanni Maria Lancisi. Nevertheless, most doctors, including very learned ones, chose not to notice and continued to adhere to the miasma doctrine because it dovetailed with the common observation that the overcrowded, filthy, stinking slums

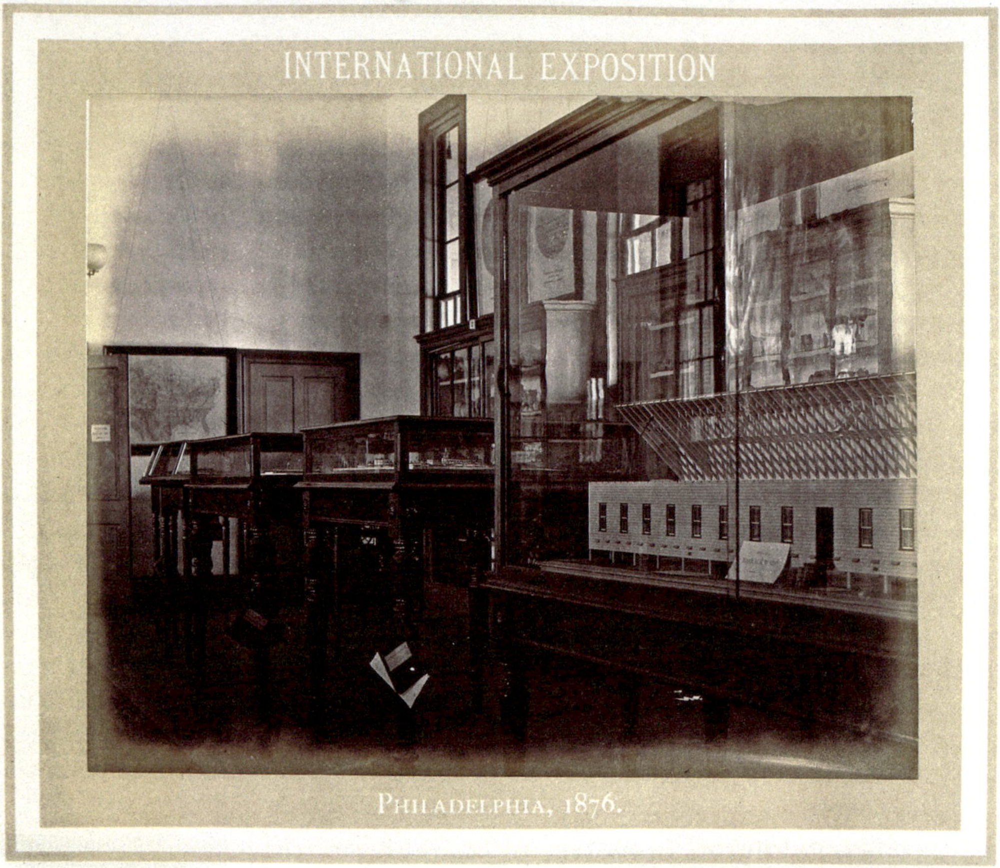

Fig. 12
Model of the US (Union) **Army** pavilion hospital **prescribed** by Surgeon **General** William Hammond, **displayed** at the Centennial **International Exhibition, Philadelphia,** Pennsylvania, **1876.** Collection: Wellcome Library, London.

inhabited by the poor had a much higher incidence of the diseases supposedly caused by miasma than the cleaner and wealthier parts of the community. "Because scientists are reasonable men, one or another argument will ultimately persuade many of them," Thomas Kuhn observed in his seminal *Structure of Scientific Revolutions* (1962). "But there is no single argument that can or should persuade them all. Rather than a single group conversion, what occurs is an increasing shift in the distribution of professional allegiances."[29] In the case of miasma vs. germs that shift was well underway in the 1880s, but it would take until World War I to be completed.

As the science concerning the etiology of infectious diseases evolved, public attitudes shifted in Europe as people just got used to the idea of a barrack civilian hospital. The thirteenth edition of the leading German encyclopedia, *Brockhaus' Conversations-Lexikon*, published between 1882 and 1887, listed the barrack system as the most advanced form of hospital design.[30] The single image that was included showed a site plan and a plan and elevation of one of the barrack patient wards of the Saint Jacob's Hospital in Leipzig.

29 Thomas S. Kuhn, *The Structure of Scientific Revolutions* (Chicago: University of Chicago Press, 1962), 158.
30 "Krankenhaus," *Brockhaus' Conversations-Lexikon*, 13th ed., 17 vols. (Leipzig: Brockhaus, 1882–87), 10:570–74.

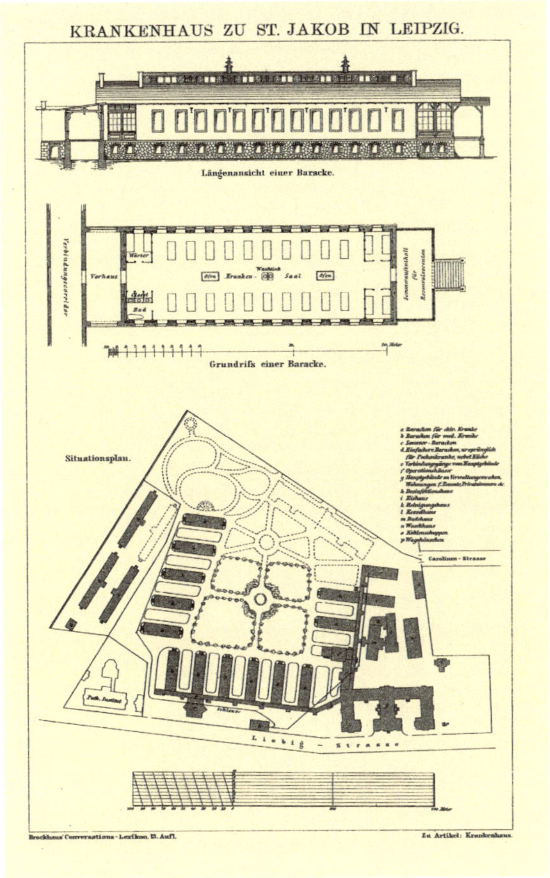

Fig. 13
Ferdinand Dost, Plan and elevation of a ward and site plan of the Saint Jacob's Hospital, 1871, from *Brockhaus' Conversations-Lexikon*, 13th ed., 1882–87. Collection: author.

The choice to illustrate the entry on hospitals with this particular institution was undoubtedly a result of its continuing fame—though the location of the *Brockhaus' Conversations-Lexikon* offices in Leipzig might also have influenced the editor's selection.

On September 18, 1888, Dr. Heinrich Curschmann, professor of medicine at the University of Leipzig, presented a public lecture entitled "What influence does today's health science, especially the recent understanding of the nature and spread of infectious diseases, have on the construction, equipment and location of hospitals?" at the fourteenth annual meeting of the Deutschen Verein für öffentliche Gesundheitspflege (German Society of Public Health), held in Frankfurt am Main. Curschmann could speak with authority on this matter. He had been director of the Moabit Hospital in Berlin, and in 1884, as medical director of the Allgemeinen Krankenhauses St. Georg (Saint George General Hospital) in Hamburg, he had initiated the construction of what was intended to be the most advanced hospital of its day: the Neue Allgemeine Krankenhaus (New General Hospital) in the Eppendorf suburb of that city.

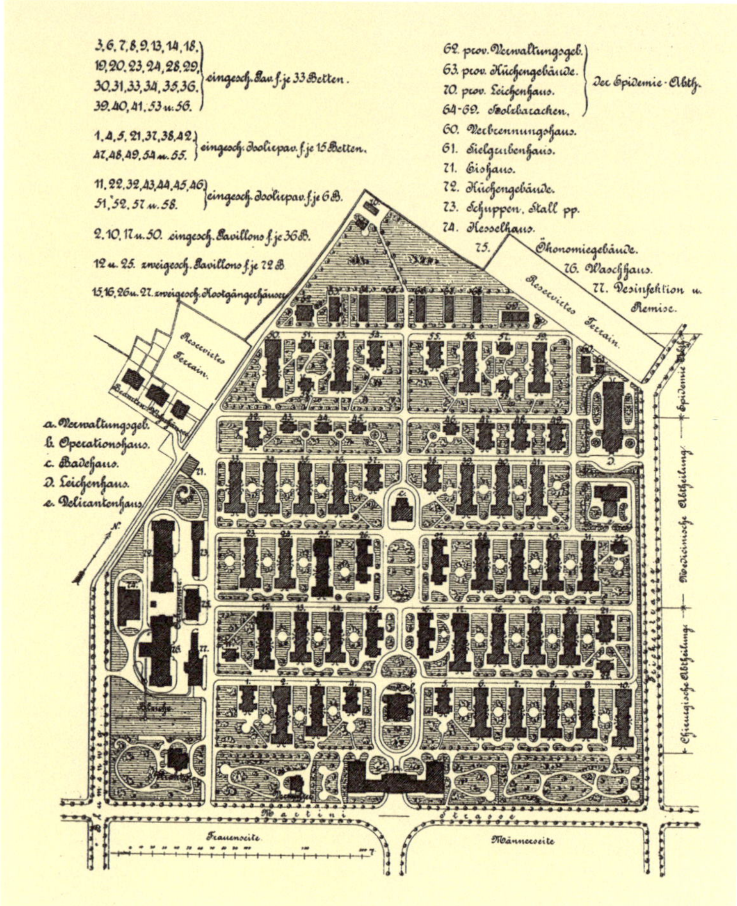

Fig. 14
Carl Johann Christian Zimmermann and Friedrich Ruppel, Plan of the Eppendorf hospital, Hamburg, Germany, 1889, from Friedrich Ruppel, *Anlage und Bau der Krankenhäuser nach Hygienisch-Technischen Grundsätzen*, 1896. Collection: author.

At the time of Curschmann's lecture, the new hospital was still under construction. Its design, initiated by Curschmann and executed by municipal architects Carl Johann Christian "Hans" Zimmermann and Friedrich Ruppel, was inspired by the Friedrichshain and Moabit hospitals in Berlin. Once completed, it was to consist of fifty-five one-story pavilions generously distributed in a park-like setting blessed with a sandy, porous soil and air as pure as could be found near the city. Intended to be a state-of-the-art institution, it was to offer 50 cubic meters of space per patient in wards equipped with ridge ventilation. Twenty-three of the pavilions were to offer isolation rooms, separated by a hall from the main sick ward. Its construction was impelled not only by the rapid growth of Hamburg's population but also by an awareness that, as a major port, the city was a gateway to epidemics. The introduction by Reich Chancellor Otto von Bismarck of a nationwide system of *Krankenkassen* (sick funds) in 1883 had created a solid financial base for hospital operations, while in 1884 a fear of a local outbreak of cholera had firmed up the resolve to begin construction.[31]

31 Carl Johann Christian Zimmermann, *Das allgemeine Krankenhaus in Hamburg-Eppendorf* (Hamburg: Ernst & Sohn, 1892).

Chapter Six, Fig. 6
→ p. 252

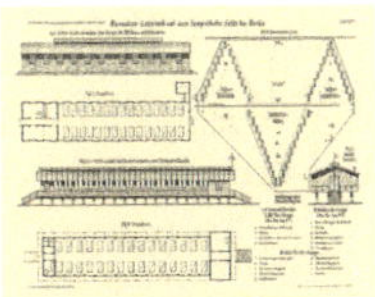

Chapter Seven, Fig. 20
→ p. 311

Chapter Eight, Figs. 1 and 2
→ p. 319

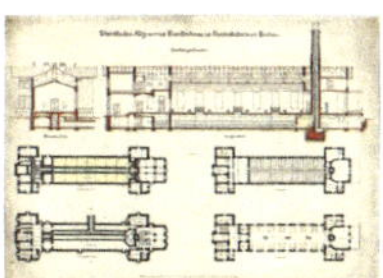

Chapter Six, Fig. 12
→ p. 259

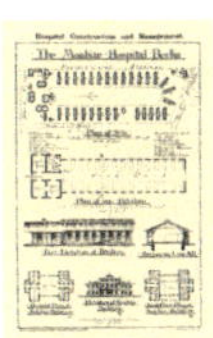

Chapter Eight, Fig. 5
→ p. 328

Curschmann began with a quick overview of the history of hospital design since the fire in 1772 at the Hôtel-Dieu in Paris, singling out the important advances made in hospital design thanks to Dr. Louis Stromeyer's tent-barracks erected during the Austro-Prussian War of 1866, Rudolf Virchow and James Hobrecht's Tempelhof hospital of 1870, the Saint Jacob's Hospital in Leipzig, and the Friedrichshain and Moabit hospitals in Berlin. At least to the lecturer, the lessons were clear: the pavilion or barrack hospital was not only the best but the only option to create hospitals that reflected current medical knowledge. Interestingly, Curschmann used the term *Pavillon* and *Baracke* interchangeably and referred to the Eppendorf complex as a *Barackenspital* (barrack hospital), even though the pavilions were permanent brick constructions. Yet his understanding that the Eppendorf was, in fact, a barrack hospital was undoubtedly shaped by the fact that it embodied what he considered to be the key principle of hospital design: "The best hospital is the one that achieves the most and the greatest perfection with the simplest of means."[32] For Curschmann this meant a design based on the repetition of many identical units—the pavilions or barracks—and simple technologies of heating and ventilation by means of operable windows and ridge ventilation.

Architect Ruppel also remained firmly committed to the lineage of hospitals that included not only the city hospitals enumerated by Curschmann in his lecture but also the American Civil War hospitals, the *Versuchsbaracke* at the Charité, and the Riga hospital. Having reviewed all of these in considerable detail, he stated in his 281-page textbook on hospital design, published in 1896 as part of the authoritative multivolume *Handbuch der Hygiene* (Handbook of hygiene): "All the experience gained so far in the field of hospital construction, and on which the present-day teachings of hospital hygiene are mainly based, indicate that the *Pavillon-Barackensystem* [pavilion-barrack system] is the most perfect construction system for hospitals to date. On the basis of this knowledge, facilities have been built in recent times which, such as the general hospital in Hamburg-Eppendorf built in 1883–1890, can be regarded as models for larger hospital facilities."[33]

On May 17, 1889, the Eppendorf hospital opened its doors. It was considered the most modern hospital of its time—and at the same time it was hopelessly outdated, given the state of knowledge on the etiology of infectious disease. But in this it reflected the conservative if not reactionary attitude of the Hamburg elite,

32 Heinrich Curschmann, "Welchen Einfluss hat die heutige Gesundheitslehre, besonders die neuere Auffassung des Wesens und der Verbreitung der Infectionskrankheiten auf Bau, Einrichtung und Lage der Krankenhäuser?," *Deutsche Vierteljahrsschrift für öffentliche Gesundheitspflege* 21 (1889), 184.

33 Friedrich Ruppel, *Anlage und Bau der Krankenhäuser nach Hygienisch-Technischen Grundsätzen* (Jena: Gustav Fischer, 1896), 10.

which was bold in its willingness to develop trade on a global scale but resisted the huge investment needed to improve public health within the city itself.

On August 16, 1892, a construction worker employed in the Hamburg port was brought to the Eppendorf hospital with cholera-like symptoms. He died within a day. Of all the infectious diseases that circulated the globe in the nineteenth century, cholera was feared the most, and not only because of its mortality—the first cholera epidemic that hit Europe in 1831–32 claimed hundreds of thousands of lives, and one in 1853 killed more than a million people in Russia. In addition, it proved a socially unacceptable disease, marked by bouts of uncontrollable diarrhea, frightening physical transformation of the body, making patients unrecognizable even to their own family members, and a terrible agony caused by muscle spasms. Since its first appearance in Europe, physicians had been convinced that cholera resulted from "contingent contagion," which means they believed that cholera originated in a contagion but acquired its catastrophic dimension in a miasmatic environment. Therefore, the key battle against the disease was to be found in destroying miasmas by cleaning up open cesspits, removing garbage, and increasing ventilation. This was the long-term approach. If cholera struck a city, then the immediate transport of the sick to a well-ventilated and isolated environment might do some good—or at least not make matters worse.[34]

The Eppendorf hospital was equipped with an isolation department that consisted of six twenty-bed barracks. These buildings had stood empty since their completion in 1884, but now they were brought into operation. It took only a couple of days before all the barracks were filled to capacity. At this time, the city authorities were still denying that there were any major problems. However, when Robert Koch, who had identified the cholera germ a decade earlier, announced that he had found cholera bacteria in the German city's water supply, the Hamburg authorities had no choice but to act boldly and to be seen to do so. On August 24 the city officially admitted the presence of an epidemic. Needing to find a culprit, the authorities turned to the easiest of scapegoats: Russian Jews who, after traveling in sealed trains from the Russian-German border, were held in a closed quarantine compound in the international part of the Hamburg port until their embarkation in the steerage section of the SS *Augusta Victoria* or another Hamburg-American Line ocean liner. Hamburg had

34 See Richard J. Evans, *Death in Hamburg: Society and Politics in the Cholera Years, 1830–1910* (Oxford: Clarendon Press, 1987), 229–30.

become a major pivot in the massive emigration of Jews from Russia to the New World, prompted by a wave of antisemitic persecution that had followed the assassination, in 1881, of Alexander II by anarchists, three of whom were Jews. The Russian government's formula for solving the Jewish problem was "one-third emigration, one-third conversion, and for one-third death." Jewish life was forcefully restricted to the Pale of Settlement, the area of Russia that had been Polish once. At the same time, the economic situation in the Pale declined, creating widespread social unrest that the government found convenient to blame on the Jews. The result was various waves of pogroms, some instigated by the government, others tolerated by it. The pogroms triggered a mass movement of unheard-of proportions; facilitated by the lack of border controls, some 2 million Jews left between the 1880s and 1914 for western Europe and America. Most of them were destitute, and the majority of Germans considered them carriers of disease—a prejudice that was certainly alive when cholera hit the city.

A small team led by city councillor Friedrich Alfred Lappenberg, Eppendorf hospital director Theodor Rumpf, and Hamburg's chief engineer, Franz Andreas Meyer, began work to create four barrack isolation compounds and one tent-and-barrack field hospital adjacent or close to existing hospitals that were to provide management, staff, and services. The 926-bed expansion of Hamburg's hospital capacity was realized within a couple of weeks, and if the continuous transports of sick people and coffins through the city and the dumping of the city's garbage in the public squares provided a spectacle of crisis and defeat, the sudden emergence of these wooden barracks in the midst of the urban environment were signs of both crisis and crisis management, for better and worse. In fact, Meyer had begun to prepare for the *Ernstfall* (emergency) of the cholera reaching Hamburg when he heard, in early August, about the outbreak of the disease in Russia, and he had at that time instructed his department to prepare designs for a barrack that measured 29 by 8 meters and which consisted of a vestibule at the center, flanked by two bathrooms and a small kitchen, leading on each side to a sick ward with ten beds, a toilet, a small isolation room with two beds, and a room that could accommodate two nurses or attendants.

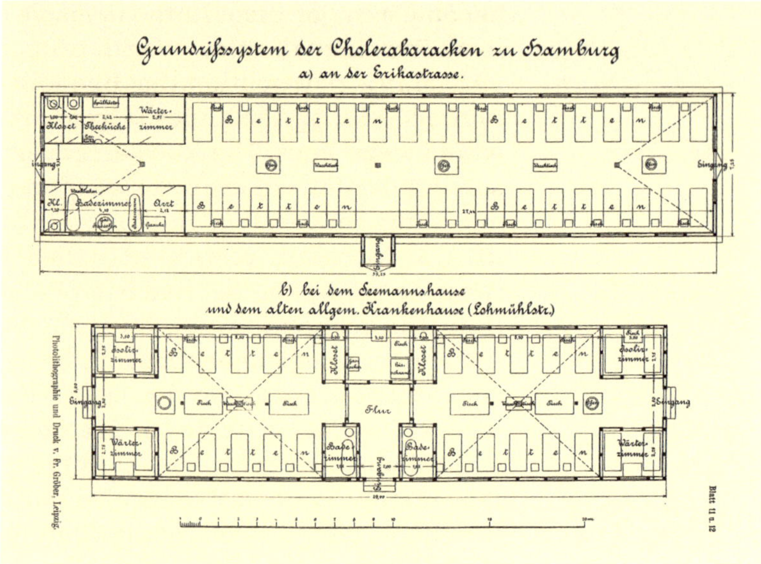

Fig. 15
Franz Andreas Meyer, Plans of the initial barrack design (bottom) and of the final design (top) adopted during the cholera epidemic in Hamburg, Germany, 1892, from Walther Lange, *Der Baracken-Bau mit besonderer Berücksichtigung der Wohn- und Epidimie-Baracken*, 1895. Collection: author.

The plans and the budget were approved, building materials secured, and contractors were put on a retainer to construct within a fortnight eight of the barracks if and when called upon to do so. Yet, in the last week of August, when Meyer issued the order to build four of these barracks next to the old Allgemeine Krankenhaus (General Hospital) and four next to the Seemannskrankenhaus (Seamen's Hospital) in the harbor, a major problem appeared: the design stipulated poured-concrete floors that could be easily cleaned and would protect the soil beneath of infectious materials, and no one had calculated that poured-concrete took four weeks to cure. Thus, at the last moment, the question of the floor became a bottleneck. The chief public health official in the city, Dr. Caspar Theodor Kraus, came forward with a solution to use wooden floors that would span over a large pit filled with peat that was to absorb the contaminants. After a few months of use, the barracks were to be burned down, and the peat, which was a common fuel for stoves, was to be burned up. This proposal was rejected as too risky from a public-health point of view, so the project remained in limbo while the physicians, engineers, and contractors argued, to settle in the end on the use of the stone pavers used in Hamburg's streets. "Mobilization plans [...] that have been worked out in detail, and which should perform mechanically when an incident occurs, can only be achieved if the anticipated event fulfills all the requirements," Meyer observed in his report on the episode published a few years later. He had learned that emergencies seldom unfolded as planned, and moreover, he had been taken by surprise, noting that he and his colleagues had been "dragged forward and backward by passionate excitement" while they tried to reconcile "the occurrence of the epidemic with their understanding of the science behind it."[35]

While the construction of the predesigned and preapproved barracks was held up, the directorate of the old general hospital approached master carpenter G. F. Lüders, who designed and constructed within a few days four utterly simple barracks (or better, sheds), of 30.8 by 6 meters, which each accommodated thirty-five beds in a single ward, at a cost of around one-fifth of the price of a bed in Meyer's barracks.

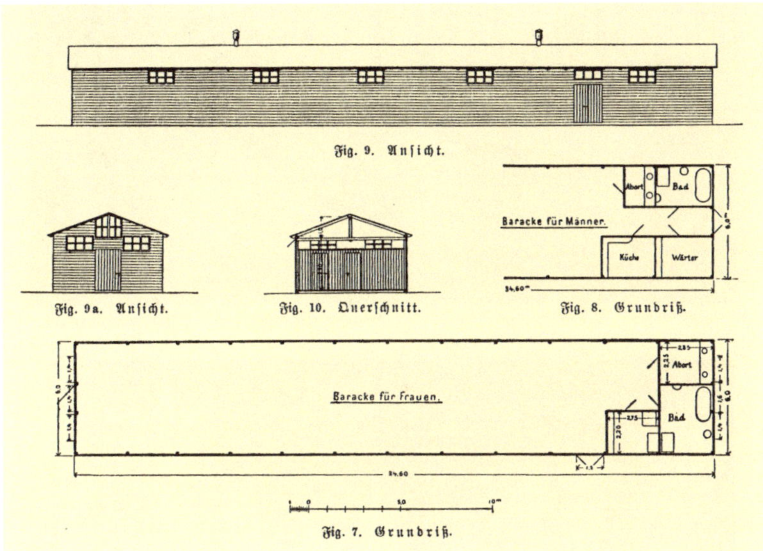

Fig. 16
G. F. Lüders, Plan, elevations, and section of a cholera barrack, from Friedrich Ruppel, "Die Cholera-Baracken in Hamburg," *Centralblatt der Bauverwaltung*, 1892. Collection: author.

But Lüders's sheds were not equipped for use in winter, and as it became clear that more emergency hospital accommodation was necessary, the city pondered whether it ought to commission more of Meyer's barracks with the modified floor or try another layout. The model barrack housed the patients in two wards of ten and two rooms of two. But the doctors who treated patients in Lüders's sheds realized that there was a definite advantage in having all the sick in a single ward, and that from a staffing perspective the maximum number of beds might be as high as thirty-six and the minimum twenty-five. As far as the width was concerned, the 6 meters offered in Lüders's sheds was too little, as it made it quite difficult to move either patients or rolling tables holding medical equipment, while the 8 meters offered in the pre-epidemic design was considered to be on the generous side. Hence, it was decided that 7 meters would do. This resulted in a redesign of Meyer's barrack, of which fourteen were constructed. Three of these were built adjacent to the Krankenhaus des Vaterländischen Frauen Hülfs Vereins (Hospital of the Aid Society of Patriotic

35 F. Andreas Meyer, "Cholera-Barackenlazarethe und Leichenhäuser sowie Nothstands-Wasserversorgung in Hamburg während der Cholera-Epidemie des Jahres 1892," *Das Auftreten der Cholera im Deutschen Reiche während des Jahres 1893*, published in Arbeiten aus der Kaiserlichen Gesundheitsamte 10 (1896), 113*.

Women) in the Schlump, four adjacent to the Marienhospital (Mary's Hospital), and seven at a site located close to the Eppendorf hospital that became known as Erikastation.

Fig. 17
Exterior of the barracks at the Erikastation, Hamburg, Germany, 1892, from August Schacht, *Rückblick auf die Cholera-Epidemie 1892 in Hamburg*, 1893. Collection: author.

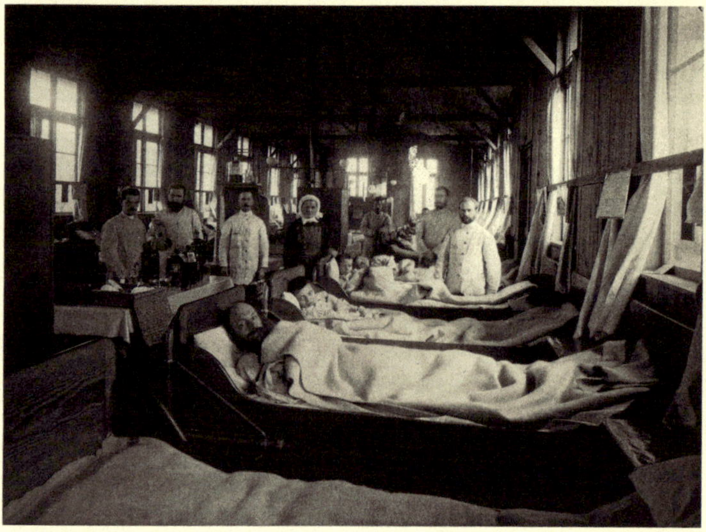

Fig. 18
Interior of a barrack at the Erikastation, 1892, from August Schacht, *Rückblick auf die Cholera-Epidemie 1892 in Hamburg*, 1893. Collection: author.

The cholera epidemic in Hamburg killed more than 8,000 people in a two-month period. In the history of the barrack, it stands as an episode in which much experience was gained, in a relatively tight feedback loop that ensured the experience led to rapid improvement in barrack design, between the beginning and the end of the epidemic. From a cost perspective, Lüders's barracks had offered a cheap and workable solution. Meyer's barracks had cost between ten and twenty times per bed. The German government had contributed a field hospital that included tents and, in addition, six prefabricated barracks, which Meyer characterized as *Feld-Baracken* (field barracks). Manufactured by the firm of Christoph & Unmack, they were universally considered at the time to be the very best in barrack design—but in Meyer's view they had not performed very well because their limited width of 5 meters had provided too little space for physicians to attend to the patients. Furthermore, the preparation of the site for the field hospital had taken too much time, and the tents and field barracks had suffered much delay in the shipping. "When enough workers are available and lumber can be easily obtained, and when larger rooms are to be created for the sick, well-constructed wooden barracks that are created even in haste are preferable to field hospitals, and even more so if they need to serve not only during the warm season but also when it gets cold," Meyer concluded after the tents and the *Feld-Baracken* had been shipped back to Berlin, and the custom-designed barracks had been pulled down. "Only where hospital tents and *Feld-Baracken* can be obtained without the need for transport—that is, they are already where they are to be used—can they be used for cholera hospitals during the summer months and when linked to the infrastructure of larger hospitals."[36]

As the epidemic was brought under control and the barracks emptied, Friedrich Ruppel, co-architect of the Eppendorf hospital, reviewed the design and construction history of the cholera barracks in an article published in the *Centralblatt der Bauverwaltung* (Central journal for building administration). Normally design, financing, approvals, and construction take time, but the project to create the barrack compounds in Hamburg had forced all involved to make decisions on the spot and act with both speed and determination. This, Ruppel noted, created enormous excitement. "Such projects offer an amazing education that allows the technician to thoroughly learn how to achieve with the simplest of means the intended goal in the speediest manner and how to distinguish between what is necessary and what is optional," he observed, ending his review with a pious wish: "May in the future such experiences and lessons be gained at more pleasant occasions, and may the sad example in Hamburg remain the only one of its kind!"[37]

Remarkably, neither Ruppel nor anyone else at that time ever raised the question concerning the capacity of the barrack to ameliorate disease through ventilation and other means—an important shift in the medical and architectural discourse concerning the barrack hospital. From now on, its design and construction was to occur outside of the discourse that, since the mid-eighteenth

36 Ibid., 122*.
37 Friedrich Ruppel, "Die Cholera-Baracken in Hamburg," *Centralblatt der Bauverwaltung* 12, no. 42 (Oct. 15, 1892), 451.

century, had defined the deployment of this building type in public health crises. In the decades to come, within the civilian sphere, the barrack was to be primarily considered as a quick means to warehouse those people from whom the public needed to be protected because they were deemed to be a threat to either the physical or social health of the community.

Between 1890 and 1910, the medical community's understanding of what made a good hospital increasingly surpassed that of the public at large. The theory of miasma, which connected visible filth and olfactory stench to disease, was now scientifically irrelevant. In his authoritative treatise on heating and ventilation, published in 1893, John Shaw Billings, who had constructed the Cliffbourne Hospital during the Civil War and played such an important role in the making of the Johns Hopkins Hospital in the mid-1870s, referred to miasma only once: "The bad results of imperfect ventilation, or of an impure air supply, are more strikingly evident in hospitals than in other buildings, owing in part to their continuous occupation, in part to the lowered vitality of their inmates, who are specially susceptible to insanitary influences, and in part to the presence of special causes of disease in the form of germs or miasms." The reference to "miasms" proved to be only lip service to that now obsolete etiology of disease, which Billings did not discuss in his text. As for bacteria, Billings was convinced that good ventilation did not aid in preventing germ-based diseases.

> The most dangerous impurity in some air, such as that contained in a hospital ward for contagious diseases, is often not gaseous, has no very marked or unpleasant odor, and cannot be detected by ordinary means of chemical analysis. It consists of minute living organisms which have the power of producing disease when they gain access to the human body under favorable circumstances. Many of these organisms, known as bacteria, have been proven to be the cause of certain specific inflammations and other diseases. The process of diluting by ventilation the air of a room which contains them does not dilute the individual bacterium or spore, and its effect in removing them from the apartment is much less than its effect upon diffused gases or vapors. Most of them are of greater specific gravity than the air, especially when adhering to particles of dust, and hence their

> tendency is to remain wherever dust can settle, and to be diffused by whatever causes the diffusion of dust in the air, such as sweeping, dusting, movements of persons, or strong air currents. It is, therefore, evident that the prevention of the entrance of the dangerous forms of micro-organisms into a building where it is possible to do so is a matter of special importance, since it is very difficult to dispose of them by ventilation alone when they have once gained entrance, and hence ventilation is no efficient substitute for proper plumbing, and the avoidance of collections of decaying organic matter within the house.[38]

However, the fully revised, fourteenth, jubilee edition of the *Brockhaus' Conversations-Lexikon*, published between 1896 and 1907, continued to praise the barrack sick wards of the Saint Jacob's Hospital in Leipzig as exemplary, and an updated plate, showing the expansion of the facilities, suggested the continued impact of this model, at least in the public imagination.[39] A photo of the interior of one of the wards, taken in 1911, suggests why. It shows a cheerful, well-lit, tidy and spotless room with friendly nurses and seemingly well-tended patients. The cross ventilation provided by the windows in the long walls, the air ducts in the floor, and the ventilation monitor in the roof might not be useful in preventing germ-based illnesses, but obviously the pleasant environment offered by the ward generated a pride of place that would have supported a regime of good hygiene that might have helped the patients recover from whatever ailed them.

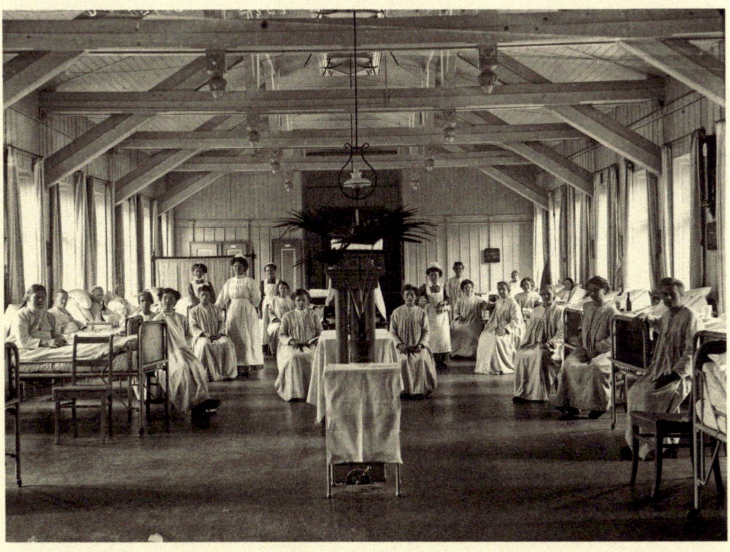

Fig. 19
Sick ward at the Saint Jacob's Hospital, 1911. Collection: Stadtgeschichtliches Museum Leipzig.

38 John S. Billings, *Ventilation and Heating* (New York: Engineering Record, 1893), 301, 25.
39 "Krankenhaus," *Brockhaus' Conversations-Lexikon*, 14th ed., 17 vols. (Leipzig: Brockhaus, 1896–1907), 10:674–77.

→ p. 373

Nine

In War and Peace

One kilometer from the point where the Neva River joins the Gulf of Finland, on Vasilyevsky Island, stands the Saint Petersburg State Budgetary Institution of Health Care Children's Infectious Diseases Hospital No. 3. Immediately adjacent to the Vasileostrovets Garden, the compound holds modern facilities and also a collection of 130-year-old structures, including two barracks of a hybrid brick-and-wood construction and three all-wood barracks.

Fig. 1
Wooden barrack of the Children's Infectious Diseases Hospital No. 3, Saint Petersburg, Russia, 1889. Photo: Alexander Veryovkin, 2021. Collection: author.

These buildings were designed in 1887 and put into operation in 1889 as the Saint Petersburg Barrack Hospital in Memory of Emperor Alexander II. Sponsored by the Saint Petersburg stock exchange, the purpose of this hospital was to serve the medical needs of dockworkers. At the time of its opening, it was famous for the fact that every room was illuminated by electric light, which generated comparisons with the emperor's fully electrified Winter Palace.

With the closure of the original Saint Petersburg stock exchange in 1917, which had remained its source of funds, the hospital became a state institution. In 1925, during a scarlet fever epidemic, it seemed a good choice for an infectious disease hospital for children, as the barrack wards made it easier to impose the necessary isolation. The original barracks still exist and are the oldest surviving examples of this remarkable building type that still function as originally intended. The barracks in Saint Petersburg suggest the unique (compared to the rest of Europe) trajectory of the adoption of wooden barracks in Russia. In western Europe, wooden barracks had ceased to be an accepted model for sick wards in civilian hospitals since the early 1870s; in Russia, they remained a viable option for another twenty years.

To understand the unique dimensions of the Russian history of the barrack, which reached its high noon in the 1870s and early 1880s, it is useful to go back to the early eighteenth century. In 1703, when Tsar Peter I (later to be dubbed "the Great") conquered the Swedish Nyenskans fortress at the confluence of the Neva and Okhta Rivers, close to the Gulf of Finland, he decided to create a new city at that location, one that was to turn Russia toward the West, toward the Atlantic world.

Since the day Tsar Peter decided to establish Saint Petersburg, the dialectic between Westernizing desire, with its trust in innovation, and Slavophile commitment to traditional moral values embodied in the city of Moscow, the Orthodox Church and the closed peasant community, has energized Russian history. The dynamic between a Westernizing push and a Slavophile pull also helped to shape a particularly Russian discourse that attempted to assimilate a culture of innovation that comes from the West by means of a narrative that rooted these imports to inventions made by often untaught Russians from rural areas. This discourse is based on a particular confusion between invention, which might be indeed the result of a single genius working in isolation, and innovation, which takes up this invention and makes it broadly relevant to society as a whole and, in the process, makes it commercially successful. For invention one needs talent, and among Russians the percentage of talented people is as great (or small) as that of other nations. But for innovation one needs a society that appreciates and nurtures change, a society that protects innovation by means of fair processes of tender, legal enforcement of patent rights, and an effective feedback loop concerning the success or failure of particular innovations represented by a freedom of speech. And this is where Russia, autocratic under the tsar-emperors, totalitarian under communism, has offered little opportunity for its talented inventors to make a difference.[1] A famous example is the story of the two-cylinder steam engine the self-taught Siberian Ivan Ivanovich Polzunov designed and constructed in 1766 to operate air pumps for steel furnaces in Barnaul, southwestern Siberia. Brilliant in conception and effective in operation, it was taken apart after three months because a cheaper alternative was available. Polzunov represents the tragic

1 See Loren Graham, *Lonely Ideas: Can Russia Compete?* (Cambridge, MA: MIT Press, 2013).

intensity of the Russian encounter with modernity, which also defines the Russian adaptation of the barrack, particularly in hospital settings.

Russia was not at the table when representatives of sixteen countries met in Geneva in 1864 to conclude an agreement on the aid to wounded soldiers in time of war. Relying on the old saying that the only allies of Russia are its army and navy, Emperor Alexander II had decided that he would not allow any curtailment in the freedom of action of the Russian forces. Two years later, in the fall of 1866, Princess Dagmar of Denmark arrived in Russia to marry the heir to the throne, Tsarevitch Alexander. Two prominent physicians, Pavel Andreevich Naranovich and Filipp Iakolevich Karel, and two ladies-in-waiting of Empress Maria Alexandrovna—Baroness Maria Petrovna Frederiks and concert pianist Martha Stepanovna Sabinina—decided that a worthy monument to the wedding would be the creation of a Red Cross society in Russia. This initiative would be successful only with support from the highest level, and there were two major obstacles: first, the emperor would have to accept that his refusal to attend the Geneva Convention in 1864 might not have been the right one; second, Metropolitan Philaret (Vasily Mikhailovich Drozdov), the archbishop of Moscow and as such the most senior clergyman in the Russian Orthodox Church, disapproved of the project. Philaret feared that a Russian Red Cross organization would cause inappropriate interaction between men and women in the various committees required to run the operation, introduce a measure of social mobility for women from the lower classes that was inappropriate to Russian traditions, and directly undermine the church's role in caring for the sick. In other words, it would represent a significant overreach of Saint Petersburg into an aspect of Russian life that was within the purview of Moscow.[2]

In a meeting, Naranovich, Karel, Frederiks, and Sabinina agreed that many of the social conditions that allowed for the formation of Red Cross societies in the West did not exist in Russia, and that "only when these ideas become fully ours, Russian, can they be implanted in our society and put to use."[3] The cabal of four decided that Frederiks and Sabinina would approach the empress with the request to extend her patronage over a Russian version of an aid society. Born in Germany as Maximiliane Wilhelmine Augusta Sophie Marie, Princess of Hesse, Empress Maria Alexandrovna was attuned to the principles of international collaboration and within

2 See Andrew J. Ringlee, "The Romanovs' Militant Charity: The Red Cross and Public Mobilization for War in Tsarist Russia, 1853–1914" (PhD diss., University of North Carolina, Chapel Hill, 2016), 62–94.

3 As quoted in ibid., 80.

days convinced her husband to reverse his earlier decision. Negotiations with the Orthodox Church were more difficult, as senior clerics certainly did not want any presence in Russia of an organization that resembled the United States Sanitary Commission. The empress, who had taken a central role in trying to massage the friction between the reformers and the conservatives, decided that the only way forward was to bow to Metropolitan Philaret's wishes on the issue of women's participation, assuming that once the organization was established, the practical need to include women at all levels would create sufficient facts on the ground to necessitate their full involvement. As a result, the charter of the Russian Aid Society for Wounded and Sick Soldiers (also known as the Russian Red Cross) not only excluded women from the main directorate but also significantly restricted their influence at lower levels of the organization. And, in another bow to Muscovite sensitivities, at least on paper, the primary commitment of the organization was not to an international effort to reduce the horror of war but to a national goal of helping Russian soldiers—one that allowed the Saint Petersburg committee to slip in the women through the back door. "The Russian people are aware of their obligation to care for those who sacrifice life and health for their defense and honor," the charter declared. "With joy they enter a union with the goal of not only satisfying Christian charity and compassion but also of fulfilling their holy duty to the defenders of the Russian land and to Russian soldiers. Russian women, of course, enter this union with joy, which gives them the capability of participating in the defense and protection of the fatherland, all the more so as this concern is truly a women's task."[4] Such nationalist language did not stand in the way of a formal relationship between the Russian Aid Society and the International Committee of the Red Cross. Emperor Alexander II signed the Geneva Convention on May 10, 1867.

In the fall of 1870, during the Franco-Prussian War, the Russian Aid Society for Wounded and Sick Soldiers dispatched a dozen surgeons to France and Germany along with a limited amount of material support. The contingent also included the two ladies-in-waiting, Frederiks and Sabinina, who would assess the effectiveness of the many women's aid societies in Prussia and the other German states; and retired military surgeon Nikolai Ivanovich Pirogov, in the company of his protégé, physician Iosif Vasil'evich Bertenson, and architect Nikolai Nikolaevich Nabokov, who would report on the medical help given to combatants in general,

4 As quoted in ibid., 93–94.

the arrangement and operation of the hospitals, and the construction of the barracks.

Pirogov had studied medicine at the University of Dorpat, a German-speaking institution located in what is today Tartu, Estonia. His education made him receptive to developments in the West, and after his graduation in 1832, he traveled to Berlin and Paris to see firsthand the newest medical developments. Subsequently, he became professor of surgery at the Imperial Medical and Surgical Academy in Saint Petersburg, and there he became an early adopter of surgery under anesthesia. In the late 1840s he was dispatched to the Caucasus, where the Imperial Russian Army was fighting an insurgency, to introduce military surgeons to this new technique. Witnessing the terrible conditions of battlefield medicine, Pirogov became a champion of a more professional approach to both the treatment of wounds and the general care of sick and wounded soldiers. At the beginning of the Crimean War, he volunteered for service in Sevastopol and worked under the most difficult circumstances in the besieged city. After the Crimean War he left the field of medicine and accepted the position of superintendent of the Odessa and Kiev (today Odesa and Kyiv) school districts with the aim of creating a system of universal education that was also open to women, Jews, Muslims, and adults—an effort that led to his dismissal and forced retirement in 1866. Settling to private life on his estate near the town of Vinnytsia (today in Ukraine), Pirogov took up the practice of medicine, now in service of the local peasant population. Yet his reputation as a military surgeon remained solid, especially after the publication, in 1864, of his treatise on the principles of war surgery. In this book he paid considerable attention to the relationship between morbidity, mortality, and hospital design, without coming to a single conclusion: "Military surgery and hospitals are unfortunately two inseparable things. Over a period of 25 years I have conducted surgery in the open field, in simple soldier tents, in peasant huts, as well as in large so-called 'well-established' hospitals. And on the basis of this experience I come to the conviction that we have to abandon the ideal of a well-designed hospital."[5] There were simply too many factors that determined the medical outcome of a sojourn in a hospital; unlike Florence Nightingale or William Hammond, Pirogov was not willing to reduce the question to a simple architectural formula.

His 1870 fact-finding mission in Germany and France convinced Pirogov that he had been right all

5 Nikolai Pirogov, *Grundzüge der allgemeinen Kriegschirurgie: Nach Reminiscenzen aus den Kriegen in der Krim und im Kaukasus und aus der Hospitalpraxis* (Leipzig: Vogel, 1864), 7.

along—large hospitals were not helpful. In a lengthy report published after his return to Russia, he stated that the Franco-Prussian War was to be the last nail in the coffin of monumental hospital architecture. Writing for a local audience, he did not fail to claim various Russian precedents for the deployment of barracks as hospital wards.

> Especially just in the last war [the Crimean War], we found everywhere temporary military hospitals that were organized according to a different system, but which we Russians justly may claim as having their origin in our society. Foreigners bury in silence the fact that the hospital tents and the wooden summer hospital buildings [*palatki*] have been in use at Russian hospitals for over fifty years, and that they took the idea from us—and we also fail to insist on our right of invention in this matter. [...] Be that as it may, we already employed barracks during the Crimean War, by which I refer to the simple wattle-and-daub huts that accommodated the wounded. During the Crimean War, both hospital tents, used in our country for a long time, and the wooden summer hospital buildings formed in the urban hospitals the best and healthiest part of our facilities for the sick.[6]

As to the prior existence of "wooden summer hospital buildings," Pirogov was referring to tents and temporary wooden pavilions, both known as *palatki*, used during the hot summer months. Little documentation survives of this popular form of patient accommodation used in Russian since the eighteenth century. The most important is a drawing of one of the four *palatki* constructed in the 1840s on the south bank of the Gulf of Finland to house patients of the Kronstadt Naval Hospital. Measuring 79 by 8.5 meters, it was constructed on stone foundations but without a basement. The *palatki* accommodated four primary wards on the ground floor, each constructed with a view to cross ventilation, and each offering room to twenty patients. The summer hospital had a total capacity of 320. The attic of the *palatki* offered extra space that proved useful in the spring, when the many sailors returning to port were suffering from scurvy, and the number of patients might exceed 500. The summer buildings of the Kronstadt Naval Hospital were certainly the most monumental form the *palatki* ever achieved.

6 Nikolai Ivanovich Pirogov, *Bericht über die Besichtigung der Militär-Sanitätsanstalten in Deutschland, Lothringen und Elsass im Jahre 1870*, trans. N. Iwanoff (Leipzig: F. C. W. Vogel, 1871), 24, 34–35.

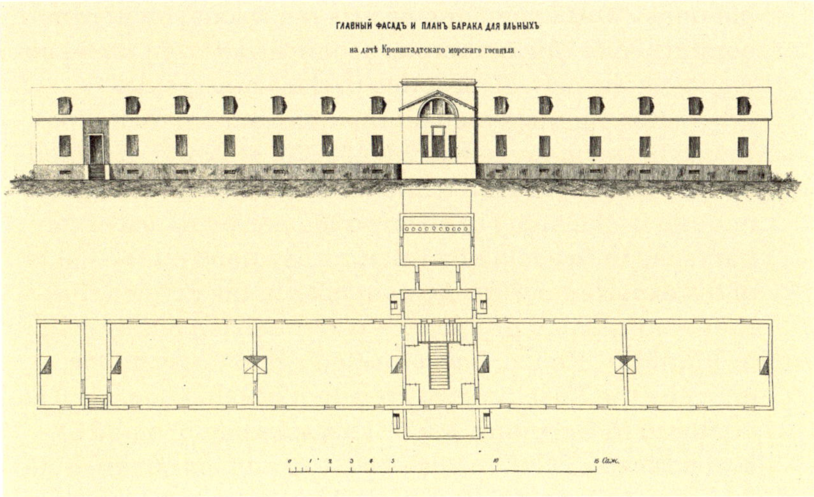

Fig. 2
Plan and elevation of a summer pavilion of the Kronstadt Naval Hospital, Lomonosov, Russia, 1846, *Meditsinskie pribavleniya k Morskomu sborniku*, 1879. Collection: Central Naval Library, Saint Petersburg.

The existence of *palatki* was not completely unknown in the West. "Each of the larger hospitals has a garden, and in those are the so-called summer-palatki," German journalist Aurelio Buddeus observed in his 1846 book on hospitals in Saint Petersburg. "They are single-story structures. [...] The summer-palatki of the hospitals are calculated to accommodate only part of the patient population at any given time, and are usually occupied from June to the end of September by different groups in rotation."[7] Yet neither Russian military men and physicians nor those from abroad had ever linked the *palatki* tradition with the discourse on emergency shelter for soldiers or the sick described in the earlier chapters of this book.

While Pirogov ensured that his report contained a claim that Russians had pioneered the barrack in the *palatki*, he did not unambiguously endorse the barrack as the best means to provide shelter for the wounded and ill. He believed that, in many cases, hospital tents offered a better solution and that the Germans had not sufficiently considered their potential before constructing barrack hospitals. "Comparing the mutual advantages of the hospital tents and the barracks," he wrote, "I come to the conclusion that the former are (1) cheaper, (2) mobile and transferable, and (3) if they are well erected, provide adequate protection from storms in summer and autumn and provide, compared to barracks, a superior level of ventilation." Barrack or tent: whatever shelter was chosen, he contended, the main principle to be observed in housing the wounded and sick was not to have more than twenty of them in the same place, and not to allow them to occupy a single space continuously. It was important to move the patients regularly into new quarters, allowing for the thorough disinfection of the

7 Aurelio Buddeus, *Zur Kenntniss von St. Petersburg im kranken Leben* (Stuttgart and Tübingen: Gotta'scher Verlag, 1846), 163–64.

old ones. "Until someone proves me wrong, I will remain committed to this principle, as it evolved from the experience in my private practice in the countryside."[8]

Having inspected all the different barrack types in use in Germany in the fall of 1870, Pirogov remained largely unimpressed. While he had not stayed long enough in Germany to observe the performance of the barracks in the cold of winter, he assumed on the basis of his experience with wooden huts in the Crimea that they would fail to protect the patients from either cold or humidity. Hence, he counseled against any major effort by the Russian army to adopt wooden barracks as deployed in Germany. As for barracks constructed of a wood frame filled in with brick, examples of which he had seen in Leipzig, Pirogov judged them to be too permanent in nature to allow for use in emergencies, while at the same time he deemed brick too porous a material to provide a healthy environment. "According to some recent, perhaps too scrupulous, opinions, brick is one of the materials that, due to its porosity, retains the air contaminated by hospital miasmas and promotes the distribution and thus the spread of these miasmas in the environment. According to these views, the barracks should be built of glass, or at least their walls should be covered with an impermeable material, such as silicon dioxide or a glaze. But such a material, even if it could be found, would be obviously too precious for temporary constructions."[9]

In a consistent back-to-basics approach, Pirogov instead advocated for adapting the southern Russian vernacular wattle-and-daub peasant hut, covered with a straw roof, for sick wards. Each of these ought to house only three or four men, and the huts should be located at a distance from one another. One physician would be responsible for ten such huts. Pirogov did not believe that these simple structures required a sophisticated ventilation system: a fire lit in a fireplace or stove, combined with some small openings in the wall, would generate the required movement of the air. As to the cost: the average expense per sickbed in one of the peasant huts had been one-eighth of that in a barrack. And Pirogov also observed that in the Russian countryside, when one considered the question from the perspective of moral equity, there could be no other choice: "One ought not construct palaces for sick people when healthy people live in huts."[10]

Pirogov's colleague Bertenson, twenty-three years younger, and the architect Nabokov, who had both accompanied him on his travels to Germany and France,

8 Pirogov, *Bericht über die Besichtigung*, 35, 39–40.
9 Ibid., 131.
10 Ibid., 135.

represented a completely different outlook on what the West had to offer—in particular, the value of the barrack for Russia. A baptized Jew, Bertenson had no particular reason to be nostalgic about a mythical Russian past from which his ancestors had been excluded, and having made a career as a physician in government service in Saint Petersburg, he missed the very experience of war and rural life that made Pirogov into a champion of the simplest of solutions in patient accommodation. When the Franco-Prussian War erupted, Bertenson was director of the cholera hospital—an institution known as either the Rozhdestvensky Hospital or the Nativity (or Christmas) Hospital, as "Rozhdestvensky" is both a family name and denotes the Feast of the Nativity—located on the grounds of the Rozhdestvensky regiment casern in Saint Petersburg. Bertenson's cash-strapped institution had been established in 1866 as a temporary hospital and housed in old buildings that had served as a fire-brigade station and a jail. A Saint Petersburg municipal architect, Nabokov was, like Bertenson, a man of the city and had no great sympathy for the relevance of peasant traditions in modern life.

During their fact-finding trip with Pirogov through Germany and German-occupied France, Bertenson and Nabokov systematically gathered material on the principles, best practices, and prospects of barrack design. Bertenson's 1871 treatise on the topic, *Barachnye lazarety v voennoe i mirnoe vremya* (Barrack hospitals in war and peace), summarized all the important developments in barrack design and their use as sick wards since the beginning of the American Civil War and offered guidance on how barracks could become an important element in Russian health care.

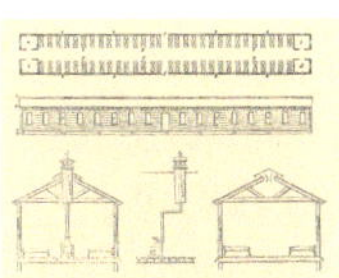
Chapter Six, Fig. 1
→ p. 237

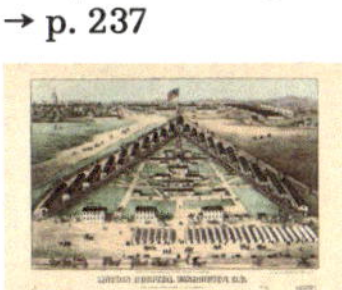
Chapter Five, Fig. 17
→ p. 225

Ignoring the British and French track records on barracks in the Crimean War, Bertenson credited the Americans with the invention of this building type and discussed the design of Surgeon General William Hammond's pavilion, the Lincoln Hospital in Washington, DC, and six other US Civil War hospitals. "The so-called American barrack system represents a substantial advance in the history of military medicine, worthy of imitation in the interests of humanity," he asserted. Yet Bertenson also believed that the case for the use of barracks as sick wards in post-Civil War civilian hospitals had not yet been made. The size, especially, of Dr. Hammond's pavilions seemed excessive. However, Bertenson's travels to France and Germany in 1870–71 had settled the issue, and he fully endorsed the barrack as a sick ward—distancing himself from Pirogov's

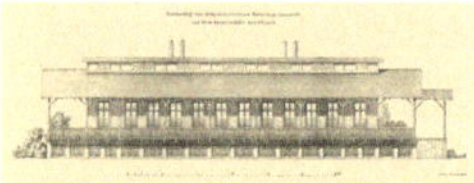

Chapter Six, Figs. 9 and 10
→ p. 257

Chapter Eight, Fig. 3
→ p. 322

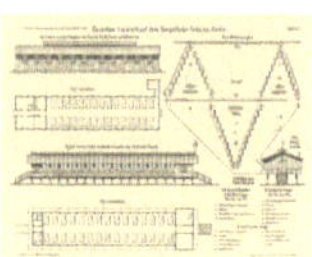

Chapter Seven, Figs. 19 and 20
→ p. 310

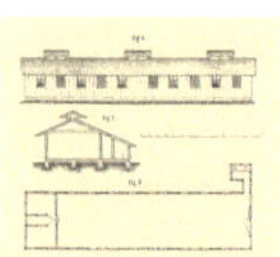

Chapter Seven, Fig. 11
→ p. 301

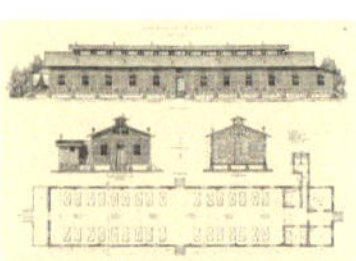

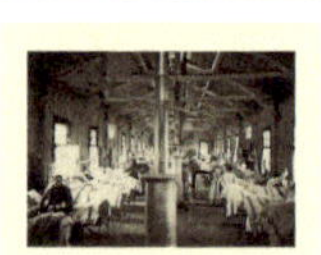

Chapter Seven, Figs. 12 and 13
→ p. 304

position on the matter: "In this war, barracks provided throughout northern and southern Germany invaluable service to the wounded and sick; the mortality statistics of this war confirm the great advantage of simple, wooden barracks over all other hospitals, those *palaces for the poor*, in which the sick are exposed to premature death resulting from both the lack and the corruption of air."[11]

As far as the theory of the barrack was concerned, Bertenson very much relied on Friedrich von Esmarch's *Ueber Vorbereitung von Reserve-Lazaretten* (On the preparation of reserve-lazarettos), published earlier in 1870 and, without doubt, the most up-to-date consideration on the topic. Further, Bertenson's main focus was on the German barrack hospitals that he had actually inspected during his trip, including the *Versuchsbaracke* at the Charité Hospital in Berlin; the barracks hospital at Mannheim, which had become well known thanks to Theodor Billroth's reports; and above all the Tempelhof hospital, which Bertenson considered in its general arrangement, with its well-considered location vis-à-vis the prevailing winds, to ensure the best possible natural ventilation, a model for future hospitals. "In general," he wrote, "all the wards of the Tempelhof infirmary have, of course, the character of temporary and quickly constructed buildings, something that was justified not only by the very speed of the military developments but also by the incredibly short interval of three weeks between the beginning and completion of the construction of such a large and well-equipped military hospital."[12] Of particular interest was the ridge ventilation.

Bertenson believed that Germany provided two types that, with some modifications, could be used in Russia. The Prussian regulation barrack of 1870 could be adopted as a sick ward to be used during the summer. The Friedrich Barrack Military Hospital in Karlsruhe provided a model for a sick ward to be occupied in the spring, summer, and fall seasons. On the basis of these conclusions, Nabokov designed a slightly modified version of the Prussian regulation barrack and a more substantial three-season barrack that included an entrance on every side, heating provided by two stoves, and ridge ventilation over the full length of the building. Both structures were designed to hold twenty-eight patients.[13]

11 Iosif Vasil'evich Bertenson, *Barachnye lazarety v voennoe i mirnoe vremya* (Saint Petersburg: O-vo popecheniya o ranennykh i bol'nykh voinakh, 1871), 35, 30.
12 Ibid., 38–39.
13 Ibid., 122–31.

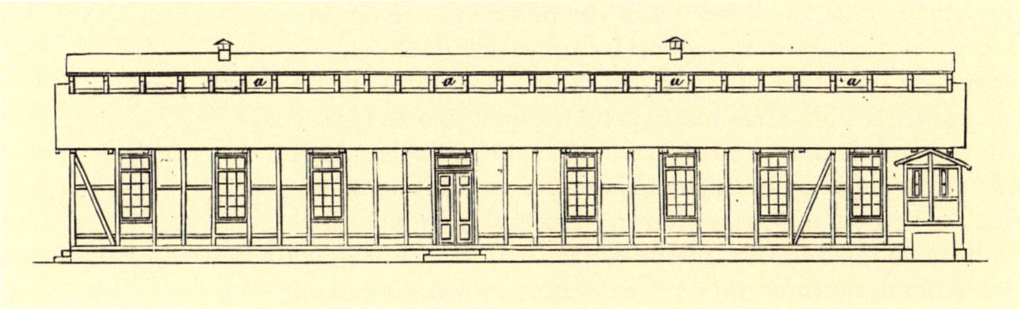

Fig. 3
Nikolai Nikolaevich Nabokov, Elevation of a three-season barrack, from Iosif Vasil'evich Bertenson, *Barachnye lazarety v voennoe i mirnoe vremya*, 1871. Collection: Białystok Technical University, Białystok, Poland.

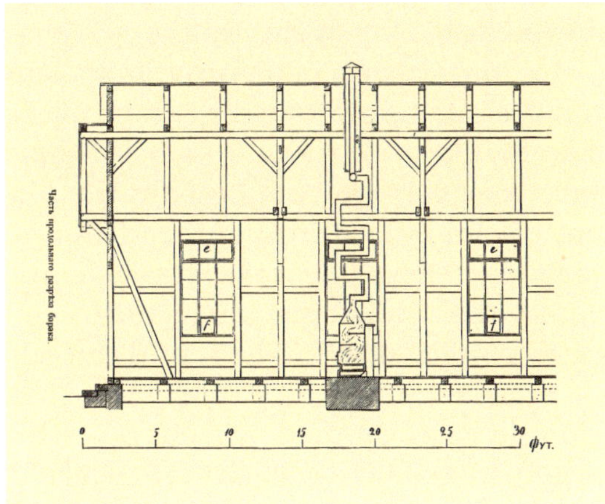

Bertenson also paid particular attention to Dr. Louis Stromeyer's tent-barrack constructed in 1866 in Langensalza and Paul Risold's design for a prefabricated barrack that could be easily assembled and disassembled, which had been commissioned by Esmarch in 1869. In a chapter on tents as shelter for the sick and wounded, Bertenson noted that German military surgeons in a tented field hospital pitched near Cologne had been content with the recovery of patients—a welcome conclusion because many of the tents had been donated by members of the Russian imperial family. But, in general, barracks remained the preferred form of accommodation.[14]

The fundamental problem that still needed to be addressed was the contradiction in the barrack's capacity to provide a space both well ventilated and, during winter, well heated. While the medical principles that had informed the architecture of the American barracks that Bertenson and Nabokov had studied and the German barracks that they had inspected in person might inform Russian practices, the specific architectural form of the American and German models could not be adapted to Russian circumstances—they were too flimsy in construction. Therefore, Russian architects would have to start from scratch. The question concerning the exact design of a barrack suited to the extremes of the Russian

Fig. 4
Nikolai Nikolaevich Nabokov, Section of a three-season barrack, from Iosif Vasil'evich Bertenson, *Barachnye lazarety v voennoe i mirnoe vremya*, 1871. Collection: Białystok Technical University, Białystok, Poland.

Chapter Six, Fig. 6
→ p. 252

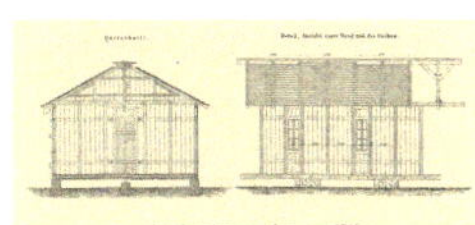

Chapter Six, Fig. 19
→ p. 269

14 Ibid., 146–48.

climate was not resolved when the book went to press. Nabokov's design that was included in the book was, obviously, not meant to be more than a first take on the problem. This also becomes clear in Bertenson's text, when he notes that the Russian barracks to be developed were to be smaller than those constructed during the Franco-Prussian War, which in turn had been smaller than those used in the United States. Quoting Pirogov as an authority in this matter, Bertenson proposed a capacity of fifteen patients per building.[15] Nabokov's design offered space for twenty-eight.

Bertenson's book provided a layout for a hospital that included nine such barracks arranged on two sides of an equilateral triangle—a parti that went back to the Harewood General and Lincoln Hospitals in Washington, DC, and the Mannheim and Tempelhof hospitals in Germany. These barracks were to connect to a covered gallery that linked the wards to a reception and administration building, a kitchen, and the building holding the pharmacy and the supply stores. The center of the triangle was occupied by a chapel, while at the apex, largely invisible to the patients, were the barracks holding the operating theater and, behind this, the morgue.

Chapter Five, Fig. 3
→ p. 200

Chapter Five, Fig. 17
→ p. 225

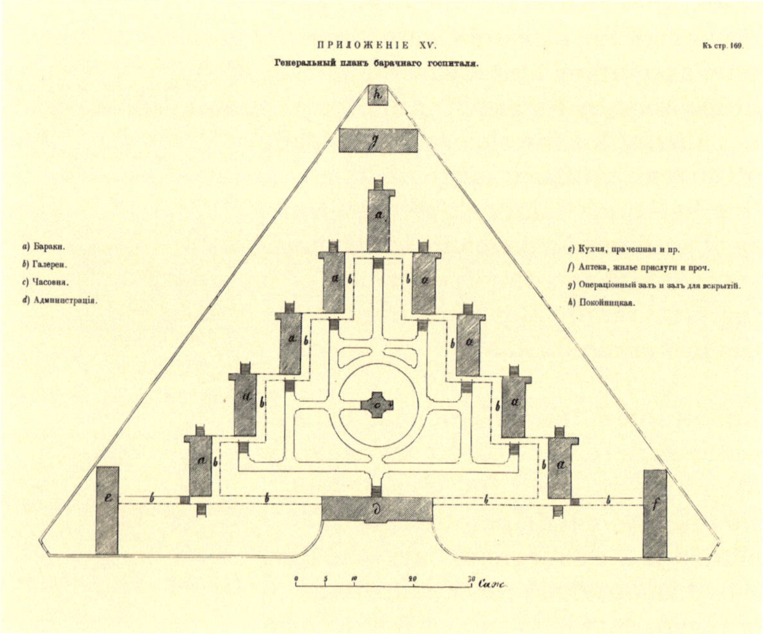

Fig. 5
Nikolai Nikolaevich Nabokov, Design for a Russian military hospital, from Iosif Vasil'evich Bertenson, *Barachnye lazarety v voennoe i mirnoe vremya*, 1871.

Legend: (a) barrack; (b) gallery; (c) chapel; (d) administration; (e) kitchen; (f) pharmacy; (g) operation room; (h) morgue.

Collection: Białystok Technical University, Białystok, Poland.

15 Ibid., 168–70.

In order to initiate a national search for one or more barrack types that would fit Russian conditions, Bertenson joined forces with the newly established Saint Petersburg Ladies' Infirmary Committee. The committee agreed to finance two different barracks, to be designed by Nabokov and constructed outside Bertenson's hospital on the grounds of the Rozhdestvensky regiment, as Russian versions of the *Versuchsbaracke* at the Charité Hospital in Berlin. As word of the initiative spread, the city government of Saint Petersburg decided to purchase a piece of land adjacent to the existing hospital, providing space for two more different barracks, to be financed by the Russian Red Cross.[16]

Each of these four distinctively designed barracks was to propose an ideal solution for a particular location and/or purpose. The parti of three of them seemed similar at first sight, but the barracks would differ in the way they were insulated, heated, and ventilated. This would allow for the investigation, over a long time, of what Bertenson considered the key problem in a barrack hospital in Russia: how to provide both sufficient heat and natural ventilation during the winter. The Mariinsky Barrack, named in honor of Empress Maria Alexandrovna, was to accommodate eighteen acute and chronic patients and aimed to offer an ideal solution for a barrack ward in central Russia. Its walls were constructed of three layers, with an air space between each layer and the next. The outer layer was a rustic-looking siding; the inside layer was tongue-and-groove, while the middle wall consisted of boards lined with felt and a coat of plaster and straw. The roof was covered with wooden shingles.

Fig. 6
Nikolai Nikolaevich Nabokov, Plans, elevations, and section of the Mariinsky Barrack, Saint Petersburg, 1871, from Iosif Vasil'evich Bertenson, *Rozhdestvenskii barachnyi lazaret*, 1891. Legend: (1) ward; (2) washroom; (3) room for a single patient; (4) bathroom; (5) room for two quarantined patients; (6) kitchen; (7) duty room; (8) porch; (9) gallery. Collection: Boris Yeltsin Presidential Library, Saint Petersburg.

16 Iosif Vasil'evich Bertenson, *Rozhdestvenskii barachnyi lazaret, Istoricheskii ocherk S.-Peterburgskogo gorodskogo Rozhdestvenskogo barachnogo lazareta, v pamyat' gosudaryni imperatritsy Marii Aleksandrovny za 1866–1890 gg* (Saint Petersburg: Shredera, 1891), 11–16.

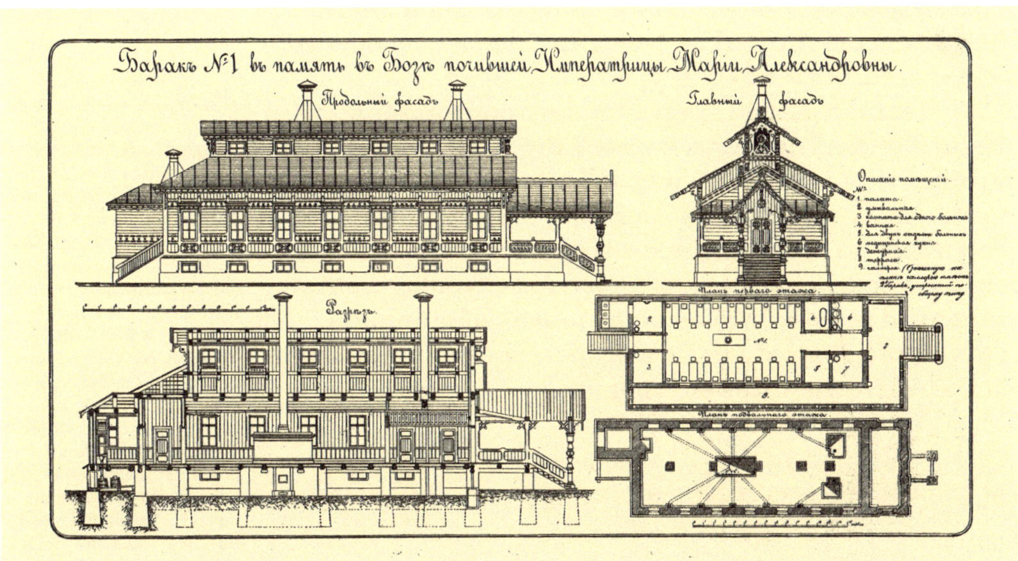

The Guboninsky Barrack, named after the entrepreneur and philanthropist Pyotr Ionovich Gubonin, was to house eighteen typhus patients and was sufficiently winterized for use in the far north. Its walls were constructed from logs, and its roof was covered with galvanized iron sheets. The Naryshkin Barrack, serving surgical patients, offered a model that was designed to provide comfortable and healthy lodgings during the hot summers of the Russian south. Its three-layer wall structure resembled that of the Mariinsky Barrack, but the middle layer lacked the insulating coat of plaster and straw, and its roof was covered with treated cardboard. Each of these three buildings was equipped with a large Finnish stove that rose through the floor into the center of the main ward and was supplied with fuel in a heating cellar. The stove pulled air from the basement and, after warming it, released it into the main ward. But the size and capacity of the stove installed varied from small (Naryshkin Barrack) to medium (Mariinsky Barrack) to large (Guboninsky Barrack). Connected to the chimney of each stove was a system of pipes that led to vents in the floor of the main ward. Using the "fire pipes" or "air pipes" principle developed a century earlier by the Englishman Samuel Sutton (see Chapter Three), the draft created by the chimney pulled the stale air from the ward. In the Mariinsky and Guboninsky barracks the pipes were made of wood that was caulked and plastered; in the Naryshkin Barrack they were made of sheet iron.[17]

The fourth barrack, named after a certain Ms. Polyakova, was to house a maternity department and provide a choice of wards for pregnant women, those in labor, postpartum women who were in good health after an uncomplicated delivery, and those who needed intensive care after delivery.

Because of the very particular requirements, the parti of the Polyakova Barrack deviated from that of the other three barracks, which centered on a single, cross-ventilated ward. No such core existed here. The design did, however, include a single monitor, which had become a characteristic part of barrack typology, above the central rooms. Connected by means of air shafts to the wards, it was to ensure proper ventilation throughout the warren of different rooms.

17 Ibid., 176–77. See also Josef Bertenson, "Les Hôpitaux-Baraques de la Société Russe," *Bulletin International des Sociétés de Secours aux Militaires Blessés* 6, no. 22 (1875), 101–02; Jean Loris-Mélikoff, *Considérations générales sur l'organisation des hôpitaux et de l'hôpital-baraque de Saint-Pétersbourg* (Paris: Ollier-Henry, 1889); Georges Dujardin-Beaumetz, *Des hôpitaux-baraques et de l'enseignement médical en Russie* (Paris: Masson, 1889); Georges Dujardin-Beaumetz, *L'Hygiène Prohylactique* (Paris: Octave Doin, 1889).

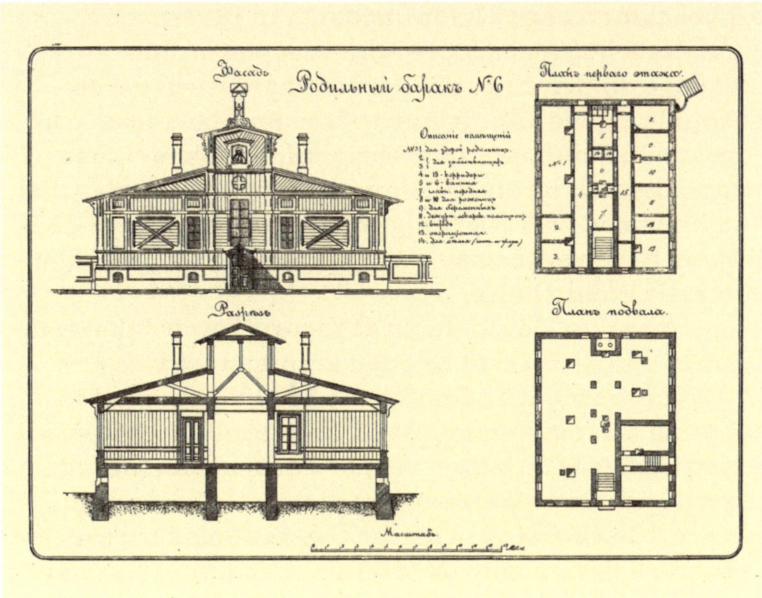

Fig. 7
Nikolai Nikolaevich Nabokov, Plans, elevations, and section of the Polyakova barrack maternity ward, Saint Petersburg, 1871, from Iosif Vasil'evich Bertenson, *Rozhdestvenskii barachnyi lazaret*, 1891. Legend: (1) ward for six healthy women who have recently given birth; (2) and (3) single room for ill women who have recently delivered; (4) and (15) corridor; (5) and (6) bathroom; (7) main hallway; (8) and (10) single room for women in labor; (9) double room for pregnant women; (11) office for medical assistants on duty; (12) exit; (13) operating room; (14) laundry room. Collection: Boris Yeltsin Presidential Library, Saint Petersburg.

In the preface to Bertenson's book, Pirogov commented on the project, which at the time was already under construction. The plans, he noted, seemed full of consideration. Yet many questions remained that could be answered only after the barracks had been put into use:

> But will it be possible, while maintaining a uniform temperature in this building, to do the same with the ventilation in winter? The question is: Will there be sufficient draft to purify the lower layers of room air, which are supposed to be withdrawn through the holes in the floor border, in the pipes into the stove? Is this draft comparable to the one in the upper layers, through the vent openings? Will the air entering the room through the stove vents of the underground be sufficiently warmed by the upper draft? How often can the air be completely freshened by this draft?[18]

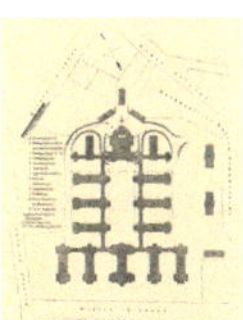

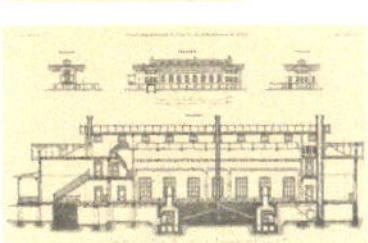

Chapter Six, Figs. 15 and 16
→ p. 262

All four barracks on the Nativity Hospital grounds showed in their execution a remarkable fusion between the most up-to-date barrack architecture as could be found in Germany, or as was being constructed in Riga, in today's Latvia, and a more traditional Russian architectural language. As such, they embodied the political possibilities and limitations in 1870s Russia; scientific and technological progress and enlightened policies of reform and modernization could succeed if framed by traditional forms and expressed in values associated with Slavic traditions. When he had sketched a general

18 Nikolai Pirogov, preface, in Bertenson, *Barachnye lazarety v voennoe i mirnoe vremya*, 16.

proposal for a barrack for inclusion in Bertenson's book, Nabokov had adopted the stripped architectural language employed in the German barrack general hospitals. In the architecture of the four barracks to be constructed at the Nativity Hospital, Nabokov competently merged the most advanced design principles that had informed barrack designs since the American Civil War with the vernacular of traditional Russian wooden domestic architecture.

Nabokov's architectural gesture toward the traditions of native Russian wooden architecture was not without precedent or context. By 1870 the interest in adopting an aesthetics derived from traditional wooden construction as an expression of Russian and Slav identity had gained a significant foothold in Russian architecture.[19] In choosing to merge the most modern concept of barrack design with decorative elements of Russian vernacular architecture, Nabokov attempted to square the proverbial circle of progress and tradition.

The Mariinsky and Guboninsky barracks opened in December 1871, during what proved to be, even by Saint Petersburg standards, a particularly cold winter. From the very beginning the project was on the receiving end of fierce criticism, much of it in anonymous articles. More than twenty years later, Bertenson was still enraged:

> The special press was extremely skeptical of the new hospital type of buildings. Among other things, it was noticed: "that the draft from top to bottom with the knee pipes, with the help of fireplaces placed at the bottom, in the basement, was very weak, and the ventilation itself barely exists, and that the constant heating of fireplaces requires a lot of fuel; that the barracks is almost a 'sieve' and cannot be heated for hospital purposes." They stressed "the excessive dryness of the air in the barracks; and the fragility, especially of the wooden buildings" and so on. As a result the first years of the existence of our barracks were taken up with polemics and repelling the almost daily attacks on our project, all as peculiar as unfounded, and above all, extremely hostile.[20]

In addition to responding to the attacks, Bertenson also initiated a two-year program of systematic measurements of temperature fluctuations, air circulation, moisture levels, carbon dioxide levels in the air of the wards, heating costs and heat loss in the wards, breakdown

19 William Craft Brumfield, *A History of Russian Architecture* (Seattle and London: University of Washington Press, 2004), 408–12, 517–18.
20 Bertenson, *Rozhdestvenskii barachnyi lazaret*, 19.

of ventilation pipes, the morbidity of staff working in those buildings, and the mortality of the patients housed within them. Obviously the Mariinsky, Guboninsky, and Naryshkin barracks performed differently, as they were constructed to different specifications, and it is no surprise that the one named after Empress Maria Alexandrovna, which was designed for central Russia, showed the overall best general performance. The polemic had attracted so much attention that in 1875 the leading Russian architectural journal, *Zodchii* (Architect), devoted a large section of its first issue of the year to the performance of the three wards. Two engineers provided page after page of data, calculations, and conclusions that clearly showed that all three buildings had performed very well, and the editors added a spread that documented the plans, façade, side elevation, and two sections of the Mariinsky Barrack.[21] As far as *Zodchii* was concerned, the matter was settled.

As for the public in general, the criticism that had enervated Bertenson did not seem to have had much impact. When the Moscow Polytechnic Exhibition opened in June 1872—officially in celebration of the two hundredth anniversary of the birth of Peter the Great, the father of Russian modernization—a large model of either the Mariinsky, Guboninsky, or Naryshkin barrack was included among the many exhibits chosen to demonstrate the latest advances in science, technology, and culture.

Fig. 8
Model of either the Mariinsky, Guboninsky, or Naryshkin barrack displayed at the 1872 Moscow Polytechnic Exhibition, *Vsemirnaya Illyustratsiya*, 1872. Collection: Russian State Library, Moscow.

Just at the time that the wooden barrack had ceased to be a viable option for use in a civilian hospital in the West, except in emergency situations, the Nativity Hospital in Russia had become a model that both connected to traditional Russian building types such as the *palatki* and the *izba* and embraced what appeared to be the most modern notions of hospital design.

21 Sil'viush Boleslavovich Lukashevich and Stepan Stepanovich Sakharov, "Issledovanie ventilyatsii barakov Rozhdestvenskoi bol'nitsy," *Zodchii* 4, no. 1 (1875), 1–9.

In 1877 Russia and Turkey were at war—again. The origin of this war was connected to the rise of Serbian, Bulgarian, and Romanian nationalism; its immediate cause was the fallout of a drought in Anatolia that led to the collapse of Ottoman tax revenues in its Asian territories. New taxes imposed by the Sublime Porte on the Orthodox inhabitants of its European possessions triggered a series of uprisings in Bosnia–Herzegovina and Bulgaria. The Ottomans responded with atrocities that, in turn, led the client states of Serbia (commonly known in English at that time as Servia) and Montenegro to declare themselves fully independent in June 1876. When Constantinople sent the army to return the Serbians into the fold, prominent Russians who were interested in the doctrine of Pan-Slavism decided that Russia should help Serbia militarily. Saint Petersburg was not willing to declare war on the Sublime Porte, yet did not stop the departure of Russians for Belgrade or a public campaign to recruit volunteers to help the Serbians militarily and medically and to raise the required funds.[22] Mikhail Grigoryevich Chernyayev, a retired Russian general and publisher of the Pan-Slav daily *Russkiy Mir* (Russian world), traveled to Belgrade, accepted Serbian citizenship, and became commander in chief of the Serbian army. Thousands of Russian volunteers followed him. "The Servian army is steadily becoming converted into a Russian one," the surgeon William McCormac reported in October 1876 after his return from a tour of duty with a unit of the National Aid Society for the Sick and Wounded, the British Red Cross society. And McCormac added to this observation a second one. "And this explains another salient feature in the position of affairs in Servia. Not only is the army a foreign one, but the medical service is so likewise. I met only two Servian medical officers during my whole stay in Servia, but Russians in great numbers, both Russian men and Russian women."[23]

Writing for the *British Medical Journal*, McCormac wisely omitted what was common knowledge to everyone who watched the Serbian-Russian cooperation from a front-row seat: Russian humanitarian intervention also served as a cover for bringing Russian military units into the country. In the fall of 1876, British nurses Emma Pearson and Louisa McLaughlin, who had served in the Franco-Prussian War and were not easily fooled, were enjoying a quiet day in Belgrade on the banks of the Danube, when they noticed that a well-known river liner, SS *Deligrad*, had arrived from the east. "We saw that her decks were crowded, and that she had two huge river

22 Astrid S. Tuminez, *Russian Nationalism since 1856: Ideology and the Making of Foreign Policy* (Lanham, MD: Rowman & Littlefield, 2000), 94–96.
23 William McCormac, "Ambulances of the Turkish and Servian Armies," *British Medical Journal* 2 (Oct. 14, 1876), 504.

barges in tow, also crowded with men. They were Russians, to the number of 2000 in all, and were all coming as ambulance attendants! A more shallow, idle pretext for sending armed men into any country was never invented, and no one believed it. [...] In all this there was a want of truth and an amount of underhand dealing unworthy of so great a country as Russia."[24]

Apart from the violation of both the letter and spirit of the Geneva Convention, McCormac did appreciate the barrack hospitals created under the auspices of the Russian Aid Society for Wounded and Sick Soldiers. The sick wards followed the vernacular developed in the US Civil War, and hence they came to be known in Russian military medical circles as "American barracks." McCormac judged the hospital created in the Serbian town of Ćuprija, which consisted of three such barracks, to be a "very complete establishment" that was "admirable in every way"—with the exception of the ventilation within the buildings, which proved poor, as in other Russian hospitals. One barrack constructed in Topčider, near Belgrade, followed the type constructed in 1871 in the Ambulance de la Grande Gerbe, the hospital in the park of Saint-Cloud, near Villeneuve-l'Etang, France, whose designer, the Austro-Hungarian physician Jaromír Freiherr von Mundy, was active in Belgrade at the same time.

Chapter Seven, Fig. 9
→ p. 296

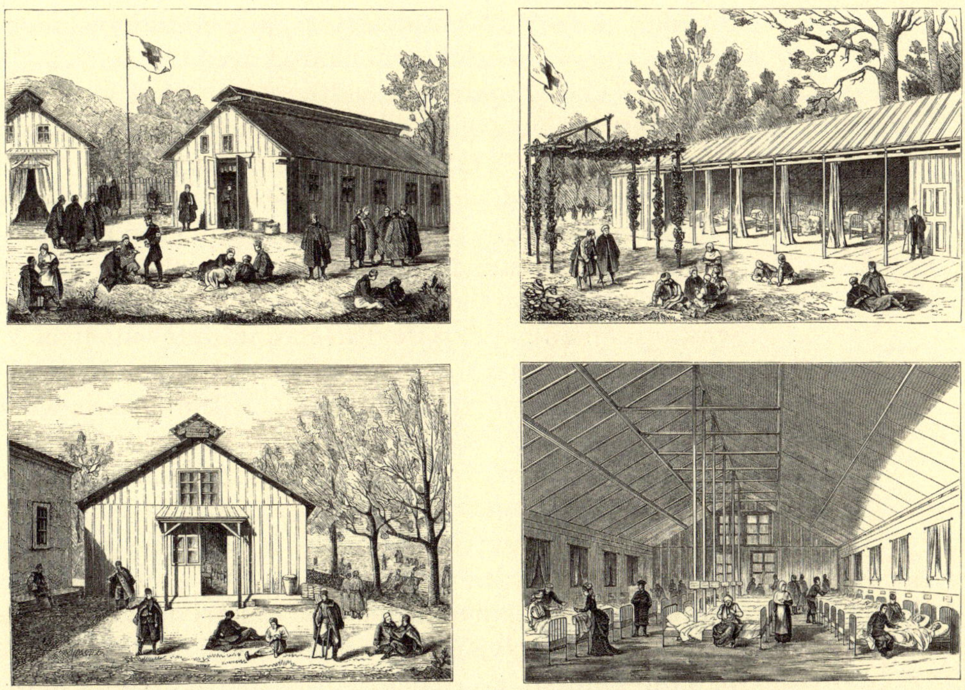

Fig. 9
Russian military hospitals in Serbia, *Vsemirnaya Illyustratsiya*, 1876. The hospital barrack shown at top right was designed by Jaromír Freiherr von Mundy and replicated the design he had developed during the Franco-Prussian War. Collection: Russian State Library, Moscow.

24 Emma Maria Pearson and Louisa Elisabeth McLaughlin, *Service in Servia: Under the Red Cross* (London: Tinsley Brothers, 1877), 206.

McCormac noticed that none of the military hospitals in Serbia contained Turkish wounded, and none of those in Turkey any Serbian soldiers. He blamed the "barbarian" custom of neither expecting quarter when captured nor giving quarter to their captives. "One thing strikes me forcibly in all this," he lamented: "That we shall not arrive at reasonable conclusions if we judge the actions of barbarous peoples solely from the standpoint of civilized Europe. When barbarians have the power and opportunity, they will be certain to commit barbarous actions, and reflect but little either upon the nature or the consequences of their acts."[25]

Once Russian volunteers were fighting under the Serbian flag, it was only a matter of time before Russian corpses began to be returned to the motherland, reinforcing public pressure on the government to conclude an official military alliance with Serbia. This happened in April 1877, after the Russian government had assured the neutrality of Austria-Hungary. Within days Bucharest, formally still under Ottoman rule, gave Saint Petersburg the right to use its territory for military operations against Constantinople, and weeks thereafter declared full independence. In this operation, the railway station of the Romanian city of Iaşi, located at the River Prut, which formed the border between Romania and Russia, played a central role. Accommodating both the standard European gauge (1,435 millimeters) and the wider Russian gauge (1,520 millimeters), the station included a large storage shed that measured over 120 meters in length and 12 meters in width and that was located on a platform between a standard-gauge track that connected to the West and a Russian-gauge track that connected to the East. Iaşi served as both an entry point of the Russian army into the Balkans and an exit point for sick and wounded soldiers. While the Russian army created a series of field hospitals in the Balkans, there was agreement among the Russian military medical establishment that the sick and wounded should be brought back to third-line hospitals within Russia whenever possible. The organization of these facilities was in the hands of an experienced provincial administrator, Nikolai Savvich Abaza.[26]

Abaza's chief designer was thirty-nine-year-old architect Maksimilian Yur'evich Arnold, who in 1877 was employed as an architectural historian at the School of Civil Engineering and the Academy of Engineering in Saint Petersburg. Arnold's presence in the rear of the army was made possible by the financial support of the

25 McCormac, "Ambulances of the Turkish and Servian Armies," 504–06.
26 Nikolai Savvich Abaza, *Krasnyi Krest v tylu deistvuyushchei armii v 1877–1878*, 3 vols. (Saint Petersburg: Rossiiskoe obshchestvo Krasnogo Kresta, 1880–82).

Saint Petersburg Society of Architects, which was eager to show its patriotism. Arnold regularly reported back to his colleagues in Saint Petersburg, creating an interesting record of the opportunities and problems he faced.[27]

One of Arnold's first tasks was the creation of a large evacuation hospital in Iaşi, one of the two principal connection points in the Russian system of evacuation.[28] The Iaşi hospital was to temporarily house the sick and wounded as they arrived from the battlefield and offer a place where military surgeons could make a decision as to each person's final destination within the Russian Empire. Arnold identified the immense freight-transfer shed as a building that, after some major modifications, could fill the role of a place of temporary rest and triage. To transform the shed into what became known as the Iaşi Evacuation Barrack, he decided to permanently close two-thirds of the twenty-four freight gates, install thirty-two stoves, and most importantly, remove a strip of roof cover along the ridge and install in its place a monitor, 100 meters long, that allowed for ridge ventilation.

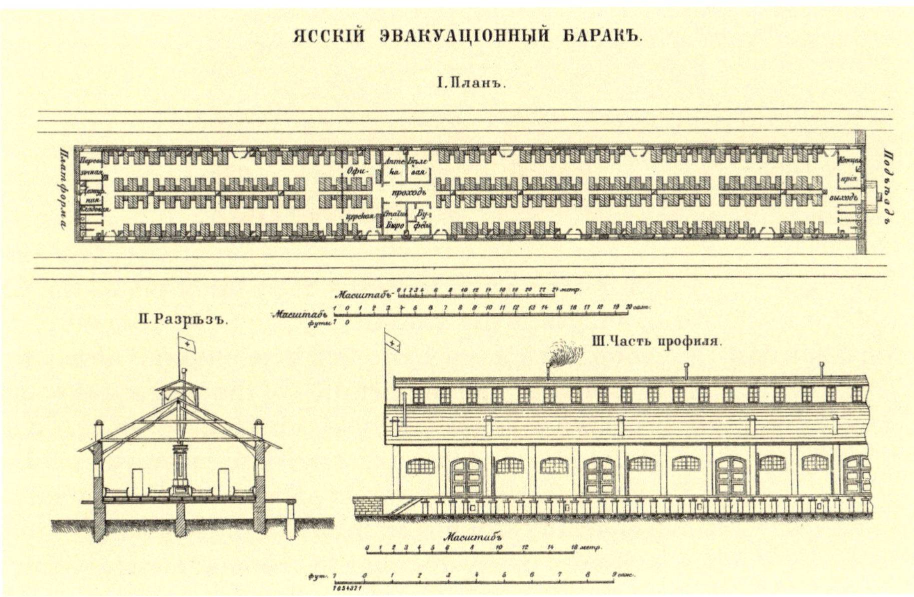

Fig. 10
Maksimilian Yur'evich Arnold, Plan, elevation, and section of the Iaşi Evacuation Barrack, Romania, 1877, from Nikolai Savvich Abaza, *Krasnyi Krest v tylu deistvuyushchei armii v 1877–1878*, 1880–82. Collection: Russian State Library, Moscow.

"In the middle of the roof, along the entire length of the building, a wooden ventilation monitor was constructed, 2.65 meters in width and 1.6 meters in height, and covered with iron sheets," a contemporary account reported. "Fifty-four windows were arranged in its walls on each side, arranged alternately (on opposite sides) and having

27 Maksimilian Yur'evich Arnold, "Obshchestvu arkhitektorov o postroike vremennykh gospitalei Obshchestva popecheniya o ranenykh i bol'nykh voinakh v tylu deistvuyushchei armii," *Zodchii* 7, no. 49 (1878), 221–22; no. 50 (1878), 225–27; no. 51 (1878), 229–31.

28 Nikolai Ivanovich Pirogov, *Das Kriegs-Sanitäts-Wesen und die Privat-Hülfe auf dem Kriegsschauplatze in Bulgarien und im Rücken der operirenden Armee 1877–78*, trans. Wilhelm Roth and Anton Schmidt (Leipzig: F. C. W. Vogel, 1882), 126–28.

a width of 0.85 meter and a height of 1 meter. The frames of these windows rotated on horizontal axes located halfway and could be very easily and conveniently opened with the help of lines and pulleys. When the windows were opened, the upper half of them opened inside the barracks, while the lower half was pushed out, so rain and snow would not fall into the barracks."[29] The result of this process of adaptation and reconstruction was a barrack that was, with a capacity of 350 beds, the largest one created to date.

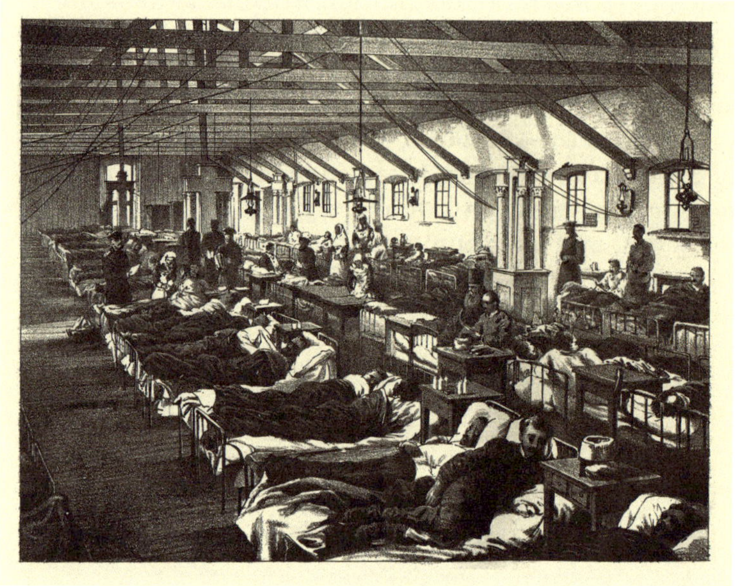

Fig. 11
Interior of the Iaşi Evacuation Barrack, 1877, from Nikolai Savvich Abaza, *Krasnyi Krest v tylu deistvuyushchei armii v 1877–1878*, 1880–82. Collection: Russian State Library, Moscow.

Both in size and in terms of its function, as the center of a nationwide system to collect and distribute sick and wounded soldiers, the Iaşi Evacuation Barrack firmly established the importance of the barrack type within Russian military medical thinking. Yet the execution of the idea to create a network of military hospitals did not follow the systematic approach taken by Surgeon General William Hammond in the American Civil War. As in Germany during the Franco-Prussian War, volunteer societies in Russia had great autonomy to design and construct general barrack hospitals how and where they saw fit. In Germany, almost all such hospitals had been erected in the cities where these societies had their headquarters; thanks to the relatively short distances between northern France and those cities, and the efficient railway system, it had not been difficult to move the sick and wounded to those general hospitals—which, at least in principle, also might serve a civilian function after the war had ended. In Russia, however, distances were much greater between the battlefields in the Balkans and the major cities where citizens had organized

29 Abaza, *Krasnyi Krest v tylu deistvuyushchei armii*, 1:70.

aid committees; for example, the Russian city of Orenburg in the southern Urals was over 3,300 kilometers from the battle lines in Bulgaria and over 2,600 kilometers from Iaşi. And railway connections were much more primitive, if they existed at all. Hence, many Red Cross societies in Russian cities in the north and east of the empire decided to sponsor the construction of hospitals in Bessarabia or the Ukraine based on a perusal of railway maps, without the benefit of any local knowledge. The executive of the Orenburg Red Cross society, for example, decided to locate a hospital at a minor railway junction between the small town of Olviopol and the hamlet of Golta (both places make up today's Pervomaisk, Mykolaiv Oblast, Ukraine), halfway between Odessa and Kiev. Accommodation was provided by thirty Kazakh yurts, a local building type in the Orenburg region. Once the hospital was in operation, architectural ambition took over, and the Orenburg committee, Red Cross commissioner Abaza, and architect Arnold decided that by the winter the yurts should be replaced with a well-designed and up-to-date hospital.

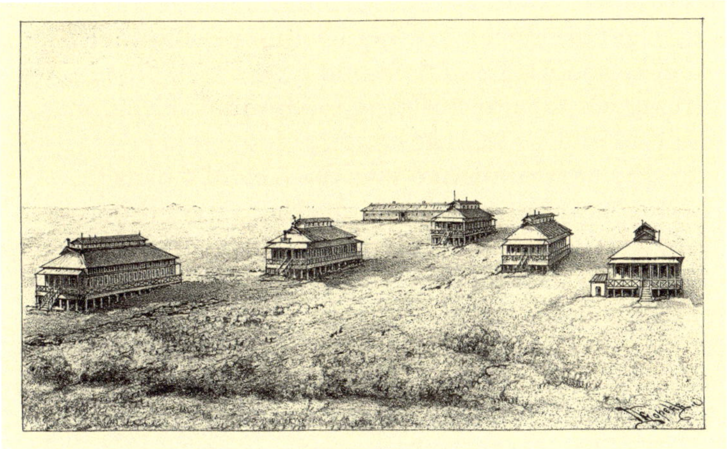

Fig. 12
View of the Olviopol hospital, Russia (today Ukraine), 1878, from Nikolai Savvich Abaza, *Krasnyi Krest v tylu deistvuyushchei armii v 1877–1878*, 1880–82. Collection: Russian State Library, Moscow.

It would follow in its general arrangement the parti pris of the model military hospital published six years earlier in Bertenson's *Barachnye lazarety v voennoe i mirnoe vremya*. The hospital was to consist of spacious, well-ventilated wards, each offering space to forty patients, inspired by those of the Nativity Hospital in Saint Petersburg, which at that time were commonly known as "American barracks." Arnold added the design and construction of the Olviopol hospital to his many other tasks, which included not only the construction of many more hospitals but also the almost impossible job to organize both building materials and labor, which were hard to come by in the steppe-like landscape of the southern Ukraine.

In early October a newsletter of the Saint Petersburg Society of Architects ran a report on the construction in the south. "The work is going on with feverish haste, and a hundred carpenters who were sent from Saint Petersburg, at the request of the authorized representative of the Saint Petersburg Society of Architects, the engineer-architect M. Y. Arnold, are barely enough to bring to execution the huge works spread out in various points." The article noted that Arnold and his men were engaged in a race with time to construct enough shelters before the onset of winter. Existing installations, such as the Iaşi Evacuation Barrack and many other barracks erected in June and designed for the conditions of summer and early fall, had to be winterized. "But the question is," the report continued, "how to do all of this? Where to get money, where to get construction materials? The builder has very little transportation capacity at his disposal in the region between Yelisavetgrad and the Danube. The existing railway is in use nonstop for the transport of troops, guns, baggage trains, and so on, and cannot be used to transport timber and bricks. And even if this problem could be solved, a new question arises: where to get builders? A difficult, difficult situation." Yet Arnold had not been defeated by the lack of supplies. Modifying vernacular building techniques, he set up a production line for boards constructed out of reeds and plaster. His next challenge was the lack of stoves to warm the many barrack hospitals that, upon their completion, were to house 2,600 patients. The greatest worry was, however, the fact that Arnold was exhausted and urgently needed a team to help him. "We fear that the Chief Builder, despite his iron energy, knowledge, and practicality, will not have the physical strength to carry out these extensive works unless he gets the help of architects who can assist him to carry out the task ahead,"[30] the newsletter stated, calling on other members of the Saint Petersburg Society of Architects to join Arnold as architect volunteers in the rear of the army.

The Olviopol hospital was exemplary from a medical and architectural perspective, and given the problems in obtaining building materials and labor, the fact that it was largely completed by the time winter arrived was a triumph of Arnold's inventiveness and organizational skills. But as Pirogov observed, this hospital and also a larger version constructed near Iaşi in Corneşti, Russia (today Moldova), represented more trouble than they were worth. He wrote:

30 "Ot obshchestva 'Krasnogo Kresta,'" *Listok arkhitekturnogo zhurnala Zodchii* 6, no. 48 (1877), 247–49.

> I do not understand why Golta was chosen for such an expensive and solid facility instead of any big city (Kishinev, Yelisavetgrad), or even a railroad station of the first class (for example Podilsk or Razdelnaya). The Olviopol barracks, as well as the Corneşti barracks in Bessarabia, clearly show the mistake of this type of construction in our country in wartime. Their construction is almost never finished in time. Neither private help nor government authorities can build American-style barracks in wartime so that they would be available in time and suitable for the winter; this is hardly possible in large cities, let alone in wood-poor areas in steppe countries. After the war, it is difficult to dispose of such expensive buildings if they are located in a desolate area. Therefore, in our local wars, the administration as well as the private help should not have the American barracks in mind but rather use transportable shelters.[31]

Fig. 13
Maksimilian Yur'evich Arnold, A barrack of the Olviopol hospital, 1878, from Nikolai Savvich Abaza, *Krasnyi Krest v tylu deistvuyushchei armii v 1877–1878*, 1880–82. Collection: Russian State Library, Moscow.

Pirogov was right: while the Olviopol hospital contributed to the care of sick and wounded soldiers during the war, it proved useless after the conflict had ended.

Another issue that raised Pirogov's ire was the fact that the civilian aid organizations did not coordinate sufficiently with the military. The Iaşi Evacuation Barrack was part of a system conceived by the medical service of the Russian army to quickly disperse sick and wounded soldiers to hospitals all over the Russian Empire. However, the Olviopol hospital was never made to fit in this scheme of dispersion. While in the US Civil War, all the military hospitals had been constructed as parts of a single integrated plan, in the Russo-Turkish War of 1877–78, no such unity of purpose existed between the military and civilian efforts to take care of casualties.[32]

31 Pirogov, *Das Kriegs-Sanitäts-Wesen*, 245.
32 Ibid., 205–10.

This, then, also undermined the operational effectiveness of the most important hutted hospital created during this last of the Russo-Turkish Wars. Located in the small town of Corneşti, between Iaşi and Chişinău, it was sponsored by the Saint Petersburg Ladies' Infirmary Committee, designed by Arnold with the input of Bertenson, and named after the Empress Maria Alexandrovna. In many ways it was meant to be a model hospital, both in its layout, which closely followed the arrangement Bertenson proposed in his 1871 book on barracks, and in the architecture of the wards, which was based on those constructed by Nabokov at the Nativity Hospital.

Fig. 14
Interior of a barrack at the Corneşti hospital, 1878, from Nikolai Savvich Abaza, *Krasnyi Krest v tylu deistvuyushchei armii v 1877–1878*, 1880–82. Collection: Russian State Library, Moscow.

However, like the Olviopol hospital, the one in Corneşti took a long time to construct, did not easily fit into the logistics of casualty dispersion adopted by the army, and after the war ended could not be adapted to another purpose. Pirogov noted with some regret in his book on the medical services during the Russo-Turkish War that this hospital might have had an important future if it had been located near the regional center of Chişinău.[33]

The Saint Petersburg Society of Architects showed its patriotism not only by sending Arnold to the south. Within days after the Russian declaration of war against the Ottoman Empire, the members of the society decided to hold an architectural competition for a prefabricated barrack for use by the army. The public announcement published on May 15, 1877, invoked a sense of national unity and praised the enormous sacrifices made by the army: "But it can't be otherwise; such truly great moments in the historical life of people require human sacrifices and now is not the time to consider it: the moment is not far off when the whole of Russia will be covered

33 Ibid., 207–08, 245–46.

with mourning. We have to be firm and carry all possible help to facilitate the relief of suffering, the sorrows of the wounded and the sick, and reduce the hardships of the combat life of our brothers." There was no doubt that the patriotic duty of architects was to design a prototype of instant shelter for the wounded. "The one from the projects received that meets its purpose will be selected and built here, in Saint Petersburg, at the expense of the Society of Architects, equipped with all that is necessary, and delivered to the theater of war."[34]

The requirements were remarkably detailed, given the fact that the society had little time to articulate them. The barrack ought to accommodate eight beds, offer a space of 18 cubic meters per person, and include a separate room for a very sick patient, a room for a nurse, a latrine, and a storage room. The building was to have a raised floor, should be equipped for use in all seasons, and provide adequate ventilation and heating. The in-house latrine should not foul the air in the main ward and should allow for easy removal of the waste. Most important, the structure should be able to withstand storms and earthquakes, yet allow for an easy and speedy assembly and disassembly, and be as light as possible in order to facilitate transport. Architects were invited to submit a set of plans that indicated not only the general appearance of the barrack but also the nature of the joints and the way it was to be put together and taken apart—an issue that was also to be explained in greater detail in an accompanying text. Entrants were specifically instructed not to bother to create presentation drawings—pencil sketches were to suffice. This advice made sense, as the deadline was a week later, on May 22.[35]

Throughout its history, Russia had never lacked for brilliant inventors, and in 1877 the members of the Saint Petersburg Society of Architects were certainly an avant-garde concerning the beneficiary potential of the prefabricated dismountable barrack. But they did not consult with the army, which did not embrace innovation—especially innovation coming from the outside. Many initiatives meant to ameliorate the conditions of sick and wounded soldiers in this war ran at cross-purposes. Moreover, the competition was irrelevant by the time architects began to draw their projects in the middle of May, as the Russian Ministry of War had decided that it had no use for prefabricated barracks, that they were more trouble than they were worth. Since the competition had been announced and architects were already at work, the society decided to go through

34 "Programma konkursa na sostavlenie proekta razbornogo perenosnogo lazaretnogo baraka," *Listok arkhitekturnogo zhurnala Zodchii* 6, no. 20 (1877), 308.
35 Ibid., 307–08.

the motions, judge the entries, award three prizes—and give the top winner the opportunity to design a permanent barrack at the Nativity Hospital, the very site that had pioneered barrack wards in Russia.

Because the competition had lost its potential significance, it did not create much of an impact in the architectural discourse. The most significant record is a short article published in *Zodchii*, and two plates that show the proposals that were awarded the first, second, and third prizes. A young and unknown architect, Nikolai Kuz'mich Reizman, earned the top award for an entry that carried the motto "A lot of things are said, but not everything is good." The design was a modified A-frame with rafters consisting of planks that were bolted together and rested on a base bolted to square pine posts, sunk a half meter into the ground, that provided the structure of the wall and the base of a secondary system of rafters. The covering of the resulting gull-wing roof—a type that has two pitches on either side of the ridge, with the first pitch shallower than the second—consisted of frames covered with boards that, in turn, were covered with waterproof canvas. The walls were made of similar frames, but instead of boards they were covered with planks on the outside and with a layer of felt and painted canvas on the inside. If a lighter version was desirable, the planks could be omitted, and the outside could also be covered with felt. A raised wooden floor, made from pine-panel frames, stretched only under the area where the beds stood; the aisles, however, did not have a floor, which according to the architect allowed for better ventilation. The gable walls contained ventilation openings that could be opened and closed.[36]

Another entrant was Dorimedont Dorimedontovich Sokolov, a well-known teacher of geodesy, heating and ventilation, civil architecture, and architectural history at various institutions of tertiary education in Saint Petersburg, as well as an architect of mainly residential buildings and a local politician. Submitted under the motto "Feasible contribution," his design, at first sight, appeared to be a relatively conventional barrack, with a structure comprising forty posts that were cross-braced with iron and connected by beams. The monitor at the center also seemed utterly conventional, as did the roof structure, consisting of boards covered with tar paper. The walls, however, were a special feature. Consisting of a series of canvas sheets to which wooden slats were attached, they could be rolled up to be stored and during transport and when in use allowed for a quick closing of the structure by simply attaching the top slat

36 Nikolai Kuz'mich Reizman, Dorimedont Dorimedontovich Sokolov, Alexei Konstantinovich Serebryakov, and Nikolai Vladimirovich Sultanov, "Konkursnye eskizy razborchatogo baraka," *Zodchii* 6, nos. 9–10 (1877), 88–92.

to the top beam, followed by an unrolling of the slatted sheet toward the bottom. It earned him the second prize.

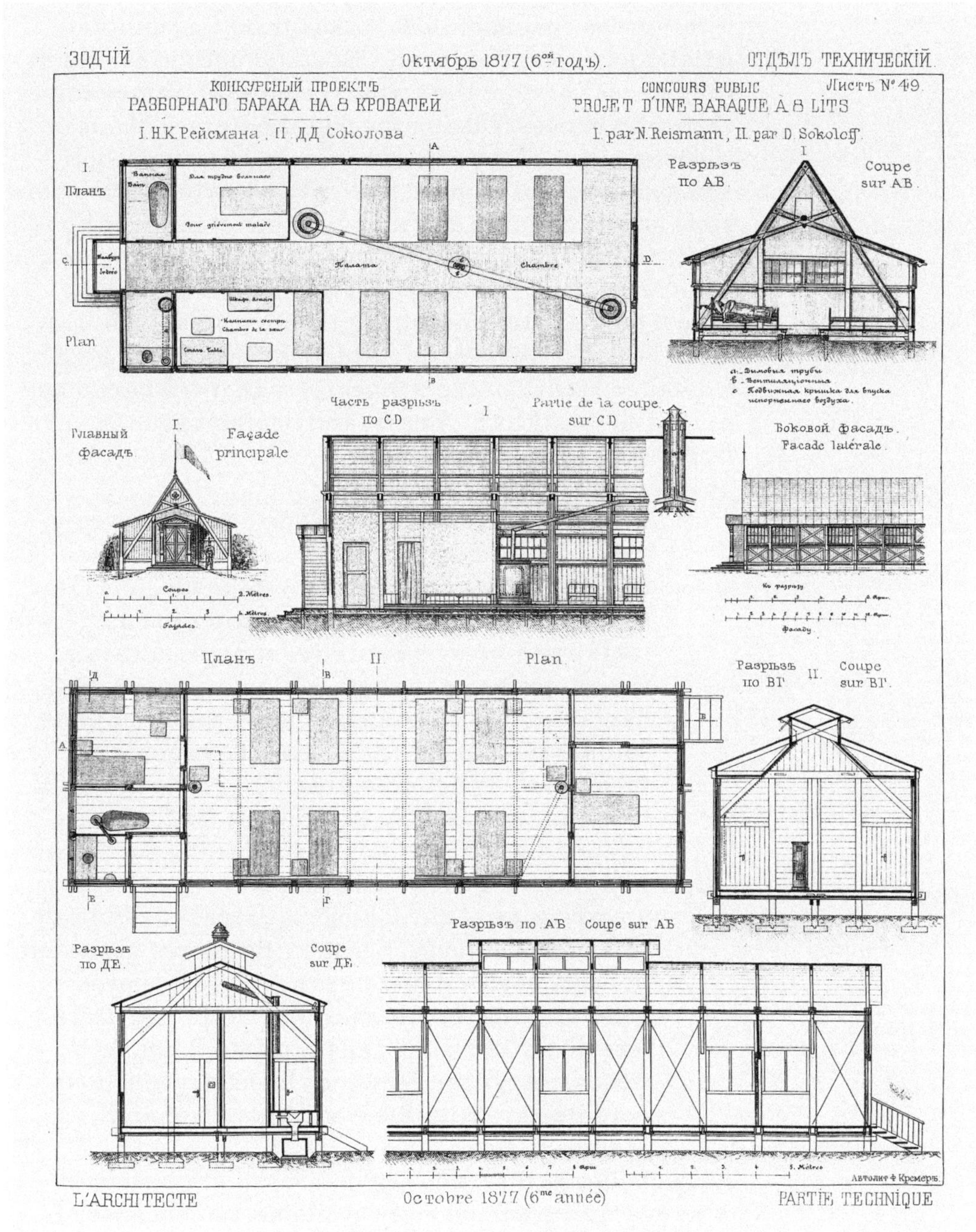

Fig. 15
Nikolai Kuz'mich Reizman (top) and Dorimedont Dorimedontovich Sokolov (bottom), Prizewinning entries in the 1877 competition for a prefabricated portable barrack organized by the Saint Petersburg Society of Architects, *Zodchii*, 1877. Collection: Russian State Library, Moscow.

Without the support of either the army or the Russian Red Cross, the competition did not have much of an impact. Yet it appears that Sokolov's design inspired a certain Mr. Johnson in Odessa—nothing is known about him—in the spring of 1878, to construct ten summer *palatki* for use at the Bender Hospital in Odessa. But in the Odessa version, the walls consisted of frames covered with canvas. During the day, the frames of one of the long sides were removed (on rare occasions, both sides). Provincial administrator Abaza, who was responsible for the creation and management of military hospitals in the Ukraine, initially believed that Johnson's structures had great promise. He noted in his final report on his activities during the Russo-Turkish War of 1877–78 that physicians at the Bender Hospital kept a detailed record of the temperature in these barracks during the months of August and September 1878, finding the range acceptable.

> It is a pity that none of the doctors consistently monitored the temperature in ordinary tents. On the basis of the few that were made, it is clear that the results were worse. During the day, tents are hotter and stuffier; at night, although the temperature in them is higher than in the barracks, this advantage is more than compensated for by the fact that barracks provide an incomparably better ventilation. While the ventilation in tents during the night is far less satisfactory than that in barracks, during rain there is none because the wet canvas does not allow for an exchange of air. Johnson's barracks eliminate this inconvenience, because the canvas is soaked in a composition that does not close its pores: when it rains the fibers do not swell, and therefore do not close the gaps between them. As a result the canvas remains almost dry and does not interfere with the free diffusion of air.[37]

Abaza believed that these structures might be useful wherever rail transport was available, but because of the relative bulkiness of the parts, they could not be used elsewhere. And, of course, no experience existed as to their performance during the late fall and winter. In the summer of 1878, when Pirogov found himself in Odessa, he also had a look at Johnson's *palatki* at the Bender Hospital. As far as a model for portable barracks to be used in emergency hospitals, he considered them at best a work in progress: "The assembly and disassembly of

37 Abaza, *Krasnyi Krest v tylu deistvuyushchei armii*, 1:47.

the frames requires great accuracy and skill, and one would need for this task specially trained staff or technicians. Hospital servants or teamsters will not be able to do it."[38]

The barrack competition had turned out to be a bit of a shambles, but to save face and make a contribution to the war effort that could be seen and admired in Saint Petersburg, the Society of Architects decided to sponsor the construction of a specially designed permanent barrack at the Nativity Hospital that was to improve on the model constructed six years earlier by Nabakov.[39] The building was to initially accommodate sick and wounded soldiers and, after the war had ended, serve as a gynecological ward. The commission went to Reizman and Sokolov, who had joined forces after winning the first and second prizes in the competition, with Sokolov becoming the senior partner in the joint effort. The barrack they designed was more compact than anything designed by Nabokov, and stylistically it was less picturesque.

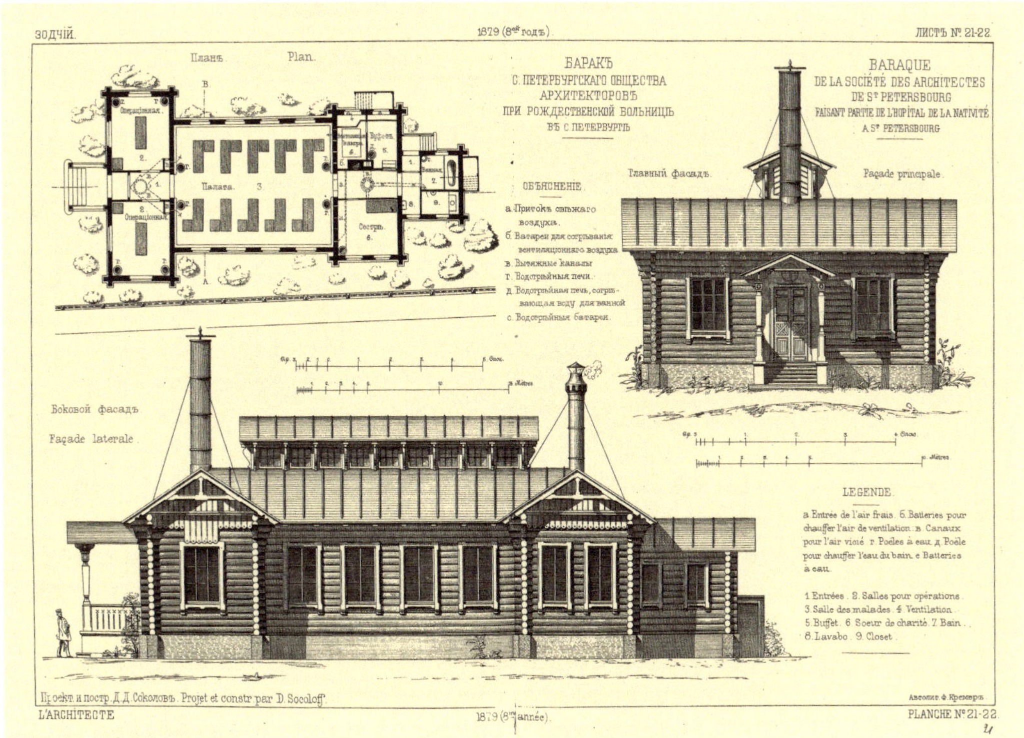

38 Pirogov, *Das Kriegs-Sanitäts-Wesen*, 217.
39 Dorimedont Dorimedontovich Sokolov, *Barak S.-Peterburgskogo obshchestva arkhitektorov, ustroennyi pri Rozhdestvenskoi bol'nitse v S.-Peterburge* (Saint Petersburg: Goppe, 1880).

Fig. 16
Dorimedont Dorimedontovich Sokolov and Nikolai Kuz'mich Reizman, Plan and elevations of the barrack sponsored by the Saint Petersburg Society of Architects at the Nativity Hospital, Saint Petersburg, *Zodchii*, 1879. Collection: Russian State Library, Moscow.

A central sick ward with a monitor that ran the whole length of the room offered space for up to twelve beds and 45 cubic meters of space per person. A furnace in the basement was the heart of a hot-water heating system that, by means of a special room designed as a heat-exchange area, was to heat up and moisten the dry fresh air coming from the outside before it was allowed to enter into the main sick ward and the two operating rooms. This time an updated version of Sutton's fire pipes provided for the evacuation of foul air by means of a ventilation shaft constructed around the smoke flue.[40]

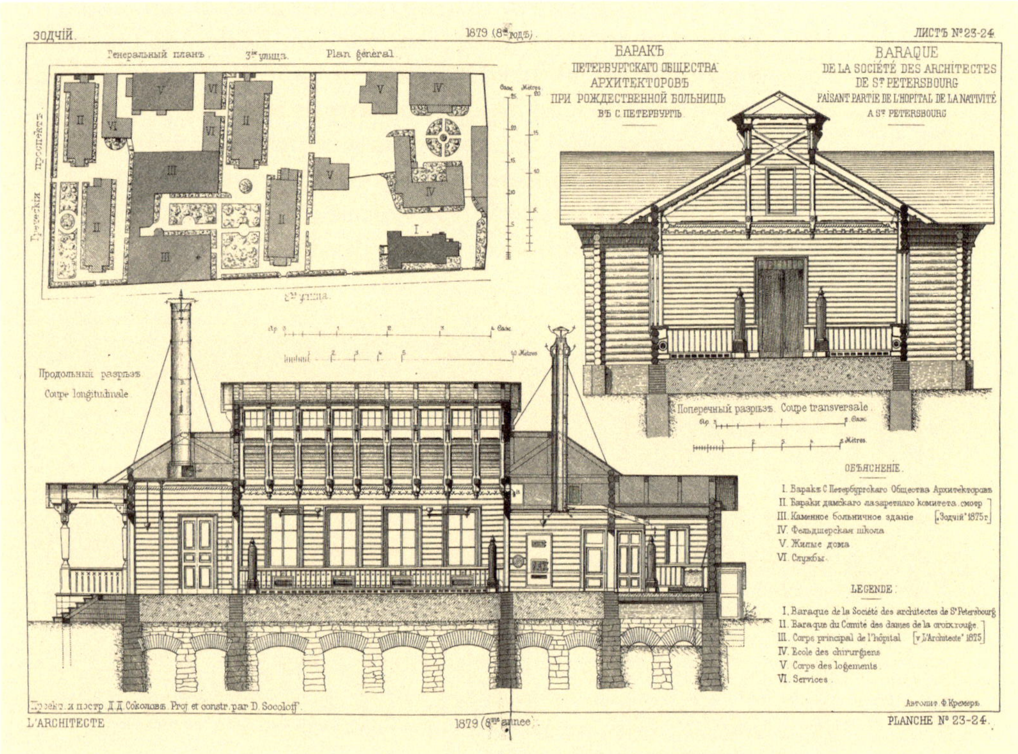

Fig. 17
Dorimedont Dorimedontovich Sokolov and Nikolai Kuz'mich Reizman, Site plan and sections of the barrack at the Nativity Hospital, *Zodchii*, 1879. Collection: Russian State Library, Moscow.

The Russo-Turkish War of 1877–78 had brought both sophisticated and more basic versions of the barrack to many different parts of eastern and southeastern Europe, yet few of these buildings were seen by anyone beyond those who worked or recovered within them. While a few books documented these buildings and their performance, they had little impact on the general architectural and medical discourse in Russia, and the military hospitals created during this period remained completely unknown outside of Russia. It certainly did not help that Pirogov, who from the beginning had been skeptical of the various claims of the beneficial if nor miraculous properties of barrack hospitals, did not find a reason to change his mind after inspecting most of the hospitals created in 1877. The most authoritative

40 Frederic J. Mouat and Henry Saxon Snell, *Hospital Construction and Management* (London: J. & A. Churchill & Co., 1883), 242–43.

voice in Russian medicine in the 1870s, Pirogov was an eminently practical man with, in his own view at least, a well-honed sense of traditional Russian values. When the Vologda committee of the Russian Red Cross decided to establish a military hospital in the Ukraine, they chose to rent all but ten of the buildings in the village of Lysaya Gora, located some 170 kilometers south of Kiev. Each dwelling typically consisted of two rooms, and the inhabitants were allowed to keep one room for themselves, while the second room was to house the sick and wounded from the war. Pirogov provided a detailed account of the conditions in this hospital, noting the low general mortality, and while he acknowledged that attending to the patients in so many different places had put a larger burden on the physicians and nurses than they would have had in a specially designed hospital, he considered it more important that the sick and wounded had felt at home. "Undoubtedly, the sick liked the life and sojourn in the huts. The homelike environment, the possibility to see the farmers at work, the children—all of that triggered pleasant memories, according to statements by the ill." The dispersal of the sick in fifty-three small buildings and the total lack of typhus cases suggested that the model chosen for the Vologda committee's hospital was medically sound. For Pirogov, however, the most important advantage remained the psychological one: "The dispersal of the sick in farmers' dwellings eliminates the painful impression of hospital life and sojourn."[41]

While hospitals made of peasant cottages might work in an emergency in the countryside, there were no comparable options for more permanent facilities in urban settings. In that context, the barrack hospital partly realized in the Nativity Hospital remained the closest approximation to Pirogov's ideal. Until 1880, the municipality of Saint Petersburg, like most other cities, had responded to the need to increase patient capacity during epidemics by requisitioning schools, hotels, and other existing buildings. They were generally death traps, and the supervisor of the municipal health service, Professor Sergey Petrovich Botkin, insisted on the construction of a permanent facility that would profit from the precedents set by the American military hospitals, the Tempelhof and Moabit hospitals in Berlin, the municipal hospital in Riga, and the Nativity Hospital in Saint Petersburg. Sokolov, who by 1877 had shown his abilities as a barrack designer, received the commission to design a 250-bed hospital, to be constructed on the

41 Pirogov, *Das Kriegs-Sanitäts-Wesen*, 253.

grounds of the Alexander Barracks in Saint Petersburg.[42] From the very beginning, the Alexander Hospital project was prepared with great care. Medical and architectural case studies of various barrack hospitals were undertaken, and a committee of physicians traveled to Riga to study the design and operation of the hospital—which, after some consideration, were deemed too expensive for the Saint Petersburg enterprise. A number of different physicians wrote reports, weighing the pros and cons of many issues, ranging from the treatment of the basement floors, to the ideal size of a ward, to the question of individual barracks standing separately or connected by galleries. In the most important American Civil War hospitals, as well as in significant military hospitals created during the Franco-Prussian War, the Saint Jacob's Hospital in Leipzig, and the Riga hospital, the wards had been connected, but in the Moabit Hospital the buildings stood alone. Because the new hospital was to specialize in infectious diseases, the question was whether or not these galleries would be conduits of disease. The champions of the galleries invoked a sense of the barrack hospital tradition. "The barracks system was born together with its connecting gallery, which connects the hospital barracks and the main economic and administrative buildings," they contended. "The irrational fear of corridors some doctors have completely ignores the huge difference between an ordinary corridor and a connecting gallery, which is a perfectly ventilated passage that is closed on both sides, and that is only connected to the barracks at a few points." The key issue, they argued, was that the concentration of infected air in the barrack wards would be low because of the superior ventilation of those spaces. As a result, "entry of such air in small quantities into well-ventilated connecting galleries is even less dangerous for anyone than staying in the barracks."[43]

The argument in favor of these galleries pivoted to whether the walls of the buildings could become saturated with infections, which framed a traditional Russian practice to regularly burn wooden buildings that had lodged patients with infectious diseases. They declared it a myth that the walls of a well-ventilated and well-maintained sick ward could become saturated with pathogens, adding that the air itself destroyed infections. "Even the most persistent infections, such as smallpox or plague, cannot resist this destructive effect of clean air, and very soon lose their infectious properties under its influence. Moreover, observations show that hospitals and barracks that have been poorly

42 See Dorimedont Dorimedontovich Sokolov, "Gorodskaya Aleksandrovskaya barachnaya bol'nitsa v S.-Peterburge," *Zodchii* 12, no. 1 (1883), 22–37, 77–82; Panteleimon Osipovich Smolenskii, *Aleksandrovskaya gorodskaya barachnaya bol'nitsa v St. Petersburg* (Saint Petersburg: Shredera, 1885).
43 Sokolov, "Gorodskaya Aleksandrovskaya barachnaya bol'nitsa," 35.

maintained for decades, thoroughly saturated with miasma, can, with good ventilation, quickly be turned into healthy rooms." Having addressed these (spurious, in their view) medical arguments against the construction of connecting galleries, their champions turned to their practical advantages of offering shelter from the rains of spring and autumn, and the slush and frosts, snow drifts and blizzards of the winter: "As a result of such considerations, it is considered necessary to arrange, following the example of American barrack hospitals, connecting galleries between the barracks of each department. The floor in these galleries should be made of asphalt, which has already been used in the Riga barracks hospital and turned out to be very convenient. It is extremely easy to transport weak patients on wheeled stretchers or chairs on the asphalt floor, moving on wheels; special wheelbarrows can transport food, underwear, bundles, mattresses, and hospital items."[44]

In spite of these very convincing arguments in favor of the construction of connecting galleries, those who insisted on ensuring the best possible isolation of patients won the day.

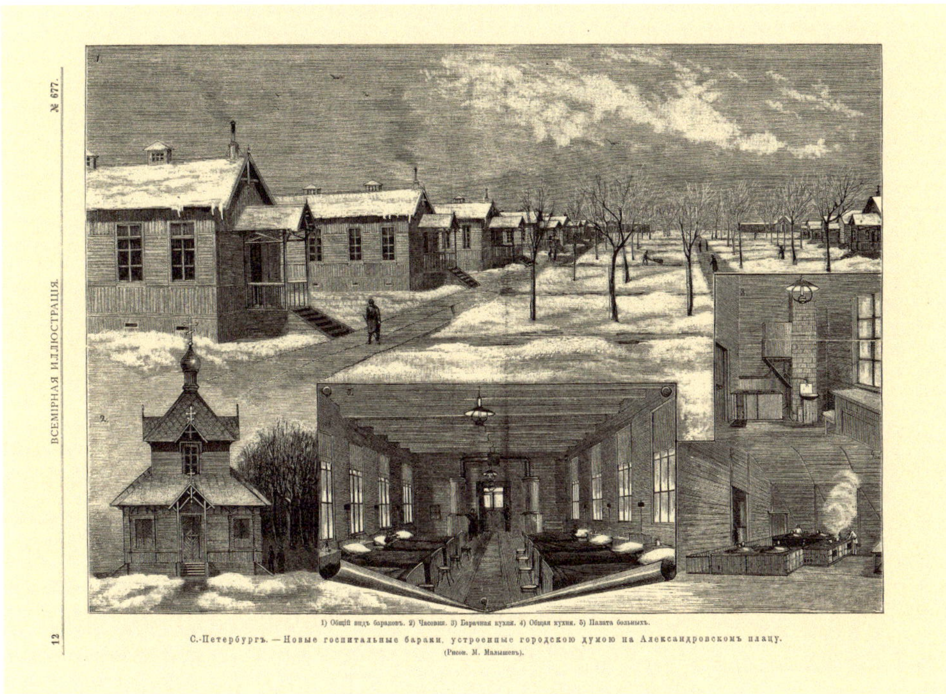

The parti pris of the Moabit Hospital became the basis of the layout, with the standard two parallel rows of eleven unconnected barracks, each with a capacity of between twelve and twenty-two patients—the lower number for those accommodating patients suffering from infectious diseases and the higher number for wards holding

Fig. 18
Composite of views of the Alexander Hospital, Saint Petersburg, *Vsemirnaya Illyustratsiya*, 1882. Collection: Russian State Library, Moscow.

44 Ibid.

noninfectious patients. Each barrack aligned on a north–south axis forming the core of the hospital. Compared to Nabokov's barracks at the Nativity Hospital, those at the Alexander Hospital were simpler, lacking the ornamental details suggesting Russian vernacular traditions. An important departure from the architecture of the barrack sick wards constructed in Saint Petersburg, Olviopol, and Corneşti was the omission of the monitor. Instead, three small roof-mounted exhaust conduits were to ensure optimal ventilation.

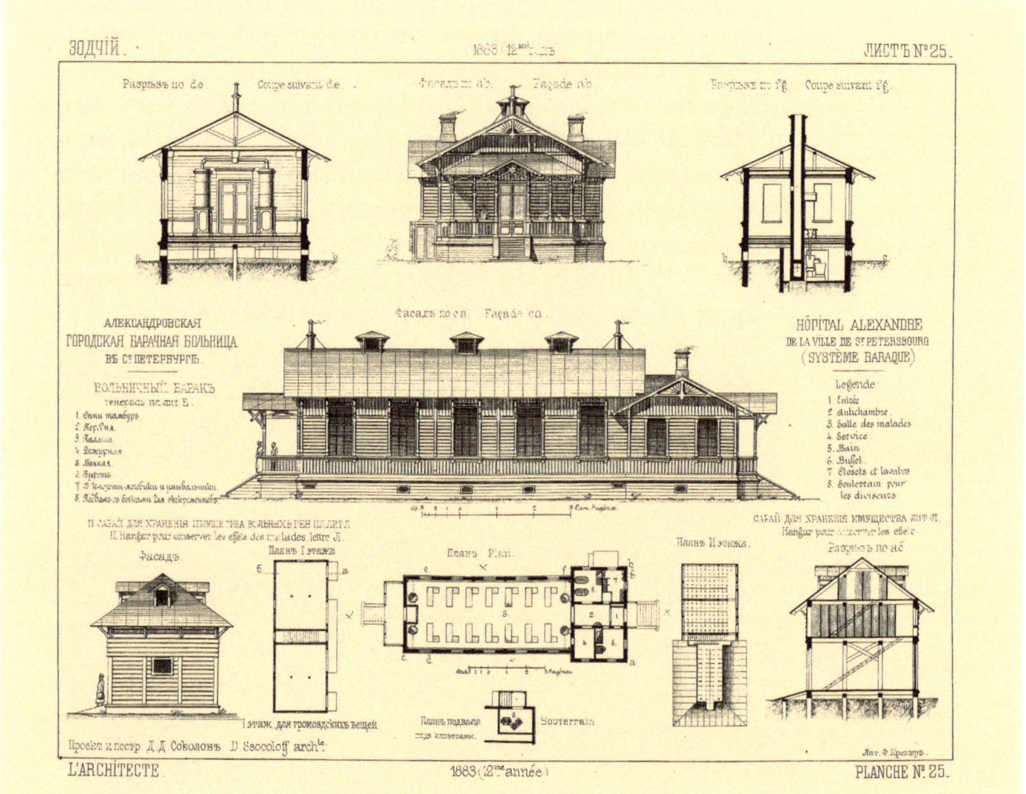

Fig. 19
Dorimedont Dorimedontovich Sokolov, Plans, sections, and elevations of a standard ward and of a storehouse of patients' belongings of the Alexander Hospital, *Zodchii*, 1883. Collection: Russian State Library, Moscow.

The entrance, reception building, pharmacy, kitchen, and two dormitories for medical staff were located to the north, and two larger double-ward buildings, each with a capacity of thirty recovering patients, to the south. The east of the site was dedicated to technical services, such as a heating plant, a laundry, a disinfection building, an incinerator for straw used in mattresses in the sick wards, a Russian bathhouse, and finally a multipurpose building that appeared from the outside to be a conventional Orthodox chapel but also extended to medical final rites by providing a morgue, an autopsy room, and a laboratory.

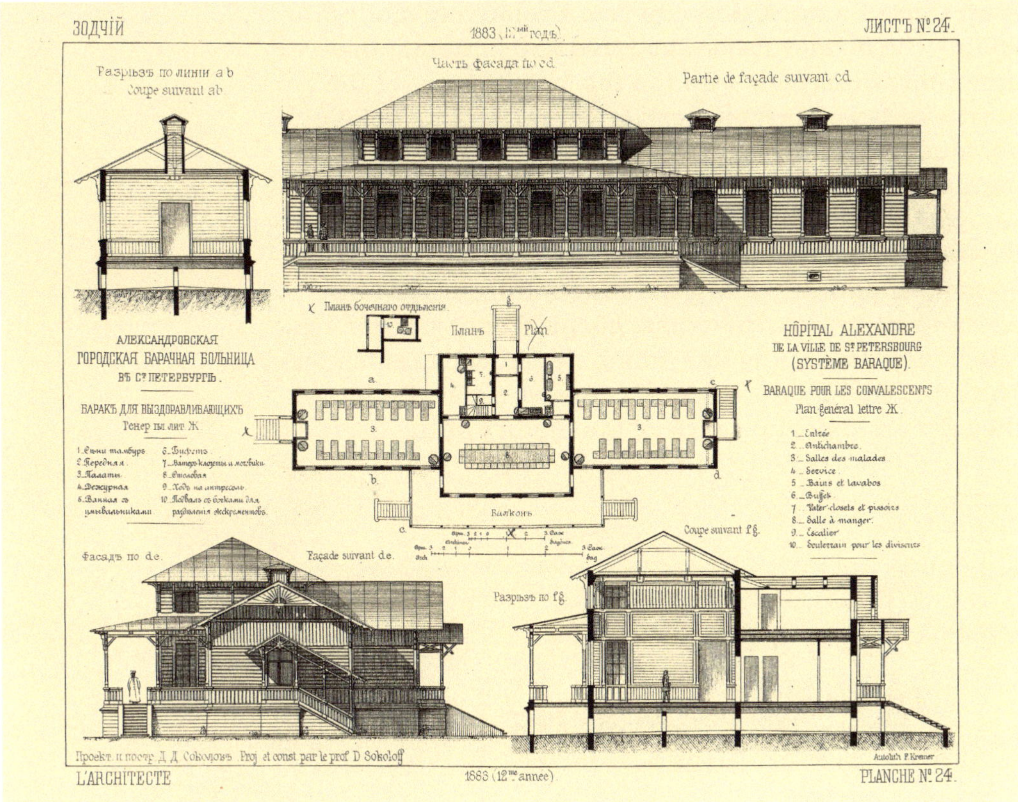

Completed in 1883, the Alexander Hospital remained unknown outside of Russia until 1887, when it was featured in German and French publications. The illustrated report that appeared in the *Centralblatt der Bauverwaltung* (Central gazette of the Construction Administration), a weekly magazine issued by the Prussian Ministry of Public Works that focused on public buildings and infrastructure projects, provided a detailed account of both the history and the architecture of the project, but it did not pass judgment on the efficacy of the hospital beyond noting that its exterior had a friendly appearance while inside the buildings were clean, manifesting a strict regime.[45]

Fig. 20
Dorimedont Dorimedontovich Sokolov, Plan, sections, and elevations of a double ward for recovering patients of the Alexander Hospital, *Zodchii*, 1883. Collection: Russian State Library, Moscow.

By the late 1880s the concept of a civilian barrack hospital also began to lose its shine in Russia. The Saint Petersburg Barrack Hospital in Memory of Emperor Alexander II, conceived in 1887 and put into operation in 1889, was the last of its kind to receive significant attention in *Zodchii*, the architectural magazine of record.[46] Both Bertenson and Sokolov were involved, as consultants to lead architect Victor Alexandrovich Schröter (also known as Shreter), a Russian of Baltic-German descent. Compared to the Alexander Hospital, which was paid for by the municipality, the privately funded Saint

45 "Das städtische Alexander-Baracken-Krankenhaus in St. Petersburg," *Centralblatt der Bauverwaltung* 7, no. 52 (1887), 503–05.
46 Victor Aleksandrovich Shreter [Schröter], "Bol'nitsa S.-Peterburgskogo Birzhevogo Kupechestva v pamyat' Imperatora Aleksandra II," *Zodchii* 20, nos. 3–4 (1891), 24–28.

Petersburg Barrack Hospital was a relatively modest affair—the former accommodated 250 patients, the latter only ninety-six—and in the architecture of the barracks, it was largely derivative. Yet, unlike Sokolov's hospital, which was pulled down to make way for ever newer incarnations of the current best and most advanced thinking in hospital design, the Saint Petersburg Barrack Hospital largely survived, which can be attributed to its apparently marginal function from 1925 onward—a children's infectious hospital does not generate much interest among late-middle-aged political leaders. Thus, the three wooden wards survive today. Together, they are an important relic of the history of the barrack.

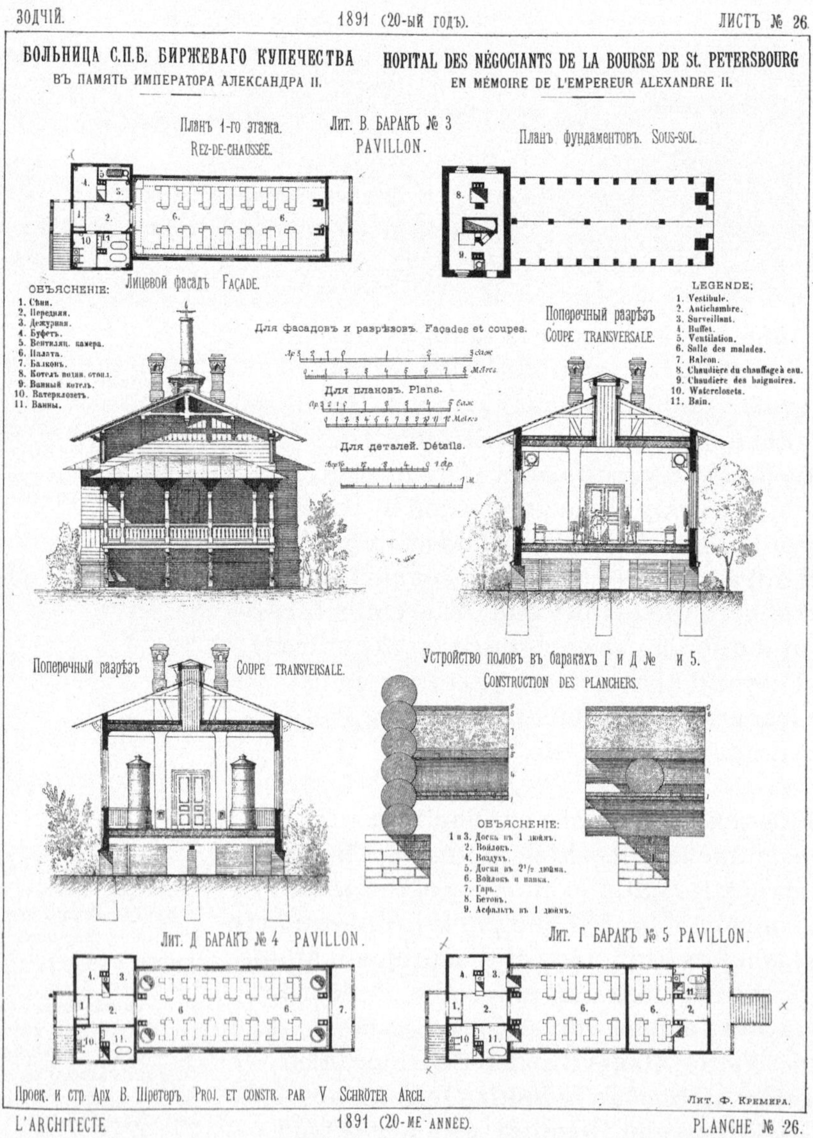

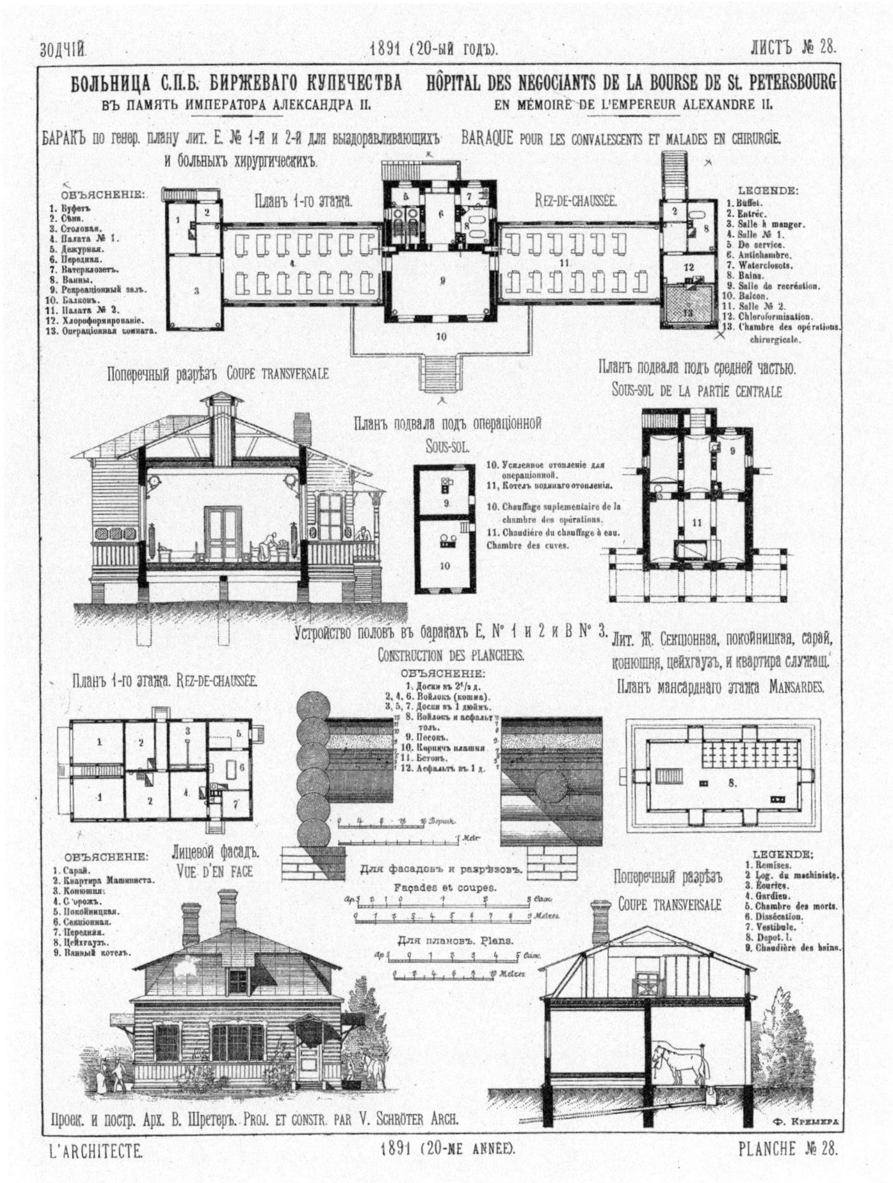

Fig. 21
Victor Alexandrovich Schröter, Plans, sections, front elevation, and construction details of a sick ward, executed in three somewhat different variations, of the Saint Petersburg Barrack Hospital in Memory of Emperor Alexander II, *Zodchii*, 1891. Collection: Russian State Library, Moscow.

Fig. 22
General view of the Saint Petersburg Barrack Hospital in Memory of Emperor Alexander II, *Zodchii*, 1891. The convalescent ward is located at the left, the sick wards in the center, and the multipurpose building to the right. The two-story building in the left background contains accommodation for the medical staff. Collection: Russian State Library, Moscow.

H. Faber del.

PRISON BARR

AT Ro

1 Stockaded Prison. 2 Prison Hospital. 3 Pest house.

→ p. 428

S AND HOSPITAL

ND ILL.

4 Barracks of the Guard. 5 Hospital for the Guard.

Ten

Whatever Is Indispensable

Deadly smallpox has been around since the Neolithic revolution introduced the beginning of permanent human settlement some 12,000 years ago. In early modern Europe the disease killed 0.4 percent of the population annually, and in the areas of the world "discovered" and settled by Europeans, especially the Americas and Australia, which had been free of smallpox until the explorers' arrival, the disease wiped out most of the indigenous populations. "The Indians were attacked by the small pox," Swedish-Finnish traveler Pehr (or Peter) Kalm reported in the mid-eighteenth century. "This disease they got from the Europeans, for they knew nothing of it before: it killed many hundreds of them and most of the Indians, of the country called New Sweden, died of it. The wolves then came, attracted by the stench of so many corpses, in such great numbers that they devoured them all, and even attacked the poor sick Indians in their huts, so that the few healthy ones had enough to do, to drive them away."[1] In the first decade of the nineteenth century, vaccination developed by the English physician Edward Jenner proved to be an effective tool in reducing the occurrence of smallpox, and the disease was in rapid decline in Europe. But the Franco-Prussian War (1870–71) triggered a major epidemic; while the German soldiers had been vaccinated against the disease, French soldiers had not. First the disease spread among them, and when infected French prisoners of war were transported to fortresses and camps in Germany, they triggered an epidemic among German civilians, which subsequently moved to other European countries.

Great Britain adopted strict quarantine measures involving the creation of isolation hospitals in the major ports that were to house those afflicted with smallpox and other infectious diseases like cholera. Where to locate these? A "not-in-my-backyard" attitude of the local citizenry forced the municipality of Lowestoft, Suffolk, to look for a creative solution: the city purchased an old barge and commissioned architect John Louth Clemence to add on top of the vessel a barrack, 15 meters long and 5 meters wide, comprising a ward for four male patients,

1 Peter Kalm, *Travels into North America*, trans. John Reinhold Forster, 2nd ed., 2 vols. (London: Lowndes, 1772), 1:223.

a ward for two female patients, a nursing station, and a kitchen. Each of the wards offered a bathtub.[2] This floating barrack hospital, moored in Lake Lothing, functioned to the great satisfaction of the city authorities, but maintenance was poor, and after a couple of years it sank.

Farther north, the Tyne port authorities followed suit, initially commissioning two floating barrack hospitals, one constructed on an old ferry accommodating fourteen patients, and a second on a flat-bottomed galliot housing ten. By 1885 both were deemed unsafe, and a third floating hospital was commissioned, to be built from scratch. Designed by civil engineer William George Laws, it consisted of three spacious barracks on a deck, measuring 43 by 21.5 meters, supported by ten cylindrical pontoons.

Fig. 1
The Tyne River floating hospital at Jarrow Slake, England, 1930. Collection: South Tyneside Libraries, South Shields, England.

When it was anchored and put in operation near the town of Jarrow, 6.5 kilometers downstream from Newcastle upon Tyne, it received much praise. The only criticism concerned the fact that the toilets dropped excrement immediately into the river. "I have not arranged any special means of treating the sewage," Laws stated in defense of his decision when he was challenged in a meeting. "We considered that, seeing the Tyne was practically an open sewer, the best plan was to have the refuse dropped at once into the river and carried away to the sea."[3]

A platform floating in an open sewer carrying three barracks filled with smallpox patients: certainly, in the history of the barrack, there have been more glorious moments, and for those who held on to the theory of miasma, the hospital must have appeared to be a quarantine station only, as the inmates would have had no chance of recovery. Yet Friedrich Ruppel, the architect of

2 W. H. Clubbe, "Floating Hospitals for Cholera Patients," *Lancet* 100, no. 2561 (Sept. 28, 1872), 468.
3 George Laws, "The Floating Hospital of the River Tyne Port Sanitary Authority," *Proceedings of the Association of Municipal and Sanitary Engineers and Surveyors* 14 (1887–88), 17.

the Eppendorf hospital in Hamburg, considered these floating barrack hospitals exemplary solutions to the quarantine problem in harbors, and he provided full documentation of two of them in his treatise on hospital design.[4] And his praise was deserved: the Tyne River hospital was to provide loyal service into old age—Mr. Laws's floating contraption remained moored near Jarrow for forty years. In the last decade of its existence, vaccination had effectively eradicated smallpox, and the barracks lacked occupants most of the time. Eventually, two of the structures were pulled down, and finally, in 1930, the platform with the final barrack was towed to the breaker's yard.

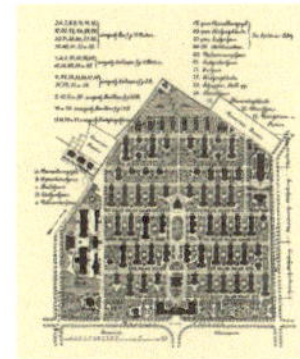

Chapter Eight, Fig. 14
→ p. 344

In early 1720 the French merchant vessel *Grand-Saint-Antoine* left the coast of Syria on its way to Marseille, which at that time was the major point of connection between the Levant and western and northern Europe. In Cyprus it picked up some cargo and a few passengers. On April 3, a passenger who had boarded in the port of Tripoli died of plague. On May 25, upon arrival in Marseille, the crew, passengers, and cargo were confined to the lazaretto in operation since 1668. Named for the beggar Lazarus mentioned in the Gospel of Luke (16:19–13), who was considered the patron saint of lepers, the lazaretto was the quarantine station for ships' crews, passengers, and cargoes suspected of infection with contagious diseases. Like almost all lazarettos constructed before the 1670s, the one in Marseille was a substantial compound sealed off from the city by a high wall. Most of the space was dedicated to the storage of goods, both in the open air and in spacious warehouses. Both the ship's crew and passengers were housed in fourteen walled courtyards, each measuring approximately 400 square meters and occupied by four huts.

→ Fig. 2

Quarantine of the *Grand-Saint-Antoine* passengers and crew did not contain the spread of plague. Within days, people in the city began to die, and soon the streets were filled with corpses.[5] The city itself was now put in quarantine, and a wall was hastily constructed to prevent transmission between Marseille and the rest of Provence. While it slowed the spread of the disease, the quarantine wall did not stop it. All over Europe, authorities and physicians looked with concern at the approach of plague and began to prepare for the worst. In Britain, the physician Richard Mead gathered

4 Friedrich Ruppel, *Anlage und Bau der Krankenhäuser nach Hygienisch-Technischen Grundsätzen* (Jena: Gustav Fischer, 1896), 216–19.
5 Patrick Mouton, *La Malédiction du "Grand-Saint-Antoine": 25 mai 1720, la peste entre à Marseille!* (Marseille: Autres Temps, 2001).

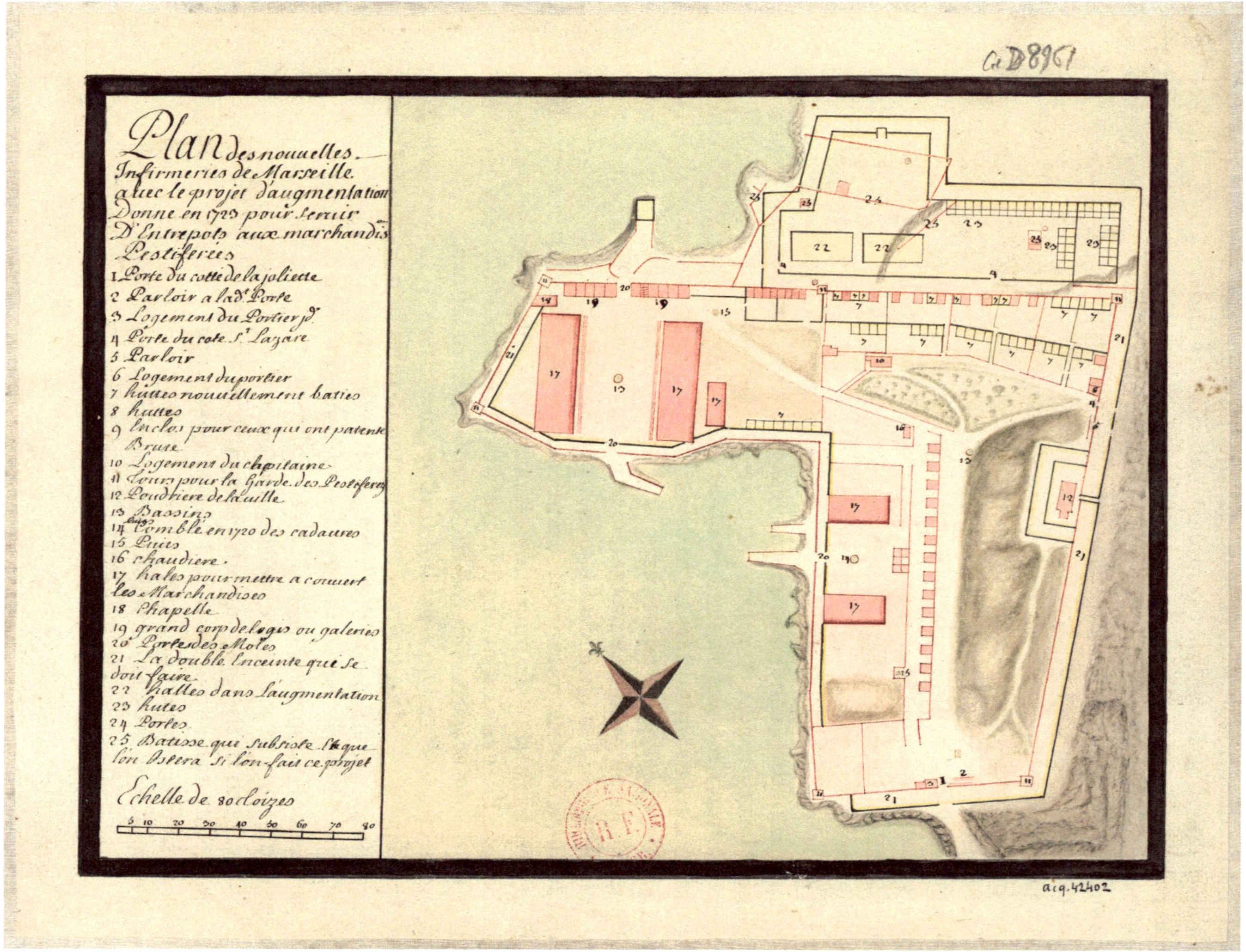

Fig. 2
Plan of the lazaretto in Marseille, France, showing the existing courtyards with huts (7) and a projected expansion with additional huts to be constructed to the northeast (23), 1723. Collection: Bibliothèque Nationale de France, Paris.

whatever information he could find about the epidemic and the various means to fight it. *A Short Discourse Concerning Pestilential Contagion, and the Method to Be Used to Prevent It* (1720) provided the scientific basis of the subsequent British Quarantine Act of 1721.

In his review of best practices, Mead was particularly impressed by the measures taken in 1712 in the Duchy of Brunswick-Lüneburg (also known as the Electorate of Hanover). In 1712, the authorities in Hanover had responded to the plague by quarantining whole villages behind quickly built walls and confining the ill in lazarettos and plague hospitals. Those who shared a household with anyone who had fallen ill but themselves escaped infection were forced to strip naked, put on special clothes provided for them, and leave for another place while a crew burned all the contents of the house deemed susceptible of contagion. "In summer," Mead wrote, "ordinary barracks (or huts) were made for those of the common people, who were obliged to quit infected houses: which barracks were afterward burned, when they had been made use of."[6] At the time when Mead wrote, the plural noun "barracks" usually referred to permanent housing for soldiers, so he took care to qualify his use of the word: "ordinary barracks (or huts)" that could be burned afterward.

In 1712, when the plague hit Hanover, its most famous resident, polymath Gottfried Wilhelm Leibniz, moved to Vienna both to research the history of the House of Guelph, which had ruled the Duchy of Brunswick-Lüneburg for centuries, and to ensure a coordination between the duke, as elector of Hanover, a key official in the constitution of the Holy Roman Empire of the German Nation, and the Habsburg dynasty, which since Maximilian I (reign 1493–1519) had held the imperial dignity. Leibniz's arrival coincided with that of plague in Vienna. He wrote a proposal for the construction of "*baraquen* or *casernen*, like those made for soldiers, in such a way that they are not connected to each other but separated, so that the air can circulate between them." He suggested they should be of the simplest log construction, as practiced by mountain people. Because streams provided a convenient way to transport logs, these plague barracks should be located adjacent to rivers. "Such *häuslein* [little houses] can be quickly put down and renovated, and the logs can be cleaned by means of water and fire, and after the contagion has come to an end, one can pull everything down."[7] Subsequently, the city created a small colony of barracks on a peninsula in the Danube—yet it brought not the sick

6 Richard Mead, "A Discourse on the Plague," in *The Medical Works of Richard Mead, M.D.* (London: Hitchs, Haws and others, 1762), ccxxix.
7 Gottfried Wilhelm Leibniz, "Über Einrichting der Lazarethe, Anstellung 'medicinalischer Observationes' und Vorsichtsmassregeln gegen die herannahende Pest," in *Die Leibniz-Handschriften der königlichen öffentlichen Bibliothek zu Hannover*, ed. Eduard Bodemann (Hanover and Leipzig: Hann'sche Buchhandlung, 1895), 274.

to the place but the homeless—and left them there to their fate.[8]

In the 1770s German physician Johann Friedrich Zückert expanded on Leibniz's proposal to use compounds with barracks as temporary lazarettos during epidemics, particularly to serve small villages. He proposed a plan for the construction of hutted isolation hospitals serving four or five villages each. Those afflicted could be held under surveillance, and physicians could carefully study the progress of the disease—something of great importance in an age devoted to reason. These barracks were not a second-best option, Zückert noted, referring to experience from recent wars: "Those who had been laying in [...] *Hütten* improved sooner and with greater ease, and [...] fewer of them died, than in the hospitals and the permanent military installations, where the sick could not breathe such free, clean, and fresh air." The barracks, he advised, should be created with some consideration of ventilation: "In the walls of those *Hütten* one creates air holes instead of windows that can be opened and closed as is needed."[9]

In 1783 the plague arrived in Dalmatia (now Croatia). Throughout the crisis, the Venetian governors of the region made use of quarantine camps to contain the situation. Nine years later Austrian officials faced the same problem in Syrmia, a region today shared by Croatia and Serbia. They authorized Franz von Schraud, professor of medicine at the Royal University of Pest (now Eötvös Loránd University), in Budapest, to take all measures to prevent the export of the disease to the rest of the Pannonian Plain by imposing a *Kontumaz* (quarantine) on the afflicted and their families and concentrating them in barracked compounds in the countryside. Convinced that his approach had general validity, Schraud made the principles and execution of the *Kontumaz* the subject of a substantial publication, which was widely read at the time.[10] Not many images of such installations survive. Perhaps the best known are two lithographs of the *Kontumaz* constructed in the spring of 1831 at the palace of Schloss Hof, located at the border between the Archduchy of Lower Austria and the Kingdom of Hungary—both crown lands of the Habsburg empire.[11]

8 Boris Velimirovic and Helga Velimirovic, "Plague in Vienna," *Reviews of Infectious Diseases* 11, no. 5 (Sept.–Oct. 1989), 821.
9 Johann Friedrich Zückert, *Von den wahren Mitteln die Entvölkerung eines Landes in epidemische Zeiten zu verhüten* (Berlin: August Mylius, 1773), 75–78.
10 Franz von Schraud, *Geschichte der Pest in Sirmien in den Jahren 1795 und 1796, nebst einem Anhange, welcher die Geschichte Pest in Ostgalizien, Vorschriften der Pestpolizei, und Ideen über die Ausrottung einiger ansteckenden Krankheiten enthält* (Pest: Trattner 1801).
11 Max Haller, *Geschichte von Schloßhof: Cultur-historische Skizze des k. u. k. Lustschlosses Schloßhof a. d. March* (Vienna: Carl von Hölzl, 1903), 96.

Fig. 3
Franz Wolf, Landscape view of the quarantine station at Schloss Hof, Austrian Empire, 1831. Collection: Österreichische Nationalbibliothek, Vienna.

Fig. 4
Franz Wolf, Courtyard view of the quarantine station at Schloss Hof, Austrian Empire, 1831. Collection: Österreichische Nationalbibliothek, Vienna.

Very rarely did an established architect get involved in the design of barracks for those who needed to be housed and quarantined. One of those few was the Englishman George Wilkinson, who in 1835 had won a high-profile competition for the design of a state-of-the-art workhouse to be built by the Thame Poor Law Union in Thame, near Oxford. An originally English institution that dated back to the Middle Ages, the workhouses became after the adoption of the Irish Poor Law Act of 1838 the principal tool to combat poverty in Ireland. Seeking to initiate the construction of workhouses that reflected "best practice" in England—which proved to be, in fact, very bad practice in terms of humanitarian impact—the Poor Law Commission hired Wilkinson, who set out to construct a workhouse in each of the 130 Poor Law unions, or districts, established by the 1838 act.[12]

In 1845 the potato blight wiped out the year's harvest in Ireland and resulted in a famine that, in turn, led to massive vagrancy, mendicancy, and overcrowding in the workhouses where the destitute obtained food and board in exchange for unpaid labor. Designed to cope with the limited number of destitute people during normal times, the hygienic conditions in Wilkinson's workhouses collapsed in 1845, and typhus, an endemic disease in Ireland and hence known as "Irish fever," took over, followed by dysentery, smallpox, and finally cholera. In order to quarantine the ill workhouse inmates, the Poor Law Commission ordered Wilkinson to construct temporary fever wards for the afflicted inmates of the workhouses. They were to be simple barracks accommodating forty patients each.[13] In early 1846 typhus spread to the Irish population at large. Despite the significant opposition of the Irish medical establishment, which saw any measures imposed by the authorities as violating the autonomy of its profession, the British government appointed commissioners of health to coordinate relief during the emergency. They were given specific powers to force local organizations charged with poor relief "to rent, hire, or procure a fitting House, Building, or Rooms, other than the Workhouse of such Union, to be used as a Hospital for the Purpose of receiving and accommodating so many poor Persons affected with Fever or any other epidemic Disease as the said Board of Health may from Time to Time think necessary."[14]

Charged as such, the health commissioners decided to establish, in addition to the existing network of both permanent and temporary fever hospitals, a few hundred others in existing buildings. Yet very few property owners were willing to lease buildings for that purpose, and the inhabitants of towns and villages generally objected to the location of fever hospitals within their communities. With no alternative but to construct such hospitals away from communities in greenfield sites, the commission asked Wilkinson to come up with a standard design for a temporary fever shed that could be rapidly constructed and, one assumes, demolished. He obliged with the design for a wood-framed barrack, separated by a brick wall containing two fireplaces into two twenty-five-bed wards, each measuring 15 by 4.5 meters.

12 See John O'Connor, *The Workhouses of Ireland: The Fate of Ireland's Poor* (Dublin: Anvil Books, 1995).

13 "Temporary Fever Wards," in Great Britain, Parliament, House of Commons, *Twelfth Annual Report of the Poor Law Commissioners, with Appendices* (London: W. Clowes and Sons, 1846), 149–52.

14 "An Act to make Provision, on the First Day of September One thousand and eight hundred and forty-seven, for the Treatment of poor Persons afflicted with Fever in Ireland," in Great Britain, *The Statutes of the United Kingdom of Great Britain and Ireland, 9 & 10 Victoriae, 1846*, vol. 18, pt. 1 (London: Her Majesty's Printers, 1846), 49.

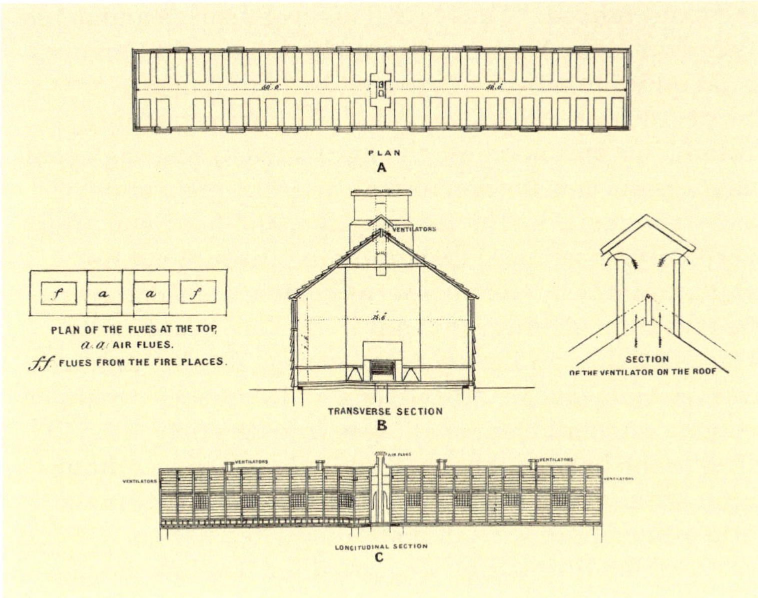

Fig. 5
George Wilkinson, Plan and sections of a temporary fever ward, from *Report of the Commissioners of Health, Ireland, on the Epidemics of 1846 to 1850*, 1852. Collection: Wellcome Library, London.

Significantly, he included a sophisticated ventilation system that was inspired by Samuel Sutton's fire pipes (or air pipes), which, when heated by a stove or fireplace, created a draft. In the explanation of his design, Wilkinson described these air pipes in some detail. "I purpose the construction of air-flues, 14 inches by 9 inches [36 by 23 centimeters], in the chimney-shaft, to be carried up from the back of each fire-place to the chimney-shaft above the roof, having an opening from the upper part of the room into the air-flue for the escape of vitiated air, which will be drawn-into it by the current of warm air in the air-flue, and be of much service in cold weather when the windows cannot well be opened."[15] Published in 1852, Wilkinson's design made history by setting, for the first time, a minimum standard in the design of civilian emergency architecture.

In April 1847, the thirty-four-year-old Anglo-Irish aristocrat Stephen de Vere embarked on an emigrant ship to Canada. Unlike most of his peers, de Vere felt a great deal of empathy for the Roman Catholic tenants on his family estate in County Limerick, a number of whom considered emigration. Driven into destitution, many of Ireland's poor had left to make a new life in North America. Reports of the terrible conditions on the emigrant ships had prompted de Vere to book a passage in steerage and observe firsthand life and death among the emigrants. In November of that same year, from the colony of Canada, he wrote a letter to the chairman of the board of the Colonial Land and Emigration Commission in England, providing a full report of what he had seen

15 George Wilkinson, Appendix A, *Report of the Commissioners of Health, Ireland, on the Epidemics of 1846 to 1850* (Dublin: Alexander Thom, 1852), 42–45.

and experienced: "The fearful state of disease and debility in which the Irish emigrants have reached Canada, must undoubtedly be attributed in a great degree to the destitution and consequent sickness prevailing in Ireland; but has been much aggravated by the neglect of cleanliness, ventilation, and a generally good state of social economy during the passage, and has been afterwards increased, and disseminated throughout the whole country by the mal-arrangements of the Government system of emigrant relief." De Vere graphically described the conditions of the voyage for the huddled masses belowdecks. "Hundreds of poor people, men, women, and children, of all ages from the drivelling idiot of 90 to the babe just born, huddled together, without light, without air, wallowing in filth, and breathing a fetid atmosphere, sick in body, dispirited in heart." Food was bad, too little water was provided to allow the passengers to wash themselves, and neither the beds, "teeming with all abominations," nor the steerage quarters were ever aired or cleaned. The result was a damp and fetid environment that was cleaned only the day before the arrival in Canada, "when all hands are required to 'scrub up,' and put on a fair face for the doctor and Government inspector."[16]

De Vere landed in Canada in June, amid a typhoid fever epidemic that raged in all the ships carrying Irish immigrants. Hence, the ship was not allowed to proceed to the port of Quebec but forced to anchor near Grosse Isle, a small island in the Saint Lawrence River some 50 kilometers northeast of Quebec, which in 1832 had been instituted as a quarantine station in an attempt to block the advance of cholera into the Americas. De Vere's ship joined some thirty other ships there. While many of the ill were forced to remain on board, those who looked particularly wretched were taken ashore and detained in wooden sheds. De Vere, who remained healthy, was given an opportunity to visit these facilities.

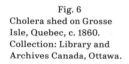

Fig. 6
Cholera shed on Grosse Isle, Quebec, c. 1860. Collection: Library and Archives Canada, Ottawa.

16 Stephen de Vere, letter, Nov. 30, 1847, in Houses of Parliament, *Papers Relative to Emigration to the British Provinces in North America, Presented . . . April 1848* (London: William Clowes and Sons, 1848), 13–14.

"The sheds were very miserable," he wrote. "So slightly built as to exclude neither the heat nor the cold. No sufficient care was taken to remove the sick from the sound, or to disinfect and clean the building after the removal of the sick to hospital. The very straw upon which they had lain was often allowed to become a bed for their successors; and I have known many poor families prefer to burrow under heaps of loose stones which happened to be piled up near the shore, rather than accept the shelter of the infected sheds."[17]

The terrible condition in the sheds was not the result of neglect. Five months earlier, Dr. George Mellis Douglas, medical superintendent of the Grosse Isle quarantine station, had called on the Executive Council on Matters of State of the Legislative Assembly of Canada to increase the budget for Grosse Isle; in 1846 the number of inmates had doubled compared to the year before, and Douglas anticipated, given the increasing numbers of destitute people leaving Ireland and the attempts by authorities in New York and other American ports to impede their landing, that Grosse Isle would be overwhelmed in the upcoming summer.[18] On May 3, Douglas sailed to Grosse Isle to prepare the existing buildings, which were typically referred to as "sheds," for the reception of the sick. Two weeks later he reported that the 200-bed hospital was filled to capacity, and he urged for the construction of an extra barrack, "as the present Sheds are insufficient, and having been put up hurriedly during the prevalence of Cholera were imperfectly built."[19]

The Executive Council made the funds available within a couple of days, but before the letter confirming the allocation had been signed, Douglas reported that seven new ships had arrived, carrying 2,778 passengers, 341 suffering from typhoid fever, and 175 dead. The ailing emigrants joined another 216 sick on four vessels moored at Grosse Isle. None of the sick could be allowed to land, Douglas explained: "I have not a bed to lay them on, or a place to put them in." Douglas asked for permission to convert all the passenger sheds into emergency hospitals, which would add 500 beds—only a fraction of what was required. "By the Quarantine Law now in force, all Passengers from a vessel in which Fever has prevailed, are to be landed on the Island with their baggage. But it will be impossible to follow to the letter the law in this particular, as thus far every vessel has arrived with Fever, and to land all the Passengers would require Sheds to accommodate from 12,000 to 15,000 people."[20]

17 Ibid., 15.
18 See André Charbonneau and André Sévigny, *Grosse Île: A Record of Daily Events* (Ottawa: Parks Canada, 1997).
19 George M. Douglas, letter, May 17, 1847, in Appendix (L.), Province of Canada, *Appendix to the Sixth Volume of the Journals of the Legislative Assembly of the Province of Canada*, session 1847 (Montreal: Legislative Assembly, 1847).
20 George M. Douglas, letter, May 21, 1847, in Appendix (L.).

Once again, the Executive Council agreed to the wish, and now a cycle began of increasingly alarming reports sent from Grosse Isle containing requests for money for the construction of extra sheds, and the funds being made available, only for the situation to dramatically worsen before even the first pole had been driven into the ground. By the end of the month, thirty-six ships carrying 12,450 passengers were anchored at Grosse Isle: 662 had died, 470 were sick on board, and 856 were in sheds on the island. By that time, 274 tents had arrived to add to the capacity, but there was no crew to erect them. Desperate to avert further landings of sick passengers at the quarantine station, Douglas begged the Executive Council to allow him to circumvent quarantine law and make the ships into somewhat viable sick wards by introducing cross ventilation. "I have ascertained," he explained, "that by making the Masters open the bow-ports, which all vessels in the Timber trade are provided with, and by likewise opening the stern-ports, knocking down all bulk-heads and midship berths, a complete current of air is passed through the hold, making it, in fact, so that a bird can fly through the vessel."[21]

While running behind events, the government continued to authorize the construction of new sheds, by the beginning of June approving seven, of which six were to be constructed on the island by a crew of carpenters managed by an agent of the Board of Works, Pierre Laurencel. The framework of one of the sheds was being prefabricated in Quebec to be assembled on the island. This worked well, and another twelve partly prefabricated sheds were ordered, requiring a construction force of 150 men for assembly. By September the quarantine station's sheds had a capacity of 5,500 people—but by that month the average daily occupancy had declined to a little over 1,300, as the immigration season was coming to an end.[22]

In spite of best efforts, the sheds at Grosse Isle remained a blot on the national consciousness of Canada. Today Grosse Isle is a national park commemorating the Irish immigration and its terrible price. From the year 1847 a cemetery survives, as does one of the prefabricated immigrant sheds. This building might well be the oldest preserved barrack in the world. Both its association with a key period in the formation of Canada and its architectural value earned it, in 1991, an official designation as a Classified Federal Heritage Building.[23]

Through the first two centuries of the history of the barrack as an object of prescription, it was used as prisoner

21 George M. Douglas, letter, May 29, 1847, in Appendix (L.).
22 Charbonneau and Sévigny, *Grosse Île*, 8–9.
23 Building 100, Classified Federal Heritage Building, Grosse-Île, Quebec, Parks Canada, Directory of Federal Heritage Designations, https://www.pc.gc.ca/apps/dfhd/page_fhbro_eng.aspx?id=4206.

accommodation only in Australia, where hutted stockades were used to house convicts. In the second half of the nineteenth century, very crude versions of the barrack also became the standard shelter in the convict colonies European powers constructed in the tropics to be permanently rid of those considered both undesirable and incapable of reform. These included not only so-called habitual criminals but also at times political opponents. Transportation to the colony was to be permanent; after an initial prison sentence, the convict was released on condition that he clear a bit of land and become a settler. A return to the European homeland was neither a theoretical nor a practical option—either because a return passage was too expensive (not to mention too hard to secure), or, as happened to be the case in tropical locations such as French Guiana, many of the deportees quickly succumbed to diseases for which they had a lower threshold of immunity than the indigenous populations. Thus, colonial powers transformed whole territories into open-air prisons, which served at the same time as dying grounds.

In general, the folks back home were to be informed about conditions in those places only through cheerful reports illustrated with views that showed the colony from a distance, in the midst of a lush landscape. The tension generated by these upbeat images and the lurid rumors about the real conditions at such dumping grounds was to provide an edge of terror, which might be useful in keeping restless populations in line. In the United States, which did not have such penal colonies, there was no reason not to provide an occasional close-up on the practices of European powers to deport superfluous people abroad. In 1853 the Boston-based magazine *Gleason's Pictorial Drawing-Room Companion* published a report on the French *bagne* (penal colony) in South America with a wood engraving illustrating the exterior elevations and internal framework of a barrack in Cayenne, French Guiana. The *bagne* had been established only a year before, and the story about its accommodations was still "news" in 1853, worthy of the attention of the middle-class public in New England.

> We are told that the treatment of the exiles is milder than that of galley slaves, and we trust so for the honor of humanity. For it must be remembered that a large proportion of the unfortunate beings now sent to Cayenne, were condemned for no other offence than that of resisting the usurpation of that consummate scoundrel, Napoleon,

> on the 2d of December. Torn from their families, associated with the vilest wretches, they are sent to die of grief and disease in the burning climate of the tropics. The barracks, which the usurper has deigned in his mercy to plan for them, would make very respectable stalls for oxen, or kennels for hounds; but what places to crowd human beings together under the relentless sun of the Equator! The horses and dogs of the prince-president are better cared for than are these unfortunate exiles.[24]

The contrast between life in the bare barrack and the comfortable drawing room in which the article was read must have given food for thought about the blessings of a truly democratic constitution.

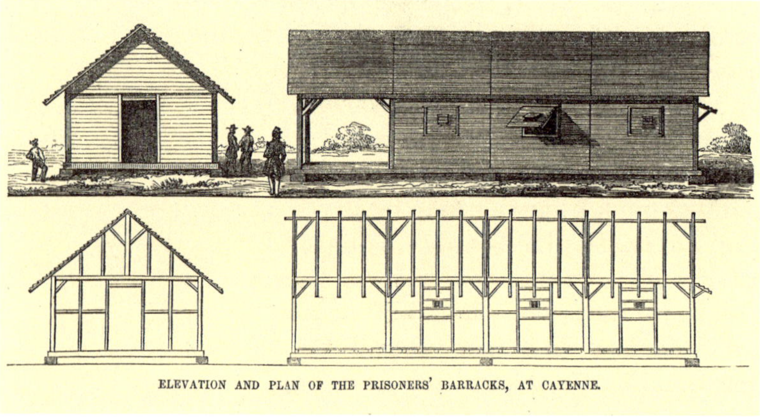

Fig. 7
Elevation and section of a prisoner's barrack in Cayenne, French Guiana, *Gleason's Pictorial Drawing-Room Companion*, 1853. Collection: author.

Gleason's Pictorial Drawing-Room Companion ceased publication in 1859, and hence its editors never had to decide whether they were willing to report on a compound filled with "undesirables" created in 1862 adjacent to Camp McClellan—the training camp in the state of Iowa for volunteers enlisting in the Union Army. In August of that year, the Dakota nation (a division of the Sioux, or Oceti Sakowin) in Minnesota rebelled after the annuity payments they were owed in exchange for lands taken from them were halted. A short but very violent war led to the death of hundreds of mostly German settlers and ended with the capture of over 1,600 Dakota people. Instead of being treated as prisoners of war, they were considered criminals, and 392 were tried for murder, in proceedings that lasted as little as five minutes and in which the accused had no lawyers. A total of 303 were convicted and sentenced to death. President Lincoln commuted the sentences of 265 of them, but thirty-eight were hanged on December 26, 1862—the largest single execution in United States history.

24 "Cayenne," *Gleason's Pictorial Drawing-Room Companion* 4, no. 25 (1853), 388.

Those who had been saved the gallows, most of them teenagers, and a group of sixteen Dakota women, who were to cook and clean, and their four children, were sent to Camp McClellan, which now included an internment camp for the Native American prisoners, Camp Kearney. Four hastily constructed barracks, without stoves to heat them in winter, were to house them: three for the young men, and one for the women, their children, and the sick. The compound in which they were set was a bare piece of ground, stripped of vegetation. No magazine ever published a picture of Camp Kearney, and only a couple of drawings survive.

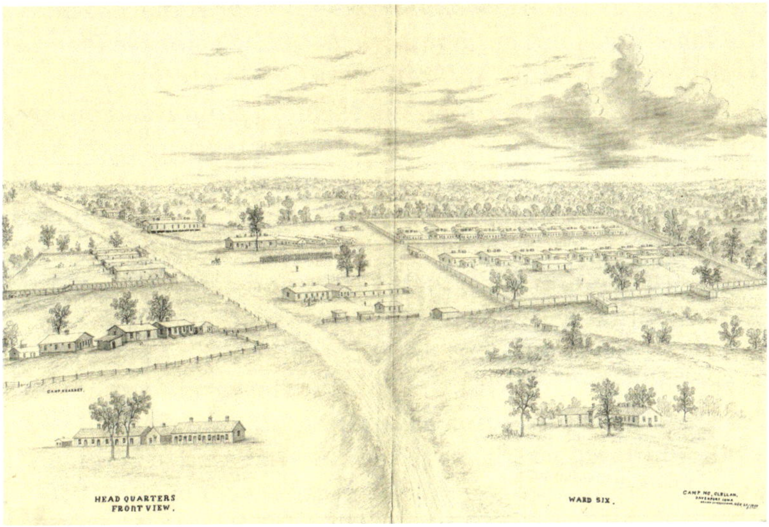

Fig. 8
W. Sharmon, The US (Union) Army's Camp Kearney (left) and Camp McClellan (right), Davenport, Iowa, 1865. Collection: US National Archives, College Park, Maryland.

But unillustrated newspaper articles made clear that the inmates did not deserve any compassion, "When at Camp McClellan, the other day, we visited the Indian pen, where they have some 365 men, women and children, real 'native Americans.' We have read something of Indian romance, but in looking at those specimens we could not see it." Thus, the *Iowa Republican* reported shortly after the prisoners' arrival. "We had the good fortune to meet the Governor and Adjutant General at the Camp, and thus gained admittance inside, among the 'animals,' and a more disgusting menagerie we never witnessed. [...] We could see no evidence of nobleness or dignity of character, but rather evidence of treachery, and cruelty."[25]

In the first two years, the men were shackled together, two by two, and all were subjected to continuous abuse by the guards and the indignity of being put on display as exotic entertainment for the locals after Sunday-morning church service. In three years, one-third of the inmates died of disease. From 1864, the inmates were able to leave the compound to work as forced labor

25 Quoted in James Edward Jacobsen, "Iowa's Rendezvous Camps, 1861–1866," unpublished report commissioned by the Iowa National Guard, 2019, 568–69, available at: http://dragonflydezignz.50megs.com/Dakota-38-plus-2/Camp%20McClellan%20777_Jacobsen_2011%20Part%207.pdf

on nearby farms. The survivors were released in 1866 and transferred to the Santee Sioux Reservation in Nebraska, the place where the rest of the Dakota people had been sent. This marked the end of the first concentration camp on American soil.[26]

In the nineteenth century, prisons, insane asylums, hospitals, workhouses, and even schools became objects of much enlightened consideration about the beneficent and reformatory ability of architectural design. "*Morals reformed—health preserved—industry invigorated—instruction diffused—public burdens lightened—Economy seated as if it were on a rock—the Gordian knot of the Poor-Laws not cut but untied—all by a simple idea in Architecture!*" Thus, in 1791, the English philosopher Jeremy Bentham initiated his idea for panoptical building that he claimed was to offer "a new mode of obtaining power of mind over mind, in a quantity hitherto without example."[27] His countryman John Haviland was inspired by Bentham's theories when, in the early 1820s, he obtained the commission to design a new penitentiary in Philadelphia, which was to be known popularly as the Cherry Hill State Prison and formally as the Eastern State Penitentiary. This prison was the product of idealism. Locked up in illuminated, heated, and, indeed, well-ventilated single-person cells that also functioned as a workshop, living in silence without an opportunity to communicate with any other inmate, each prisoner was to be given many years of opportunity to learn to listen to his inner voice of conscience.

Prison camps have generally escaped the (from a humanitarian perspective) embarrassing idealization that has accompanied the designs of so many penitentiaries in the past 200 years. Even if the general arrangement of a series of barracks in a guarded compound might be less off-putting than the claustrophobic environment of a typical prison cellblock—after all, the similarities between a military training camp and a prison camp are many—the fact remains that a hutted prison camp is considered at best a temporary solution to the problem of warehousing undesirables. In its architecture, the late eighteenth- or nineteenth-century prison invoked the medieval castle, a building type with pedigree that encompasses both a monstrous and majestic of the dimension. The prison camp evokes, at best, a kind of squalid efficiency.

This, then, hints at the extraordinary character of three articles describing an American prisoner-of-war camp, published in April 1865, in *Our Young Folks:*

26 Sarah-Eva Ellen Carlson, "They Tell Their Story: The Dakota Internment at Camp McClellan in Davenport, 1862–1866," *Annals of Iowa* 63, no. 3 (2004), 251–78; Linda M. Clemmons, "'The young folks [want] to go in and see the Indians': Davenport Citizens, Protestant Missionaries, and Dakota Prisoners of War, 1863–1866," *Annals of Iowa* 77, no. 2 (2018), 121–50.

27 Jeremy Bentham, *Panopticum: Postscript; Part I: Containing Further Particulars and Alterations Relative to the Construction Originally Proposed; Principally Adopted to the Purpose of a Panopticon Penitentiary-House* (London: T. Payne, 1791), i–ii.

An Illustrated Magazine for Boys and Girls. The first lines certainly ought to have caught the attention of both young and old.

> Most people consider it a great disgrace to get into prison, and think, too, that all prisons are very bad places; but that is not so. Some of the best men that ever lived have passed years in dungeons; and the prison I have been in is one of the most comfortable places in the world, a great deal more comfortable than the houses that one half of its inmates have been accustomed to living in. So, one cold morning, not a great while ago, with my eyes wide open, and knowing very well what I was about, I walked into it. All of you have heard of this famous prison, for it is talked about all over the world.[28]

The author, James Roberts Gilmore, under the pen name Edmund Kirke, had written various books on life in the Southern states that had helped convince Northerners to accept no compromise on the issue of slavery. In January 1865, Gilmore traveled to Chicago to spend three days at Camp Douglas, a former Union Army assembly camp that had been transformed into a huge prisoner-of-war depot holding more than 8,000 captured Confederate soldiers. His enthusiastic report on the camp was meant to counter allegations that conditions were concerning and to support the moral superiority of the Union cause. This was particularly clear in his comment on the camp's hospital facilities: "nicely battened and whitewashed" wooden buildings offered ample wards "with plastered walls, clean floors, and broad, cheerful windows, through which floods of pure air and sunshine pour in upon the dejected, homesick prisoners." He estimated that "about five hundred are always here, and four or five of them are borne out daily to the little burial-ground just outside the walls." A yearly mortality of roughly 20 percent was, of course, scandalous, but Gilmore contrasted this with prisoner-of-war camps in the South, such as the Belle Isle prison camp near Richmond, Virginia. "Compare this mortality with that of our own men in the Confederate prisons! When only six thousand were at Belle Isle, eighty-five died every day; and when nine thousand—about the average number confined at Camp Douglas—were at Salisbury, Mr. Richardson [Albert D. Richardson published an account of his ordeal in the improvised Confederate prison created at a textile mill in Salisbury, North Carolina, in *The New York Times* in early February

28 Edmund Kirke, "Three Days at Camp Douglas," *Our Young Folks: An Illustrated Magazine for Boys and Girls* 1 (Apr. 1865), 252.

1865] reports that *one hundred and thirty* were daily thrown into a rude cart, and dumped, like decayed offal, into a huge hole outside the camp."[29]

Gilmore continued, in a reassuring voice, providing American boys and girls with further details about Camp Douglas, which was located 5 kilometers from Chicago on the shore of Lake Michigan. Enclosed by a high wooden fence, it was so large that one could not see it all at once; *Our Young Folks* thus offered an engraved bird's-eye view of the whole camp, showing a train track to the left and, toward the center, a gate with access to compounds housing the garrison, the administrative offices, the bakery, and the hospital. To the right is the prisoners' compound, filled with row upon row of barracks.

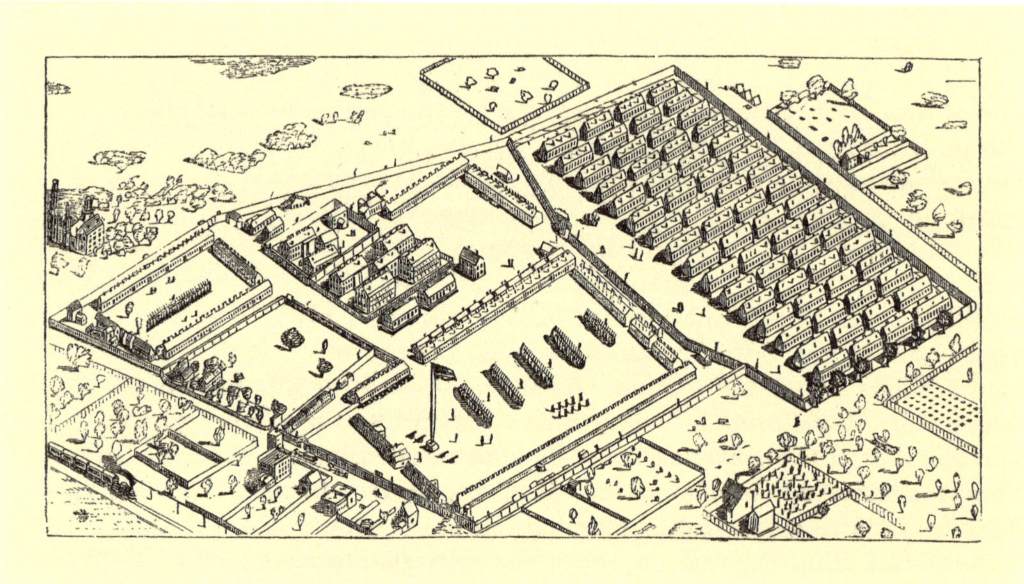

Fig. 9
Bird's-eye view of the US (Union) Army's Camp Douglas, Chicago, Illinois, *Our Young Folks*, 1865. Collection: Baldwin Library of Historical Children's Literature, George A. Smathers Libraries, University of Florida, Gainesville.

Gilmore described the layout: "The prison-yard is an enclosure of about twenty acres [8 hectares], surrounded by a board fence fourteen feet [4.3 meters] high and guarded by thirty sentinels, who are posted on a raised platform just outside the fence, and pace the rounds at all hours of the day and night." He added, "Inside the enclosure, and thirty feet [9 meters] from the fence, is a low railing entirely surrounding the camp. This is the dead line. Who so goes beyond this railing, at any hour of the day or night, is liable to be shot down without warning."[30]

Gilmore noted that most of the prison yard was divided into streets lined with barracks: "The streets are fifty feet [15 meters] wide, and extend nearly the whole length and breadth of the enclosure. They are rounded up in the middle, and have deep gutters at the sides, so

29 Ibid., 254–55.
30 Ibid., 255–56.

that in wet weather the rain flows off, and leaves them almost as dry as a house floor. The barracks are one-story wooden buildings, ninety feet [27.4 meters] long and twenty-four feet [7.3 meters] wide, and stand on posts four feet [1.2 meters] from the ground. They are elevated in this manner to prevent the prisoners tunneling their way out of camp." Taking his readers inside the barracks, he wrote, "Each barrack is divided into two rooms; one a square apartment, where the prisoners do their cooking; the other a long hall, with three tiers of bunks on either side, where they do their sleeping. The larger rooms are furnished with benches and a stove, have several windows on each side, and ventilators on the roof, and are as comfortable places to stay in as one could expect in a prison."[31]

Camp Douglas did not have a barbed-wire fence—the first patent for barbed wire was issued in the same month that Gilmore's article appeared in *Our Young Folks*. Nor did it have guard towers to facilitate control of the perimeter; rather, a continuous *chemin de ronde* (sentry walk) located on the outside of the high fence allowed for surveillance.[32] Yet, even without barbed-wire fences and guard towers, Camp Douglas eerily foreshadowed one of the settlement forms that was to define the twentieth century.[33] It also marked a bold departure in the history of the barrack by showing the full potential of that building type within the context of forced confinement.

Before the early modern period, the housing of prisoners of war was not a significant military concern. In the Greco-Roman world, captured warriors were normally killed, mutilated, enslaved, drafted into the victorious armies, or exchanged. In the Middle Ages, prisoners of war were usually ransomed, in mostly ad hoc agreements in which public interest (of the monarch) and private interest (of the individual captor and, possibly, his commanding officer or feudal lord) often clashed.[34] In the early seventeenth century, the Dutch legal scholar Hugo de Groot (known also as Hugo Grotius) suggested that prisoners of war should be treated humanely and exchanged or ransomed according to accepted procedures. His advice reflected the formal cartel devised by Spain and the Dutch Republic, according to which all prisoners of war were exchanged, equal rank by equal rank, within twenty-five days of capture, and any surplus prisoners were ransomed at the equivalent of one month's pay. From the mid-seventeenth century onward, formal cartels became the conventional way of dealing with

31 Ibid., 256–57.
32 See Henry D. and Frances T. McCallum, *The Wire That Fenced the West* (Norman: University of Oklahoma Press, 1965); Olivier Razac, *Barbed Wire: A Political History* (New York: New Press, 2002); and Reviel Netz, *Barbed Wire: An Ecology of Modernity* (Middletown, CT: Wesleyan University Press, 2004).
33 In 1995, the sociologist Zygmunt Bauman labeled the twentieth century "The Age of the Camps." See *Life in Fragments: Essays in Postmodern Morality* (Oxford, UK, and Cambridge, MA: Blackwell, 1995), 192–206.
34 Maurice Keen, *The Laws of War in the Late Middle Ages* (London: Routledge & Kegan Paul, 1965), 137–85; Rémy Ambühl, *Prisoners of War in the Hundred Years War: Ransom Culture in the Late Middle Ages* (Cambridge: Cambridge University Press, 2013).

prisoners of war in Europe. These cartels stipulated not only the time frame in which the exchange had to take place but also the prisoners' relative exchange value. As a result, prisoners were kept for only short times and were held in requisitioned barns, stables, churches, or other public buildings until they could be exchanged.[35]

In the war that was triggered by the American Revolution, this exchange system came under pressure. First, King George III had declared the members of the Continental Army traitors. The usual punishment for treason was hanging, but this policy could not be pursued due to the threat of reprisals, with Americans hanging captured British soldiers. Secondly, the British captured many more Americans than vice versa. Finally, George Washington was not interested in exchanging prisoners, as he would release highly trained British professional soldiers in return for ragtag American volunteers. Hence, exchanges proved difficult, and both sides had to find ways to deal with prisoners of war. Washington had no difficulty offering them a conditional release, or parole, and sending them to help out on American farms. The British, however, were unwilling to extend such courtesy to their prisoners: in their view, parole could be offered only to "men of honor"—which rebels, by definition, were not.

Instead, the British created floating prisons in decommissioned warships, or "hulks," moored in British-held ports like Brooklyn. "Man took one of the most beautiful objects of his handiwork and deformed it into a hideous monstrosity," a British historian observed more than a century later.[36] These hulks, shorn of masts and rigging, painted black and burdened with ugly superstructures to increase prisoner capacity, not only looked terrifying—they also proved to be death traps. A July 1778 report in the *Connecticut Gazette* recounted the imprisonment and escape of an American soldier from one of the British ships. When he was led below-decks, "the steam of the hold was enough to scald the skin and take away the breath—the stench enough to poison the air all around. [. . .] A little epitome of hell—about 350 men confined between decks." Within the hulk, the report continued, "the heat [was] so intense (the hot sun shining all day on deck) that they were all naked, which also served the well to get rid of vermin, but the sick were eaten up alive. Their sickly countenances and ghastly looks were truly horrible."[37]

35 Ernst Friedrich Gurlt, *Zur Geschichte der internationalen und freiwilligen Krankenflege im Kriege* (Leipzig: Vogel, 1873), 10–30; *The Consolidated Treaty Series*, ed. Clive Parry, 231 vols. (Dobbs Ferry, NY: Oceana, 1969–86), 12:457–61; 13:379–91; 19:79–93; 47:291–94, 299–301; Geoffrey Parker, *The Army of Flanders and the Spanish Road, 1567–1659: The Logistics of Spanish Victory and Defeat in the Low Countries' Wars* (Cambridge: Cambridge University Press, 1972), 169–70.

36 Francis Abell, *Prisoners of War in Britain, 1756 to 1815: A Record of Their Lives, Their Romance and Their Sufferings* (Oxford: Oxford University Press, 1914), 37.

37 In Henry Onderdonk, *Revolutionary Incidents of Suffolk and Kings Counties: With an Account of the Battle of Long Island and the British Prisons and Prison-ships at New York* (New York: Leavitt & Company, 1849), 227–28.

Having pioneered hulks as prisoner-of-war accommodation in the American Revolutionary War, the British used them again during the wars that followed the fall of the French monarchy. It proved very difficult to create a cartel after the National Constituent Assembly abolished the hierarchies of the *ancien régime*, proclaimed the principle of human equality and, as a result, refused to honor the old conventions regarding the relative value of officers and the rank and file, and instead insisted on an exchange rate of one to one, irrespective of rank. As the British government rejected those terms, from 1794 onward it was left with prisoners who could not be exchanged, and their accommodation became an issue. French, Dutch, and Danish officers, who were still considered gentlemen, often obtained parole that allowed them to live in England in rented quarters, but those from the ranks were thought not to be bound by a code of honor and could not be paroled—they had to be interned.[38] Floating prisons consisting of rows of hulks became a common sight in major English harbors.

Fig. 10
Ambroise-Louis Garnerey, Prison hulks in Portsmouth Harbour, England, 1808. A French privateer, Garnerey was captured by the British in 1806 and imprisoned on hulks for eight years. Collection: National Maritime Museum, Greenwich, London.

As hulks had become a cause of public concern, the Royal Navy's Transport Board, which was responsible for supplying the fleet and for the prisoner-of-war hulks, decided to build the first prisoner-of-war depot on land. It selected a site at Norman Cross, Huntingdonshire, which was located some 125 kilometers north of London along the major road leading to Scotland, in easy reach of two ports and close to a town that could provide a workforce and supplies.[39] Constructed in a few months,

38 See Abell, *Prisoners of War in Britain, 1756 to 1815*; Paul Chamberlain, *Hell upon Water: Prisoners of War in Britain, 1793–1815* (Stroud, UK: Spellmount, 2008); and Michael Lewis, *Napoleon and His British Captives* (London: Allen & Unwin, 1962).

39 See Thomas James Walker, *The Depot for Prisoners of War at Norman Cross, Huntingdonshire, 1796 to 1816* (London: Constable, 1913).

the depot consisted of four compounds of some 2 hectares each. Each compound contained four wooden two-story "caserns" of 30.5 by 6.7 meters.[40] These caserns were a kind of hybrid, with an architectural lineage that combined military barracks, warehouses, and naval hulks used as prisoner-of-war depots. The prison yards were surrounded by wooden stockades and divided by four avenues that converged on a central blockhouse. All of this was surrounded by a brick wall.

Fig. 11
Captain John Durrant, View of one of the four prisoner compounds of the Norman Cross prison depot, England, 1803. Collection: Hampshire Cultural Trust, Winchester, England.

"Nothing could be less romantic than the appearance of these Norman Cross Barracks," an observer noted. "They looked from outside exactly like a vast congeries of large, high, carpenters' shops, with roofs of glaring red tiles, and surrounded by wooden palisades, very lofty and of prodigious strength. In fact, the place was like an entrenched camp of a rather more permanent type. But if there was no architectural beauty, there was the perfection of security. It looked like business."[41] The interiors of the caserns were also businesslike. Each floor was divided into three bays; the outer bays were 2.4 meters wide, the center bay was 1.8 meters wide, and a series of closely placed posts separated the three bays. Between these posts and the wooden walls, the prisoners slept in hammocks. On the first floor, hammocks were mounted in three tiers, and on the second floor in two, creating space for 500 prisoners in each of the caserns, or 2,000 in each compound.

The Norman Cross depot had been built as a temporary facility, and when it seemed there would be no more European wars in the foreseeable future, the

40 "Casern | Caserne," in *The Oxford English Dictionary*, ed. John A. Simpson and Edward S. C. Weiner, 2nd ed., 20 vols. (Oxford: Clarendon Press, 1989), 2:937–38.
41 Arthur Brown, *The French Prisoners of Norman Cross: A Tale* (London: Hodder, 1895), 10.

Transport Board decided to sell the caserns in lots. On August 31, 1816, a local newspaper announced their sale by auction: "The very extensive and substantial TIMBER BUILDINGS, comprising Three Hundred and Ninety-six Lots, of various dimensions, suitable to the purposes of all classes of persons, to whom the Premises are now open for inspection."[42] On October 2, the Norman Cross site was sold. The caserns, which had been brought to the site in prefabricated form, proved still usable as workshops, stables, or barns, and were re-erected at various locations in the county.[43]

After 1815, prisoner-exchange cartels again became common practice in Europe, but when the Civil War broke out in the United States, the federal government did not want to recognize Confederate soldiers as legal combatants. "At first the prevailing opinion was in favor of hanging as traitors every prisoner captured by the government," a contemporary account of the war observes. "The rebellion was regarded as an insurrection [...] and it seemed derogatory to the national dignity to recognize the belligerent rights of rebels by negotiations with them of any sort."[44] Yet, when the Confederate States Army threatened to reply in kind, politicians decided to adopt the usual conventions. There was also good legal opinion to support this. In August 1861, *The New York Times* carried a letter to the editor, signed with the initials "F. L.," that argued that in wartime, leaders should recognize realities rather than rights: "According to our opinion the exchange of prisoners involves no question of acknowledgment of right, but is a simple recognition of fact and reality; and nothing remains to be decided except the expediency or advantage, which we leave to the proper authorities. They must decide, in each case, whether it is advisable or not. There is no obligation to exchange prisoners, either in civil or other wars; but, be it repeated, there is no other consideration to be consulted but that of prudence and advantage."[45]

In February 1862, the Union Army captured Fort Donelson near Dover, Tennessee, taking between 12,000 and 15,000 Confederate prisoners, and had no place to house them. Colonel Joseph H. Tucker, commanding officer of Camp Douglas near Chicago, volunteered to take in prisoners. In the fall of 1861, Tucker had established Camp Douglas to facilitate the mobilization and training of volunteer regiments from Illinois—as such, it was not much different from Camp Dennison in Ohio, or Camp McClellan in Iowa.[46] He designed the camp to accommodate 8,000 men and commissioned the 56th

42 "Norman Cross Barracks and Depots for Prisoners of War," *Colchester Gazette, and General Advertiser for Essex, Suffolk, Norfolk, Cambridgeshire, and Herts*, Aug. 31, 1816, 1.
43 Abell, *Prisoners of War in Britain*, 1756 to 1815, 154.
44 Alfred H. Guernsey and Henry Mills Alden, *Harper's Pictorial History of the Civil War*, 2 vols. (Chicago: McDonnell Bros., 1866–68), 2:792.
45 "The Disposal of Prisoners: Would the Exchange of Prisoners Amount to a Partial Acknowledgment of the Insurgents as Belligerents, According to International Law?," *The New York Times*, Aug. 19, 1861.
46 On the history of Camp Douglas, see Dennis Kelly, *A History of Camp Douglas Illinois, Union Prison, 1861–1865* (Atlanta, GA: United States Department of the Interior, National Park Service, Southeast Region, 1989); and George Levy, *To Die in Chicago: Confederate Prisoners at Camp Douglas, 1862–1865* (Gretna, LA: Pelican Publishing Company, 1994).

Illinois Infantry Regiment, which consisted largely of carpenters, builders, and engineers, to build the barracks using the vernacular balloon-frame construction invented thirty years earlier in Chicago.[47]

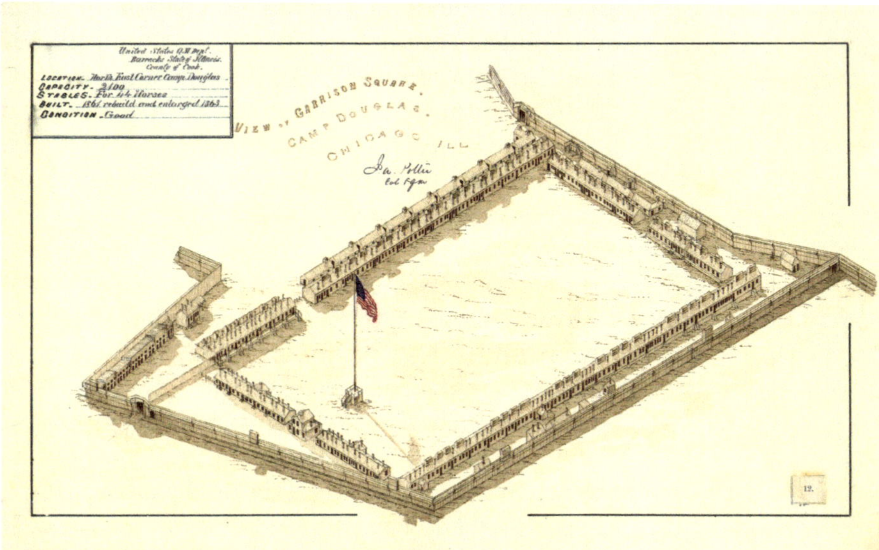

Fig. 12
Isometric drawing of the original part of Camp Douglas, 1865. Collection: US National Archives, College Park, Maryland.

By November 15, 1861, Camp Douglas housed about 4,222 Union Army volunteers, but as soldiers left for the front, Tucker realized the camp might soon be empty—hence his offer to take in the prisoners of war. He received an initial batch of 4,459, and in the spring the number of inmates swelled to almost 9,000.

One of those captured at Fort Donelson and brought to Camp Douglas was nineteen-year-old Mississippi native Milton Asbury Ryan. The first thing that struck him upon his arrival, was the camp's standing as a major source of entertainment for the local population. "It seemed that they never tired of looking at us. They visited the prison everyday in great crowds until an order was issued prohibiting it. Then some enterprising Yankee built an observatory just outside the prison wall. It was crowded with people from morning until night." As far as the camp itself was concerned, Ryan had few complaints at first. "Every thing looked new and clean," he recollected, some fifty years later. "I think that we were the first arrival of prisoners. Each barracks had a capacity of 125 prisoners. On each side of the barracks there were three tiers of bunks, one above another, with a narrow hall between and a heater in the center. The prison was laid off in squares and had the appearance of a little town. It had a plank wall around it 15 ft. [4.5 meters] high with a 3 ft. [1 meter] walk on top for the guards to walk on. There was a commissary in the center where our rations were kept and issued every morning."[48]

47 "The State Camp of Instruction," *Chicago Tribune*, Nov. 16, 1861.
48 Milton Asbury Ryan, "Experience of a Confederate Soldier in Camp and Prison in the Civil War 1861–1865," ms., Civil War Times Illustrated Collection, United States Army Military Institute, Carlisle, PA.

Growing into the largest prisoner-of-war depot in the Union, Camp Douglas became an increasingly unhappy place as hygienic conditions worsened. "The amount of standing water, unpoliced grounds, of foul sinks, of unventilated and crowded barracks, of general disorder, of soil reeking miasmatic accretions, of rotten bones and emptying of camp kettles, is enough to drive a sanitarian to despair," the president of the US Sanitary Commission reported to Lieutenant Colonel William Hoffman, the commissary general of prisoners. "The absolute abandonment of the spot seems to be the only judicious course. I do not believe that any amount of drainage would purge that soil loaded with accumulated filth or those barracks fetid with two stories of vermin and animal exhalations. Nothing but fire can cleanse them."[49]

Soon it seemed the situation might change for the better. In December 1861, Congress had asked President Lincoln to introduce a general prisoner-exchange agreement, and a cartel was signed on July 22, 1862. Known as the Dix–Hill cartel for its signatories, Major General John Adams Dix of the Union and Major General Daniel Harvey Hill of the Confederacy, this agreement stipulated that all prisoners of war would be discharged within ten days after their capture, "and the prisoners now held, and those hereafter taken, to be transported to the points mutually agreed upon, at the expense of the capturing party. The surplus prisoners not exchanged shall not be permitted to take up arms again, nor to serve as a military police or constabulary force." Both sides agreed to keep each other informed about the parole status of released prisoners. The final article of the agreement stipulated that when problems were to arise, "it is mutually agreed that such misunderstanding shall not interrupt the release of prisoners on parole as herein provided, but shall be made the subject of friendly explanation, in order, that the object of this agreement may neither be defeated nor postponed."[50]

In the wake of the Dix–Hill cartel, the depots were emptied. "Sometime in September after our capture in February we, to our unspeakable joy received notice that we would soon be exchanged and sent back to dear old Mississippi," Ryan recalled. "We were this time marched to the railroad and packed in horse and cattle cars which were filthy in the extreme; but that was all right. It was a joy ride for us. We laughed, sang, and shed tears of joy at our release from prison."[51] While the great majority of those released and sent home were captured soldiers, some were political prisoners. A well-known example was Dr. Alfred Hughes, a respected physician practicing

49 In Kelly, *A History of Camp Douglas*, 26.
50 In Guernsey and Alden, *Harper's Pictorial History of the Civil War*, 2:794.
51 Ryan, "Experience of a Confederate Soldier."

in Wheeling, Virginia, and a friend of General Robert E. Lee. In May 1861 Hughes voted in favour of secession. However, Unionist sentiment prevailed in Wheeling, as it did in all the counties west of the Allegheny Mountains, and when this part of the state formally refused in June 1861 to obey the secessionist government in Richmond, declaring loyalty to the Union, Hughes was one of a small number of prominent members of Wheeling society who opposed the de facto break off of the western part of the state. In May 1862 he and eleven other Southern sympathizers were arrested and, after a second and third refusal to take the oath of allegiance, were sent, as political prisoners, to a Union prison hastily set up in a stockade filled with thirty-seven barracks at the edge of Camp Chase, a large recruitment and training camp established by William Dennison on the outskirts of Columbus, Ohio.

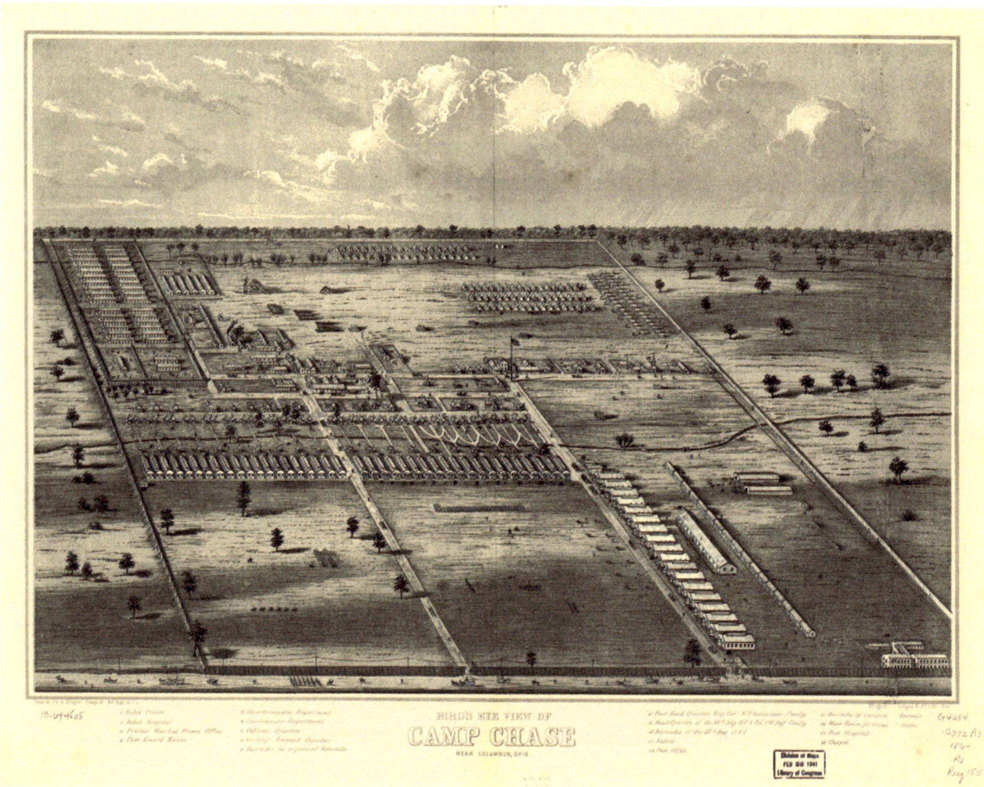

Fig. 13
Albert Ruger, Bird's-eye view of the US (Union) Army's Camp Chase, Columbus, Ohio, c. 1862. The four-partite stockade for the prisoners and the adjacent stockade with the prison hospital are located in the top-left corner of this view of the camp. While the barracks housing Union soldiers are equipped with ridge ventilation, those housing prisoners are not, graphically illustrating a lesser concern for the health of the captives. The 1929 Geneva Convention establishing the rights of prisoners of war aimed to address this situation. "Prisoners of war shall be lodged in buildings or huts which afford all possible safeguards as regards hygiene and salubrity. [...] As regards dormitories, [...] the conditions shall be the same as for the depot troops of the detaining Power." Collection: Library of Congress, Washington, DC.

There, their presence proved something of an embarrassment to the military authorities charged with managing the Union Army's prisoner-of-war camps, and they were happy to see them leave in December 1862, when a prisoner exchange could be arranged within the context of the Dix–Hill cartel—in Hughes's case with the brother of a well-known Philadelphia physician held in the Salisbury Prison in North Carolina. After his release, Hughes made his way to Richmond, the capital of the Confederacy, where he became the personal physician of Mary Anna Custis Lee, the wife of his friend Robert. Respected for his martyrdom at Camp Chase, he became a well-known member of Richmond society and was elected to the Virginia Legislature.

In the meantime, "F. L.," who had written the August 1861 letter to the editor of *The New York Times* that counseled governments to be led by prudence when considering what to do with prisoners of war, had been working hard to codify rules of war. Francis Lieber, a German-born historian and political scientist, had become very interested in the rules of war when the Civil War broke out, as the hastily organized Confederate States Army seemed to violate many of them. He wrote a paper on the topic in early 1862 and began to work on a code, eventually adding up to 157 articles, which the federal government adopted in April 1863. A key document in formalizing the rules of war, it established for the first time the status of combatants. Moreover, the Lieber code made it clear that prisoners of war and those who participate in a lawful war by serving in duly established armies are not criminals when they kill and destroy in the course of their duties but "public enemies," who cannot be treated or judged as criminals when captured.[52]

The Lieber code included a few articles that carried particular importance in the US Civil War. They concerned the fact that in war, international law, which is the law of nature, has a higher standing than national law. For example, article 42 stipulated, "Slavery, complicating and confounding the ideas of property, (that is of a thing,) and of personality, (that is of humanity,) exists according to municipal or local law only. The law of nature and nations has never acknowledged it." And article 58 read, "The law of nations knows of no distinction of color, and if an enemy of the United States should enslave and sell any captured persons of their army, it would be a case for the severest retaliation, if not redressed upon complaint. The United States cannot retaliate by enslavement; therefore death must be the

52 United States, United States Army, Adjutant-General's Office, *Instructions for the Government of Armies of the United States in the Field*, prepared by Francis Lieber (New York: Van Nostrand, 1863), 15, 17, 20, 26–28, 30.

retaliation for this crime against the law of nations."[53] To put the matter simply: any black soldier serving in the US Army had to be treated as an ordinary prisoner of war when captured. He could not be enslaved, even if he had been once been enslaved and had escaped this condition through flight to the North. These issues became crucially important, because on January 1, 1863, President Lincoln had proclaimed the freedom of all enslaved persons in the states that were still in rebellion and allowed them to enroll in Union Army. The Confederate government responded to the Emancipation Proclamation by denying both captured black soldiers and their commanding officers prisoner-of-war status.[54] The Union Army ceased to engage in prisoner exchanges, the Dix–Hill cartel broke down, and both sides faced again the task of housing prisoners of war.

Now Lieutenant Colonel Hoffman decided to reopen former depots, including Camp Douglas. After its last prisoners of war had been released, in October 1862, the camp had served as a holding ground for Union soldiers who had been captured by the Confederates and released on parole. Enraged that, after captivity in the South, they found themselves locked up again by their own side, these soldiers had set fire to the barracks.[55] Expecting a great influx of Confederate prisoners, Hoffman applied to Secretary of War Edwin McMasters Stanton for funds to rebuild the facility. In early November, Hoffman got his answer: "The Secretary of War is not disposed at this time, in view of the treatment our prisoners of war are receiving at the hands of the enemy, to erect fine establishments for their prisoners in our hands. Whatever is indispensable, however, to prevent suffering, whether from the effects of the weather or other causes, will be provided by commanding officers of prison establishments if ordinary means fail."[56]

The acting medical inspector of prisoners of war, Dr. Augustus M. Clark, had written a critical report on the conditions at Camp Douglas. "All the prisoners barracks are greatly in need of repair; there is not a door and hardly a window among them; a large proportion of the bunks are so mutilated as to be useless; much of the flooring and siding is removed and the open fire-places in the cook-houses are in a dilapidated condition; the roofs of all require repairs," he wrote. As to the ventilation, he observed: "An attempt at ventilation seems to have been made when the barracks were built by making two small openings about twenty by eight inches [50 by 20 centimeters] in the ridge of each roof; this is utterly insufficient, or will be so when the barracks are repaired.

53 Ibid., 15–16, 20.
54 United States, War Department, *The War of the Rebellion: A Compilation of the Official Records of the Union and Confederate Armies*, 70 vols. (Washington, DC: Government Printing Office, 1880–1901), ser. 1, vol. 28, pt. 2, 235.
55 In United States, United States Army, Surgeon General, *The Medical and Surgical History of the War of the Rebellion*, 2 vols. in 6 pts. (Washington, DC: Government Printing Office, 1875–88), vol. 1, pt. 3, 49.
56 William Hoffman, letter to Colonel Thomas, Sept. 23, 1863; and James A. Hardie, memo to War Department, Nov. 7, 1863, in United States, War Department, *The War of the Rebellion*, ser. 2, vol. 6, 314–15.

Some approved mode of ventilation should be adopted, especially in the hospitals, otherwise when cold weather sets in a large increase in cases of pneumonia will have to be looked for."[57]

Upon receipt of this report, Hoffman immediately ordered the commander of Camp Douglas, Colonel Charles Victor DeLand, to attend to the issues Dr. Clark had raised.[58] In response, DeLand reported that twenty-six prisoners locked up in the camp prison had escaped: they had cut a hole through the plank floor and dug a tunnel to the outside. Complaining that he did not have enough resources to prevent escapes, DeLand noted that the design of the camp did not allow him to keep control: "I tell you frankly this camp has heretofore been a mere rookery; its barracks, fences, guard-houses, all a mere shell of refuse pine boards; a nest of hiding places instead of a safe compact prison." In a later letter, after another escape, he noted that "the large spaces under the barracks afford ample room to store away the dirt and render detection difficult," and, as such, he had "ordered all the floors removed from the barracks and cook-houses and the spaces filled with dirt even with the top of the joist."[59]

DeLand's complaint that the original layout of Camp Douglas did not make for a well-run prison was justified, and Hoffman knew it. After the collapse of the Dix–Hill cartel, he and the quartermaster general, Brigadier General Montgomery C. Meigs, had set out to create prisoner-of-war camps from scratch, and decided that Rock Island, Illinois, a 383-hectare island in the Mississippi River, would serve as an ideal location. On July 14, 1863, Meigs ordered Captain Charles A. Reynolds to proceed to Rock Island and oversee the construction of a prisoner-of-war depot based on plans from the Quartermaster General's Office.[60] It is not clear who prepared the materials Captain Reynolds used as the basis for his design, yet it is clear that Meigs was a hands-on manager, and he might have been the author.

Shortly after Reynolds arrived at Rock Island, he received a letter from Meigs reminding him that "the barracks for prisoners at Rock Island should be put up in the roughest and cheapest manner, mere shanties, with no fine work about them, and the work should, if possible, be done by contract and in the shortest possible time."[61] Reynolds responded by proposing modifications in the design of the camp, and Meigs, after consulting with Hoffman, endorsed them.

57 Augustus M. Clark, "Report of Inspection of Camps and Field Hospitals at Camp Douglas, Chicago, Ill.," Oct. 9, 1863, in United States, War Department, *The War of the Rebellion*, ser. 2, vol. 6, 372–73.
58 William Hoffman, letter to Charles V. De Land, Oct. 24, 1863, in United States, War Department, *The War of the Rebellion*, ser. 2, vol. 6, 417.
59 Charles V. DeLand, letters to William Hoffman, Oct. 28, 1863, and Dec. 3, 1863, in United States, War Department, *The War of the Rebellion*, ser. 2, vol. 6, 434–35, 637–38.
60 Montgomery C. Meigs, letter to Charles A. Reynolds, July 14, 1863, in United States, War Department, *The War of the Rebellion*, ser. 2, vol. 6, 115.

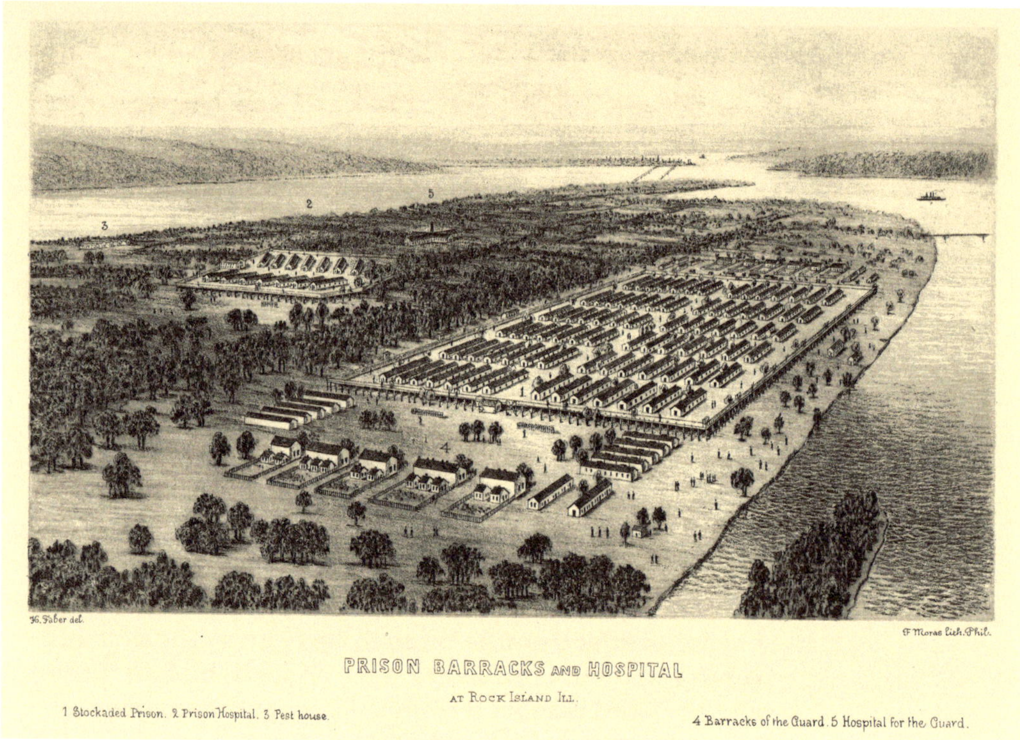

H. Faber del.
F. Moras Lith. Phil.
PRISON BARRACKS AND HOSPITAL
AT ROCK ISLAND ILL.
1 Stockaded Prison. 2 Prison Hospital. 3 Pest house.
4 Barracks of the Guard. 5 Hospital for the Guard.

Fig. 14
Barracks at the US (Union) Army's Rock Island, Illinois, prison camp for Confederate soldiers, 1864. Collection: Library of Congress, Washington, DC.

The camp consisted of a compound measuring some 400 by 275 meters surrounded by a 3.6-meter-high stockade supplied with a sentry walk and sentry boxes located every 30 meters. On the inside, parallel to the stockade, was either a ditch or a row of stakes that marked the deadline. Eighty-four barracks, each intended to accommodate 120 men, stood within this boundary.

In February 1864, Dr. Clark provided a full description of the barracks:

> They are arranged in blocks of 7 each, fronting on streets 100 feet [30 meters] wide, with two main avenues, 130 feet [40 meters] wide, intersecting the camp in the center. [...] The barracks have each 2 ridge ventilators and 12 windows, with 2 doors. These would afford abundantly sufficient ventilation were it not for the difficulty in having the windows kept open, and in view of this difficulty I have suggested that the ridge ventilation be carried the full length of the barrack. This can be done by prison labor and at trifling expense. Each barrack is 100 by 22 by 12 feet [30 by 6.7 by 3.7 meters] in dimensions. [...] The barracks are sufficiently heated by two coal stoves in each. The bedding is well aired each day, and the police and discipline, as well as the general condition of the men, is admirable.[62]

62 August M. Clark, letter to William Hoffman, Feb. 13, 1864, in United States, War Department, *The War of the Rebellion*, ser. 2, vol. 6, 948–49.

Ridge ventilation had been developed in the Crimean War, and less than a decade after its invention, it was seen as an excellent device to obtain good ventilation without draft and loss of heat. Yet Meigs chose not to approve Dr. Clark's recommendations.

Secretary of War Stanton, who had become convinced that DeLand was not up to the task of running Camp Douglas, decided to appoint Brigadier General William Ward Orme as commanding officer of the military district of Chicago, and gave him specific orders to take care of Camp Douglas. In the fall, Orme conducted a three-week inspection tour of twelve prisoner depots, and in his generally upbeat report on the conditions in the camps, he noted that at Camp Douglas, the 5,964 prisoners exceeded the capacity of the barracks, "which are long, wooden, one-story buildings, with bunks on either side, and stoves in the passageway between the bunks." As to Rock Island, he noted: "There were no prisoners at this point November 30, but arrangements were being rapidly perfected for their reception. The capacity of the barracks will be 10,000 men."[63]

The design of Rock Island was to inspire Orme to make some radical changes in the layout of Camp Douglas. Two of Camp Douglas's three units were to be united into one large prisoner compound, and in this compound, barracks were to be arranged in parallel rows. On February 2, 1864, Dr. Clark, who had been dispatched to Camp Douglas to report on its hygienic condition, reported to Hoffman that Orme had "proposed to remove the prisoners' barracks entirely into the western division of the camp, leaving the eastern division for Federal troops and the hospitals." Dr. Clark added that Orme wanted to take this opportunity to raise the barracks on posts 60–90 centimeters high, "so as to afford a clear view beneath them and allow the prisoners the advantage of a floor."[64] A week later, Orme shared his ideas with Hoffman: he proposed recycling the existing barracks, which were over 100 meters long, by cutting them into pieces about 27 meters long and moving these pieces to a new location within a grid. Rock Island was the model.

Orme's plan reflected the advantage offered by balloon-frame construction: it allowed buildings to be easily transported. In the 1860s in Chicago, development was so rapid, with land values rising so quickly, that the rental return on two-story balloon-frame houses, shops, and other businesses was not enough to pay increased property taxes. Balloon-frame structures were moved to the newly laid-out suburbs, where land was still cheap.

63 William M. Orme, letter to Edwin M. Stanton, Dec. 7, 1863, in United States, War Department, *The War of the Rebellion*, ser. 2, vol. 6, 660–63.
64 August M. Clark, letter to William Hoffman, Feb. 2, 1864, in United States, War Department, *The War of the Rebellion*, ser. 2, vol. 6, 909.

Orme undoubtedly knew this and reasoned that he could rearrange the camp in such a way that it could be easily policed.

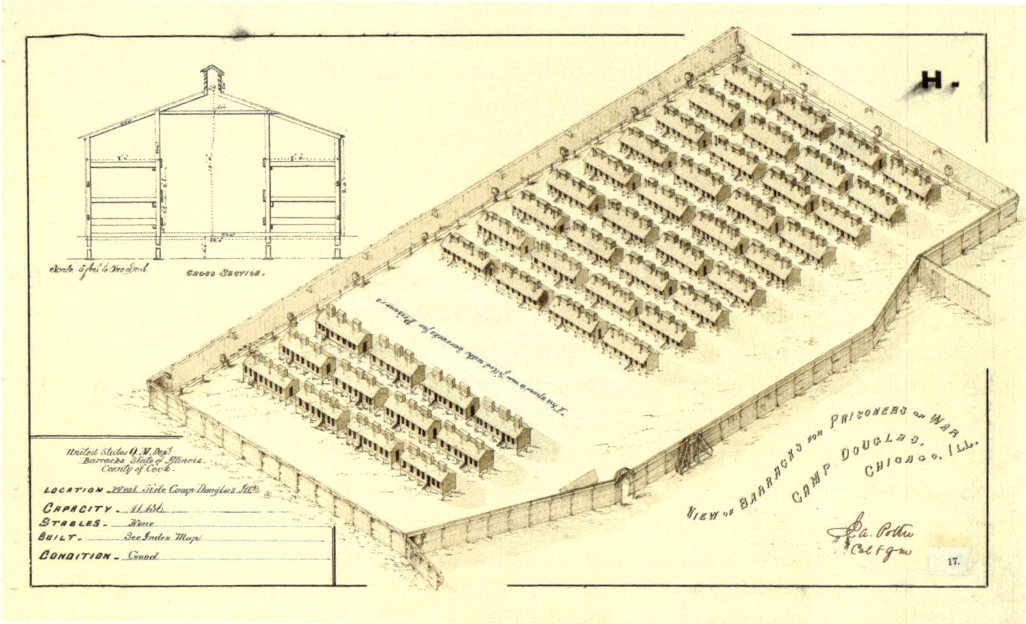

Fig. 15
Isometric view of the new prisoner-of-war compound at Camp Douglas, 1865. Collection: US National Archives, College Park, Maryland.

Before the first barrack was moved, Orme's deteriorating health forced him to resign; his successor was Colonel Benjamin J. Sweet, who completed the rebuilding of the camp following Orme's design. The result was the arrangement that was illustrated in Gilmore's propagandic article published in *Our Young Folks*.
In June 1864, Sweet reported to Hoffman:

> I have the honor respectfully to report that the grounds at Camp Douglas have been thoroughly policed and drained, nearly all the barracks in the prisoners' square, which were in long lines around the square, on the ground with floors ripped up, cut in lengths of ninety feet [27 meters] to each barrack, moved, ranged on streets fifty feet [15 meters] wide, four and five barracks on each street, with an alley twenty-five feet [7.5 meters] between the ends, streets graded, and barracks whitewashed inside and out, floors laid, and barracks raised and firmly placed on blocks four feet [1.2 meters] from the ground to prevent burrowing. [...] It leaves the grounds handsomely arranged, clean, and commodious, and clears somewhat more than half of the ground formerly occupied by the same barracks from incumbrance.

He went on to recommend that "thirty-nine more barracks be constructed on the plan according to which those now in the square are arranged. The changes which have been made make great improvement in the appearance and sanitary condition of the camp, as well as assistant in enforcing better discipline."[65]

In the following days, realizing that the funds for these new barracks might not be forthcoming, Sweet suggested to Hoffman that he also could recycle the barracks used by the garrison, which were to be vacated in the near future.[66] "They can be raised and moved into the prisoners' square without incurring large expense," he wrote. "We have apparatus for moving and raising on hand, and if you desire to fill up the prisoners' square will, of course, lessen the expense in proportion to the number of men they will hold."[67]

As Hoffman considered Colonel Sweet's request, prisoner-of-war accommodation became front-page news. When the Dix–Hill cartel came to an end in July 1863, the Confederate army had only limited resources to devote to managing an influx of prisoners. Brigadier General John Henry Winder, who was in charge of prisoners of war, decided to build a large depot in Andersonville, Georgia, consisting of a compound surrounded by a stockade that was to be filled with log cabins. The construction of the stockade was straightforward, as pine trees were abundant and labor was available: a large crew of enslaved men had been pressed into military service for sixty days. But by the time the stockade was finished, they had to return to the slaveholders' estates to work the fields. Captain Richard B. Winder, who was supervising the construction, wrote to his uncle, Brigadier General Winder, noting that "plank houses can be built much more rapidly and at less expense to the Government than log ones." He asked that "this matter be left to my discretion and that I be allowed to use logs or plank, as the occasion requires."[68]

But Captain Winder was unable to get the boards he needed, and the depot created near Andersonville, which was given the name Camp Sumter, ended up as a large, empty site surrounded by a double stockade but without any cabins, barracks or tents.[69] Originally intended to hold a maximum of 10,000 inmates, the site held 33,000 Union Army prisoners by October 1863. Crowded together in a little over 10.5 hectares, the prisoners bivouacked amid an increasing accumulation of mud and filth—including their own excrement. Of the 45,000 men imprisoned at Andersonville, 13,000 died.

65 Benjamin J. Sweet, letter to William Hoffman, June 1, 1864, in United States, War Department, *The War of the Rebellion*, ser. 2, vol. 7, 184–85.
66 Benjamin J. Sweet, letter to William Hoffman, June 4, 1864, in United States, War Department, *The War of the Rebellion*, ser. 2, vol. 7, 195.
67 Benjamin J. Sweet, letter to William Hoffman, June 6, 1864, in United States, War Department, *The War of the Rebellion*, ser. 2, vol. 7, 201–02.
68 Robert E. Lee, letter to James E. Seddon, Oct. 28, 1863; and Richard B. Winder, letter to John H. Winder, Feb. 17, 1864, in United States, War Department, *The War of the Rebellion*, ser. 2, vol. 6, 438, 965.
69 On the history of Camp Sumter, see Ovid L. Futch, *History of Andersonville Prison*, rev. ed. (Gainesville: University Press of Florida, 1999).

Conditions in Andersonville became known in the North in the late summer of 1864, after the Confederate States Army allowed for the release of four inmates who had been deputized by the prisoners to present a petition to President Lincoln. It is likely the Confederates had released the captives with the express intention of publicizing the conditions at Andersonville, so that the federal government would be forced to resume prisoner exchanges. By the fall of 1864, the putrid swamp of Andersonville had made the issue of prisoner-of-war camps politically sensitive, and Hoffman gave Sweet his approval to build new barracks at Camp Douglas. “You are authorized to erect buildings in the prison square, on the ground which is now vacant on the place, and arrange after the manner of those now up, except in the elevation of the floor from the ground, which I think is unnecessarily high,” he wrote. He also demanded that Sweet “make the expense as much under the estimate of $500 to the building as possible, and let the work be completed with as little delay as possible.”[70] By January 1865, the camp was finished, and a report summed up the result:

> The prisoners of war are confined within an area of about forty acres, surrounded by a strong oaken barricade twelve feet [3.7 meters] in height, surmounted by a railed platform for sentinels. The prison barracks are one-storied, ridge-ventilated buildings erected on posts four to six feet [1.2 to 1.8 meters] from the ground, to prevent escape by burrowing. These barracks are sixty-four in number, four of which are for convalescents exclusively: thirty-one have been built since January, 1864. They are arranged in streets of suitable width, and are all of the same dimensions, viz: 90 feet [27.4 meters] long, 24 feet [7.3 meters] wide and about 12 feet [3.7 meters] to eaves.

A remarkable element of the design of the barracks is that each building contained not only a dormitory, measuring 21.5 by 7.3 meters, but also a kitchen, measuring 6 by 7.3 meters. Given the always present danger of wooden barracks burning down, the decision of including a kitchen in each building is unusual, but it did not warrant any explanation in the report. After describing how each dormitory was fitted with three-tier bunks, the report noted that each barrack housed 165 men, “each having a cubic space of 142 [4 cubic meters] and a superficial area of 10 square feet [1 square meter].”[71]

70 William Hoffman, letter to Benjamin J. Sweet, Sept. 13, 1864, in United States, War Department, *The War of the Rebellion*, ser. 2, vol. 7, 834–35.

Such statistics, suggesting a healthy amount of air for every inmate, mattered: in 1865, the barrack stood for a resolve to provide, despite difficult circumstances, shelter that measured up to some minimum standards of humanity. And it appears that, in general, the administrators of Camp Douglas proved able to limit overcrowding to less than 20 percent above the official capacity.

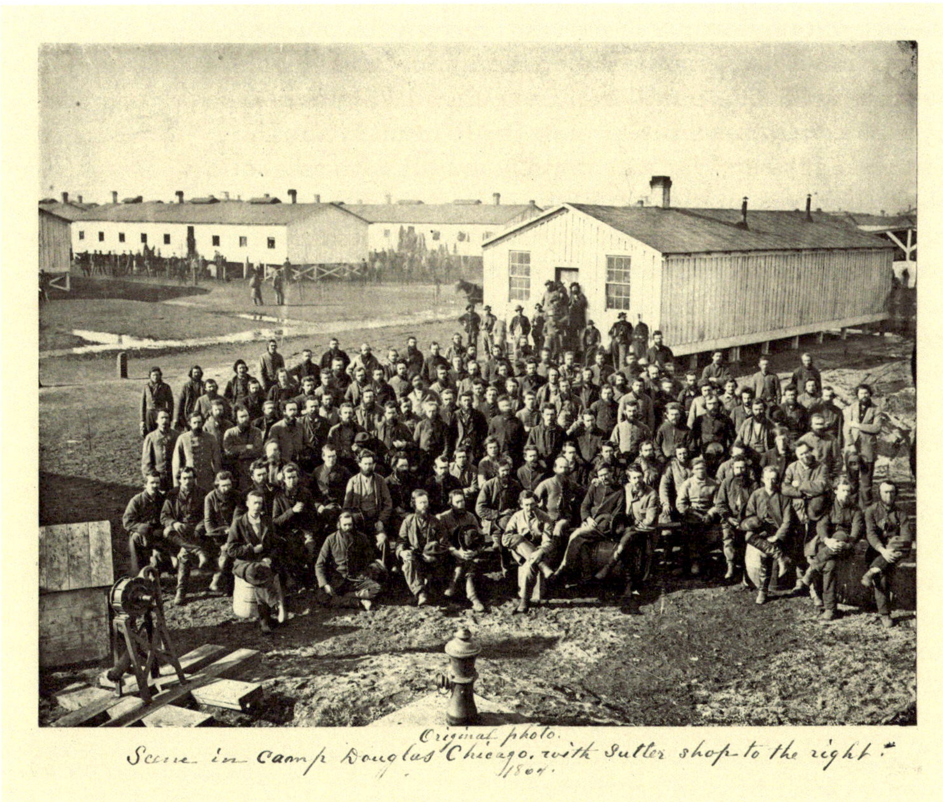

Fig. 16
Prisoners of war in the prison compound of Camp Douglas, 1865. Collection: Chicago Historical Museum.

Camp Douglas showed that a mobilization camp could easily be transformed into a prison camp: one needed only to construct a wall around the barracks, and perhaps a wall between the dormitory and the kitchen, which is, in all places where people are confined, the focus of much attention. It was "Yankee ingenuity" at its best—or perhaps, given the legacy of Camp Douglas—at its worst.

In the second half of the 1860s, the Germans had been willing to learn from the United States when it came to the construction of hospitals. In the fall of 1870, during the Franco-Prussian War, they also took inspiration from places like Rock Island and Camp Douglas. In the wake of the French surrender at Sedan and Metz, the German armies were dealing with increasing numbers

71 In United States, United States Army, Surgeon General, *The Medical and Surgical History of the War of the Rebellion*, vol. 1, pt. 3, 19.

of captured soldiers. While members of the Garde Mobile (nonprofessional soldiers) were typically released and sent home, on the condition that they abstain from further military service until the end of the war, almost 12,000 officers and over 370,000 noncommissioned officers and men of the regular forces were taken by rail to Germany and divided over the various German states, each one obliged to take a share of the prisoners proportional to its population. Prussia took 65 percent of the prisoners, Bavaria 13 percent, Saxony 8.5 percent, Württemberg 5 percent, Baden 3 percent, and so on. By contrast, the total number of German military captured by the French was a little below 8,000 men. While the Franco-Prussian War was fiercely fought with all available resources on the battlefields, neither of the parties in the conflict had a sense of absolute righteousness and an all-or-nothing attitude about each particular outcome. In addition, the International Committee of the Red Cross had official standing in the conflict, and while the ICRC was decades away from obtaining a formal jurisdiction over prisoners of war (secured only by means of the second Hague Convention, in 1907), it was clear to both sides that it had an informal authority to ensure the captured soldiers and officers received lodgings, clothing, food, and medical care of a quality commensurate with their rank—that is, similar to those enjoyed by a person of equivalent rank in the army that held them captive. Also, civil society organizations such as the Oeuvre des Prisonniers Français en Allemagne (Work of the French Prisoners in Germany) were routinely given access to prisoners and the opportunity to support their lives in captivity.[72]

As a rule, officers were permitted to stay in hotels or rent private quarters within the assigned town or city and were given a per diem to support their expenses, which included the services of an orderly. They could live relatively freely and socialize with the local population. Interaction between the lower ranks of the French army and German civilians was not encouraged, perhaps because German civilians in general showed sympathy for the captured soldiers in their communities, taking a special interest in the so-called *Turcos* (Turks), colonial troops from Algeria, Morocco, and Senegal. For most Germans, this was their first encounter with non-Europeans.

72 Manfred Botzenhart, "Französische Kriegsgefangene in Deutschland, 1870/71," *Francia, Forschungen zur Westeuropäischen Geschichte* 2, no. 3 (1994), 13–28.

PRISONNIERS FRANÇAIS DANS LES BARRAQUEMENTS DE FRANCFORT. — Croquis de M. W. A. Beer.

Fig. 17
Wilhelm Amandus Beer, *Turcos* and other French prisoners of war, Prussian guards, and German civilians mixing in the Frankfurt prisoner-of-war depot, *L'Illustration*, 1871. Collection: author.

The captured noncommissioned officers and privates were housed in existing military quarters in fortresses and permanent barracks, which were largely empty as their regular inhabitants were fighting in France. When the capacity of the military infrastructure proved not enough, those charged with taking care of the prisoners began to use government-owned warehouses and stables and even to requisition monasteries that were largely empty because of the dwindling number of monks or friars. After all existing spaces had been filled, the army began to pitch tents to accommodate newly arrived prisoners and, as the cold season approached, to construct barracks in compounds that were at times surrounded by a palisade, or a fence, or in the case of Lechfeld in Bavaria, only by a series of guard posts located at a considerable distance from each other.

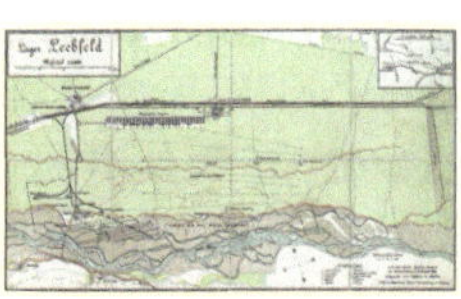

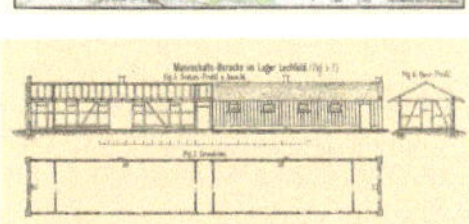

Chapter Four, Figs. 18 and 19
→ p. 183

The city of Koblenz, located in the Rhineland province of Prussia, received the largest concentration of French prisoners of war. In October 1870, 12,000 prisoners arrived to be housed in a tent camp on the Karthause, a hill to the west of the city named after a Carthusian abbey that had stood there for many centuries until its demolition in 1818. A month later, another 10,000 prisoners had arrived, and a second depot equipped with barracks was laid out around and adjacent to two bastions known as Feste Franz (Francis Fortress) on the Petersberg, a steep hill located on the north side of the Mosel river.

→ Fig. 18

At the same time, the Prussian army also commissioned the construction of barracks at the Karthause depot, ensuring that the prisoners would survive the winter. The camp was divided into two compounds, each with its proper barrack. The largest part served as the main depot and contained seventy-six regular barracks that served as dormitories, each for 100 prisoners. They were of a simple design and did not have ridge ventilation. The interior of the barracks had a highly original arrangement: a series of tables and benches, located parallel to and at some distance from the walls, provided each prisoner with his own place to sit; his bed stretched out under the table to the wall. The *Lazareth* (sick bay) was equipped with a more sophisticated barrack, modeled on the one officially prescribed by the Prussian War Ministry. This structure was equipped with ridge ventilation at three locations.

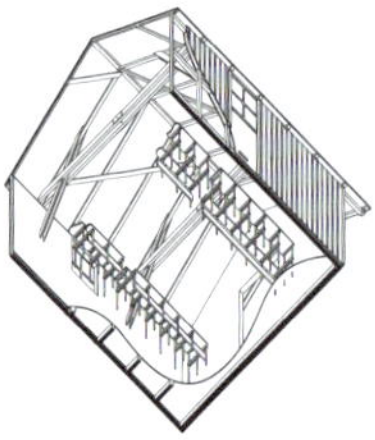

Drawings,
Koblenz Barrack
→ p. 520

→ Fig. 19

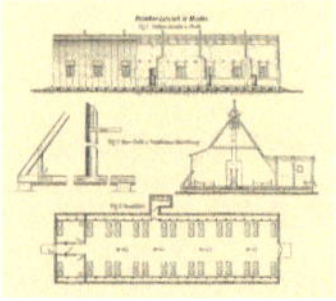

Chapter Eight, Fig. 4
→ p. 327

In the nineteenth-century discourse on the barrack, those created to house the French prisoners in Koblenz and elsewhere were ignored—with one exception. The Prussian fortress town of Minden also became a destination for French prisoners of war. To accommodate sick prisoners, the army constructed a hospital consisting of thirteen barracks based on an A-frame design. While cheap to construct, these barracks had been designed with a highly efficient ventilation system (inspired by Hermann Blankenstein's *Versuchsbaracke* at the Charité Hospital in Berlin), based on the presence of a large air chamber located below the floor. Openings in the wainscoting close to the beds connected to this plenum, and four iron pipes, which were heated by four stoves, created an efficient air movement to pull the foul air from the beds, through the wainscoting into the air chamber, and from there up to the ridge.[73] Thanks to its impressive design, the Minden hospital barrack found a place in many subsequent books on hospital design, including what became, by the end of the nineteenth century, the German-language bible on the topic: Friedrich Oswald Kuhn's *Krankenhäuser* (Hospitals).[74] In addition, and more importantly, the Minden barrack

73 Prussia, Royal Prussian Ministry of War, *Der Sanitätsdienst bei den deutschen Heeren im Kriege gegen Frankreich 1870/71* (Berlin: E. S. Mittler & Sohn, 1884), 392–93.
74 Friedrich Oswald Kuhn, *Handbuch der Architektur, Vierter Theil, 5. Halb-Band, Gebäude fur Heil- und sonstige Wohlfahrts-Anstalten, 1. Heft: Krankenhäuser* (Stuttgart: Arnold Bergsträsser, 1897), 612–14.

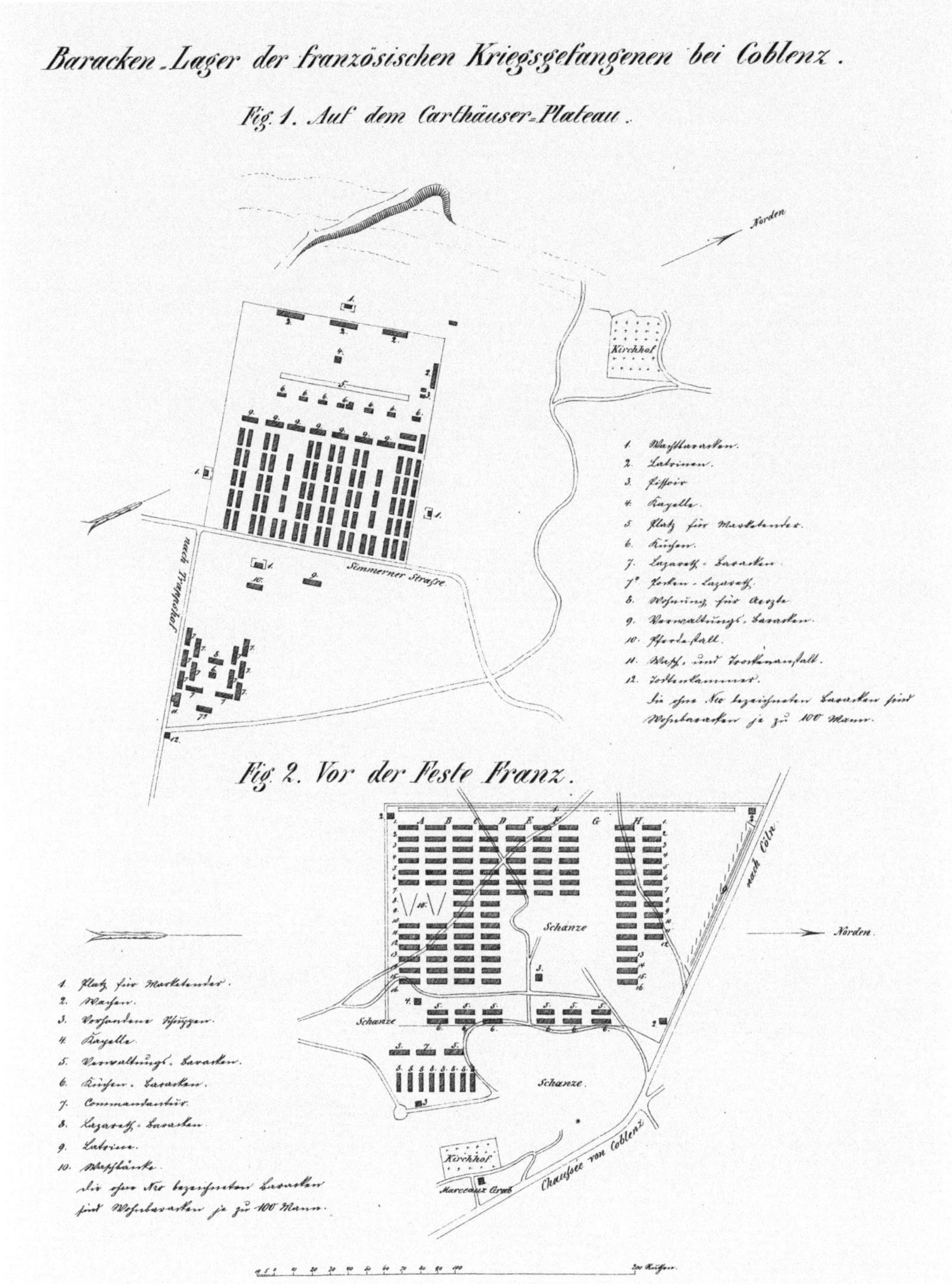

Fig. 18
Plan of the prisoner-of-war depots on the Karthause and the Petersberg, Koblenz, Kingdom of Prussia, 1870. Collection: Landesbibliothekszentrum Rheinland-Pfalz / Rheinische Landesbibliothek, Koblenz, Germany.

came to occupy an important place in the history of this building type—the destruction by fire of five of the barracks on February 27, 1871, confirmed in the eyes of many that the barrack had no future in civilian hospital architecture.

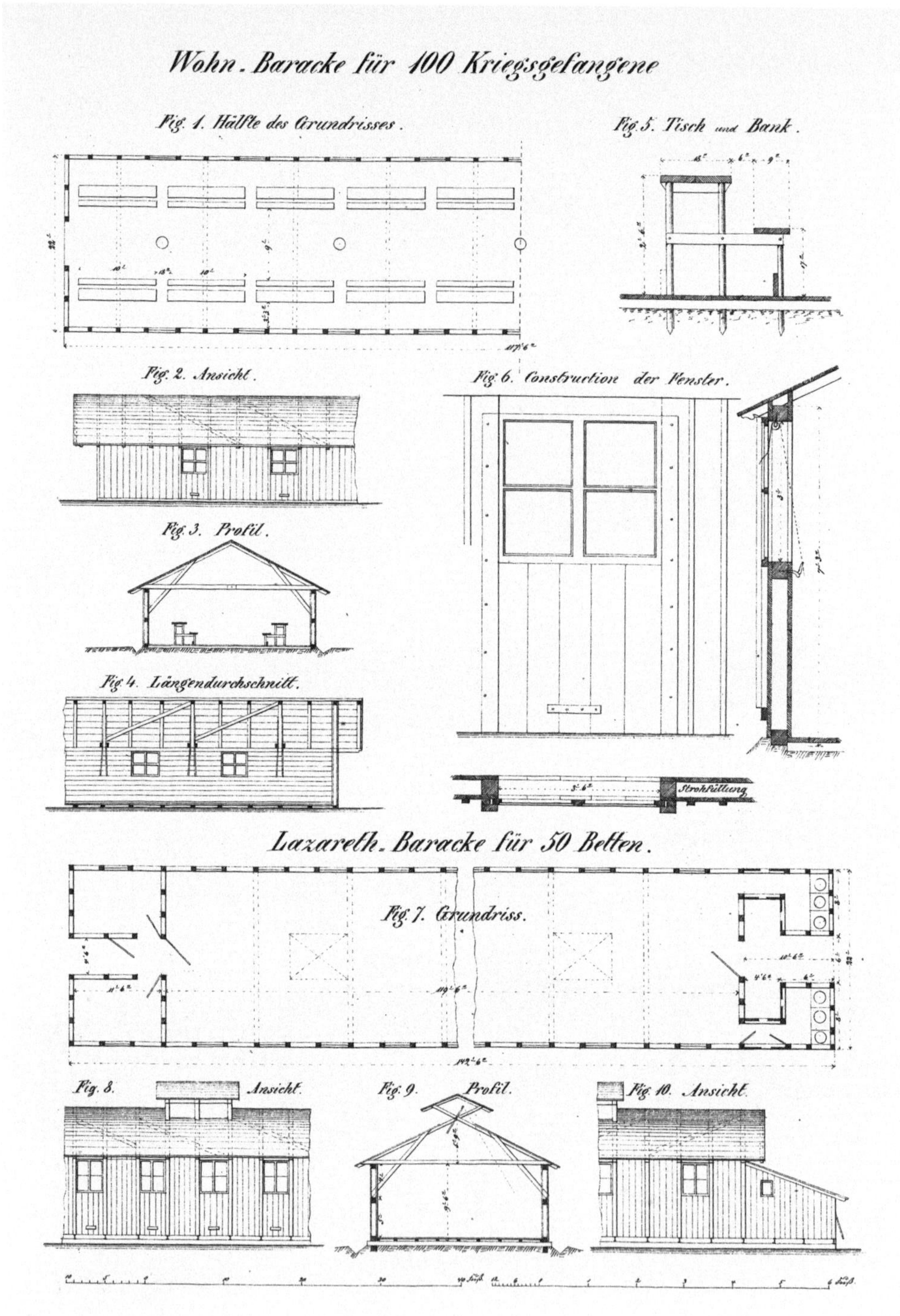

Fig. 19
Plans, sections, and elevations of a prisoner barrack and a hospital barrack of the Karthause prisoner depot, 1870. Collection: Landesbibliothekszentrum Rheinland-Pfalz / Rheinische Landesbibliothek, Koblenz, Germany.

Situations-Plan eines transportabe
Central-Comité der Deutscher
Tracé general d'un Hôpital de pavillons portatifs pour 200 malades.
Le Comité central des associations allemandes de la Croix Rouge (Dr. Menger).
Plan of situation of a p
Central Committee of the
Personal-Baracke.
Pavillon des personnes attachées au service.
Staffs hut.
Баракъ для службы.
Barak for Personalet.
Operations-Baracke.
Pavillon d'operation.
Operation hut.
Операціонный баракъ.
Operations Barak.
10 Kranken-Baracken (No. 1
10 Pavillons de malades (nos. 1—10).
10 Patients huts (No. 1—10.)
10 больничныхъ барако
10 Syge Barakker (N
Pferdebahn.
Tramway.
Tramway.
Конная желѣзная дорога.
Sporvej.
CHR
ХРИСТОФЪ И УНМА

→ p. 475

Baracken-Lazareths für 200 Kranke.

vom Rothen Kreuz (Dr. Menger).

ospital for 200 patients.

associations (Dr. Menger).

Ситуаціонный планъ переноснаго барачнаго лазарета для 200ти больныхъ.

Центральный Комитетъ Германскихъ Обществъ Краснаго Креста (Дръ. Менгеръ).

Situations-Plan over et transportabelt Barak-Hospital for 200 Syge.

Central Komiteen for den tyske Afdeling for Rode Kors (Dr. Menger).

D. Löwenstein, Berlin C.

4 Wirthschafts-Baracken (No. 11-14).

4 Pavillons d'économies (nos. 11–14).
4 Economy huts (No. 11—14)

4 хозяйственные бараки.
4 Economi-Barakker (No. 11—14).

٤ عدد لوازم باراقه لری

Personal-Baracke.

Pavillon des personnes attachées au service.
Staffs hut.
Баракъ для службы.
Barak for Personalet.

(ب) خدمه

Küchen-Baracke.

Pavillon de cuisine.
Kitchen hut.
Кухонный баракъ.
Kökken Barak.

(ب) مطبخ

Desinfection.

Désinfection.
Disinfection.

Дезинфекція.
Desinfection.

& UNMACK.

قريستوفل واونماق

Eleven

The Most Perfect Portable Structures Ever Invented for the Purposes Intended

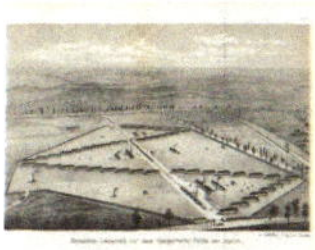

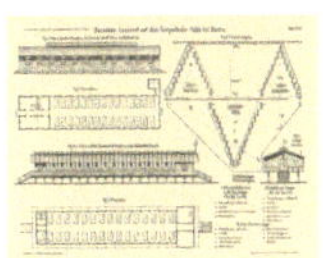

Chapter Seven, Figs. 19 and 20
→ p. 310

Berlin, December 21, 1891. Four volunteer military hospital attendants gather in the early morning frost at the Tempelhof grounds, the onetime site of the famous emergency hospital constructed during the Franco-Prussian War. The men were part of a government pilot program to create a cadre of civilians that could be quickly mobilized for service in military hospitals during war.

→ Fig. 1

The training facility was a hutted hospital consisting of six so-called Doecker barracks manufactured by Christoph & Unmack, a firm originally from Copenhagen but now with a new branch in the German town of Niesky, some 200 kilometers southeast of Berlin.[1] Three of the barracks were sick wards with a capacity of sixteen beds each; one barrack contained an operating room, a pharmacy, a bathroom, and a room for female nurses; one contained an office for the doctors and administrators, two supply rooms, and a lodging for male nurses; the last barrack contained a kitchen, a laundry, and a messroom. The walls and roofs of three of the barracks were made from a material known as *carton-feutre*, or felt cardboard. The remaining structures were covered with a double layer of sailcloth. The purpose of the hospital was to scientifically test, in real-world conditions, the performance of the portable barrack type that had prevailed in a big worldwide competition organized by the International Committee of the Red Cross six years earlier. Did these buildings provide comfort to the patients in all four seasons? What were the comparative

1 The Doecker barrack had been invented by the Danish tentmaker Johan Gerhard Clemens Døcker and marketed in Denmark under its inventor's name. Because the letter *ø* exists only in Danish, Norwegian, and Faroese, it is commonly transcribed as the digraph *oe* or, in the case of German, Swedish, Finnish, Estonian, Hungarian, Turkish, and some other languages, as *ö*. This book refers to the maker of this barrack as "Doecker" and to his creation as the "Doecker barrack."

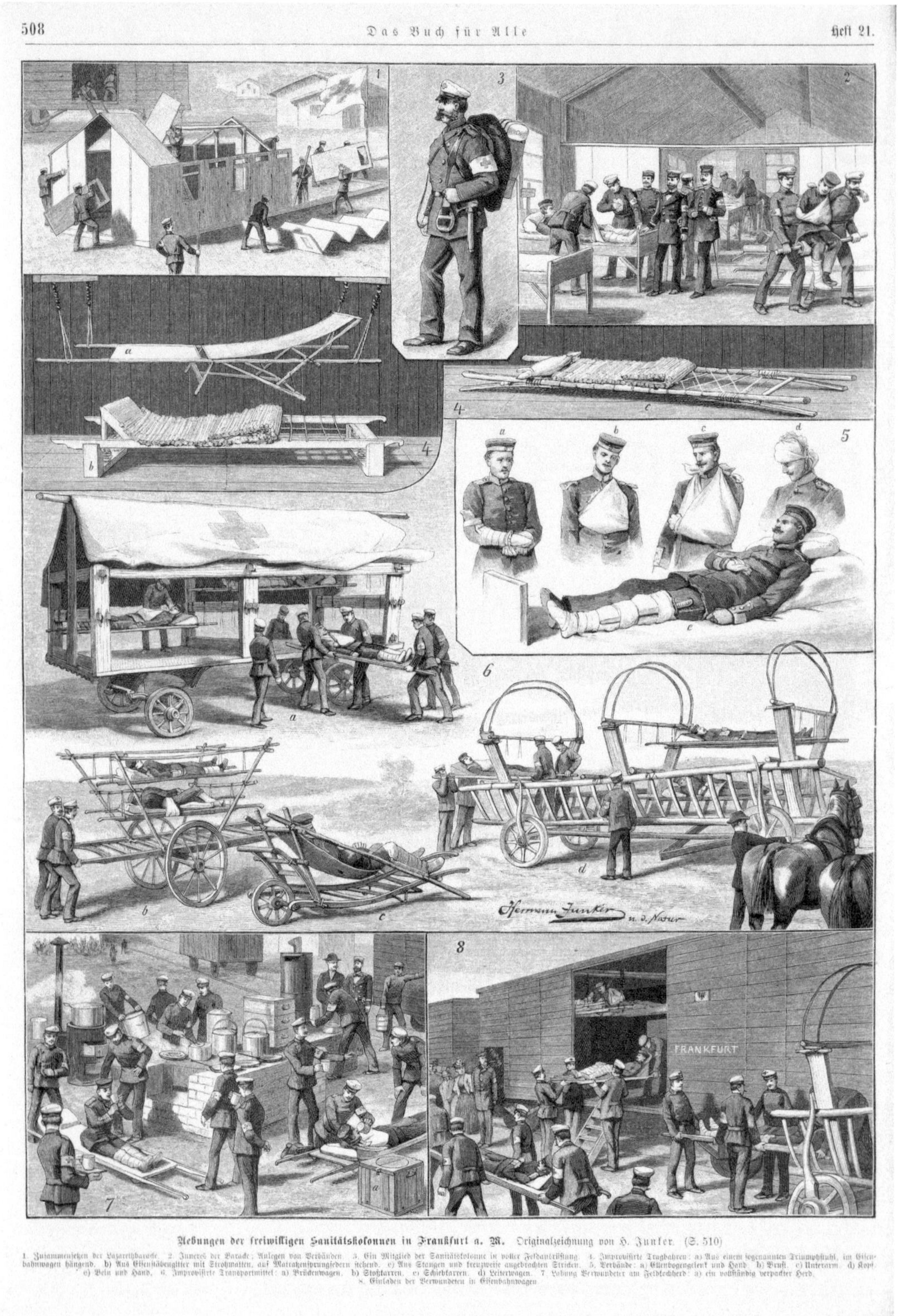

Fig. 1
Hermann Junker, Composite image showing exercises of volunteer military hospital attendants held in Frankfurt am Main. Image 1 shows the assembly of a Doecker barrack. *Das Buch für alle: illustrierte Blätter zur Unterhaltung und Belehrung für die Familie und Jedermann*, 1893. Collection: Bayerische Staatsbibliothek, Munich.

advantages and disadvantages of the felt-cardboard and sailcloth versions? And, very important, could one trust the claim made by the manufacturer that these buildings could be easily put together and taken apart by unskilled labor?[2]

By the middle of December, it had become clear that the barracks were eminently suitable for hospital use, with the ones covered in sailcloth performing somewhat better in the summer, and those in felt cardboard in winter. But the question concerning assembly, disassembly, and reassembly remained. And therefore the four men were to take one of the barracks apart with only the written instructions of the manufacturer as their guide and only a few tools at their disposal. They would then pack the pieces and load them onto three horse-drawn wagons, which would transport them over a 20-kilometer trajectory, consisting of both cobblestone roads and uneven field paths, that would loop back to Tempelhof. There, after their return, the crew was to reconstruct the barrack. One impartial observer was to monitor the whole operation and make a detailed record.[3]

Dismantling the structure proved surprisingly easy: the crew began work at 9:00 a.m., and all the pieces of the building were neatly stored on the site by 3:10 p.m. The next day, it took them from 7:00 a.m. to noon to load and secure the pieces on the wagons; the journey lasted six hours. It took the crew the whole of December 23 and the morning of December 24 to re-erect the building in its original location—it was noted that their reuse of the original foundations did speed up the process of reconstruction. On December 29 and 30, the experiment was partially repeated, when the crew dismantled a barrack covered with *carton-feutre*, which had used the specially designed packing cases for the parts as floorboards. While the disassembly proceeded easily, the crew faced problems with the storage of the parts: after six months of use as floorboards, the packing cases had warped somewhat and did not close tightly anymore. It was clear that Christoph & Unmack had some more work to do.[4]

The disassembly, transport, and reassembly exercise held at Tempelhof capped a two-decade-long search for a workable portable knockdown barrack that had been underway since the Franco-Prussian War. This conflict had been marked by far-reaching technological changes: a dense network of railroads allowed for an unprecedented volume, reach, and speed of mobilization; conscription allowed for an almost unlimited supply of soldiers;

2 Henry Menger, *Das transportabele Baracken-Lazareth zu Tempelhof vom 1. Juli bis 31. Dezember 1891* (Berlin: Central-Comité der deutschen Vereine vom Rothen Kreuz, 1892).
3 Ibid., 29–31.
4 Ibid.

industrialization provided an almost unlimited supply of ever-more destructive arms and ammunition; and the telegraph allowed for fast-moving military operations involving hundreds of thousands of soldiers. The expectation to defeat the enemy with what would be labeled a *Blitzkrieg* (lightning war) in the twentieth century necessitated the concentration of masses of soldiers in relatively tight areas in the crucial weeks before a major attack. In such conditions, there was little opportunity to billet soldiers with civilians, and many soldiers had to spend weeks in open-air bivouacs, where the breakdown in sanitation and personal hygiene, malnutrition, fatigue, and exposure to the elements led to smallpox, dysentery, and typhus epidemics. In the late summer and early fall of 1870, when the 160,000-man Prussian force besieged the French city of Metz, German soldiers began to fall ill in masses; by the middle of October more than 60,000 were too sick to fight. To house the sick and the still healthy, the Prussians began to construct crude huts, but a lack of building materials limited the amount of shelter that could be created. Would that outcome have differed if the frontline force had been equipped with portable knockdown barracks?[5]

Dr. Bernhard von Langenbeck, director of the Clinical Institute for Surgery and Ophthalmology at Berlin's Charité Hospital, served as a military surgeon at the front in 1870. Langenbeck realized that the army's preferred solution to the accumulation of sick and wounded in the area of military operation—evacuation to barrack hospitals in Germany—carried the danger of triggering epidemic diseases among the civilian population.[6] Hence, it was better to quarantine and treat the soldiers where they had fallen ill. Yet very few of the spaces available were suited for use as military hospitals. During the siege of Paris, the palace of Versailles had become a German military hospital, and from many perspectives the spacious building provided ideal conditions: the lofty palace chambers, halls, and galleries offered the 2,000 inmates much air space, and Langenbeck's surgical staff had maintained the highest standards of hygiene. Nevertheless, there had been a progressive increase of pyemia and septicemia, causing 59 percent of all deaths.[7] A final complication was the fact that the military surgeons and medics could not rely on support from the men in the fighting units. Key to Prussian military tactics was speed, and if in earlier days frontline units remained for a shorter or longer time in the same area as the wounded, now they quickly moved on, in a war of movement. When surgeons and

5 See Adolph Goetze, *Feldzug 1870–71: Die Thätigkeit der deutschen Ingenieure und technischen Truppen in deutsche-französischen Kriege 1870–71* (Berlin: Mittler und Sohn, 1872), 158–59; G. Paulus, *Die Cernirung von Metz: Auf Befehl der K. General-Inspection des Ingenieur-Corps und der Festungen unter Benutzung amtlicher Quellen bearbeitet* (Berlin: Schneider, 1875).

6 During the 1870–71 campaign, the Germans suffered 5,000 cases of smallpox, 39,000 cases of dysentery, and almost 75,000 cases of typhus. See Bernhard von Langenbeck, Alwin Gustav Edmund von Coler, and Friedrich Emil Otto Werner, *Die transportable Lazareth-Baracke*, 2nd ed. (Berlin: Hirschwald, 1890), 39.

7 Carl Kirchner, *Aerztlicher Bericht über das königlich preussische Feld-Lazareth im Palast zu Versailles während der Belagerung von Paris vom 19. September 1870 bis 5. März 1871 von seinem Chefarzte* (Erlangen: Enke, 1872), 17.

medics began to organize the housing and treatment of casualties, they found themselves dependent on their own resources.

Managing the crisis as well as he could, Langenbeck did not articulate at that time a solution to the problem. But Russian physician Nikolai Ivanovich Pirogov had become convinced that medical units assisting the wounded had to be completely self-reliant. In the fall of 1870, he traveled as an observer of the Russian Red Cross to Germany and France. After his review of all that had happened, Pirogov came to a simple conclusion: "International help either arrives at the battlefield fully equipped—that is, with its own field hospitals, doctors, nurses, and aides—or it should stay away." This meant that aid societies like the Red Cross had to stockpile tents for summer use and portable barracks for winter use in peacetime. Pirogov noted that such preparations might also carry dividends when there were no hostilities, as nations also faced catastrophes during peace, such as railway accidents, epidemics, and so on. "In summary," Pirogov wrote, "may the societies undertake the organization of such a mobile hospital building that can be easily kept in any locality, and that can be easily transported to wherever there is a need."[8]

Chapter Ten, Figs. 3 and 4
→ p. 405

The concept that temporary hospitals might play a key role during emergencies such as epidemics had been around since the 1770s, and the precedent of the hutted quarantine stations as *Kontumaz* erected in the Pannonian Plain in the 1790s and elsewhere in the Austrian Empire afterward was well known. In Britain, which was at the forefront in recognizing that prevention of epidemics was a significant if not critical responsibility of the state, the Public Health Act (1848), the Nuisances Removal and Diseases Prevention Consolidation and Amendment Act (1855), and the Contagious Diseases Act (1864) had created the legal, financial, and physical infrastructure that obliged physicians and officials to immediately report any outbreak of epidemic disease, and to sequester the afflicted—in their own dwellings if possible but otherwise in isolation wards in general hospitals, in isolation pavilions built on the grounds of general hospitals, in isolation hospitals that accommodated patients from all infectious diseases, or in isolation hospitals that specialized in one infectious disease. By 1870 a network of mostly smaller isolation hospitals had begun to arise in Britain.[9] Pirogov knew of these developments, but he pushed the envelope by insisting on the creation of stockpiles of appropriate tents and prefabricated barracks, which would allow for a

8 Nikolai Ivanovich Pirogov, *Bericht über die Besichtigung der Militär-Sanitätsanstalten in Deutschland, Lothringen und Elsass im Jahre 1870*, trans. N. Iwanoff (Leipzig: F. C. W. Vogel, 1871), 138, 142.

9 See Iacob Félix, "Sur la nécessité et l'installation des hôpitaux d'isolement," *VI. Internationaler Congress für Hygiene und Demographie zu Wien 1887, Heft 15: Arbeiten der hygienischen Sectionen* (Vienna: Verlag der Organisations-Commission des Congresses, 1887), 1–48; Great Britain, Hospitals Commission, *Report of the Commissioners Appointed to Inquire Respecting Small-Pox and Fever Hospitals* (London: Eyre and Spottiswoode, 1882).

planned construction of temporary hospitals at short notice, instead of the common, reactive, and utterly frantic attempts to cobble together, as Antoine Demoget had done in Metz, an emergency hospital with whatever lumber, canvas, or corrugated metal might be at hand. Implied in his proposal was a technical requirement that earlier designers and manufacturers of prefabricated barracks such as the Gloucester contracter William Eassie had not faced before: they had to be shelters that could be easily assembled from prefabricated parts, disassembled, and most importantly, reassembled at another place without any loss of their performance.

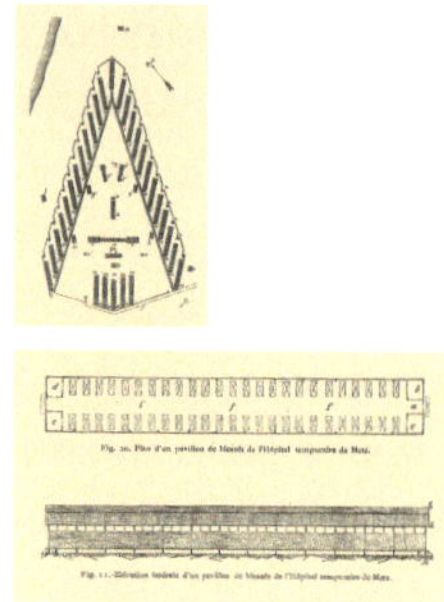

Chapter Seven, Figs. 2 and 3
→ p. 283

At the time when Pirogov articulated this idea, Johann Friedrich August von Esmarch urged various builders to develop designs for a prefabricated barrack that could be deployed at short notice. Paul Risold had produced an at first sight viable concept, but no prototype had been constructed. The Dutch Red Cross, established in 1867, had commissioned the design and production of such a prefabricated portable barrack, which had shown great success during a typhus epidemic in the Dutch coastal village of Egmond aan Zee in 1871 (discussed in Chapter Eight).[10] However, the costs associated with this structure's deployment were deemed to have been unacceptably high. A senior member of the Dutch Red Cross, Hendrik N. C. Baron van Tuyll van Serooskerken, who in 1870 had led a team deployed to provide medical assistance in the Franco-Prussian War, doubted the viability of a prefabricated barrack as a tool of humanitarian intervention. "It served well during the epidemic, but I must not mince my words, and I must be frank to those who love barracks and who believe that when you have such a building, and have paid the bills, the disease will be defeated." The reality of the deployment of the Red Cross barrack had been fraught, he recalled. Not only were the costs of transport and construction much steeper than anticipated, but in addition there was "the expense of dismantling again, the journey back, storage, disinfecting, and a complete reconstruction with repairs, which again generated bills *that make one tremble*, and when one adds up all the expenses, our *barak* cost so much, that for the same amount of money, three of them could be constructed from scratch in a few days."[11] Unable to carry the escalating costs of the barrack, the Dutch Red Cross decided that it had better get rid of the building and successfully transferred it to the municipality of The Hague, which re-erected it as a permanent isolation pavilion for infectious diseases.

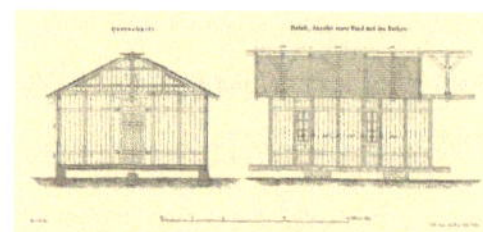

Chapter Six, Fig. 19
→ p. 269

10 Hendrik Linse, Martin Fredrik Onnen, and Nicolaas Bernhard Donkersloot, *De Waarde der Barakken, als Tijdelijke of Duurzame Verblijfplaats ter Verpleging van Zieken* (Dordrecht: H. R. van Elk, 1872), 12.

11 Hendrik Nicolaas Cornelis Baron van Tuyll van Serooskerken, *Waarschuwende Stem aan mijn Vaderland* (The Hague: M. M. Couvée, 1873), 13–14.

Yet within the Dutch Red Cross, there were still some who believed that a prefabricated barrack was a magical solution to the problem of health care during war and epidemics, and that one should have another try, creating an improved version of the type deployed at Egmond. Tuyll told the board to forget it. The Dutch Red Cross had no business spending any more money trying to perfect an inherently flawed concept. "If it comes down to it, I will, with the help of a few agile carpenters, build you in a couple of days an efficient barrack, and in the days that follow I'll provide you with models galore to make your choice from. So save your money: it can be spent more usefully."[12]

Pirogov's view was not much different: he also believed that it didn't make sense to seek to develop a perfect prefabricated barrack on the basis of the standard types deployed in the past decade. Instead, he proposed, the Central Asian yurt might provide a perfect model: "In a difficult and complicated situation, such as the accommodation of the sick during war, one cannot look down on any means, no matter how crude and *original* it may be."[13] In 1870–71 Pirogov did not know the yurt from his own experience. But at that time he did know that, consisting of a self-supporting wooden circular lattice frame carrying a set of rafters covered with wool felt, it could be assembled and disassembled in a couple of hours. As the felt was dimensionally stable, it did not need to be in tension to provide an effective cover, and hence a felt-covered yurt didn't require the ropes and tent poles that provide structure to the fabric, allowing it to keep its shape and withstand loads.

During the Russo-Turkish War of 1877–78, Pirogov, then sixty-seven years old, volunteered his services, which included conducting many hundreds of surgical operations and organizing field hospitals. One day he found himself in the company of Colonel Alexander Vasilyevich, Baron von Kaulbars, who had served the preceding decade in the Central Asian regions of the Russian Empire. Pirogov remembered the yurt and began to question him about his experience with that form of shelter. Kaulbars responded that he had spent many winter months in yurts, found them warm and comfortable, and offered to send a telegram to the governor of the Orenburg district, 1,500 kilometers southeast of Moscow, to obtain some yurts. Pirogov accepted the offer, and half a year later yurts began to arrive at both the Bulgarian and Anatolian fronts. They proved a great success, and when Grand Duke Sergei Alexandrovich, son of Tsar Alexander II, sojourned in a yurt during the

12 Ibid., 15.
13 Pirogov, *Bericht über die Besichtigung*, 143.

campaign, they were seen as positively fashionable. Pirogov now became an informed advocate of their use: "Based on all these facts, I think it is necessary that in the future, the Medical Administration [of the army] and the society of the Red Cross will own in their depots a constant and large supply of yurts."[14]

However, the deployment of yurts was not without its critics. The regional Red Cross commissioner Nikolai Savvich Abaza, who had organized medical services in what is today southern Ukraine, remembered them as a poor solution to the problem of providing instant shelter. "Kyrgyz yurts, so persistently recommended by N. I. Pirogov, were used in our district only in the Orenburg-sponsored infirmary, and only for a short time, from August to October. We can therefore say nothing about their practical suitability and will confine ourselves to one observation made by us, that during and long after the rain, their ventilation is even more unsatisfactory than in tents; but besides, wet felt emits a rather strong and nasty smell, which of course cannot be listed among the advantages of yurts."[15] The structures may have had a bad odor, but in 1882 when the Russian Red Cross contributed a special pavilion at the All-Russia Industrial and Art Exhibition in Moscow, it displayed yurts at its entrance.

14 Nikolai Ivanovich Pirogov, *Das Kriegs-Sanitäts-Wesen und die Privat-Hülfe auf dem Kriegsschauplatze in Bulgarien und im Rücken der operirenden Armee 1877–78*, trans. Wilhelm Roth and Anton Schmidt (Leipzig: F. C. W. Vogel, 1882), 20.

15 Nikolai Savvich Abaza, *Krasnyi Krest v tylu deistvuyushchei armii v 1877–1878*, 3 vols. (Saint Petersburg: Rossiiskoe obshchestvo Krasnogo Kresta, 1880–82), 1:47.

Fig. 2
Yurts to be used for emergency hospitals displayed at the Red Cross pavilion at the 1882 All-Russia Industrial and Art Exhibition, Moscow, *Niva*, 1882. Collection: National Library of Russia, Moscow.

An article published in *Niva* magazine explained: "These yurts are the most ordinary, well known, portable dwellings of nomads, only inside they are furnished and adapted to serve as infirmaries for the sick and wounded. Undoubtedly, they have a huge advantage over tents and canvas barracks."[16]

The 1882 exhibition did not include a portable barrack inspired by the yurt, which could and ought to have been a game changer. In the mid-1870s, the Russian military engineer in charge of the Caucasus region, Major General Pyotr Fyodorovich Rerberg, was working on a design for a prefabricated barrack that offered space for ten patients, was usable in both summer and winter, was resistant to storms, allowed for long storage without any deterioration, and was light and low-cost. This barrack measured 7 by 7 meters in plan, with walls 2.6 meters high and a total height of 5.6 meters.

Fig. 3
Pyotr Fyodorovich Rerberg, Plan, section, and details of a design for a prefabricated barrack, 1875, from his *Perenosnyi barak dlya bol'nykh*, 1896. Collection: National Library of Russia, Moscow.

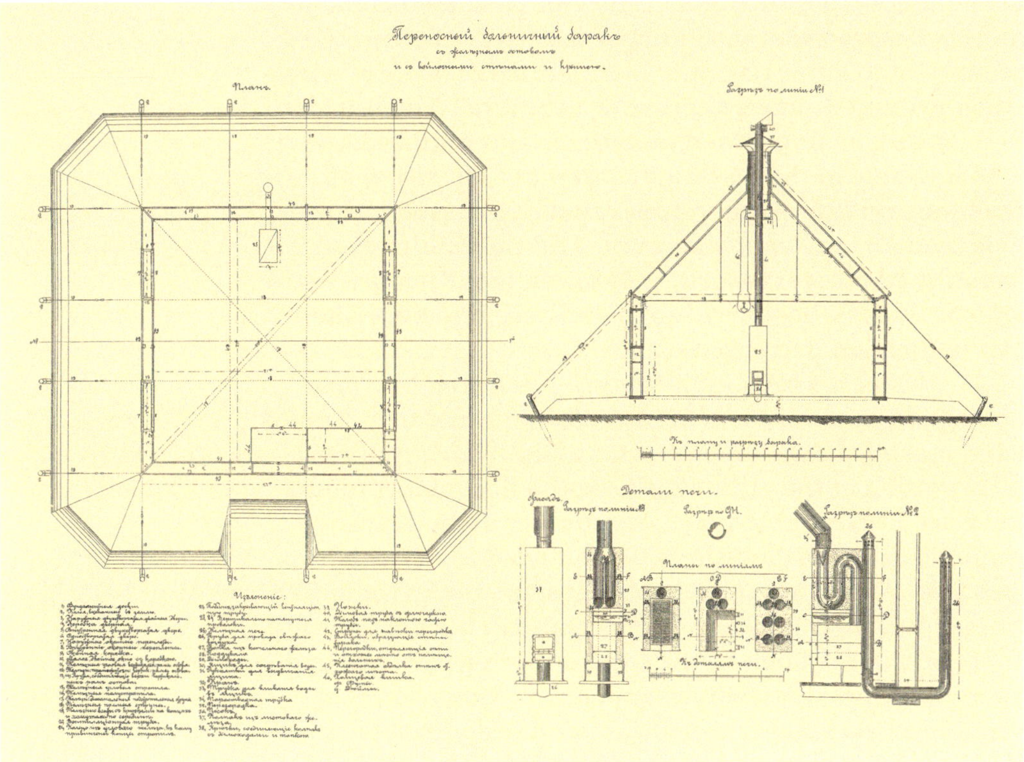

Its inspiration in size and in structure was the yurt, but it had a square plan rather than a circle and a wire mesh grate taking the place of the latticework that provided the structure of the walls onto which the felt cover was attached. While in a yurt the lattice wall was not only self-supporting but also strong enough to carry the rafters and the roof, in Rerberg's version the wire-mesh grate did not have such structural strength and had to be supported by an assembly of twelve iron frames that

16 "Vserossiiskaya promyshlenno-khudozhestvennaya vystavka," *Niva* 13 (1882), 666.

were bolted together and screwed on four foundation boards. Two layers of wire-mesh grating, one on the outside and one on the inside, covered this structure, and fastened to each of these two layers were large panels of felt: four triangular ones for the roof, and one for each of the walls, with windows and the door cut out. Canvas strips sown to the felt panels allowed them to be firmly tied to the wire mesh. The inner felt layer could be painted white, which made the surface washable, or covered with white canvas, which could be removed for disinfection. Offering 14 cubic meters of space per patient, the barrack met minimum medical standards, while it was both relatively light and inexpensive. The elements of one barrack could be transported on two four-wheeled carts, while those of four barracks fit into one railway freight wagon.[17]

In 1875 Rerberg constructed two prototypes at his headquarters in Tbilisi, Georgia. The only problem he encountered was a sagging of the felt roof when the accumulated snow began to melt. An extra layer of wire-mesh grating seemed to provide a solution. The Russian Red Cross was impressed with the result and selected it as its entry in the 1876 International Exposition of Hygiene and Life-Saving Apparatus in Brussels, where it earned an honorable mention. And then it dropped from the historical record, only to reappear twenty years later in a small book written by Rerberg and published by the Russian Red Cross.

Rerberg's revolutionary prefabricated barrack, employing an unprecedented combination of iron frame, wire-mesh grating, and felt, was a highly original reinterpretation of the yurt. It offered the first viable model for a prefabricated barrack. Its sudden disappearance would create the conditions that allowed the Doecker barrack to become, more than a decade later, in the 1880s, a market leader. Rerberg did not publish his design until 1896, and in his book he did not mention why there had been no follow-up twenty years earlier. However, the sad fate of the hasty competition for a prefabricated portable barrack organized by the Saint Petersburg Society of Architects in May 1877 (see Chapter Nine) explains the silence: without the endorsement of the Russian Ministry of War, it had proven to be a pointless exercise.

One of the outcomes of the Russo-Turkish War was the Austro-Hungarian occupation of Bosnia–Herzegovina—an act that created Serbian resentment, which would lead to the 1914 assassination of the Habsburg heir Archduke Franz Ferdinand and his wife by a Serbian

17 Pyotr Fyodorovich Rerberg, *Perenosnyi barak dlya bol'nykh* (Saint Petersburg: Rossiiskoe obshchestvo Krasnogo Kresta, 1896), 6–12.

nationalist in Sarajevo: shots that triggered World War I. In the summer of 1878, when the 80,000-man-strong Austro-Hungarian army got orders to occupy the territory, it was badly prepared for what turned out to be an unusually cold and wet fall. The military planners in Vienna had assumed that the army would bivouac under the heavens until the onset of winter and had not prepared for other accommodation in the sparsely populated and mountainous territory. While there were Turkish military buildings in the larger towns, they were in a very bad state of repair and did not offer enough space. Because of the hostility of the majority of the population, billeting appeared irresponsible.

The Austro-Hungarian army was to construct barracks. However, in addition to a lack of building materials, especially lumber, there were no workers to cut wood or mills to saw it. With winter approaching, the Ministry of War in Vienna decided to investigate the option of using prefabricated barracks.[18] Austrian civil engineer Carl Völckner had developed on paper a system that used as its key element a bent iron I beam that, bolted to a second one, produced an oval-shaped arch with a width of 6.5 meters and a height of 4.4 meters.

18 Franz Rieger, "Ueber den Bau von Baracken in Bosnien und der Herzegowina während der ersten Periode der Occupation dieser Länder," in *Mittheilungen über Gegenstände des Artillerie- und Genie-Wesens, herausgegeben vom k. k. technischen und administrativen Militär-Comite* 14 (1883), 327–92; also Paul Myrdacz, *Sanitätsgeschichte und Statistik der Occupation Bosniens und der Hercegowina im Jahre 1878* (Vienna and Leipzig: Urban and Schwarzenberg, 1882).

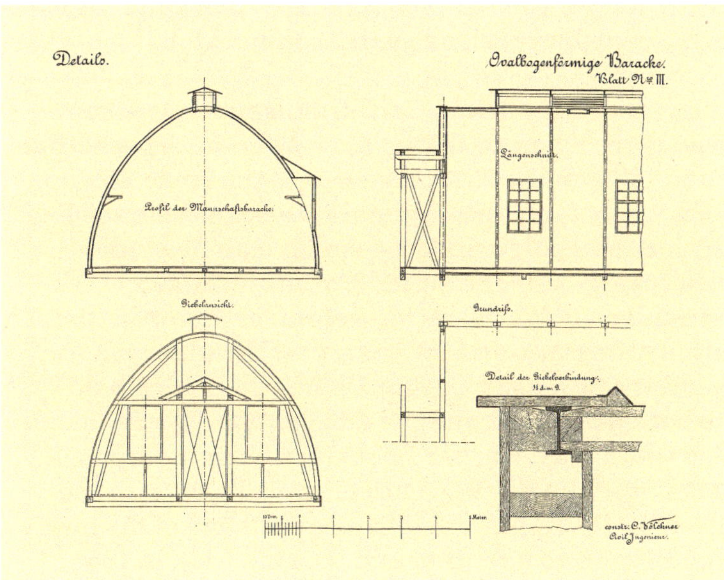

Fig. 4
Carl Völckner, Partial plan, elevation, sections, and construction detail of the second version of a portable barrack, from his *Die ovalbogenförmige Kriegsbaracke der k. k. österreichischen Armee*, 1878. Collection: Medizinische Universität Wien.

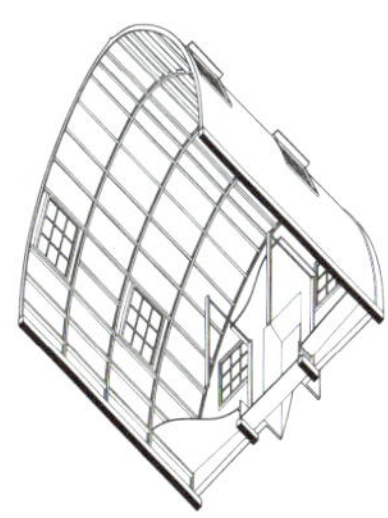

Drawings, Völckner Barrack
→ p. 520

Twenty-one arches, connected by I beams and erected at 1.5 meters distance from each other, were to make an iron skeleton for a barrack, 31.4 meters in length, housing eighty soldiers. The construction did not use the tie beams and struts that commonly strengthen the open roof structure in conventional barracks. Völckner noted that their top surfaces collected dust, which easily produced dust clouds, infecting the air inside. Hence the vaulted interior of his barrack was to provide a much healthier environment than ordinary types did.

Völckner assumed the army would locally source boards to provide a skin. Yet it quickly became clear that this might be difficult, and that the roof materials would have to be included in the shipment, increasing the total weight of all the elements for a single barrack to 30,000 kilograms. Völckner now designed a second version that used much lighter I beams and came with a covering made of jute panels soaked in rubber—a product undoubtedly inspired by the waterproof fabric developed half a century earlier by the Scottish chemist Charles Macintosh for use in raincoats. This version of the barrack weighed a "mere" 14,000 kilograms. Both the heavy and light versions were equipped with windows and ridge ventilation. The Ministry of War ordered sixty-nine of the heavy barracks and a greater number of those covered with jute, but delays in production and delivery meant that a whole division found itself without decent shelter when winter arrived in Bosnia–Herzegovina. This experience led Völckner to a simple conclusion: prefabricated barracks should be produced before the need arose for them, so that they could be dispatched by train, barge, and cart when required. Despite his best efforts, he never received such a commission.[19]

Danish tentmaker Johan Gerhard Clemens Doecker proved more adept in selling his invention in peacetime. Born in 1828 on the Nissumgaard estate, some 25 kilometers west of Aarhus, Denmark, Doecker belonged to the landed gentry, and as a young man he studied agriculture in Aalborg. In 1848, at the outbreak of the First Schleswig War, Doecker volunteered for the Danish Army. By the war's end he was a first lieutenant in the cavalry. It was a good war for Denmark—which held on to both Schleswig and the adjacent Duchy of Holstein. It also was a good war for Doecker, who found himself billeted near the Schleswig town of Padborg with the Jensen family. Doecker fell in love with one of his host's daughters, Anne Kristina, and they married in 1851.[20] At the end of the war, the couple bought a small estate in Schleswig. The Doeckers lived a relatively tranquil life until 1863, when Denmark's king, Frederik VII, who was also Duke of Schleswig and Duke of Holstein, died without a son. In the dynastic confusion that followed his death, the pro-German Frederik August, Duke of Augustenburg, proclaimed himself Duke of Schleswig-Holstein, an act that was resisted by the new king of Denmark, Christian IX, who considered himself the rightful heir

19 Carl Völckner, *Die ovalbogenförmige Kriegsbaracke der k. k. österreichischen Armee: Ein Beitrag zur Lösung der Barackenfrage* (Vienna: Carl Gerold's Sohn, 1878).
20 Knud Peter Petersen and Laurits Christian Petersen, *Slægtsbog og Slægtstavler* (Odense: Petersen, 1918); "Johan Gerhard Clemens Døcker," *Dansk Biografisk Lexikon*, ed. Povl Engelstoft and Svend Dahl, 2nd ed., 27 vols. (Copenhagen: Gyldenhal, 1933–34), 6:170.

to Schleswig and Holstein. In response to Frederik August's proclamation, Christian IX signed a new constitution that fully incorporated within the Danish kingdom the hitherto autonomous Duchy of Schleswig. The German Confederation had a *casus belli*, and on February 1, 1864, Prussian and Austrian troops invaded Schleswig. As it had sixteen years earlier, the Danish army rushed to strengthen the ancient Danevirke defense line with hastily constructed hutted camps that followed the proven designs taught in the military academy.

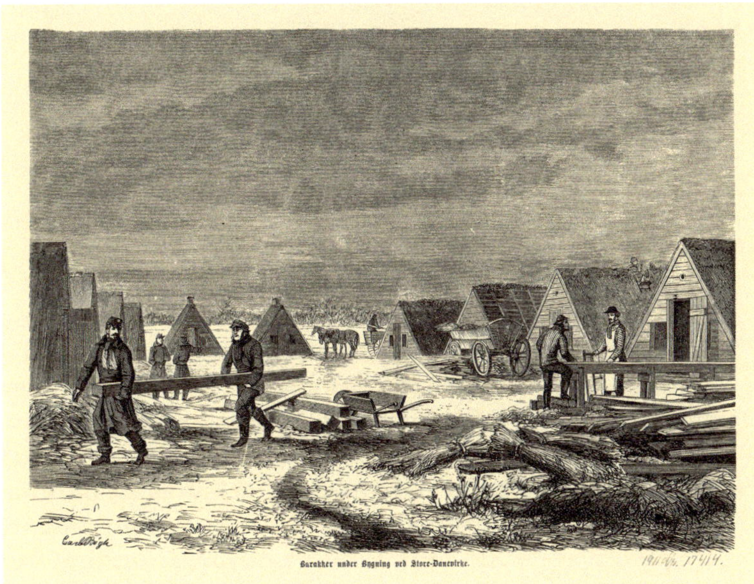

Fig. 5
Carl Henrik Bøgh, Barracks under construction at Danevirke, Schleswig, Denmark (today Schleswig-Holstein, Germany), *Illustreret Tidende*, 1864. Collection: Kongelige Bibliotek, Copenhagen.

Thirty-five-year-old Doecker rejoined the Danish army and fought with distinction. But his gallantry did not prevent a catastrophe for Denmark: it lost the Duchies of Schleswig and Holstein. Demobilized, with the honorary rank of *Ritmester* (cavalry captain), Doecker found himself now under Prussian rule. He decided to move to Copenhagen. After selling his estate at a huge loss, he faced poverty, with only a small army pension as a regular source of income. However, as a former military officer, he knew something about tents and established the Døckerske Teltbyggeri (Doecker's Tent Construction), which for the first decade of its operation proved a marginal business. A lack of financial success did not lessen Doecker's ambition. Knowing the needs of the army well, he began to investigate the possibility of creating some hybrid of a tent, a yurt, and a barrack, to be used by the army's medical corps. Doecker's *filttelt* (felt tent) consisted of rectangular frames, 80 centimeters by 190 centimeters, that could be clipped together by a system of rabbeting, screw fastenings, and clamps, all numbered according to the sequence in which they should be applied.

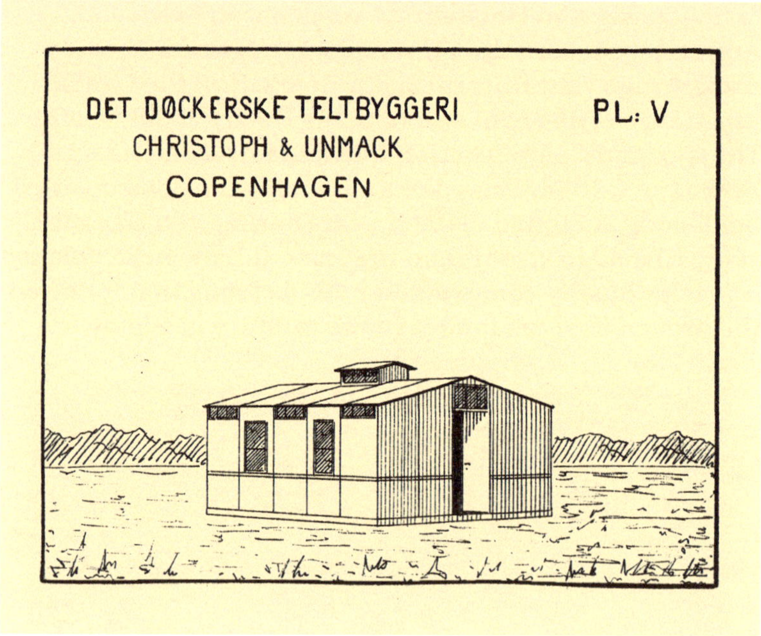

Fig. 6
Johan Gerhard Clemens Doecker, Perspective of the first-generation *filttelt* (felt tent), 1880s. Collection: Geheimes Staatsarchiv Preussischer Kulturbesitz, Dahlem, Berlin.

The frames were covered with *carton-feutre* (felt cardboard)—a lightweight but very rigid sheet of highly dense felt pressed on a base of canvas and impregnated with linseed oil. This material combined the thermal qualities of felt with the rigidity of thick cardboard or plywood and, with a few coats of linseed oil, was not only waterproof but also easily cleaned. In the wake of Sir John Simon's observation that the rate of infectious diseases such as erysipelas and hospital gangrene had dropped after the hospital ship HMS *Dreadnought* was replaced by a ship that had not been used to house the sick, physicians had come to the conclusion that unpainted wood was not a proper material for barracks designed for medical use. And painted wooden surfaces still offered a problem at the tongue-and-groove joints between the individual boards, where infectious substances were believed to hide. The smooth, linseed-oil impregnated sheets of *carton-feutre* used by Doecker did not have any grooves and also could be easily wiped down. The antimicrobial properties of linseed oil were, at that time, not known.[21]

Chapter Three, Fig. 15
→ p. 145

There were additional advantages. Doecker's *filttelt* was easy to set up, dismount, and transport. Because the structures were self-supporting, they did not need the ropes or cables that provide stability to tents but also increase the space each tent occupies. Without the need of such guylines, a field of a given size could accommodate significantly more people when they were housed in Doecker barracks instead of ordinary tents. In 1881 Doecker applied for a patent.[22] A year later,

21 Christan Rudolf Unmack, "Døcker Sygebarakker," *Ugeskrift for Laeger* 16 (1887), 318–19.
22 Kristian Grøn, "Notiser fra Kjøbenhavn of Strassburg," *Norsk Magazin för Laegevidenskapen* 13 (1883), 516.

his *filttelt* earned a gold medal at the agricultural exhibition in Aalborg, and Danish magazines and newspapers began to pay attention to Doecker's obviously useful invention.[23]

As a tent manufacturer, Doecker had shown his inventiveness by moving away from canvas to felt as the key material of his tent-barrack hybrid. But he had no equipment to bring the building into production. For this purpose he approached the firm of Christoph & Unmack. Born in 1846 in Southern Jutland, Denmark, Christian Ferdinand Christoph belonged to the Moravian brothers Protestant sect and, like many Moravian brothers, had trained as a carpenter. In the mid-1860s he worked as a journeyman in the Netherlands and Germany, but he returned to Denmark and, in 1869, opened a furniture workshop in Copenhagen. Christoph went into partnership with Christian Rudolf Unmack, a master carpenter and architect who specialized in the design of farm buildings and small manor houses. In the summer of 1882, Christoph & Unmack helped Doecker manufacture twenty-five barracks for trial use at the Danish military base on Amager, an island located in the Sound (Øresund). At this time, Doecker's barrack was still extremely simple, comprising identically sized panels, containing either a full window, a small ventilation window, or no window at all, that could be combined to create the side walls, while the gables consisted of two different trapezoidal panels (corner and connecting) and a central panel containing a door with a window above it. The barracks passed the test: they were erected in a few hours by unskilled labor, proved sturdy and comfortable, and were easily taken down.

Now the de facto collaborative of Doecker and Christoph & Unmack began to move boldly ahead. In 1883 the partners decided to move onto the international stage by exhibiting a *filttelt* at the International Fisheries Exhibition in London. There it attracted the attention of English civil engineer Robert Rawlinson, who during the Crimean War, together with Dr. John Sutherland, had undertaken an in-depth study of the performance of William Eassie's barracks. Rawlinson was more than impressed. He noted in a lecture: "To my belief, the Doecker hospital huts are, so far as I know, the most perfect portable structures ever invented for the purposes intended."[24] Rawlinson's endorsement was welcome, but the enthusiastic response to the exhibition of the Doecker *filttelt* at the Allgemeine Deutsche Ausstellung auf dem Gebiete der Hygiene und des Rettungswesen (General German Exhibition of Hygiene and Safety) in

23 A basic text on the evolution of the Doecker barrack is Heinrich Wurm, "Die Industrialisierung des Holzhausbaues: Christoph und Unmack," *Tradition: Zeitschrift für Firmengeschichte und Unternehmerbiographie* 14, nos. 3–4 (July 1969), 198–211.
24 Robert Rawlinson, as quoted in "New Inventions, Article 3166: Doecker's Patent Portable Hospitals," *London Medical Record* 12 (1884), 419.

Berlin made all the difference. The building earned a gold medal, and Doecker received a medal.[25]

In his review of the exhibition, one of the most prominent military surgeons in Germany, Wilhelm August Roth, expressed particular admiration for Doecker's barrack. Roth's opinion mattered; he had followed barrack development since the Franco-Prussian War, and he knew the problems with the building type. Ease and speed of construction were essential to the utility of the prefabricated barrack. "Depending on the number of people, assembly and disassembly of the building, including unpacking and packing, takes between ½ and 3 hours; it is even possible to do so when wet, thanks to the air spaces between the frames." Referring to Pirogov's account of Mr. Johnson's *palatki* (summer hospital barracks, discussed in Chapter Nine), built in Odessa during the Russo-Turkish War of 1877–78, Roth noted that the Johnson barracks were easily damaged when setting up and pulling down, and had required trained labor. By contrast, the Danish barracks did not seem to need white-glove service. Roth noted that it appeared that the various claims made by the manufacturer were probably justified: compared to canvas tents, the felt tents were superior in providing a completely waterproof environment that was warmer in winter and cooler in summer, and allowed for a precisely controlled ventilation. In addition, the lack of tent ropes made it possible to put the barracks close together, leaving unobstructed passages between them. Finally, while more expensive than tents, they were more durable. "The advantages of this type of felt-barrack, which is a more correct designation than felt-tent, are obvious," Roth observed, but he added that they also had some glaring defects. "In my view, the felt-barracks are very useful when used on a small scale, especially for the isolation of infectious patients. Yet the insufficient air space of seven cubic meters per sick person suggests that they should not be adopted as transportable hospital accommodation for a whole army. In addition, their weight [...] makes it difficult to take along enough of them to serve as accommodation for the sick."[26]

Responding to the criticism that the amount of air space was too low, Doecker, Christoph, and Unmack developed a version that used a somewhat larger frame as its basic unit, increasing both the width and the height by 20 percent. A barrack using the same number of the larger-size elements would have a 40 percent larger floor space than the original version and provide almost double the volume. With 14 cubic meters of space

25 "Namen-Liste der auf der Allgemeinen Deutschen Austellung für Hygiene und Rettungswesen zu Berlin, 1883, Preisgekrönten," *Hygiene-Ausstellungs-Zeitung* 46 (July 3, 1883), 2.

26 Wilhelm August Roth, "Allgemeine Deutsche Ausstellung auf dem Gebiete der Hygiene und des Rettungswesen zu Berlin im Sommer 1883: Militär- und Marine-Sanitätswesen," *Deutsche Vierteljahrschrift für öffentliche Gesundheitspflege* 16 (1884), 222–24.

per person, the Doecker barrack became a contender. Indeed, in the wake of this modification, the Medical Department in the Prussian Ministry of War bought two Doecker barracks for trials at the Augusta Hospital in Berlin. The remaining question concerned whether the barrack could be winterized. The original version could not accommodate a heater, as the *carton-feutre* was at best fire-resistant but not fireproof. The application on the inside of a fabric coated with sodium silicate, or water-glass—a tested means of fire protection when used in a dry environment—provided a solution.[27]

At the same time, Professor Karl August Thomsen of the Polytekniske Læreanstalt (Polytechnic Institute) in Copenhagen tested Doecker barracks on behalf of the Danish Ministry of Justice, which considered using them in a quarantine station. In March 1884 he conducted a series of measurements in temperatures that ranged from 7° to 2° C and in various wind and snow conditions. The Doecker barrack performed well, but the ministry ultimately did not adopt it; a separate report, written by an architect, determined that while its use might produce initial savings, these would turn into a loss when one included the costs of storage of the parts and of the repeated inspection, assembly, and disassembly.[28] Yet this episode in the development of the Doecker barrack did generate a very important endorsement of Sextus Meyer, chief of the Københavns Brandvæsen (Copenhagen Fire Department), who had concluded after various tests that it was much more fireproof than a wooden barrack.[29]

By the time the Danish Ministry of Justice decided not to purchase Doecker's barracks, their inventor had lost control of the product. From the beginning of their collaboration, Christoph & Unmack had provided capital, technological expertise, materials, and labor, in exchange for an increasing share of future earnings. In August 1883, the firms of Christoph & Unmack and Doecker's Tent Construction entered into a close financial relationship when they jointly established health insurance for their workers.[30] Within a year, Christoph & Unmack had absorbed Doecker's premises and inventory into its own operations and convinced Doecker, who was close to bankruptcy, to sell the patent in exchange for 40,000 kroner and the promise that, for all eternity, the Døckerske Teltbyggeri Christoph & Unmack (Doecker's Tent Construction Christoph & Unmack) was to market the structure as the Døckerske Barakker.

27 Langenbeck, Coler, and Werner, *Die transportable Lazareth-Baracke*, 95.
28 "Forholdsregler mod smitsomme og epidemiske Sygdomme," in *Det kongelige Sundhedskollegiums Forhandlinger i Aaret 1883*, ed. Emil Madsen (Copenhagen: Reizels, 1883), 285–93.
29 Christoph & Unmack, *Portable Hospitals and Huts: Doeker System, Christoph & Unmack, Owners of the Patents and Manufactures, Copenhagen* (London: Doecker Hopsitals and Huts Factory, 1886), 7.
30 Sygekassen for Arbejderne hos d'Hrr. Christoph & Unmack samt det Døckerske Teltbyggeri, *Love for Sygekassen for Arbejderne hos d'Hrr. Christoph & Unmack samt det Døckerske Teltbyggeri, stiftet d. 1. Aug. 1883* (Copenhagen: author, 1884).

A short time after Christoph & Unmack had taken full control of Doecker's invention, an announcement appeared of a high-profile design competition for a prefabricated barrack organized by the International Committee of the Red Cross (ICRC).[31] Unlike the competition held in 1877 by the Saint Petersburg Society of Architects, this one was backed by both civilian and military establishments, and the German empress, Augusta, who had sponsored the Berlin barrack hospital named after her in the late 1860s, was the competition's patron. Heavily involved with the German Red Cross since its establishment twenty years earlier, Empress Augusta had a close relationship with Dr. Langenbeck of Berlin's Charité Hospital, who in early 1884 convinced her to make available a significant amount of money and a gold medal and, in so doing, to make a major contribution to the improvement of medical services in time of war. Delegates at the Third International Conference of the Red Cross Societies, held in Geneva in September 1884, endorsed a motion, probably drafted by Langenbeck but presented by the vice president of the ICRC, Louis Micheli–de la Rive, "that a competition is held to create a model type (full size) of a barrack for a mobile ambulance" and "that a commission, appointed by the meeting of the delegates, decides on the program of this competition before December 1, 1884." Micheli's motion got traction, especially after it received the endorsement of Swiss military surgeon Louis Appia, who was an ICRC founding member. "If the proposal of Mr. Micheli is adopted, one ought to organize an exhibition where prototypes of the barracks of the mobile ambulances are sent," Appia proposed, adding: "These should be full-size prototypes, supplied with all necessary equipment, bedding, supplies, etc., and with means of ventilation and heating." The delegate of the Belgian society, Joseph Tasson, immediately followed with a suggestion: "The [International] Exposition to be held in Antwerp from May to October 1885 is the ideal venue for it."[32] Langenbeck endorsed Appia's and Tasson's suggestions, and contacted the Belgian government and the city of Antwerp, which made space available in the exhibition hall of the Exposition Universelle d'Anvers for drawings and models and on the grounds for the erection of the full-size prototypes.

Chapter Six, Fig. 11
→ p. 258

On February 3, 1885, the ICRC issued the official brief of the competition.[33] Four weeks later the *British Medical Journal* gave an overview of the competition, noting that it was "likely to lead to results of much advantage in civil life, on the occurrence of epidemics,

31 See, for example, "Concours: Modèle-type de baraque d'ambulance mobile," *Gazette des Architectes et du Batiment*, 2nd ser., 14 (1885), 94; "Preis-Auschreiben für eine transportable Lazareth-Baracke," *Gesundheits-Ingenieur* 8, no. 7 (1885), 207–10.

32 Red Cross, Third International Conference, *Troisième Conférence Internationale des Sociétés de la Croix-Rouge tenue a Genève du 1er au 6 Septembre 1884: Compte Rendu* (Geneva: International Committee of the Red Cross, 1885), 226–28; see also Thomas Longmore, "Report on the Conference Held at Geneva between the 1st and 6th of September 1884 by the Representatives of Various Governments and National Aid Organizations at the Invitation of the Red Cross International Committee of Geneva," *Army Medical Department Report for the Year 1883* (London: Eyre and Spottiswoode, 1885), 314.

33 See Red Cross, Third International Conference, *Troisième Conférence Internationale des Sociétés de la Croix-Rouge*, 434–38.

as well as for military hospitals in time of war."[34] The barrack was to be capable of being rapidly assembled and made ready for use; function both as a standalone unit or as part of a larger field hospital; be available as prefabricated pieces that can be easily transported by rail, on main roads, and even country lanes; be stable and able to resist the normal range of weather conditions that occur in temperate climates; and be usable in both summer and winter. The competition program also stipulated a number of special conditions. The barrack ought to keep out the rain and, as far as possible, be incombustible. It had to contain at least twelve beds and provide 12 cubic meters for each patient—incidentally, this amount of space per person was an eighth of that provided in the barracks erected in the Luxembourg Palace gardens in 1870 and a third of the minimum required for military hospitals in Prussia. It should have good ventilation, even when, during the winter, doors and windows were closed. In the winter, the barrack should have such a system of heating that a temperature of 18.75° C could be maintained. For the assembly and disassembly, one should not need skilled workmen. Finally, "considering the large number of barrack-ambulances that may be required, and the advantage of having such as may be destroyed without scruple after they have been some time in use, reduction in weight and cost as far as possible should be kept in view."[35] Competitors were to send plans and sections drawn at scale 1:25, details at 1:10 or 1:5, and a model at 1:5 or a prototype of the barrack at scale 1:1. The deadline was September 1.

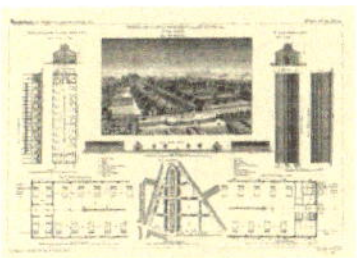

Chapter Seven, Fig. 7
→ p. 293

Messrs. Christoph and Unmack knew they had a winning proposition—not only because the Doecker barrack fulfilled the principal requirements and its design had been tested, but also because, in its appearance, it was conventional enough to appeal to people of ordinary tastes. In fact, the match between the competition brief and the Doecker barrack was so close that one might wonder whether the very public display of the barrack at the General German Exhibition of Hygiene and Safety of 1883 had, consciously or unconsciously, shaped Langenbeck's view of what might be needed. Whatever may have been the case, Christoph and Unmack decided to throw everything at it; they would submit not one but two entries, each including a full prototype. The first one was constructed from the large frames developed in the wake of the German hygiene exhibition, while the second one used the smaller panels of the original design. They provided the required air space per

34 "Conditions of the Prize Offered by the Empress of Germany for the Best Form of Movable Hut-Hospital," *British Medical Journal* 1885, no. 1 (Feb. 28, 1885), 459.
35 "Conditions of the Prize Offered by the Empress of Germany," 459–60.

person. Each weighed 3,490 kilograms; of this, the base and floor absorbed more than a third of the weight—and it was made clear that the barrack could be built without the base. Convenience was the key theme of the two entries. All the parts were numbered and packed in custom-designed boxes or cases.

An extensive, well-written document that addressed all the issues raised in the competition brief accompanied the submission. It explained why a hybrid like the Doecker barrack was superior to tents and tent-barracks (safe shelter during bad weather; no ropes, which allows for a more economic use of space; easy to heat) and to wooden barracks (ease of transport, construction, and demounting; can be handled by anyone; easy to disinfect, as it can be taken apart, all the parts thoroughly disinfected separately, and put together again). "We put a special emphasis on the comfort of the sick, so that they will feel in our barracks as well as in the best permanent hospitals, without running the risk that our barracks, like ordinary portable or provisional barracks, become the carriers of infectious materials."[36] In addition, a thorough engineering report on the thermal behavior of the Doecker barrack provided scientific backup to many of the claims made in the submission. It was clear: on the basis of reading the Christoph & Unmack submission, there ought to be no doubt that the firm had not only pursued the holy grail of the perfect demountable building but actually achieved it.

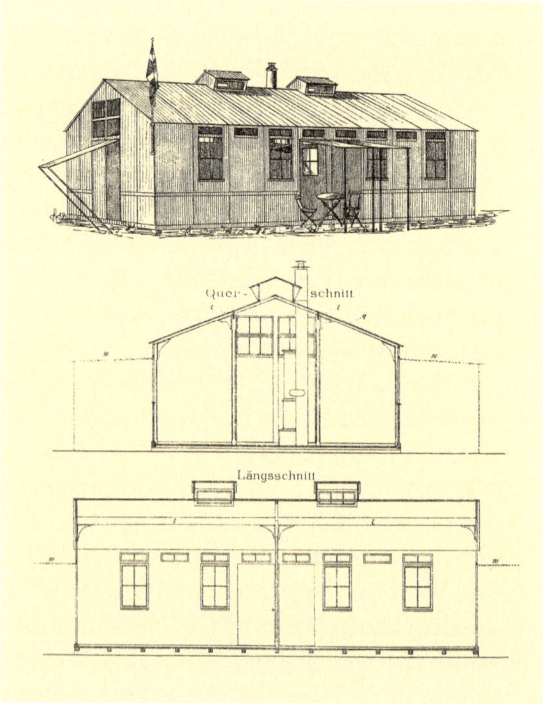

Fig. 7
Christoph & Unmack, Perspective view and sections of the larger of the two Doecker barracks the firm entered in the Red Cross competition at the 1885 Exposition Universelle in Antwerp, Belgium, from Bernhard von Langenbeck, Alwin Gustav Edmund von Coler, and Friedrich Emil Otto Werner, *Die transportable Lazareth-Baracke*, 2nd ed., 1890. Collection: author.

36 Christoph & Unmack, *Transportable Baracken (Döckersches System)* (Copenhagen: Axel E. Aamodt, [c. 1895]), 5–6.

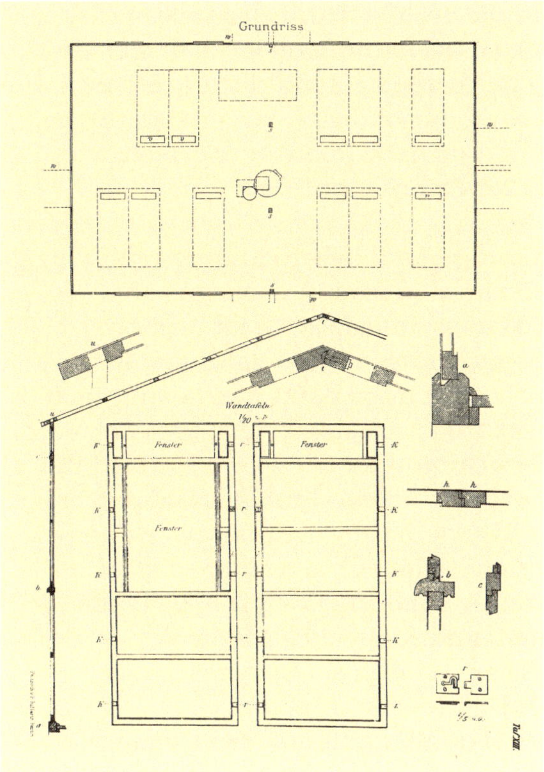

Fig. 8
Christoph & Unmack, Plan and construction details of the larger of the two Doecker barracks the firm entered in the Red Cross competition at the 1885 Exposition Universelle in Antwerp, from Bernhard von Langenbeck, Alwin Gustav Edmund von Coler, and Friedrich Emil Otto Werner, *Die transportable Lazareth-Baracke*, 2nd ed., 1890. Collection: author.

Of the sixty entries, thirteen included full-size prototypes, thirty-six included models at scale 1:5, and eleven consisted of drawings only. Early in its deliberations, the jury determined that both the quantity and quality of the entries exceeded their expectations and that more medals were warranted. Langenbeck convinced Empress Augusta to fund a second gold medal and ten silver medals. In addition, the jury decided that the results of the competition warranted an extensive, illustrated publication of all the major entries. Three members of the jury, Langenbeck, Alwin Gustav Edmund von Coler, a senior physician in the Medical Department of the Prussian Ministry of War, and Albert Ellissen, a French engineer who was also secretary of the French Red Cross Society, were to take charge of this publication, in collaboration with Friedrich Emil Otto Werner, a colleague of Coler.[37]

The first gold medal and a cash prize of 5,000 francs went to the two entries submitted by Christoph & Unmack. "The general aspect of the two huts from the outside was very similar to the appearance of the wooden huts which are common in our standing camps," the British member of the jury, Surgeon General Thomas Longmore (a veteran of the Crimean campaign who had represented Britain at the Geneva Convention of 1864), observed in his report of the competition published in the *Army Medical Department Report for the Year 1884.*

37 Gustave Moynier and Albert Elissen, "Rapport du jury du concours d'Anvers," *Bulletin International des Societes de Secours aux Militaires Blesses* 16 (1885), 130–37.

There is no doubt that the architectural elegance of the Doecker barracks created the foundation for their success. Yet, in addition, they performed splendidly on all the key issues set in the competition brief. Summarizing the jury's reasons for awarding both Doecker barracks with a shared gold medal, Longmore identified:

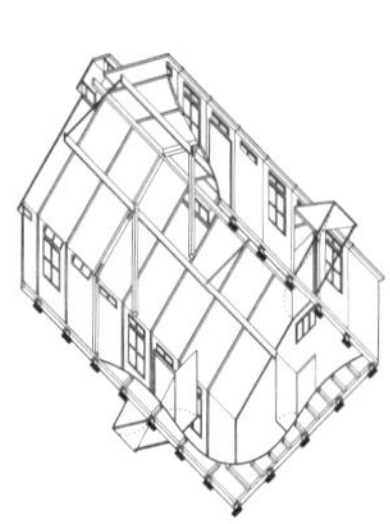

Drawings, Doecker Barrack
→ p. 521

> (*a*) the panel arrangement by which the parts were enabled to be placed in packages of convenient shapes and sizes for transport by road or railway, and protected against injury;
> (*b*) the manner in which the parts composing each hut were prepared for being fitted together;
> (*c*) the methodical arrangement which enabled the assembled parts to be manipulated and put systematically together by ordinary workmen for the erection of the hut in a single day or less, and equally enabling the hut to be taken down, packed, and removed elsewhere;
> (*d*) the compactness, stability, and serviceable qualities of the hut when erected;
> (*e*) the waterproof quality and moderate weight, of the substance employed for covering the panels and forming the principal part of the walls of the hut;
> (*f*) the adequacy of the means of light, aeration, and heating;
> (*g*) and, lastly, the ease with which the walls, roof, and floor of the hut could be cleansed and disinfected when necessary.[38]

Longmore noted that, while some of the other entries exhibited a superior performance in one or two of the categories listed, "none appeared to combine the whole of the qualities above enumerated to the same extent as the Doecker huts."[39]

The second gold medal, which was not accompanied by a cash prize, went to a rather futuristic design produced by the French engineer Casimir Tollet, who by 1885 was well known as a designer of the recently completed hospitals at Saint-Denis, Bourges, and Montpellier. Each of these provided single-room sick wards that followed in plan the principles established by Florence Nightingale, but also showed in elevation a concrete vault that began at the floor and had a section of a pointed, or ogival, arch. This form was considered to be not only incombustible but also hygienic, as it allowed for a more perfect ventilation and for easy cleaning of the interior surface of the ward, if necessary

38 Thomas Longmore, "Report on the Competitive Exhibition of Movable Hut-Hospitals at Antwerp in September 1885, Together with a Descriptive Account of the Pattern to Which the Principal Prize Was Awarded," *Army Medical Department Report for the Year 1884* (London: Eyre and Spottiswoode, 1886), 361, 364.
39 Ibid., 364.

with the aid of a water hose. For the competition, Tollet submitted a prototype for a barrack that was a modified version of a hospital tent he had brought into production. It consisted of an arched iron frame covered with wooden panels covered with a sheet of zinc. The design won the admiration of the jury, but with many projects at hand, Tollet had neither the time nor the financial need to capitalize on the gold medal earned in Antwerp, and as a result his design remains a footnote in the history of the barrack.

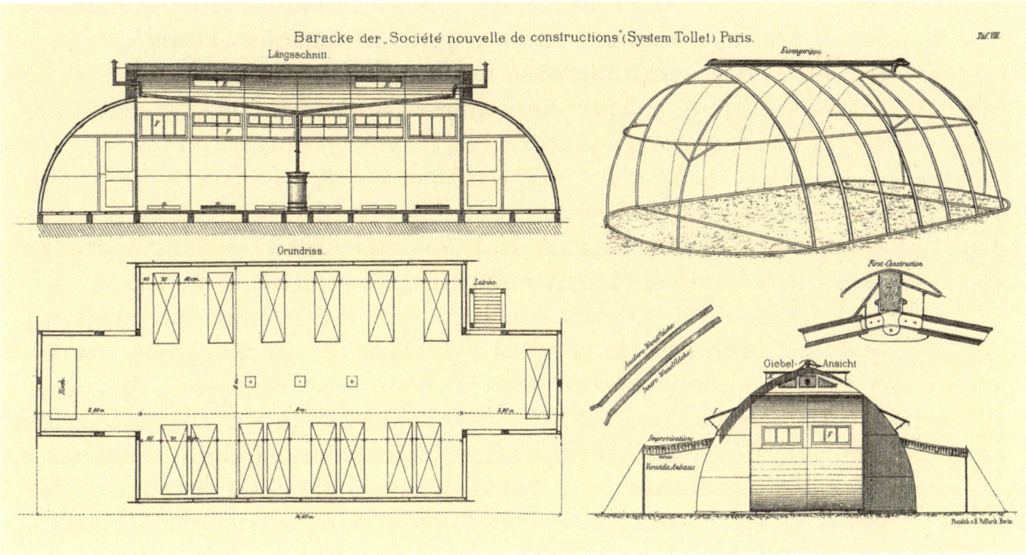

Fig. 9
Casimir Tollet, Plan, elevation, section, construction detail, and perspective view of a barrack entered in the Red Cross competition at the 1885 Exposition Universelle in Antwerp, consisting of an iron frame covered with wooden panels covered with a sheet of zinc, from Bernhard von Langenbeck, Alwin Gustav Edmund von Coler, and Friedrich Emil Otto Werner, *Die transportable Lazareth-Baracke*, 2nd ed., 1890. Collection: author.

The future of Christoph & Unmack fully depended on the firm's ability to make the Doecker barrack into a popular consumer product, and the firm did not lose any time capitalizing on the results. It rushed out illustrated catalogues to market its products. The English-language version, entitled *Portable Hospitals and Huts: Doeker [sic] System, Christoph & Unmack, Owners of the Patents and Manufacture, Copenhagen*, clearly established the key facts. After listing all the medals and awards earned by the barrack, the narrative continued:

> The *Portable Hospitals and Houses*, which form the subject of the following remarks, are the invention of Capt. *v. Doecker*, of the Danish Army, and have been further improved by Messrs. *Christoph &. Unmack*, of Copenhagen, the owners of the patents.
>
> The houses consist of wooden frames covered with specially prepared paper felt or other waterproof material, and afford perfect shelter not only against wind and rain but also against heat and cold.

The construction varies according to the uses for which the houses are intended.

For *Military or other tents* the frames are only covered on the outside with a waterproof covering.

For *Hospital and Military barracks* the frames may be covered on both sides, leaving between the two coverings a space of one inch, which may be either left as an air space or be filled with wood, cork, silicate of cotton, or any other bad conductor of heat. The covering on the inside is made fireproof by being impregnated to that effect.

The floors are of planed boards and varnished.[40]

Marketing the barracks in a country with large dominions, Christoph & Unmack described Doecker barracks as appropriate homes emigrants might take along on their Atlantic passage as they "can be packed so as to take up very small space." Yet their primary uses were as soldiers' accommodation and hospital wards. As catalogues need to provide information about prices, *Portable Hospitals and Huts* provided not only a detailed price list but also sample calculations to show the great savings that could be obtained when using a Doecker barrack instead of a more permanent building. For example, comparing the cost per bed of the new Blegdam Hospital in Copenhagen with that of a typical Doecker hospital barrack, the latter could provide a bed at 39 percent of the cost of the former. Somewhat perversely the catalogue suggested that the savings might be much greater. "Considering the great ease with which the barracks can be disinfected and ventilated, the risk of admitting even the double number of sick would not be great, which makes the difference so much greater."[41] Who could refuse a shelter that housed the sick, be it in cramped conditions, at 20 percent of the usual cost?

The competition, and the display of the thirteen prototypes and thirty-six models in the high profile setting of the Antwerp exhibition, brought enormous attention to portable knockdown barrack design. The subsequent publication of the results in journals worldwide kept the issue alive. One publication stood out for its size and impact: in 1886, Langenbeck, Coler, and Werner published a 154-page article in *Archiv für klinische Chirurgie* (Archive of clinical surgery), a major medical journal edited by Langenbeck. It contained a sixty-three-page

40 Christoph & Unmack, *Portable Hospitals and Huts*, 1.
41 Ibid., 8.

historical overview of the use of barracks for military hospitals and, in addition, lengthy descriptions filled with much detail about the construction and materials proposed. Twenty-three large lithographed plates recorded the key designs in detail. This article remains one of the key documents in the history of barrack architecture.[42] At the time, it was considered to be a standard text on the topic, and four years later an expanded version appeared as a 511-page monograph.[43]

The popular press also carried articles about the competition. The cover of the June 26, 1886, issue of *Scientific American* featured a number of wood engravings showing a horse-drawn wagon heavily loaded with wooden building parts; perspective views of a barrack both under construction and in completed state; various orthogonal drawings of the gable, side panel, and other elements; and a medal carrying an equilateral cross in a presentation case marked by a crown.

→ Fig. 10

The caption read: "Ducker's Portable Barrack and Field Hospital." The Ducker referred to was not Johan Gerhard Clemens Doecker but American builder William M. Ducker—no relation—who lived in Brooklyn, New York. The accompanying text told of the Red Cross competition. "A circular containing these requirements having come into the possession of Mr. Wm. M. Ducker, of Brooklyn, he addressed himself to the solution of the problem, and in a short time produced a structure in accordance with the specifications of the society." The article noted that at the Antwerp world's fair, Ducker's proposal had encountered much interest: "It is a representative American invention, for it combines in an eminent degree lightness and portability with strength and convenience." After reporting that Ducker's design had been awarded a silver medal it noted: "He is now in correspondence with several European governments, with reference to the adoption of his 'baraque' in their respective countries."[44] The article did not mention that the jury had issued no fewer than ten silver medals, so the honor bestowed on Ducker's design was not, as it appeared, a single step from victory.

The *Scientific American* write-up was both the first and the last that honored a design of a barrack with front-page status in a general interest publication. It described Ducker's portable knockdown barrack in great detail, noting, among other things: "Two men can erect the baraque without the least difficulty, and in little more than an hour's time, as all the parts lock into each other

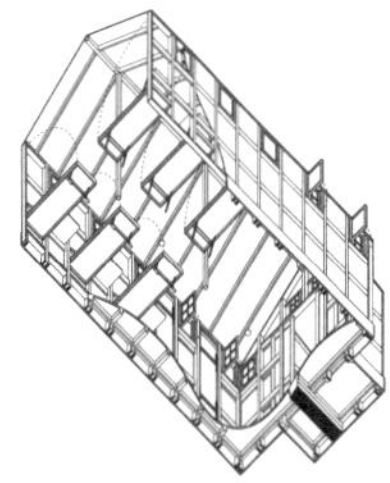

Drawings,
Ducker Barrack
→ p. 521

42 Bernhard von Langenbeck, Alwin Gustav Edmund von Coler, and Friedrich Emil Otto Werner, "Die transportable Lazareth-Baracke: Mit besonderer Berücksichtigung der von Ihrer Majestät der Kaiserin und Königin Augusta hervorgerufenen Baracken-Ausstellung in Antwerpen im September 1885," *Archiv für klinische Chirurgie* 33 (1886), 781–934.
43 Langenbeck, Coler, and Werner, *Die transportable Lazareth-Baracke*.
44 "Ducker's Portable Barrack and Field Hospital," *Scientific American* 54, no. 26 (June 26, 1886), 400, 404.

SCIENTIFIC AMERICAN

[Entered at the Post Office of New York, N. Y., as Second Class Matter.]

A WEEKLY JOURNAL OF PRACTICAL INFORMATION, ART, SCIENCE, MECHANICS, CHEMISTRY, AND MANUFACTURES.

Vol. LIV.—No. 26. [NEW SERIES.] NEW YORK, JUNE 26, 1886. $3.20 per Annum. [POSTAGE PREPAID.]

DUCKER'S PORTABLE BARRACK AND FIELD HOSPITAL.

The Society of the Red Cross in Europe has, for several years, given particular attention to the subject of portable field hospitals and other improved appliances for the care of sick and wounded soldiers. Though the more humane method of settling international differences by arbitration is appealing each year with increasing earnestness to the conscience of Christendom, there is still an immense field for the ministrations of those who seek the conservation of life in the midst of its military destroyers. Despite the deadliness of modern instruments of warfare, it is conceded that a greater proportion of soldiers die from lack of sufficient care and from exposure than from the immediate effects of the

(*Continued on page* 404.)

DUCKER'S PORTABLE BARRACK AND FIELD HOSPITAL.

Fig. 10
William M. Ducker, Various views of a design for a prefabricated barrack entered in the Red Cross competition at the 1885 Exposition Universelle in Antwerp, *Scientific American*, 1886. Collection: author.

and are perfectly interchangeable." Pull-down beds, tables, and chairs offered great convenience and security, as they could not get lost when in use. Finally: "Every provision has been made for the comfort of the invalid. A rope suspended from the rafter over the bed permits him to raise himself; a chair back is provided when he wishes to sit up; a small slate is tacked over the bed to receive any memoranda the physician or nurse may want to make. In short, the baraque is remarkably complete."[45]

Ducker got his publicity, but if he had any hope to sell his portable knockdown barrack to the US Army, he must have been disappointed: for another twenty years, prefabricated barracks were not considered essential to its anticipated operations. In Germany, by contrast, the Prussian Ministry of War decided to purchase fifty Doecker barracks in order to submit them to a series of practical tests. Yet at this phase, it did not want to dismiss all the other designs; one problem with the Christoph & Unmack product was that it was patented, and the ministry did not want to be wholly dependent on a single product that might be vital in time of war. For these reasons, therefore, it also identified another fourteen barrack designs submitted in the competition that might serve its purposes. These included the ones proposed by: Tollet, which proved to be the most expensive per bed; retired military surgeon Wilhelm Eltze, the cheapest; brothers Peter and Jean-Baptiste Adt (pâpier-maché manufacturers from Forbach, France), the heaviest; and the Hanover firm of Vogler and Noah, a corrugated iron barrack that proved to be the lightest.

45 Ibid., 404.

Fig. 11
Vogler and Noah, Plan, sections, dimetric view, and construction detail of a barrack entered in the Red Cross competition at the 1885 Exposition Universelle in Antwerp, consisting of a foldable wooden frame that was covered by three layers of cloth: an outer one that was watertight, a middle one that provided insulation, and an inner one that was fire resistant, from Bernhard von Langenbeck, Alwin Gustav Edmund von Coler, and Friedrich Emil Otto Werner, *Die transportable Lazareth-Baracke*, 2nd ed., 1890. Collection: author.

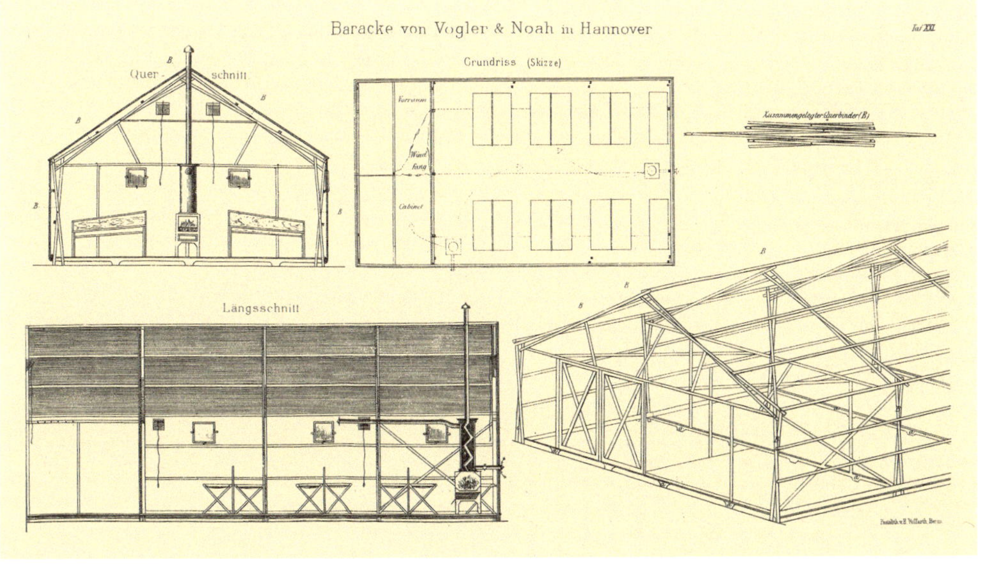

The Doecker barrack constructed from the larger panels was in the middle range in these categories, but when all performance standards were considered together, it proved to represent what later generations were to characterize as the Goldilocks Principle, providing just the right amount of space, structural integrity, comfort, and convenience, for just the right price.[46] Most importantly, the Doecker barrack was the easiest to construct: the manufacturer claimed that hospital attendants were able to put the structures together and take them apart without any problem, while all other designs required experienced carpenters or builders. Hence the Prussian Ministry of War decided in the end to adopt the Doecker barrack as the main type for its military hospitals, but insisted on an important design modification, especially where it concerned the heavy base. The floor joists and floorboards made up more than one-third of the weight of the barrack, and Christoph & Unmack had argued that, in principle, one could procure the materials for the floor locally, and that hence the practical weight of the barrack was only 2,200 kilograms. The ministry refused to accept this argument; even if it were true, it would take time to buy or requisition the building materials at the place where the barrack was to be erected, and this defeated the whole purpose of the barrack as a speedy solution to the problem of shelter. Consequently, the ministry proposed that Christoph & Unmack modify the design of the eleven boxes in which the parts of the barrack were transported—four boxes for the wall panels, four for the roof panels, two for the end walls and the roof ventilators, and one for the steps leading to the entrance, screws, and tools. They were now to be constructed in such a manner that they could be taken apart, and their elements could be used to construct the floor.

Fig. 12
Diagram showing the construction of the floor from the boxes in which the various elements of the Christoph & Unmack Doecker barrack were transported, from Bernhard von Langenbeck, Alwin Gustav Edmund von Coler, and Friedrich Emil Otto Werner, *Die transportable Lazareth-Baracke*, 2nd ed., 1890. Collection: author.

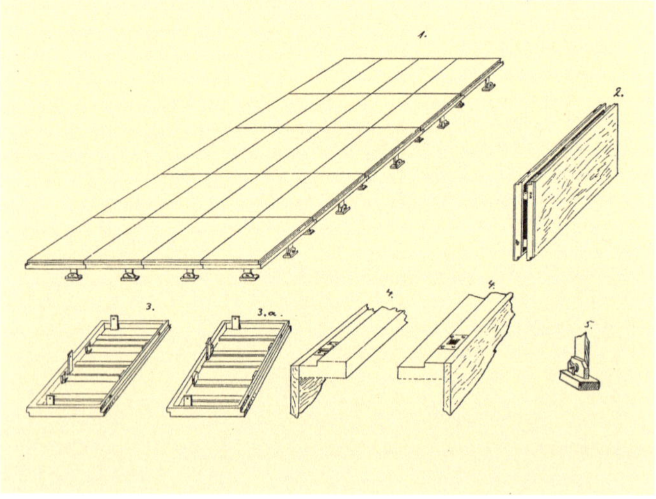

46 Langenbeck, Coler, and Werner, *Die transportable Lazareth-Baracke*, 114.

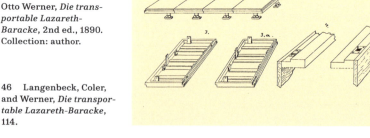

An added advantage was that, used as a base, the boxes would not get stolen while the barrack was in operation. After all, there was always a great need for firewood.[47]

The Prussian Ministry of War also ordered a couple of variations that might perform better in different circumstances. One, which offered extra insulation by means of a peat filling between the felt-cardboard layers, did not pass the test. One that provided a surface of waterproof canvas instead of the linseed-impregnated felt cardboard carried great promise. The problem with the felt-cardboard was that each of the many linseed-oil coats took a week to dry, slowing down production significantly. The canvas version allowed for unlimited mass production in time of emergency. Both the felt-cardboard and canvas versions were submitted to many tests that focused on questions of heating and ventilation, and in which the performance of the Prussian medical tent was used as a control. The six-month trial held at Tempelhof between the beginning of July and the end of December 1891 was the longest of these tests. After considering questions of cost, packaging, transport, resilience against damage, tightness of the walls, insulation, ventilation, and so on, it had become clear that nothing surpassed the Doecker barrack. A final modification concerned size. The barracks shown in Antwerp had a length of 10 meters, but an enlargement to 15 meters seemed optimal, as it allowed for an increase of the capacity from twelve to between eighteen (in winter) and twenty (in summer) beds, which was the maximum a single nurse could handle. Moreover, all the materials to build two 15-meter-long barracks would just fit into one standard railway freight car.

The orders from Berlin came with the promise for larger orders in the future and with an important condition: the manufacture of the barracks was to take place in Prussia. Christian Ferdinand Christoph contacted his cousin Johannes Ehregott Christoph, who lived in the Moravian brothers' community in Niesky, located some 200 kilometers southeast of Berlin. Johannes owned a factory producing boilers and railway engines. An added advantage was that Niesky was close to large forests that could be commercially logged. Thus the Döcker'sche Barackenfabrikation Christoph & Unmack (Doecker's Barrack Manufacturer Christoph & Unmack) came to be built next to Maschinenfabrik J. E. Christoph A. G. (Machine Factory J. E. Christoph Inc.).

In 1891 the Doecker was to see its first deployment in a substantial crisis. On May 1, workers demonstrated in the French textile town of Fourmies, located some

47 Ibid., 177–80.

70 kilometres north of Reims, in favor of an eight-hour workday. A day earlier Paris had dispatched a regiment of infantry to the town. As tensions increased, more soldiers arrived, leading in the late afternoon to a confrontation. Soldiers fired into the crowd, killing nine, and wounding thirty-five. The fusillade de Fourmies (shootout of Fourmies) became a charged marker in the history of the workers' movement in France. In addition, it also proved an important moment in the history of the Doecker barrack: more than a week after the shooting, the Ministry of War set up a temporary military hospital consisting of two Doecker barracks. It was the first use of these structures in the wake of lethal violence. Yet their deployment was not without criticism: not only had these structures arrived late, but also the patients consisted of soldiers only. Obviously as far as the wounded were concerned, the spirit of *Tutti fratelli* (All are brothers), which had given birth to the Red Cross, did not prevail that year in Fourmies.

→ Figs. 13, 14

In the early 1890s Christoph & Unmack expanded its European sales network into a global one. Its product line also increased: the firm could deliver not only barracks but also the furnishings and all the tools and supplies to produce an instant hospital wherever needed. A competition organized by the German Red Cross in 1888 for furnishings and equipment for a Doecker barrack that served as a sick ward and another that provided kitchen and laundry facilities had generated a plethora of designs for foldable beds, foldable stools, chairs, tables, wash basins, storage units, kitchen equipment, stoves, easily transportable boxed sets of surgery tools, foldable operating tables, and boxed pharmacies.[48] As a result, it had become possible to order a prefabricated Doecker barrack with all its fittings and tools—purchasing, in essence, an instant hospital.

Frederick William Elsner, an Australian physician of German origin, became the firm's voice in the United States. As ships filled with poor immigrants were arriving at US ports on a daily basis, the American public had become very worried about epidemics. A typhus epidemic that had erupted in 1892 in the Lower East Side of New York had been traced back to the steerage passengers of a transatlantic liner that had arrived a few weeks earlier. This incident led to an increase in the powers of the federal government to detain ships and immigrants, which was confirmed in the National Quarantine Act (1893). During the typhus epidemic, a temporary quarantine

48 Langenbeck, Coler, and Werner, *Die transportable Lazareth-Baracke*, 289–511.

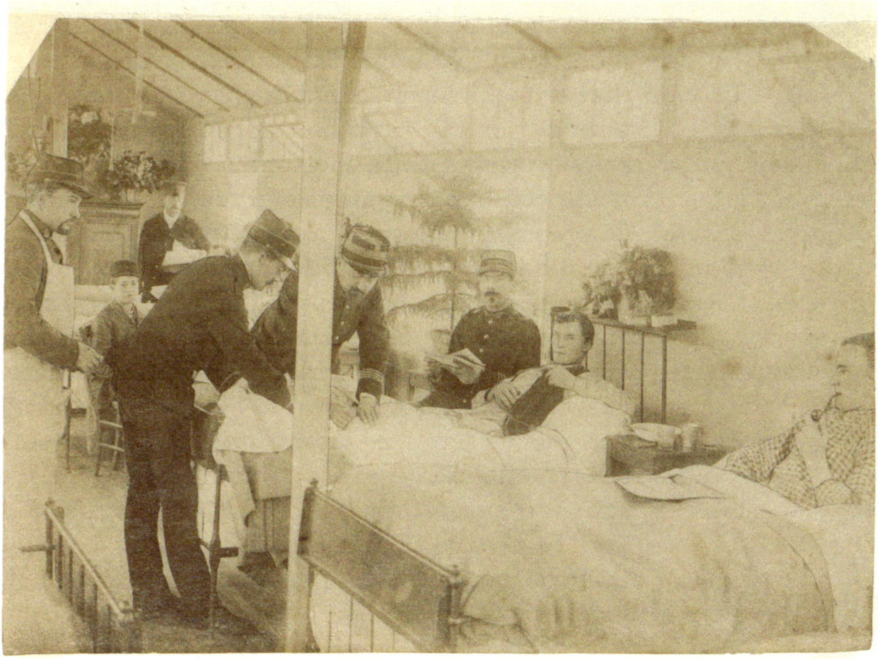

Fig. 13
Exterior of the two Doecker barracks erected in Fourmies, 1891. Collection: Ecomusée de l'Avesnois, Fourmies.

Fig. 14
Interior of one of the Doecker barracks erected in Fourmies, 1891. Collection: Ecomusée de l'Avesnois, Fourmies.

station established on North Brother Island, located in the East River not far from Rikers Island, had used tents, but Christoph & Unmack were not in the tent business anymore—and hence Elsner's first job was to discredit these as public health tools. "Infectious diseases are not for treatment under canvas," Elsner noted in an article that he published twice in 1894, qualifying his statement with the provision, "unless one is prepared to burn the canvas when the epidemic is stamped out, or something is invented to render it fire-proof and germ-resisting, or capable of disinfection by germicides. [...] The life of a canvas hospital is that of a butterfly; for when you have used it once, it is done for."[49] After providing testimony about how the mortality of typhus patients in a tented isolation hospital in the Australian city of Melbourne had been initially low but increased as time went on—suggesting that the canvas of the tents had become incubators of the disease—Elsner turned to the alternative. "Now, what have we in the Doecker Hospital? A building composed of material that is germ-proof, fire-proof, and capable of disinfection, *ad infinitum*, by chemicals. A building that is cool in summer and warm in winter; that is portable and capable of being put up or taken down by a few men in a few hours; capable of being carried by railway, wagon, or pack-horses, and which will provide twenty beds in winter or eighteen beds in summer time, at a moment's notice." Noting that a Doecker hospital could be supplied with all the necessary medical and hospital equipment, it provided an instant solution in any emergency. "All you have to do is to wire to headquarters for one, two, or more hospitals, which on arrival are unpacked and erected at once. Fill them with patients as required, and when your epidemic is stifled, take them down again, disinfect and repack them, and return to headquarters." And if the users had become attached to the Doecker barracks, they could purchase them as a more permanent hospital. "Level your site, asphalt it if you like, and drain well; then erect your hospital and put a fence around it. It is storm-proof and will resist a tornado; it is more water-proof than a brick house, and if any moisture should appear, simply wipe the walls down with a dry, aseptic cloth. Can anything be more simple?"[50]

If there was any doubt that the Doecker barrack was a universal and lasting tool for the relief of suffering, the large-format, atlas-size and handsomely illustrated sales brochure published a year later made clear that there was no choice but to contact the Christoph & Unmack company in Niesky and allow the firm to outfit

49 Frederick William Elsner, "Portable Hospitals for Use in the Field and in Epidemics," *Annals of Hygiene: A Journal of Health* 9 (1894), 691.
50 Ibid., 692.

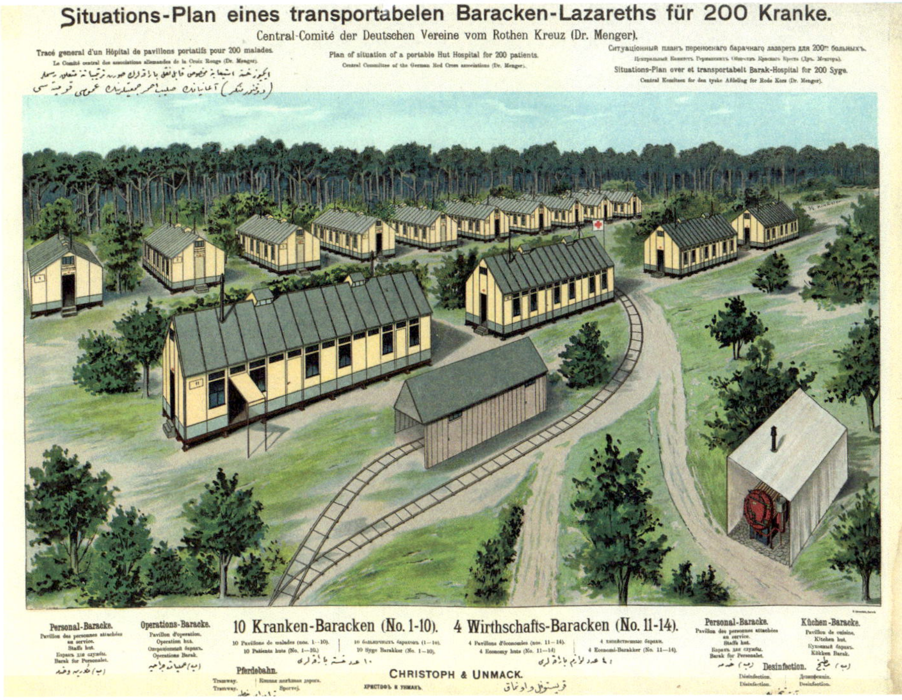

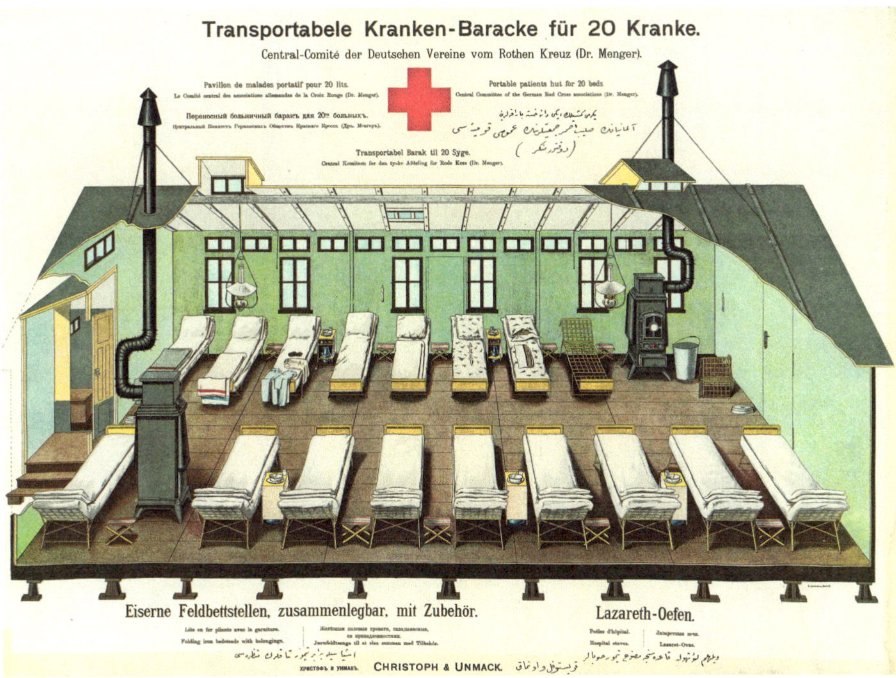

Fig. 15
Military hospital for 200 patients composed of Doecker barracks, from Christoph & Unmack, *Transportabeles Baracken-Lazareth*, 1895. Collection: Staatsbibliothek zu Berlin.

Fig. 16
A hospital sick-ward barrack, from Christoph & Unmack, *Transportabeles Baracken-Lazareth*, 1895. Collection: Staatsbibliothek zu Berlin.

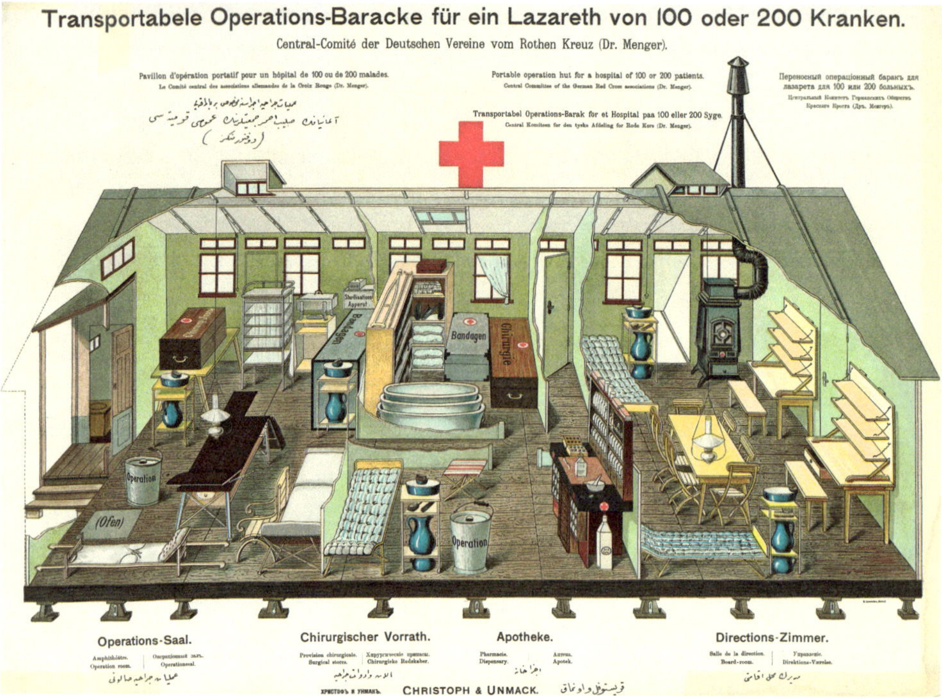

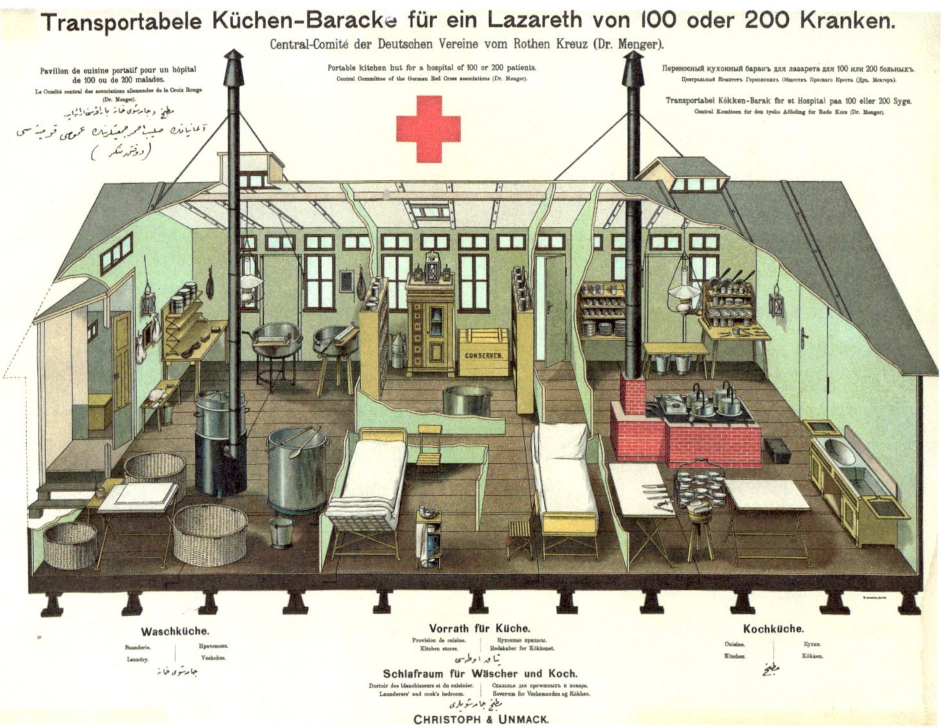

Fig. 17
An operating room barrack, from Christoph & Unmack, *Transportabeles Baracken-Lazareth*, 1895. Collection: Staatsbibliothek zu Berlin.

Fig. 18
A hospital kitchen barrack, from Christoph & Unmack, *Transportabeles Baracken-Lazareth*, 1895. Collection: Staatsbibliothek zu Berlin.

one's armed forces or public health service with the best of the best. *Transportabeles Baracken-Lazareth für 200 Kranke* (Portable barrack hospital for 200 patients) presented in four large, cheerfully colored plates that were captioned in six languages (German, French, English, Russian, Danish, and Ottoman Turkish), a bird's-eye view of a typical military hospital for an army division and interior views of a ward barrack, an operation barrack, and a kitchen barrack.

← Figs. 15–18

The book did not need any explanatory text. The pictures, especially those showing the three interiors as if they were dollhouse versions, not only invoking a sense of simplification, domestication, perfection, and purity but also giving the viewer—that is, the client—the opportunity to immediately grasp, assess, and apprehend it both as a building that might do some good in the world and as a compensatory, wish-fulfilling fantasy that reduces the terrors of war and pestilence to manageable proportions.[51]

By the mid 1890s Christoph & Unmack faced many competitors who aimed to have a share in what appeared to be an ever-expanding market in Germany. Yet Christoph & Unmack remained the market leader. Energetic, savvy, and utterly ruthless, Christian Ferdinand Christoph and Christian Rudolf Unmack created a major construction empire out of the Doecker barrack. By the beginning of the twentieth century their company offered three major product lines. The first supplied, as stated in one of its catalogues, "demountable, portable, *light-weight* so-called *flying* Döcker barracks for provisional use" and was based on the improved version of the barrack that had won the 1885 Red Cross competition. The firm distinguished between versions to be used (1) for the military; (2) by the Red Cross; (3) as isolation hospitals; (4) as tuberculosis sanatoria; (5) as schools, spas, and so on; (6) as temporary hospital sick wards; (7) as shelters for those made homeless by earthquakes, floods, and fires; (8) for travel use by the *Allerhöchsten Kriegsherrn* (supreme warlord)—that is, the Kaiser—and his staff; and (9) as accommodation in the colonies during research expeditions, the construction of railways, and so forth.[52]

51 See Susan Stewart, *On Longing: Narratives of the Miniature, the Gigantic, the Souvenir, the Collection* (Durham, NC: Duke University Press, 1994), 47–67.
52 Christoph & Unmack, *Verwendungsformen von zerlegbaren, transportabelen Döcker-Bauten* (Munich: Wolf & Sohn, n.d.), 1.

Fig. 19
Standing in front of a Doecker barrack, Empress Augusta Victoria, known as Dona, photographs the German Kaiser, Wilhelm II, and his retinue in the German camp outside of Jerusalem, 1898. The trip of the imperial couple to the Holy Land was to serve German global ambition, which included the creation of a Jewish homeland in Palestine as a German Protectorate under Ottoman suzerainty. This project had been proposed in early 1898 by the Zionist visionary Theodor Herzl, and initially found support in Berlin. "To live under the protection of this strong, great, moral, splendidly governed, tightly organized Germany can only have the most salutary effect on the Jewish national character," Herzl recorded in his diary. "Also at one stroke we would obtain a completely ordered internal and external legal status. The suzerainty of the Porte and the protectorate of Germany would certainly be sufficient legal pillars." On his way to Jerusalem, Kaiser Wilhelm met the Sultan in Constantinople. The latter rejected this scheme as it implied surrender of Muslim territory to infidels, and by the time Herzl met the Kaiser in the shadow of a Doecker barrack in Jerusalem, the plan was dead. History was to prove that Germany was to have a very different role in the formation of a Jewish state in Palestine. Collection: Imperial War Museum, London.

The second series, which was the largest, offered "demountable, portable, soldiers' barracks 'Model Döberitz,' demountable portable pavilions and homes of stronger and strongest Doecker construction and pure wood-construction, System Christoph & Unmack, for continuous use." It listed forty-six different versions that included a more permanent version of all but one of those provided in the flying barrack form—no solid barrack was offered for continuous use by the Kaiser—and also horse stables, "ordinary" homeless shelters, worker shanties, railway waiting rooms, station buildings, freight sheds, offices, summer cottages, homes, garden sheds, garages, artist ateliers, beach huts, mountain huts, clubhouses, guest cabins at beach hotels, and more. And, of course, as Germany was developing its newly acquired colonies in Africa and the Pacific, it offered a full line of tropical houses, offices, hospitals, schools, churches, and "prayer rooms."[53] In fact, the line of barracks for the tropics was quite important to the Niesky enterprise, as it was there that the firm could expect to have a near monopoly on construction to house both German institutions and individuals. With little construction capacity—or at least construction capacity that was taken seriously by the German colonizers—the newly established colonies Deutsch-Westafrika (German West Africa, today

53 Ibid., 1–3.

Cameroon, Togo, and part of Ghana), Deutsch-Südwestafrika (German Southwest Africa, today Namibia), Deutsch-Ostafrika (German East Africa, today Tanzania, Rwanda, and Burundi), Deutsch-Neuguinea (German New Guinea, today northern Papua New Guinea), various Micronesian archipelagoes, and the Kiautschou (Jiaozhou) colony that centered on Tsingtao (Qingdao), China. The quick development of these colonies was to partly depend on prefabricated architecture, and Christoph & Unmack believed it could fully exploit that market.

Fig. 20
Walther Dobbertin, Treatment of an injured construction worker at a Christoph & Unmack barrack first-aid station in German East Africa, c. 1910. The barrack is protected by a double roof, with a vented air space between the two layers. Collection: Bundesarchiv, Berlin.

The third series, "German Wooden Houses, System Christoph & Unmack," presented prefabricated homes, "in a great variety of styles," to be manufactured "for every possible use."[54] A fifteen-point questionnaire to be filled out by the customer was to help the architects and salespeople at Christoph & Unmack to match need to both the general product on offer and the many different options for foundations, insulation, roofing, and heating. It required the location of the site where the building was to be erected and its distance to the nearest station, the address of which had to be supplied. The second to last question concerned labor: Christoph & Unmack was to supply one mechanic, but the customer was to provide a number of helpers to assist him. The last question concerned the date of delivery.[55] But no attempt was made to indicate what it might mean to own, live in, and raise a family in a Christoph & Unmack home.

Christoph & Unmack was a successful firm, but despite its ambitions to become a leader in German single-family residential construction, it never was more than a niche player. It was held back by the fact that,

54 Ibid., 3.
55 Ibid., 4–7.

while wooden single-family houses had a certain romantic appeal, building lots were relatively expansive and suburban German residential construction used brick. Traditional fears of the flammability of wooden houses also played a part. And Christoph & Unmack did not offer financing. Perhaps most important was the fact that the firm did not try to make a connection to what Germans might perceive as their core values, be they those of the Protestant north, which are aptly expressed in the notion of *Pünktlichkeit* (punctuality), or those of the Roman Catholic south, which center on *Gemütlichkeit* (comfortableness). Technologically Christoph & Unmack was a remarkable enterprise, but culturally it had a tin ear. This becomes clear when one compares the track record of Christoph & Unmack to those of two American companies, which became giants in the field of prefabricated construction. The Aladdin brand, produced by the Michigan-based North American Construction Company, sold over 75,000 mail-order kit houses between 1900 and 1940. The Chicago-based mail-order and retail firm Sears, Roebuck and Co. sold over 100,000 prefabricated homes. Both of these firms succeeded not so much because of the technological sophistication of their products but because of their ability to produce financing, smart logistics, and brilliant advertising that made the purchase and construction of a prefabricated home a key part of living the American Dream, which was embodied in a do-it-yourself attitude that recalled the life of pioneers on the frontier. "This new movement, or idea, of 'building things yourself,' has been fully vindicated," a catalogue of prefabricated homes issued by the Aladdin Company in 1908 proclaimed. "You don't need the skill. If you can hit a nail with a hammer, you can put up an 'Aladdin' knocked-down house. You do not need a saw. Not even a rule or square, because you do not have to make any measurements. It is as simple as a b c. A bright boy can put an 'Aladdin' house together."[56] The Aladdin brand was meant to be a moral force in the country, and buying one of its home kits meant not only to associate oneself with a force for good. "Integrity means *moral soundness*; it means *honesty*; it means *freedom from corrupting influence or practice*; it means *strictness in the fulfillment of contracts, uprightness, square dealing*."[57] To do business with Aladdin meant to help make the world a bit better. Christoph & Unmack never made "integrity" into the core of its sales strategy—and given the way Messrs. Christoph and Unmack had treated *Ritmester* (ret.) Doecker, who died a penniless man in 1904, it might be just as well.

56 Aladdin Company, *"Build It Yourself": Aladdin Knocked-Down Houses* (Bay City, MI: North American Construction Company, 1908), 1.
57 Aladdin Company, *Aladdin Homes: "Built in a Day,"* cat. no. 29 (Bay City, MI: Aladdin Company, 1917), 3.

→ p. 504

Twelve

Heimatlich, *Heimlich*, and *Unheimlich*

The nineteenth century saw itself as an age of progress, and therefore continuous self-improvement through education was an important part of social life. In Europe, the Americas, and in the clubs of white settlers and officials in the colonies, professional presenters, who traveled from venue to venue, and local academics, teachers, or members of the clergy, educated and entertained audiences of all ages with illustrated lectures on a variety of topics, including religion, history, ethnography, medicine, and zoology. The main tool of this trade was the magic lantern (projector) and a box of slides or plates. Most of these slides, which displayed a transparent image that was either custom-made or based on an existing illustration or photograph, were produced in large quantities by special companies and could be rented or purchased through catalogues. In a special category were the lectures given by celebrity explorers who had returned from journeys to exotic places with tall tales to tell and slides to show of newly made photographs of hitherto unknown places and life-forms. Magic lantern slide presentations were an essential marketing tool to raise funds for future expeditions. Others who had traveled far and believed they had a story to share and a cause to serve, albeit with a more modest claim on the attention of the world, went on the lecture circuit with a couple of boxes of slides in their carpetbag or valise. One of these was a German woman, Elisabeth von Oettingen née Schambach, who had spent the winter of 1904–05 in Manchuria as part of the Livonia Voluntary Hospital dispatched from Riga. Her presentations contained reflections, illustrated by hand-colored slides, of her experiences within a Doecker barrack.

→ Fig. 1

Born in Weimar in 1875, Elisabeth grew up in an upper-middle-class family. Her father, a senior civil servant, was overseer of the Thuringian Railway Company. In her early twenties she began training to become a nurse at

Fig 1
Elisabeth and Walter von Oettingen (center right) and members of the Lutheran community in Mukden standing in front of the Doecker barrack of the Livonia Voluntary Hospital in Manchuria, 1905. Collection: Heinrich Heine Universität, Düsseldorf.

the Charité Hospital in Berlin. There she met Walter Joachim Georg von Oettingen, a 28-year-old physician. They married after a two-year courtship.

Born in Russia, Walter belonged to the aristocracy of Livonia—a territory located on the eastern shore of the Baltic Sea that encompasses today's Estonia and Latvia. Colonized by Germans in the thirteenth century, this territory had been ruled by Poland and Sweden, then in 1710 became an autonomous part of the Russian Empire, with the German aristocrats remaining in charge of the administration of the territory, and German remaining the official language. Walter studied medicine at the University of Dorpat, but before he had finished his degree, his father, a famous physicist who taught at the same university, was forced into early retirement as part of a process of both administrative and cultural Russification initiated by Emperor Alexander III. The aim of such action was to make the multiethnic population of the Baltic provinces into an integral part of the Russian people—a policy that also led to the suppression of other cultures within the Russian Empire, including that of the Ukrainian people farther to the south. Oettingen Senior resisted the Russian violation of old liberties, paid the consequences, and moved to the country of his ancestors' ancestors to continue his academic career at the University of Leipzig. Walter decided to follow him, and he finished his medical studies at the universities of Leipzig and Berlin. He was something of an adventurer, and after his graduation worked for a time as a ship's doctor on one of the liners connecting Germany to German East Africa. Afterward he specialized in surgery and established himself at the Charité, where he met Elisabeth in 1901.

The couple's relationship to Russia was complicated. Walter had left Livonia when his father chose exile, but Livonia had not left him, and he was loyal to the land, its unique culture, and its peoples. And Elisabeth also learned to love that land, through stories told, personal artifacts kept, family traditions maintained. While Russia was not an altogether benign factor in that familial memory, it had been an integral part of Livonian existence for almost two centuries, and the territory's German elite had contributed much to Russian history, providing the empire with many government ministers, high officials, generals, intellectuals, physicians, and so on. And so, in 1904, when units of the Japanese navy attacked a Russian naval squadron at Port Arthur in the Far East, triggering a war between the two states, both Walter and Elisabeth decided to come to Russia's aid—a decision that brought them to oversee a military hospital in Manchuria that centered on a Doecker barrack. It was this adventure that became the topic of a memoir written by Elisabeth after the war's end, and the occasion for many magic lantern slide presentations she gave in Berlin to raise funds for the German Red Cross. In these talks she referred often to the Doecker barrack, its technology, and the way it had given her a sense of her German *Heimat* (home, homeland) in the otherwise not so home-like Far East. It must have given her audience extra motivation to contribute money to the humanitarian organization that had been a major force in the worldwide success of the invention by *Ritmester* (ret.) Doecker.

The Russo-Japanese War had its root in the rapid ascent, during the last two decades of the nineteenth century, of Japan as a new hegemon in East Asia. Nervous of its ability to defend eastern Siberia, Moscow sought to improve its strategic position by constructing the Trans-Siberian Railroad, connecting Moscow to the Pacific port of Vladivostok, a town founded in the 1860s. Originally the railroad was only to traverse Russian territory, but the rugged topography east of Lake Baikal and the trajectory of the border provided major obstacles for a rapid completion of the project. A more-or-less straight line from the Russian town of Chita to Vladivostok ran through the relatively easy terrain of the Chinese province of Manchuria and was 500 kilometers shorter. Hence Moscow negotiated with Beijing an eighty-year concession for a railway corridor through Manchuria and added a second one to the harbor of Lüshun, located on the southern tip of the Liaodong Peninsula. Also leased to the Russian government, Lüshun was better known at the time as Port Arthur—named so after an English naval officer who had surveyed the site in 1860. An ice-free harbor even in winter, Port Arthur was to be the base of the Russian squadron in the Pacific. In addition, China permitted the Russians to construct Russian-run cities along the way—causing a de facto colonization of Manchuria. The most important of these cities was Harbin, located at the railway junction where the tracks from Chita, Vladivostok, and Port Arthur met.

As Russia was consolidating its strength in Manchuria, Japan decided to challenge it, and on February 8, 1904, launched a surprise raid, using torpedo boats to charge Russian battleships anchored at Port Arthur. The attack triggered a bloody war that included the Battle of Mukden (Shenyang), the largest military engagement fought between 1813 and 1916. When news of the raid reached Saint Petersburg, the Russian Red Cross began to plan for the creation of bandage stations and field hospitals in Manchuria. As usual, women volunteers assumed a central role in this operation. One field hospital was to be organized and dispatched from Riga by the Livonian branch of the Russian Red Cross. In a rush of Livonian patriotism, the Oettingens decided that they wanted to be involved in the creation and operation of what was to be known as the Livonia Voluntary Hospital. Walter offered to become its medical director—an offer that was accepted—and Elisabeth was to accompany him and assist him as a nurse. Before they left Berlin for Riga, they went on a shopping spree in the German capital to buy the necessary medical equipment, which included all the paraphernalia to set up a state-of-the-art operating room, disinfection and sterilization apparatus, an X-ray machine, and an electrical generator. The Oettingens also sought to purchase a full Doecker barrack hospital, with sick wards, a kitchen-laundry building, and the operating theater barrack, but the committee back in Riga had doubts that they would offer enough protection under the arctic conditions of the Manchurian winter, and the result was a compromise: the Oettingens got permission to purchase a single Doecker barrack that was to house an operating theater, a room with sterilization equipment and medical supplies, an X-ray room, and a darkroom. Having a choice between different models, they decided on the version with felt-cardboard panels. They also purchased a Goerz-Anschütz hand camera that was specially designed for taking photos of people or objects in movement, and 288 photographic plates consisting of a thin sheet of glass coated with a light-sensitive emulsion of silver halides.

They then traveled with their purchases to Riga, where the Livonian branch of the Russian Red Cross was busy.[1]

On April 17, 1904, a train consisting of two passenger carriages carrying five doctors, fourteen nurses, and twenty-four medics, and eleven freight wagons carrying the Doecker barrack, tents, hospital equipment, and medical supplies, left Riga on what proved to be a very slow journey to the Far East. In June the group endured a forced break in their journey in a small Siberian settlement 80 kilometers east of Chita. With time on their hands, Walter decided that it might be useful to have a trial run at erecting the Doecker barrack. "Construction began at 6 am and by 10 pm the proud building was complete," Elisabeth wrote on June 14 in her diary.

> The graceful house, with twelve windows, two large and three small rooms, looked so pretty that one would have liked to move in immediately. The next day we equipped the operation room. We covered the floor with linoleum and installed the chimneys for the sterilization and cooking equipment, so that we would be able to erect at future occasions the barrack in eight hours. One commences with "Gable 1," and after three hours, when the first third part stands, one can commence operating, while others finish the remaining two thirds of the house in the next five hours.[2]

→ Fig. 2

On June 23 they received the order to immediately travel to Harbin, which served as the headquarters of the Russian army in the east. Yet, as they began to pack the train and prepare to take down the barrack, they received a second telegram telling them to postpone their departure for another ten days, as the single-track railway line couldn't cope with the traffic. "This allowed us to take apart the barrack without haste," Elisabeth noted that same day in her diary. They reached Harbin only to be told to proceed farther east to Eho, where there they found a half-ready hospital that received a steady supply of wounded soldiers but did not have an operating room. With a solution to this problem at hand, they re-erected the barrack in eight hours, this time also installing the electrical generator in a small wooden shed next to it. Surgeries commenced the next day.

→ Fig. 3

1 Elisabeth von Oettingen, *Unter dem Roten Kreuz im Russisch-Japanischen Kriege* (Leipzig: Wilhelm Weicher, 1905), 6–7.
2 Ibid., 52–53.

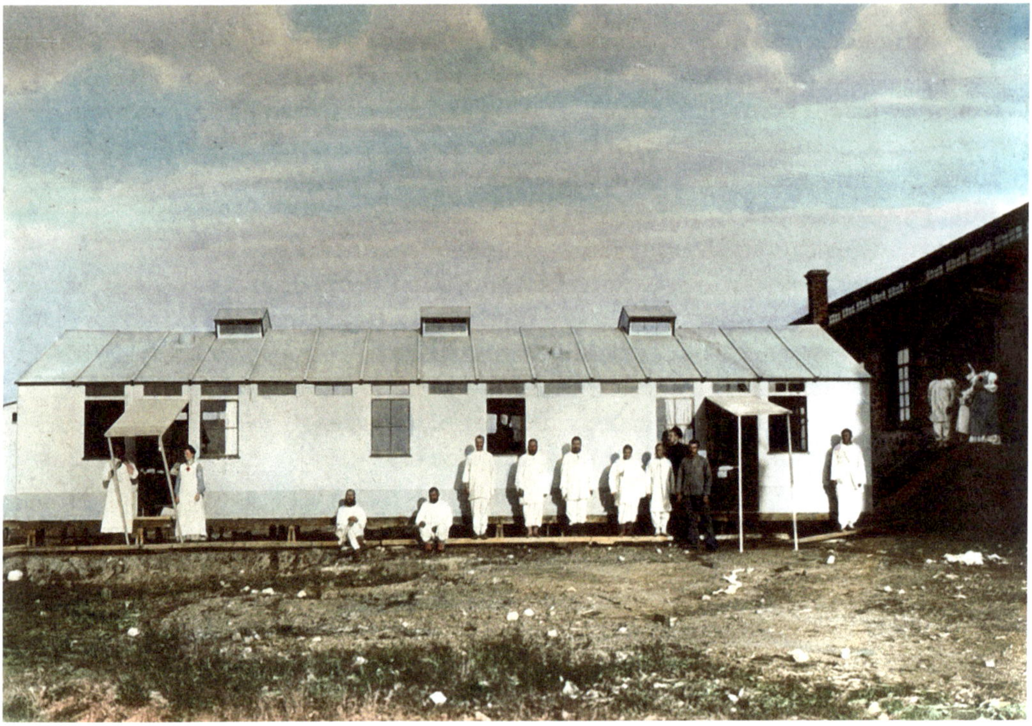

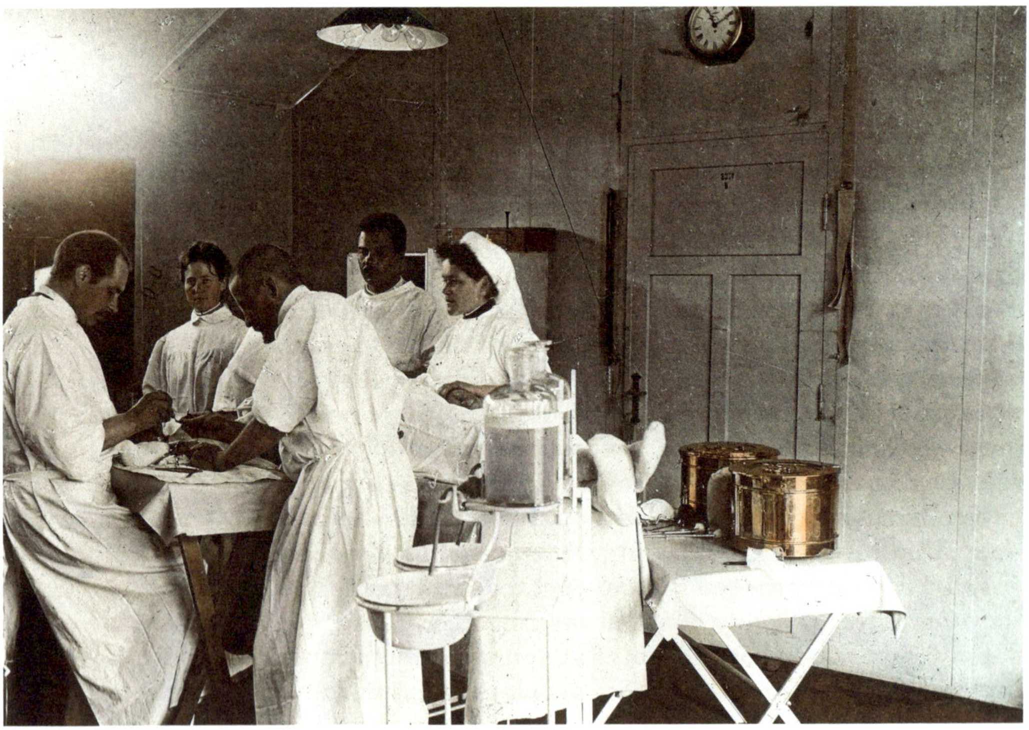

Fig. 2
The Doecker barrack of the Livonia Voluntary Hospital in Eho, Manchuria, 1904. Collection: Heinrich Heine Universität, Düsseldorf.

Fig. 3
Operation in the Doecker barrack of the Livonia Voluntary Hospital, 1904. Collection: Heinrich Heine Universität, Düsseldorf.

The building was used continuously from the end of July until September 12, when a storm, combined with a sudden soil movement caused by unceasing rain, damaged the structure. "Windows and doors gaped, the rain seeped through, and we had to refrain, willy-nilly, from any operational activity," Elisabeth reported. The Oettingens now feared that the Doecker barrack might not be much good during the winter. Yet the couple were given a leave to visit Vladivostok at this time, and when they returned, the barrack had been repaired. They used it until the end of October, when it became too cold. In early November, the Red Cross instructed them to move the hospital to Mukden, which was closer to the front. They were given only two freight wagons to transport the utmost necessary, and despite some disappointment with the performance of the Doecker barrack during the storm, the Oettingens decided that it was worth the space of half a wagon. Upon arrival in Mukden, the Livonian Voluntary Hospital was given a site right next to the station, adjacent to two enormous earth huts, half buried in the earth, which provided spaces for 600 people each. In contrast to the extremely primitive conditions in these earth huts, the Doecker barrack represented a remarkable level of luxury. "This time the construction took many days, as we aimed to make the little cardboard house useable in the winter," Elisabeth noted in her diary. "We created an earth bank around it, installed the double windows that we had purchased in Berlin, applied a layer of felt to the walls and, with care, closed all cracks. [...] Finally two iron stoves were installed in the barrack which, together with the sterilization equipment and the Berlin kerosene heater, heated the whole area with ease." Standing amidst the most primitive of shelters, the Doecker barrack acquired a profound symbolic significance as an anchor of stability in a very uncertain environment. In Elisabeth's words, it was "a piece of the *Heimat* that had traveled to the Far East."[3]

The German Red Cross had followed the war from its very beginning, and in the spring of 1904 had shipped seventy-two freight wagons of medical supplies to its Russian and Japanese sister organizations. In the summer of that year, both the Russian and Japanese Red Crosses approached their German counterpart with the request for a field hospital, and on November 23, a train with twenty-four wagons loaded with the necessary personnel and equipment to create a hospital for 100 to 120 patients left Berlin for the long journey to Manchuria.

3 Ibid., 106, 147–48, 159.

The transport included all the materials to construct two Doecker barracks. No decision yet had been taken about where the hospital was to be constructed: Irkutsk and Chita were considered and rejected. Finally, instruction came that a recently completed business college in Harbin would host the hospital. The college building proved a perfect fit, and thus the Doecker barracks were not really of vital importance to the core operation of the hospital—but they did fulfill a useful function as isolation wards for patients with infectious diseases.[4]

The German Red Cross dispatched a second hospital to Japan, which included four Doecker barracks. It arrived in the port of Yokohama in late February 1905. Alexander Georg Moslé, a German national who was a well-known representative of German arms manufacturers in Japan and who also served as consul of Belgium, made his house and garden in the Sendagaya district of Tokyo and his country house in the seaside resort of Kamakura available as sites, believing that this might strengthen German–Japan relations. The layout of the Sendagaya hospital followed the principle first adopted in the American Civil War hospitals: a covered walkway provided a spine, and attached to it were three of the four barracks shipped from Germany and a number of barracks constructed from scratch by Japanese carpenters using the local vernacular.

→ Fig. 4

The German physician in charge, Dr. Adolf Henle, noted that the Japanese structures performed well: they were cooler in the summer and also were large and spacious, offering a much greater amount of space per patient. "On the whole," he summarized, "the Japanese barracks were very functional structures, which can by no means replace Doecker's with their easy transportability, but where there is plenty of wood available, as in Japan, these can be improvised in a short time." In other words, the Germans might have saved themselves trouble and money if they had assessed the need to send prefabricated demountable barracks to Japan. Henle added an observation that echoed one that Michel Lévy, the physician responsible for medical care of the French army in the Crimean War, had made fifty years earlier. Lévy noticed that there was no need to ship prefabricated *baraques* from England and France to the Levant and the Black Sea, given the capacity of Turkish carpenters to apply the construction techniques used in Ottoman residential architecture to construct perfectly fine barrack-like sick wards for use in the French military hospitals. Henle

4 Central Committee of the German Red Cross, *Beiträge zur Kriegsheilkunde aus der Hilfstätigkeit der Deutschen Vereine vom Rothen Kreuz während des Russisch-Japanischen Krieges 1904–05* (Leipzig: Friedrich Engelmann, 1908), xvi–xix, 1–16.

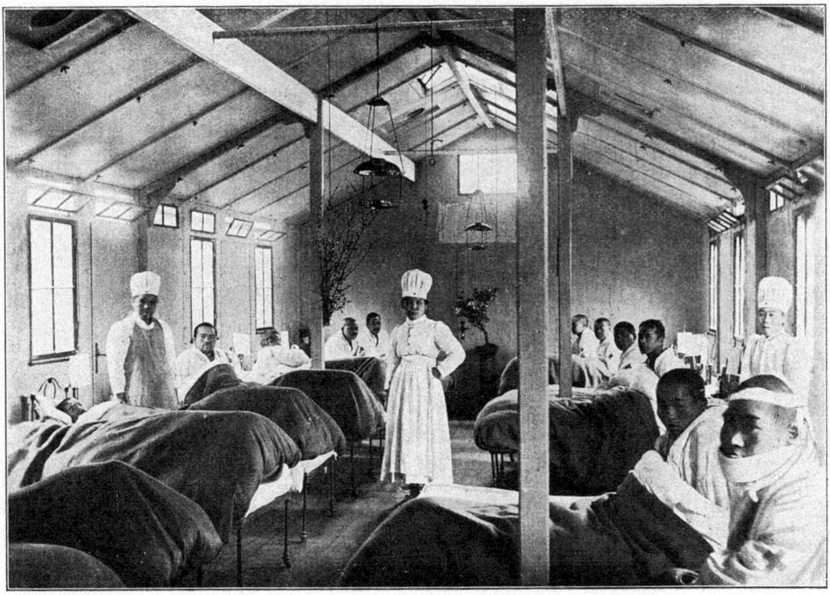

Fig. 4
A view of the hospital in Sendagaya, Tokyo, showing the covered walkway, a Doecker barrack, and in the rear a Japanese barrack under construction, from Central Committee of the German Red Cross, *Beiträge zur Kriegsheilkunde*, 1908. Collection: ZB Med: Informationszentrum Lebenswissenschaften, Bonn and Cologne.

Fig. 5
Interior view of a Doecker barrack of the Sendagaya hospital, from Central Committee of the German Red Cross, *Beiträge zur Kriegsheilkunde*, 1908. Collection: ZB Med: Informationszentrum Lebenswissenschaften, Bonn and Cologne.

observed, “Incidentally, the entire building art of the Japanese consists essentially of barrack construction. Almost the entire population lives in more or less solidly constructed barracks, which is made possible by the mild climate and has the advantage of cheapness. Finally, these buildings have a relatively high resistance to the very frequent earthquakes.” He believed that the Japanese constructions performed better as sick wards than the German imports. But having installed the operating room in one of the Doecker barracks, Henle did in the end modify his judgment so that German honor was not lost: “Although, as I said, the Japanese hospital barracks offered great advantages over Doecker’s for the special situation we found in Tokyo, I have to admit also that I liked our operating barracks considerably better than corresponding Japanese improvisations. The light was better, the walls, floors, and ceiling were easier to keep clean due to their smoothness, and the entire room layout corresponded more to that of a well-equipped permanent clinic.”[5]

← Fig. 5

By the time the three Doecker barracks arose in Moslé’s gardens in Sendagaya, and one at his seaside home at Kamakura, the barrack that had provided a sense of “home” (*Heimat*) in Mukden to the Oettingens and their colleagues had already been destroyed. In February 1905, the Russian positions in Manchuria collapsed after a battle in which 640,000 soldiers participated, 164,000 were wounded or killed, and the Japanese and Russian armies each used up more ammunition in ten days than the German armies had in the 191 days of the Franco-Prussian War. Recognized at the time as the greatest battle in the world’s history, this extremely violent encounter initiated the twentieth century, foreshadowing not only the destruction of World Wars I and II but also the defeat of the Russian army. Its ignominious retreat to the west after the Battle of Mukden caused a decisive humiliation of the tsarist regime, fueling over a decade of civil unrest, which, combined with more defeats in World War I, was to end in first the overthrow of the Romanovs in March 1917 and then, in October of that year, the establishment of the Bolshevik regime.

→ Fig. 6

5 Dr. Adolf Henle, as quoted in ibid., 326, 329.

Fig. 6
Carl Hassman, "Home, Sweet Homeski!," *Puck*, 1905. Collection: Library of Congress, Washington, DC.

The collapse of the Russian position at Mukden forced the Livonia Voluntary Hospital into a quick evacuation. There was neither time to pack up the Doecker barrack nor space to transport it in the last evacuation train, and so it was to be abandoned. The Mukden station had been the location not only of the hospital but also of stores of ammunition, food, and fodder, and Russian soldiers torched everything as part of a scorched-earth policy to be enacted upon retreat. "In one passenger carriage we found the last free space," Elisabeth recalled in her memoir. "All corridors were filled, with the wounded on the floor, and luggage reached to the ceiling. Slowly the train left the old imperial city, and from our window we had a last gaze at the Doecker *Baracke* in which we had experienced since the new year so many wonderful hours of useful work, and which was now illuminated by the fire. Very saddened, we left that now beloved piece of the *Heimat* amidst the Manchurian earth to the Japanese."[6]

A parting photograph Elisabeth took of the burning hospital symbolizes not only defeat but a major turning point in the history of the world. Japan's victory over Russia, which centered on the Battle of Mukden, fought on land, and the Battle of Tsushima, fought a month later at sea, marked the first instance in modern times that an Asian power had defeated a major European one, undermining the whole narrative of the innate superiority of the West, setting in motion a sequence of events that led not only to the aforementioned disintegration of tsarist rule in Russia but also the breakdown of the colonial system established by Europeans in Africa, Asia, and the Pacific.

Fig. 7
The destruction of the Livonia Voluntary Hospital, 1905. Collection: Heinrich Heine Universität, Düsseldorf.

6 Oettingen, *Unter dem Roten Kreuz im Russisch-Japanischen Kriege*, 223–24.

For Elisabeth von Oettingen, the Doecker barrack had been a piece of the German *Heimat* in Manchuria, a home amid confusion and a symbol of the assumed improvement of the lot of humankind in an age of scientific, technological, and social progress. And, without doubt, in the fifty years that separated the Crimean War and the Russo-Japanese War, the barrack had been a key element in one of the greatest leaps forward in the history of civilian and above all military medicine—one of the few tokens of progress wrought as a result of the otherwise toxic nationalism that created increasingly destructive armed conflicts between the nation-states. But the burning barrack at Mukden also opened another, darker reality, which was to dominate the history of that building type for the next forty years—one that was to be finally consumed, amid fanfare, in the ritual burning, attended by a large crow of British soldiers and recorded by journalists, of the last barrack of the Belsen concentration camp, Germany, in May 1945.

Fig. 8
The burning of the last barrack of the Bergen-Belsen concentration camp, Germany, 1945. Collection: author.

In terms of numbers, those four decades saw the production of millions of barracks, by many of the world's major nations—and while many served what seemed to be, at first encounter, relatively benign purposes, like housing proletarian children suffering from tuberculosis in day camps in pine forests near big cities or putting unemployed men back to work in land reclamation or reforestation projects during the Great Depression, many more were to be erected in compounds surrounded by barbed-wire fences. This is the period in which tens if not hundreds of millions of people, many of whom were civilians, were forced to live in barracks, as refugees, as expellees, as civilian internees, as forced laborers, as prisoners of war, as concentration camp prisoners, and as people made homeless by the destruction wrought by war. This is the epoch in which the barrack acquired an uncanny—or as it is known in German, *unheimlich*—reputation.

Unheimlich suggests two meanings at the same time: *Heim* is home, and thus the concept suggests that the uncanny is the unhomely. But as *heimlich* also means what is concealed or secret, it suggests, as Freud argued, the return of the repressed—the painful stuff we have unconsciously removed from our awareness but that continues to lie in wait in our unconscious, often for decades, ready to reappear in odd behaviors, tics, phobias, or slips of the tongue. Every barrack carries the signature of displacement, and hence of waiting, of biding one's time until the return to one's home or the arrival at the desired destination. The soldier's job is to be sent into battle, and possibly sacrifice his life, and the promise that comes with it is comradeship, adventure, and possibly glory, most often collective, scarcely ever individual. The true home of the soldier is the battlefield, and most soldiers will reach that place on only the rarest occasions, if at all. This creates a lack of fulfillment in the daily life of the soldier, which will be packed with drills, exercises, and parades, while officers are occupied with upholding the etiquette that comes with being a respected member of the middle and upper reaches of the social hierarchy. But for all such activity, the soldier's life is one of standing by and marking time. The patient's life is also marked by waiting—in fact, the noun "patient" derives from the adjective "patient," which originally referred to the ability of enduring pain, affliction, or inconvenience without discontent or complaints, and quickly also acquired the meaning of calmly waiting in quiet expectation.

The barrack is quite literally *unheimlich* in the way that it's a building of the periphery, while the home always denotes a center, ideally symbolized by the heart. It is also *unheimlich* in the way that it does not provide a sense of permanence; nor does it seem, in its most generalized character, particularly suitable for any specific human activity, or attempt to express in its architectural form any notable idea or ideal. An embodiment of bare necessity, it may offer, by means of a simple space, a shelter for one's body, and in the presence of comrades or chamber fellows—often those with whom one happens to share the same room—a temporary haven in a usually bleak condition. Or it may function as a sick ward, or an office space—as a shop, workshop, messroom, or almost any other function. In 1859, an anonymous report on Aldershot ironically listed all the different functions the otherwise identical barracks fulfilled: "There is a bread-hut, a meat-hut, and a library-hut . . ."[7] And during the Second World War, from 1942 onward in the bombed cities of Europe, barracks provided a roof over every possible human activity—in the forests of East Prussia (now Poland), where the infamous *Wolfsschanze* (Wolf's Lair) was located, it even was the home of the management of the war itself.

But in providing a universal solution to the problem of emergency accommodation, the barrack does not offer any orientation in the world—geographically, as a church steeple or a barn may provide direction to a traveler in the countryside; or politically, in the way that it provides information about power relations and one's ability to engage them to both insiders, like citizens, and outsiders, like recent arrivals from far away. The primary civic purpose of architecture is to allow buildings to become beacons in an otherwise confusing reality, signposts that both project the powers that are *and*, perhaps paradoxically, empower everyone by allowing habits to emerge in the negotiation of one's physical, social, and political environment.

The barrack resists the primary role of architecture to provide orientation by means of some specific and at the same time familiar form that is recognized as both normal and self-evident for the purpose served except in pointing to the circumstance of its presence: emergency.

→ Fig. 9

Hence, it is unable to provide orientation beyond amplifying an awareness of predicament and calamity that its users will already possess without the symbolic mediation provided by the architecture of the barrack. The German psychologist Ernst Jentsch was the first to apply the adjective *unheimlich* to both the state and the shade of disorientation that arises when people find themselves in a situation that ought to provide orientation but in fact creates confusion—when the identity of a thing encountered is neither distinct nor manifest.[8]

7 Anonymous, "Aldershott Town and Camp," *All the Year Round* 1 (1859), 405.

8 Ernst Jentsch, "On the Psychology of the Uncanny" (1906), *Angelaki* 2, no. 1 (Jan. 1, 1997), 7–16.

Fig. 9
The construction of a barrack on the Île de la Cité, Paris, 1919. This barrack, originally designed and manufactured for use by the American Expeditionary Forces in France, was reconstructed in Paris on the orders of the Sous-Secrétaire d'État au Ravitaillement (Under-Secretary of State for Food Supply) Ernest Vilgrain as a temporary government-run food store. Throughout 1919, many dozens of so-called Baraques Vilgrain were an essential part of the Paris urbanscape and a vital link in the city's food supply. Collection: Bibliothèque Nationale de France, Paris.

Sometimes the emergence of the uncanny from the appearance of a human artifact is welcome—for example, in a horror movie or a magician's performance—or it can be useful to the powers that be, when, for either solicitous or malign reasons, a group of people needs to be transitioned from the particularity and discernment of each person's civilian existence into the undifferentiated, undiscriminating, and compliant unity of comradeship, captivity, or both. But in general, it is considered a liability.

In its anonymity, the architectural form of the barrack has an *unheimlich* dimension that is amplified by the typical environment in which the barrack is located. While a regular building almost always stands on a site that has been graded and supplied with dry wells to provide drainage, a barrack that provides temporary accommodation typically stands on an undeveloped site that, after a cloudburst, is bound to turn into sludge. And when the soil is disturbed by the impact of shelling, as happens close to the front line, or has been trampled by too many feet, as in a situation of overcrowding, light rain will be enough to transform the ground into a squalid, *uncanny* mudscape, into an abject world that carries close associations with slime and shit.

Before Elisabeth von Oettingen bade farewell to her Doecker home, the abhorrent dimension of the barrack had been largely kept in check by the sense of achievement this building type represented as it entered the public sphere. But this spirit was to disappear in 1914, as the barrack became one of the primary symbols of the *unheimliche Welt* (world) of the new century, one that has been identified as the Age of the Camps. This dimension was well articulated by another woman who had volunteered as a nurse. As we saw in the Introduction, in 1914 the twenty-eight-year-old Mary Borden established a frontline hospital in France, which she helped to run while keeping a record of her experiences in prose and poetry. One of the most famous of her poems was "The Song of the Mud," published in 1917. Here, the first stanza: "This is the song of the mud, / The pale yellow glistening mud that covers the hills like satin; / The grey gleaming silvery mud that is spread like enamel over the valleys; / The frothing, squirting, spurting, liquid mud that gurgles along the road beds; / The thick elastic mud that is kneaded and pounded and squeezed under the hoofs of the horses; / The invincible, inexhaustible mud of the war zone."[9]

9 Mary Borden-Turner, "The Song of the Mud," *English Review* 25, no. 2 (Aug. 1917), 99.

In the book that sealed her reputation as a first-rank writer, *The Forbidden Zone*, Borden evoked the Hôpital d'Evacuation de Mont-Notre-Dame (Evacuation Hospital of Mont-Notre-Dame) as a postapocalyptic city of identical barracks set in a desert of mud: "What is this city that sprawls in the shallow valley between the chalk hills? Why are its buildings all alike, gaunt wooden sheds with iron roofs? Why are there no trees, no gardens, no pleasant places? The sheds are placed on top of the muddy ground like boxes, row after row of them, with iron rails down the centre where the main street of the town should be. But there are no streets. There are only tracks in the mud and wooden walks laid across the mud from one shed to the other, and a railway line." The site where the hospital stood appeared like a mudflat along the shore from which a great wave had just receded. "Whoever built this city on this slippery waste, built it quick, at ebb tide, between tides, to serve some queer purpose between low and high tide. They put up these sheds in a hurry, covered them with sheets of corrugated iron, pinned them to the mud somehow, anyhow, knowing that a roaring surge would rise again, come rolling back over the hills to carry them away again. Then all these new buildings, all this timber and these sheets of iron will be broken up, and will rush down in a torrent." She racked her brain for a comparison—perhaps a mining town in Colorado or a logging camp farther north? But the appearance of the hospital was without a precedent she knew, except, perhaps, the one she had been taught in Sunday school: the terrible appearance the earth must have offered to Noah after the waters of the Great Flood receded. "Perhaps a new race of men has been hatched out of the mud, hatched like newts, slugs, larvae of water beetles. But slugs who know horribly, acutely, that they have only a moment to live in between flood tides and so built this place quickly, a silly shelter against the wrath of God."[10] Borden had no illusions: the barracks—those "gaunt wooden sheds" surrounded by mud—framed a savage dimension of life that might, at best, have been exhilarating for a young woman struggling to free herself from the limitations imposed by society. But in the end, they were the building blocks of a landscape of almost biblical perdition wrought by the destructive power of modern war and, from the 1930s onward, totalitarian domination.

10 Mary Borden, *The Forbidden Zone* (London: William Heinemann, 1929), 109–13.

Fig. 10
Exterior of field Hospital at Cugny, France, c. 1916. Wooden walkways were to ensure safe and clean passage between the barracks during the rainy season. Collection: Library of Congress, Washington, DC.

Borden's interpretation of the radically *unheimlichen* dimensions of the barrack became the dominant understanding of this architectural type in the twentieth century—one that arose out of the story of the more gentle, and perhaps even gentile, origins sketched in the foregoing pages. Of those origins, sadly, very few remnants survive as part of the built world. The loss of the Doecker barrack transported all the way from the factory in Niesky, Germany, to Mukden stands for the loss of almost all the other examples of this building type constructed from its beginnings in the early modern era up to 1914. The few exceptions include a quarantine shed on an island in the Saint Lawrence River near Quebec City, three sick wards in a hospital in Saint Petersburg, and one Doecker barrack constructed in 1912 as a single-barrack hospital to serve the construction of the Pallars Jussà hydroelectric power dam, located at an elevation of 1,300 meters in the Spanish Pyrenees, created to supply Barcelona with electricity. Its cardboard-wall technology quickly failed in the mountain climate, and after a few years the hut was abandoned by the medics, to be appropriated by farmers as a shed.

Forgotten for almost a century, the Pyrenean Doecker barrack was discovered a few years ago by Catalan architect Sígrid Remacha Acebrón, and in 2019 was made the center of an intense forensic photographic exploration by artists Carlos Bunga and Primož Bizjak, in collaboration with curator Ainhoa González Graupera.

Chapter Ten, Fig. 6
→ p. 408

Chapter Nine, Fig. 1
→ p. 357

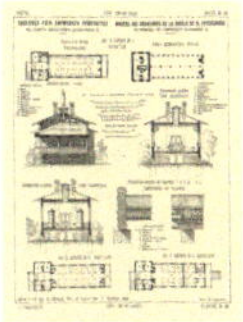

Chapter Nine, Fig. 21
→ p. 395

Fig. 11
Hospital de cartón, La Vall Fosca, Pallars Jussà, Catalonia, Spain, 2019. Photo: Ainhoa González Graupera.

The focus was not the structure but the decaying cardboard skin of the building, which the artists saw as a metaphor of the fragility of human achievement, human life.

Fig. 12
Hospital de cartón, 2019. Photo: Ainhoa González Graupera.

Fig. 13
Hospital de cartón, 2019. Photo: Carlos Bunga.

In September 2020, in the midst of the Covid-19 pandemic, an exhibition of their work opened at Galería Elba Benítez in Madrid, under the title *Hospital de cartón* (*Cardboard Hospital*). "Today the Hospital is an unwell organism, no more than skin and bones," González Graupera wrote in the press release. "Today, to consider this type of architecture—prefabricated, modular, low-cost, emergency-based and ephemeral yet still existing—is anachronistic, a voyage to the past in real time; and to document it, the desire to retain it outside of the passage of time, even as it is disappearing." Yet what might have appeared an anachronism in 2019, when Bunga and Bizjak began their project, had become all too current a year later, as the curator notes: "The post-production phase of *Hospital de cartón* coincided with the arrival of the current pandemic, forcing both artists to work from their homes. As the *Hospital de cartón* resisted collapse, new prefabricated field hospitals were being installed in Wuhan, China, in fewer than ten days each."[11]

Within weeks after the opening of the exhibition, Madrid went into a total lockdown, and the rooms of Galería Elba Benítez emptied, providing an uncanny echo of the empty barrack in the mountains—a projection screen of all our anxieties and fears. Yet, amid the despair and suffering, opportunity beckoned also—at least for me. As the world was reduced to a small apartment filled with binders holding research notes, I realized that I had run out of excuses not to complete the genealogy of the very building documented in that silent gallery in Madrid, and I set to work to finish the first part of a project begun in Monowice eight years earlier.

11 Ainhoa González Graupera, "Hospital de cartón, Primož Bizjak-Carlos Bunga. September–November 2020," press release, Galería Elba Benítez, Madrid, n.d.

Drawings

Note on the Worm's-Eye Views of Selected Barracks

The discovery of Ka-Be, a ruined Auschwitz hut, in December 2012 triggered my interest in the barrack, as a visit to Amiens Cathedral fifty years earlier had triggered my love for architecture. But my fascination with architectural history began in 1968 during a five-month stay in a tiny hospital room. A small library provided a fellowship of sorts, and my chosen companion was John Mansbridge's *Graphic History of Architecture* (1967). While all Mansbridge's illustrations proved both captivating and instructive, a series of "worm's-eye" views proved my favorites. Showing buildings as if they were suspended in space, offering a viewpoint, located below the ground plane, that looked upward toward the vaults, these oblique projections managed to unify in a single drawing the technical information embodied in plan, elevation, and section, as well as a sense of the resulting tectonic space as it can be experienced subjectively. Several worm's-eye views of buildings of a similar type and style, when drawn at the same scale and placed in juxtaposition, facilitated not only an instant apprehension of similarities and differences but also a sense of the historical development that connected them as a family. Thus, the page that set side-by-side oblique projections of a single bay of the cathedrals of Noyon (1150–55), Paris (1163–1235), Chartres (1194–1260), Amiens (1220–88), and Beauvais (1225–72) prompted a detailed comparative study of these buildings that, a decade later, I confirmed during a journey to northern France in which I visited them all. By that time, I was a student of architectural history and had graduated from the worm's-eye views drawn by Mansbridge to their inspiration, found in the iconic graphic language of French architectural historian Auguste Choisy's *Histoire de l'architecture* (1899).

When I began to collect material on the history of the barrack, it became clear that the very ideal of standardization of constructive elements, spatial modules, and their disposition, which informed the development of this architectural type, seemed to have a natural affinity to the systemized worm's-eye views constructed by Choisy and Mansbridge. Because almost all of the barracks had disappeared, and because too many had been developed, constructed, used, and demolished without leaving visual evidence of the interiority that would have provided a sense of shelter of their occupants, it appeared useful to construct such views—they would allow for a comparison of constancies and variations in the history of the barrack as an architectural type and also provide a sense of how it might have felt to be inside them.

This project was begun in collaboration with University of Waterloo architecture student Victor Tulceanu, who initially developed the graphic language to be used, expanded in collaboration with Waterloo architecture students Suhaib Bhatti, Mark Clubine, and Anna Longrigg, and brought to a provisional conclusion by Waterloo architecture alumnus Zaven Titizian, who created the final views, edited all the images, and prepared them for publication.

Koefoed's Danish Standard Barrack

→ p. 39

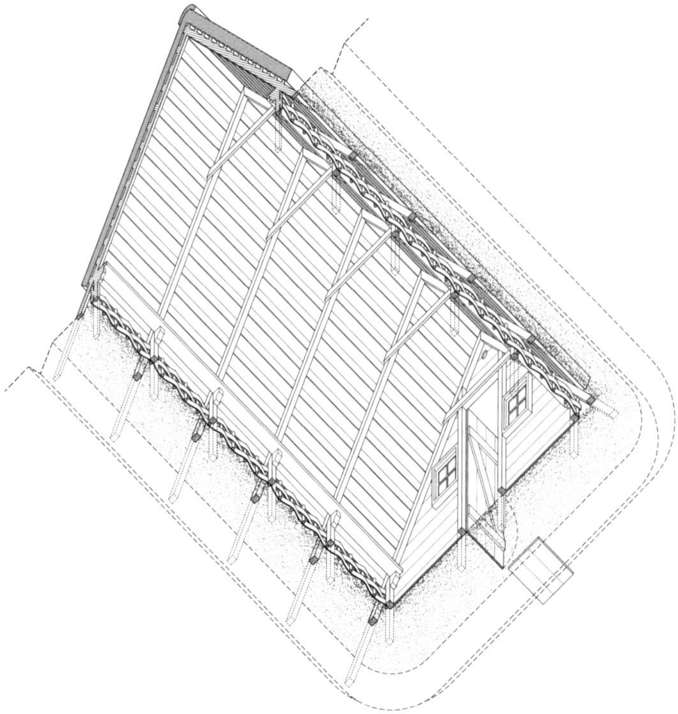

Lomet des Foucaux's Barrack

→ p. 63

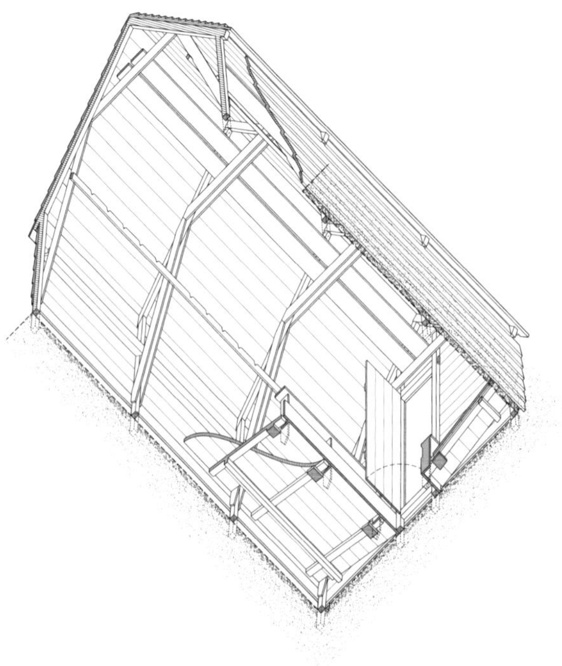

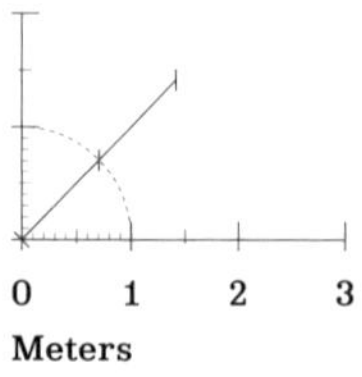

Gloucester Soldiers' Hut

→ p. 88

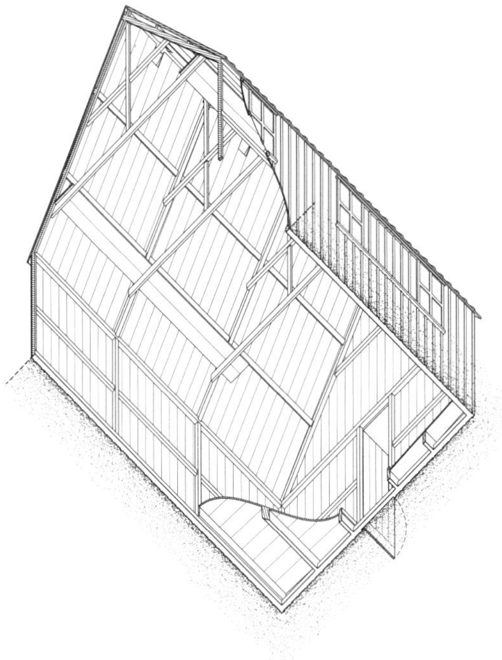

Wooden Hut for Fifty Men

→ p. 93

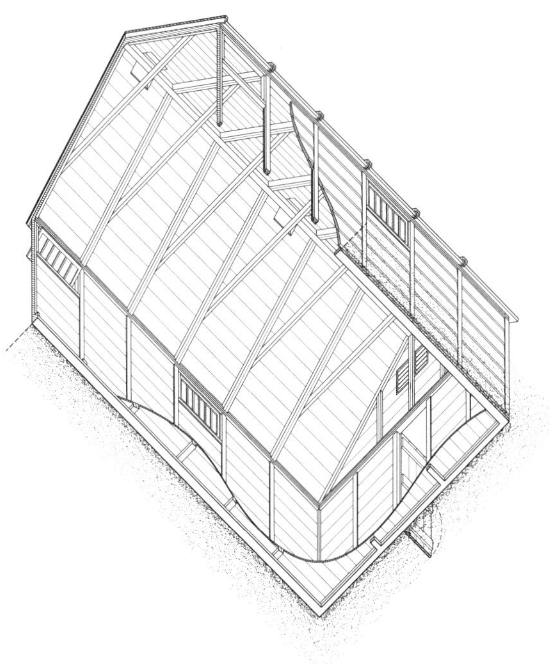

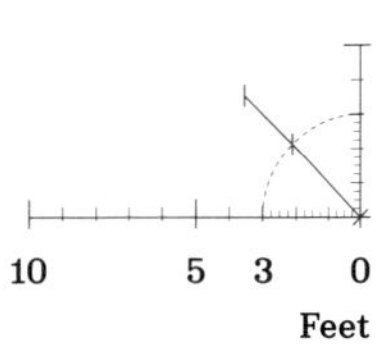

→ p. 109

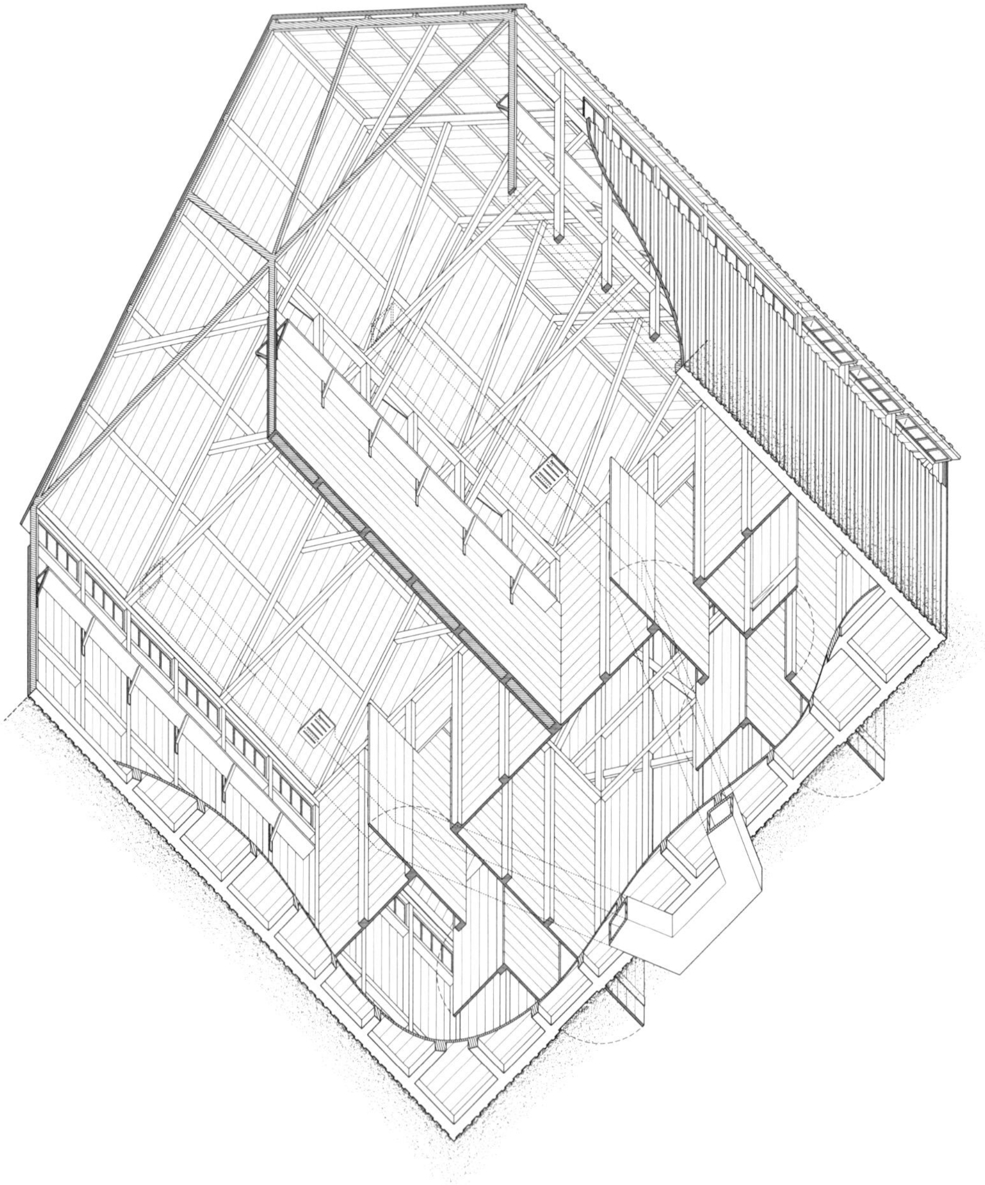

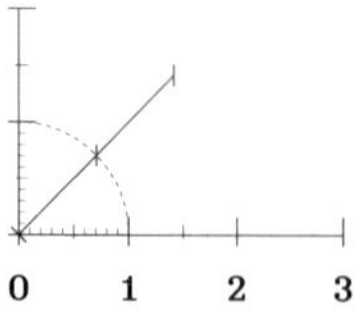

Curragh Officers' Quarters

→ p. 166

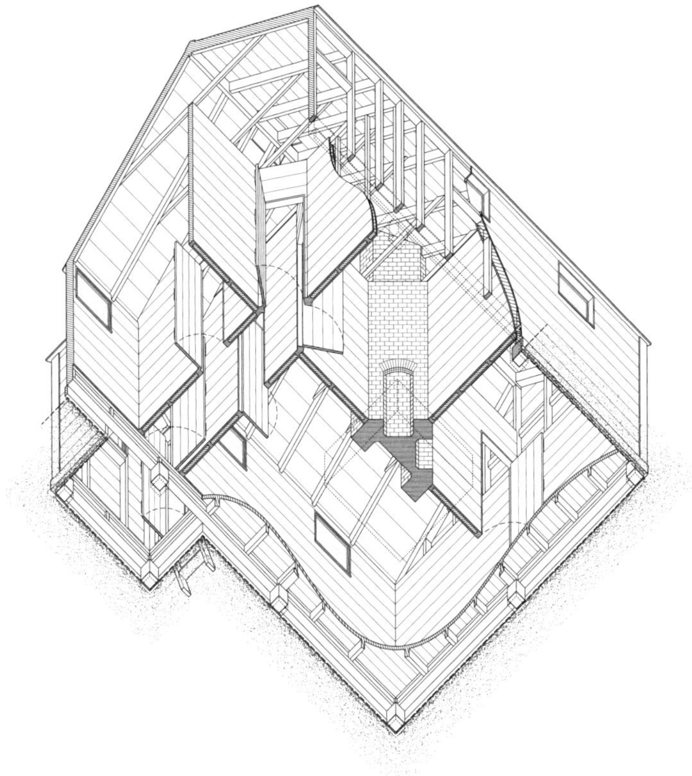

Curragh Soldiers' Quarters

→ p. 167

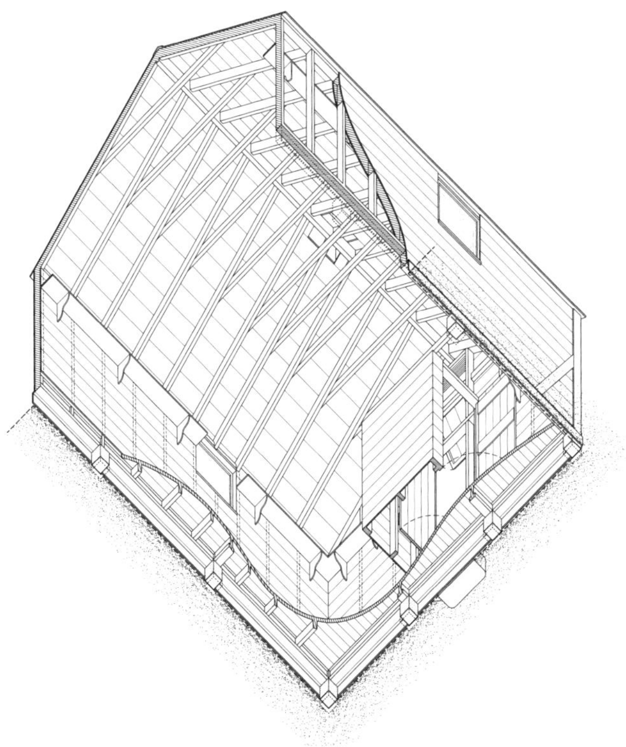

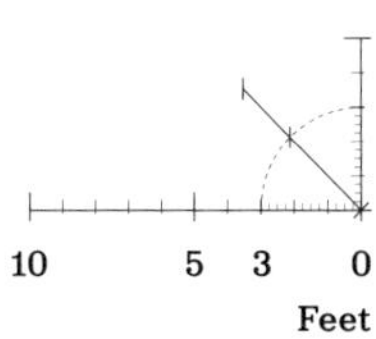

→ p. 223

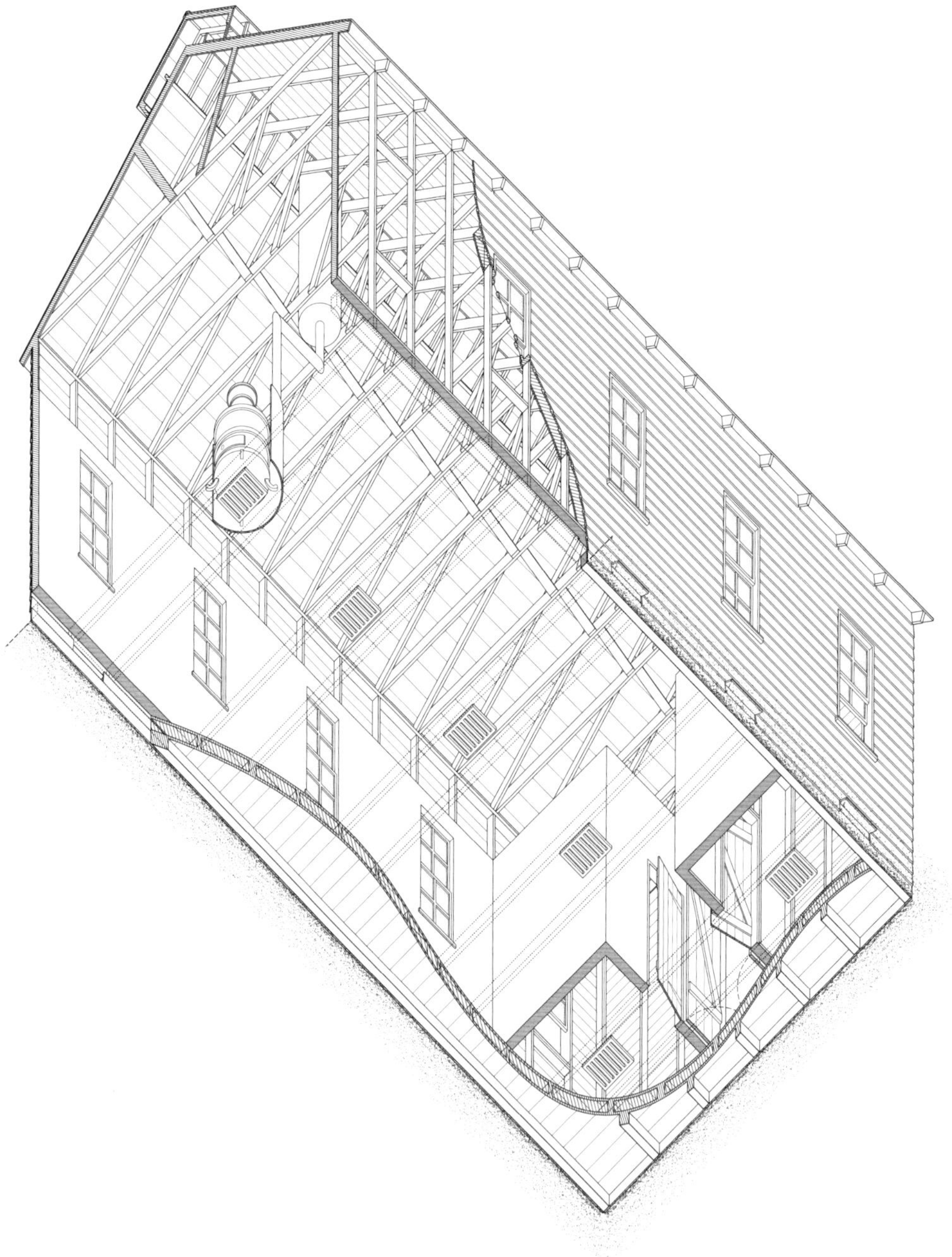

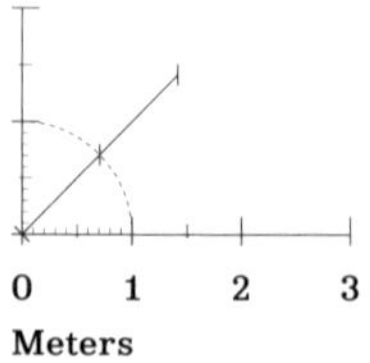

→ p. 256

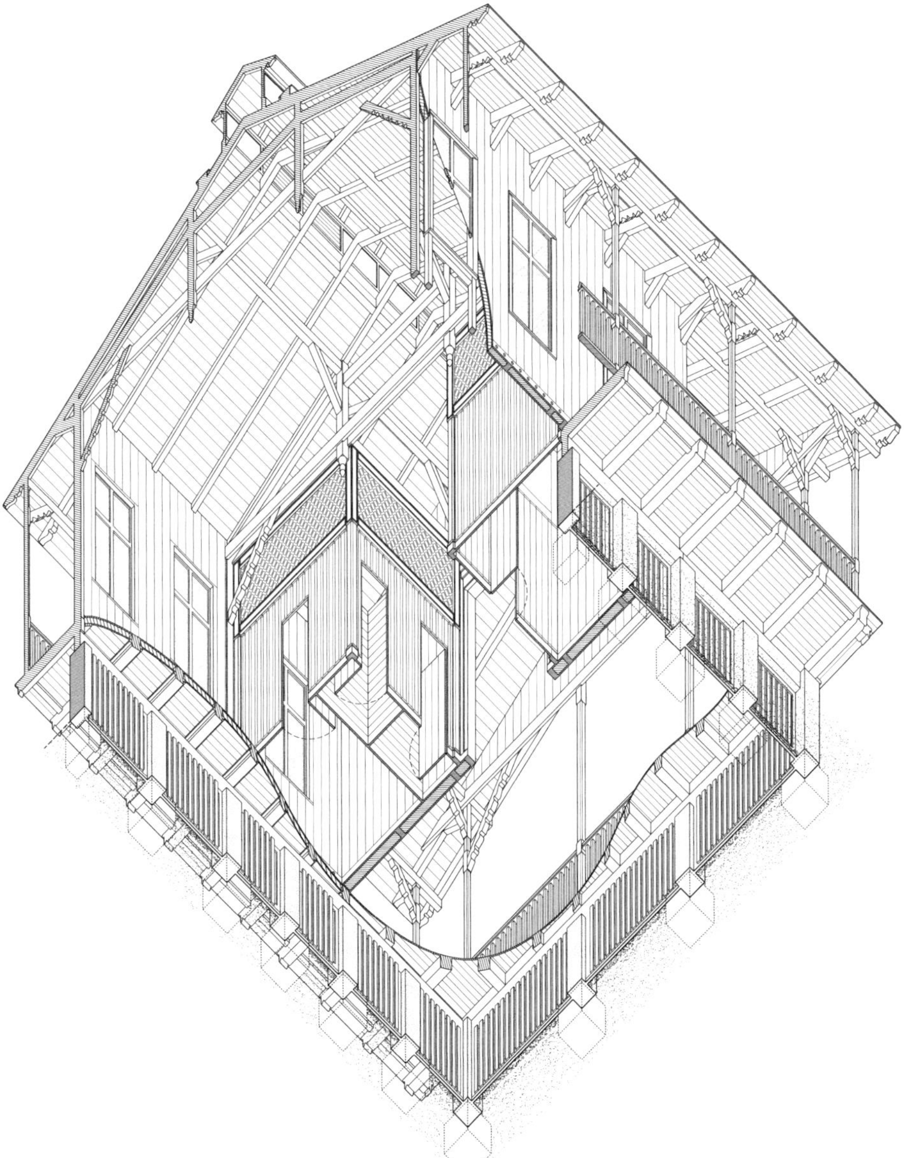

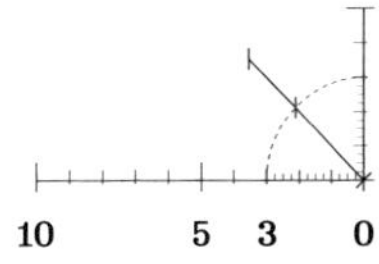

→ p. 263

→ p. 263

→ p. 269

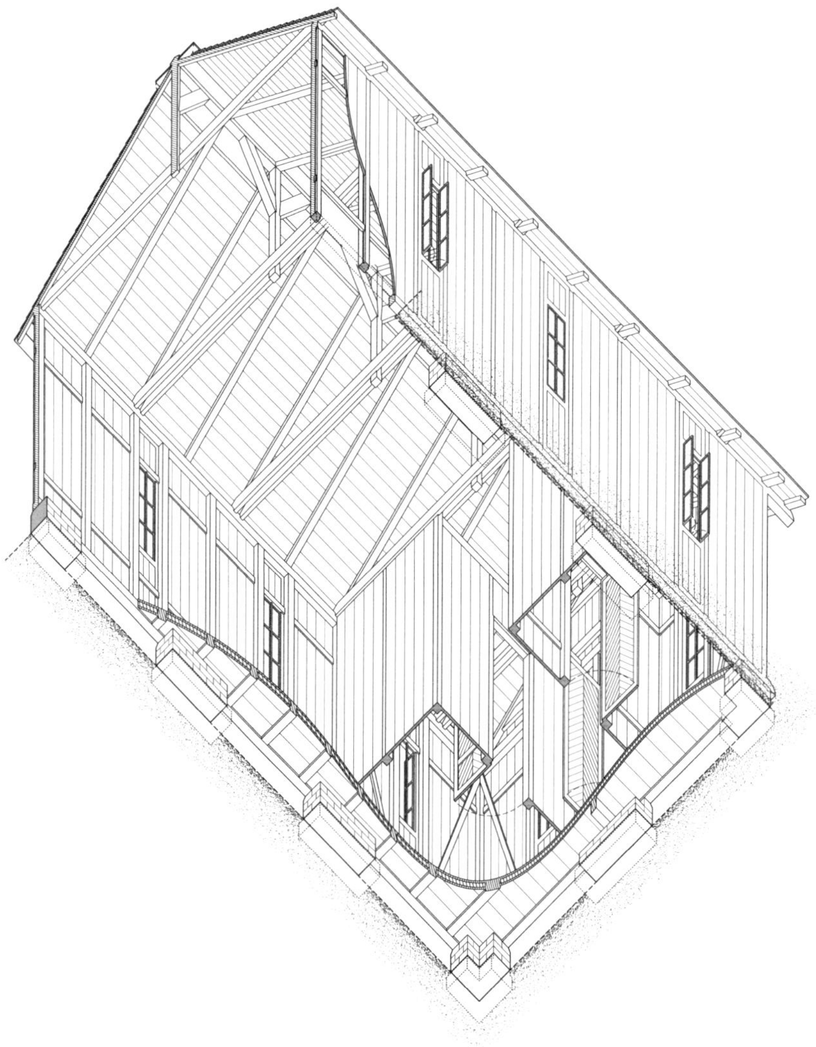

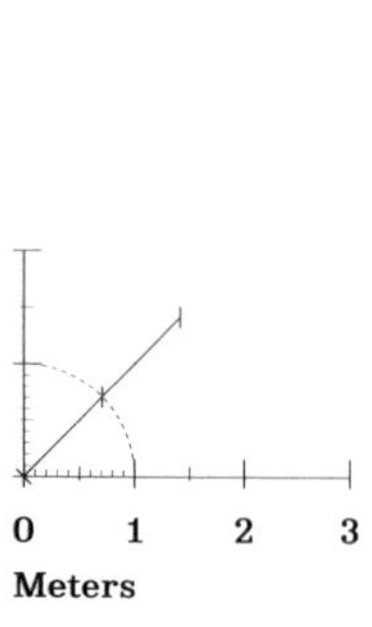

Stromeyer's Tent-Barrack

→ p. 252

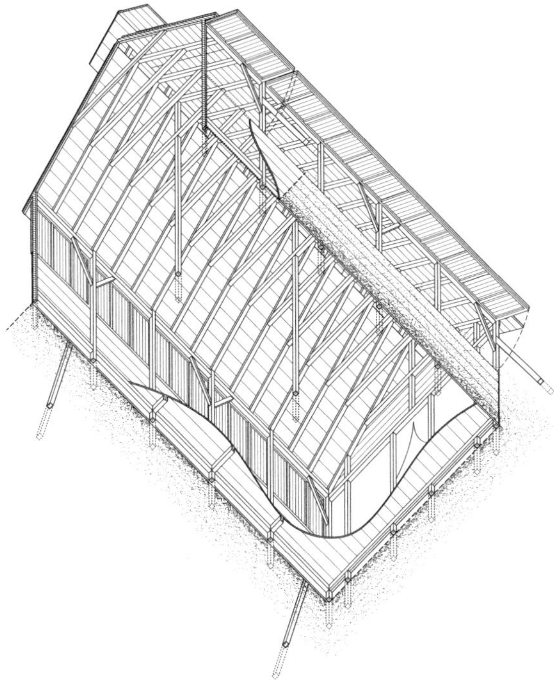

Metz Hospital Barrack

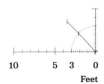

→ p. 284

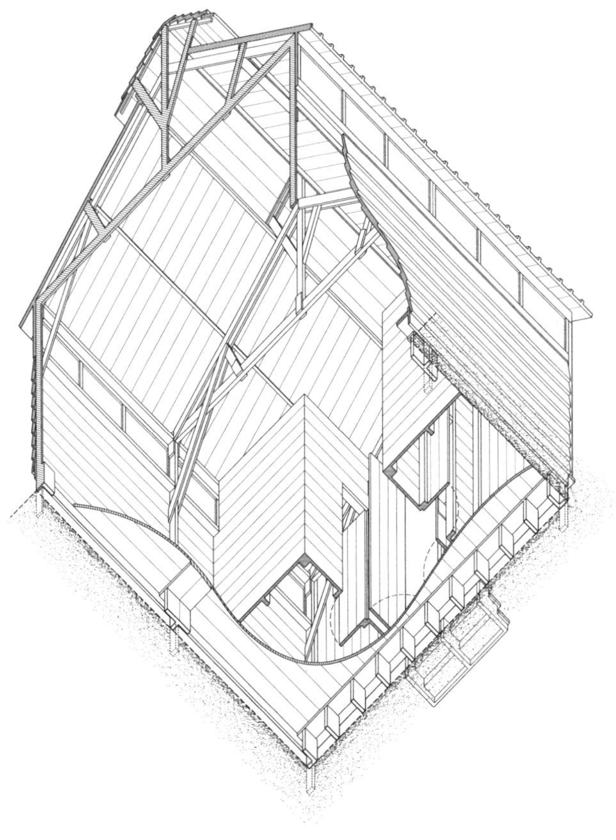

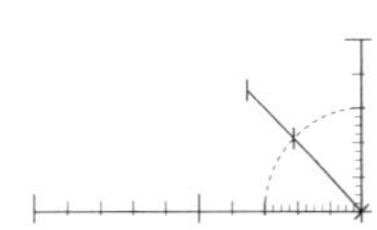

→ p. 292

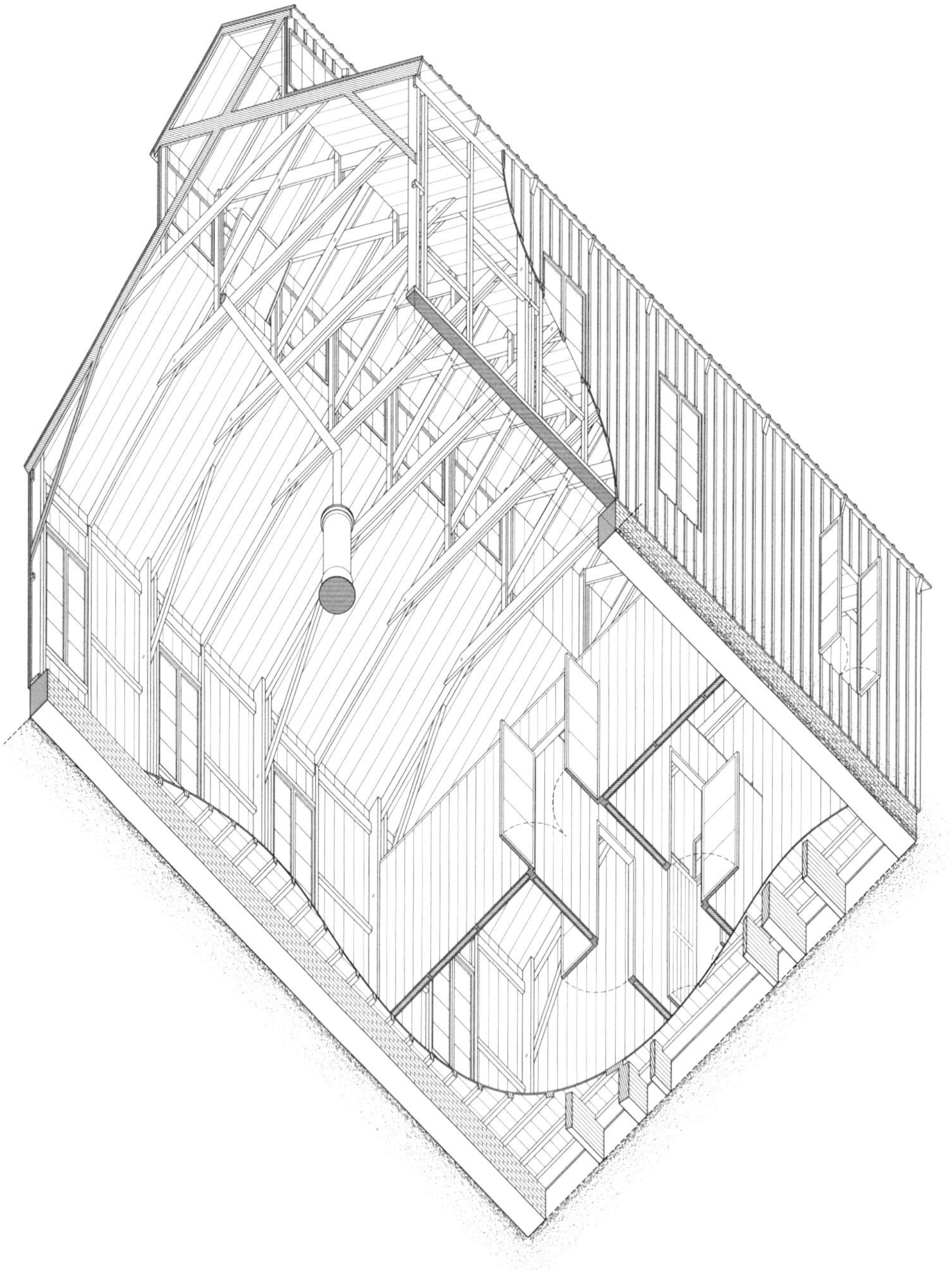

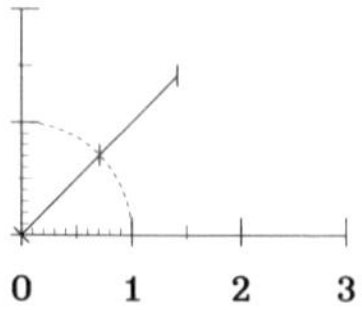

→ p. 308

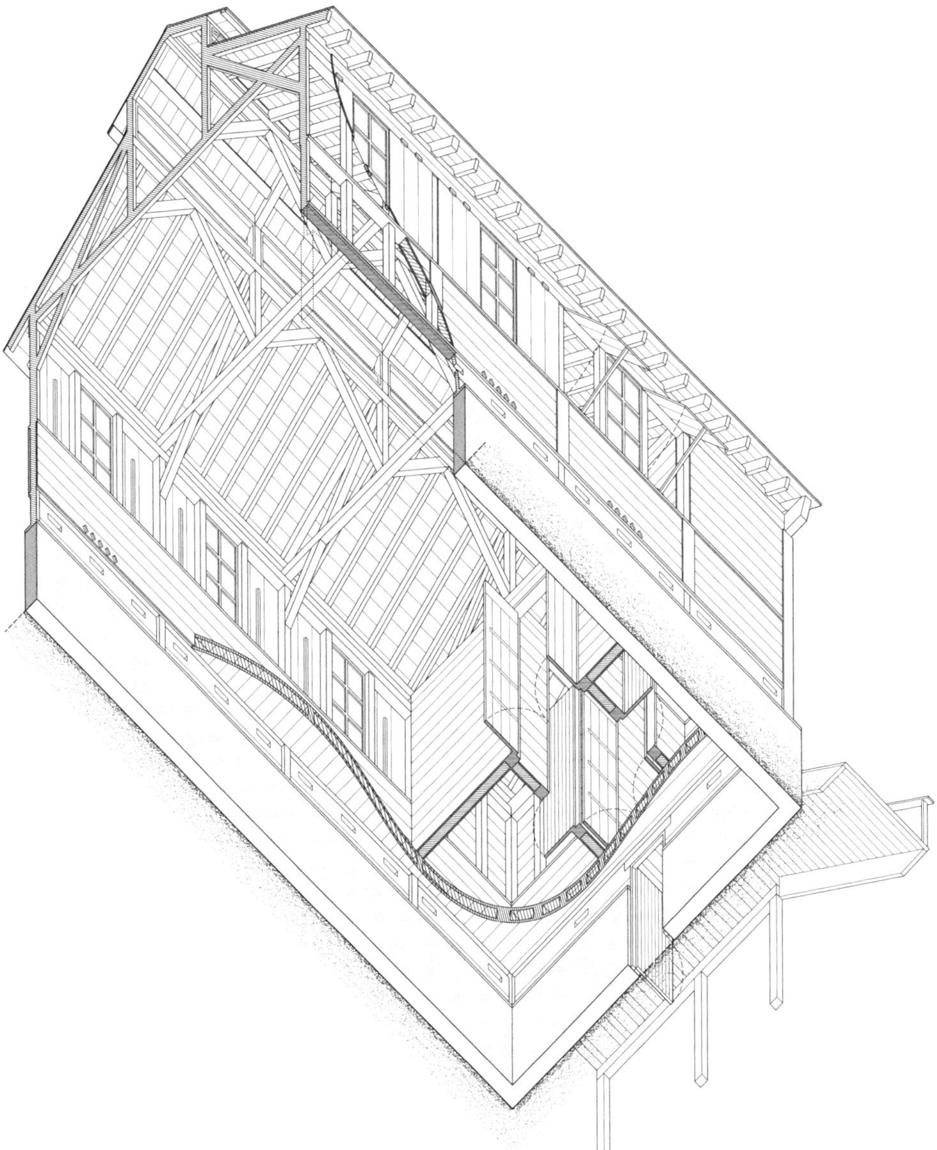

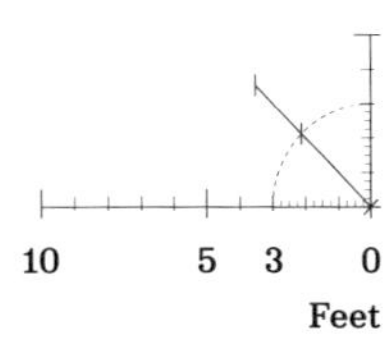

Koblenz Barrack

→ p. 436

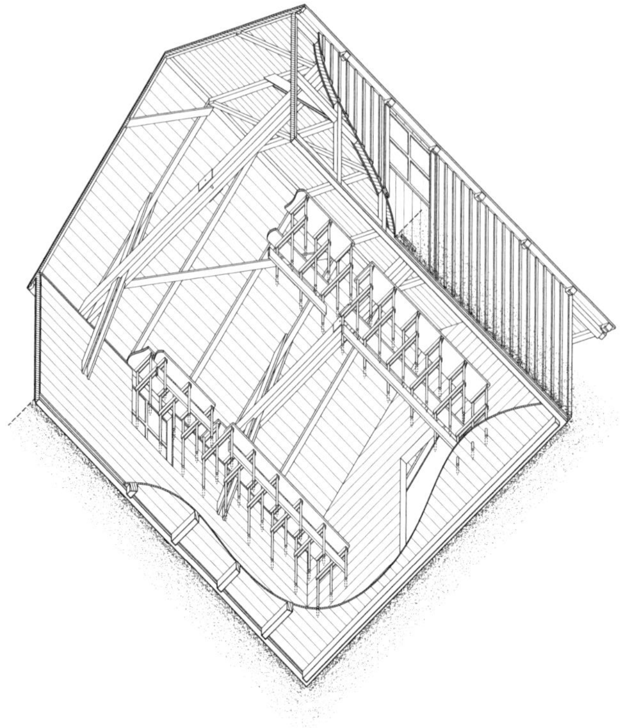

Völckner Barrack

→ p. 453

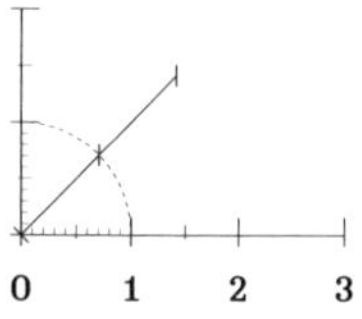

Doecker Barrack

→ p. 464

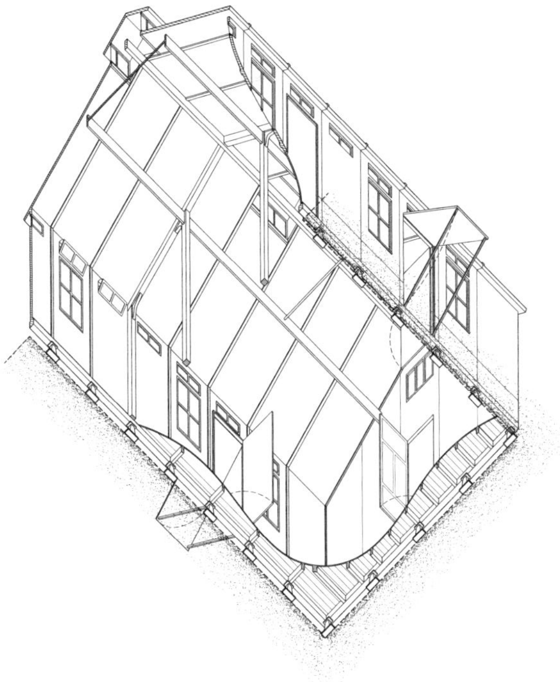

Ducker Barrack

→ p. 467

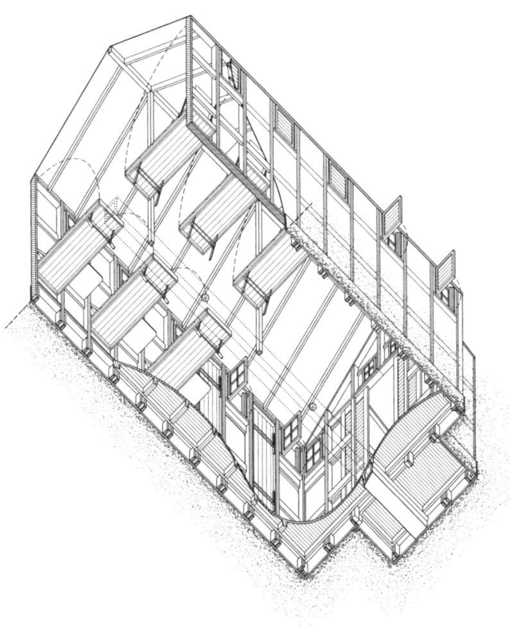

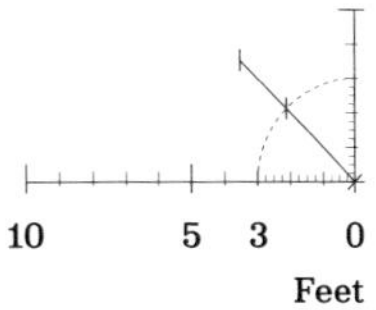

Index

A

B

C

D

Imprint

Author:
Robert Jan van Pelt

Editor:
Miriam Greenbaum

Copy editing:
Claire Crighton
Amy Hughes

Proofreading:
Colette Forder

Indexing:
Dave Prout

Design:
Bureau Sandra Doeller
(Sandra Doeller, Merle Petsch)

Drawings:
Zaven Titizian, in collaboration with
Suhaib Bhatti, Mark Clubine,
Anna Longrigg, and Victor Tulceanu

Image processing, printing, and binding:
DZA Druckerei zu Altenburg

Park Books
Niederdorfstrasse 54
8001 Zurich
Switzerland
www.park-books.com

Park Books is being supported by the Federal Office
of Culture with a general subsidy for the years
2021–2024.

ISBN 978-3-03860-365-8